ARGUMENT AND ANALYSIS
Reading, Thinking, Writing

ARGUMENT AND ANALYSIS
Reading, Thinking, Writing

LynnDianne Beene
University of New Mexico

Krystan V. Douglas
University of New Mexico

Holt, Rinehart and Winston, Inc.

New York   Chicago   San Francisco   Philadelphia
Montreal   Toronto   London   Sydney   Tokyo

Library of Congress Cataloging-in-Publication Data

Argument and analysis : reading, thinking, writing / [compiled by]
LynnDianne Beene, Krystan Douglas.
    p.   cm.
    Includes index.
    ISBN 0-03-009743-6
    1. Literature—Collections. 2. Rhetoric. I. Beene, Lynn.
II. Douglas, Krystan.
PN6014.A66 1988
808'.0427—dc19   88-9039
                                                   CIP

0-03-009743-6

Request for permission to make copies of any part of the
work should be mailed to:
Permissions, Holt, Rinehart and Winston, Inc., Orlando, FL 32887
PRINTED IN THE UNITED STATES OF AMERICA

9012 016 9 8 7 6 5 4 3 2 1

Holt, Rinehart and Winston, Inc.
The Dryden Press
Saunders College Publishing

For David W. Frizzell and Shelley G. Douglas,
who cared about us and
had the good sense to keep their heads
above water when we could not.

———————

If we think of it, all that a University, or final highest School, can do for us is still but what the first School began doing—teach us to *read*.

—Thomas Carlyle, "The Hero As Man of Letters," *On Heroes and Hero Worship* (1841)

Preface

Argument and Analysis: Reading, Thinking, Writing is an anthology of readings designed to supplement a full rhetoric for a second-semester freshman composition course. We have supplied students with an overview of critical reading, argumentative techniques, and writing and revising strategies in the first part. This overview augments, rather than takes the place of, a complete discussion of reading and writing. We chose the readings to illustrate to students some of the strategies used in writing effective "academic" prose. Read in the context of our suggestions in the introduction (Part One), these essays encourage students to think seriously about a variety of issues and, eventually, write analyses and arguments using their own ideas on these issues.

We followed two principles in designing this anthology. First, we determined that essays representing the various disciplines would both appeal to students and provide a wide range for the teachers. We based the mixture of essay types on our experience as composition teachers, where we have learned that, no matter what majors students intend to pursue, they will have to write analytic and argumentative essays for academic and professional audiences. We also found that teaching analysis and argumentation with only literary models is less successful than using a variety of types of essays. Therefore, we selected not only quality literary examples but also essays from business, the humanities, and science. Additionally, we have added several student essays to the anthology which serve as positive examples of writing techniques for students.

Second, we know that students need a textbook that stresses text considerations such as audience, situation, context, and coherence. To this end we have included an introductory discussion of methods on how to create reader-based analytic and argumentative essays. This introduction discusses critical reading and thinking, elements of logic and argumentation, fallacious reasoning, audience identification, elements of essay construction (e.g., topic identification, thesis statements), and revision and editing in terms of the strategies student writers can use. We also include, as an appendix, a discussion of the research paper and a glossary of terms familiar to composition teachers and their students.

Books aren't written without the help of many people—people whose names never appear on the title page nor in the reviews. Even the following short list cannot include everyone who gave us their expertise, offered suggestions about readings, tested readings and assignments in their classes, assured us at every step, ran for coffee, or listened to our fears. It would take a book to thank each one.

We wish to express our gratitude to our colleagues and the students at the University of New Mexico. Their assistance and support made this book a reality. Most particularly we wish to thank Katherine Martin, Denise Warren, JoAnne Altrichter, and Gwen FitzGerald, friends without whom this book would have been much more difficult to complete. In addition, we want to thank Lee Bartlett, Michael J. Hogan, Antonio Marquez, Mary Power, Patricia Clark Smith, and Scott P. Sanders for suggesting some of the better readings we included in this anthology. Thanks are also due to Juliette Cunico, Bill Balassi, David Kammer, Elaine McCullough, and Katherine Marsters for suggesting editorial changes to smooth out our prose and for testing readings and writing topics in their classes. We didn't always incorporate their suggestions, but we always valued their ideas. We also thank Jonathan Briggs and David Kleinfeld for duty above and beyond the call. We want to thank Hector Torres for patiently translating portions of Gloria Anzaldúa's text for us, and Edward Pate of the Anne Plumb Gallery and Manuel Lujan, Representative of New Mexico, for their help. Special thanks to all the people at Holt, Rinehart and Winston who helped make this book a reality, especially Paula Cousin.

Finally, we thank the following reviewers for their ideas and constructive criticism: Carol Barnes, Kansas State University; Nancy Bent, Ithaca College; Thomas Bucholz, University of Wisconsin, Stevens Point; Sandra Clark, Anderson College; Linda Doran, Volunteer State Community College; Leslie Harris, Georgia State University; Claudia Hutchison, Clackamus Community College; Janet McCann, Texas A & M University; Paul Meyer, Texas A & M University; Michael Moran, University of Rhode Island; Patricia Morgan, Louisiana State University; Larry Perkins, Jefferson Community College; Margot Soven, LaSalle University; Elaine Toia, Rutgers University; and Paul Yoder, Louisiana State University.

To the Student

What You Wished You'd Learned in English 101

David R. Pichaske

College students don't write as well as they once did.

You hear teachers, grad school admissions officers and employers lament this almost weekly in the news media. Test scores on entrance exams confirm the decline in writing skills. Between 1963 and 1975 the average score on SAT verbal exams fell from 478 to 434. Between 1965 and 1975 ACT verbal scores dropped from 19.9 to 18.7.

All of this, of course, is bad news to educators. But it need not be bad news to you. The student ambitious enough to work on improving his writing skills—at a time when the writing of others is getting worse—has an obvious advantage.

Writing competent prose is no trickier now than a decade ago. Plus, the competition is not as stiff. What got your older brother, sister or second cousin a "C" back then might get you a "B," maybe even an "A," now. A little work will put you well ahead of the pack.

Writing isn't difficult, really. Anybody, even people with −273 degrees of raw talent, can learn to write acceptable prose. You needn't wait for the winds of inspiration to blow upon the strings of your soul—writing is no happy accident, but the result of deliberate, sensible choices among options of subject and presentation. All you need is common sense, a little thought, a little work.

Here are ten suggestions for improving your writing.

1. Read

All writers read. Original ideas are, after all, few and far between, and writers know that reading is the best way to pick up both ideas and the tricks of the writing trade: clever introductions, nicely turned phrases, quotations and examples, even details of punctuation and grammar. This is not plagiarism, it is common sense, and it's something you ought to be doing regularly.

When you read, remember you're in college now. If you read the *Reader's Digest*, you will inevitably sound and even (heaven forbid) think like the *Reader's Digest,* which will not get you very far with your professors. Read what your prof reads: *Atlantic, New Republic,* the kind of books that get reviewed in the *New York Times* book review section.

Learn from what you read. Pick up content: paper topics, anecdotes, ideas, quotations. Pick up style: vocabulary, phrasing, organization, introductions, and conclusions. Imitate the models you read.

Reading is the best way I know to improve your writing . . . and your mind.

2. Be interesting

Your paper is one of 30, 40, maybe 70 or 80 other papers your instructor has to read. He'll read them because he's obligated to read them, but you can imagine the attitude with which he drags himself to a stack of themes.

What will he think when he gets to yours? A lot depends on your topic. Give him a break; make it interesting.

If you write on an assigned topic, look for an angle ("energy conservation and the little man"), an adversary position ("censorship is justifiable, even in America"), or a unique approach ("women's lib: the conservative revolution").

If you choose your own subject, remember that an interesting topic compensates for mediocre style. Pick a topic that compels you (you'll not write well unless *you're* interested), but also remember your audience. Most college professors are not interested in your high school pompom squad, family vacations, fraternity rush, last Friday's drinking party. In fact, unless you climbed Mt. Kilimanjaro at 16 (a coed I once knew actually did), you had best ignore yourself entirely.

Write about people (but not your roommate). Write about issues, events, ideas. Write movie reviews. Write about things writers in *Atlantic* write about.

Set yourself a test: "If this theme were a novel, would I pay $2.50 to read it?" If not, put the thing back in your pocket.

3. Look professional

In writing, as in everything else, appearances are often deceiving, even to the experts. A few years back, somebody hired a professional actor to be introduced as Dr. Wiseacer, Ph.D., and deliver to an assemblage of learned educators what you call in the dorm a load of "b.s." He made absolutely no sense at all, but he had the form, the title, and the appearance.

Naturally everybody was fooled: "Very educational," people said. "Informative." "Definitely worthwhile." It made all the newspapers.

I'm not advocating "b.s.," but you might suspect that a paper scrawled in Bic banana on paper torn from a spiral notebook arouses expectations very different from those awakened by an essay typed in crisp black ribbon on virginal white bond, paper clip in the left-hand corner.

Give yourself every possible advantage.

There are limitations and degrees, of course, but for most of your college work you'll want to type your papers—avoiding handwritten corrections, worn ribbons, and dirty type. An electric machine is more impressive than a manual. For very important items (a dossier, a senior thesis) you might even consider carbon ribbon. Always avoid art deco title pages, script type face, and red/black ribbons. All smell of amateurism.

4. *Get organized*

No good writing ever sprang from a typewriter fresh and clean on the first draft. Occasionally a very adept fiction writer takes a character, puts him in a situation, and lets it develop. This may work for him, but if you sit down and type off an unpremeditated essay on the Congressional elections, Bach's *Passacaglia and Fugue in C Minor* or (yikes!) your high-school pompom squad, you will get bopped.

A paper, like a painting, emerges gradually from conceptualization to finished product. It must be blocked out, and once it's written it can be touched up, even completely redone. Good writing requires much revision before rough edges are worn away and the thing comes clean.

Again there are steps and degrees. Initially you would be wise to do even your thinking on paper, letting the essay grow from a topic to a thesis to an arrangement of arguments and examples to a fully developed outline to a rough draft to a second draft to a finished product. As you become more experienced, you might perform *some* of these steps mentally. But nobody can skip from idea to finished draft.

I use an outline and two rough drafts before a finished piece. An outline is one method of forcing yourself to think where you're headed before you set out. The first revision will allow you to incorporate any new ideas and gee-I-wish-I'd-thought-of-that-thens that always crop up. A second revision cleans up style, grammar, and mechanics.

Always revise. Your work will be one-half to a full letter grade better than unrevised writing knocked out off the top of your head.

5. *Be concrete*

Most readers prefer concrete examples. Consequently you will find your writing appealing (and, probably, persuasive) in direct proportion to its concretion. Avoid fuzzy words like *concept, idea, thought,* and the vague *this* and *that*. Use direct quotations instead of paraphrases. Use the specific *Sony portable* instead of the more general *television set*. Use examples, especially in introductions and conclusions.

6. Buy and use a dictionary

Medieval scribes spelled pretty much as the spirit moved them: *land* in one line, *lond* three lines down. Not so today. Now there's a right way and a wrong way, and you're stuck with it.

You're also stuck with the fact that people who can't spell are generally regarded as stupid. Nothing says "moron" louder than bad spelling.

Especially if the misspelled word is one of the basics: *it, it's, there, their, they're, your, you're, allot, a lot, to, two, too*. Straighten these words out and bind them upon your forehead. When you proofread, watch for them.

While you're at it, watch for a lost *ed* in past tenses and participles ("a prejudic*ed* person," "was suppos*ed* to"), missing apostrophes (and question marks) and plural nouns you might think are singular *(media, phenomena, graffiti)*.

7. Avoid common mechanical errors

Everyone has his own carefully cultivated grammatical and mechanical bad habits. And every instructor allows latitude somewhere while stomping down hard somewhere else. I know professors who dangle modifiers regularly but foam at the mouth over comma splices, fragments or split infinitives.

The truth is that I can take almost any issue of *Atlantic, Harper's, Esquire* or *Playboy* you hand me and find examples of all four, but no nevermind. Learn your teacher's rules and play by them. As papers return all reddened up, make a list of your own bad habits. Then work to correct them.

Meanwhile, buy yourself a handbook and turn immediately to the following sections: dangling and misrelated modifiers, agreement *(somebody, everyone, each, nobody*, etc., all take *his* instead of *their*, and singular verbs as well), sentence fragments, comma splices, parallelism (especially "reason is *that*," not "reason is *because*"), and semicolons (used less frequently than you think). These six items represent 50 percent of the grammatical and mechanical errors I see daily in freshman composition.

Any handbook will explain them in detail. None is especially mysterious, and some can be straightened out in ten minutes or less. Clean them up and your writing will improve half a letter grade. Trust me.

8. Vary the length of your sentences

One day try an experiment. Take a piece of writing published in any of the magazines mentioned in item seven and count the words in each sentence of each paragraph. Then take an average. Then do the same thing to one of your papers.

Probably you will find two things: first, the professional's average sentence will be longer than your average sentence; second, his longest *and* shortest sentences will be longer and shorter than yours. He writes this way because variety is variety and monotony is monotony and *Playboy* will not pay him for being monotonous.

Neither would your teacher. Avoid the "Dick and Jane" style: work consciously to vary the length of your sentences. Usually this means building bigger sentences to sprinkle among the short ones. Do this not by stapling together medium sentences with an *and* or a *but*, but by using subordinate clauses, phrases, dashes, parentheses, and colons. In fact, one thing to watch in your reading is sentence variety and the way good writers mix types and lengths of sentences. You will soon observe that this is the high road to a professional writing style.

9. Avoid empty words

English is full of empty words, sometimes called "function words," and the fewer of them the better. Replace *of the government* with *government's*. Instead of "there are many who would argue," write "many would argue." Avoid the passive voice. Substitute "because" for "the reason for this is that" and "medieval scribes spelled" for "in the middle ages scribes spelled." Unless you want to sound like a Watergate co-conspirator, say "now" instead of "at this point in time." Omit the definite article *(the)* whenever possible. Don't use "proceeded to," "it seems to me that" or "I believe that."

Cram maximum idea into minimum words. Condense.

10. Practice

Writing is a skill, and a good writer learns to write the way a basketball star learns to play basketball. He may watch a lot of games, read a lot of books, memorize a lot of diagrams, but in the last analysis it's practice that does it. He shoots 50 free throws a day. He runs fast breaks up and down the court. He plays plenty of basketball. If he doesn't practice, you can bet the rest is for nothing.

The same is true of writing: you can't improve if you don't practice. The more you write, the better you will become. Just for practice, write five different drafts of one paper. Write three, six, 10 different versions of a couple of sentences. Write a diary. Write letters to your friends. Write letters to the editor.

The effort will pay off, because writing is a game worth playing well. It won't become obsolete, and it's useful in any number of situations. And while the ability to write won't take you very far if you've nothing to say, all the ideas in the world will get you nowhere unless you get them out of your head and down on paper clearly—usually in triplicate, with copies to supervisory personnel.

Contents

Rhetorical Contents

Revision

Analogy

Argumentation

Causal Analysis

Definition, Classification, and Generalization

Style

ARGUMENT AND ANALYSIS
Reading, Thinking, Writing

PART ONE

An Introduction to
Reading, Thinking,
and Writing

READING CRITICALLY

The Right Tools

Readers—like artists, scientists, and craftspeople—know that having the right tools makes a job easier. Therefore, the first step in **critical reading** is the easiest and the most obvious: collect the tools necessary to help you read. Make sure you have a dictionary, a pencil or pen, and a notebook with you; look up words you may not understand and write the definitions either in the text you are reading or in the notebook. Knowing what words mean, both their **denotative,** or dictionary meaning, and **connotative,** or emotionally colored meaning, helps you to understand an essay or story better when you reread it. Also, use a notebook to jot down concepts or **ideas** you agree with or find questionable, as well as unfamiliar concepts or ideas that you wish to explore.

The second step in critical reading is knowing something about the writer and about the text. Begin your reading by looking at obvious clues. If the text is introduced by a biographical statement or preface about the author or the writing, read that information carefully. Who is the author? When did this author live? What makes the writer interested in or qualified to write about the topic? Being familiar with the writer's life, background, education, and interests can help you place the essay or story in historical context or detect potential biases.

Next, look at the essay's title. Does the title suggest the essay's topic, the writer's attitude about the topic, or the type of writing you can expect? Does the title imply that the writer is being **ironic,** creating a contrast between the words the writer uses and the writer's intentions? Pichaske uses this technique in his essay "To the Student: What You Wish You'd Learned in English 101." Or does the writer use the title to pose his own questions, as Thomas does in "Is Corporate Executive Compensation Excessive?" or argue a minority opinion, as Feynman does in "Personal Observation on the Reliability of the [Challenger] Shuttle," or explain a seeming contradiction, as Wade does in "What Science Can Learn from Science Frauds." The title may also tell you something about the kind of text you are about to read. "The Erosion of American Education" or "Fenimore Cooper's Literary Offenses" sound like analyses of problems, whereas "Why Are Americans Afraid of Dragons?" and "The Way We Act" sound like examples of expository writing, writing that supplies definitions and explanations of concepts.

The most important step in critical reading is reading: critical readers read every word in a text looking for connections among words, sentences, paragraphs, and sections of the text. Ignoring unfamiliar words, skimming through the sentences, or skipping whole sections is not reading for understanding. If you come across a word or name you do not know, circle it and look it up before you reread the essay. If you read a sentence or two, or a paragraph, and realize that your mind is wandering, that you are beginning to daydream, or that you are outlining a project for another class, you are reading superficially rather than critically. Go back and start the section again. If your attention still wanders, try reading the work aloud because hearing a writer's words may help you identify what the writer's ideas are and how the writer organizes support for the ideas. A writer's meaning, the shape of the argument, and the effectiveness of the **essay** are matters of discovery and seldom are found in a single reading. You should plan time to reread any text.

The best way to develop critical reading skills is to know how to look for information when you read and to annotate the essay or story you are studying with your questions and reactions. As you read, look for obvious mechanical devices, such as different type fonts or styles of print, headings and subheadings, italicized words, or charts and diagrams. Writers use such devices to direct their readers' attention to certain ideas. Their intent is to have their readers question why an idea receives emphasis. For example, Rodriguez in "The Achievement of Desire" uses capital letters to make his advice clear. He wants readers to remember his lessons: "OPEN THE DOORS OF YOUR MIND WITH BOOKS," "READ TO LEARN," "CONSIDER BOOKS YOUR BEST FRIENDS." At other times writers will emphasize certain carefully selected words in an effort to persuade readers to accept controversial or unpopular ideas. Again, Rodriguez provides a ready example. To highlight the potentially controversial lesson his experiences taught him, he italicizes the following sentence: *A primary reason for my success in the classroom was that I couldn't forget that schooling was changing me and separating me from the life I enjoyed before becoming a student.*

Writers also select their words and phrases carefully either to qualify an idea or, often, to engage their readers' emotions. Turco and his co-authors use qualifying words such as *normally* and phrases such as *has been generally assumed* and *our initial results* to suggest objectivity and thus appeal to readers' intellect or reason; Sagan, on the other hand, appeals directly to readers' emotions using words such as *unprecedented, immense,* and *horrifying* and phrases such as *except for fools and madmen* and *by far the most dire.* Finally, the first few sentences of a story or essay can forecast the writer's **attitude** toward the topic. For example, a story that begins with a "Once upon a time" statement suggests a fantasy. If it begins with a description of a **character** or a character speaking, such as Paul in Cather's "Paul's Case," it suggests a psychological portrait; activities or actions, such as the opening football pass in Shaw's "The Eighty-Yard Run," suggest **conflict.** If the reading is a letter or a series of letters like Nurse's "Too Many Rejections," ask yourself who the writer and addressee are and why the writer thought a letter, rather than an essay or a speech, would be more influential for this **audience,** a particular type of reader. If the reading is an essay, the writer may begin by stating the **purpose** or reason for writing the essay, as Peters and Waterman do in "Analytic Ivory Towers," or by putting the main issue of the essay in historical or cultural context as Kennedy does in "Who Killed King Kong?"

Reread the Text Several Times

As you reread an essay or story, look for **thesis statements** (an essay's controlling or purpose statement) and **topic sentences** (a paragraph's controlling statement). By locating these sentences you can outline a writer's major points, patterns of development, and arrangement of ideas. A writer may present a **thesis** directly by introducing a controversy and either giving readers a proposed solution to that controversy, as Jefferson and his coauthors do in "The Declaration of Independence," or explaining why a ready-made solution is difficult, if not impossible, as Catton does in "The Way of the Liberated." Or, like Asimov in "The Shape of Things," a writer may delay this presentation, giving readers the situation or context that gave rise to the text. Often a writer who wants to persuade readers that a specific stance is the only prudent one will use an organizational pattern such as **narration** (see "The Romance of Scholarship"), **classification** (see "America's Gunpowder Women"), **comparison** and **contrast** (see "Rock as Folk Art"), or **definition** (see "Richard Nixon Is Back") to explain a situation or present an argument because these patterns make the writer's line of reasoning easy to follow. Persuasive writers know that the more understandable their essays are for their readers, the more likely it is that the readers will accept their opinions. Thus, when Catton in "The Way of the Liberated" wants to persuade his readers that historical change can be abrupt and unsettling, he uses a **narrative** or time sequence pattern. In "How Many Sheep Will It Hold?" Toelken, on the other hand, does not want his readers to concentrate on the process of discovering differences between Anglo and Indian cultures but, instead, on those differences themselves. Therefore, he uses a comparison/contrast pattern.

Look also for devices such as **allusions, anecdotes, images, metaphors,** or varieties of language (e.g., **clichés, jargon, colloquialisms,** formal **diction**). These devices help you identify a writer's **style** and **tone** and assess whether a writer is appealing to your emotions or your intellect and reason. For example, Gould begins his essay "Were Dinosaurs Dumb?" with an anecdote about Muhammed Ali, both so that his readers can put his discussion into a contemporary context and so he can establish an informal style for an otherwise erudite debate.

Annotate the Text

Whether you are reading an essay, a story, or a poem, underline the writer's main point, purpose statement, key phrases, or important details and support. The writer's main point may not always appear in the first paragraph; in fact, often writers ease into their topics by presenting a situation or context for their essays *before* they present their thesis statements. In "Design As Revision," Petroski begins with an image familiar to all writers: "the writer staring at a blank sheet of paper in his typewriter beside a wastebasket overflowing with crumpled false starts at his story." Petroski's thesis isn't that writers are slow or wasteful; rather, he wants to explain how writing is like the practice of engineering. His thesis is most clearly stated in paragraph 8:

> The work of the engineer is not unlike that of the writer [summary thesis statement and topic sentence for paragraph 8]. How the original design for a new bridge comes to be may involve as great a leap of the imagination as the first draft of a novel. The designer may already have rejected many alternatives, perhaps because he could see immediately upon their conception that they would not work for this or that reason. Thus he could see immediately that his work would fail. What the engineer eventually puts down on paper may even have some obvious flaws, but none that he believes could not be worked out in time.

Other writers force readers to assume what their theses are. Nicolson, for instance, never tells her audience directly that scholarship is an activity essential to their growth as individuals; nevertheless, she implies that thesis throughout the essay.

Good writers not only use thesis statements to organize their essays overall, they also organize the individual paragraphs around topic sentences. Whereas external, or text, organization helps readers recognize a writer's major ideas, internal, or paragraph, organization helps readers understand specific points a writer uses to support the essay's ideas. For each paragraph, underline the topic sentence and evaluate how the topic sentence advances the thesis statement and how the remaining sentences in the paragraph explain the topic sentence. Supporting sentences develop or illustrate a writer's topic sentence; topic sentences comment on a writer's thesis or position on a question. For instance, in the Petroski paragraph just quoted his main point is his first sentence ("The work of the engineer is not unlike that of a writer"). Petroski balances subsequent sentences in the paragraph by mentioning first the engineer's work and then, by comparison, the writer's work. By using this method, called **analogy,** both here and throughout his essay, Petroski uses the paragraph's structure to support his comparative thesis.

Another method many readers use to understand an essay is to find a sentence that is well written or an image that is striking, underline it, and write in the margin why it is memorable. But this is not the only way to annotate an essay. Rather than leave their thinking behind when they leave their reading, some readers memorize the text's main point or a memorable sentence, a repeated word or phrase that summarizes the writer's point, one idea, several key words, or an important phrase. Jefferson, for instance, wanted to move the colonists to radical action; consequently, he constructed phrases that would metaphorically ring in their ears, such as "We hold these truths to be self-evident." By memorizing, you will have something about the essay or story to ponder at times when you are not actually studying it.

Locating the writer's thesis statement and topic sentences helps you to summarize—paragraph by paragraph—the writer's main ideas, the evidence offered as support for the ideas, and any repeated information. **Summaries** are a form of taking notes or making an index of a text: you are classifying where and how often information appears so that you can review that information and evaluate it. Your notes also allow you to reproduce quickly and efficiently for yourself what the writer actually argued rather than depending solely upon your memory.

When you reread an essay or story, ask yourself questions about its organization, about the writer's ideas and evidence, and about your reactions to those ideas and evidence. You may not, for instance, initially understand what Nicolson means by preserving old values. This dilemma needs sorting out before you can fully understand her address. Put questions in the margins to remind yourself of your opinions, but remember that writing questions does not guarantee discovering answers. We most often find answers once we have learned how to ask the right questions. As you read, use questions such as the following to guide your understanding.

Questions about situation: What situation or **issue** caused this writer to develop this text? What do I know about this situation? What do I already believe about this issue? Has this situation changed since the writer completed this text? Has the issue been resolved or become more complex since the text was written? Why or why not? What was the resolution? What are the complexities? Can this situation or issue ever be settled? What, for example, prompted academician Marjorie Hope Nicolson to decide on scholarship as a commencement address topic rather than some other seemingly more appropriate topic? What possible controversies can scholarship imply? What resolutions can Nicolson present?

Questions about audience: What audience did the writer have in mind? Am I a part of this audience? Would the audience in this situation be offended or appeased? How did the writer appeal to the audience? What techniques did the writer use to bring me into the text? How does the writer make this text relate to me? What convinces me that I should or should not be the audience for this text? Nicolson's topic in "The Romance of Scholarship" seems appropriate for her intended audience, graduating seniors. However, is the essay as appropriate for a student beginning a college career as Nicolson obviously believes it is for her audience?

Questions about purpose: What questions does the writer pose for me to answer? Why does the writer think these questions are important? Why should I be concerned about these questions? If I am concerned, what answers do I already have? What answers do I find from this writer? What happens if these questions are not answered? Nicolson poses a series of **rhetorical questions** throughout her address. But many of her questions imply other equally intriguing questions she never directly states. For instance, she asks, "Is there, I wonder, any greater charm to a lover of the past than is found in manuscripts?"; however, the implied question is Why be a lover of the past? What does Nicolson believe old manuscripts can contribute to contemporary issues?

Questions about organization: What is the writer's main point? Where does the writer make this point? Does the writer develop this point throughout the text or change emphasis? What sub-ideas does the writer use to advance this point? How does the writer structure the ideas in the essay? How is this structure appropriate for the audience? The situation? The writer's purpose? Because she is presenting a speech rather than writing an argument, Nicolson uses narration or storytelling as her primary organizational technique. However, each incident in her narrative is a type of sub-idea used to persuade her audience that her thesis is reasonable and worth serious consideration.

Questions about logic: If the writer presents information as factual, are the statements true? If the writer presents information as an interpretation, is the interpretation the only possible one? What **reasons** does the writer present to support the main point? Are these reasons obvious or do they depend upon one another? How does the writer tie these reasons to the text's conclusion? Does the writer abandon **logic** and embrace emotion? How does the writer's logic influence me? How would emotional responses influence me? For example, the facts in Nicolson's story cannot be disputed because they are events that happened to the writer. Yet, Nicolson takes care to present the incidents with emotional language appropriate to a storyteller.

Questions about support: What evidence does the writer offer to convince me? Examples? Statistics? Anecdotes? Evidence from other **authorities?** Who are these authorities? Is the writer's evidence appropriate? Why? Are the facts, statistics, or references to other writers believable or incredible? Do I want to believe the writer's evidence because I accept the writer's position or because the writer has persuaded me? Nicolson obviously is her own authority in "The Romance of Scholarship" because she is relating experiences that happened to her. Part of the persuasiveness of her address depends on how closely readers associate their own experiences with the type of experience Nicolson had.

Questions about the writer's character or persona: What kind of person is this writer? What does the writer want me to think about him or her? How does the writer present himself or herself? Would I want to get to know this writer? Why or why not? If I like the writer, how does that influence my thinking about the text? If I find the writer pompous and distant, should I reject the text's main point? Throughout her address, for example, Nicolson takes care to present herself not only as an authority but as someone who understands her audience's point of view. This joining of the writer's interests with the readers' is a compelling, persuasive technique.

Questions about your reactions: How does this text confirm or refute my beliefs? Does the text change my mind about my position? Is it persuasive enough for me to adjust my own ideas? Should I look into this situation and question further? What do I hope to discover from further investigation? What should I do about the writer's main point? Does the writer want me to do something? What? Do I believe I can do something about this issue? Readers finishing an essay like "The Romance of Scholarship" need to ask themselves how Nicolson's thesis has relevance in their lives. Although she does not call for immediate action, as Brown does in "The Road Back" or Sagan in "Nuclear Winter," Nicolson nevertheless wants to influence her audience to take action—to learn, study, read, and understand the past—as a means of understanding the present.

The last step in critical reading is taking stock. Review your annotations and organize or outline them. Try to write a **paraphrase** of the essay or story and compare your paraphrase with the original. Consider whether you have fairly represented the writer's ideas, as well as reacted to them. When you paraphrase you repeat the writer's ideas, methods of organization, and major evidence in your words—not the writer's. When you react, you scrutinize ideas and evaluate a writer's position without bias, alertly seeking patterns of ideas in order to accept some, reject others, but question everything.

A Case in Point: Reading "The Romance of Scholarship"

"The Romance of Scholarship" provides a ready example of how to use these suggestions for critical reading. First, background information on the writer, the context, and the intended audience can be found in the headnote to the essay. From the headnote, you know that Nicolson was a scholar who received many honorary degrees and awards. Her background suggests that scholarship for Nicolson was a calling worthy of a life's work and that her own scholarship was, and still is, highly esteemed. In addition, Nicolson refused to accept others' opinions of what her place as a woman should be in a traditionally male-dominated society. She used quiet persuasion rather than rebellion when she championed women's rights by gaining her colleagues' respect through her research and writing. Her academic background, honors, and influence imply that readers should not only respect Nicolson's opinions but try to see the world of academics and scholarship through her eyes. However, accepting or rejecting a writer's position *only* because of education or background can limit readers' comprehension and may lead casual readers not to understanding but to unexamined beliefs. Would you dismiss a writer's ideas on politics because his or her professional training or early interests were in another field, such as the theater? Therefore, although Nicolson's credentials speak for accepting her position, critical readers demand more; the text, in addition to the writer's credentials, must justify the writer's **assertions.**

Second, the headnote and the introductory paragraph also tell you something about the context and audience for Nicolson's essay. Nicolson's text, a college commencement address, was commissioned by the school's current president, a former fellow graduate student. She identifies her audience, graduating seniors, by acknowledging that they are thinking more about their futures than the past. Furthermore, she anticipates that her audience will believe scholarship is boring and that her address is, at best, ironic or paradoxical. This background material establishes the context and the audience. The essay's title, "The Romance of Scholarship," implies the challenge Nicolson's topic, context, and audience present: Nicolson wants to convince a possibly disinterested audience that her topic is not only provocative but adventuresome and, inevitably, crucial for their intellectual growth. She must invite her audience to suspend their own beliefs and, for a time, to experience scholarship through her eyes, as a romantic pursuit rather than a dull occupation. Nicolson is inviting both her immediate audience and her readers to try out her interpretation and to enlarge their vision of scholarship, romance, and adventure by taking on her role as a struggling young scholar. Her essay, therefore, is less an argument with premises and conclusions than a persuasive document, and her strategies must depend less on logic and deductive reasoning than on subtlety and inductive reasoning.

Third, critical reading means looking for the obvious clues a writer uses to alert readers to important points. Notice, for example, the obvious mechanical devices, the free use of *I*, and Nicolson's informal word choice in the essay's first paragraph. Notice, also, that early in the essay Nicolson sets up part of her purpose—to convince her audience of the adventure scholarship promises—and her two primary organizational techniques, narration and comparison/contrast.

compare/contr. in title, speaker and aud., age, and intent

irony: contrast of words and meaning
paradox: also a contrast

contrast def.: light vs. heavy words

compare/contr. then and now. Beginning of a story: when we were young

compare/contr. school life with outside world

nostalgia: longing for things not present but past

The Romance of Scholarship

From the undergraduate point of view, I am sure, the title I have chosen will seem either *irony* or *paradox*. At your age you should and do know a great deal about "romance," but one of the last things with which you are likely to associate it is "scholarship." "Romance" is a light, charming word. In spite of teachers whom you admire and respect, "scholarship" is likely to seem a heavy word. I appreciate your point of view so much that I would not have attempted what I shall try to do now were it not for your president. Many years ago President Hard and I were fellow-students in the graduate school of the Johns Hopkins University where both of us discovered that there was romance in scholarship. He has asked me to describe to you another kind of romance than that you already know. I find my task an easier one here than it would be in many places, because the world in which you few, you happy few at Scripps, live has always seemed to me an enchanted land, one to which I return whenever I can with *nostalgia*. Here on the most exquisite campus in America, you should be able to understand enchantment.

However, it is not until readers have finished her essay that they discover her full purpose. Although she begins by telling the audience that her task is "to try to show you that 'scholarship' is not all baldness and spectacles and old age and great erudition" (paragraph 3), this is not Nicolson's full purpose. She is attempting to convince her audience the value of perseverance in the face of discrimination (paragraph 14), of knowing the past to understand the present (paragraphs 15 and 17), and of trusting ability no matter what the frustrations or prejudices (paragraphs 5, 6, 9–17). Her main point does not appear in a specific statement but in several key words or phrases, such as *opportunities unheard of in my generation, persistence,* and *goodly fellowship* and in sentences that compare her searches and discoveries to contemporary issues (paragraph 15): *"It was an age when men everywhere, emerging from a narrower, more circumscribed, safer world were questioning their beliefs; when the boundaries of the universe were enlarging as never before as the 'new astronomy' destroyed those* flammantia moenia mundi *of the past, when a man, looking through a telescope, discovered universes of which men had never dreamed, when new philosophy called all in doubt, and men, finding their old values challenged, strove to build new values."* These words and sentences should be highlighted, circled, or connected with arrows or numbers so that in rereading the essay you can trace her argument through her stories.

Nicolson uses various persuasive tactics throughout the essay to identify herself and her interests with her audience and their interests so she can compare her life with theirs and contrast her life as a scholar with the **stereotype**. She tells the Scripps students of her love for the small, private college, "an enchanted land" that she returns to often and "with nostalgia," a campus that defines enchantment and romance. As she mentions in paragraph 2, others, certainly not Scripps College's graduates, associate *scholar* with *pedant,* a person whose undue attention to books and knowledge obscures practical sense. Without fully understanding what *pedant* means, readers will miss Nicolson's ironic contrast and fail to see how Nicolson sets her audience up to believe scholarship is enjoyably adventuresome.

Nicolson's organization does not stop with a comparison/contrast. She entrances her audience with her uncommon narrative, using the effective technique of storytelling to advance her position. She tells about her European trip as if it were an intrigue where her part was to search for missing persons long dead and, for many, long forgotten. She uses the mainstays of classic detective fiction: scattered clues, conflicting testimonies, red herrings, missed opportunities, serendipitous discoveries, circular trails, and, eventually, solutions to interlocking mysteries. Others, such as the owner of Ragley Hall, may marvel at Nicolson's knowledge, but her audience knows, as detective fiction readers always know, how the sleuth solved the case.

A first reading tells you much about Nicolson's essay, her point of view, and her persuasive strategies:

1. She puts important words either in quotation marks ("romance," "scholarship") or in italics (e.g., *lived, adventure, fun*). When giving her speech, she would have verbally emphasized these words. When reading her speech, you should recognize this emphasis.

2. She uses her background and the specific situation that gave rise to her speech to strengthen connections between speaker and audience.

3. She uses several obvious assumptions about her audience including their approximate ages (early twenties), educational status (at least four years of college), and presumed interests (leaving a secure environment

for new challenges) to compare and contrast their expectations and her evaluation. Her **rhetorical** technique encourages her audience to view scholarship as an adventure that should be continued throughout life.

4. Nicolson uses her ability to tell good stories to illustrate the adventures that scholarship promises. Her stories are filled with twisted paths and human intrigues, and she draws her conclusion as subtly out of her stories as a preacher would draw the moral out of a parable.

5. Nicolson organizes her essay using comparison and contrast. She plays with contrasts, such as her undergraduate years and her audience's more contemporary college experiences; the comfortable world of a private, liberal arts school and the outside world where people must make a living; the scholar's adventure world in British libraries and the dusty Public Records' Office and the teacher's world at Goucher College; the search of a young enthusiast and the reluctance of her sources to yield information. Nicolson encourages readers to see these opposites by purposely contrasting not only situations but words such as *charming* with *heavy*, *enchanted*, *nostalgia*, and *exquisite* with *hard* and *pedant*.

A first reading will also alert you to terms that need definitions and names that need identification. What do the words *erudition* (paragraph 3), *grizzled*, *corpulent*, *reticule* (paragraph 5), *acrimoniously* (paragraph 8), *calomel*, *peremptorily* (paragraph 9), *folio*, *repository* (paragraph 10), *rostrums* (paragraph 11), and *bole* (paragraph 17) mean? More than their denotative meaning, what are these words' connotations? Who are, or were, [Robert] Browning, Samuel Johnson, [Samuel Taylor] Coleridge, [Charles] Lamb, Karl Marx, and Mark Twain? What purpose does Nicolson's mention of them serve in her speech? Is she just dropping names, or do these names carry significance for her audience and her topic? Nicolson also gives references that are, on a first reading, unclear. Who is the Scholar Gypsy, or what are the Elgin Marbles? What do *Wanderjahr* and *flammantia moenia mundi* mean? When was the Century of Revolutions, and how does that Century compare to today's? A good dictionary and sourcebook like *The Dictionary of British Biography* or *The Dictionary of American Biography* will answer some of these questions. A knowledge of German and Latin—or a friend taking one of these languages—will net you a rough translation of *Wanderjahr* (a year of wandering) and *flammantia moenia mundi* (world's flaming ramparts).

You will also want to ask yourself what you believe about Nicolson's topic and why you believe as you do. Are you convinced by Nicolson's logic? Does she present factual information or speculations? How does she support her main points? What reasons does she give for believing that scholarship is romantic? Are her reasons too obvious? Too obscure? Is she more emotional than logical? Does Nicolson present herself as a reliable speaker in this essay? Is she pompous and distant or friendly and nurturing? Does the way she presents herself, the way she creates her *persona*, influence whether you believe her? Does Nicolson's essay have any relevance for you as a student? If so, what? If not, how have times changed education and perhaps diminished Nicolson's position?

To help you see how these definitions, questions, and annotations look in an essay, we have annotated several paragraphs of Nicolson's essay. With each reading, more ideas came to mind. Even now the section is not fully annotated because you can pose more questions than the ones we have suggested. As you read the following annotations, consider what other points you feel need explanation.

sets tone—
descriptive and
fun adventures

secrets locked but
available to those
who look

antiquarian: one
who deals w/ old
books
rector: Episcopal
priest supported
by the parish

curmudgeon:
cranky person

itinerant: one
who travels and
works (see
Wanderjahr
below)

discrimination
disappears with
common goals

From London my pursuit of lost letters led me to many parts of England. Sometimes I stopped in small towns or villages to read parish registers, in small libraries in churches—in some of which I found the old "locked" books (often Bibles) fastened with chains so they could be read but not taken from the library. More than once I was fortunate enough to find one of those *antiquarians*—often a local *rector* who knew the local history of the parish, inheriting much of it from oral tradition that had come down for generations. Small libraries as well as great ones: in nearly all *I had the same experience of being received with courtesy and kindness*. Once in a while, to be sure, I found a dour old *curmudgeon* who objected to taking books from the shelves—largely, I gathered, because he thought that books belonged on the shelves and not in the hands of *itinerant* scholars—but that was rare indeed. More and more I came to realize *the goodly fellowship of scholars*; that I was an unknown young person from a foreign country (and *of the wrong sex) mattered not at all* to most of them. *I was a "scholar,"* and they—scholars in their way—did everything they could to further my pursuit. And always along the way came adventures and amusement.

begins tales of
"amusement and
adventure"
discrimination
theme again

equals as
scholars—
brought together
by interests

ties history to
today: we learn
from the past

humor—giving/
taking among
scholars

SJ: 1709–84,
author, language
scholar

I like to remember a day at Christ's College, Cambridge, after I had found my letters and had settled in and finally broken down the *prejudices of the old librarian*, so that *he no longer objected to my youth or sex or nationality*, but even shared his fire with me. I was waited upon by the college architect with a request that I visit one of the halls which had been built before the Civil War, all the records of which had been lost at the time the soldiers were quartered there in the 1640s. Because I had been reading so many letters of the period, he thought it possible that I might be able to identify some of the initials which students *then as now* had cut into the woodwork, or give him other clues as to who had lived in which room in the seventeenth century. All the fellows and dons were there to greet me; in twenty-three different rooms I was regaled with twenty-three cups of tea and twenty-three slices of what seemed the same tea-cakes. I know of Samuel Johnson's capacity for tea, which was greater than mine. I know too, that since that day I have never drunk a cup of tea if I could possibly avoid it.

So the year went on and gradually *my story book* took on form and shape. From a chaos of crumbling letters, petitions, bills, and order books, from torn and faded journals and diaries, from wills, from commonplace books and college records, scattered throughout England, one character after another emerged in clear outline against a background of stirring events. It was a tale told against the background of one of the greatest periods of history, when the cannon thundered and England beheaded a king; when plague and pestilence and the Great Fire threatened to put an end to the London of the past, when that gallant city rose like a Phoenix from the ashes, as she was to rise from more terrible devastation in the twentieth century. It was an age when men everywhere, emerging from a narrower, more circumscribed, safer world were questioning their beliefs; when the boundaries of the universe were enlarging as never before as the "new astronomy" destroyed those *flammantia moenia mundi* of the past, when a man, looking through a telescope, discovered universes of which men had never dreamed, when new philosophy called all in doubt, and men, finding their old values challenged, strove to build new values. Repercussions of all the many revolutions in that Century of Revolutions I found in my papers and letters. But all these things I had known before. What was new to me was *the human side* of a great century. As time went on these men and women of the past became as real to me as any friends of the present— more real perhaps because I knew them more intimately than one knows most friends. I had known that Lady Conway was a philosopher; I discovered her now as a woman—a woman who proudly made new curtains for her bedroom, only to find them too short so that she had to piece them; a woman who was pleased as any woman of her age with her new "muffle and cambrick." I knew all the medical treatments that were used for those excruciating headaches of hers, and followed with sympathy the gradual change in her handwriting as "fitt" after "fitt" of devastating illness laid her low. I knew that each coach her husband ordered that she might take the air had to be specially made, each one "softlier" than the one before, until the time came when she could no longer leave her house. I was with her when she became a Quaker—a shocking matter for a lady of quality in her day, and when she surrounded herself with Quaker handmaids, because, as she poignantly said, they were a "suffering" people and they were a "quiet" people. I seemed to be at her great home in Ragley when death came gradually, and a steward who loved her—as everyone who knew her loved her—set down day by day, then hour by hour, the account of her last illness. I knew how the great van Hel-

---

Margin notes:

good description

history: the story of people

G. Fire: 1660s destroyed most of London

two world wars (1913–18; 1939–45)
change in world's beliefs

fmm: from Lucretius, *De Rerum Natura* (55 BC) "world's flaming ramparts"
18th C

good point—memorize

people seem real because they faced same problems
humorous story set against sadness

language different from today

softlier? a real word?

discrimination against Quakers

suffering and discrimination

discrimination disappears with love

old values
disappear—how
do we keep
values?
moving story of
L. Conway's
death

mont preserved her body in "spirits of alcohol" in a glass coffin so that her husband—abroad in Ireland—might see her again and how she was finally laid to rest in the little village cemetery in a plain leaden casket on which someone scratched her only epitaph: "Quaker Lady."

These annotations are no more magical than Nicolson's stories. As she dug in bundles of documents for meaning, so you as a critical reader can dig through writers' statements to find both meaning and knowledge. With annotations like the preceding ones written in the margins, you gain a better sense of what an essay is about and have an easier time writing your own essay based on your reading. It may take you two or three readings to feel you have mastered an essay; thus, your annotations may be in layers with some comments answering questions you have posed earlier, other comments connecting the essay you are reading to others you know, and still other annotations introducing questions you feel demand answers.

THINKING CRITICALLY

Critical thinking, like careful reading, is the ability to recognize a carefully constructed **argument** and to distinguish it from a fallacious, fraudulent, or unreasonable one. However, before you can think about an argument, you need to understand what it is, what its parts are, and how those parts contribute to an essay. Strictly speaking, argument is one strategy or means by which a writer tries to persuade readers. In a persuasive essay, a writer argues for a **conclusion,** a proposition that the writer wants readers to accept, by presenting evidence in clauses or sentences called **premises,** the propositions a writer presents as grounds for accepting a conclusion. In persuasive writing, the conclusion is often the writer's purpose, the thesis that the writer feels is important enough to present, argue, and support; the premises are the most convincing points the writer can present to support a conclusion. Although some writers make the connections between their conclusion and premises obvious, most writers make their readers assume these connections. Critical thinking, as a result, includes the ability to make appropriate inferences between propositions presented in an essay. As a brief definition, then, an argument is a group of propositions including premises and a conclusion that are related by inference and are used in writing as a means of persuasion. A series of premises and conclusions form an argument somewhat like metal loops linked together form a chain. If the premises and conclusions are connected logically, the argument is said to be *valid;* if the links of a chain are connected tightly, the chain is *sound.*

To be a persuasive technique in an essay, an argument must be complete and the writer's reasoning must be correct. Correctness in this context means logically connected: if the argument is acceptable, the conclusion reached must follow directly from the premises presented. If the premises are false, missing, or do not relate to the proposed conclusion or if the conclusion fails to follow the premises or requires premises that are missing, flawed, or assumed rather than stated, the argument is faulty or suspect and detracts from the essay's persuasiveness. On the other hand, if a conclusion can be reasonably inferred from the premises, the argument contributes to the essay's persuasiveness. Critical readers and thinkers are seldom persuaded by incomplete arguments or by arguments with questionable conclusions or premises.

Readers seldom distinguish fallacious or invalid arguments from reasonable or valid ones when they first read an essay. Instead, they read for the writer's general concept and to see if they like the writer's approach to the topic. When they study a text, critical readers look beyond merely liking or disliking a writer's generalizations; they scrutinize the writer's ideas to decide whether those ideas are rational and defensible. They want to know whether the writer's conclusion follows logically from the premise or starting point, whether all of the writer's premises can be evaluated, and whether all of the premises support the conclusion. However, some people are convinced by flawed arguments or may remain unconvinced by logical arguments. For instance, a writer may outline a flawed argument using highly emotional language. Unexamined, this argument could be persuasive. Or, a writer may have an argument that offends some readers' beliefs; nevertheless, the argument can still be sound, yet less persuasive for some readers, if the writer has carefully linked the premises to prove the conclusion. With or without the technical rules of logic, evaluating arguments is a skill developed with practice in critical reading. Evaluation comes from recognizing the elements of an argument, separating those elements from emotional appeals, and then applying your own common sense to both the arguments and the appeals.

Writers often fail to state the connection between a conclusion and its premises in an obvious way because they want readers to infer how the proposed conclusion relates to the presented premises. Thus, identifying premises and conclusions and the inferences that connect them takes practice. Although few shortcuts or obvious clues always work to pinpoint the parts of an argument, responsible readers find the following four-step system often works in helping them think about a writer's argument:

1. figuring out what the conclusion is;
2. finding what the premises are;
3. tracing the relationship between the conclusion and the premises;
4. evaluating that relationship and its impact on the writer's essay.

One way to develop your critical thinking skills is to study the techniques that writers use to relate ideas to one another and to the conclusions or concepts they want you to accept. For instance, writers frequently begin with a conclusion and then present their premises. They often tip off readers by using words such as *therefore, consequently, thus,* and *so* to introduce the conclusion and *because, since, in as much as,* and *for* to point to premises. Brown uses these techniques throughout his essay "The Road Back." Specifically, when he introduces a series of facts, such as the level of trichloroethylene found in well water and the economic versus human impact of these levels, he signals readers what conclusions the facts imply: "Therefore individuals who owned their own wells or who were attached to small municipal systems would not, based on economic considerations, be provided the proper protection."

Generally, writers structure premises and conclusions in arguments in one of two ways: **inductively** or **deductively**. The differences between the two types of reasoning have to do with the relationship between the premises and the conclusion and not with how convincing the argument can be. Whatever strategy a writer uses, you can determine and evaluate the argument being promoted by sorting out which statements are the writer's premises, which the conclusions, and what relationships between them the writer presents.

Deductive Arguments

A deductive argument claims to provide conclusive grounds for accepting its conclusion. Moreover, when it is valid, a deductive argument's conclusion must be true if its premises are true. Deductive reasoning assumes that ideas and propositions can be shaped into certain "forms," including **syllogisms**. Arguments using deductive reasoning must be carefully worded to be valid. When writers argue syllogistically, they employ logical sequences that present conclusions inferred from **major** and **minor premises,** because deductive reasoning often strengthens argumentative writing. For example, a writer who wants to argue that dictatorship is an unacceptable form of government may suggest that dictators are ruthless, like Joseph Stalin, or that dictators do not compare favorably to elected officials like U.S. president John F. Kennedy. Both cases attempt to support the contention that dictators and dictatorship are undesirable. But, to test the strength of this argument, you should take the text apart, find the reasoning buried in the words, and evaluate it.

Deductive arguments, particularly the traditional syllogisms, are evaluated as they correspond to forms. When taken out of an essay and stated as a form, a syllogism begins with a statement, the major premise, that designates all or more members of a group or objects in a class. For example, when talking about a class like *dictators* you may want to generalize about them by asserting that a quality reasonably describes them or by naming another group that seems similar but is excluded from the class because it will not fit the categorization. You might write that

Major Premise: All dictators are ruthless.
or
No U.S. presidents are dictators.

The second statement in our examples, the minor premise, specifies a member of the named class or a person who cannot be a member of the named class because he belongs to the excluded group.

Minor Premise: Stalin was a dictator.
or
John F. Kennedy was a U.S. president.

The conclusion asserts relationships between forgoing subcategories and categories and should seem inevitable. In other words, the premises and conclusion must be so closely related that readers cannot infer the truth of one without the other also being true. Furthermore, if a proposition is true about the category, it must also be true about the subcategory.

Conclusion: Therefore, Stalin was ruthless.
or
Therefore, John F. Kennedy was not a dictator.

Graphically, the two preceding valid syllogisms would look like the following models:

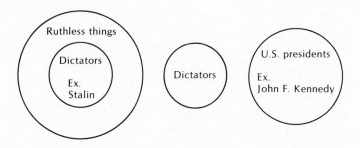

In the first example, Stalin is in the subclass *dictators*, and dictators, as a class, are designated as ruthless. Because he is an example of the subclass, Stalin also exemplifies the class. In the second example, John F. Kennedy is in the subclass that was specifically excluded from the

class of dictators. Therefore, John F. Kennedy cannot be an example of a class he does not represent. The two syllogisms are valid.

Moreover, the two syllogisms make sense. Additional reading about Joseph Stalin confirms that under his dictatorship thousands of Russian citizens were brutally murdered. The adjective *ruthless* is factual. In the second case, John F. Kennedy could not, as president of the United States, be a dictator because the Constitution outlines a check and balance system designed to prevent dictatorships. Both syllogisms are valid, reasonable, and also sound; that is, their conclusions are supported by historical reality.

Unfortunately, not all deductive arguments are so obvious or so simple. Nor are all valid syllogisms sound or sensible. Consider the following exchange between Alice and the Cheshire Cat in *Alice in Wonderland.*

> "How do you know I'm mad," said Alice.
> "You must be," said the Cat, "or you wouldn't have come here."

When phrased as a syllogism, the Cat's argument meets the standards outlined in formal logic for validity:

Major Premise: People who come here [the woods near the Mad Hatter's House] are mad.

Minor Premise: Alice came here.

Conclusion: Alice is mad.

Graphically, the Cat's argument matches the valid arguments on Stalin and Kennedy outlined earlier.

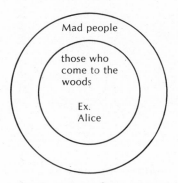

As in the argument using Stalin as an example of ruthless dictators and Kennedy as an example of the excluded class, Alice is an example of mad people who come to the Mad Hatter's woods. However, the Cat's argument, though valid, is neither sound nor reasonable. It depends on readers accepting the Cat's major premise that people who come to Wonderland's forest must be mad—a premise Lewis Carroll intended his readers to see as humorous.

Writers using deductive reasoning as a strategy seldom confine themselves to syllogisms. Consider the following two arguments, one from Lewis Carroll and the other a possible thesis statement for an argumentative essay. After rejecting but not refuting the Cat's argument that she is mad, Alice turns the tables on the Cat asking "And how do you know that you're mad?" The Cat again tries deductive reasoning.

> "To begin with," said the Cat, "a dog's not mad. You grant that?"
>
> "I suppose so," said Alice.
>
> "Well, then," the Cat went on, "you see a dog growls when it's angry and wags its tail when it's pleased. Now *I* growl when I'm pleased and wag my tail when I'm angry. Therefore, I'm mad."

The problem here is easily understood but difficult to dissect. Has the Cat used syllogistic reasoning to advance its argument? If so, is the Cat's argument valid? In other words, does the Cat's conclusion logically follow his premises, making the Cat's argument valid? If you read the Cat's argument carefully you find that he's using deduction but has too many premises for a syllogism. Even though the Cat's argument will not fit conveniently into a syllogism, it can still be evaluated using the types of reasoning that syllogisms promote. When readers take the Cat's pattern of reasoning apart and examine the premises and conclusion, they find his argument is invalid, not because he's not mad—he may be— but because his premises are faulty and fail to support his conclusion. The Cat states one questionable premise, assumes two more, and draws his clever but unreasonable conclusion from them. The first premise is clearly stated:

No dogs are mad [where *mad* is assumed to mean *insane* or *hydrophobic*].

The second premise is *implied* but not stated:

Cats and dogs respond identically.

The third premise is a simple fact:

Dogs growl when angry and wag their tails when happy.

The conclusion is:

Because the Cat responds in an opposite way from dogs, he must be mad.

Critical readers and thinkers can hardly accept the first two premises as factual because they know of many counterexamples. Further, the Cat uses "madness" to mean "insanity" in the first and last premises, but uses "anger" to mean "madness" in the third premise. Changing definitions this way in an argument is known as **equivocation** (discussed in further detail on page 31).

Readers can easily recognize an unsound argument or unreasonable conclusion when it is presented in so obvious a way as the Cat presents his. Consider, however, a more complex argument whose conclusion is that all actors are politically liberal. One might support this thesis by arguing that actors have, historically, lived in close contact with a wide variety of people. This close association causes actors to develop tolerance. Additionally, actors must play a variety of roles, which makes them sensitive to and understanding of the problems people face.

This thesis and its supporting statements or premises may appear, superficially, to be valid and reasonable. Simplified, the thesis argument is as follows:

Premise: All actors live in close contact with people having different lifestyles and philosophies.

Premise: All actors are sensitive and understanding.

Premise: All actors play a variety of roles.

Premise: All people who live like actors develop tolerance.

Premise: All political liberals have tolerance.

Conclusion: Therefore, all actors are political liberals.

Like the Cat's complex argument, this thesis could yield several syllogisms. For example, one conclusion implied by this argument is that actors are tolerant people because their work puts them in contact with many people having different lifestyles and ways of thinking. When written as a syllogism, this part of the argument clearly fails readers' test for validity:

Major Premise: Tolerant people are persons who are in close contact with many people having different lifestyles and philosophies.

Minor Premise: Actors are persons who are in close contact with people having different lifestyles and philosophies.

Conclusion: Therefore, all actors are tolerant people.

Graphically, this syllogism fails to follow the patterns for validity:

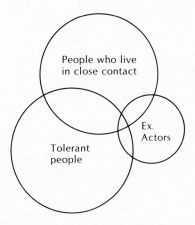

Furthermore, flaws in the reasoning and problems with the premises that force you as a critical reader and evaluator to reject the conclusion become apparent when you give the argument careful thought and analysis. Among the flaws are the equation of *actors, tolerant people,* and *political liberals,* the **assumption** that what happened historically applies today, and the assumption that playing a role demands understanding of and empathy with the character being portrayed. In addition, the use of terms such as *liberal, lifestyles, philosophies,* and *tolerance* is open to question because none of them are defined.

Inductive Arguments

Unlike a deductive argument's premises, the premises of an **inductive argument** only provide some grounds for accepting a conclusion. Inductive arguments work in at least two ways. First, inductive arguments enumerate or count specifics to present systematically evidence and draw conclusions. Second, inductive arguments list incidents or details and draw conclusions about similar events. The enumeration can be anything from simply counting—that is, every incidence of an event witnessed by a writer—to complex statistics. From the enumerated specifics, writers conclude that a statement is reasonable.

Inductive arguments maintain that by presenting evidence from several members of a class or group a writer can present conclusions about *all* members of that class or group. Rather than a connected but limited series of premises, inductive reasoning depends on a piling up of evidence. An argument using inductive reasoning would look like the following:

Data: The first raven I saw was black.

Data: The second raven I saw was black.

Data: The third raven I saw was black.

Data: Every raven I have ever seen has been black.

Therefore (conclusion), even though I have not seen every raven alive, I contend that all ravens are black.

Writers using inductive reasoning cannot claim they have conclusively proved a point, merely that they have confirmed a conclusion by citing numerous supporting incidents. They are arguing that their evidence provides reasonable grounds for accepting a conclusion as worthwhile. Inductive arguments are frequently used when the class of objects is too great to survey. It would be impossible to watch every sunrise and every sunset, but it is not impossible to conclude that the sun will rise tomorrow morning in the east and set tomorrow evening in the west. We could not drop every object on earth from the top of a tower, yet we can argue for gravitation. In a curious inversion, inductive arguments can easily be challenged by only one counterexample. After all, a writer who finds one raven that *isn't* black cannot fairly conclude that all ravens are black. But this writer can confirm the negative side of the claim: the one nonblack raven makes the proposition *not all ravens are black* certain and impossible to refute.

Inductive arguments form the mainstay of much scientific writing. In fact, the scientific method—the process of gathering data, drawing inferences from that data, and presenting hypotheses based on the data and inferences—is an inductive method. Science writers generally use induction to propose arguments by analogy. These arguments are commonplaces for anyone who reads the newspapers, science magazines, or any government reports. For example, government scientists cite the results of various studies done over many years to argue the connection between smoking and lung cancer. Although many of these experiments used animals rather than humans, the scientists argue that, since these animals share important characteristics with humans, their claims for humans are reasonable. In addition, government scientists present statistics for the number of people who smoked and eventually contracted lung cancer. By analogy and enumeration, these scientists conclude that smoking is a serious health risk.

However, the debate continues. Scientists for tobacco companies also present studies that claim other factors—heredity, lifestyle, or environment—cause or contribute to lung cancer and that a simple correlation between laboratory experiments with animals and cigarette use by humans is not conclusive. Furthermore, they list people who have smoked for many years and have not contracted the disease. By claiming the discovery of counterexamples, these scientists call into question the previous scientists' hypotheses and arguments.

Critical readers and thinkers challenge all inductive arguments, not to prove the arguments are necessarily unsound, but to test the arguments' strength and to develop their own abilities with inductive reasoning. Critical readers will ask themselves "Is there an exception to the class this writer is describing?" or "How can a hypothesis be applicable to me?" If there are no exceptions or if readers accept that the class is so large it cannot be completely enumerated, then readers accept the writer's argument as strong and the conclusion as warranted. However, relevant counterexamples call the writer's generalization into question. With any inductive argument, exceptions do not prove the rule; they make the argument suspect.

Logical Fallacies

Reducing a writer's thesis to a syllogism is sometimes misleading because writers seldom limit themselves to syllogisms or deductive or inductive arguments. Instead, writers use the richness that ordinary language affords to convince readers. Thus, trying to compress an entire essay into two premises and a conclusion in order to evaluate the essay is limiting. Instead, recognizing when a writer is presenting conclusions by using emotional appeals or ambiguous language helps you criticize the writer's position. Carefully used, strategies such as emotional appeals or ambiguity convince casual readers and impress critical readers by their cleverness; carelessly used, such strategies defeat writers who would otherwise expect their words to reinforce their messages.

You may hear people discussing how a speaker or writer's argument is unacceptable because it is based on a fallacy or on fallacious reasoning. Typically these discussions hinge on unstated assumptions about the definition of the word **fallacy,** a term used in various ways. In ordinary language a fallacy designates any idea or belief that is shown to be mistaken or false when it is judged against fact. For example, although it is comforting to believe that all people receive equal treatment in our legal system, examining the facts leads to a different conclusion. At times, guilty people are freed and innocent people are jailed; at other times, people receive different sentences for the same crime. Such **facts** argue that the belief "all people receive equal treatment in our legal system" is mistaken and, in a general sense of the word, fallacious.

However, strictly speaking, a **logical fallacy** is not a belief or idea proved unacceptable by facts but a type of incorrect or flawed argument. Beliefs are not subject to analysis; they are concepts or convictions accepted by trust rather than evaluation. Thus, when Parker tells readers that Good Souls, unlike the rest of civilization, "are fated to go through life, congenital pariahs," she is basing her humorous conclusion on her

outcast

beliefs rather than on careful reasoning. She uses emotional language *expressively* to persuade readers through an emotive appeal to accept her characterization. Arguments, on the other hand, are constructs that demand analysis. When Gaustad tells readers that "dissent, therefore, is not a social disease," he is basing his conclusion on his reasoning. He uses dispassionate language *informatively* to persuade readers through a reasoned argument to accept his thesis. Readers should think carefully about how Gaustad constructed his argument and whether the reasoning and appeals he provides for the argument violate the principles of formal reasoning.

When viewed as an aspect of arguments, the broadest category of logical fallacy is called the **informal fallacy**. Informal fallacies are errors in reasoning in an argument's structure used by writers to appeal to readers' emotions. Typically writers indulge in informal fallacies when they are careless about what is being written, pay little attention to the subject matter, or are misled by some ambiguity common in ordinary language. In other words, informal fallacies may arise from writers ignoring relevant questions or indulging potential ambiguities. However, they may also be conscious choices that writers make to strengthen an otherwise shaky argument by using emotional appeals or to expose a position that contradicts the argument they are advancing. Thus, informal fallacies can detract or empower depending upon the writer's skill in using them.

Informal fallacies are usually divided into *fallacies of relevance* and *fallacies of ambiguity*. Fallacies of relevance are generally found in arguments where the writer uses premises that are logically irrelevant to the conclusion; fallacies of ambiguity occur in arguments where the writer uses words or phrases that have multiple interpretations and allows those words to shift meaning throughout the argument from one definition to another. The following is only a partial list of fallacies of relevance and ambiguity. They are ones you should be most alert for when you read and, eventually, write and revise your own argumentative essays. However, when you study the list remember that informal fallacies are easier to spot when they are isolated from the full context of an essay. When you first read an essay, you may miss how a writer uses a fallacious appeal in an argument. You should, with practice, be able to find and, at times, enjoy how these appeals affect your understanding of issues and texts.

Fallacies of Relevance

PETITIO PRINCIPII.   *Petitio principii* is also known as **begging the question**. *Petitio* (Latin for *claim*) *principii* (Latin for *at the beginning*) means arguing in a circle or literally assuming that a premise in an argument can also be the argument's conclusion. An argument that appeals to readers already convinced of the conclusion often uses the conclusion as a major premise. When the premise and the conclusion are stated in the same words, the fallacy is so glaring that no reader could miss it. For example, if someone offered the argument that the contra rebels must be right in their cause because President Reagan supports them; after all, President Reagan only supports the right political cause, the fallacy would be obvious. However, usually the premise and conclusion are sufficiently different that their similarity escapes casual evaluation.

Sophisticated instances of *petitio principii* include the teacher's instructions to her students in Hughes' poem and the context Le Guin outlines for her speech in "Why Are Americans Afraid of Dragons?" The compact language of the teacher's instructions implies that the student should write what is true because only what that student writes will be true. It is this circular appeal that Hughes answers in the poem. Le Guin takes another tactic. Asked to address a conference on the topic of fantasy, she tells about a librarian who keeps "escapist literature" like *The Hobbitt* in the adult collection, away from children, because escapism is not good for children. Adults, Le Guin fears, do not accept fantasy because they had little experience with it as children. What was unacceptable for them in youth became unattainable in adulthood. Le Guin's purpose in her speech is not to degrade the librarian but to call attention to a circular, defeating policy.

CONVERSE ACCIDENT. *Converse accident* is also known as **hasty generalization**. Often writers who are presented with facts, statistics, events, or incidents are asked to shape these data into a coherent statement and to make assumptions based on the patterns they discern. This process of generalizing is essentially an inductive process that requires reviewing the evidence, forming (consciously or unconsciously) questions about implied relationships, and answering those questions by proposing generalities. However, when a generalization rests on only incident or fact or on only atypical cases or unusual incidents, hasty rather than considered generalizations result. Hasty generalizations are not always obvious, even to great numbers of people. The prohibition amendment to the U.S. Constitution was, in effect, a hasty generalization. Based on evidence about people who overindulged in alcohol, lawmakers drew the conclusion that all liquor harmed all people and should, therefore, be banned. The typical cases were irrelevant; they could not support the hastily drafted legislation.

ARGUMENTUM AD HOMINEM. **Argumentum ad hominem** is also known as appeal directed against the person. An *argumentum ad hominem* appeal attacks, usually by innuendo, the person making an argument in an attempt to discredit the argument by discrediting the person. This fallacy diverts readers' attention from the issue under discussion to their often unstated biases or prejudices about the person raising the issue. *Ad* *hominem* appeals can be either abusive, that is directed to the person through his individual actions, or circumstantial, that is directed to the person through his associations (also called guilty association). For example, a candidate for political office may have his or her candidacy called into question by an opponent if it is revealed that the candidate voluntarily underwent psychiatric treatment. The abusive *ad hominem* appeal here is to voters' uneasiness about a person's loss of control rather than the candidate's qualifications. If, however, a candidate for office has his candidacy called into question because he is a member of a conservative group, such as the Heritage Foundation, or a liberal group, such as Americans for Democratic Action, the appeal is circumstantial not evidential. A circumstantial *ad hominem* appeal assumes that the individual subscribes to all the values of the group. The candidate is "guilty" not for his actions but for his associations.

Because *ad hominem* appeals excite audiences, some writers use them as rhetorical devices, means to interest an audience rather than as means of establishing credibility. Thomas, in "Is Corporate Executive Compensation Excessive?" begins his argument that executives receive appropriate rather than excessive compensation for their work by attacking Ralph Nader, the critic who raised the issue, rather than by attacking Nader's evidence. Thomas's attack comes early in his essay and is designed to stir his audience's emotions before he presents more substantial support for his position.

ARGUMENTUM AD VERECUNDIAM. **Argumentum ad verecumdiam** is also known as appeal to authority. Closely related to an *ad hominen* appeal, it is based on someone's authority rather than the merits of an argument. At times readers are more willing to accept a writer's argument if the writer is a noted authority. Turco and his associates (TAPPS), authors of "The Climatic Effects of Nuclear Winter," enjoy a scientific prestige based on their education and professions that encourages readers to accept their positions on nuclear winter. To accept TAPPS's argument primarily because of the authors' scientific reputations is to indulge in a version of the *ad verecundiam* appeal. However, to argue that Thomas's environmental arguments in "The Hazards of Science" or Brown's in "The Road Back" should be dismissed because Thomas is a "popular" rather than a "serious" scientist or Brown a journalist rather than a scientist is not to reverse the appeal to authority but to indulge in an *ad hominem* appeal. It is the argument—its construction, justification, and execution—that should influence readers more than its writer's credentials.

ARGUMENTUM AD IGNORANTIAM. **Argumentum ad ignorantiam** is also known as appeal from ignorance. Appeals from ignorance are not arguments proposed by ignorant or uneducated people. *Argumentum ad ig-*

norantiam is an appeal that alleges that a conclusion must be accepted because it cannot be proved or disproved; that is, there is no clear-cut evidence for or against the argument. People who argue that poltergeists and other ghosts must exist because no one can prove they do not, are using *ad ignorantiam* appeal. Likewise, arguing that poltergeists cannot possibly exist, again because no one has shown otherwise, is an *ad ignorantiam* appeal. But *ad ignorantiam* appeals appear in essays by the best writers, particularly when the writers are seeking to sway readers' emotions, while proposing their arguments. Thomas in "The Hazards of Science" uses an appeal to ignorance when he says "it does seem to me that in the biological and medical sciences we are still far too ignorant to begin making judgments about what sorts of things we should be learning or not learning."

ARGUMENTUM AD POPULUM.   **Argumentum ad populum** is also known as appeal to the people. *Argumentum ad populum* appeals, also called bandwagoning appeals, seek to enlist readers' agreement by implying that everyone with any credibility accepts a certain position regardless of the evidence presented for or against that position. Used frequently by political speech writers and salespersons, *ad populum* appeals include suggesting that all right-thinking Americans are antisocialists or that all sexually attractive people use toothpaste that makes their teeth "whiter than white, brighter than bright." FitzGerald exposes an *ad populum* appeal used to justify the misinformation in 1950s' textbooks.

> To my generation—the children of the fifties—these texts appeared permanent just because they were so self-contained. Their orthodoxy, it seemed, left no handholds for attack, no lodging for decay. Who, after all, would dispute the wonders of technology or the superiority of the English colonists over the Spanish? Who would find fault with the pastorale of the West or the Old South? Who would question the anti-Communist crusade? There was, it seemed, no point in comparing these visions with reality, since they were the public truth and were thus quite irrelevant to what existed and to what anyone privately believed. They were—or so it seemed—the permanent expression of mass culture in America.

POST HOC ERGO PROPTER HOC.   **Post hoc ergo propter hoc** is also known as false cause. Arguments using cause and effect sometimes present false or irrelevant causes as evidence for an effect. At times such arguments become obvious superstitions, such as the idea that tossing salt over your shoulder after spilling some will help you avoid bad luck. However, the two actions—tossing salt and future bad luck—are either coincidentally or chronologically rather than causally related. *Post hoc ergo propter hoc,* inferring that one event causes another merely because one occurred before the other, is a common danger in any inductive argument or essay based on scientific inquiry. Feynman, in his minority view of the Challenger tragedy, reveals an example of post hoc thinking when he points out that "The argument that the same risk was flown before without failure is often accepted as an argument for the safety of accepting it again. Because of this, obvious weaknesses are accepted again and again, sometimes without a sufficiently serious attempt to remedy them or to delay a flight because of their continued presence."

FALSE DILEMMA. **False dilemma** is also known as black and white fallacy or an either-or assumption. A false dilemma, at its most obvious, is an oversimplification that uses an either-or structure. When faced with a true dilemma, people generally search for as many possible choices as they can. Claims of conscience are balanced against claims of expediency. However, a false dilemma catches us "between the devil and the deep blue sea" because with false dilemmas, all potentially relevant solutions are reduced to only two possibilities. For example, a salesperson could appeal to a customer by arguing that either the customer buys a product immediately or loses any chance of getting the sale price. Left out of such a situation are the possibilities that other stores may offer the product at a cheaper price, that the customer may not need this particular product, or that the product may go on sale later.

Bennett in "What Value Is Values Education?" poses a version of a false dilemma—a situation posed in some values-education classes—to expose its limitations.

> All right class. Your husband or wife is a very attractive person. Your best friend is attracted to him or her—presumably one or the other. How would you want him or her to behave? The choices are: (a) maintain a clandestine relationship so you wouldn't know about it; (b) be honest and accept the reality of the relationship; or (c) proceed with a divorce.

By limiting the range of solutions rather than allowing the participants to explore the problem fully, the example represents a false dilemma. Bennett finds this form of values education impoverished because it includes too few and too trivial a set of options. The argument, presented as a false dilemma, is suspect.

FALSE ANALOGY. Closely related to false dilemma is the appeal based on **false analogy,** another form of **oversimplification** that credits an analogy as evidence rather than illustration. Analogy rests on similarities between differing items. For example, political opponents are often compared to sparing partners boxing in a political rather than sporting ring. Like boxers the opponents come at each other varying their attacks and strategies and seeking to "knock out" the opposition. Government officials serve in this analogy as referees keeping the combatants within the rules set out for the contest. However illustrative it may be, any analogy carried too far results in a suspect appeal rather than a convincing argument.

   Analogy is a persuasive strategy in writing because it draws attention
to a new or previously misunderstood concept and encourages readers to
see the concept in terms of knowledge they already have. Petroski in
"Design As Revision" draws an at first unusual analogy between the
books and engineering structures. Having introduced his topic using this
analogy, Petroski goes on to acknowledge the important differences between the practice of writing and the profession of structural engineering. In "Can a Bee Behave Intelligently?" James and Carol Gould reject
as a false analogy the comparison of animal intelligence and mechanical
brains. Like Petroski's use of analogy, this rejection of false analogy advances the Goulds's argument.

Fallacies of Ambiguity

EQUIVOCATION.   Most words have not only denotative meanings but
more than one connotative meaning. For example, most people know
that a *clip* that fastens items together (like a *paper clip*) is not the same
clip meant in a haircut or in a football penalty. Differences in meaning
such as these are acceptable as long as the meaning in the text stays
constant. However, confusing the different meanings of a word in a single context or situation is equivocating; when the context is an argumentative essay, the equivocation is a logical or argumentative fallacy.
One humorous example of equivocation already mentioned is the
Cheshire Cat's argument to Alice where he uses the word *mad* to mean,
alternately, *angry* and *insane*. Gould's use of *dumb* in his essay "Were
Dinosaurs Dumb?" is an effort to point out to readers how the term is
an equivocation. Gould's purpose in this essay is to satisfactorily define
a commonly misapplied term by making its vagueness and ambiguity
understandable.

COMPOSITION AND DIVISION.   **Composition** fallacies are generalizations
that ask readers to transfer their acceptance of specific points to the essay's generality; the fallacy resides in agreeing that whatever is true
about the individual parts must also be true of the whole. Stated more
informally, the composition fallacy assumes that the individual value of
the members of the group conclusively demonstrates the value of the
group. For instance, just because all the starters on a basketball team are
individually good shooters cannot serve as conclusive evidence that they
will work well as a team. The individuals could compete with one another rather than concentrate on competing as a team.
   Division, the opposite of composition, appeals to readers by arguing
from generality to specifics. Arguments using division ask readers to assume that what is true of the whole will be true of the parts. Consider,
for example, the basketball example in the preceding paragraph. Because
the team has a winning season does not mean that every player on the

team is a star shooter. One team member could excel in rebounding while another could lead the defense. Instead of individual star players, the team could be a cohesive group set on working toward the goal of winning games rather than winning individual honors.

Clemens plays humorously with both composition and division in his essay "Man the Irrational." Throughout the essay he presents specifics, such as men's preferences for mates and for quiet; he later argues that since his audience now has the facts, it knows "what the human race enjoys, and what it doesn't enjoy." For Clemens's speaker, the individual incidents validate these generalizations. This is an appeal using composition. On the other hand, Clemens explains that "only about two men in 100 can play upon a musical instrument, and not four in a hundred have any wish to learn how." This assertion does not demonstrate conclusively that mankind is not musical.

Questioning a writer's assumptions or premises allows you to understand the nature of the conclusion and determine the validity or soundness of the argument. Studying and questioning writers' arguments help you to develop your critical thinking skills. Practicing both activities with other writers' texts will help you understand how you as a writer can evaluate the patterns of reasoning in your own analytic or argumentative essays and revise your text to present convincing arguments.

WRITING PERSUASIVELY

Reading and rereading an essay, poem, or short story and questioning the main ideas in that text and your reactions to those ideas are the methods by which you evaluate and judge an essay. You are searching for the writer's main ideas, your agreement or disagreement with those ideas, and experiences you have had that support or contradict the writer's ideas. You also are questioning the writer's style, the way the ideas are presented, and the number and quality of the examples or details. Asking yourself questions about an essay or story you read not only helps you understand and judge the writer's main points, it also suggests ideas you can use when you compose. Just as identifying general ideas in an essay or story is not enough for critical readers, presenting your ideas without judging them by the same standards is insufficient. You need to inventory your reactions to a reading or a subject, assess your audience, determine your purpose in writing, and write and revise your essay. In other words, you need to compose your own argumentative essay.

Most successful argumentative writing comes from writers' opinions, often strongly held ones, that demand written attention. Yet not all opinions necessarily prompt effective arguments. Matters of taste or style, for instance, seldom merit formal arguments. If your roommate loves blue but you prefer red, there is little room for argument. But, if your roommate wants to redecorate your shared apartment in blue and you disagree, there are grounds for discussion, argument, and eventually compromise. Your roommate will want to present reasons why blue is preferable to the apartment's current color scheme and why blue is preferable to any other color. The disagreement, perhaps a heated one, can be argued, whereas personal preferences cannot.

Similarly, if you read an essay or story and find that you disagree with the writer's main point, the way the writer supported the essay's points, or the implications the writer draws from the presented evidence, you have formed an opinion and have begun the process of gathering information to use in your writing. Examine your disagreement carefully to ensure that you either know enough about the topic or that you can find enough information about the topic to begin writing. Without sufficient information, you may have difficulty deciding on a topic, forming and narrowing a thesis statement, creating appropriate generalizations, and providing sufficient support.

Finding Thesis Statements

A thesis statement is a proposition or assertion—sometimes one sentence, often more than one sentence—that will guide your audience through your argument or discussion. Thesis statements respond to a situation or propose a responsible solution for a question posed by another writer, event, predicament, or inquiry by describing to your readers what your essay is about, what position you are committed to and so are arguing for, and how you will present evidence for that position.

When you write an essay, you should remember that most readers are more interested in the journey than the destination *if they are sure of what that destination is;* they care more about how you reach your conclusion than what that conclusion is. Without a statement of your thesis, your argument or analysis will seem purposeless to your readers. They will sense what you may already know: that you are writing either for yourself or writing just to be writing. Thus, to satisfy your audience you as a writer need to forecast your destination (narrow and focus your topic), select the route your readers will follow (formulate your thesis statement), and identify points of interest (organize and support the main ideas).

Drafting a Thesis Statement

Although it guides readers through arguments and analyses, the thesis statement is seldom the first sentence in an essay nor the first statement you as a writer will compose. In fact, you may find yourself devising your thesis near the end of your first or second **draft** after you have put the problem you are evaluating on paper so you can examine it more systematically and objectively. Rough drafts are the necessary raw material of any writing—not the essays themselves. Drafts seldom have thesis statements because they are discovery documents for a private audience: you as a writer are discovering your positions, searching for the edge you can take on a question, inquiring of yourself how you can responsibly convince yourself. Rough drafts force you to decide what point is actually at issue and what you can or cannot support about a topic. In a rough draft you discriminate between opinion and an arguable statement; you reject the form so you can shape the latter into a tentative thesis statement, one that in your final draft tells your readers what your observations, deductions, and evidence will prove.

In order to write an essay in response to a particular text, you will have to narrow and clarify your focus to those responses, ideas, and feelings that seem most important to *you*. The ability to move from a broad subject to a defined topic and from this topic to a specific thesis statement is a problem-solving strategy essential to the writing process. Such strategies are closely allied to the processes of finding an issue in an essay (i.e., critical reading), of recognizing reasoning techniques (i.e., critical thinking), and of evaluating readers (i.e., analyzing audiences). Problem solving, whether in reading, thinking, or writing, involves your interests, your curiosity, and the responses that your curiosity prompts.

Problem-solving strategies require that you ask questions and propose solutions to those questions. Therefore, to narrow a subject and focus on a topic, you begin by asking yourself what problems a particular subject suggests and deciding what your solutions are to those problems. Some of the questions you will want to consider as you begin to draft your essay and its thesis statement include questions about topic, point of view, and goals.

Questions about topics: Are there opposing ideas about this topic? Does the topic imply any further problems? Could readers have different points of view about this topic?

Questions about your position: What do I believe about this topic? Is my belief an opinion, formed from my personal preferences, or an arguable statement, formed from my reasoning and evaluation of this issue? What is my point of view about it? Is this point of view based on my experiences, on other people's experiences, or on my thinking about the topic?

Questions about goals: What do I want my readers to understand about my point of view? What evidence do I have that will convince my audience that I have an argument or an analysis rather than an unsupported belief? Do I want my readers to change their point of view to fit mine, to include my point of view in theirs, or to reject their position in favor of mine?

Narrowing a Subject

Suppose your political science professor assigns you a short evaluative essay on a topic of your choice. The instructor provides you with several essays about governments to read and asks you to write about an aspect of "government" that engenders argument. After reading the essays you realize that government cannot be your topic because it is obviously too broad. In fact, government is not a topic; it's a complex subject with unlimited possible topics. You must immediately begin to narrow that broad subject to something you know enough about to discuss in a short analytic essay. Start by asking yourself questions about your reading and what interested you or confused you in that reading. With pencil in hand, write down your responses, queries, doodles, misgivings, assertions, "what ifs," frustrations, and—most importantly—reactions. Initially you may narrow this broad subject by considering some of the ideas in government such as the differences between economic philosophies behind governments. Two such philosophies would be capitalism and communism. However, a thesis statement such as "Capitalism and communism are competing economic philosophies" is still too broad, complex, and undefined for a short analysis. Trying to define *capitalism* or *communism* indicates the problem: pure capitalism or communism seems not to exist. In fact, many different governments can be called capitalistic or communistic. Perhaps the forms of government that may appear under one or both systems would be less cumbersome. An essay, perhaps, on military dictatorship, oligarchy, technocracy, representative democracy, monarchy? These are better subjects because they are more focused, but they are still too broad to be dealt with in a short essay.

Focusing on a Topic

What you have done is to question and to simplify the broad subject and to identify narrower subjects. You have a sense of direction. One way to proceed now is to pick one of these more restricted subjects and outline what you know about this subject. But this process leads to exposition: you will end up describing for your readers what this topic is and not why this topic or your position on it should interest them. Another way to proceed is to take a restricted topic, such as representative democracy, and ask yourself not only what do you know about it but what about this form of government would make it appealing or unappealing. As you consider representative democracy, you will quickly realize that it has several components. Which ones interest you the most? Its structure? Function? Processes? If you chose its processes, which ones? Electoral? Legislative? Enforcement? At this stage trying to form a thesis statement is helpful as long as you realize that the assertion you write probably will not be the thesis statement you decide on. A thesis statement such as "Representative democracy answers the needs of its people better than other forms of government" restricts the original subject (government) to a more manageable one (representative democracy) and presents an opinion (your preference for this system), but you still need to narrow your **focus.** If you write down your reactions to this tentative thesis, you find you must still define broad concepts such as *representative democracy, other forms of government,* and *needs.* Question yourself more carefully, uncritically writing down your responses.

After thinking about the concept of representative democracy, you may decide that the heart of such a concept is the process by which our ideas become the laws that govern not only ourselves but others. In an expository essay you might detail how this process happens, how bills become laws, or, perhaps, the nature of laws within the legislative system. In an analytic essay, you might take one of these subtopics and evaluate the procedure in your home state. However, your audience, the political science professor, wants an argumentative essay, a **document** that takes a side in a governmental debate and persuades the audience that one position *must* supersede another. You are still at the drawing board, sketching with bolder lines your essay's topic.

When you think about how bills become laws in your state, you might question your reaction to the process. Do you approve or disapprove of the process or the results? Do the results justify the process? Whose interests are mainly served in the legislative process? Is your legislature paternalistic, managing citizens' affairs as a father would his child's? If it is, is paternalistic legislation always a bad thing? Is it better for citizens to be guided by the government or for them to make their own decisions? At this point, you have discovered your topic ("representative democracy"), the idea within the broad subject ("government"), and focused on an aspect of that topic ("paternalistic legislation") which contains an arguable statement, the outline of your thesis statement.

Forming a Working Thesis Statement

Writing down your initial reactions to paternalistic legislation should cause you to recognize that you still have some narrowing to do. You have defined the concept for yourself, but you must identify your attitude toward the topic and present that attitude as a reasoned, objective thesis and not a personal, subjective opinion. Opinions in arguments are superficial responses such as "Yes, I agree with paternalistic legislation" or "No, I don't like such legislation." You cannot prove opinions; you can merely have them. But you can reshape your opinions into statements that help your reader to focus on the real issue in your essay: the reasons why you feel the way you do and the criteria, or standards, you are using to make your judgment. Are your standards factual or based on logic? If factual, for example, you will want to devise a thesis that systematically summarizes the specific points you will make. More helpful than an absolute statement such as "Paternalistic legislation is always a bad thing" is a statement that qualifies your judgment and indicates to your reader how you will present your points of view. An example of a working thesis statement, one that can change as you develop your essay, is:

Paternalistic legislation can be a bad system *because* it reduces to a common denominator all activity without regard to special circumstances and *because* it implies that adults cannot make decisions for themselves.

Graphically, the process you have followed looks like this:

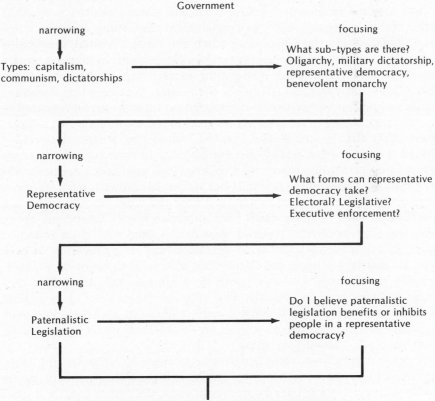

Now you have a specific thesis that states your attitude toward an idea and indicates why you hold that attitude; you have simplified a very complex idea to a few relatively manageable ones. You have narrowed a broad subject, "government," to a narrow subject, "representative democracy," to a topic, "legislation," to a restricted topic, "paternalistic legislation," to, finally, a thesis giving your judgment and reasons for that judgment.

Determining Your Audience

Whatever you write will be read by someone. Whoever that person is will want your prose to make sense, that is, to communicate. Thus, one important technique that informs good writing is knowing who the audience is for your writing.

At first it seems superficial to speculate about what an audience is or how you identify your audience. Obviously, your audience is whoever reads your writing. However, the concept of audience is complicated. There are no formulas or "recipes" that will always identify your audience correctly because each writing situation is unique. In some cases your audience may be yourself, as when you write a journal, keep notes for class, or write a rough draft for a class assignment. In journals, notes, or rough drafts you write down your ideas, trying to organize them quickly so that you can understand them later. You are a real audience, an actual person whose need for information must be accommodated.

At other times you need to write for other real audiences, specific persons other than yourself. For example, when you write a letter to a friend or a relative, a report or memorandum to your supervisor, or an essay or examination answer for a college class, you have a defined audience who knows some of the facts but who needs either further information about a subject or to understand how the facts are related to one another. In each of these cases your audience knows something about you and expects certain types of information from you. Your friend or relative will want to know what you have been doing recently or how you are enjoying school; your supervisor will want to know what information will help him or her complete a project; your instructor will want to know how successfully you have integrated your ideas or how well you have understood someone else's ideas. In each instance your audience has specific needs—either for information or for confirmation that you have learned something.

Understanding how your perspective changes in your writing from emphasizing your own needs to emphasizing another person's needs helps you develop a keener awareness of audience. Other equally important considerations about audience quickly follow. A letter to your parents, for instance, describing a party you attended last weekend is not the same letter you would send to a friend or to a lawyer describing the same party. The structures, examples, tone, and emphasis you use for your parents are not the ones that best communicate your situation to your lawyer. These different audiences expect different things.

Your other audiences may be more ambiguous and more difficult to characterize. When you write a letter to the editor of your local newspaper or school newspaper, the audience is ostensibly the editor. However, the actual audience is a much larger one: all possible readers of the newspaper. When you write a report about your company, the audience may be the chief executive officer, the board of directors, the managers and administrators, the company's stockholders, or even people interested in investing in the company or seeking employment with the company. Although you know much less about public audiences than you do about the audience for a letter, a college assignment, or a specific memorandum, public audiences are not complete mysteries. Not knowing their names or their preconceived ideas does not diminish your responsibility to evaluate them or to speculate on their prejudices. Public audiences are extensions of general readers; they demand that you put yourself in their place, asking every question you can about a topic, evaluating every answer for them, and presenting your thinking as if it were clearly their own. In general, remember that the less you know about your audience, the more demanding the assignment becomes and the more you must try to become your audience.

Audiences are especially important when you are writing arguments or analyses because these modes of discourse seek to influence by changing readers' minds about a topic or to inform by showing readers how to interpret a concept. In writing arguments or analyses the audience you are addressing determines which aspect of an issue warrants your attention. An audience that accepts your point of view, that does not want to be convinced, or that already understands a concept sufficiently will not require carefully detailed evaluations. Your essay confirms rather than challenges their viewpoints. Because they need little convincing, familiar audiences depend more on key words and phrases than on lengthy background explanations. Additionally, this audience will welcome jargon, **generalizations,** and, if used judiciously, some informality.

However, an audience that hold views opposing yours or that actively seeks information challenges your abilities as a writer. This skeptical, inquiring audience—the critical readers we have already outlined—is neither wrongheaded, ignorant, nor necessarily careless. They are unfamiliar with you or your topic and, consequently, less trusting; because they are more critical, they require detailed evidence and carefully structured arguments. To reach a skeptical or unfamiliar audience demands that you as a writer know why you accept an assertion; that you anticipate the evidence that refutes your position; that you offer counterarguments, concessions, and concrete examples of your position; and that you present your argument or analysis in a thoughtful, fair-minded style. Persuading skeptical audiences requires thought rather than belligerence, selectivity rather than bombast, planning rather than confusion.

Analyzing Audience Profiles

To judge their similarities or differences, writers have traditionally analyzed potential audiences by inventing profiles of them. Writers ask themselves questions about their readers' backgrounds, such as probable socioeconomic level, age, education, occupation, and level of intelligence. Whether accurate or speculative, reader profiles assist writers when they draft and revise in much the same way that asking questions while reading helps critical readers evaluate a text. As a critical reader your questions about the writer's **point of view,** organization, and support draw you into the writer's world; they allow you to see a situation or problem and its proposed solution through another's eyes. As a writer the profiles you create draw you into the readers' world; they assist you in anticipating what questions or objections readers could have and in answering those concerns before they are asked. Audience profiles are merely assumptions that writers make about their readers' expectations. The more complete you are in determining the attributes of your audience, the more likely you will understand what information and form of presentation your readers demand.

Although there are no foolproof strategies for analyzing your audience, knowing something about your audience's background, attitudes, and requirements can help you to identify who your audience is, to anticipate what you will have to tell that audience, and to structure your essay so it communicates effectively. Further, your assumptions about your audience can suggest how best to organize your material, how many and what types of support you should include, and what tone you should adopt.

BACKGROUND AND KNOWLEDGE. If you and your audience have read the same essay, seen the same movie, or heard the same lecture, then you share some common ground. You both were presented with the same facts although you may not share the same impressions of those facts. Thus, although it should refer to this shared experience, your essay must detail your responses to the experience rather than retell it. Using your shared experience, you can show your readers why they should agree with your response to an essay, what they should understand about the characters or the action in a movie, or how they should react to the ideas presented in a lecture.

ATTITUDE.   If you and your readers see an issue the same way, such as where the best vacation spots are or who should be the next president of your school, then you share a certain attitude about the issue with your audience. The more your audience's attitudes agree with yours, the easier the essay is to write. You are retelling, with more discussion and detail, what you believe about an issue. However, the more your audience's attitudes differ from yours, the more formidable the essay is to write. You are changing someone else's point of view, so you will need to explain your position, exemplify it, and organize your reasoning for it carefully.

NEEDS.   If your audience is expected to take action based on your document, then that audience's needs are very clear. For example, if you are applying for a job, your audience needs to know who you are, what job you are applying for, and what qualifications you have for the job. Your audience may also be interested in what you think about your school or in your career goals, but their primary interest is in what you can do. Your writing will tell this audience whether it can expect to gain a good worker if you are hired.

In your English composition class, your audience's needs may seem less concrete than a potential employer's, but that audience has specific needs too. In any writing class, essay assignments are designed to teach you something either about a topic (such as art, music, or politics) or about a type of writing (such as analysis or argumentation). Thus, your teacher approximates a potential employer: both are real audiences with specific needs. Your teacher needs to know if you are learning specific skills; the potential employer needs to know if you can do a certain job. Each needs—and expects—certain information and is disappointed when that information is obscured.

Consider, as an example of background, attitudes, and needs, your English composition instructor as your audience and the problem to be solved an assignment to argue who should be the next president of your college. The problem is twofold: you must decide what your solution to the question is, and you must determine how best to argue your point of view with an audience that may have already evaluated this problem and arrived at a different conclusion. Reaffirming mutual beliefs is comparatively simple; convincing an audience that may not already share your attitude toward a subject requires critical thinking and anticipating possible prejudices and counter-responses. You are literally putting yourself in your audience's place and trying to second guess what that audience thinks. For example, if you believe that your school should hire someone from private business as its next president but you are unsure of what your instructor believes, you should ask yourself what objections could be raised about your position. Possible questions your audience could pose are the following: Why would a business executive be a good choice? What expertise could this person provide that would benefit the students and faculty? What would the new president need to know about education and, specifically, your school? Is this knowledge best gained as an insider, someone who has worked for educational institutions, or from someone with a broader or more various perspective? Asking and answering questions such as these forces you to see a topic from your audience's point of view, anticipate what attitudes that audience might have, form a position that can persuade your audience, and present that position in terms of your audience's needs.

Before you draft a text—whether it is a letter home, a job application, an essay examination, a formal report, or an argumentative or analytic essay for a college instructor—consider questions such as the following:

Questions about audience's background: Who is my audience? How well do they know me? How well do I know them? If I drew a composite picture of my audience's personality, what would it be? What is my audience's political, social, or educational background? How does this background fit my subject? How much background information does my audience share with me about the topic? What will my audience not know about the subject or my position on it?

Questions about audience's knowledge: Is my audience interested in this subject or interested in how I approach this subject? Why should my readers be interested in my subject? Do my readers need to have simple information about a subject, to have their opinions reinforced, or to have their views on a subject expanded? If my audience knows a great deal about my subject, how much explanation should I include? If they know very little about my subject, what should I tell them to make it clearer?

Questions about audience's attitude: What are my readers' basic attitudes toward my topic and my stand on that topic? Is my audience formal, informal, or casual? Is it demanding or easily pleased? What details or examples can I include in my essay that will speak to their political, social, or educational background? If my audience expects certain vocabulary, organization, or style because of its background, what will be their attitude if I vary these stylistic elements?

Questions about audience's needs: What are my audience's needs? What do they need to gain from reading my essay? What do I hope they will learn? What do they need to know about the subject? If someone else were writing on my subject, what would I want them to say to me as their audience? What would my expectations as a reader be?

Advancing Arguments and Analyses Through Examples

Essays are convincing when they present generalizations supported by specific examples. Knowing when to provide an **example** is a matter of knowing your audience. In at least the four basic instances that follow you should give readers examples:

1. writing about general concepts for public audiences
2. writing about complex ideas for critical readers
3. writing about controversial subjects for all audiences
4. writing about subjects outside your professional expertise

General Concepts Defined for Public Audiences

If your audience is an unfamiliar one, one that either does not know you or your position, you should provide examples for them that you believe would be familiar to any interested reader. Without such examples, your readers may dismiss your assertions as hasty generalizations, conclusions reached without sufficient study or interpretation of events, data, or evidence. For example, when Edwin S. Gaustad in "A Delineation of Dissent" (pp. 113–117) states that "all societies, even those that cry out against all change, require a mechanism for change," his statement is too broad to be easily understood. Without examples, Gaustad invites readers to reject his assertion because, for instance, he has failed to define *mechanism for change* and so left the concept open for multiple and possibly incorrect interpretations. However, he avoids this criticism by clarifying *mechanism for change* through exemplification when he writes "if the written law resembles that of the Medes and Persians, then there must be an oral law, a livelier tradition, a juicier commentary. . . ." With this statement Gaustad not only explains and defines what he means by "mechanism for change," he also places his assertion in an historical and cultural context by forcing critical readers to consult their dictionaries and encyclopedias and refresh their knowledge on Medes, Persia, and oral legal traditions.

Complex Ideas Made Understandable

If you are defining or evaluating a complex idea, you should clarify it by many examples because complex ideas may be new or confusing to your audience. Although most critical readers welcome the mental challenges a complex idea presents, they embrace the idea more readily when the writer illustrates it. For instance, in Ethan Canin's short story "The Emperor of the Air" (pp. 363–374), the **narrator** feels that his neighbor Mr. Pike has no soul. But the definition of *soul* often gets confused with the word's connotations and with the religious, moral, or ethical background readers impose on it. To understand Canin's presentation of Mr. Pike, readers need to understand what Canin, through his narrator, means by soul. Canin illustrates his concept of soul by contrasting Pike's repeated complaints about the elm tree, his insistence on a bomb shelter, and his blunt statements with his amateurish attribution of fanciful, imaginative names for the traditional scientific names of the constellations. Readers—and the narrator—discover, of course, that Mr. Pike indeed has a soul; but this discovery does not come through moralizing statements but rather through a provocative, specific event. Interestingly, if readers were unfamiliar with the terms *fanciful* and *imaginative,* they would find Mr. Pike's names give the terms substance and definition.

Furthermore, if examples are to succeed in clarifying complex ideas, they must be familiar to the audience and appropriate for the writing context. Again, Canin's short story provides an excellent example. Mr. Pike's names for the constellations are relevant examples for Canin's protagonist because he is an astronomer. Through the narrator's understanding, the readers come to the same understanding. Like Canin, Michael Guillen also uses familiar examples in "The Familiar Faces of Change" (pp. 485–493) as signposts to help his readers understand his ideas. Guillen assumes an interested general reader, rather than a scientist, when he picks examples such as balloon inflation and "toy metal frogs" to expand his scientific definition of *catastrophe.*

Controversial Ideas Demand Persuasive Illustration

If you are writing about a contemporary controversy, you should define it objectively so you can avoid offending readers who may not understand either the idea or your position. Critical readers or an audience you suspect disagrees with your viewpoint will expect more illustrations to support a thesis on a controversial issue than a sympathetic audience would. Yet, even with several illustrations, you may not be able to convince a hostile audience. Thomas Jefferson, for example, filled the Declaration of Independence (pp. 118–122) with examples of King George III's transgressions. Although he knew British readers would never be swayed to his position, Jefferson was convinced that his real audience, the other colonists, needed justifications for rebellion. In the late eighteenth century, Jefferson's contemporaries generally believed in the divine right of kings and in a clear hierarchy or ruling order. By arguing for the overthrow of a recognized authority (that is, King George and his representatives), Jefferson risked offending his readers, for what he proposed was the uprooting of their value system. Thus, Jefferson's details in the Declaration of Independence support his radical ideas. He not only gives the colonists specific reasons why they should indeed change their way of life, he also gives them substantive examples of the crown's exploitation of the colonies and a tyrant to rebel against in the person of George III. Thus, for the sake of emphasis and to build solidarity, he begins the first twelve points of the Declaration with *He*. Jefferson's technique is a common rhetorical strategy used to persuade. Edwin Guastad, perhaps remembering Jefferson's powerful examples, uses a similar technique in his essay when he summarizes events from the American Revolution to illustrate part of his argument.

Reasoned Evaluations Require Details

If you are writing about a topic new to you or about which you have limited knowledge, you will need to provide examples to show your readers that you have investigated and understood the basics of that topic. A good rule of thumb to remember is unless you are a recognized expert in a professional field it is difficult for critical readers to accept your statements on faith. Most readers, for example, will accept Carl Sagan's assertions about environmental issues or ecological or geologic changes because of his reputation as a scientist. However, the same readers require numerous examples from Sagan before they accept his claims on other topics such as political incompetence, critical thinking, or cultural change because they do not immediately credit Sagan as an expert on these topics. Readers' requirements from students learning a discipline are even more demanding. If your audience is to believe your assertions, therefore, you must support them with concrete evidence. Expanding an assertion by examples provides proof in an argument or analysis because examples refer to objective evidence.

Michael Brown's use of examples illustrates how a journalist not recognized as a scientific authority can write convincingly about an environmental controversy. In "The Road Back," an analysis of businesses and toxic chemicals excerpted from *Laying Waste*, Brown asserts that "[chemical] manufacturers not only downplayed the dangers [of toxic chemicals] but on occasion covered them up or kept them from entering newspapers." This statement is not necessarily believable without substantiation. Brown thus gives his readers a series of examples to support his point beginning with his least convincing example, the silence maintained by the Manufacturing Chemists Association, and ending with his most convincing example, the Stanford study. The latter clinches Brown's argument because it has dates, suggests relationships between two institutions, and mentions specific areas of knowledge, reports, and public understanding. Later in his essay, Brown again cites example after example to persuade his readers of both his credibility as a writer (i.e., his *persona*) and his argument that the public can force manufacturers to pay for their excesses in creating toxic waste sites. His examples identify specific steps that businesspeople, scientists, and citizens can take to eliminate the danger present in current waste sites and to minimize the health hazards to humans.

In addition to knowing when to use examples, you need to decide what type of examples to use. The best examples for your essays are shaped by an understanding of what you want your audience to accept and arise from information you know, experiences you have had, or data you can collect. Rather than believing that you have no examples or knowledge, question yourself about what you know and how you know it. Ask yourself questions such as the following:

What are typical attitudes, beliefs, or ideas that most people share about this topic?

Are there representative people or events that support this position?

Is there information available in newspapers, magazines, or books that would provide good examples?

What statistics advance the argument?

Knowing when to give your readers examples and what type of examples to provide will make your analyses clearer and your arguments more persuasive.

Revising and Editing: Making an Essay Understandable

Many writers draft their texts by jotting down all their thoughts on a topic, weeding through the ideas for the ones that hold the most promise, organizing those ideas into an outline, carefully composing an introduction, and, finally, completing the text by tying the points listed in the outline to the thesis suggested by the introduction. Other writers are less methodical. They may also begin by jotting down ideas and sorting the most promising ones from the least, but instead of outlining their thoughts these writers begin by drafting their essays. Often these writers will rewrite their drafts four, five, six or more times, each time adding new ideas, deleting inappropriate ones, rearranging others. At this point, some writers turn to a variety of revision aids. For example, some people review handbook rules to check sentence grammar and dictionaries to verify spelling. Others look at style manuals to check tone and language standards; still others look at college rhetorics to refresh themselves about possible organizational patterns. But, as you may have noticed, not all of these aids are really revision aids. Most of them help writers fix the words and sentences; in other words, they help writers edit or draft or evaluate the style. None of these aids help writers revise an essay.

As the previous paragraph implies, revising is more than just editing although editing is a part of revising. When you revise an essay, you rethink and reshape the ideas you are explaining; you resolve the differences between what you had in mind to write and what the essay actually says; you rethink your stand on an issue as well as the content and form of the essay. **Editing** an essay, on the other hand, is evaluating grammar, sentence structure, spelling, and handwriting to ensure that your usage is consistent with the accepted standards of written English; it is **proofreading,** standardizing your text so that you can communicate with your audience through the shared dialect of written English. Furthermore, revising and editing are not superfluous activities designed to take time away from other assignments. They are part of a process that begins with critical reading and characterizing your audience and continues through planning your ideas, organizing your thoughts, writing your first draft, and, finally, reformulating that draft. Thus your essay can be coherent and informative if you plan carefully, evaluate your writing critically, and revise the draft conscientiously.

Revising and Rethinking

After your first draft, your **revision** depends on your concept of audience. When you first start to write an essay, you have an audience in mind, one that will eventually read the final draft. You started with ideas and support for these ideas, fragmented bits and pieces of information that had to be fitted together in some order. In this rough draft, you put pieces together initially so that they made sense to you. Then you expanded them, provided additional examples and support, and perhaps rearranged some of them so that you could make your view of an issue understandable to another reader. Now you need to revise your initial attempt into a draft that will make your readers believe that your ideas and prose flow as smoothly as if they had never been fragmented at all.

Successful revisions are cyclical processes, sequences rather than hastily done, one-time events. In your first revision evaluate the information you have given your readers. You should give them all the information they need to understand your position—and only the information they need. Thus you need to reconsider your position on a topic and what facts prove your case. It is not sufficient to state your position: you have to prove to your readers that yours is a rational, supportable position. Without support and a rational organization, your prose implies that you are guessing about your stand.

To evaluate the **evidence** in your essay, ask yourself such questions as Do I need to add details to support a complex or controversial idea?

Have I used the same example to support two different ideas? Have I included ideas that do not develop my main point? Have I included ideas my readers already know or accept? Have I omitted ideas that my readers need to understand if they are to accept my analysis or argument? Have I included information that is of interest primarily to me?

Revising, however, is not just a matter of adding or deleting ideas and details. You have to direct the flow of information systematically. An argument, for example, is a controlled statement, not a catalog of every possible position. Outline your essay to find its main point. Circle this idea. Ask yourself whether your thesis statement, your position in the essay, is too broad or too narrow. Next, try to determine if you have subdivided your thesis statement into its related aspects. Find a sentence in each of the remaining paragraphs of your draft that restates, elaborates, or evaluates your main point. If these sentences are already in your draft, consider what they tell the reader about your thesis. Are these the points you think are most important? Are there alternatives to any of these sentences that would identify your position better? If these sentences are not in your draft, how can you provide them?

Once you are sure you have an identifiable thesis statement and clear subdivisions that support it, consider each subdivision. Is there a logical organization in the subdivision? For example, do your ideas move from least to most important, from most obvious to least obvious, from least controversial to most controversial? If you move the subdivisions around, will it strengthen your thesis? By looking at your draft in sections, rather than trying to revise and edit it all at once, you can easily identify where your organization might be disrupted, which sections need additional detail, and what details demand rearrangement.

After you have arranged the subdivisions of your draft into a logical sequence, look at the individual paragraphs in the draft. Joining sentences in a paragraph effectively means matching what you want to say—the paragraph's content—with a clear organization—the paragraph's structure. Structurally, sentences in a paragraph should be organized around a central topic so that the sentences string ideas about the topic together. But, just as there is no ideal length for a paragraph, there is no perfect organization for one either. Although writers are free to organize paragraphs in a variety of ways, one basic organization many writers use introduces a topic (T), restricts that topic (R), then illustrates or discusses that topic (I). The paragraph follows a pattern much like the one outlined for narrowing a subject to a thesis statement. In this organization, the topic appears in a sentence, usually called the **topic sentence,** stating the general subject matter of the paragraph. The restriction states the specific point of the paragraph, and the illustration gives readers evidence developing that restriction. Gould uses this pattern in the following paragraph from "Were Dinosaurs Dumb?":

If behavioral complexity is one consequence of mental power, then we might expect to uncover among dinosaurs some signs of social behavior that demand coordination, cohesiveness, and recognition. Indeed we do, and it cannot be accidental that these signs were overlooked when dinosaurs labored under the burden of a falsely imposed obtuseness. Multiple trackways have been uncovered, with evidence for more than twenty animals traveling together in parallel movements. Did some dinosaurs live in herds? At the Davenport Ranch sauropod trackway, small footprints lie in the center and larger ones at the periphery. Could it be that some dinosaurs traveled much as some advanced herbivorous mammals do today, with large adults at the borders sheltering juveniles in the center?

Gould's paragraph gives readers the topic (behavioral evidence for mental power) and its restriction (signs of that complexity) in the topic sentence. The remaining sentences in the paragraph develop the topic restriction by giving examples of and posing rhetorical questions about the "social behavior[s] that demand coordination, cohesiveness, and recognition." Characteristic of most tightly constructed essays, the topic and restriction of this paragraph refers to an idea advanced in the previous paragraph (i.e., that brain size is not correlated with mental capacity). The illustrations he cites prepare readers for the next paragraph, a discussion of seemingly useless behavior that, when analyzed, implies an intricate social system characteristic of intelligent beings.

Each paragraph in your essay should center on a particular issue raised in your thesis statement. As you revise the individual paragraphs, ask yourself whether the paragraph proves that you have read observantly, probed ideas deeply, considered implications carefully, and included specifics beyond the most obvious ones. If a paragraph has a general statement and two or three sentences illustrating that statement, readers assume that the writer included the paragraph for illustration only. If your paragraphs provide illustration without discussion, your readers may feel you have not investigated your topic sufficiently. However, if you create topic sentences for your paragraphs that not only support part of your thesis but also point out evidence for further implications, you create convincing, textured paragraphs.

Revising for Style

The term *style* is a much overused and even more misunderstood concept. Some people believe that writers add style to their texts the way dress designers add style to their collections—by changing a hemline or adding an accessory. Others believe that style is superfluous language added to divert readers' attention from unpleasant information. Still others see style as a set of features that can be evaluated in counting sentences in paragraphs, words in sentences, and syllables in words.

However, style actually designates the range of choices all writers have when they compose, choices that determine not only how writers give readers meaning but, in many cases, just what that meaning will be.

One important aspect of style is an understanding of where writers place information in their sentences and how this placement promotes or disrupts the coherence of their writing. Consider as an example the following paragraph from Gould's essay "Were Dinosaurs Dumb?":

> The discovery of dinosaurs in the nineteenth century provided, or so it appeared, a quintessential case for the negative correlation of size and smarts. With their pea brains and giant bodies, dinosaurs became a symbol of lumbering stupidity. Their extinction seemed only to confirm their flawed design.

Gould's audience for this paragraph is you, a general reader somewhat interested in this topic but without specialized knowledge or background in paleontology. His purpose is to interest his readers in his topic and to set up his argument that perceptions about size and intelligence may not be consistently accurate. We could revise Gould's style by simply manipulating his sentences, changing active voice verbs for passive ones or elevating the formality of his word choice. However, such manipulation does more than change Gould's style; it would also obscure or change his meaning. For example, changing the verbs in the paragraph makes it awkward:

> A quintessential case for the negative correlation of size and smarts was provided in the nineteenth century by the discovery of dinosaurs. Lumbering stupidity was symbolized by dinosaurs with their pea brains and giant bodies. Their flawed design was only confirmed by their extinction.

The revision presents readers with an unacceptable and inappropriate style not because the sentences in the paragraph are grammatically incorrect but because they are awkward. Readers no longer understand the meaning because they cannot sort out easily what information is important. All readers have certain expectations for sequences of sentences: they want sentences to follow one another logically. To help readers follow their discussions, most writers follow a common stylistic strategy: they introduce a *topic* in a sentence and then *comment* on it.

A sentence topic typically corresponds to the sentence's subject and introduces the writer's topic or concept for the sentence. It is "old" or "given" **information** that a writer assumes readers already understand or that a writer intends to discuss in the rest of a paragraph. A sentence comment is usually the sentence predicate and functions as an elaboration of the writer's concept. It is the "new" information that adds to readers' knowledge of the topic by commenting on the topic, illustrating it with details, suggesting comparisons for it, or presenting a rationale for it. Language theorists claim that information in the comment section of a sentence, like the final clincher paragraph of an argument, carries the greatest emphasis for readers.

Writing stylistically effective sentences, therefore, is a matter of placing information where readers expect to find it. Two helpful rules to use for this placement are

1. start sentences with "old" information keeping the topics of sentences in your paragraphs consistent
2. put information at the end of your sentence that is new to your readers, that is important to your argument, or that you want to emphasize

In other words, you as the writer control completely what a reader will remember as important information because whatever words you place at the ends of your sentences will by their placement be given emphasis.

To see how topics and comments appear, consider how information is placed in Gould's paragraph and in the stylistically unacceptable revision. Gould's first sentence emphasizes for readers that dinosaurs seem to confirm the idea that size does not equal intelligence. Gould's second sentence balances the first by beginning with a specific example of size ("their pea brains") and smarts ("giant bodies"), information found in the comment section of the first sentence, and by moving to his comment on this topic, the dinosaurs' presumed "lumbering stupidity." His third sentence begins with common knowledge (i.e., that dinosaurs are extinct) and introduces an explanation for that knowledge (i.e., that they were flawed designs). Gould's paragraph links information by consistently flowing from common knowledge to less common assertions based on that knowledge. His style makes his assertions clear and meaningful.

The revision confuses this flow of information. The first sentence of the revision implies that the discovery of dinosaurs rather than the correlation between size and intelligence should be important. Yet the second sentence begins with information about lumbering stupidity rather than discovery. The third sentence seems to connect with the previous sentence because "flawed design" could relate to "lumbering stupidity"; however, the paragraph ends by emphasizing extinction rather than discovery and leaves readers confused rather than interested.

As these brief examples show, writers should review where they have placed information and remember that most readers expect older, more familiar information before newer, less well known or understood information. When these expectations are met, readers adjust comfortably to the writer's presentation and style. When these expectations are not met (if, for example, the commentary appears before the subject or if a writer includes additional information by varying syntactical patterns), then readers are required to work harder to understand ideas and may find the writer's style obtuse and inappropriate.

A second and equally important stylistic consideration is **diction,** the kind of words a writer chooses to communicate an idea. Making the diction of an essay stylistically appropriate does not mean substituting a fancy word for a plain one. Such substitutions typically frustrate meaning and readers. Instead, appropriate diction means providing the level of language that meets your audience's expectations. For example, if an audience needs technical information about a topic, that audience will expect technical jargon, terminology specific to a field of study. If, however, your audience expects you to analyze an article you have read or to present your position on a theory, that audience expects formal prose, diction free of **colloquial language** (e.g., *a lot of, sort of*), slang, or regional expressions.

Consider the paragraph from Gould's essay again. Gould prefers a mixture of formal but identifiable words (e.g., *quintessential, negative correlation*) with informal yet descriptive ones (e.g., *smarts, pea brains, lumbering*). Making the word choice more formal by including more scientific terms would limit the audience appeal: the more technical the terminology, the smaller the audience for the text. For example, in a revision *smarts* might become *intelligence, intellectual capacity, sagacity,* or *mental ratio; pea brains* might become *mental deficiency, stupidity,* or *hebetude.* These revisions, substituting more complex words for simpler ones, are perfectly appropriate in some contexts. However, making such substitutions for a general audience inflates the text's style and, consequently, discredits the author. On the other hand, making the word choice less formal would also limit the audience and call the writer's credibility into question because readers could interpret such informal diction as the writer's flippancy or disregard for the topic. Either choice has stylistic consequences.

Editing the Draft

Two other aspects of revision, providing **transitions** and reviewing **syntax,** complete the revision process by focusing on sentences. Indicating transitions means more than using conjunctions such as *therefore, however, in conclusion, in addition,* or *consequently.* To show your audience what connections you determine exist between and among sentences, you can use grammatical strategies such as appropriate word choice, consistent verb sequences, and clear pronoun references.

Consistent verb sequence simply means that, in a series of sentences, actions that occur at the same time appear in the same tense. Such consistency not only ties sentences in a paragraph together, it also moves your readers through your prose. Readers follow ideas more easily if they do not have to reread sections to understand a time sequence or determine whether something is a cause or an effect.

Establishing clear references for pronouns is important because pronouns have no real meaning of their own. They depend upon nouns, their antecedents, for their meaning. Thus, if a pronoun does not refer to a noun near it in the text, readers have difficulty following the prose. As you edit your sentences, circle any pronouns you find. Draw a line between the pronoun and the one word it refers to. If you cannot find an antecedent for a pronoun, either provide one, rewrite the sentence to eliminate the pronoun, or substitute a noun for the circled pronoun.

The final step in any revision process is to proofread the sentences in the draft. Read each sentence of your draft aloud. Does the sentence sound stilted, confused, unreasonable, overly complex or simple? Do the subject and verb agree? Have you followed accepted standards for punctuation? Are there any misspellings? Punctuation, sentence mechanics, and spelling are surface features of prose. Correcting the sentences will polish a well-organized detailed analysis or argument. By themselves, the surface features of sentences are no substitute for adequate content, appropriate form, or a clear stand on an issue. However, sentences that are easy for readers to understand help make an analysis or argument more convincing.

A Final Encouragement

No writer writes perfectly the first time. All good writers must revise. Although some writers are tempted to call the rough version of their ideas the final copy, most writers know that by rewriting their prose they make their ideas clear, understandable, and readable. Revising an essay is not a penalty for writing poorly the first time. It is an opportunity for you as a writer to manipulate the meaning in an essay so that the discourse says what you want it to say. Words do not control writers; writers control words.

PART TWO

Controversies
in the
Disciplines

INTRODUCTION TO THE ANTHOLOGY

Argument and Analysis presents essays and stories in eight sections. Each section focuses on a central issue that we believe holds intrinsic interest for all readers. The selections within each section can be read as differing opinions on a controversial theme. Viewed this way, the readings within any section encourage readers to see an issue both broadly and narrowly, that is, to see the larger picture but also see the discrete specifics of the picture. The readings have been selected to complement one another and promote productive questioning rather than provide definitive solutions. Resolving the perplexing issues raised by the various readings or suggesting easy resolutions was never our intent. The essays and stories are not texts with simple themes but ones that explore the multiple ideas clustered around any complex issue. Other thematic groupings are clearly possible. These themes have been chosen because they are speculative and suggestive, open-ended rather than limiting.

Yet the issues posed by the selections must never overshadow their usefulness as examples of writing. Beyond their value as explorations of controversies, the selections illustrate the tactics of argumentation. The information contained within them should stimulate discussion and debate—the basics of brainstorming that lead writers to compose. Readers gain when they inquire into the ideas, strategies, and techniques used by experienced writers. Such inquiry helps each reader to write by suggesting ideas about topics, controversial stands, and stylistic variations. Each writer represented in *Argument and Analysis* addresses an audience with a specific purpose in mind; each selects a tone appropriate to the issue under discussion; and each projects a persona, a voice to be trusted or questioned, through word choice (diction), sentence construction (syntax), and organization of the essay or story. For example, Benjamin Franklin's essay criticizes the idea of financing government service. The essay rewards careful inquiry into Franklin's use of inductive and deductive reasoning as persuasive techniques. It also illustrates the stylistic changes English has undergone since the eighteenth century. Samuel L. Clemens's critical review not only provides a template for assessing one type of literature but is also an interesting example of satire employed as literary criticism. Thus, throughout the anthology, the content of each reading is complemented by the writers' techniques for presentation. To guide readers of the anthology, a brief summary of each section follows, along with some suggestions for readings that work well together.

Section 1: Controversies in Education

This section is entitled "Controversies in Education" because each of the readings defends a position taken about education or analyzes a problem in education that differs in some degree from popularly held views. Marjorie Hope Nicolson's "The Romance of Scholarship," for example, challenges a popularly held view of the scholar, as well as the assumption that "education" ends with graduation. William J. Bennett and the members of the President's Commission on Education challenge the opinions of "experts" who have shaped American education. Like so many of the essays in *Argument and Analysis*, the selections in this section address additional questions. Nicolson, Langston Hughes, John Barth, and Plato, for instance, ask "Why learn?" and argue that the value of learning is related to the individual's sense of self-worth.

On the other hand, David Pichaske, (whose essay appears in To the Student), the members of the President's Commission, Secretary of Education Bennett, and Frances FitzGerald look at what should be taught. In the introduction to student readers, Pichaske offers a humorous analysis of how to learn to write competently. This essay can be read along with the commission's report, which—unlike Pichaske—blames student failure on administrators. Bennett discusses the failure of education to teach appropriate values, and FitzGerald's essay analyzes the values that surround and promote changes in the presentation of history. Each essay identifies a different culprit in the failure of American education.

In their presentations of unpopular or unexpected views, the authors represented here echo the views of the writers included in the sections on "Business Ethics," "Rights and Responsibilities," and "Controversies in Science." Each part of the text forces readers to think carefully about such pertinent questions as, What do we as a society value? What responsibilities do individuals have to preserve political or religious rights? What influences how people learn?

Section 2: Dissent: Rights or Responsibilities?

This section broadly addresses the issue of what makes a democratic society work. The essays identify certain societal boundaries and explore the ways in which people test these boundaries. Despite the rupture that can result from this testing, dissent is most commonly associated with the positive expansion of human rights and government responsibility. Jonathan Swift's "A Modest Proposal" attacks an economic and political system that destroys itself by allowing the subjugation, even brutalization, of a population. Richard P. Feynman's essay about the *Challenger* disaster exposes the breakdown of responsible decision making in a bureaucracy. Although separated by more than two centuries, Swift and Feynman both show how irresponsible government has dire consequences for the public.

Edwin Scott Gaustad and Thomas Jefferson address the need for citizens to fight the limits of government and the status quo. Their aim is to keep the human spirit alive. The *New Yorker* essay "Richard Nixon Is Back," Clemens's "Man the Irrational," Bruce Catton's "The Way of the Liberated," and Elizabeth Cady Stanton's "Address to the Temperance Society" can be read together to show how old boundaries can be changed.

Other essays in the book establish or realign boundaries. Some of these are Bennett's "What Value Is Values Education?," Adam Smith's "Why Not Call Up the Economists?," Carl Belz's "Rock As Folk Art," and Gloria Anzaldúa's "Movimientos de rebeldía y las culturas que traicionan." Each of these essays examines an aspect of culture and asks that we consider it in new and perhaps unfamiliar ways—each asks that we change the boundaries.

Section 3: Business Ethics

The readings in this section challenge widely held attitudes about business in various ways. In general, they show how typical business concerns can be at variance with the public interest, and they illustrate the way business ethics support "business as usual." In particular, Robert Thomas's "Is Corporate Executive Compensation Excessive?" and Franklin's "Reasons for Opposition to the Payment of Salaries to the Executive Branch" address the issue of salaries, with each coming to a radically different conclusion. Robert Samuelson's "The Budget Masquerade" and Peters's and Waterman's "Analytic Ivory Towers" warn of the dangers of ignoring key aspects when finding obvious solutions to a problem. In a similar vein, David Vogel's "Business without Science" and Smith's "Why Not Call Up the Economists?" decry doing business by relying on only one method of gaining information or setting strategies.

Overreliance on only one point of view is not just a problem in business, however. It is examined in a number of other works in the anthology that are not concerned with business. Among them are H. Beam Piper's "Omnilingual," Frances FitzGerald's "America Revised," Michael Brown's "The Road Back," and Mark Shapiro's "The Excludables."

Section 4: Gender and Culture

This section asks that we think about what makes up a culture. It particularly examines the diversity of American culture. Most of the essays deal with people who are separated from the mainstream by ethnic origin or gender. As a foundation, Hector St. John de Crèvecoeur provides us with an overview of what has come to be known as "American Character." Barre Toelken's "How Many Sheep Will It Hold?" and Joseph Little's "Whispers from a Dead World" explore the confrontation between mainstream America and the American Indian. Richard Rodriguez's "The Achievement of Desire" and Gloria Anzaldúa's "Movimientos de rebeldía y las culturas que traicionan" look at the pain associated with leaving their Hispanic culture behind in the process of assimilating to the mainstream. Piper's 'Omnilingual" and Pearl S. Buck's "America's Gunpowder Women" depict women who struggle to be accepted as part of the mainstream despite their gender. Finally, Dorothy Parker's "Good Soul" shows us that we reject some people precisely because they are too mainstream—caricatures of those traits considered essential to American character.

Elsewhere in the anthology, Clemens's essay eclipses Parker by presenting society's attitude toward those who are too good. Loren Eiseley's "The Bird and the Machine" forces readers to examine the problems of those who find their familiar ways being torn away; likewise, Ethan Canin's "The Emperor of the Air" describes a person wrenched out of his comfortable existence.

Section 5: Literary Analysis

This section presents a number of short stories that provide the opportunity for literary analysis. More importantly, the stories explore themes already encountered in the anthology; for example, the conflict between mainstream culture and ethnic identity, the need to take responsibility for our actions, and the conflict between an individual's rights and a society's demands. One purpose of literature is to present these issues and experiences in new, strange, and, therefore, exciting ways, and thus to make us better aware of the human condition.

The first work in this section, Clemens's "Fenimore Cooper's Literary Offenses," offers a classic piece of effective literary analysis. The remaining works are short stories, each representing in its own fashion the frailities of the human spirit. Irwin Shaw's "The Eighty-Yard Run" and Stephen Crane's "The Bride Comes to Yellow Sky" both show characters who find themselves in worlds in which they are not comfortable. Alexander Miller's "The 'Western'—A Theological Note," provides a provocative religious framework for interpreting Crane's story. Hortense Calisher's "Il Plœr Dä Mõ Kœr" and Willa Cather's "Paul's Case" illustrate what happens to characters who naively move out of their familiar worlds into worlds for which they are unprepared. Shirley Jackson's "The Possibility of Evil" and Canin's "The Emperor of the Air" reveal the darker side of human nature. This dark side is found in other works in the text: X. J. Kennedy's "Who Killed King Kong?" reveals one aspect of it and Jonathan Swift's "A Modest Proposal" another.

Section 6: Environmental Issues

The essays in this section have as a common theme the need to more fully understand our relationship with our environment. Yet the readings approach this theme very differently. Carl Sagan's "The Nuclear Winter" and TAPPS's "The Climatic Effects of Nuclear Winter" contrast a popular and a scientific discussion of the possibility of nuclear destruction of the environment. Blending a popular approach with scientific and legal approaches, Brown's "The Road Back" also addresses the fragile balance necessary in a healthy environment and the measures that must be taken to protect it.

Henry Petroski, Oscar Newman, Alfred Russel Wallace, and Loren Eiseley define environment somewhat differently. Petroski's "Design As Revision" and Newman's "Defensible Space" discuss the need to shape our environment to reflect our needs and interests, both on an individual and a societal level. Wallace's "The Importance of Dust" and Eiseley's "The Bird and the Machine" emphasize the importance of becoming more sensitive to aspects of our environment that we may have taken for granted.

The essays here share themes with other essays in the book. Brown raises some of the same concerns as Feynman, Franklin, FitzGerald, and Bennett, specifically, the consequences citizens incur when their representatives fail to act for the public good and to uphold the public faith. Newman and Petroski focus on an issue also raised in Canin's short story, that is, the need to make our world safe and comfortable.

Section 7: Controversies in Science

Like "Controversies in Education" or "Environmental Issues," this section offers essays about science that may run counter to popular conception or provide unexpected views. Stephen Jay Gould's "Were Dinosaurs Dumb?" offers a view of paleontology and dinosaurs that contradicts prevalent opinion. Yvonne Baskin's "The Way We Act" and James and Carol Gould's "Can a Bee Behave Intelligently?" use seemingly uncomplicated examples of behavior to show that our common understanding could be in error. These examples encourage us to reevaluate the logic we use to assess human motivation. Nicholas Wade's "What Science Can Learn from Science Frauds" and Lewis Thomas's "The Hazards of Science" lead readers to question the mystique that surrounds science. Michael Guillen's "The Familiar Faces of Change" and Isaac Asimov's "The Shape of Things" invite us to take inventory of our world, as a business executive would audit a company to determine its future.

Section 8: The Arts

In this section we find discussions of literature, film, painting, and music. These essays, like so many others in *Argument and Analysis*, provide unexpected approaches to their subjects. X.J. Kennedy's "Who Killed King Kong?" does more than simply review the 1932 movie; it also provides a surprising and effective sociological commentary. Shapiro's "The Excludables" and Ursula K. Le Guin's "Why Are Americans Afraid of Dragons?" address the issue of American society's unwillingness to accept ideas that run counter to commonly held views, a theme repeated in many of the essays on science and culture. Robin Longman's "Can a Figurative Work of Art Be Libelous?" portrays the frustrations of the artist in America; Patricia Nurse does something similar in a comic way in "One Rejection Too Many." Together, Belz's "Rock As Folk Art" and Aaron Copeland's "How We Listen" explore our responses to music. The essays motivate readers to reexamine the role of music in our lives. Further, applying Copeland's template to Belz's review of rock music tests both the logic of their arguments and their analyses of music. The questions of responsibility Longman raises are related to those Feynman raises in his speculations about the space shuttle, while Le Guin provides a view of American character that enlarges on the perceptions found in Crèvecoeur's "American Character," Toelken's "How Many Sheep Will It Hold?," and Buck's "America's Gunpowder Women."

Section 1

CONTROVERSIES IN EDUCATION

The Romance of Scholarship

Marjorie Hope Nicolson

Marjorie Hope Nicolson (1894–1981) was born in Yonkers, New York, the daughter of a newspaper editor and a homemaker. She received her early education in Halifax and attended the University of Michigan, earning her B.A. in 1914. Nicolson taught in the public school system in Detroit before completing her master's degree at Michigan and her Ph.D. at Yale University in 1920. She began her career as a university professor and researcher at the University of Minnesota. In 1926 Nicolson won a Guggenheim Fellowship that allowed her to spend a year in Europe, browsing through libraries and discovering old letters and documents. This experience, along with her university studies, confirmed her love of research.

In 1929 Nicolson was appointed dean at Smith College and later was made a professor of English and the chair of the English and comparative literature department at Columbia University. Nicolson's considerable achievements arose from her commitment to education. She was awarded sixteen honorary degrees from various institutions and was the first woman to win the Jon Addison Porter Prize from Yale University for original scholarship. She was also the first woman to be vice president of the Modern Language Association and the first woman to head Phi Beta Kappa, the distinguished honorary scholastic fraternity. Nicolson considered research and library work enjoyable challenges. In "The Romance of Scholarship," a commencement address to the 1952 graduating class of Scripps College, Nicolson retells her adventures, setbacks, and final successes as a young scholar in England. This essay, published in *The Humanities at Scripps College* (1952), explores the rewards any young scholar may find by digging into the past for the treasures it holds.

1   From the undergraduate point of view, I am sure, the title I have chosen will seem either irony or paradox. At your age you should and do know a good deal about "romance," but one of the last things with which you are likely to associate it is "scholarship." "Romance" is a light, charming word. In spite of teachers whom you admire and respect, "scholarship" is likely to seem a heavy word. I appreciate your point of view so much that I would not have attempted what I shall try to do now were it not for your president. Many years ago President Hard and I were fellow-students in the graduate school of the Johns Hopkins University where both of us discovered that there was romance in scholarship. He has asked me to try to describe to you another kind of romance than that you already know. I find my task an easier one here than it would be in many places, because the world in which you few, you happy few at Scripps, live has always seemed to me an enchanted land, one to which I return whenever I can with nostalgia. Here on the most exquisite campus in America, you should be able to understand enchantment.

2   "Scholarship," I have said, seems a hard word. The layman has inherited from literature, particularly from satire, a picture of the scholar as pedant, an elderly man (usually with thick glasses) spending his life in a dusty library, reading books which only a bookworm has visited before him, a man, as has often been said, who devotes his life to knowing more and more about less and less, perhaps like Browning's Grammarian:

> He settled *Hoti*'s business—let it be!—
>   Properly based *Oun*—
> Gave us the doctrine of the enclitic *De*,
>   Dead from the waist down.

I am told that Browning is a forgotten poet today. My own college generation was enthusiastic about him, and I am quite sure that some of my undergraduate feeling about the scholar as a learned pedant came from "A Grammarian's Funeral":

> So, he gowned him,
> Straight got by heart that book to its last page;
>   Learnèd we found him.
> Yea, but we found him bald too, eyes like lead,
>   Accents uncertain:
> . . . .
> Back to his book then: deeper dropped his head:
>   *Calculus* racked him:
> Leaden before, his eyes grew dross of lead:
>   *Tussis* attacked him.

One need not understand Browning's classico-medical puns to get a clear picture of the Grammarian. But even in youth I realized that the old scholar was a symbol of something else to the disciples who carried him to his grave on the mountain top, chanting the exultant last lines:

> Here's the top-peak; the multitude below
> Live, for they can, there;
> This man decided not to Live but Know—
> Bury this man there?
> ....
> Loftily lying,
> Leave him—still loftier than the world suspects,
> Living and dying.

3   In spite of what the world believed, the Grammarian *lived* and lived richly. But it is not that type of scholar with which I am primarily concerned, but with lesser fry like myself, as I set out on my task to try to show you that "scholarship" is not all baldness and spectacles and old age and great erudition. Within the last year or so a book appeared which some of you, I think, would enjoy and which in the future will bring back to you many memories of your English classes, *The Scholar Adventurers* by Richard Altick. It is the title even more than the book which I have in mind at the moment. There is no one of your teachers who does not know that scholarship is *adventure*—even more, that it is often *fun*.

4   Many years ago I set out on my first adventure which opened up to me a world of enchantment. I had taken my doctor's degree at Yale and had been teaching at Goucher and studying at the Hopkins, where your president and I met, when I read in the newspapers about a new Foundation established by Senator Guggenheim in memory of his dead son: the Guggenheim Foundation, which offered fellowships for foreign travel and study to young scholars. Today fellowships and scholarships are common, and foreign study and travel within the reach of many. It is not uncommon for undergraduates to spend "the Junior Year Abroad"; every year hundreds of young men and women just out of college receive Fulbright Fellowships; and other great Foundations—like the Rockefeller, the Ford, the American Council of Learned Societies—offer all sorts of opportunities unheard of in my generation. I could not believe what I read in that newspaper announcement, and I still did not believe it when I ventured to apply for a fellowship. The competition was less keen then than now, but it was still with a feeling that it was all incredible that I read the letter saying that I had been appointed. I wonder whether you can imagine how it seemed to me: in those days Guggenheim Fellowships paid twenty-five hundred dollars—more than the to-

tal annual salary I was receiving as an assistant professor. It was all incredible and overwhelming, and even when the letter-of-credit arrived, I still felt there must be some mistake. "This could not be I!" We have become so accustomed to the vast generosity of Foundations today that there are some who take such generosity for granted: someone owes them a living, someone owes them a fellowship. I myself have never forgotten, and I hope I shall never forget, the fact that the Guggenheim Foundation owed me nothing—and it gave me everything that was to matter in my professional life.

5 I had been to Europe once before. As a tourist I had seen the cities and countryside, paintings and sculpture, cottages and cathedrals. This time I saw all these again, to be sure, but most of my time was spent in buildings which the tourist seldom sees—libraries. The tourist, to be sure, usually visits the British Museum if for nothing else than to see the Elgin Marbles. But the path of the tourist ends where that of the scholar-adventurer begins: at those swinging doors marked "FOR READERS ONLY." Long before the tourists arrive in the morning, even before the great outer doors of the Museum open, the scholars begin to congregate on the steps, each eager to be the first arrival in order that he may claim the seat he feels his own—and woe betide any unwary casual reader who happens to take the seat of a "regular reader"! I can see them yet in my memory—the motley crew of early-morning scholars of my own *Wanderjahr*, some of them familiar to generations of Museum readers. Some of your teachers will remember them as vividly as do I. There was, for instance, the elderly Negro (his hair was grizzled in my time) who, rumor said, had never missed a day at his desk in fifteen years, during which time he drew out daily the same pile of books, all on elementary arithmetic. There was the very corpulent priest who, we knew, was compiling a bibliography, who seemed never to read books but only to read their titles in those great folio volumes which constitute the catalogue of the British Museum. Evidently he was as nearsighted as he was tall, so that he bent double over the volumes. He has gone down in history in an amusing caricature of "a reader finding his way through the catalogue by sense of *smell* only!" My own favorite was a demure little elderly woman in bonnet and shawl who might well have been a returned missionary of the Victorian era. She carried an old-fashioned reticule, and every hour-on-the-hour she drew out a flask from which she gulped a satisfying draught of something that certainly was not tea.

6 One could understand the little bonneted woman better as the winter days set in, the Museum daily colder, the pea-souper fog outside settling into the reading room so that the domed roof was obscured, spoiled Americans shivering as they looked forward to teatime when they might feel a momentary warmth. But there was not one of us reading there, I am sure, who did not feel the romance of that place even in the worst

possible weather. Sometimes I would stop my work, flexing my fingers, which were stiff with cold and cramped with copying, to think of that great host of readers of the past who had preceded us—for the library is far more venerable than the present building, which was a century old when I was working there. I thought of Lamb and Coleridge, who had used some of the books I myself was using. On more than one occasion I had found those characteristic marginalia of Coleridge, in the writing of which he enriched the library by breaking all library rules. Where, I wondered, had Karl Marx sat when he was developing the ideas which were to revolutionize the world far more than we realized in the 1920s? Surely even Marx must have been grateful for the wealth of the British Museum. Around me in dim recesses which I had never penetrated, stretched, I knew, some fifty-five miles of shelves, bearing more than three million volumes of that fabulous library. For a time I was content with the treasures I was finding in books. Later I was to discover even greater romance in the great manuscript collection of that library.

7   Is there, I wonder, any greater charm to a lover of the past than is found in manuscript? Nothing in my undergraduate or graduate training had prepared me for the excitement that was to come as I began to discover and piece together the correspondence of men and women who had lived nearly three centuries before.

8   The subject on which I was engaged was of little importance to anyone except myself—"scholarly" projects usually are not! I was seeking the correspondence of a minor philosopher of the seventeenth century, Henry More, the Cambridge Platonist. Many of his letters were in the British Museum—that much I knew. I shall not forget my shock when a volume of his manuscript letters was laid before me. I opened them eagerly—only to realize that I could not read a word of them! At no time in my graduate training had I ever worked with manuscripts, and my knowledge of different "hands" was only theoretical. The "Elizabethan hand," for example, is as unintelligible at first glance as is German script—and while More himself did not write an Elizabethan hand, his predecessors—equally necessary for my purposes—did. I had to stop and put myself to school all over again, studying until at length I could decode those handwritings. When I came back to my manuscripts, I discovered that the real trouble with Henry More's writing was one I shared—for my correspondents speak acrimoniously about what President Neilson used to call my "interesting but entirely illegible writing." Not only was Henry More's writing almost illegible, but—thrifty as he was—he wrote all over the margin of his pages, and sometimes turned the paper upside down and wrote between the lines. He had another habit which I shared until he cured me of it—he seldom dated his letters, other than to write "Monday" or "Wednesday," so that his letters were in no logical or chronological order, but had to be dated by internal

evidence, with blood, sweat, and tears on my part. Gradually, however, his hand became as familiar to me as that of any of my friends; gradually, too, order began to emerge from the chaos of his letters, and I could begin to surmise the richness of the story I had discovered. Here was a tale of Platonic love between a philosopher and a noble lady who were perhaps the last people in history who really understood what "Platonic love" meant. Here was a story of adventure and travel, of discovery of things but even more of ideas, bringing together on a broad canvas poets and philosophers, Quakers and charlatans, spiritists and scientists: William Harvey, discoverer of the circulation of the blood, Sir Theodore Mayerne, who introduced calomel into England and was the physician of three kings; scientists such as Robert Boyle, Thomas Willis, Isaac Newton, philosophers such as Descartes, Hobbes, Leibniz, Cudworth; Quakers such as William Penn, George Fox, George Keith; not least, one of the most universal characters of an age of universality, Francis Mercury van Helmont, alchemist, chemist, philosopher, adventurer, and the original Scholar Gypsy. Always in the midst of them, the center of the whole group, was a great lady, a woman who suffered from an incurable malady all her life, yet wrote an original philosophical treatise praised by the leading philosophers of her day, the Lady Anne Conway.

9   It is not the story that is of importance, however. What I remember best is the excitement of the chase, as I sought throughout England for the missing letters that would complete the story I could only guess from the one-sided correspondence with which I started. It was then that I came to understand the excitement and the adventure of the scholar's life—which often seems so drab and dull to the world outside the library. It was then, too, that I discovered the frustration, the hours of toil that seemingly led to nothing, the dead-end streets ending in a sign: "Turn back; no passing here." Let me give you an example. I started with known letters of Henry More, which he wrote to others; but what of the letters others wrote to him? I knew he had kept them—particularly those of Lady Conway—for they were mentioned in his will. But I could find no record of them in any college catalogue. Since he spent his whole life as a Fellow of Christ's College in Cambridge, it seemed as if some of his papers should be there—and there I started that part of my search. The librarian of Christ's was an elderly man who felt little need of a catalogue—since his memory *was* the catalogue. He assured me peremptorily (for he did not approve of women-scholars, particularly American barbarians) that there were no More manuscripts in the Christ's College Library. For four months I sought to track those manuscripts down, going to Somerset House to read wills, studying old catalogues of sales of books and manuscripts, using every device I could think of to find those missing links. At last I tracked some of the papers

down to the beginning of this century, at which time they had been in
the possession of someone named Robinson, of whom I knew nothing
except that he was a clergyman. I wrote to dozens of clergymen of the
name of Robinson, and finally after many weeks discovered that the person I sought was a very distinguished gentleman indeed, Dean Armitage
Robinson of Wells Cathedral. Eagerly I went to see him. Had he by
chance purchased any letters written to or by Henry More? He had, indeed. Breathlessly I asked what had become of them. "Oh," replied Dean
Robinson, "naturally I put them where they belonged—in the library of
Christ's College!" Four months after I had begun my search I was back
right where I started. The librarian still insisted he had no such papers,
but his insistence was surpassed only by my persistence. I found my
dust-covered papers where they had fallen on the shelf behind some old
folio volumes. I had no reason to regret the lost time, which was not
wasted, in part because I had learned by practical experience much that
I could never have learned in a classroom, in part because the chase had
led me from library to library throughout the length and breadth of England and had all been fun and excitement.

10   I wish there were time to tell you many of those adventures that made
the whole experience exciting, but I must deliberately limit myself only
to one or two. I wish I could take some of you with me to the Public
Record Office in London, that great repository of all state papers. For
years it was the natural Mecca of students of political history, but only
in my own generation has it become a haunt of students of literature. It
was there that Professor Leslie Hotson discovered the legal papers which
finally solved a three-hundred-year-old mystery which might be called
"The Strange Case of the Death of Christopher Marlowe." I remember
vividly the paper Professor Hotson wrote for *The Atlantic Monthly* in
which he described his emotions late one afternoon when after a search
of many months he held in his hands a legal document which gave the
clue to the mystery of the death of the great poet-dramatist who was
killed in a tavern brawl. Just as he started to read it the bell rang, indicating the end of the day at the Public Record Office—a sound as final
as that of the Trump of Doom. Without having had time to read the document, out staggered the professor, afraid to walk along the streets for
fear he might be hit by a car or bus before he knew the answer to the
puzzle, afraid even to go to bed that night since, as Mark Twain said,
most people die in their beds, spending the longest night of his life waiting until the Record Office reopened in the morning. Morning came at
last and with it the end of a chapter and the end of a search and an answer to the problem that had teased scholars for nearly three centuries.

11   The Public Record Office is not imposing. Indeed, at first sight it
seems very small in comparison with the reading room of the British
Museum. The press of scholars is to be there early enough to get near

the fire which heats the chilly rooms. At high rostrums stand scholars working in early fields whose materials come in long rolls—like gargantuan ticker tape. The manuscripts used by workers in fields like mine come to the reader in "bundles"—just bundles tied up in strong butcher-paper, wrapped with cord that always seems perversely to knot itself in fancy sailors' knots. One opens the bundle with growing excitement: certain political papers, one knows in advance, will be there, for they have been "calendared" (that is, published in brief digest form in the *Calendars of State Papers*). It is not for the "calendared" papers that the literary student looks, but for all sorts of other documents which may or may not be there, far more interesting to us than the political papers. Let me give you an example. The father-in-law of my Lady Conway, the first Viscount Conway, had been twice Secretary of State. I knew from the *Calendars* that many of his political papers were in the Public Record Office: it was my hope that included with them might be letters and documents of a much more personal nature.

12   I was richly rewarded, for in bundle after bundle I found the personal letters of a most charming and amusing gentleman who corresponded with a host of people, who seemed to have known everyone worth knowing in his day, who was a gourmet, and who had an eye for the ladies. Here were his order books, kept by a steward who ordered from abroad all sorts of gifts for the ladies, every kind of delicacy that could be imported. My Lord Conway liked the rich foods he ordered so lavishly; that was clear, for as the food-orders grew so too did Lord Conway, as I discovered when the steward noted that the tailor reported he must make his Lordship's breeches two inches larger than before. Lord Conway's was an impish humor, as his correspondents knew, and his personal letters sparkle with wit and irony. Among his correspondents was Sir Walter Raleigh's son, Garew, who had been with his father in the Tower during the imprisonment. On one occasion the younger Raleigh sent Conway a bundle of old medical recipes which he said had been his father's, and on another occasion he mentioned having in his possession many "verses and other discourses" of his father's—papers which have now disappeared, probably forever. The most amusing letters in my bundles were those Lord Conway exchanged with that extraordinary character Sir Kenelm Digby, scientist, philosopher, man of letters, great lover and Exhibitionist-in-Chief of the seventeenth century, who, married to the most beautiful woman of the time, sought to preserve her beauty by strange brews until—rumor said—he killed what he loved, inadvertently poisoning his wife. Dozens—even hundreds—of personal letters with their human stories of past ages lie in the Public Record Office, unpublished and often unread since their authors penned them and their correspondents received them two or three centuries ago.

13   From London my pursuit of lost letters led me to many parts of En-

gland. Sometimes I stopped in small towns or villages to read parish registers, in small libraries in churches—in some of which I found the old "locked" books (often Bibles) fastened with chains so they could be read but not taken from the library. More than once I was fortunate enough to find one of those antiquarians—often a local rector—who knew the local history of the parish, inheriting much of it from oral tradition that had come down for generations. Small libraries as well as great ones: in nearly all I had the same experience of being received with courtesy and kindness. Once in a while, to be sure, I found a dour old curmudgeon who objected to taking books from the shelves—largely, I gathered, because he thought that books belonged on shelves and not in the hands of itinerant scholars—but that was rare indeed. More and more I came to realize the goodly fellowship of scholars; that I was an unknown young person from a foreign country (and of the wrong sex) mattered not at all to most of them. I was a "scholar," and they—scholars in their way—did everything they could to further my pursuit. And always along the way came adventures and amusement.

14   I like to remember a day at Christ's College, Cambridge, after I had found my letters and had settled in and finally broken down the prejudices of the old librarian, so that he no longer objected to my youth or sex or nationality, but even shared his fire with me. I was waited upon by the college architect with a request that I visit one of the halls which had been built before the Civil War, all the records of which had been lost at the time the soldiers were quartered there in the 1640s. Because I had been reading so many letters of the period, he thought it possible that I might be able to identify some of the initials which students then as now had cut into the woodwork, or give him other clues as to who had lived in which room in the seventeenth century. All the fellows and dons were there to greet me; in twenty-three different rooms I was regaled with twenty-three cups of tea and twenty-three slices of what seemed the same tea-cakes. I know of Samuel Johnson's capacity for tea, which was greater than mine. I know, too, that since that day I have never drunk a cup of tea if I could possibly avoid it.

15   So the year went on and gradually my story book took on form and shape. From a chaos of crumbling letters, petitions, bills, and order books, from torn and faded journals and diaries, from wills, from commonplace books and college records, scattered throughout England, one character after another emerged in clear outline against a background of stirring events. It was a tale told against the background of one of the greatest periods in history, when the cannon thundered and England beheaded a king; when plague and pestilence and the Great Fire threatened to put an end to the London of the past, when that gallant city rose like a Phoenix from the ashes, as she was to rise from more terrible devastation in the twentieth century. It was an age when men everywhere,

emerging from a narrower, more circumscribed, safer world were questioning their beliefs; when the boundaries of the universe were enlarging as never before as the "new astronomy" destroyed those *flammantia moenia mundi* of the past, when a man, looking through a telescope, discovered universes of which men had never dreamed, when new philosophy called all in doubt, and men, finding their old values challenged, strove to build new values. Repercussions of all the many revolutions in that Century of Revolutions I found in my papers and letters. But all these things I had known before. What was new to me was the human side of a great century. As time went on these men and women of the past became as real to me as any friends of the present—more real perhaps because I knew them more intimately than one knows most friends. I had known that Lady Conway was a philosopher; I discovered her now as a woman—a woman who proudly made new curtains for her bedroom, only to find them too short so that she had to piece them; a woman who was pleased as any woman of any age with her new "muffle and cambrick." I knew all the medical treatments that were used for those excruciating headaches of hers, and followed with sympathy the gradual change in her handwriting as "fitt" after "fitt" of devastating illness laid her low. I knew that each coach her husband ordered that she might take the air had to be specially made, each one "softlier" than the one before, until the time came when she could no longer leave her house. I was with her when she became a Quaker—a shocking matter for a lady of quality in her day, and when she surrounded herself with Quaker handmaids, because, as she poignantly said, they were a "suffering" people and they were a "quiet" people. I seemed to be at her great home in Ragley when death came gradually, and a steward who loved her—as everyone who knew her loved her—set down day by day, then hour by hour, the account of her last illness. I knew how the great van Helmont preserved her body in "spirits of alcohol" in a glass coffin so that her husband—abroad in Ireland—might see her again and how she was finally laid to rest in the little village cemetery in a plain leaden casket on which someone scratched her only epitaph: "Quaker Lady."

16   And so at last I came to the end of my year—the end of my search. I had left until the last the great hall at Ragley which was her home, and which I seemed to have seen built, as she watched its building. It was a Sunday afternoon when a member of the family that now owns Ragley (the Conway line was extinct in the seventeenth century) took me into the house. I went into the bedroom where once had hung those curtains, pieced because they were too short. I went into the library and took down one after another books that I knew would be there. I stopped particularly over the volumes of his works which Henry More had sent her, each in its special binding ("volumes something handsomelyer bound up for your Ladiship"). I recognized some pieces of furniture she had bought, saw some familiar pictures on the walls and missed others that

had once been there. I had come home to a great hall which long was home to Anne Conway, which was the home-from-home of Henry More, who spent all his vacations there, which was a home too to such Quakers as William Penn and George Keith and George Fox. The shadow of the Scholar Gypsy—who had ceased his roving life for many years to minister to the comfort of a sick woman—was always around me.

17   Perhaps my guide became weary of my reminiscences which he could not share. At all events, at the end of the afternoon, he took me to a room I did not know—a room built in modern times, where no shadow of philosopher or lady or Scholar Gypsy could fall. It was a room in which they would not have been interested—a modern gun-room, filled with trophies of hunting and fishing. In the center of the room on a table was a glass case containing the skeleton of a tiny animal. "Here," said my guide, "is one mystery I wish you could solve." A few years before, he said, one of the greatest oaks at Ragley had been struck by lightning, and had been cut down. In the bole of that tree, preserved for many years, they found the skeleton of this little animal, which the curators of a great museum had told the family was that of a small dog, not native to England, a skeleton they estimated as being more than two hundred years old. Standing there in a modern gun-room of a great English estate, a young scholar from a foreign land experienced to the full the poignance, the mystery, the enchantment of scholarship which makes past and present one. My memory went back across dead centuries, as I realized that only I—and men and women dead for more than two hundred years—could know that that was Anne Conway's pet dog, which her brother had sent her from Italy, which had wandered away and been lost. I did not know whether it was recognition or remembrance, as I said: "That? Why that is Julietto."

Content Questions

1. Is Nicolson's title ironic and paradoxical?
2. From where do we derive our ideas about scholars?
3. Why was Nicolson's first hurdle in researching her ideas a problem?
4. Why can the circumstances surrounding Lady Conway's death be described as "romantic"?
5. What does Nicolson conclude is the value of scholarship?

Questions on Presentation

1. Why does Nicolson quote so extensively from Browning's poem? Would a summary of it be as effective? Why or why not?

2. In paragraph 4 Nicolson changes her tone and rhetorical approach. What is the new tone and approach? Why does she adopt these?
3. Why does Nicolson tell her audience about the other readers in the British Museum reading room?
4. How does Nicolson create a sense of adventure in her essay?
5. This is, in part, an essay of extended definition. Is Nicolson's definition of "scholarship" effective?

Theme for English B

Langston Hughes

Langston Hughes (1902–1967), poet, lyricist, playwright, and novelist, was born in Joplin, Missouri. After graduating from Lincoln University in 1929, Hughes went to work as a seaman. These early experiences gave him the background for his first autobiographical work *The Big Sea* (1940). In 1925 Hughes was the first black writer to win *Opportunity* magazine's poetry prize for his poem "The Weary Blues." He went on to win various awards including a Guggenheim Fellowship (1935), the Rosenwald Fellowship (1940), an American Academy of Arts and Letters Grant (1947), and the Ainsfield-Wolfe Award (1954) for the best book on race relations. In addition to his more serious works, such as *Montage of a Dream Deferred* (1951), Hughes also wrote the humorous collections *Simple Speaks His Mind* (1950) and *Simple Takes A Wife* (1953). Hughes' issues come from the experience of black Americans and his expression from the "blues." Although many of his poems are protests of blacks' second-class citizenship, Hughes' work is filled with sardonic humor. In this poem he explores one aspect of the variety of human experiences.

1 The instructor said,
    Go home and write
    a page tonight.
    And let that page come out of you—
    Then, it will be true.

2 I wonder if it's that simple?
I am twenty-two, colored, born in Winston-Salem.
I went to school there, then Durham, then here
to this college on the hill above Harlem.
I am the only colored student in my class.
The steps from the hill lead down into Harlem,

through a park, then I cross St. Nicholas,
Eighth Avenue, Seventh, and I come to the Y,
the Harlem Branch Y, where I take the elevator
up to my room, sit down, and write this page:

3 It's not easy to know what is true for you or me
at twenty-two, my age. But I guess I'm what
I feel and see and hear, Harlem, I hear you:
hear you, hear me—we two—you, me, talk on this page.
(I hear New York, too.) Me—who?

4 Well, I like to eat, sleep, drink, and be in love.
I like to work, read, learn, and understand life.
I like a pipe for a Christmas present,
or records—Bessie, bop, or Bach.
I guess being colored doesn't make me *not* like
the same things other folks like who are other races.
So will my page be colored that I write?
Being me, it will not be white.
But it will be
a part of you, instructor.
You are white—
yet a part of me, as I am a part of you.
That's American.
Sometimes perhaps you don't want to be a part of me.
Nor do I often want to be a part of you.
But we are, that's true!
As I learn from you,
I guess you learn from me—
although you're older—and white—
and somewhat more free.

5 This is my page for English B.

Content Questions

1. What conclusion does the speaker draw about the teacher's assignment?
2. What should the instructor learn from the speaker?
3. How will the speaker's essay be a part of both the speaker and his audience, the instructor?
4. Does the speaker's "essay" satisfy the requirements that the instructor set out for the essay?

Questions on Presentation

1. Stanzas in poems are frequently equated with paragraphs in an essay. What are the topics of each of Hughes' "paragraphs"?
2. As mentioned in the headnote, Hughes' work is filled with sardonic humor. What is sardonic humor? Where do you find examples of it in this poem?
3. Why does Hughes use shorter lines in stanza 4 but not in other stanzas?

What Value Is Values Education?

William J. Bennett

William J. Bennett was born in Brooklyn in 1943 and earned his doctorate in philosophy from the University of Texas at Austin and his law degree from Harvard University. He directed the National Humanities Center in Research Triangle Park, North Carolina, and is currently Secretary of Education in the Reagan administration. In the following essay, originally published in *The American Educator*, Bennett takes aim at current educational programs designed to teach students values and morals. Bennett argues that, no matter what disclaimers are made, values education cannot be impartial and objective.

1   Within the myriad values education programs available in our schools today, there is the common assertion that traditional values and traditional methods of teaching values won't do the job anymore. The world has changed so much, say the values educationists, that the old ways of teaching values do not apply to a world of new moral challenge.

2   Further, it is said that efforts to apply these old methods, to apply modeling or teaching by example, lead to the most awful thing in the world—indoctrination. Indoctrination is held to be a violation of the child's autonomy and his ability to think for himself. There is also the assertion that the teacher should be neutral about his or her values and should proceed by using neutral exercises—dilemmas and simulations that stress the child's need to come to his own values by himself.

3   The result of all this, however, is that values education programs in today's classrooms range from the inadequate and impoverished to the intolerable and detestable. Most of them are a waste of time.

4   Why do I believe this is so? First of all, values education programs are not at all neutral, in subject matter or technique. While they purport to

be objective and impartial, they are, in fact, biased in favor of particular ideologies. These ideologies most often are either inarticulate left-wing communitarianism or an equally inarticulate right-wing libertarianism. Interestingly, none of the biases I have observed are biased toward conservative values or toward the mixed liberal realism of the founding fathers. Rather, it seems that they are always biased toward what one might call the "trendy" ideologies.

5   It is certainly legal and constitutionally permissible to be left-wing communitarian or right-wing libertarian or trendy or Woodstockian, but one shouldn't be any of those things when one has promised to be neutral. Political values are values, and so is trendiness a value. In many values education exercises, for example, authority is identified over and over again with authoritarian. That is a mistake. Conventions of practice, for example, in marriage or in parent-child relationships, competition, or other values of liberal democratic societies, are always put to the burden of proof. Thus, in short, these programs fall by their own charge; that is, they are indoctrinative, if covertly so.

6   Values education programs also provide an impoverished view of morality. The materials recommended for use in values education programs—multiple choices, little paragraph dilemmas, and games—offer a severely diminished vision of students' and elders' moral lives and limit students to insufficient intellectual moral options. Values education exercises consistently present students with narrow choices and options and inadequate information in order to be able to make a good decision. From Sidney Simon, a leading values educationist, is an example of what I am talking about. Consider what is left in, and what is left out, of this example:

> All right class. Your husband or wife is a very attractive person. Your best friend is attracted to him or her—presumably one or the other. How would you want him or her to behave? The choices are (a) maintain a clandestine relationship so you wouldn't know about it; (b) be honest and accept the reality of the relationship; or (c) proceed with a divorce.

7   That's it—that's all the options. That is why they are impoverished. It is ironic that in a movement that stresses the child's freedom to make his own choices and create his own values, so much of the material ends up putting the child in a kind of moral straitjacket.

8   Because values educationists view moral life principally as a matter of making decisions about dilemmas in morally problematic matters, the ethically significant collapses into the ethically problematic. The problematic approach denies the most important part of morality, which is not the development of decision-making capacities, but the development of what used to be called, and can still be called, character—that is, dispositions and habits of mind and heart. A moral educationist's

model moral person is one who is always in doubt, in dilemma, tearing his hair out, trying to get clear about what to do. The moral individual, however, is rarely presented as a conscientious person, a person of character and equanimity, who, because of his character, doesn't have to face hard choices every ten minutes or every ten days.

9   Further, in the emphasis on games, role-playing, simulations, and the like, the assumption is made that one can become a better person by practicing in make-believe situations. At best, such exercises may disclose possibilities of action not previously considered by a student. At worst, these exercises do not test the character of students, because nothing is at stake. They are not a test of anybody's character; they are most often a test of a person's ability to think of possibilities. In assessing a person's behavior, we do not normally ask, "What possibilities did you think of?" The principal question is, "What did you do, and why?" The games and simulations played in values classes thus are a kind of failsafe. There is nothing to them in a true moral sense.

10   It is clear enough, for example, that professors of philosophy don't become better persons by studying philosophy. That's a different kind of exercise. What we are concerned with is the moral growth of children, and it may be that it is not moral philosophy that we want, but something else. Someone becomes more thoughtful not by these kinds of simulations but by acting more thoughtfully and by being encouraged and taught to do so in actual situations in which one finds oneself.

11   It is ironic that efforts are made to simulate moral situations when, in every school I have ever seen, there is an abundance of real situations involving right and wrong—matters and difficulties that invite real students and real teachers to address together.

12   It is certainly wrong to tell teachers not to tell students what their opinions are at appropriate times and not to tell students what they think they should do. That is why teachers have entered the profession in the first place—because they thought they could make a positive difference in the lives of students. Why must teachers, who have the students' best interests at stake, be silenced? Why are they to silence themselves when the rest of the world—people outside the school, pushers, street-corner flakes, etc.—are not similarly muzzled? If we stop teaching values, the task will simply pass to others.

13   Again, the values educationists have it backward. They attack indoctrination. There are things of value to be learned from the reflections, judgments, and opinions of men and women of principle; however, there are blessings from teaching, from indoctrination in the form of adults talking to children and telling them what they know and believe.

14   Nothing can make my final point of criticism of values educationists better than the words and practices of one of the leading values educa-

tion practitioners himself, Howard Kirschenbaum. In a book entitled *Advanced Value Clarification*, in a section called "Frequently Asked Questions About Our Practice," Kirschenbaum deals with the following question:

> "What about discipline, Professor Kirschenbaum? Supposing a fight breaks out in class. Do we do values clarification there? Is that the student's free choice?" Kirschenbaum answers, "Not in my classroom. Nor is cheating or ridiculing others allowed in my classroom. I put a stop to those right away. I do not pretend that that is values clarification. This is discipline."

15   A sweet whiff of reality. When it counts, when it matters, when something is at stake, values clarification comes up empty. That is the ruse, the fraudulence, and the scandal.

Content Questions

1. What is "values education"?
2. Why are current values education programs impoverished?
3. What is a substitute for values education?

Questions on Presentation

1. How convincing is Bennett in presenting his position that problems in education stem from parents' lack of concern about the moral growth of their children?
2. How would you characterize Bennett's audience?
3. How successful is Bennett in condemning "values educationists"?
4. Where does Bennett state his thesis?
5. Bennett uses words such as communitarianism (4), indoctrinative (5), Woodstockian (5), and equanimity (8) to convince his audience of his position. What do these words mean, and do they contribute to or detract from Bennett's thesis?

Welcome to College—and My Books

John Barth

When not writing or teaching at Johns Hopkins University, American novelist John Barth (b. 1920) sails the Chesapeake Bay. Barth was born in Cambridge, Maryland, and educated at the Juilliard School of Music and Johns Hopkins. In his fiction Barth humorously diagnoses the plight of modern people by exaggerating characters and situations. The narrator of Barth's first book, *The Floating Opera* (1956), uses the metaphor of a play staged on a boat flowing down the Chesapeake River to tell readers his autobiography and to imply how his condition is like their lives. Barth has also written books as diverse as the macabre *The End of the Road* (1958); *The Sot-Weed Factor* (1960), a re-creation of *Candide* reminiscent of *Robinson Crusoe, Moll Flanders, Tarzan,* and the Keystone cops; *Giles Goat-Boy* (1966), a biography of a boy raised by goats who aspires to be a Grand Tutor at the university; *Lost in the Funhouse* (1968), a collection of short fictions; *Chimera* (1973), a collection of novellas that won Barth the National Book Award; and *Sabbatical* (1982), an inventive extension of spy fiction. Barth continues his use of surprise, grotesquerie, and humor in his latest novel, *Tidewater Tales* (1987).

   This selection, reprinted from *The New York Times Book Review,* is an amended text of Barth's "orientation lecture" for entering undergraduates to Washington University in St. Louis, Missouri. Barth expanded his original lecture to make it an orientation for himself and his readers to his fiction and his views on education.

1   We meet this morning under a mutual misapprehension. You had been led to expect that I would read from and talk about my fiction; I had been led to believe that I'd be addressing the new freshman class as part of their orientation program, and that is what I originally prepared to do. I shall now see if I can do both at once.

2   As to my orienting university freshpeople to their new academic environment, it is the blind leading the blind. I know very little about Washington University beyond the fact that there are on its faculty at least two excellent writers of fiction and two excellent poets—William Gass, Stanley Elkin, Howard Nemerov and Mona Van Duyn—all of whom are reported to be fine teachers as well. Enroll in their courses before you graduate. As they are also quite famous, hit them for letters of recommendation for your job placement files, and you'll be a shoo-in to graduate school if that is whither you incline. But do this only after you have done brilliant, even astonishing work in their courses; otherwise take your C and don't be pushy.

3   Speaking more generally, I remind you that orientation literally means determining which way is east, whether for architectural purposes (if you're building a medieval Christian church, you aim it in that direction), or for funerary purposes (a well-oriented corpse lies with its feet to the rising sun). Apparently it wasn't until the end of the 19th century that orientation came to mean getting one's bearings, literally or figuratively, and not until well into the 20th that it was used specifically to name the project of suggesting to new American college students that they're not high school kids any longer, but responsible young adults commencing a major phase of their intellectual apprentice-

ship; taking a tour as it were of the lunchrooms and classrooms, lavatories and laboratories of the Western cultural conglomerate.

4   In short, the word orientation came to mean finding out where in the Occidental world we are as more and more of us came to suspect we didn't know. I feel on familiar ground. Indeed, when I set about to find something from my fiction suitable for this occasion, I realized that the general project of orientation—at least the condition of *dis*orientation which the project presumes—is my characteristic subject matter, my fictionary stock in trade. Intellectual and spiritual disorientation is the family disease of all my main characters—a disease usually complicated by ontological disorientation, since knowing where you're at is often contingent upon knowing who you are.

5   It is a malady, of course, epidemic in the literature of the last 100 years: one of its *orientations*, you might say, as the term is used in crystallography. What's more, the specific malaise of *academic* disorientation I find recurring from book to book of mine like a flu virus one had thought oneself done with. William Carlos Williams remarks in his autobiography that after years and years as both a practicing physician and a practicing poet, it occurred to him one day in a brow-slapping swoop of insight that the word venereal is related to the goddess Venus! It was a connection too obvious for him to have noticed. In the same way, I hadn't quite realized how *academic*, in this special sense, my life's work as a writer of stories has been. All of my books, I see now, are in the genre the Germans call *Erziehungsromane*: "upbringing-novels," education novels—a genre I had not found especially interesting after "David Copperfield" except as a vehicle for satire or an object of parody.

6   More dismaying, when I reviewed my literary offspring under this aspect, I realized that what I've been writing about all these years is not only orientation and education (rather, disorientation and education), but imperfect or unsuccessful or misfired education at that; not *Erziehungsromane* but *Herabziehungsromane*: "down-bringing novels." That I failed to recognize this before now is exemplary: I am obliged to reorient myself to my own bibliography, as one must occasionally revise one's view of oneself retrospectively in the light of some new self-knowledge, usually bad news.

7   The themes of my work, I suppose, are regression, re-enactment and reorientation. Like an ox-cart driver in monsoon season or the skipper of a grounded ship, one must sometimes go forward by going back. As an amateur sailor and navigator myself, I like the metaphor of dead reckoning: deciding where to go by determining where you are by reviewing where you've been. Aeneas does that; many of the wandering heroes of mythology reach an impasse at some crucial point in their journey, from which they can proceed only by a laborious retracing of their steps. This

is the process, if not the subject, of my novel-in-*re*gress, and it is the substance of this orientation talk.

8   Todd Andrews, the hero of my first novel, "The Floating Opera," goes to college originally in order to fulfill his father's expectations more than his own. His own expectation is to drop dead before he finishes this sentence, from a certain kind of heart disease he learned he had while serving in the army in World War I. It takes him most of his undergraduate career (and most of a chapter) to discover what on earth he's doing there in the university; his orientation period, you might say, lasts almost to the baccalaureate. Even postgraduately, he is given to unpredictable shifts of life style: In successive decades he plays the role of a libertine, an ascetic, a practicing cynic; he ends up at 54 (his present age in the novel) a sexually feeble small-town nihilist lawyer with an ongoing low-grade prostate infection and subacute bacteriological endocarditis tending to myocardial infarction, writing long letters to his father, who committed suicide a quarter-century since. The fruit of his education, formal and informal, is one valid syllogism:

1. There is no ultimate justification for any action.
2. Continuing to live is a variety of action.
3. Therefore etc.

9   Whence he **moves**, less validly, to the resolve not only to kill himself that very evening, but to take a goodly number of townspeople, friends, lovers and such with him: He means to blow up the showboat of the novel's title by opening some acetylene gas tanks under the stage. The attempt fails; the show goes on; Todd Andrews's deductive faculty is restored, perhaps by the gas, and he understands (but neglects to inform Albert Camus) that, given his premises, he's likely to go on living because—in his case, at least—there's finally no more reason to commit suicide than not to.

10   If this sounds to you like the thinking more of a 24-year-old than of a 54-year-old, that is because the author was 24 at the time. Todd Andrews is a moderately successful lawyer but he couldn't have done better than a gentleman's C+ in Logic 1, and he must have flunked the Chemistry of Gases cold. I hope your education will be more successful.

11   Novel No. 2, "The End of the Road," is set on and around the campus of a seedy little state teachers college at the opening of the fall term. (In the film version, the campus sequences were shot at Swarthmore.) The central character is a grad school dropout and ontological vacuum named Jacob Horner, who is subject to spells of paralysis because he suffers from the malady *cosmopsis*, the cosmic view. He is teaching English grammar on orders from his doctor, as a kind of therapy; but the prescription fails, as did his education. He becomes involved with a col-

league's wife, a kind of nature-girl on the wrong trail: Nature may abhor a vacuum, but she shows her abhorrence by rushing to fill it. The novel ends with an illegal and botched abortion fatal to the young woman (this was the 1950's) and a final abdication of personality on Horner's part. I see now, however, that it was not the clinical abortion but Horner's aborted education that originally wound the mainspring of the plot: his total disorientation in the concourse of Baltimore's Penn Station, where he first becomes immobilized because he can't think of any reason to go anywhere—and, apparently, can't go anywhere without a reason.

12   Those two novels make a little duet: a nihilist comedy and, if not a nihilist tragedy, at least a nihilist catastrophe. I am a twin—an opposite-sex twin—and I see in retrospect that I've been oriented as a writer to the same iteration-with-variation that my sister and I exemplify: a sort of congenital redundancy.

13   There followed a pair of very long novels, "The Sot-Weed Factor" and "Giles Goat-Boy," each of whose heroes begins with a radically innocent orientation of which he is disabused in successive chapters. Ebenezer Cooke, the hero of "The Sot-Weed Factor," matriculates at Cambridge University near the end of the 17th century; he has been ruinously disoriented by a tutor who professes *cosmophilism*, the sexual love of everything in the world: men, women, animals, plants, algebra, hydraulics, political intrigue. Cooke, like Jacob Horner, tends toward paralysis; he copes with the tendency by a radical assertion of his innocence and his fondness for versifying: He declares himself programmatically to be a virgin and a poet, as one might choose a double major, and sets out for the New World with a commission as Poet Laureate of the Province of Maryland. But the commission is spurious, his talent is questionable, the New World isn't what he'd been led to suspect and commissioned to eulogize; his innocence grows ever more technical and imperfect.

14   In the end Cooke has to marry a whore and contract a social disease in order to regain the estate he didn't recognize as his until he'd lost it. His poetry gets a little better, but it's written figuratively in red ink— his own blood—and it is admired for the wrong reasons. By the time he is legitimately appointed Poet Laureate, he couldn't care less. Ebenezer Cooke would recommend that you choose some other major than Innocence, which he comes to see he has been guilty of.

15   Giles Goat-Boy, raised by the goats on one of the experimental stock-farms of an enormous, even world-embracing university, takes as *his* orientation program the myth of the wandering hero: He majors, as it were, in mythic heroism. It is not a gut course, though Giles has to descend into the very bowels of knowledge, and of the Campus, in order to earn his degree. After nearly 800 pages, the main thing he seems to have learned is that what he has learned can't be taught: In his attempts to eff the ineffable, his truths get garbled, misconstrued, betrayed by ver-

balization, institutionalism. He almost ceases to care—as, I'm sure, many serious teachers do. But the *almost* is important.

16   After those two long books came a pair of short ones. Both are about orientation, disorientation, reorientation. Both involve wandering heroes from classical mythology, usually lost. (One reason why classical mythic heroes need to know which way is east is that they traditionally travel west. But they *always* lose their way.) The first book of the pair is a series of fictions for print, tape and live voice called "Lost in the Funhouse." Orientationwise, the title speaks for itself. The other consists of three novellas, called "Chimera." "Dunyazadiad," the opening panel of the "Chimera" triptych, is a reorchestration of one of my favorite stories in the world: the frame-story of "The Thousand and One Nights." You know the tale: how King Shahryar is driven so mad by sexual jealousy that he sleeps with a virgin every night and has her killed in the morning, lest she deceive him; and how that wonderful young woman Scheherazade, the vizier's daughter, beguiles him with narrative strategies until he comes to his senses. For a time, I regarded the "Nights" as an insightful early work of feminist fiction: Scheherazade is called *specifically* "the Savior of Her Sex"; the king's private misogyny is shown to be dangerous not only to his women but to his own mental health and, since he's the king, to the public health as well. Later in my own education as a writer, I came to regard the story as a metaphor for the condition of narrative artists in general, and of artists who work on university campuses in particular, for a number of reasons:

1.   Scheherazade has to lose her innocence before she can begin to practice her art. Ebenezer Cooke did, too; so do most of us.
2.   Her audience—the king—is also her absolute critic. It is "publish or perish," with a vengence.
3.   And her talent is always on the line. Never mind how many times she has pleased the king before; she is only as good as her next piece. So are we all.
4.   But this terrifying relationship is also a fertilizing one; Scheherazade bears the king three children over those 1,001 nights, as well as telling all those stories. Much could be said about those parallel productions.
5.   Which, however, cease—at least her production of stories ceases—as soon as the king grants her the "tenure" of formal marriage. So it goes.

17   My version of the story, told by Scheherazade's kid sister, Dunyazade, echoes some of these preoccupations:

18   "Three and a third years ago, when King Shahryar was raping a virgin every night and killing her in the morning, and the people were praying that Allah would dump the whole dynasty, and so many parents had fled the country with their daughters that in all the Islands of India and China there was hardly a young girl, my sister was an undergraduate arts-

and-sciences major at Banu Sasan University. Besides being Homecoming Queen, valedictorian-elect, and a four-letter varsity athlete, she had a private library of a thousand volumes and the highest average in the history of the campus. Every graduate department in the East was after her with fellowships—but she was so appalled at the state of the nation that she dropped out of school in her last semester to do full-time research on a way to stop Shahryar from killing all our sisters and wrecking the country.

19   "Political science, which she looked at first, got her nowhere. Shahryar's power was absolute; by sparing the daughters of his army officers and chief ministers ... he kept the military and the cabinet loyal enough to rule out a *coup d'état*. Revolution seemed out of the question, because his woman-hating, spectacular as it was, was enforced more or less by all our traditions and institutions, and as long as the girls he was murdering were generally upper-caste, there was no popular base for a guerrilla war.

20   "So we gave up poly sci and tried psychology—another blind alley.... She grew daily more desperate: the body-count of deflowered and decapitated Moslem girls was past 900, and Daddy was just about out of candidates.... When nothing else worked, as a last resort she turned to her first love, unlikely as it seemed, mythology and folklore, and studied all the riddle/puzzle/secret motifs she could dig up. 'We need a miracle, Doony,' she said (I was braiding her hair and massaging her neck as she went through her notes for the 1,000th time), 'and the only genies *I've* ever met were in stories, not in Moormen's-rings and Jews'-lamps. It's in words that the magic is—Abracadabra, Open Sesame, and the rest—but the magic words in one story aren't magical in the next. The real magic is to understand which words work, and when, and for what; the trick is to learn the trick.' "

21   In other words—as Dunyazade and Scheherazade and the Author come to learn in the pages that follow—the *key* to the treasure may *be* the treasure.

22   The tuition for that sort of lesson can be very high. Retracing one's steps—"becoming as a kindergartener again," as the goat-boy puts it—may be necessary to a fruitful reorientation, but one runs the risk of losing oneself in the past instead of returning to the present equipped to move forward into the future.

23   Perseus (in the second "Chimera" novella, called "Perseid") understands this, though he's not sure for a while what to do with his understanding. He too has retraced his heroical route, recapitulated his mythic exploits, and not for vanity's sake, but for reorientation. As he says one night to the nymph Calyxa, as she and he are making love:

"Well, now perhaps it was a bit vain of me to want to retrace my good young days; but it wasn't *just* vanity; no more were my nightly narratives:

Somewhere along that way I'd lost something, took a wrong turn, forgot some knack, I don't know; it seemed to me that if I kept going over it carefully enough I might see the pattern, find the key."

"A little up and to your left," Calyxa whispered.

24 Perseus' research is successful: he finds the key and moves on to his proper destiny, which is to become a constellation in the sky, endlessly reenacting his story in his risings and settings. Perseus "makes it" because his vocation is legitimate: He doesn't major in Mythic Heroism; he happens to *be* a mythic hero, whose only problem is what to do for an encore.

25 More cautionary is the lesson of Bellerophon, the hero of the final "Chimera" novella. Like Giles the goat-boy, Bellerophon aspires to be a mythic hero; it is his only study. When Perseus reaches middle age, he researches his own history and the careers of other mythic heroes in order to understand what brought him to where he is, so that he can go on. Young Bellerophon's orientation, on the other hand, is that by following perfectly the ritual pattern of mythic heroes—by getting all A's and four letters of recommendation, as it were—he will become a bona fide mythic hero like his cousin Perseus. What he learns, and it is an expensive lesson, is that by perfectly imitating the pattern of mythic heroism, one becomes a perfect imitation of a mythic hero, which is not quite the same thing as being Perseus the Golden Destroyer. Hence the novella's title, "Bellerophoniad." Something similar may befall the writer too fixated upon his/her distinguished predecessors; it is a disoriented navigator indeed who mistakes the stars he steers by for his destination.

26 He is not, my Bellerophon, entirely phony, however: He is too earnest for that; too authentically dedicated to his profession, whatever the limits of his gift. What's more, he really does kill the Chimera—that fictive monster or monstrous fiction—to the extent that it ever really existed in the first place. Bellerophon's immortality is of a more radically qualified sort: What he becomes is not the story of his own exploits, as Perseus does up there among the other stars, but the *text* of the story "Bellerophoniad." Pegasus, the winged horse of inspiration on which Bellerophon has flown, gets to heaven (in fact, he's one of the constellations in the Perseus group); his rider is thrown at the threshold of the gate, falls for a long time (long enough to tell his long tale), and is transformed just in the nick of time into the pages, the sentences, the letters of the book "Chimera." To turn into the sound of one's own voice is an occupational hazard of professional storytellers; even more so, I imagine, of professional lecturers.

27 That brings us to the present. Now: All these retracements, recapitulations, rehearsals and reenactments really would be simply regressive if they didn't issue in reorientation, from which new work can proceed. But that, as Scheherazade says, is another story.

Postscript 1984, For the Class of 1988

28   The novel "Letters," published shortly after that orientation lecture, centers upon an enormous (and hypothetical) third-rate American university, Marshyhope State, constructed for my purposes on the freshly filled salt marsh of my native Dorchester County, in Maryland. The year is 1969, the heyday of American academic imperialism and gigantism. Marshyhope's architectural symbol and intended beacon to the world, The Tower of Truth, on the eve of its dedication already shows signs of subsiding into the fenlands whence it sprang, like the Hancock Tower into Back Bay Boston. "All great cultures," the critic Leslie Fiedler once remarked, "arise from marshes"—and not a few thereto return.

29   As R. D. Laing rationalizes schizophrenia, at least in certain cases, as a sane response to a deranged but inescapable set of circumstances, so the cautionary example of Marshyhope State suggests that—in certain cases, at least—the fault of disorientation may lie not in ourselves, Horatio, but in our alma maters and paters. To disoriented undergraduates I say: By all means allow for that possibility—but do not jump to that conclusion, as it is most likely mistaken.

30   My little novel, "Sabbatical: A Romance" (1982), carries the Laingian scenario farther. Todd Andrews in "The Floating Opera" (and again in "Letters") wonders sentence by sentence whether his heart will carry him from subject to predicate; in "Sabbatical," set on Chesapeake Bay in 1980, the background question is whether the world will end before the novel does.

31   More specifically, the question is whether one can responsibly bring children into the disoriented powder keg wherein we dwell. The prospective parents in "Sabbatical" are literal navigators, of a seaworthy cruising sailboat (she is a proper young academic, on sabbatical leave; he is a decent, middle-aged ex-C.I.A. officer, between careers). *They* are oriented; the course they steer is accurate, if not always straightforward. What's more, after years of marriage and trials large and small they remain happily in love with each other. In an oriented world, their landfall—and progeny—would be assured. In the troubled and dangerous waters through which they, like the rest of us, necessarily sail, however, no degree of skill in navigation or of seaworthiness in the vessel guarantees that our destination will still be there at our Estimated Time of Arrival.

32   This being the more or less apocalyptic case—the Sot-Weed Factor supplanted as it were by the Doomsday Factor—why set a course at all, whether toward graduation or procreation or distinguished career or further fiction? This is the approximate subject of my next effort at self-orientation: my novel presently in the works. But that, as Scheherazade says, is another story, for another night.

33   I wish you good luck in your own orientation. East is over that way.

Content Questions

1. What "mutual misapprehension" brings Barth and the students together?
2. Why is the literal meaning of the word *orientation* important to Barth?
3. What are the themes of Barth's works?
4. How did Barth turn Scheherazade's story into a story of a college student?
5. Why couldn't Bellerophon follow the same path his cousin Perseus takes?

Questions on Presentation

1. Why does Barth mention writers such as William Gass, Stanley Elkin, Howard Nemerov, and Mona Van Duyn?
2. Is Barth's style and approach appropriate to his subject?
3. Is the discussion of architecture in paragraph 3 useful? Why or why not?
4. What does Barth's use of words such as misapprehension (1), ontological (4), crystallography (5), malaise (5), ascetic (8), syllogism (8), nihilistic (12), cosmophilism (13), and misogyny (16) tell you about his attitude toward his audience?
5. Barth explores one way of viewing a college education. How does his view compare to Nicolson's or Hughes'?

Rites of Passage

Claude H. Muller

A sociology major, Claude Muller is interested in the ways people adapt to changing circumstances. Responding to Barth's essay, he explores the changes students may face in college and defines the stages any student may go through in the course of a college career.

1   All cultures have what are called rites of passage, rituals that mark an individual's transition from one status to another. When analyzed, each transition or stage in a ritual has its own set of requirements and demands that can leave the individual disoriented and confused. For example, while in school, a college student usually goes through three rites of passage: the Rite of Separation, in which an individual is removed from his or her familiar environment; the Rite of Transition, in which an individual is between statuses; and the Rite of Incorporation, in which an individual assumes a new status and position in life. In college students can experience the Rite of Separation when they move from

high school life to college life. They can experience the Rite of Transition when they transfer from one degree-granting college to another. Upon graduation they will experience the Rite of Incorporation.

2   Many students find the transition from high school to college a frightening experience because they don't know what personal, social, and economic responsibilities are expected of them. Personal responsibility begins to develop when the students' parents are no longer around to take care of them and they realize they have to rely upon themselves. For instance, they now have to ensure that they wake up when the alarm goes off and that they don't live on just snack food. Attending classes and completing assignments promptly become every student's personal responsibility. In addition to personal responsibility, new students come to realize that to be successful in college work they must gain social responsibility. Therefore, while they know that proper conduct in class, such as not smoking, eating, or talking, is expected behavior, they may not understand that in college their part in a collaborative project is a social responsibility. For example, to complete their science laboratory report, both the student and his or her lab partner must complete their share of the project on time. Finally, the desperation inherent in learning economic responsibility is easily seen in the message "Mom, Send Money" on placards students wave at televised college games. Since Mom and Dad aren't immediately available for a loan, new students must learn to manage their money. The Rite of Separation is an uneasy period when students learn to accept personal, social, and economic responsibilities necessary for the transition from high school to college.

3   The majority of students attending college usually experience a Rite of Transition that requires an academic reorientation toward a new major or field of study. This reorientation may center upon the transfer from one degree-granting college within a university to another. A student may enter college unsure of what field of study to pursue. Fortunately, during freshman year a student will attend a variety of classes in several academic fields. This exposure to different programs will help the undecided student determine which academic field to enter. In addition, this diversity helps a student fulfill certain academic requirements needed to enter the college of his or her choice. However, students who are still undecided after the first few semesters of college go through a period of reorientation. They must carefully scrutinize what courses they have already taken; they must seek encouragement and direction from academic advisors; and they must take time to search their desires, intentions, and goals. The Rite of Transition is the most critical one a student must pass through, for, if prolonged, it may end with the student forced out of school, frustrated by unmet goals or unformed ambitions.

4   Any student graduating from college experiences a Rite of Incorpora-

tion, a reorientation that revolves about the transition from student to employee. Students must reframe learned skills to become productive skills, follow rigid work schedules, and adhere to dress codes. For example, students entering the business world find that this new environment is production and profit oriented. These new employees, or ex-students, are expected to demonstrate their learned skills in a productive way. Their knowledge is tested not on paper but in practice. This testing can be traumatic for them because in school they proved their knowledge and skills through theoretical not practical demonstration. New college graduates must reorient themselves. They find that changing from flexible class schedules, which allowed time for relaxation or study during the day, to rigidly scheduled business hours is a difficult task. Dressing properly for work may also be new. The denim jeans and tennis shoes the students wore in college are not appropriate to the business world where business suits and wingtip shoes or heels are expected. Once the graduates have reoriented themselves to these new requirements the Rite of Incorporation is complete; they can now assume their new status.

5   There are at least three times when college students must reorient themselves. The first is when they enter college; the second is when they change degree programs; and the last is when they graduate. The key to understanding and accomplishing these rites is to satisfy the demands of each reorientation. Rites of Passage—you may call them stages of life—are universal; they are present in almost all aspects of our lives. Students pass through these rites only to find they must experience them again in other forms, for the end of one Rite of Passage is the beginning of a new Rite of Passage. It is a cycle which perpetuates a challenging but neverending process of life.

The Erosion of American Education: A Nation at Risk

President's Commission on Education

"A Nation at Risk," the 1983 report from the National Commission on Excellence in Education, horrified many educators, politicians, and citizens because the commission warned the nation that "mediocre educational performance" will undermine our prosperity and security. Since the report's publication, individuals and state and national panels have repeated the criticisms. While they may agree on an outline for the nation's educational deficiencies, critics still disagree on the solution.

1   Our Nation is at risk. Our once unchallenged preeminence in commerce, industry, science, and technological innovation is being overtaken by competitors throughout the world. This report is concerned with only one of the many causes and dimensions of the problem, but it is the one that undergirds American prosperity, security, and civility. We report to the American people that while we can take justifiable pride in what our schools and colleges have historically accomplished and contributed to the United States and the well-being of its people, the educational foundations of our society are presently being eroded by a rising tide of mediocrity that threatens our very future as a Nation and a people. What was unimaginable a generation ago has begun to occur— others are matching and surpassing our educational attainments.

2   If an unfriendly foreign power had attempted to impose on America the mediocre educational performance that exists today, we might well have viewed it as an act of war. As it stands, we have allowed this to happen to ourselves. We have even squandered the gains in student achievement made in the wake of the Sputnik challenge. Moreover, we have dismantled essential support systems which helped make those gains possible. We have, in effect, been committing an act of unthinking, unilateral educational disarmament.

3   Our society and its educational institutions seem to have lost sight of the basic purposes of schooling, and of the high expectations and disciplined effort needed to attain them. This report, the result of 18 months of study, seeks to generate reform of our educational system in fundamental ways and to renew the Nation's commitment to schools and colleges of high quality throughout the length and breadth of our land.

4   That we have compromised this commitment is, upon reflection, hardly surprising, given the multitude of often conflicting demands we have placed on our Nation's schools and colleges. They are routinely called on to provide solutions to personal, social, and political problems that the home and other institutions either will not or cannot resolve. We must understand that these demands on our schools and colleges often exact an educational cost as well as a financial one.

5   On the occasion of the Commission's first meeting, President Reagan noted the central importance of education in American life when he said: "Certainly there are few areas of American life as important to our society, to our people, and to our families as our schools and colleges." This report, therefore, is as much an open letter to the American people as it is a report to the Secretary of Education. We are confident that the American people, properly informed, will do what is right for their children and for the generations to come.

6   History is not kind to idlers. The time is long past when America's destiny was assured simply by an abundance of natural resources and

inexhaustible human enthusiasm, and by our relative isolation from the malignant problems of older civilizations. The world is indeed one global village. We live among determined, well-educated, and strongly motivated competitors. We compete with them for international standing and markets, not only with products but also with the ideas of our laboratories and neighborhood workshops. America's position in the world may once have been reasonably secure with only a few exceptionally well-trained men and women. It is no longer.

7   The risk is not only that the Japanese make automobiles more efficiently than Americans and have government subsidies for development and export. It is not just that the South Koreans recently built the world's most efficient steel mill, or that American machine tools, once the pride of the world, are being displaced by German products. It is also that these developments signify a redistribution of trained capability throughout the globe. Knowledge, learning, information, and skilled intelligence are the new raw materials of international commerce and are today spreading throughout the world as vigorously as miracle drugs, synthetic fertilizers, and blue jeans did earlier. If only to keep and improve on the slim competitive edge we still retain in world markets, we must dedicate ourselves to the reform of our educational system for the benefit of all—old and young alike, affluent and poor, majority and minority. Learning is the indispensable investment required for success in the "information age" we are entering.

8   Our concern, however, goes well beyond matters such as industry and commerce. It also includes the intellectual, moral, and spiritual strengths of our people which knit together the very fabric of our society. The people of the United States need to know that individuals in our society who do not possess the levels of skill, literacy, and training essential to this new era will be effectively disenfranchised, not simply from the material rewards that accompany competent performance, but also from the chance to participate fully in our national life. A high level of shared education is essential to a free, democratic society and to the fostering of a common culture, especially in a country that prides itself on pluralism and individual freedom.

9   For our country to function, citizens must be able to reach some common understandings on complex issues, often on short notice and on the basis of conflicting or incomplete evidence. Education helps form these common understandings, a point Thomas Jefferson made long ago in his justly famous dictum:

> I know no safe depository of the ultimate powers of the society but the people themselves; and if we think them not enlightened enough to exercise their control with a wholesome discretion, the remedy is not to take it from them but to inform their discretion.

10   Part of what is at risk is the promise first made on this continent: All, regardless of race or class or economic status, are entitled to a fair chance and to the tools for developing their individual powers of mind and spirit to the utmost. This promise means that all children by virtue of their own efforts, competently guided, can hope to attain the mature and informed judgment needed to secure gainful employment and to manage their own lives, thereby serving not only their own interests but also the progress of society itself.

11   The educational dimensions of the risk before us have been amply documented in testimony received by the Commission. For example:

- International comparisons of student achievement, completed a decade ago, reveal that on 19 academic tests American students were never first or second and, in comparison with other industrialized nations, were last seven times.
- Some 23 million American adults are functionally illiterate by the simplest tests of everyday reading, writing, and comprehension.
- About 13 percent of all 17-year-olds in the United States can be considered functionally illiterate. Functional illiteracy among minority youth may run as high as 40 percent.
- Average achievement of high school students on most standardized tests is now lower than 26 years ago when Sputnik was launched.
- Over half the population of gifted students do not match their tested ability with comparable achievement in school.
- The College Board's Scholastic Aptitude Tests (SAT) demonstrate a virtually unbroken decline from 1963 to 1980. Average verbal scores fell over 50 points and average mathematics scores dropped nearly 40 points.
- College Board achievement tests also reveal consistent declines in recent years in such subjects as physics and English.
- Both the number and proportion of students demonstrating superior achievement on the SATs (i.e., those with scores of 650 or higher) have also dramatically declined.
- Many 17-year-olds do not possess the "higher order" intellectual skills we should expect of them. Nearly 40 percent cannot draw inferences from written material; only one-fifth can write a persuasive essay; and only one-third can solve a mathematics problem requiring several steps.
- There was a steady decline in science achievement scores of U.S. 17-year-olds as measured by national assessments of science in 1969, 1973, and 1977.
- Between 1975 and 1980, remedial mathematics courses in public 4-year colleges increased by 72 percent and now constitute one-quarter of all mathematics courses taught in those institutions.
- Average tested achievement of students graduating from college is also lower.
- Business and military leaders complain that they are required to spend

millions of dollars on costly remedial education and training programs in such basic skills as reading, writing, spelling, and computation. The Department of the Navy, for example, reported to the Commission that one-quarter of its recent recruits cannot read at the ninth grade level, the minimum needed simply to understand written safety instructions. Without remedial work they cannot even begin, much less complete, the sophisticated training essential in much of the modern military.

12   These deficiencies come at a time when the demand for highly skilled workers in new fields is accelerating rapidly. For example:

- Computers and computer-controlled equipment are penetrating every aspect of our lives—homes, factories, and offices.
- One estimate indicates that by the turn of the century millions of jobs will involve laser technology and robotics.
- Technology is radically transforming a host of other occupations. They include health care, medical science, energy production, food processing, construction, and the building, repair, and maintenance of sophisticated scientific, educational, military, and industrial equipment.

13   Analysts examining these indicators of student performance and the demands for new skills have made some chilling observations. Educational researcher Paul Hurd concluded at the end of a thorough national survey of student achievement that within the context of the modern scientific revolution, "We are raising a new generation of Americans that is scientifically and technologically illiterate." In a similar vein, John Slaughter, a former Director of the National Science Foundation, warned of "a growing chasm between a small scientific and technological elite and a citizenry ill-informed, indeed uninformed, on issues with a science component."

14   But the problem does not stop there, nor do all observers see it the same way. Some worry that schools may emphasize such rudiments as reading and computation at the expense of other essential skills such as comprehension, analysis, solving problems, and drawing conclusions. Still others are concerned that an over-emphasis on technical and occupational skills will leave little time for studying the arts and humanities that so enrich daily life, help maintain civility, and develop a sense of community. Knowledge of the humanities, they maintain, must be harnessed to science and technology if the latter are to remain creative and humane, just as the humanities need to be informed by science and technology if they are to remain relevant to the human condition. Another analyst, Paul Copperman, has drawn a sobering conclusion. Until now, he has noted:

Each generation of Americans has outstripped its parents in education, in literacy, and in economic attainment. For the first time in the history of our country, the educational skills of one generation will not surpass, will not equal, will not even approach, those of their parents.

15   It is important, of course, to recognize that *the average citizen* today is better educated and more knowledgeable than the average citizen of a generation ago—more literate, and exposed to more mathematics, literature, and science. The positive impact of this fact on the well-being of our country and the lives of our people cannot be overstated. Nevertheless, *the average graduate* of our schools and colleges today is not as well-educated as the average graduate of 25 or 35 years ago, when a much smaller proportion of our population completed high school and college. The negative impact of this fact likewise cannot be overstated.

16   Statistics and their interpretation by experts show only the surface dimension of the difficulties we face. Beneath them lies a tension between hope and frustration that characterizes current attitudes about education at every level.

17   We have heard the voices of high school and college students, school board members, and teachers; of leaders of industry, minority groups, and higher education; of parents and State officials. We could hear the hope evident in their commitment to quality education and in their descriptions of outstanding programs and schools. We could also hear the intensity of their frustration, a growing impatience with shoddiness in many walks of American life, and the complaint that this shoddiness is too often reflected in our schools and colleges. Their frustration threatens to overwhelm their hope.

18   What lies behind this emerging national sense of frustration can be described as both a dimming of personal expectations and the fear of losing a shared vision for America.

19   On the personal level the student, the parent, and the caring teacher all perceive that a basic promise is not being kept. More and more young people emerge from high school ready neither for college nor for work. This predicament becomes more acute as the knowledge base continues its rapid expansion, the number of traditional jobs shrinks, and new jobs demand greater sophistication and preparation.

20   On a broader scale, we sense that this undertone of frustration has significant political implications, for it cuts across ages, generations, races, and political and economic groups. We have come to understand that the public will demand that educational and political leaders act forcefully and effectively on these issues. Indeed, such demands have already appeared and could well become a unifying national preoccupation. This unity, however, can be achieved only if we avoid the unproductive tendency of some to search for scapegoats among the victims, such as the beleaguered teachers.

21   On the positive side is the significant movement by political and edu-

cational leaders to search for solutions—so far centering largely on the nearly desperate need for increased support for the teaching of mathematics and science. This movement is but a start on what we believe is a larger and more educationally encompassing need to improve teaching and learning in fields such as English, history, geography, economics, and foreign languages. We believe this movement must be broadened and directed toward reform and excellence throughout education.

22 We define "excellence" to mean several related things. At the level of the *individual learner*, it means performing on the boundary of individual ability in ways that test and push back personal limits, in school and in the workplace. Excellence characterizes a *school or college* that sets high expectations and goals for all learners, then tries in every way possible to help students reach them. Excellence characterizes a *society* that has adopted these policies, for it will then be prepared through the education and skill of its people to respond to the challenges of a rapidly changing world. Our Nation's people and its schools and colleges must be committed to achieving excellence in all these senses.

23 We do not believe that a public commitment to excellence and educational reform must be made at the expense of a strong public commitment to the equitable treatment of our diverse population. The twin goals of equity and high-quality schooling have profound and practical meaning for our economy and society, and we cannot permit one to yield to the other either in principle or in practice. To do so would deny young people their chance to learn and live according to their aspirations and abilities. It also would lead to a generalized accommodation to mediocrity in our society on the one hand or the creation of an undemocratic elitism on the other.

24 Our goal must be to develop the talents of all to their fullest. Attaining that goal requires that we expect and assist all students to work to the limits of their capabilities. We should expect schools to have genuinely high standards rather than minimum ones, and parents to support and encourage their children to make the most of their talents and abilities.

25 The search for solutions to our educational problems must also include a commitment to life-long learning. The task of rebuilding our system of learning is enormous and must be properly understood and taken seriously: Although a million and a half new workers enter the economy each year from our schools and colleges, the adults working today will still make up about 75 percent of the workforce in the year 2000. These workers, and new entrants into the workforce, will need further education and retraining if they—and we as a Nation—are to thrive and prosper.

26 In a world of ever-accelerating competition and change in the condi-

tions of the workplace, of ever-greater danger, and of ever-larger opportunities for those prepared to meet them, educational reform should focus on the goal of creating a Learning Society. At the heart of such a society is the commitment to a set of values and to a system of education that affords all members the opportunity to stretch their minds to full capacity, from early childhood through adulthood, learning more as the world itself changes. Such a society has as a basic foundation the idea that education is important not only because of what it contributes to one's career goals but also because of the value it adds to the general quality of one's life. Also at the heart of the Learning Society are educational opportunities extending far beyond the traditional institutions of learning, our schools and colleges. They extend into homes and workplaces; into libraries, art galleries, museums, and science centers; indeed, into every place where the individual can develop and mature in work and life. In our view, formal schooling in youth is the essential foundation for learning throughout one's life. But without life-long learning, one's skills will become rapidly dated.

27   In contrast to the ideal of the Learning Society, however, we find that for too many people education means doing the minimum work necessary for the moment, then coasting through life on what may have been learned in its first quarter. But this should not surprise us because we tend to express our educational standards and expectations largely in terms of "minimum requirements." And where there should be a coherent continuum of learning, we have none, but instead an often incoherent, outdated patchwork quilt. Many individual, sometimes heroic, examples of schools and colleges of great merit do exist. Our findings and testimony confirm the vitality of a number of notable schools and programs, but their very distinction stands out against a vast mass shaped by tensions and pressures that inhibit systematic academic and vocational achievement for the majority of students. In some metropolitan areas basic literacy has become the goal rather than the starting point. In some colleges maintaining enrollments is of greater day-to-day concern than maintaining rigorous academic standards. And the ideal of academic excellence as the primary goal of schooling seems to be fading across the board in American education.

28   Thus, we issue this call to all who care about America and its future: to parents and students; to teachers, administrators, and school board members; to colleges and industry; to union members and military leaders; to governors and State legislators; to the President; to members of Congress and other public officials; to members of learned and scientific societies; to the print and electronic media; to concerned citizens everywhere. America is at risk.

29   We are confident that America can address this risk. If the tasks we set forth are initiated now and our recommendations are fully realized

over the next several years, we can expect reform of our Nation's schools, colleges, and universities. This would also reverse the current declining trend—a trend that stems more from weakness of purpose, confusion of vision, underuse of talent, and lack of leadership, than from conditions beyond our control.

Content Questions

1. Why does the Presidential Commission feel the nation is at risk?
2. How do current citizens today compare to citizens twenty-five to thirty years older?
3. What is the Learning Society? Why is it "an ideal"?
4. Why is history "not kind to idlers"?
5. What is necessary for a country to function?

Questions on Presentation

1. How convincing is the commission in its presentation of risks to the country?
2. Why does the commission quote Jefferson in its report?
3. How did the writers achieve a clear definition of excellence?
4. How does the commission present the case for the need for balance in education?
5. Why is paragraph 28 presented in the way it is?

America Revised

Frances FitzGerald

New Yorker Frances FitzGerald (b. 1940) graduated magna cum laude from Radcliffe with a degree in Middle Eastern studies and went on to study Chinese and Vietnamese history and culture. She used her knowledge of these topics as a freelance journalist in Vietnam in the late 1960s, contributing articles on politics for *Atlantic Monthly*, *The New York Times*, and the *Village Voice*. Upon her return to the United States, she won the Overseas Press Club award for interpretative reporting (1967). FitzGerald took five years to research and write her first book *Fire in the Lake: The Vietnamese and the Americans in Vietnam* (1972); the book won her the Pulitzer Prize for contemporary affairs writing, the National Book Award, and the Bancroft Prize for History. Since this first book, Fitz-Gerald has continued to write on conflicts prompted by the clash of politics, history, and culture. Her recent book *America Revised* (1979), from which the following selection was taken, evaluates American history textbooks by analyzing how American culture and history are changed not so much by events as by publishers, educators, and politicians.

1   Those of us who grew up in the fifties believed in the permanence of our American-history textbooks. To us as children, those texts were the truth of things: they were American history. It was not just that we read them before we understood that not everything that is printed is the truth, or the whole truth. It was that they, much more than other books, had the demeanor and trappings of authority. They were weighty volumes. They spoke in measured cadences: imperturbable, humorless, and as distant as Chinese emperors. Our teachers treated them with respect, and we paid them abject homage by memorizing a chapter a week. But now the textbook histories have changed, some of them to such an extent that an adult would find them unrecognizable.

2   One current junior-high-school American history begins with a story about a Negro cowboy called George McJunkin. It appears that when McJunkin was riding down a lonely trail in New Mexico one cold spring morning in 1925 he discovered a mound containing bones and stone implements, which scientists later proved belonged to an Indian civilization ten thousand years old. The book goes on to say that scientists now believe there were people in the Americas at least twenty thousand years ago. It discusses the Aztec, Mayan, and Incan civilizations and the meaning of the word "culture" before introducing the European explorers.[1]

3   Another history text—this one for the fifth grade—begins with the story of how Henry B. Gonzalez, who is a member of Congress from Texas, learned about his own nationality. When he was ten years old, his teacher told him he was an American because he was born in the United States. His grandmother, however, said, "The cat was born in the oven. Does that make him bread?" After reporting that Mr. Gonzalez eventually went to college and law school, the book explains that "the melting pot idea hasn't worked out as some thought it would," and that now "some people say that the people of the United States are more like a salad bowl than a melting pot."[2]

4   Poor Columbus! He is a minor character now, a walk-on in the middle of American history. Even those books that have not replaced his picture with a Mayan temple or an Iroquois mask do not credit him with discovering America—even for the Europeans. The Vikings, they say, preceded him to the New World, and after that the Europeans, having lost or forgotten their maps, simply neglected to cross the ocean again

for five hundred years. Columbus is far from being the only personage to have suffered from time and revision. Captain John Smith, Daniel Boone, and Wild Bill Hickok—the great self-promoters of American history—have all but disappeared, taking with them a good deal of the romance of the American frontier. General Custer has given way to Chief Crazy Horse; General Eisenhower no longer liberates Europe single-handed; and, indeed, most generals, even to Washington and Lee, have faded away, as old soldiers do, giving place to social reformers such as William Lloyd Garrison and Jacob Riis. A number of black Americans have risen to prominence: not only George Washington Carver but Frederick Douglas and Martin Luther King, Jr. W. E. B. Du Bois now invariably accompanies Booker T. Washington. In addition, there is a mystery man called Crispus Attucks, a fugitive slave about whom nothing seems to be known for certain except that he was a victim of the Boston Massacre and thus became one of the first casualties of the American Revolution. Thaddeus Stevens has been reconstructed—his character changed, as it were, from black to white, from cruel and vindictive to persistent and sincere. As for Teddy Roosevelt, he now champions the issue of conservation instead of charging up San Juan Hill. No single President really stands out as a hero, but all Presidents—except certain unmentionables in the second half of the nineteenth century—seem to have done as well as could be expected, given difficult circumstances.

5   Of course, when one thinks about it, it is hardly surprising that modern scholarship and modern perspectives have found their way into children's books. Yet the changes remain shocking. Those who in the sixties complained of the bland optimism, the chauvinism, and the materialism of their old civics texts did so in the belief that, for all their protests, the texts would never change. The thought must have had something reassuring about it, for that generation never noticed when its complaints began to take effect and the songs about radioactive rainfall and houses made of ticky-tacky began to appear in the textbooks. But this is what happened.

6   The history texts now hint at a certain level of unpleasantness in American history. Several books, for instance, tell the story of Ishi, the last "wild" Indian in the continental United States, who, captured in 1911 after the massacre of his tribe, spent the final four and a half years of his life in the University of California's museum of anthropology, in San Francisco. At least three books show the same stunning picture of the breaker boys, the child coal miners of Pennsylvania—ancient children with deformed bodies and blackened faces who stare stupidly out from the entrance to a mine. One book quotes a soldier on the use of torture in the American campaign to pacify the Philippines at the beginning of the century. A number of books say that during the American Revolution the patriots tarred and feathered those who did not support

them, and drove many of the loyalists from the country. Almost all the present-day history books note that the United States interned Japanese-Americans in detention camps during the Second World War.

7   Ideologically speaking, the histories of the fifties were implacable, seamless. Inside their covers, America was perfect: the greatest nation in the world, and the embodiment of democracy, freedom, and technological progress. For them, the country never changed in any important way: its values and its political institutions remained constant from the time of the American Revolution. To my generation—the children of the fifties—these texts appeared permanent just because they were so self-contained. Their orthodoxy, it seemed, left no handholds for attack, no lodging for decay. Who, after all, would dispute the wonders of technology or the superiority of the English colonists over the Spanish? Who would find fault with the pastorale of the West or the Old South? Who would question the anti-Communist crusade? There was, it seemed, no point in comparing these visions with reality, since they were the public truth and were thus quite irrelevant to what existed and to what anyone privately believed. They were—or so it seemed—the permanent expression of mass culture in America.

8   But now the texts have changed, and with them the country that American children are growing up into. The society that was once uniform is now a patchwork of rich and poor, old and young, men and women, blacks, whites, Hispanics, and Indians. The system that ran so smoothly by means of the Constitution under the guidance of benevolent conductor Presidents is now a rattletrap affair. The past is no highway to the present; it is a collection of issues and events that do not fit together and that lead in no single direction. The word "progress" has been replaced by the word "change": children, the modern texts insist, should learn history so that they can adapt to the rapid changes taking place around them. History is proceeding in spite of us. The present, which was once portrayed in the concluding chapters as a peaceful haven of scientific advances and Presidential inaugurations, is now a tangle of problems: race problems, urban problems, foreign-policy problems, problems of pollution, poverty, energy depletion, youthful rebellion, assassination, and drugs. Some books illustrate these problems dramatically. One, for instance, contains a picture of a doll half buried in a mass of untreated sewage; the caption reads, "Are we in danger of being overwhelmed by the products of our society and wastage created by their production? Would you agree with this photographer's interpretation?"[3] Two books show the same picture of an old black woman sitting in a straight chair in a dingy room, her hands folded in graceful resignation;[4] the surrounding text discusses the problems faced by the urban poor and by the aged who depend on Social Security. Other books present current problems less starkly. One of the texts concludes sagely:

Problems are part of life. Nations face them, just as people face them, and try to solve them. And today's Americans have one great advantage over past generations. Never before have Americans been so well equipped to solve their problems. They have today the means to conquer poverty, disease, and ignorance. The technetronic age has put that power into their hands.[5]

Such passages have a familiar ring. Amid all the problems, the deus ex machina of science still dodders around in the gloaming of pious hope.

9   Even more surprising than the emergence of problems is the discovery that the great unity of the texts has broken. Whereas in the fifties all texts represented the same political view, current texts follow no pattern of orthodoxy. Some books, for instance, portray civil-rights legislation as a series of actions taken by a wise, paternal government; others convey some suggestion of the social upheaval involved and make mention of such people as Stokely Carmichael and Malcolm X. In some books, the Cold War has ended; in others, it continues, with Communism threatening the free nations of the earth.

10   The political diversity in the books is matched by a diversity of pedagogical approach. In addition to the traditional narrative histories, with their endless streams of facts, there are so-called "discovery," or "inquiry," texts, which deal with a limited number of specific issues in American history. These texts do not pretend to cover the past; they focus on particular topics, such as "stratification in Colonial society" or "slavery and the American Revolution," and illustrate them with documents from primary and secondary sources. The chapters in these books amount to something like case studies, in that they include testimony from people with different perspectives or conflicting views on a single subject. In addition, the chapters provide background information, explanatory notes, and a series of questions for the student. The questions are the heart of the matter, for when they are carefully selected they force students to think much as historians think: to define the point of view of the speaker, analyze the ideas presented, question the relationship between events, and so on. One text, for example, quotes Washington, Jefferson, and John Adams on the question of foreign alliances and then asks, "What did John Adams assume that the international situation would be after the American Revolution? What did Washington's attitude toward the French alliance seem to be? How do you account for his attitude?" Finally, it asks, "Should a nation adopt a policy toward alliances and cling to it consistently, or should it vary its policies toward other countries as circumstances change?"[6] In these books, history is clearly not a list of agreed-upon facts or a sermon on politics but a babble of voices and a welter of events which must be ordered by the historian.

11   In matters of pedagogy, as in matters of politics, there are not two sharply differentiated categories of books; rather, there is a spectrum. Politically, the books run from moderate left to moderate right; pedagogically, they run from the traditional history sermons, through a middle ground of narrative texts with inquiry-style questions and of inquiry texts with long stretches of narrative, to the most rigorous of case-study books. What is common to the current texts—and makes all of them different from those of the fifties—is their engagement with the social sciences. In eighth-grade histories, the "concepts" of social science make fleeting appearances. But these "concepts" are the very foundation stones of various elementary-school social-studies series. The 1970 Harcourt Brace Jovanovich series, for example, boasts in its preface of "a horizontal base or ordering of conceptual schemes" to match its "vertical arm of behavioral themes."[7] What this means is not entirely clear, but the books do proceed from easy questions to hard ones, such as— in the sixth-grade book—"How was interaction between merchants and citizens different in the Athenian and Spartan social systems?" Virtually all the American-history texts for older children include discussions of "role," "status," and "culture." Some of them stage debates between eminent social scientists in roped-off sections of the text; some include essays on economics or sociology; some contain pictures and short biographies of social scientists of both sexes and of diverse races. Many books seem to accord social scientists a higher status than American Presidents.

12   Quite as striking as these political and pedagogical alterations is the change in the physical appearance of the texts. The schoolbooks of the fifties showed some effort in the matter of design: they had maps, charts, cartoons, photographs, and an occasional four-color picture to break up the columns of print. But beside the current texts they look as naïve as Soviet fashion magazines. The print in the fifties books is heavy and far too black, the colors muddy. The photographs are conventional news shots—portraits of Presidents in three-quarters profile, posed "action" shots of soldiers. The other illustrations tend to be Socialist-realist-style drawings (there are a lot of hefty farmers with hoes in the Colonial-period chapters) or incredibly vulgar made-for-children paintings of patriotic events. One painting shows Columbus standing in full court dress on a beach in the New World from a perspective that could have belonged only to the Arawaks. By contrast, the current texts are paragons of sophisticated modern design. They look not like *People* or *Family Circle* but, rather, like *Architectural Digest* or *Vogue*. One of them has an Abstract Expressionist design on its cover, another a Rauschenberg-style collage, a third a reproduction of an American primitive painting. Inside, almost all of them have a full-page reproduction of a painting of the New York school—a Jasper Johns flag, say, or "The

Boston Massacre," by Larry Rivers. But these reproductions are separated only with difficulty from the over-all design, for the time charts in the books look like Noland stripe paintings, and the distribution charts are as punctilious as Albers' squares in their color gradings. The amount of space given to illustrations is far greater than it was in the fifties; in fact, in certain "slow-learner" books the pictures far outweigh the text in importance. However, the illustrations have a much greater historical value. Instead of made-up paintings or anachronistic sketches, there are cartoons, photographs, and paintings drawn from the periods being treated. The chapters on the Colonial period will show, for instance, a ship's carved prow, a Revere bowl, a Copley painting—a whole gallery of Early Americana. The nineteenth century is illustrated with nineteenth-century cartoons and photographs—and the photographs are all of high artistic quality. As for the twentieth-century chapters, they are adorned with the contents of a modern-art museum.

13   The use of all this art and high-quality design contains some irony. The nineteenth-century photographs of child laborers or urban slum apartments are so beautiful that they transcend their subjects. To look at them, or at the Victor Gatto painting of the Triangle shirtwaist-factory fire, is to see not misery or ugliness but an art object. In the modern chapters, the contrast between style and content is just as great: the color photographs of junkyards or polluted rivers look as enticing as *Gourmet*'s photographs of food. The book that is perhaps the most stark in its description of modern problems illustrates the horrors of nuclear testing with a pretty Ben Shahn picture of the Bikini explosion, and the potential for global ecological disaster with a color photograph of the planet swirling its mantle of white clouds.[8] Whereas in the nineteen-fifties the texts were childish in the sense that they were naïve and clumsy, they are now childish in the same sense that they are polymorphous-perverse. American history is not dull any longer; it is a sensuous experience.

14   The surprise that adults feel in seeing the changes in history texts must come from the lingering hope that there is, somewhere out there, an objective truth. The hope is, of course, foolish. All of us children of the twentieth century know, or should know, that there are no absolutes in human affairs, and thus there can be no such thing as perfect objectivity. We know that each historian in some degree creates the world anew and that all history is in some degree contemporary history. But beyond this knowledge there is still a hope for some reliable authority, for some fixed stars in the universe. We may know journalists cannot be wholly unbiased and that "balance" is an imaginary point between two extremes, and yet we hope that Walter Cronkite will tell us the truth of things. In the same way, we hope that our history will not change—that we learned the truth of things as children. The texts,

with their impersonal voices, encourage this hope, and therefore it is particularly disturbing to see how they change, and how fast.

15   Slippery history! Not every generation but every few years the content of American-history books for children changes appreciably. Schoolbooks are not, like trade books, written and left to their fate. To stay in step with the cycles of "adoption" in school districts across the country, the publishers revise most of their old texts or substitute new ones every three or four years. In the process of revision, they not only bring history up to date but make changes—often substantial changes—in the body of the work. History books for children are thus more contemporary than any other form of history. How should it be otherwise? Should students read histories written ten, fifteen, thirty years ago? In theory, the system is reasonable—except that each generation of children reads only one generation of schoolbooks. That transient history is those children's history forever—their particular version of America.

16   The nature of the influence that these textbooks have on children is, of course, another matter. Many studies have been done on the question of what seventeen- or eighteen-year-old Americans know about their history and their political system, with uniformly depressing results. A recent survey by the National Assessment of Educational Progress showed that forty-seven percent of the nation's seventeen-year-olds did not know that each state has two United States senators.[9] A wholly unscientific survey of my own would show that few American adults can remember as much as the name of the history textbook they "had" in secondary school. And the sight of an old textbook is much less likely to bring back the sequence of Presidents or the significance of the Hawley-Smoot Tariff Act than it is to evoke the scene of an eighth-grade classroom: the sight of, say, Peggy, one long leg wrapped around the other, leaning forward on the scarred green bench, or Stevie talking a mile a minute and excitedly twirling his persistent cowlick. Rabbits, it is said, cannot remember pain or fear for more than sixty seconds. Perhaps human beings cannot remember things that bored them. Memory has its own antidotes. On the other hand, the fact that one cannot remember the order of the Presidents does not mean that all is lost. Amid the telephone numbers, nursery rhymes, and advertising jingles that we carry around in our heads, there are often snatches of textbook history. My own snatches consist of visual images detached from their context: Balboa on his peak in Darien; the supporters of Andrew Jackson celebrating his first election by tromping over the White House furniture in their muddy boots. Other people have more literary memories. "I had Muzzey," one friend told me recently. "Wonderful book. I'll never forget the scene of Lincoln after the Battle of Gettysburg looking over the graves in the cemetery and a voice crying out to him, 'Calhooon! Calhoooon!' " The memory of my friend was not, as it turned out, per-

fectly accurate, for in David Saville Muzzey's *American History* William Lloyd Garrison is speaking at a banquet in Charleston after the war, and about him Muzzey asks rhetorically, "Did the echoes of his voice reach a grave over which stood a marble stone engraved with the single word 'Calhoun'?"[10] Still, my friend had remembered the dramatic irony, and that was surely the essence of this particular passage.

17   In some general sense, this may be the truth of the matter: what sticks to the memory from those textbooks is not any particular series of facts but an atmosphere, an impression, a tone. And this impression may be all the more influential just because one cannot remember the facts and arguments that created it. In the fifties, we learned from our texts—math and English as well as history—that Americans were a tolerant people, full of common sense, practical, industrious, democratic, civic-minded, and generally homogeneous. That we, then or later, read about Cotton Mather, slavery and the Civil War, Thoreau, the Molly Maguires, and vigilante rule in San Francisco somehow did not cause us to alter this impression. It was only the events of the nineteen-sixties that changed it. To learn that Americans were also violent, idealistic, and divided by race and culture was not just to learn something new but to undergo a re-education. What the current texts say about the American Revolution or the Vietnam War may therefore have some importance: though the memory of children may reduce much of it to white sound, some may remain as a tone of voice, a definition of the register.

Notes

[1]Wood, Leonard C., Ralph H. Gabriel, and Edward L. Biller, *America: Its People and Values*. New York: Harcourt, Brace, Jovanovich, 1975, p. 3. [Eds.]

[2]King, David C. and Charlotte C. Anderson, *The United States*, sixth level. Boston: Houghton Mifflin Social Studies Program, 1976, pp. 15–16. [Eds.]

[3]Sellers, Charles G., et al., *As It Happened: A History of the United States*. New York: McGraw-Hill, 1975, p. 812. [Eds.]

[4]Graff, Henry F., *The Free and the Brave: The Story of the American People*, Second Edition. Chicago: Rand McNally, 1973, p. 696. Graff, Henry R. and John A. Krout, *The Adventure of the American People*, Second Edition. Chicago: Rand McNally, 1973, p. 784. [Eds.]

[5]Wood, Gabriel, and Biller, *America* (1975), p. 812.

[6]Fenton, Edwin, gen. ed., *A New History of the United States: An Inquiry Approach*. New York: Holt, Rinehart and Winston, 1969, p. 170. [Eds.]

[7]Brandwein, Paul Franz, et al., *The Social Sciences: Concepts and Values*. 6 vols., seven levels, kindergarten through grade six. New York: Harcourt, Brace Jovanovich, 1975. [Eds.]

[8]Ver Steeg, Clarence L. and Richard Hofstadter, *A People and a Nation*. New York: Harper & Row, 1974, pp. 722–723. [Eds.]

[9]*New York Times*, January 2, 1977.

[10]Muzzey, David Saville, *An American History*. Boston: Ginn, 1936, p. 420. [Eds.]

Content Questions

1. How do textbooks of the 1950s differ from contemporary textbooks?
2. Why is Columbus now a "minor character"?
3. How do contemporary history textbooks view science?
4. What types of illustrations were typical in history textbooks of the 1950s?
5. What is ironic about the use of art and high-quality design in history textbooks?
6. What "sticks in the memory" from old history texts?

Questions on Presentation

1. How do you believe FitzGerald views her audience in paragraph 1?
2. FitzGerald uses a series of rhetorical questions in paragraph 7. Why does she use them? What is their effect on the reader?
3. FitzGerald uses comparison/contrast to present part of her argument. Is it convincingly detailed or not?
4. Define vindictive (4), technetronic (8), deus ex machina (8), gloaming (8), pedagogy (11), and punctilious (12).
5. Does FitzGerald's level of diction contribute to or detract from her essay?

The Parable of the Cave

Plato

Although he lived during one of the richest literary and philosophic periods, Greek philosopher Plato (c. 427 B.C.–c. 347 B.C.) was seldom mentioned by contemporaries such as Isocrates, Dionysius, or Aristotle. Born to a wealthy family, Plato probably served in the cavalry during the war against Sparta. When the democratic cause prevailed in Athens, Plato, an aristocrat, found himself without political influence. His political prospects took a further turn for the worse when his teacher, Socrates, was executed in 399 B.C. for "impiety" or "irreligion"; shortly afterward, Plato and other students of Socrates took refuge in Megara, an ancient city in east central Greece. Plato traveled extensively in Egypt and Sicily before establishing his Academy in 387 B.C. Plato's Academy differed from earlier forms of education in several ways. Previously, there were no organized institutions of higher education; instead, young men were taught individually, by tutors, skills they would subsequently need in their careers. The Academy had a many-sided curriculum and, consequently, several different teachers. In addition, it trained students in academics rather than for vocations such as orator or politician. Despite these seeming similarities, Plato's Academy was not the equivalent of modern universities: the Academy did not give examinations or degrees, probably did not have a library, and did not employ different ranks of instructors. Whether the Academy ever charged its students fees is unknown; however, we do know that, shortly before Plato's death at age eighty-one, the Academy became an endowed foundation.

As a philosopher, Plato wrote dialogues, dramatic addresses in which he sought a truth about a topic by examining and overcoming the contradictions of an argument. As a writer, Plato filled his prose with a rich vocabulary, high drama, humor, irony, bluntness, and metaphor. In the following selection, taken from Book VII of *Republic*, Plato skillfully compares people destitute of philosophy to prisoners in a cave.

1   Next, said I, here is a parable to illustrate the degrees in which our nature may be enlightened or unenlightened. Imagine the condition of men living in a sort of cavernous chamber underground, with an entrance open to the light and a long passage all down the cave. Here they have been from childhood, chained by the leg and also by the neck, so that they cannot move and can see only what is in front of them, because the chains will not let them turn their heads. At some distance higher up is the light of a fire burning behind them; and between the prisoners and the fire is a track[1] with a parapet built along it, like the screen at a puppet-show, which hides the performers while they show their puppets over the top.

2   I see, said he.

3   Now behind this parapet imagine persons carrying along various artificial objects, including figures of men and animals in wood or stone or other materials, which project above the parapet. Naturally, some of these persons will be talking, others silent.[2]

4   It is a strange picture, he said, and a strange sort of prisoners.

5   Like ourselves, I replied; for in the first place prisoners so confined would have seen nothing of themselves or of one another, except the shadows thrown by the fire-light on the wall of the Cave facing them, would they?

6   Not if all their lives they had been prevented from moving their heads.

7   And they would have seen as little of the objects carried past.

8   Of course.

9   Now, if they could talk to one another, would they not suppose that their words referred only to those passing shadows which they saw?

10   Necessarily.

11   And suppose their prisoner had an echo from the wall facing them? When one of the people crossing behind them spoke, they could only suppose that the sound came from the shadow passing before their eyes.

12   No doubt.

13 In every way, then, such prisoners would recognize as reality nothing but the shadows of those artificial objects.

14 Inevitably.

15 Now consider what would happen if their release from the chains and the healing of their unwisdom should come about in this way. Suppose one of them set free and forced suddenly to stand up, turn his head, and walk with eyes lifted to the light; all these movements would be painful, and he would be too dazzled to make out the objects whose shadows he had been used to see. What do you think he would say, if someone told him that what he had formerly seen was meaningless illusion, but now, being somewhat nearer to reality and turned towards more real objects, he was getting a truer view? Suppose further that he were shown the various objects being carried by and were made to say, in reply to questions, what each of them was. Would he not be perplexed and believe the objects now shown him to be not so real as what he formerly saw?

16 Yes, not nearly so real.

17 And if he were forced to look at the fire-light itself, would not his eyes ache, so that he would try to escape and turn back to the things which he could see distinctly, convinced that they really were clearer than these other objects now being shown to him?

18 Yes.

19 And suppose someone were to drag him away forcibly up the steep and rugged ascent and not let him go until he had hauled him out into the sunlight, would he not suffer pain and vexation at such treatment, and, when he had come out into the light, find his eyes so full of its radiance that he could not see a single one of the things that he was now told were real?

20 Certainly he would not see them all at once.

21 He would need, then, to grow accustomed before he could see things in that upper world. At first it would be easiest to make out shadows, and then the images of men and things reflected in water, and later on the things themselves. After that, it would be easier to watch the heavenly bodies and the sky itself by night, looking at the light of the moon and stars rather than the Sun and the Sun's light in the day-time.

22 Yes, surely.

23 Last of all, he would be able to look at the Sun and contemplate its nature, not as it appears when reflected in water or any alien medium, but as it is in itself in its own domain.

24 No doubt.

25 And now he would begin to draw the conclusion that it is the Sun that produces the seasons and the course of the year and controls everything in the visible world, and moreover is in a way the cause of all that he and his companions used to see.

26 Clearly he would come at last to that conclusion.

27   Then if he called to mind his fellow prisoners and what passed for wisdom in his former dwelling-place, he would surely think himself happy in the change and be sorry for them. They may have had a practice of honouring and commending one another, with prizes for the man who had the keenest eye for the passing shadows and the best memory for the order in which they followed or accompanied one another, so that he could make a good guess as to which was going to come next. Would our released prisoner be likely to covet those prizes or to envy the men exalted to honour and power in the Cave? Would he not feel like Homer's Achilles, that he would far sooner 'be on earth as a hired servant in the house of a landless man' or endure anything rather than go back to his old beliefs and live in the old way?

28   Yes, he would prefer any fate to such a life.

29   Now imagine what would happen if he went down again to take his former seat in the Cave. Coming suddenly out of the sunlight, his eyes would be filled with darkness. He might be required once more to deliver his opinion on those shadows, in competition with the prisoners who had never been released, while his eyesight was still dim and unsteady; and it might take some time to become used to the darkness. They would laugh at him and say that he had gone up only to come back with his sight ruined; it was worth no one's while even to attempt the ascent. If they could lay hands on the man who was trying to set them free and lead them up, they would kill him.

30   Yes, they would.

31   Every feature in this parable, my dear Glaucon,[3] is meant to fit our earlier analysis. The prison dwelling corresponds to the region revealed to us through the sense of sight, and the fire-light within it to the power of the Sun. The ascent to see the things in the upper world you may take as standing for the upward journey of the soul into the region of the intelligible; then you will be in possession of what I surmise, since that is what you wish to be told. Heaven knows whether it is true; but this, at any rate, is how it appears to me. In the world of knowledge, the last thing to be perceived and only with great difficulty is the essential Form of Goodness. Once it is perceived, the conclusion must follow that, for all things, this is the cause of whatever is right and good; in the visible world it gives birth to light and to the lord of light, while it is itself sovereign in the intelligible world and the parent of intelligence and truth. Without having had a vision of this Form no one can act with wisdom, either in his own life or in matters of state.

Notes

[1]The track crosses the passage into the cave at right angles, and is *above* the parapet built along it.

[2]A modern Plato would compare his Cave to an underground cinema, where the audience watch the play of shadows thrown by the film passing before a light at their backs. The film itself is only an image of 'real' things and events in the world outside the cinema. For the film Plato has to substitute the clumsier apparatus of a procession of artificial objects carried on their heads by persons who are merely part of the machinery, providing for the movement of the objects and the sounds whose echo the prisoners hear. The parapet prevents these persons' shadows from being cast on the wall of the Cave.

[3]Plato's brother, son of Ariston. Plato uses Glaucon to make this monologue appear to be a dialogue. [Eds.]

Content Questions

1. In what ways are the prisoners unwise?
2. How will the released prisoner gain happiness from pain?
3. What sort of person is compelled to return to the cave and help the other prisoners?
4. Why will the released prisoner have difficulty convincing the other prisoners to leave the cave?

Questions on Presentation

1. How does Plato use analogy to advance his argument?
2. Plato uses dialogue, often in the form of questions and answers, to develop this essay. Is this device effective? How do you, as a reader, respond to this rhetorical device?
3. Does the detailed discussion Plato provides in paragraphs 15, 17, 19, and 21 make the argument easy or difficult to follow? Why?
4. Why does Plato make the parallels in paragraph 31 so obvious?

Questions for Discussion and Writing

1. As many critics have noted, contemporary history textbooks hint that American history has had some unpleasant events but that the writers "change" history by eliminating any unpleasantness. How will events currently in the news, such as the president's proposed Strategic Defense Initiative or the economic status of the country, likely be reported in history textbooks? Do you think that any "unpleasantness" connected with these issues should be recorded? Will such information help future students understand the event better or will such information obscure the important facts of the event?
2. In different ways, several of the essays in this section address questions about educational values. Some of the writers imply what values their

readers should admire. Others discuss who should be charged with teaching these values. Do high schools or colleges consciously teach values to their students? Should schools teach values? If not, where should values be taught? If students should receive such education, when should it begin? Elementary school? High school? College? Should it be part of the regular coursework or an extra-curricular activity?

3. How is the apparent lack of appropriate values in education manifested today? Do you see it in business? in sports? in industry? in science? What can be done to correct this lack?

4. Assume, for the moment, that schools are appropriate settings in which to teach values. What values should be taught in schools? Should students receive instruction in ethical questions such as how to assess human worth? If so, how will they be taught to make such assessments? Should they assess worth by money? by accomplishments? by other criteria?

5. Many of the essays in this section are concerned with the subjects being taught. For example, one of the assertions found in the report by the President's Commission is that "learning is the indispensable investment required for success in the 'information age' we are entering." For many people, this statement implies that knowledge of science and technology is important while knowledge of art and music is not. Is a knowledge of art and music dispensable or indispensable in the coming "information age"?

Section 2

DISSENT: RIGHTS OR RESPONSIBILITIES?

A Delineation of Dissent

Edwin Scott Gaustad

Edwin Scott Gaustad (b. 1923), a professor of history at the University of California at Riverside, is the author of several books including *Dissent in American Religion*, the first volume in the Chicago History of American Religion series edited by Martin E. Marty. In this selection, Gaustad introduces one of his major themes in *Dissent in American Religion*, the essential part dissent plays in America's religious character.

1   In America religious dissent is as vital as it is elusive. Like the secretions of the pituitary, the juices of dissent are essential to ongoing life even if we do not always know precisely how, when, or where they perform their task. And the not knowing—the flimsy, filmy elusiveness—is supremely characteristic of America's expressions of religious dissent. For in the United States no stalwart orthodoxy stands ever-ready to parry the sharp thrust or clever feints of dissent. No National Church resists or restrains the indigenous as well as the imported gift for schism. Of course, there are fashions, there are hucksterings of consent. Slogans do prevail for a time, and self-evident maxims receive widespread assent until another generation perversely fails to perceive their self-evidence. But the altars and idols revolve, court favorites fall, once noble churches stand in ruins, dogmas are defoliated and die. If only consensus stood still, dissent would be so much easier to locate, tag, and train.

2   That consensus—and society—do not stand still is the business and burden of dissent. All societies, even those that cry out against all

change, require a mechanism for change. If the written law resembles that of the Medes and Persians, then there must be an oral law, a lively tradition, a juicier commentary, a freer oracle to make flexible and timely that which is "unchanging and eternal." All these mechanisms, however much a creature of the establishment they appear to be, hear and respond to the strident, impatient voices of dissent. It is true that societies often call for the silencing of dissent. Should a society actually succeed, however, in suffocating all contrary opinion, then its own vital juices no longer flow and the shadow of death begins to fall across it. No society—ecclesiastical or political, military or literary—can afford to be snared by its own slogans.

3   Dissent, therefore, is not a social disease. While this proposition presents no particular difficulty when read in the library, its reception is different in the marketplace or on the march, in the town meeting or within the church council, at the political forum or even around the family hearth. For dissent seen as live action rather than as safe replay can be, and generally is, irritating, unnerving, pig-headed, noisy, and brash. It can also be wrong. And if often wrong, is not the suffering it provokes too keen to compensate for its now-and-then stumble into the right? That earnest, poignant question will not down. Its answer determines how firm or fine that line between a society that is open and one that is closed, a society that is virile and creative as opposed to one that is sterile and decadent. To steal a rhythm from Reinhold Niebuhr, consent makes democracy possible; dissent makes democracy meaningful.

4   In most of Western Civilization's history, religious dissent has presented few problems of definition—whatever other problems it has brought in its wake. One recited the common creed and counted the recalcitrants who refused to join in its intoning. Or, one stood within the established church and readily categorized all who were cast from that visible, much-favored body. Or, one studied the law to see who enjoyed the sanction and protection of public authority, and who did not. Dissent's flag flew high, calling a few to its redoubt, warning more against a treacherous, often fatal bog. Outcasts knew without question of their despised and lowly estate; a few eccentrics may even have reveled in it. The Establishment on the other hand bore with dignity the burdens that leadership, power, and wisdom impose. Divisions were clear: the lions knew whom to devour.

5   The American experiment, the American folly, was to place both orthodoxy and dissent upon the same shifting platforms of public favor and public support. Throughout so much of American history, it has been distressingly difficult to separate the "ins" from the "outs": What was stubborn schism in Massachusetts was quiet conformity in Virginia; what was doctrinal sobriety in Pennsylvania was intolerable "enthusiasm" in Connecticut; what was proper churchmanship in Rhode

Island was arrogant pretension almost everywhere else. E pluribus unum in early America? Hardly. Not only was there wild diversity in space, there was unsettling instability in time. The conformity so rigidly demanded in the seventeenth century was largely forgotten in the eighteenth. What was theological terror for one generation was for the next a vaguely disquieting dream. That which one age was willing to die for another age was not prepared to live for. And then deliberate disestablishment with the adoption of the First Amendment in 1791, further confounding the contrary categories of orthodoxy and dissent, or respectability and heresy, of decency and order against impropriety and sectarian novelty. The lions might be thirsty for blood, but where should they turn? So the confusions concerning good order, right opinion, and agreeable behavior continued until the vices of dissent were seen as virtues and the glories of pluralism were heralded as the American Way of Life. Up to a point.

6   For if society is diverse, flexible, adaptive, and pragmatic, why do we still hear quarrelsome cries of dissent? Why cannot everybody cooperate, get along, play the game, work within the system? Why multitudes still so unmelted, still so unwashed? Why the long lines of detractors and despisers, the sweaty crowds of nay-sayers and protesters? Is it possible that dissent is something more than flexible adaptability, that the abandonment of "creeds outworn" is not its full message? Is it possible to gain the "free world" and nonetheless lose one's soul? Dissent cannot be understood simply in terms of whines against oppression, resistance to organizational corruption, demurrers against the affirmations of others. To view dissent in these terms is to suppose that when all external restraints are removed and all ecclesiastical authority stilled, then dissent falls flat on its face never to rise again. This could be the case only if dissenters were merely noisy nay-sayers.

7   But history hones dissent to a fine edge: sharp, severe, unyielding. While it is true that restraint and oppression frequently give dissent its cohesion and therefore its strength as a mass movement, it is not true that, apart from these external forces, the dissenter is without aim or energy or nerve. Rather, the dissenter is a powerful if unpredictable engine in the service of a cause. Though he is prone to many sins, sloth is not his crime. The path of greatest resistance is frequently the very one that the dissenter sets himself upon. He may cast out demons dwelling in others; himself he cannot save.

8   One might argue that the above describes not the dissenting man but the religious man, *homo religiosus*. This observation has some validity. Religion in its essence is already offbeat, irregular, asymmetric. It confronts and attempts to cope with the unexpected and the unexplained. That which conforms, that which is balanced, that which is orderly and precise does not require the ministrations of cult or clergy, of ritual or

myth. The profoundly religious man resists the routine, defies the machine, confounds the computer. In Abraham Heschel's terms, he is concerned not with process but with event. Yet, as everyone knows, religious institutions do make their peace with the world, they do themselves become part of the regular order. So the prophet contends against the priest, protests the accommodations, calls forth fresh energies, and challenges the unfeeling stones within existing structures. This reform of religion in the name of religion, this growing edge, this refusal to let well enough alone, is the role of dissent. In Christian history even monasticism began as a form of dissent—a protest against a hardening of ecclesiastical arteries that even by the third century had already set in.

9   If dissent is a distillation of the religious quest, it may also be a manifestation of the unfettered human spirit. The dissenter is autonomous and inner-directed, displaying all of the pompous arrogance or heroic sacrifice of which a free spirit is capable. Like any fanatic, the dissenter can be a threat to civilization; like some fanatics, he may be the restorer or the inspirer of civilization. If cultural peaks are scaled only when a delicate balance between chaos and order obtains, dissent's contribution to one side of that balance is clear. The liberal, so often seen as the major instrument of progress and change, may in fact be the major voice for accommodation and consent. He sees the cultural train as something that all right-thinking persons should get aboard. The dissenter, on the other hand, may indicate that he really does not care for the way the tracks are laid, nor does he have much confidence that adjustments in throttle settings will give society a sense of direction or purpose. Long before counter-culture became a cliché, the dissenter was in the business of resisting a tyrannous majority, disturbing an establishment's peace, and breaking the bondage to a moderating, mollifying, debilitating civility.

10   In his *Genealogy of Morals,* Friedrich Nietzsche (1844–1900) vented his scorn upon a society grown soft and slavish. A political system, namely democracy, extols comfort, fashion, and mediocrity, while a religious system, namely Christianity, venerates meekness and reverence and all that is sickly and hanging on a cross. Together, he argued, they destroy the bold, free, creative spirit, replacing it with that "pink of modernity, who 'bites no longer,' shakes hands politely in a fashion that is at least instructive, the latter exhibiting a certain facial expression of refined and good-humored indolence, tinged with a touch of pessimism and exhaustion; as if it really did not matter to take all those things—I mean moral problems—so seriously." What Nietzsche missed in the world around him was a spirit of dissent.

11   That same hollowness disturbed Sören Kierkegaard (1813–1855). With biting wit, the Danish theologian no less than the German philosopher was prepared to lay much blame at the door of the Christianity of his

time and place. Kierkegaard's *Attack Upon "Christendom"* was, in the spirit of religious dissent, an attack upon a false, compromised, tame religion for the sake of a true, absolute, ever-discontented, ever-dissenting faith. The New Testament has nothing in common, he wrote, with all this "twaddle, twattle, patter, smallness, mediocrity, playing at Christianity, transforming everything into mere words." This is why in nineteenth-century Europe the New Testament seems unable "to punch a blow at real life." No one takes Christianity with sufficient seriousness even to attack it or dissent from it. ". . . for one certified hypocrite there are 100,000 twaddlers; for one certified heretic, 100,000 nincompoops." In this polite pink of modernity, one finds no absolute commitment, no unconditional surrender to a cause, but only a tentativeness, a pledge of trust "to a certain degree." This calculating caution is the disease that must be cured. If, however, the world sets about to cure itself, the chances are that it will seek to do so only "to a certain degree." A Swedish priest, Kierkegaard noted, dismayed by his sermon's effect on the congregation, added soothingly, "Children, do not weep; the whole thing might be a lie." Kierkegaard, too, missed the bold presence of dissent.

12   America, like nineteenth-century Europe, has had its theoreticians of dissent, but in far greater abundance has it had its practitioners. Dissenters against the structure and authority of ecclesiasticism, dissenters against the rigidity or folly or sterility of religious ideas, dissenters against the hopes and the messianic pretensions of the social order. Dissenters in such number and variety as to suggest that not all Americans surrendered to good-humored indolence or to mediocre twaddle. Not all resigned themselves to the awesome power of churches, of creeds, of cultural captivities. Rather, they engaged in and took up the banner of "dissent."

13   Still the word has not been neatly defined. It is easier to describe where the wind blows and what effects it has than it is to declare the precise nature of the wind. Dissent, we have already observed, is elusive and erratic; religious dissent, far from being an exception to that rule, is an exaggeration of it. Religious dissent can be illustrated and typed; the "sins" against love, against faith, against society can be described. All this, however, is illustrative, not exhaustive. If it were possible totally to box and compass religious dissent, its very character would be transformed. True dissent has too many moods, too many guises, too many brief incarnations.

14   The enemy, on the other hand, is in a sense always the same: Procrustean beds of any make, shibboleths in any form. Thus the religious dissenter cries out against absurd confinements in manners and morals, against the fatuous kowtowing of body or of mind, against the circumscribing of vision or of aspiration, against the evil that men do in the

name of good, against indifference, insensitivity, and inertia. Sometimes the dissenter turns out to be a saint, more often he does not. Sometimes he prevails, more often he does not. Sometimes it is safe to ignore him, more often it is not. Society's and religion's problem is that amid the clanging cymbals of consensus it is frequently difficult to hear what the dissenter is trying to say. One has to make a special effort to listen. He that has ears to hear, said a dissenter of ancient days, let him hear.

Content Questions

1. What is the nature of the "American experiment"?
2. How is dissent the "manifestation of the unfettered human spirit"?
3. How do Nietzsche's and Kierkegaard's positions compare to Gaustad's?

Questions on Presentation

1. Gaustad's essay is likely to be offensive to a number of people, especially those who, as "ins" are repelled and threatened by dissent from the "outs." This being so, how does Gaustad create his causal discussion to make his argument acceptable, even convincing, to any audience?
2. In paragraph 3 Gaustad uses a variety of metaphors and images to describe dissent. Are these effective? Why or why not?
3. What do the allusions in paragraph 5 say about Gaustad's perception of his audience?
4. Gaustad often uses balanced or parallel constructions in his sentences. What effect do these choices have on his argument?
5. How does the argument as developed in paragraphs 10 and 11 advance Gaustad's thesis?

The Declaration of Independence

Thomas Jefferson et al.

Thomas Jefferson (1743–1826), a Virginia farmer, architect, inventor, and writer, graduated from the College of William and Mary in 1763, studied law, and was admitted to the bar in 1767. After serving in the House of Burgesses in Williamsburg, he entered the Continental Congress in 1775. The Continental Congress selected Jefferson, with colleagues such as Benjamin Franklin and John

Adams, to write a declaration of independence. The final document, primarily Jefferson's work, was hotly debated by the Congress before its acceptance. From 1779 to 1781 Jefferson was governor of Virginia, succeeding Patrick Henry. He went on to negotiate several treaties with France and later became minister to France. When he returned from Europe in 1787, the Constitution had already been written. Because of his objections to the document, the Continental Congress added the Bill of Rights. Elected president of the United States in 1800, Jefferson doubled the nation's area and secured access to the Pacific with the Louisiana Purchase in 1803. After retiring from political life, Jefferson not only renewed his interests in farming and inventing, he also founded the University of Virginia. Jefferson died in Virginia on July 4, 1826, the same day as his contemporary and friend John Adams. His extensive library, sold to the U.S. Congress in 1814, became the core for the Library of Congress.

Jefferson's vision of democracy is not drawn from the British Federalist view but from the French Republicans. For Jefferson, government should be based on the ideal of self-reliant agrarianism and rules best when it protects the general welfare of its citizens. In the Declaration of Independence (1776), Jefferson recounts the grievances that the colonists had against British rule and argues for a government created not by foreign rule but by the consent of the governed. Thus, not only are individuals' rights and freedoms more important than institutions, but individuals have the obligation to destroy institutions if the institutions no longer serve the people's needs.

1   When in the Course of human events it becomes necessary for one people to dissolve the political bands which have connected them with another, and to assume among the powers of the earth, the separate and equal station to which the Laws of Nature and of Nature's God entitle them, a decent respect to the opinions of mankind requires that they should declare the causes which impel them to the separation.

2   We hold these truths to be self-evident, that all men are created equal, that they are endowed by their Creator with certain unalienable Rights, that among these are Life, Liberty and the pursuit of Happiness. That to secure these rights, Governments are instituted among Men, deriving their just powers from the consent of the governed. That whenever any Form of Government becomes destructive of these ends, it is the Right of the People to alter or to abolish it, and to institute new Government, laying its foundation on such principles, and organizing its powers in such form, as to them shall seem most likely to effect their Safety and Happiness. Prudence, indeed, will dictate that Governments long established should not be changed for light and transient causes; and accordingly all experience hath shewn, that mankind are more disposed to suffer, while evils are sufferable, than to right themselves by abolishing the forms to which they are accustomed. But when a long train of abuses and usurpations, pursuing invariably the same Object, evinces a design to reduce them under absolute Despotism, it is their right, it is

their duty, to throw off such Government, and to provide new Guards for their future security. Such has been the patient sufferance of these Colonies; and such is now the necessity which constrains them to alter their former Systems of Government. The history of the present King of Great Britain is a history of repeated injuries and usurpations, all having in direct object the establishment of an absolute Tyranny over these States. To prove this, let Facts be submitted to a candid world.

3 He has refused his Assent to Laws, the most wholesome and necessary for the public good.

4 He has forbidden his Governors to pass Laws of immediate and pressing importance, unless suspended in their operation till his Assent should be obtained; and when so suspended, he has utterly neglected to attend to them.

5 He has refused to pass other Laws for the accommodation of large districts of people, unless those people would relinquish the right of Representation in the Legislature, a right inestimable to them and formidable to tyrants only.

6 He has called together legislative bodies at places unusual, uncomfortable, and distant from the depository of their public Records, for the sole purpose of fatiguing them into compliance with his measures.

7 He has dissolved Representative Houses repeatedly, for opposing with manly firmness his invasions on the rights of the people.

8 He has refused for a long time after such dissolutions, to cause others to be elected; whereby the Legislative powers, incapable of Annihilation, have returned to the People at large for their exercise; the State remaining in the meantime exposed to all the dangers of invasion from without, and convulsions within.

9 He has endeavoured to prevent the population of these States, for that purpose obstructing the Laws of Naturalization of Foreigners, refusing to pass others to encourage their migrations hither, and raising the conditions of new Appropriations of Lands.

10 He has obstructed the Administration of Justice, by refusing his Assent to Laws for establishing Judiciary powers.

11 He has made Judges dependent on his Will alone, for the tenure of their offices, and the amount and payment of their salaries.

12 He has erected a multitude of New Offices, and sent hither swarms of Officers to harass our people, and eat out their substance.

13 He has kept among us, in times of peace Standing Armies, without the Consent of our legislatures.

14 He has affected to render the Military independent of and superior to the Civil power.

15 He has combined with others to subject us to a jurisdiction foreign to our constitution, and unacknowledged by our laws; giving his Assent to their Acts of pretended Legislation: For quartering large bodies of armed troops among us: For protecting them by a mock Trial from punishment

for any Murders which they should commit on the Inhabitants of these States: For cutting off our Trade with all parts of the world: For imposing Taxes on us without our Consent: For depriving us in many cases of the benefits of Trial by Jury: For transporting us beyond Seas to be tried for pretended offenses: For abolishing the free System of English Laws in a neighbouring Province, establishing therein an Arbitrary government, and enlarging its Boundaries so as to render it at once an example and fit instrument for introducing the same absolute rule into these Colonies: For taking away our Charters, abolishing our most valuable Laws and altering fundamentally the Forms of our Governments: For suspending our own Legislatures, and declaring themselves invested with power to legislate for us in all cases whatsover.

16   He has abdicated Government here by declaring us out of his Protection and waging War against us.

17   He has plundered our seas, ravaged our Coasts, burnt our towns, and destroyed the lives of our people.

18   He is at this time transporting large Armies of foreign Mercenaries to complete the works of death, desolation and tyranny, already begun with circumstances of Cruelty and perfidy scarcely paralleled in the most barbarous ages, and totally unworthy of the Head of a civilized nation.

19   He has constrained our fellow Citizens taken Captive on the high Seas to bear Arms against their Country, to become the executioners of their friends and Brethren, or to fall themselves by their Hands.

20   He has excited domestic insurrections amongst us, and has endeavoured to bring on the inhabitants of our frontiers, the merciless Indian Savages, whose known rule of warfare is an undistinguished destruction of all ages, sexes and conditions. In every stage of these Oppressions We have Petitioned for Redress in the most humble terms. Our repeated Petitions have been answered by repeated injury: A Prince, whose character is thus marked by every act which may define a Tyrant, is unfit to be the ruler of a free people. Nor have We been wanting in attentions to our British brethren. We have warned them from time to time of attempts by their legislature to extend an unwarrantable jurisdiction over us. We have reminded them of the circumstances of our emigration and settlement here. We have appealed to their native justice and magnanimity, and we have conjured them by the ties of our common kindred to disavow these usurpations, which would inevitably interrupt our connections and correspondence. They too have been deaf to the voice of justice and of consanguinity. We must, therefore, acquiesce in the necessity, which denounces our Separation, and hold them, as we hold the rest of mankind, Enemies in War, in Peace Friends.

21   WE, THEREFORE, the Representatives of the UNITED STATES OF AMERICA, in General Congress, Assembled, appealing to the Supreme Judge of the world for the rectitude of our intentions, do, in the Name

and by authority of the good People of these Colonies solemnly publish and declare That these United Colonies are and of Right ought to be FREE AND INDEPENDENT STATES; that they are Absolved from all Allegiance to the British Crown, and that all political connection between them and the State of Great Britain, is and ought to be totally dissolved; and that as Free and Independent States, they have full Power to levy War, conclude Peace, contract Alliances, establish Commerce, and to do all other Acts and Things which Independent States may of right do. And for the support of this Declaration, with a firm reliance on the protection of divine Providence, we mutually pledge to each other our Lives, our Fortunes, and our sacred Honor.

John Hancock

Button Gwinnett
Lyman Hall
George Walton
William Hooper
Joseph Hewes
John Penn
Edward Rutledge
Thos. Heyward Jr.
Thomas Lynch Jr.
Arthur Middleton
Samuel Chase
William Paca
Thomas Stone
Charles Carroll of Carrollton
George Wythe
Richard Henry Lee
Thomas Jefferson
Benjamin Harrison
Thos. Nelson Jr.
Francis Lightfoot Lee
Carter Braxton
Robert Morris
Benjamin Rush
Benjamin Franklin
John Morton
Geo Clymer
James Smith
George Taylor

James Wilson
George Ross
Caesar Rodney
George Read
Thomas McKean
William Floyd
Philip Livingston
Francis Lewis
Lewis Morris
Richard Stockton
John Witherspoon
Francis Hopkinson
John Hart
Abraham Clark
Josiah Bartlett
William Whipple
Samuel Adams
John Adams
Robert Treat Paine
Elbridge Gerry
Stephen Hopkins
William Ellery
Roger Sherman
Samuel Huntington
William Williams
Oliver Wolcott
Matthew Thornton

Content Questions

1. Why should a dissenting people make clear the nature of their dissent?

2. What forces prevent people from altering or abolishing their government?

3. What does Jefferson hope to gain by writing this statement of dissent?

Questions on Presentation

1. Jefferson presents a long list of abuses by King George III. Which of these examples is the most effective? Why?

2. Why does Jefferson feel it necessary to define the nature of government in paragraph 2? What techniques does he use to define it?

3. Would an objective audience be convinced by this argument? The colonists? The British? Whom do you believe Jefferson intended as his audience?

4. What tone do words such as usurpations (2), candid (2), inestimable (5), perfidy (18), consanguinity (20) create in the Declaration?

5. How does the sentence structure of the Declaration, written in an earlier century, compare or contrast to contemporary sentence structure?

A Modest Proposal for Preventing the Children of Poor People in Ireland from Being a Burden to Their Parents or Country, and for Making Them Beneficial to the Public

Jonathan Swift

Jonathan Swift (1667–1745), one of England's greatest satirists, was born to English parents and educated in Dublin. In 1689 Swift became Sir William Temple's secretary, a position he held off and on until Temple's death in 1699. His duties for Temple exposed Swift to the politics and literary life of contemporary London. Swift began writing satires on political and religious subjects including *The Tale of a Tub* (1704) and *Battle of the Books* (1704). However, with Temple's death, Swift had to support himself and his writing, so in 1700 he became the vicar of Laracor. In 1713 Swift was appointed Dean of St. Patrick's Cathedral, Dublin, and served in this position for most of his life. In the 1720s Swift became a vociferous supporter of Ireland, decrying English exploitation of his homeland. For this effort as for other social ills he identified, Swift wrote pamphlets and journal articles marked by sharp wit and ironic satire. His most famous book, *Gulliver's Travels* (1726), is an adult satire written as a children's book. Originally published in 1729 as a pamphlet, *A Modest Proposal* employs one of Swift's favorite literary devices: the supposedly unsentimental author coolly proposing heartless solutions for society's problems.

1   It is a melancholy object to those who walk through this great town[1] or travel in the country, when they see the streets, the roads, and cabin doors, crowded with beggars of the female-sex, followed by three, four, or six children, all in rags and importuning every passenger for an alms. These mothers, instead of being able to work for their honest livelihood, are forced to employ all their time in strolling to beg sustenance for their helpless infants, who, as they grow up, either turn thieves for want of work, or leave their dear native country to fight for the Pretender[2] in Spain, or sell themselves to the Barbadoes.

2   I think it is agreed by all parties that this prodigious number of children in the arms, or on the backs, or at the heels of their mothers, and frequently of their fathers, is in the present deplorable state of the kingdom a very great additional grievance; and therefore whoever could find out a fair, cheap, and easy method of making these children sound, useful members of the commonwealth would deserve so well of the public as to have his statue set up for a preserver of the nation.

3   But my intention is very far from being confined to provide only for the children of professed beggars; it is of a much greater extent, and shall take in the whole number of infants at a certain age who are born of parents in effect as little able to support them as those who demand our charity in the streets.

4   As to my own part, having turned my thoughts for many years upon this important subject, and maturely weighed the several schemes of other projectors,[3] I have always found them grossly mistaken in their computation. It is true, a child just dropped from its dam may be supported by her milk for a solar year, with little other nourishment; at most not above the value of two shillings,[4] which the mother may certainly get, or the value in scraps, by her lawful occupation of begging; and it is exactly at one year old that I propose to provide for them in such a manner as instead of being a charge upon their parents or the parish, or wanting food and raiment for the rest of their lives, they shall on the contrary contribute to the feeding, and partly to the clothing, of many thousands.

5   There is likewise another great advantage in my scheme, that it will prevent those voluntary abortions, and that horrid practice of women murdering their bastard children, alas, too frequent among us, sacrificing the poor innocent babes, I doubt, more to avoid the expense than the shame, which would move tears and pity in the most savage and inhuman breast.

6   The number of souls in this kingdom being usually reckoned one million and a half, of these I calculate there may be about two hundred thousand couple whose wives are breeders; from which number I subtract thirty thousand couples who are able to maintain their own children, although I apprehend there cannot be so many under the present distresses of the kingdom; but this being granted, there will remain an hundred and seventy thousand breeders. I again subtract fifty thousand for those women who miscarry, or whose children die by accident or disease within the year. There only remain an hundred and twenty thousand children of poor parents annually born. The question therefore is, how this number shall be reared and provided for, which, as I have already said, under the present situation of affairs, is utterly impossible by all the methods hitherto proposed. For we can neither employ them in handicraft or agriculture; we neither build houses (I mean in the country) nor cultivate land. They can very seldom pick up a livelihood by stealing till they arrive at six years old, except where they are of towardly[5] parts; although I confess they learn the rudiments much earlier, during which time they can however be looked upon only as probationers, as I have been informed by a principal gentleman in the country of Cavan, who protested to me that he never knew above one or two instances under the age of six, even in a part of the kingdom so renowned for the quickest proficiency in that art.

7   I am assured by our merchants that a boy or a girl before twelve years old is no salable commodity; and even when they come to this age they will not yield above three pounds, or three pounds and half a crown[6] at most on the Exchange; which cannot turn to account either to the parents or the kingdom, the charge of nutriment and rags having been at least four times that value.

8   I shall now therefore humbly propose my own thoughts, which I hope will not be liable to the least objection.

9   I have been assured by a very knowing American of my acquaintance in London, that a young healthy child well nursed is at a year old a most delicious, nourishing, and wholesome food, whether stewed, roasted, baked, or boiled; and I make no doubt that it will equally serve in a fricassee or a ragout.

10   I do therefore humbly offer it to public consideration that of the hundred and twenty thousand children, already computed, twenty thousand may be reserved for breed, whereof only one fourth part to be males, which is more than we allow to sheep, black cattle, or swine; and my reason is that these children are seldom the fruits of marriage, a circumstance not much regarded by our savages, therefore one male will be sufficient to serve four females. That the remaining hundred thousand may at a year old be offered in sale to the persons of quality and fortune through the kingdom, always advising the mother to let them suck plen-

tifully in the last month, so as to render them plump and fat for a good table. A child will make two dishes at an entertainment for friends; and when the family dines alone, the fore or hind quarter will make a reasonable dish, and seasoned with a little pepper or salt will be very good boiled on the fourth day, especially in winter.

11   I have reckoned upon a medium that a child just born will weigh twelve pounds, and in a solar year if tolerably nursed increaseth to twenty-eight pounds.

I grant this food will be somewhat dear, and therefore very proper for landlords, who, as they have already devoured most of the parents, seem to have the best title to the children.

12   Infant's flesh will be in season throughout the year, but more plentiful in March, and a little before and after. For we are told by a grave author, an eminent French physician,[7] that fish being a prolific diet, there are more children born in Roman Catholic countries about nine months after Lent than at any other season; therefore, reckoning a year after Lent, the markets will be more glutted than usual, because the number of popish infants is at least three to one in this kingdom; and therefore it will have one other collateral advantage, by lessening the number of Papists among us.[8]

13   I have already computed the charge of nursing a beggar's child (in which list I reckon all cottagers, laborers, and four fifths of the farmers) to be about two shillings per annum, rags included; and I believe no gentleman would repine to give ten shillings for the carcass of a good fat child, which, as I have said, will make four dishes of excellent nutritive meat, when he hath only some particular friend or his own family to dine with him. Thus the squire will learn to be a good landlord, and grow popular among the tenants; the mother will have eight shillings net profit, and be fit for work till she produces another child.

14   Those who are more thrifty (as I must confess the times require) may flay the carcass; the skin of which artificially[9] dressed will make admirable gloves for ladies, and summer boots for fine gentlemen.

15   As to our city of Dublin, shambles[10] may be appointed for this purpose in the most convenient parts of it, and butchers we may be assured will not be wanting; although I rather recommend buying the children alive, and dressing them hot from the knife as we do roasting pigs.

16   A very worthy person, a true lover of his country, and whose virtues I highly esteem, was lately pleased in discoursing on this matter to offer a refinement upon my scheme. He said that many gentlemen of this kingdom, having of late destroyed their deer, he conceived that the want of venison might be well supplied by the bodies of young lads and maidens, not exceeding fourteen years of age nor under twelve, so great a number of both sexes in every county being now ready to starve for want of work and service; and these to be disposed of by their parents, if alive, or otherwise by their nearest relations. But with due deference

to so excellent a friend and so deserving a patriot, I cannot be altogether in his sentiments; for as to the males, my American acquaintance assured me from frequent experience that their flesh was generally tough and lean, like that of our schoolboys, by continual exercise, and their taste disagreeable; and to fatten them would not answer the charge. Then as to the females, it would, I think with humble submission, be a loss to the public, because they soon would become breeders themselves; and besides, it is not improbable that some scrupulous people might be apt to censure such a practice (although indeed very unjustly) as a little bordering upon cruelty; which, I confess, hath always been with me the strongest objection against any project, how well so ever intended.

17   But in order to justify my friend, he confessed that this expedient was put into his head by the famous Psalmanazar, a native of the island Formosa, who came from thence to London above twenty years ago, and in conversation told my friend that in his country when any young person happened to be put to death, the executioner sold the carcass to persons of quality as a prime dainty; and that in his time the body of a plump girl of fifteen, who was crucified for an attempt to poison the emperor, was sold to his Imperial Majesty's prime minister of state, and other great mandarins of the court, in joints from the gibbet, at four hundred crowns. Neither indeed can I deny that if the same use were made of several plump young girls in this town, who without one single groat[11] to their fortunes cannot stir abroad without a chair,[12] and appear at the playhouse and assemblies in foreign fineries which they never will pay for, the kingdom would not be the worse.

18   Some persons of a desponding spirit are in great concern about that vast number of poor people who are aged, diseased, or maimed, and I have been desired to employ my thoughts what course may be taken to ease the nation of so grievous an encumbrance. But I am not in the least pain upon that matter, because it is very well known that they are every day dying and rotting by cold and famine, and filth and vermin, as fast as can be reasonably expected. And as to the younger laborers, they are now in almost as hopeful a condition. They cannot get work, and consequently pine away for want of nourishment to a degree that if at any time they are accidentally hired to common labor, they have not strength to perform it; and thus the country and themselves are happily delivered from the evils to come.

19   I have too long digressed, and therefore shall return to my subject. I think the advantages by the proposal which I have made are obvious and many, as well as of the highest importance.

20   For first, as I have already observed, it would greatly lessen the number of Papists, with whom we are yearly overrun, being the principal breeders of the nation as well as our most dangerous enemies; and who stay at home on purpose to deliver the kingdom to the Pretender, hoping

to take their advantage by the absence of so many good Protestants, who have chosen rather to leave their country than to stay at home and pay tithes against their conscience to an Episcopal curate.

21   Secondly, the poorer tenants will have something valuable of their own, which by law may be made liable to distress,[13] and help to pay their landlord's rent, their corn and cattle being already seized and money a thing unknown.

22   Thirdly, whereas the maintenance of an hundred thousand children, from two years old and upwards, cannot be computed at less than ten shillings a piece per annum, the nation's stock will be thereby increased fifty thousand pounds per annum, besides the profit of a new dish introduced to the tables of all gentlemen of fortune in the kingdom who have any refinement in taste. And the money will circulate among ourselves, the goods being entirely of our own growth and manufacture.

23   Fourthly, the constant breeders, besides the gain of eight shillings sterling per annum by the sale of their children, will be rid of the charge of maintaining them after the first year.

24   Fifthly, this food would likewise bring great custom to taverns, where the vintners will certainly be so prudent as to procure the best receipts for dressing it to perfection, and consequently have their houses frequented by all the fine gentlemen, who justly value themselves upon their knowledge in good eating; and a skillful cook, who understands how to oblige his guests, will contrive to make it as expensive as they please.

25   Sixthly, this would be a great inducement to marriage, which all wise nations have either encouraged by rewards or enforced by laws and penalties. It would increase the care and tenderness of mothers toward their children, when they were sure of a settlement for life to the poor babes, provided in some sort by the public, to their annual profit instead of expense. We should see an honest emulation among the married women, which of them could bring the fattest child to the market. Men would become as fond of their wives during the time of their pregnancy as they are now of their mares in foal, their cows in calf, or sows when they are ready to farrow; nor offer to beat or kick them (as is too frequent a practice) for fear of a miscarriage.

26   Many other advantages might be enumerated. For instance, the addition of some thousand carcasses in our exportation of barreled beef, the propagation of swine's flesh, and improvement in the art of making good bacon, so much wanted among us by the great destruction of pigs, too frequent at our tables, which are no way comparable in taste or magnificence to a well-grown, fat, yearling child, which roasted whole will make a considerable figure at a lord mayor's feast or any other public entertainment. But this and many others I omit, being studious of brevity.

27   Supposing that one thousand families in this city would be constant

customers for infants' flesh, besides others who might have it at merry meetings, particularly weddings and christenings, I compute that Dublin would take off annually about twenty thousand carcasses, and the rest of the kingdom (where probably they will be sold somewhat cheaper) the remaining eighty thousand.

28   I can think of no one objection that will possibly be raised against this proposal, unless it should be urged that the number of people will be thereby much lessened in the kingdom. This I freely own, and it was indeed one principal design in offering it to the world. I desire the reader will observe, that I calculate my remedy for this one individual kingdom of Ireland and for no other that ever was, is, or I think ever can be upon earth. Therefore let no man talk to me of other expedients: of taxing our absentees at five shillings a pound: of using neither clothes nor household furniture except what is of our own growth and manufacture: of utterly rejecting the materials and instruments that promote foreign luxury: of curing the expensiveness of pride, vanity, idleness, and gaming in our women: of introducing a vein of parsimony, prudence, and temperance: of learning to love our country, in the want of which we differ even from Laplanders and the inhabitants of Topinamboo:[14] of quitting our animosities and factions, nor acting any longer like the Jews, who were murdering one another at the very moment their city was taken: of being a little cautious not to sell our country and conscience for nothing: of teaching landlords to have at least one degree of mercy toward their tenants: lastly, of putting a spirit of honesty, industry, and skill into our shopkeepers; who, if a resolution could now be taken to buy only our native goods, would immediately unite to cheat and exact upon us in the price, the measure, and the goodness, nor could ever yet be brought to make one fair proposal of just dealing, though often and earnestly invited to it.

29   Therefore I repeat, let no man talk to me of these and the like expedients, till he hath at least some glimpse of hope that there will ever be some hearty and sincere attempt to put them in practice.

30   But as to myself, having been wearied out for many years with offering vain, idle, visionary thoughts, and at length utterly despairing of success, I fortunately fell upon this proposal, which, as it is wholly new, so it hath something solid and real, of no expense and little trouble, full in our own power, and whereby we can incur no danger in disobliging England. For this kind of commodity will not bear exportation, the flesh being of too tender a consistence to admit a long continuance in salt, although perhaps I could name a country[15] which would be glad to eat up our whole nation without it.

31   After all, I am not so violently bent upon my own opinion as to reject any offer proposed by wise men, which shall be found equally innocent, cheap, easy, and effectual. But before something of that kind shall be advanced in contradiction to my scheme, and offering a better, I desire the

author or authors will be pleased maturely to consider two points. First, as things now stand, how they will be able to find food and raiment for an hundred thousand useless mouths and backs. And secondly, there being a round million of creatures in human figure throughout this kingdom, whose sole subsistence put into a common stock would leave them in debt two millions of pounds sterling, adding those who are beggars by profession to the bulk of farmers, cottagers, and laborers, with their wives and children who are beggars in effect; I desire those politicians who dislike my overture, and may perhaps be so bold to attempt an answer, that they will first ask the parents of these mortals whether they would not at this day think it a great happiness to have been sold for food at a year old in the manner I prescribe, and thereby have avoided such a perpetual scene of misfortunes as they have since gone through by the oppression of landlords, the impossibility of paying rent without money or trade, the want of common sustenance, with neither house nor clothes to cover them from the inclemencies of the weather, and the most inevitable prospect of entailing the like or greater miseries upon their breed forever.

32   I profess, in the sincerity of my heart, that I have not the least personal interest in endeavoring to promote this necessary work, having no other motive than the public good of my country, by advancing our trade, providing for infants, relieving the poor, and giving some pleasure to the rich. I have no children by which I can propose to get a single penny; the youngest being nine years old, and my wife past childbearing.

Notes

[1]Dublin, Ireland. [Eds.]

[2]James Edward Stuart (1688–1766), son of King James II (1633–1701), the first Roman Catholic ruler of England (1685–1688) since Mary Tudor ("Bloody Mary" 1516–1558). After King James was deposed in the Protestant revolution, his son was barred from succession. He fled Great Britain for exile in France and Spain where he and many Irish Catholic sympathizers attempted unsuccessfully to regain the throne. [Eds.]

[3]Schemers. [Eds.]

[4]A shilling was worth approximately twenty-five cents. [Eds.]

[5]Favorable to or advantageous. [Eds.]

[6]A pound was worth about 20 shillings; a crown, about 2½ shillings. [Eds.]

[7]François Rabelais (1494?–1553), French humanist and writer. [Eds.]

[8]Papists are Roman Catholics strongly supportive of the Pope and his edicts. [Eds.]

[9]Artfully or skillfully. [Eds.]

[10]Slaughterhouses. [Eds.]

[11]An English silver coin used between the 14th and 17th centuries and worth about four pennies. [Eds.]

[12] A seat carried around on poles, also called a sedan chair. [Eds.]
[13] To hold someone's property for the payment of that person's debts. [Eds.]
[14] Laplanders are inhabitants of Lapland, a region in the extreme northern part of Europe. Topinamboo is in Brazil. [Eds.]
[15] England. [Eds.]

Content Questions

1. Why is the proposal necessary?
2. Why is Swift's one objection to his proposal an "unrealistic" one?
3. What does Swift recommend his opponents do about the Irish famine?
4. Is Swift's proposal logical? What type of argumentative structure does he use?

Questions on Presentation

1. In this essay Swift assesses the relative value of the individual versus the value of society. Does he favor the individual or society? Is his position on the issue clear to contemporary readers? If so, what techniques does he use to make his position clear? If not, what prevents contemporary readers from understanding Swift's viewpoint?
2. What techniques does Swift use to make his satiric tone apparent?
3. Swift's satiric approach is so broadly done that the essay seems almost to be a parody. Could Swift's essay be effectively parodied? What would be most easy to parody and what most difficult?
4. What use does Swift make of statistics? Are they effective?
5. How does Swift make the narrator seem a reasonable man?
6. Swift mentions other writers' beliefs and other countries' customs. Do his references strengthen his argument, detract from it, or contribute to it?

A Modest Proposal for Helping Society
David Kleinfeld

David Kleinfeld is a professional writing major in the English Department at the University of New Mexico. His career goals include entering the publishing field as an editor or reviewer. Like many writing majors, Kleinfeld is concerned with what limits are imposed on the rights of individuals. In this essay he parodies Swift's "Modest Proposal," making a proposal of his own regarding the treatment of prisoners. Notice how Kleinfeld echoes Swift's structure and approach, although the specifics in his essay differ from Swift's.

1   It's a discouraging situation. People are being raped, murdered, assaulted, and abused every day, but criminals aren't punished or rehabilitated. For the past thirty years I have worked in the prison system and seen it fail. The current system fails in four ways. First, the criminal receives no serious punishment. Prison has become an acceptable way of life for many convicts. Most prefer jail to the outside world, which makes perfect sense for a criminal who knows he is going to live a better life behind bars than he would outside. In prison, the convict knows he will receive food, clothing, and a bed. This leads to the second problem. Taxpayers are putting too much money into the penal system without getting any results. It takes more than $20,000 a year to feed, clothe, and house one convict. Third, prisoners are not being rehabilitated, which makes them hard to employ after their incarceration. And fourth, the current prison system is failing to work as a deterrent. This becomes evident when one sees how many repeat offenders there are in any penitentiary.

2   Aside from working as a prison psychologist for the past thirty years, I have also spent thousands of hours, with the help of my spouse, researching the penal system. The proposal that follows is the result of my experience and professional research. I have devised a system that would punish the convict, and at the same time be cost effective, rehabilitating, and serve as a deterrent.

3   I propose that once a criminal has been sentenced as a felon he should be taken to a processing center where he will receive an orientation about the prison system. Immediately after orientation he will undergo surgery. It will be a simple operation with little risk to the patient. The procedure is known as a frontal lobotomy.

4   My proposed system will serve to punish without being inhumane. In the past, punishments ranged from hideous forms of torture to solitary confinement. At present, prisons use various forms of restriction as a means of punishment, such as not allowing the inmates to watch television. The lobotomy will be a stern punishment without being cruel. Although it will leave the criminal without a brain to speak of, it will also allow him to live a contented life. Opponents of my proposal will argue that turning a living, breathing criminal into a living, breathing vegetable is cruel and unusual punishment; but this won't be the case. At present, prisoners are forced to live a life of guilt in overcrowded cells, but after surgery they won't be able to understand the concept of guilt, let alone pronounce the word *cell*.

5   Under this new system, taxpayer's money will go much further. As I mentioned earlier, it costs $20,000 to maintain one inmate for a year. The new system will make it possible to house twenty prisoners for the same price. At present this can't be done because prisoners complain about unfair living conditions. The ideal inmate will not have a functioning brain so he will not mind living in an $8 \times 8 \times 10$ cell with nine other inmates. The food and clothing cost will be a fraction of what it is now. Convicts won't ask for new clothes, and they won't receive them. Instead of three relatively good meals a day, they'll receive one nutritional supplement in the morning. There will no longer be a need for one prison guard for every ten inmates. Instead there will be one caretaker for every fifty sedate, institutionalized, rehabilitated persons. No more money will need to be spent on expensive security systems or luxurious recreational facilities because the inmate of the future will no longer have the mental strength to open a door or turn on a radio.

6   Opponents of this system will say that rehabilitation will be impossible because the inmates won't be able to do anything but sit and stare into space. But that's the beauty of my system. Where there was once a hardened psychotic criminal there will now be a content individual who causes no harm to himself or society. This is the ultimate rehabilitation.

7   Finally, society will have a prison system that will serve as a deterrent to criminals everywhere. Who wants to risk losing their brain for $43.16 in a convenience store holdup? As always the opponents of my system will look for a weakness. They'll say that anyone who is willing to commit a serious crime is already missing half a brain, and, thus, this system will not act as a deterrent. Even if this were true, once the criminal is caught and incarcerated the chance that he would commit a serious crime after a frontal lobotomy is inconsequential.

8   This system was designed for the good of society not for the good of the criminal. However, with this system the prisoner will be more content and happier than ever before.

Richard Nixon Is Back

The New Yorker

Richard M. Nixon (b. 1913) was born in Yorba Linda, California, and graduated from Whittier College in 1934 and Duke University Law School in 1937. Soon after the outbreak of World War II, Nixon enlisted in the navy and served as an aviation ground officer in the Pacific. After the war Nixon returned to his law practice but was soon attracted to politics. In 1947 and 1949 he was elected to the House of Representatives; in the 1952 presidential election, he was selected as Dwight D. Eisenhower's running mate because of his anti-Communist reputation. After serving eight years as vice president, Nixon challenged John F. Kennedy for the presidency but narrowly lost the election. He retired from politics until the late 1960s when he won election as the thirty-seventh president of the United States. Elected to his second term of office by an overwhelming margin, Nixon, faced with almost certain impeachment, was forced to resign from office on August 4, 1974. Nixon admitted that he had conspired to conceal facts about the break-in and wiretapping of the Democratic National Headquarters in the Watergate complex and had directed the Federal Bureau of Investigation away from his White House staff and supporters. Although his successor Gerald R. Ford pardoned him shortly after his resignation, Nixon was disbarred from legal practice.

For many years after his resignation, Nixon retired from public view, content to write his memoirs and infrequently comment on the political health of the nation. However, as the author of this article from *The New Yorker* explains, Richard M. Nixon is back.

1   Richard Nixon is "back." So we learn from *Newsweek*, on whose recent cover we find a picture of him, smiling broadly. To be "back," of course, you must have first been somewhere, then gone somewhere else, and then returned. The most notable spot that Nixon once occupied and then departed from, we recall, was the Presidency of the United States. But he hasn't returned *there*. In that sense, he's not back. To what is he "back," then? Well, he's written an article for *Foreign Affairs, Newsweek* tells us by way of partial explanation. Also, when he stopped in at a Burger King not long ago a lot of people asked him for his autograph. In other words, there are signs that he's acceptable again to the public in some way or other, and hence to the mass media—including, above all, *Newsweek*, which puts him on its cover with the caption "He's Back." The statement in this context makes itself true: if *Newsweek* says he's back, he is. That still leaves the question of where he was until he came back. *Newsweek* says that since "Watergate" he has been in "exile." This exile, however, is evidently different from what we ordinarily mean by exile. When Napoleon was in exile, he was confined to a small island in the Atlantic. Today, Solzhenitsyn is barred from returning to his beloved Russia. But Nixon has been right here in the United States—in California, in New York City, and, lately, in Saddle River, New Jersey—free to come and go as he pleased. (*Newsweek* refers to him as the Sage of Saddle River.) "Exile" in the *Newsweek* story seems to mean something like exile from the mass media, from celebrity—a thoroughly modern definition, and one that makes an exile of almost everyone. Implicit in the use of the terms "back" and "exile" is a sort of story—a version of what "Watergate" was. In this version,

there is a man called Richard Nixon who was once a great celebrity. Then "Watergate" occurred, and, like a television performer whom the public no longer cares to look at, he disappeared from view. But now "Watergate" has faded from people's minds, and his days in the shadows—in "exile" from public acclaim—are over, and he is again a great celebrity, appearing on the cover of *Newsweek*. He's back.

2   Missing from this implicit story, of course, is any notion of just what the "Watergate" episode was about: of why the whole country occupied itself with it for more than two years, and why its consequence was a phenomenon unprecedented in our history—the resignation of a President under active threat of impeachment. The feeling of something missing is intensified by two other words that come up in the *Newsweek* story: "rehabilitation" and "redemption." The first is used by one of President Reagan's senior aides, who says, "As far as this White House is concerned, his rehabilitation is complete. There's tremendous respect for him around here." The second is used by *Newsweek*, which comments, "It's hard to say what finally signifies redemption for a disgraced President." Both words have in them the idea of coming back: in the one case, coming back to good citizenship, and, in the other, coming back, presumably, into God's grace—or, at least, to some better moral condition. Rehabilitation occurs when someone shows that he understands that what he has done is wrong, and resolves not to do it again. Nixon, we continue to trust, will never again get a chance to abuse the powers of the Presidency, but he may still someday show an understanding of what he has already done. So far, he shows not the slightest glimmering of it. In an interview accompanying the *Newsweek* story, the Sage of Saddle River had this to say when he was asked about Watergate: "It was a very mishandled thing. Churchill said his study of history showed that great leaders more often stumble on little things than on big things. And this is not an excuse but it is to a certain extent a reason. Seventy-two was a busy year: My God, we went to Russia, we were winding down the war in Vietnam. . . . The deed itself was a nonsense thing. It didn't produce anything." And there you have it—a busy man who was occupying himself with great things overlooked a few details and suddenly found himself out of a job. Redemption moves in the same direction as rehabilitation, but invisibly, on a spiritual plane. It is not given to us to know whether one or another of us is redeemed or not. All we can say is that if Richard Nixon has redeemed himself he has done it without rehabilitating himself. Either way, his "comeback" has been a purely individual matter, having no reference to the meaning of his acts for the nation.

3   It's true that some people with a less insouciant view of Watergate—*Newsweek* calls them "diehard critics"—are given a say. One is the political scientist James David Barber. He said, "What I'm resisting is the

reduction of all Nixon's shenanigans to Watergate, and the reduction of Watergate to one break-in, and the reduction of all that—as he would dearly love us to think—to a few tapes, a little indiscretion." Barber's comments point, indirectly, to the actual dimensions of the crisis: the full-scale assault by a President and his Administration on the Constitution, and therefore on our system of government. Its significance was described often and well at the time of the crisis by those whose responsibility it became to weigh the facts and move the country toward a decision on the fate of the Nixon Presidency. We remember some words spoken by a mild, gentlemanly representative from South Carolina, a Democrat called James R. Mann, during the House Judiciary Committee hearings on impeachment. Mann's district had voted overwhelmingly for Nixon in the previous election, but Mann had now decided to vote in favor of the first of the articles of impeachment. He said, in part:

> You know, Americans revere their President, and rightly they should, because they know that by his oath he is supposed to preserve, protect, and defend the Constitution; to enforce the Bill of Rights, which is their heritage—your rights and mine—whether I am a Democrat or a Republican, rich or poor; and that he will see that the laws are faithfully executed; and that the individual liberties of each of us are protected.... And so, as Thomas Paine wrote, "those who expect to reap the blessing of freedom must, like men, undergo the fatigue of supporting it." And in this situation, as we look at how the office of the Presidency has been served by an individual, I share the remarks of Representative George Danielson that it is not the Presidency that is in jeopardy from us. We would strive to strengthen and protect the Presidency. But if there is no accountability, another President will feel free to do as he chooses. But the next time there may be no watchman in the night.

Content Questions

1. How does Nixon's exile differ from Napoleon's or Solzhenitsyn's?
2. What are the implicit definitions of "back" and "exile"?
3. What are the articles of impeachment?
4. Why was it difficult for Rep. James R. Mann to vote for the articles of impeachment?

Questions on Presentation

1. *The New Yorker* writer draws a distinction between "rehabilitation" and "redemption," suggesting that one is preferable to the other. What is this writer's distinction? Which concept does he believe is preferable and why?

2. The writer generalizes about Nixon's return by using the idea of Nixon's being "back" in several different ways. In what ways does this writer present Nixon as "back"?
3. How would you describe the tone of this essay? Is the tone appropriate for the topic? Why or why not?

Man the Irrational

Samuel L. Clemens

Samuel Langhorne Clemens (1835–1910), American humorist and author of novels, short stories, and travel sketches, wrote using the pseudonym Mark Twain. Born in Florida, Missouri, Clemens grew up in Hannibal, Missouri, and left school at age twelve when his father died. He worked in various parts of the country as a printer until 1856 when he decided to go to South America to seek his fortune. But instead of becoming a wealthy man in South America, Clemens became a riverboat pilot on the Mississippi. When the Civil War broke out, Clemens volunteered as a Confederate soldier but was later convinced by his brother to go to Nevada where he prospected, without success, for gold. Clemens soon found himself work as a reporter for newspapers in Nevada and California and adopted the pen name "Mark Twain," the riverboat pilots' cry for "two fathoms deep." "The Celebrated Jumping Frog of Calaveras County" (1865) made Clemens famous but not rich. His investments in publishing companies and in a typesetting machine finally forced Clemens into bankruptcy in 1894; however, within four years, he made enough money through lectures and writing to pay off his creditors. Perhaps because of his financial setbacks, his failing health, and the deaths of his wife and two daughters, Clemens became in his latter years a pessimistic satirist.

As a satirist, Clemens portrayed humans according to his deterministic outlook and growing, bitter pessimism. The following selection is taken from *Letters from the Earth*, unpublished until 1962. In the letters, Satan has been banished from heaven for confidential, but satiric, remarks he made about a few of the "Creator's sparkling industries." He investigates how the human race is doing and writes home to his friends, St. Michael and St. Gabriel, about its progress.

1   "I have told you nothing about man that is not true." You must pardon me if I repeat that remark now and then in these letters; I want you to take seriously the things I am telling you, and I feel that if I were in your place and you in mine, I should need that reminder from time to time, to keep my credulity from flagging.

2   For there is nothing about man that is not strange to an immortal. He

looks at nothing as we look at it, his sense of proportion is quite different from ours, and his sense of values is so widely divergent from ours, that with all our large intellectual powers it is not likely that even the most gifted among us would ever be quite able to understand it.

3   For instance, take this sample: he has imagined a heaven, and has left entirely out of it the supremest of all his delights, the one ecstasy that stands first and foremost in the heart of every individual of his race—and of ours—sexual intercourse!

4   It is as if a lost and perishing person in a roasting desert should be told by a rescuer he might choose and have all longed-for things but one, and he should elect to leave out water!

5   His heaven is like himself: strange, interesting, astonishing, grotesque. I give you my word, it has not a single feature in it that he *actually values*. It consists—utterly and entirely—of diversions which he cares next to nothing about, here in the earth, yet is quite sure he will like in heaven. Isn't it curious? Isn't it interesting? You must not think I am exaggerating, for it is not so. I will give you details.

6   Most men do not sing, most men cannot sing, most men will not stay where others are singing if it be continued more than two hours. Note that.

7   Only about two men in a hundred can play upon a musical instrument, and not four in a hundred have any wish to learn how. Set that down.

8   Many men pray, not many of them like to do it. A few pray long, the others make a short cut.

9   More men go to church than want to.

10   To forty-nine men in fifty the Sabbath Day is a dreary, dreary bore.

11   Of all the men in a church on a Sunday, two-thirds are tired when the service is half over, and the rest before it is finished.

12   The gladdest moment for all of them is when the preacher uplifts his hands for the benediction. You can hear the soft rustle of relief that sweeps the house, and you recognize that it is eloquent with gratitude.

13   All nations look down upon all other nations.

14   All nations dislike all other nations.

15   All white nations despise all colored nations, of whatever hue, and oppress them when they can.

16   White men will not associate with "niggers," nor marry them.

17   They will not allow them in their schools and churches.

18   All the world hates the Jew, and will not endure him except when he is rich.

19   I ask you to note all those particulars.

20   Further. All sane people detest noise.

21   All people, sane or insane, like to have variety in their life. Monotony quickly wearies them.

22   Every man, according to the mental equipment that has fallen to his

share, exercises his intellect constantly, ceaselessly, and this exercise makes up a vast and valued and essential part of his life. The lowest intellect, like the highest, possesses a skill of some kind and takes a keen pleasure in testing it, proving it, perfecting it. The urchin who is his comrade's superior in games is as diligent and as enthusiastic in his practice as are the sculptor, the painter, the pianist, the mathematician and the rest. Not one of them could be happy if his talent were put under an interdict.

23   Now then, you have the facts. You know what the human race enjoys, and what it doesn't enjoy. It has invented a heaven, out of its own head, all by itself: guess what it is like! In fifteen hundred eternities you couldn't do it. The ablest mind known to you or me in fifty million aeons couldn't do it. Very well, I will tell you about it.

24   1. First of all, I recall to your attention the extraordinary fact with which I began. To wit, that the human being, like the immortals, naturally places sexual intercourse far and away above all other joys—yet he has left it out of his heaven! The very thought of it excites him; opportunity sets him wild; in this state he will risk life, reputation, everything—even his queer heaven itself—to make good that opportunity and ride it to the overwhelming climax. From youth to middle age all men and all women prize copulation above all other pleasures combined, yet it is actually as I have said: it is not in their heaven; prayer takes its place.

25   They prize it thus highly; yet, like all their so-called "boons," it is a poor thing. At its very best and longest the act is brief beyond imagination—the imagination of an immortal, I mean. In the matter of repetition the man is limited—oh, quite beyond immortal conception. We who continue the act and its supremest ecstasies unbroken and without withdrawal for centuries, will never be able to understand or adequately pity the awful poverty of these people in that rich gift which, possessed as we possess it, makes all other possessions trivial and not worth the trouble of invoicing.

26   2. In man's heaven *everybody sings*! The man who did not sing on earth sings there; the man who could not sing on earth is able to do it there. This universal singing is not casual, not occasional, not relieved by intervals of quiet; it goes on, all day long, and every day, during a stretch of twelve hours. And *everybody stays*; whereas in the earth the place would be empty in two hours. The singing is of hymns alone. Nay, it is of one hymn alone. The words are always the same, in number they are only about a dozen, there is no rhyme, there is no poetry: "Hosannah, hosannah, hosannah, Lord God of Sabaoth, 'rah! 'rah! 'rah! siss!—boom! . . . a-a-ah!"

27   3. Meantime, every person is playing on a harp—those millions and millions!—whereas, not more than twenty in the thousand of them could play an instrument in the earth, or ever wanted to.

28   Consider the deafening hurricane of sound—millions and millions of voices screaming at once and millions and millions of harps gritting their teeth at the same time! I ask you: is it hideous, is it odious, is it horrible?

29   Consider further: it is a *praise* service; a service of compliment, of flattery, of adulation! Do you ask who it is that is willing to endure this strange compliment, this insane compliment; and who not only endures it, but likes it, enjoys it, requires it, *commands* it? Hold your breath!

30   It is God! This race's God, I mean. He sits on his throne, attended by his four and twenty elders and some other dignitaries pertaining to his court, and looks out over his miles and miles of tempestuous worshipers, and smiles, and purrs, and nods his satisfaction northward, eastward, southward; as quaint and naïve a spectacle as has yet been imagined in this universe, I take it.

31   It is easy to see that the inventor of the heavens did not originate the idea, but copied it from the show-ceremonies of some sorry little sovereign State up in the back settlements of the Orient somewhere.

32   All sane white people hate noise; yet they have tranquilly accepted this kind of a heaven—without thinking, without reflection, without examination—and they actually want to go to it! Profoundly devout old gray-headed men put in a large part of their time dreaming of the happy day when they will lay down the cares of this life and enter into the joys of that place. Yet you can see how unreal it is to them, and how little it takes a grip upon them as being fact, for they make no practical preparation for the great change: you never see one of them with a harp, you never hear one of them sing.

33   As you have seen, that singular show is a service of praise: praise by hymn, praise by prostration. It takes the place of "church." Now then, in the earth these people cannot stand much church—an hour and a quarter is the limit, and they draw the line at once a week. That is to say, Sunday. One day in seven; and even then they do not look forward to it with longing. And so—consider what their heaven provides for them: "church" that lasts forever, and a Sabbath that has no end! They quickly weary of this brief hebdomadal Sabbath here, yet they long for that eternal one; they dream of it, they talk about it, they *think* they think they are going to enjoy it—with all their simple hearts they think they think they are going to be happy in it!

34   It is because they do not think at all; they only think they think. Whereas they can't think; not two human beings in ten thousand have anything to think with. And as to imagination—oh, well, look at their heaven! They accept it, they approve it, they admire it. That gives you their intellectual measure.

35   4. The inventor of their heaven empties into it all the nations of the earth, in one common jumble. All are on an equality absolute, no one of them ranking another; they have to be "brothers"; they have to mix to-

gether, pray together, harp together, hosannah together—whites, niggers, Jews, everybody—there's no distinction. Here in the earth all nations hate each other, and every one of them hates the Jew. Yet every pious person adores that heaven and wants to get into it. He really does. And when he is in a holy rapture he thinks he thinks that if he were only there he would take all the populace to his heart, and hug, and hug, and hug!

36   He is a marvel—man is! I would I knew who invented him.

37   5. Every man in the earth possesses some share of intellect, large or small; and be it large or be it small he takes a pride in it. Also his heart swells at mention of the names of the majestic intellectual chiefs of his race, and he loves the tale of their splendid achievements. For he is of their blood, and in honoring themselves they have honored him. Lo, what the mind of man can do! he cries; and calls the roll of the illustrious of all the ages; and points to the imperishable literatures they have given to the world, and the mechanical wonders they have invented, and the glories wherewith they have clothed science and the arts; and to them he uncovers, as to kings, and gives to them the profoundest homage, and the sincerest, his exultant heart can furnish—thus exalting intellect above all things else in his world, and enthroning it there under the arching skies in a supremacy unapproachable. And then he contrives a heaven that hasn't a rag of intellectuality in it anywhere!

38   Is it odd, is it curious, is it puzzling? It is exactly as I have said, incredible as it may sound. This sincere adorer of intellect and prodigal rewarder of its mighty services here in the earth has invented a religion and a heaven which pay no compliments to intellect, offer it no distinctions, fling to it no largess: in fact, never even mention it.

39   By this time you will have noticed that the human being's heaven has been thought out and constructed upon an absolutely definite plan; and that this plan is, that it shall contain, in labored detail, each and every imaginable thing that is repulsive to a man, and not a single thing he likes!

40   Very well, the further we proceed the more will this curious fact be apparent.

41   Make a note of it: in man's heaven there are no exercises for the intellect, nothing for it to live upon. It would rot there in a year—rot and stink. Rot and stink—and at that stage become holy. A blessed thing: for only the holy can stand the joys of that bedlam.

Content Questions

1.   Why would the audience for this letter be interested in Satan's observations?
2.   Why is man "a marvelous curiosity"?

3. Why is man's concept of heaven illogical? Why is the writer's logical?
4. What will happen to human intellect in heaven?

Questions on Presentation

1. Does the letter form allow the author to present information with greater impact than an essay or narrative form would? Why or why not?
2. What is the effect of the use of imperatives in paragraphs 6 and 7?
3. What is Clemens' tone here? How does he create it?
4. What is the effect of the numerous short paragraphs between paragraphs 6 and 22?

Personal Observations on the Reliability of the Shuttle

Richard P. Feynman

In January of 1986, the space shuttle Challenger was destroyed 75 seconds into its flight. All seven astronauts, including one civilian schoolteacher (Christa McAuliffe), were killed. President Ronald Reagan appointed a special commission to investigate the disaster and to determine, if possible, the exact cause of the explosion. When the report from the President's Commission on the Space Shuttle Challenger accident was issued, Richard P. Feynman, a member of the commission, appended to the lengthy document a sharply worded criticism of NASA and its handling of the space shuttle program. Feynman (1918–1988) was a professor of theoretical physics at the California Institute of Technology. A graduate of Massachusetts Institute of Technology, Feynman began researching quantum electrodynamics, the part of quantum mechanics that deals with electromagnetic interactions, in the 1940s. For his extensive research, he was awarded the 1965 Nobel Prize for physics along with Julian S. Schwinger and Sin-Itiro Tomonaga.

Feynman was not only a notable teacher of physics, he was also a colorful, sometimes controversial, character and a precise writer. Throughout his professional career, Feynman insisted on clear exposition of abstract matters and refused to accept obscure language. These demands, coupled with his concern for accuracy and critical evaluation, forced him to write the following dissent to the commission's main report. Although many of his statements found their way into the main report, Feynman's conclusions were his own and did not represent those agreed to by all the commission members. Feynman's personal observations show his argumentative style and use of specific details to indict NASA officials for their errors in judgment.

1   It appears that there are enormous differences of opinion as to the probability of a failure with loss of vehicle and of human life. The estimates range from roughly 1 in 100 to 1 in 100,000. The higher figures come from working engineers, and the very low figures from management. What are the causes and consequences of this lack of agreement? Since 1 part in 100,000 would imply that one could put a Shuttle up each day for 300 years expecting to lose only one, we could more properly ask "What is the cause of management's fantastic faith in the machinery?"

2   We have also found that certification criteria used in Flight Readiness Reviews often develop a gradually decreasing strictness. The argument that the same risk was flown before without failure is often accepted as an argument for the safety of accepting it again. Because of this, obvious weaknesses are accepted again and again, sometimes without a sufficiently serious attempt to remedy them or to delay a flight because of their continued presence.

3   There are several sources of information. There are published criteria for certification, including a history of modifications in the form of waivers and deviations. In addition, the records of the Flight Readiness Reviews for each flight document the arguments used to accept the risks of the flight. Information was obtained from the direct testimony and the reports of the range safety officer, Louis J. Ullian, with respect to the history of success of solid fuel rockets. There was a further study by him (as chairman of the launch abort safety panel (LASP)) in an attempt to determine the risks involved in possible accidents leading to radioactive contamination from attempting to fly a plutonium power supply (RTG) for future planetary missions. The NASA study of the same question is also available. For the history of the Space Shuttle Main Engines, interviews with management and engineers at Marshall, and informal interviews with engineers at Rocketdyne were made. An independent (Cal Tech) mechanical engineer who consulted for NASA about engines was also interviewed informally. A visit to Johnson [Space Center] was made to gather information on the reliability of the avionics (computers, sensors, and effectors). Finally there is a report "A Review of Certification Practices Potentially Applicable to Man-rated Reusable Rocket Engines," prepared at the Jet Propulsion Laboratory by N. Moore, et al., in February, 1986, for NASA Headquarters, Office of Space Flight. It deals with the methods used by the FAA and the military to certify their gas turbine and rocket engines. These authors were also interviewed informally.

Solid Fuel Rockets (SRB)

4   An estimate of the reliability of solid fuel rockets was made by the range safety officer by studying the experience of all previous rocket

flights. Out of a total of nearly 2,900 flights, 121 failed (1 in 25). This includes, however, what may be called early errors, rockets flown for the first few times in which design errors are discovered and fixed. A more reasonable figure for the mature rockets might be 1 in 50. With special care in the selection of the parts and in inspection, a figure of below 1 in 100 might be achieved but 1 in 1,000 is probably not attainable with today's technology. (Since there are two rockets on the Shuttle, these rocket failure rates must be doubled to get Shuttle failure rates from Solid Rocket Booster failure.)

5   NASA officials argue that the figure is much lower. They point out that these figures are for unmanned rockets, but since the Shuttle is a manned vehicle "the probability of mission success is necessarily very close to 1.0." It is not very clear what this phrase means. Does it mean it is close to 1 or that it ought to be close to 1? They go on to explain "Historically this extremely high degree of mission success has given rise to a difference in philosophy between manned space flight programs and unmanned programs; i.e., numerical probability usage versus engineering judgment." (These quotations are from "Space Shuttle Data for Planetary Mission RTG Safety Analysis," pages 3-1, 3-2, February 15, 1985, NASA, JSC.) It is true that if the probability of failure was as low as 1 in 100,000 it would take an inordinate number of tests to determine it (for you would get nothing but a string of perfect flights from which no precise figure, other than that the probability is likely less than the number of such flights in the string so far). But, if the real probability is not so small, flights would show troubles, near failures, and possibly actual failures with a reasonable number of trials, and standard statistical methods could give a reasonable estimate. In fact, previous NASA experience had shown, on occasion, just such difficulties, near accidents, and accidents, all giving warning that the probability of flight failure was not so very small. The inconsistency of the argument not to determine reliability through historical experience, as the range safety officer did, is that NASA also appeals to history, beginning "Historically this high degree of mission success. . . ." Finally, if we are to replace standard numerical probability usage with engineering judgment, why do we find such an enormous disparity between the management estimate and the judgment of the engineers? It would appear that, for whatever purpose, be it for internal or external consumption, the management of NASA exaggerates the reliability of its product to the point of fantasy.

6   The history of the certification and Flight Readiness Reviews will not be repeated here. The phenomenon of accepting for flight seals that had shown erosion and blow-by in previous flights is very clear. The Challenger flight is an excellent example. There are several references to flights that had gone before. The acceptance and success of these flights is taken as evidence of safety. But erosion and blow-by are not what the

design expected. They are warnings that something is wrong. The equipment is not operating as expected, and therefore there is a danger that it can operate with even wider deviations in this unexpected and not thoroughly understood way. The fact that this danger did not lead to a catastrophe before is no guarantee that it will not the next time, unless it is completely understood. When playing Russian roulette the fact that the first shot got off safely is little comfort for the next. The origin and consequences of the erosion and blow-by were not understood. They did not occur equally on all flights and all joints; sometimes more, and sometimes less. Why not sometime, when whatever conditions determined it were right, still more, leading to catastrophe?

7   In spite of these variations from case to case, officials behaved as if they understood it, giving apparently logical arguments to each other often depending on the "success" of previous flights. For example, in determining if flight 51-L was safe to fly in the face of ring erosion in flight 51-C, it was noted that the erosion depth was only one-third of the radius. It had been noted in an experiment cutting the ring that cutting it as deep as one radius was necessary before the ring failed. Instead of being very concerned that variations of poorly understood conditions might reasonably create a deeper erosion this time, it was asserted there was "a safety factor of three." This is a strange use of the engineer's term "safety factor." If a bridge is built to withstand a certain load without the beams permanently deforming, cracking, or breaking, it may be designed for the materials used to actually stand up under three times the load. This "safety factor" is to allow for uncertain excesses of load, or unknown extra loads, or weaknesses in the material that might have unexpected flaws, etc. If now the expected load comes on to the new bridge and a crack appears in a beam, this is a failure of the design. There was no safety factor at all; even though the bridge did not actually collapse because the crack only went one-third of the way through the beam. The O-rings of the Solid Rocket Boosters were not designed to erode. Erosion was a clue that something was wrong. Erosion was not something from which safety can be inferred.

8   There was no way, without full understanding, that one could have confidence that conditions the next time might not produce erosion three times more severe than the time before. Nevertheless, officials fooled themselves into thinking they had such understanding and confidence, in spite of the peculiar variations from case to case. A mathematical model was made to calculate erosion. This was a model based not on physical understanding but on empirical curve fitting. To be more detailed, it was supposed a stream of hot gas impinged on the O-ring material, and the heat was determined at the point of stagnation (so far, with reasonable physical, thermodynamic laws). But to determine how much rubber eroded it was assumed this depended only on this

heat by a formula suggested by data on a similar material. A logarithmic plot suggested a straight line, so it was supposed that the erosion varied as the .58 power of the heat, the .58 being determined by a nearest fit. At any rate, adjusting some other numbers, it was determined that the model agreed with the erosion (to depth of one-third the radius of the ring). There is nothing much so wrong with this as believing the answer! Uncertainties appear everywhere. How strong the gas stream might be was unpredictable; it depended on holes formed in the putty. Blow-by showed that the ring might fail even though not, or only partially, eroded through. The empirical formula was known to be uncertain, for it did not go directly through the very data points by which it was determined. There was a cloud of points, some twice above and some twice below the fitted curve, so erosions twice predicted were reasonable from that cause alone. Similar uncertainties surrounded the other constants in the formula, etc., etc. When using a mathematical model careful attention must be given to uncertainties in the model.

Liquid Fuel Engine (SSME)

9   During the flight of 51-L the three Space Shuttle Main Engines all worked perfectly, even, at the last moment, beginning to shut down the engines as the fuel supply began to fail. The question arises, however, as to whether, had it failed, and we were to investigate it in as much detail as we did the Solid Rocket Booster, we would find a similar lack of attention to faults and a deteriorating reliability. In other words, were the organization weaknesses that contributed to the accident confined to the Solid Rocket Booster sector or were they a more general characteristic of NASA? To that end the Space Shuttle Main Engines and the avionics were both investigated. No similar study of the Orbiter or the External Tank was made.

10   The engine is a much more complicated structure than the Solid Rocket Booster, and a great deal more detailed engineering goes into it. Generally, the engineering seems to be of high quality and apparently considerable attention is paid to deficiencies and faults found in operation.

11   The usual way that such engines are designed (for military or civilian aircraft) may be called the component system, or bottom-up design. First it is necessary to thoroughly understand the properties and limitations of the materials to be used (for turbine blades, for example), and tests are begun in experimental rigs to determine those. With this knowledge large component parts (such as bearings) are designed and tested individually. As deficiencies and design errors are noted they are corrected and verified with further testing. Since one tests only parts at a time these tests and modifications are not overly expensive. Finally one works up

to the final design of the entire engine, to the necessary specifications. There is a good chance by this time that the engine will generally succeed, or that any failures are easily isolated and analyzed because the failure modes, limitations of materials, etc., are so well understood. There is a very good chance that the modifications to the engine to get around the final difficulties are not very hard to make, for most of the serious problems have already been discovered and dealt with in the earlier, less expensive, stages of the process.

12   The Space Shuttle Main Engine was handled in a different manner, top down, we might say. The engine was designed and put together all at once with relatively little detailed preliminary study of the material and components. Then when troubles are found in the bearings, turbine blades, coolant pipes, etc., it is more expensive and difficult to discover the causes and make changes. For example, cracks have been found in the turbine blades of the high-pressure oxygen turbopump. Are they caused by flaws in the material, the effect of the oxygen atmosphere on properties of the material, the thermal stresses of startup or shutdown, the vibration and stresses of steady running, or mainly at some resonance at certain speeds, etc.? How long can we run from crack initiation to crack failure, and how does this depend on power level? Using the completed engine as a test bed to resolve such questions is extremely expensive. One does not wish to lose entire engines in order to find out where and how failure occurs. Yet, an accurate knowledge of this information is essential to acquire a confidence in the engine reliability in use. Without detailed understanding, confidence cannot be attained.

13   A further disadvantage of the top-down method is that, if an understanding of a fault is obtained, a simple fix, such as a new shape for the turbine housing, may be impossible to implement without a redesign of the entire engine.

14   The Space Shuttle Main Engine is a very remarkable machine. It has a greater ratio of thrust to weight than any previous engine. It is built at the edge of, or outside of, previous engineering experience. Therefore, as expected, many different kinds of flaws and difficulties have turned up. Because, unfortunately, it was built in the top-down manner, they are difficult to find and to fix. The design aim of a lifetime of 55 mission equivalent firings (27,000 seconds of operation, either in a mission of 500 seconds or on a test stand) has not been obtained. The engine now requires very frequent maintenance and replacement of important parts, such as turbopumps, bearings, sheet metal housings, etc. The high-pressure fuel turbopump had to be replaced every three or four mission equivalents (although that may have been fixed now) and the high-pressure oxygen turbopump every five or six. This is at most ten percent of the original specification. But our main concern here is the determination of reliability.

15   In a total of about 250,000 seconds of operation, the engines have failed seriously perhaps 16 times. Engineering pays close attention to these failings and tries to remedy them as quickly as possible. This it does by test studies on special rigs experimentally designed for the flaw in question, by careful inspection of the engine for suggestive clues (like cracks), and by considerable study and analysis. In this way, in spite of the difficulties of top-down design, through hard work, many of the problems have apparently been solved.

16   A list of some of the problems follows. Those followed by an asterisk are probably solved:

- Turbine blade cracks in high-pressure fuel turbopumps (HPFTP). (May have been solved.)
- Turbine blade cracks in high-pressure oxygen turbopumps (HPOTP).
- Augmented Spark Igniter (ASI) line rupture.*
- Purge check valve failure.*
- ASI chamber erosion.*
- HPFTP turbine sheet metal cracking.
- HPFTP coolant liner failure.*
- Main combustion chamber outlet elbow failure.*
- Main combustion chamber inlet elbow weld offset.*
- HPOTP subsynchronous whirl.*
- Flight acceleration safety cutoff system (partial failure in a redundant system).*
- Bearing spalling (partially solved).
- A vibration at 4,000 Hertz making some engines inoperable, etc.

17   Many of these solved problems are the early difficulties of a new design, for 13 of them occurred in the first 125,000 seconds and only three in the second 125,000 seconds. Naturally, one can never be sure that all the bugs are out, and, for some, the fix may not have addressed the true cause. Thus, it is not unreasonable to guess there may be at least one surprise in the next 250,000 seconds, a probability of 1/500 per engine per mission. On a mission there are three engines, but some accidents would possibly be contained and only affect one engine. The system can abort with only two engines. Therefore let us say that the unknown surprises do not, even of themselves, permit us to guess that the probability of mission failure due to the Space Shuttle Main Engine is less than 1/500. To this we must add the chance of failure from known, but as yet unsolved, problems (introduced by asterisk in the list above). These we discuss below. (Engineers at Rocketdyne, the manufacturer, estimate the total probability as 1/10,000. Engineers at Marshall estimate it as 1/300, while NASA management, to whom these engineers report, claims it is 1/100,000. An independent engineer consulting for NASA thought 1 or 2 per 100 a reasonable estimate.)

18   The history of the certification principles for these engines is confusing and difficult to explain. Initially the rule seems to have been that two sample engines must each have had twice the time operating without failure, as the operating time of the engine to be certified (rule of 2x). At least that is the FAA practice, and NASA seems to have adopted it, originally expecting the certified time to be 10 missions (hence 20 missions for each sample). Obviously the best engines to use for comparison would be those of greatest total (flight plus test) operating time— the so-called "fleet leaders." But what if a third sample and several others fail in a short time? Surely we will not be safe because two were unusual in lasting longer. The short time might be more representative of the real possibilities, and, in the spirit of the safety factor of 2, we should only operate at half the time of the short-lived samples.

19   The slow shift toward decreasing safety factor can be seen in many examples. We take that of the HPFTP turbine blades. First of all the idea of testing an entire engine was abandoned. Each engine number has had many important parts (like the turbopumps themselves) replaced at frequent intervals, so that the rule must be shifted from engines to components. We accept an HPFTP for a certification time if two samples have each run successfully for twice that time (and of course, as a practical matter, no longer insisting that this time be as large as 10 missions). But what is "successfully"? The FAA calls a turbine blade crack a failure in order, in practice, to really provide a safety factor greater than 2. There is some time that an engine can run between the time a crack originally starts until the time it has grown large enough to fracture. (The FAA is contemplating new rules that take this extra safety time into account, but only if it is very carefully analyzed through known models within a known range of experience and with materials thoroughly tested.) None of these conditions apply to the Space Shuttle Main Engine.

20   Cracks were found in many second stage HPFTP turbine blades. In one case three were found after 1,900 seconds, while in another they were not found after 4,200 seconds, although usually these longer runs showed cracks. To follow this story further we shall have to realize that the stress depends a great deal on the power level. The Challenger flight was to be at, and previous flights had been at, a power level called 104% of rated power level during most of time the engines were operating. Judging from some material data it is supposed that at the level 104% of rated power level, the time to crack is about twice that at 109% or full power level (FPL). Future flights were at this level because of heavier payloads, and many tests were made at this level. Therefore dividing time at 104% by two, we obtain units called equivalent full power level (EFPL). (Obviously, some uncertainty is introduced by that, but it has not been studied.) The earliest cracks mentioned above occurred at 1,375 EFPL.

21   Now the certification rule becomes "limit all second stage blades to a maximum of 1,375 seonds EFPL." If one objects that the factor of 2 is lost, it is pointed out that the one turbine ran for 3,800 seconds EFPL without cracks, and half of this is 1,900 so we are being more conservative. We have fooled ourselves in three ways. First we have only one sample, and it is not the fleet leader, for the other two samples of 3,800 or more seconds had 17 cracked blades between them. (There are 59 blades in the engine.) Next we have abandoned the 2x rule and substituted equal time. And finally, 1,375 is where we did see a crack. We can say that no crack had been found below 1,375, but the last time we looked and saw no cracks was 1,100 seconds EFPL. We do not know when the crack formed between these times; for example, cracks may have formed at 1,150 seconds EFPL. (Approximately ⅔ of the blade sets tested in excess of 1,375 seconds EFPL had cracks. Some recent experiments have, indeed, shown cracks as early as 1,150 seconds.) It was important to keep the number high, for the Challenger was to fly an engine very close to the limit by the time the flight was over.

22   Finally it is claimed that the criteria are not abandoned, and the system is safe, by giving up the FAA convention that there should be no cracks and considering only a completely fractured blade a failure. With this definition no engine has yet failed. The idea is that since there is sufficient time for a crack to grow to fracture we can insure that all is safe by inspecting all blades for cracks. If they are found, replace them, and if none are found we have enough time for a safe mission. This makes the crack problem not a flight safety problem but merely a maintenance problem.

23   This may in fact be true. But how well do we know that cracks always grow slowly enough that no fracture can occur in a mission? Three engines have run for long times with a few cracked blades (about 3,000 seconds EFPL) with no blades broken off.

24   But a fix for this cracking may have been found. By changing the blade shape, shot-peening the surface, and covering with insulation to exclude thermal shock, the blades have not cracked so far.

25   A very similar story appears in the history of certification of the HPOTP, but we shall not give the details here.

26   It is evident, in summary, that the Flight Readiness Reviews and certification rules show a deterioration for some of the problems of the Space Shuttle Main Engine that is closely analogous to the deterioration seen in the rules for the Solid Rocket Booster.

Avionics

27   By "avionics" is meant the computer system on the Orbiter as well as its input sensors and output actuators. At first we will restrict ourselves

to the computers proper and not be concerned with the reliability of the input information from the sensors of temperature, pressure, etc., nor with whether the computer output is faithfully followed by the actuators of rocket firings, mechanical controls, displays to astronauts, etc.

28   The computing system is very elaborate, having over 250,000 lines of code. It is responsible, among many other things, for the automatic control of the entire ascent to orbit and for the descent until well into the atmosphere (below Mach 1) once one button is pushed deciding the landing site desired. It would be possible to make the entire landing automatically (except that the landing gear lowering signal is expressly left out of computer control and must be provided by the pilot, ostensibly for safety reasons) but such an entirely automatic landing is probably not as safe as a pilot-controlled landing. During orbital flight it is used in the control of payloads, in displaying information to the astronauts, and the exchange of information to the ground. It is evident that the safety of flight requires guaranteed accuracy of this elaborate system of computer hardware and software.

29   In brief, the hardware reliability is ensured by having four essentially independent identical computer systems. Where possible each sensor also has multiple copies, usually four, and each copy feeds all four of the computer lines. If the inputs from the sensors disagree, depending on circumstances, certain averages or a majority selection is used as the effective input. The algorithm used by each of the four computers is exactly the same, so their inputs (since each sees all copies of the sensors) are the same. Therefore at each step the results in each computer should be identical. From time to time they are compared; but, because they might operate at slightly different speeds, a system of stopping and waiting at specified times is instituted before each comparison is made. If one of the computers disagrees or is too late in having its answer ready, the three which do agree are assumed to be correct and the errant computer is taken completely out of the system. If, now, another computer fails, as judged by the agreement of the other two, it is taken out of the system, and the rest of the flight canceled, and descent to the landing site is instituted, controlled by the two remaining computers. It is seen that this is a redundant system since the failure of only one computer does not affect the mission. Finally, as an extra feature of safety, there is a fifth independent computer, whose memory is loaded with only the programs for ascent and descent, and which is capable of controlling the descent if there is a failure of more than two of the computers of the main line of four.

30   There is not enough room in the memory of the main line computers for all the programs of ascent, descent, and payload programs in flight, so the memory is loaded about four times from tapes by the astronauts.

31   Because of the enormous effort required to replace the software for

such an elaborate system and for checking a new system out, no change has been made in the hardware since the system began about fifteen years ago. The actual hardware is obsolete; for example, the memories are of the old ferrite core type. It is becoming more difficult to find manufacturers to supply such old-fashioned computers reliably and of high quality. Modern computers are very much more reliable, can run much faster, simplifying circuits and allowing more to be done, and would not require so much loading of memory, for their memories are much larger.

32   The software is checked very carefully in a bottom-up fashion. First, each new line of code is checked; then sections of codes or modules with special function are verified. The scope is increased step by step until the new changes are incorporated into a complete system and checked. This computer output is considered the final product, newly released. But completely independently there is an independent verification group, which takes an adversary attitude to the software development group, and tests and verifies the software as if it were a customer of a delivered product. There is additional verification in using the new programs in simulators, etc. A discovery of an error during the verification testing is considered very serious, and its origin studied very carefully to avoid such mistakes in the future. Such unexpected errors have been found only about six times in all the programming and program changing (for new or altered payloads) that has been done. The principle that is followed is that all the verification is not an aspect of progam safety, it is merely a test of that safety, in a non-catastrophic verification. Flight safety is to be judged solely on how well the programs do in the verification tests. A failure here generates considerable concern.

33   To summarize then, the computer software checking system and attitude are of highest quality. There appears to be no process of gradually fooling oneself while degrading standards so characteristic of the Solid Rocket Booster or Space Shuttle Main Engine safety systems. To be sure, there have been recent suggestions by management to curtail such elaborate and expensive tests as being unnecessary at this late date in Shuttle history. This must be resisted for it does not appreciate the mutual subtle influences and sources of error generated by even small changes on one part of a program on another. There are perpetual requests for changes as new payloads and new demands and modifications are suggested by the users. Changes are expensive because they require extensive testing. The proper way to save money is to curtail the number of requested changes, not the quality of testing for each.

34   One might add that the elaborate system could be very much improved by more modern hardware and programming techniques. Any outside competition would have all the advantages of starting over, and whether that is a good idea for NASA now should be carefully considered.

35   Finally, returning to the sensors and actuators of the avionics system, we find that the attitude to system failure and reliability is not nearly as good as for the computer system. For example, a difficulty was found with certain temperature sensors sometimes failing. Yet 18 months later the same sensors were still being used, still sometimes failing, until a launch had to be scrubbed because two of them failed at the same time. Even on a succeeding flight this unreliable sensor was used again. Again reaction control systems, the rocket jets used for reorienting and control in flight, still are somewhat unreliable. There is considerable redundancy but a long history of failures, none of which has yet been extensive enough to seriously affect a flight. The action of the jets is checked by sensors, and, if they fail to fire, the computers choose another jet to fire. But they are not designed to fail, and the problem should be solved.

Conclusions

36   If a reasonable launch schedule is to be maintained, engineering often cannot be done fast enough to keep up with the expectations of originally conservative certification criteria designed to guarantee a very safe vehicle. In these situations, subtly, and often with apparently logical arguments, the criteria are altered so that flights may still be certified in time. They therefore fly in a relatively unsafe condition, with a chance of failure of the order of a percent (it is difficult to be more accurate).

37   Official management, on the other hand, claims to believe the probability of failure is a thousand times less. One reason for this may be an attempt to assure the government of NASA perfection and success in order to ensure the supply of funds. The other may be that they sincerely believe it to be true, demonstrating an almost incredible lack of communication between themselves and their working engineers.

38   In any event this has had very unfortunate consequences, the most serious of which is to encourage ordinary citizens to fly in such a dangerous machine, as if it had attained the safety of an ordinary airliner. The astronauts, like test pilots, should know their risks, and we honor them for their courage. Who can doubt that McAuliffe was equally a person of great courage, who was closer to an awareness of the true risk than NASA management would have us believe?

39   Let us make recommendations to ensure that NASA officials deal in a world of reality in understanding technological weaknesses and imperfections well enough to be actively trying to eliminate them. They must live in reality in comparing the costs and utility of the Shuttle to other methods of entering space. And they must be realistic in making contracts, in estimating costs, and the difficulty of the projects. Only realistic flight schedules should be proposed, schedules that have a reasonable chance of being met. If in this way the government would not support

them, then so be it. NASA owes it to the citizens from whom it asks support to be frank, honest, and informative, so that these citizens can make the wisest decisions for the use of their limited resources.

40   For a successful technology, reality must take precedence over public relations, for nature cannot be fooled.

Content Questions

1. What system did NASA use to assess the reliability of vital shuttle parts (such as the solid fuel rockets, liquid fuel engine, or computer systems)?
2. What systems would Feynman prefer to see NASA use to assess reliability?
3. Why did NASA officials use the success of previous missions as arguments for future missions?

Questions on Presentation

1. Why does Feynman cite his sources of information?
2. What is Feynman's thesis? How does he present it?
3. Statistics are often unreliable, and Feynman identifies several instances of such statistics. Yet he also uses other statistics as support. What is the effect of identifying some statistics as unreliable on his own use of statistics?
4. How does Feynman demonstrate inconsistencies in NASA's arguments?
5. How does Feynman's reference to Russian roulette (6) enhance his argument?

The Way of the Liberated

C. Bruce Catton

Charles Bruce Catton (1899–1967) was born in Petoskey, Michigan, and educated at Oberlin College. His fascination with the Civil War began in his childhood when he would listen to the stories Civil War veterans told children in Catton's hometown. Young Catton absorbed the traditions and emotional experiences this war gave the United States through these veterans' stories and his own reading about the Civil War. In the early 1920s Catton worked as a reporter for newspapers in Boston and Cleveland; in 1926 he became the Washington correspondent for the Newspaper Enterprise Association, a position he held until

1941 when he went to work for the federal government as an information specialist. Although he worked as a writer and novelist, Catton's desire to write about the Civil War never waned. Instead, it grew through his years as a journalist, information director for the Department of Commerce, and editor of *American Heritage.*

Catton first tried to chronicle the Civil War in fiction; his first three novels, *War Lords of Washington* (1948), *Mr. Lincoln's Army* (1951), and *Glory Road* (1952), were well received by critics but not by the public. However, in 1953 Catton published the Pulitzer prizewinning *A Stillness at Appomattox,* an evaluation of the last years of the Civil War that combines history with poetic insight. Catton saw history as a journalist would: not as great or sweeping changes but as the sum of victories won and losses suffered by individuals. In the following selection, taken from his *Never Call Retreat* (1965), Catton discusses the effect of the Emancipation Proclamation on the course of the Civil War.

1   The trouble was that events were moving too fast. The Emancipation Proclamation[1] had been nothing more than a statement of intent, written by a man who supposed that there would be time to make all necessary adjustments. What was happening in Missouri was a case in point: the people of this state were trying to work out a slow transition, and the President was willing to allow a margin for trial-and-error expedients in the hope that other slave states would fall in line. But emancipation came with such a rush that there was no time to adjust anything. Men found that they were living with it while they still wondered whether it ought to happen at all.

2   In his notable speech Congressman Vallandigham[2] warned that nothing of the kind could possibly occur. The institution had too many roots and the roots went down too far in too many hearts. Sudden change was out of the question.

3   "You cannot abolish slavery by the sword; still less by proclamations, though the President were to 'proclaim' every month," he cried. "Neither, sir, can you abolish slavery by argument. As well attempt to abolish marriage, or the relation of paternity."[3]

4   This was a perfectly logical argument, robbed of its meaning by the fact that what Vallandigham considered impossible was actually being done. Slavery *was* being abolished by the sword and by proclamation, by fire and by sudden uprising of the spirit; perhaps because there was no other earthly way to do it. The greatest single change in American life arrived without the benefit of any advance planning.

5   To begin with, the proclamation was taken with deadly seriousness by the people most concerned, the Negroes themselves. To others it might be no more than a piece of paper that would mean much or nothing depending on how the war went; to the Negroes it was the parting of the Red Sea. It meant freedom now and everywhere, as fast as the

word could travel, and the Negroes acted on this belief. Even though it had always been buttressed by unlimited force, slavery in America really existed by the consent of the governed. This consent, to be sure, came largely because the governed were utterly helpless, but it was a basic element in the institution, and the worst nightmares of slaveholding society arose from the fear that consent might some day be withdrawn, with violence. Now, almost overnight, the consent was gone. The Negro was using no violence; he just was not consenting anymore, and he never would consent again no matter what happened because he had at last been told that he did not have to.

6   The lack of violence may have been at least partly due to the fact that the proclamation had been issued. The feeling that the Federal government was on their side relieved the Negroes from the desire to start the war for freedom on the plantations; dreadful nightmares failed to come true because the slaves believed that they were or soon would be under the protection of the United States Army. Some time earlier Mr. Lincoln had told an acquaintance that the proclamation was essentially conservative, sparing the slaveowners possible horrors and making servile insurrection unnecessary.[4] Now events were bearing him out.

7   Because the Negro response was so strong, Mr. Lincoln began to see that the problems that came with freedom would have to be solved in America. His long-held idea that it might be possible to avoid these by transferring the Negroes en masse to some far-off colony began to fade when he realized that the colored folk not only wanted freedom but wanted to be Americans, enjoying their freedom in America and not elsewhere. He still gave the colonization project some support but he no longer really fought for it; the place he had suddenly taken in the Negroes' hearts made it impossible. On January 1, just after the signing of the final draft of the proclamation, the abolitionist Benjamin Rush Plumly wrote to him to tell how the free Negroes of Philadelphia had held watch-night services in their churches, praying, singing, weeping, and displaying "the solemn joy of an old Jewish Passover." Plumly, who had attended some of the meetings, tried to tell the President how these people felt:

8   "The Black people trust *you*. They believe that you desire to do them justice. They do not believe that *you* wish to expatriate them, or to enforce upon them any disability, but that you cannot do *all* that you would . . . Someone intimated that you might be forced into some form of colonization. 'God won't let him,' shouted an old woman. 'God's in his *heart*,' said another, and the response of the Congregation was emphatic.

9   "Another thought there must be some design of God in having your name 'Abraham,' that if you were not the 'Father' you were to be the 'Liberator' of a people. One minister advised them to thank God that He

had raised up an honest man for the White House, whereupon they broke, five hundred strong, into that ringing hymn, 'The Year of Jubilee.' "[5]

10   In the deep South the slaves held no prayer meetings of celebration. They simply walked away from the plantation whenever they heard that there was a Federal army within range and presented themselves to their liberators with a touching faith that a new day had come; beginning thus a tragic pilgrimage that cost many thousands of them their lives and plunged all of them deep into utter misery but that did not quite destroy the appeal of the vision that led them on. Before the winter was out the army in the Mississippi Valley area alone was caring for 30,000 or 40,000 of them—men and women and children whose helplessness was absolute, who had no resources except impossible expectations, and for whom no one on earth was really responsible.[6]

11   The army was giving them atrocious care because it had been taken completely by surprise; and so had government, President, War Department, and everyone else. To turn nearly 4,000,000 slaves into free people demanded long-range planning if anything ever did, partly because the problems of transition were so intricate and partly because meeting these problems would inevitably set patterns that would affect Negro life for generations to come. If there had been plenty of time the administration doubtless would eventually have created a special department to handle all of this, with expert planners, a suitable appropriation and a man of cabinet rank to take charge; but that word "eventually" fell out of the language the moment the other word, "freedom," went down the lanes and the grapevine telegraph to the slave cabins, and everything that was done had to be improvised by men whose real concern was something quite different.

12   There was no way out of it. The soldiers in the field had to do the job simply because they themselves stood where the Red Sea waves had parted. The chaplain of an Ohio regiment in Grant's army wrote that the in-gathering of fugitive Negroes was "like the oncoming of cities." Some of the slaves had fled from their masters and some were adrift because the masters themselves had fled, and all of them were waifs in a baffling world where the only certainties they had ever known were gone forever. They came to the army camps because for the moment they were totally helpless, self-reliance and initiative being traits which had gone undeveloped under slavery. They came because they could think of no other place to go and knew only that they had to be on their way somewhere; as the chaplain said, "a blind terror stung them and an equally blind hope allured them, and to us they came."[7] The army had to take some sort of care of them because otherwise the army itself would be swamped.

13   So the army set up concentration camps, whenever and wherever they seemed to be needed; near enough to be under army protection, remote enough to be out of the army's way. For shelter there were condemned army tents, or makeshift cabins improvised out of stray bits of lumber. Army rations were issued, supplemented by foodstuffs gathered in the neighborhood and later by produce from little vegetable plots cultivated by the Negroes themselves. Sometimes army blankets and clothing could be had; more often, as the business got organized, such things were sent to the camps by charitably minded folk in the North. There were armed guards, to keep order, and at least in theory medical care was available. This was nearly always inadequate, sanitary arrangements barely existed, and a representative of the Western Sanitary Commission, after inspecting a chain of these camps in the Mississippi Valley, wrote that many of the inmates were a good deal worse off than they had been under slavery.

14   The death rate, naturally, was appalling. By the middle of the summer a camp near Natchez, Mississippi, was having from fifty to seventy-five deaths every day—rather more than half the number recorded at notorious Andersonville Prison in its worst days, although the Natchez camp held only a fraction of the number confined at Andersonville. Part of this came because the whole operation was done on the spur of the moment, with the left hand, and part of it came because so many of the refugees were physically unfit to begin with. Early in the winter Grant[8] notified Halleck[9] that most of the planters who moved South took their healthy, able-bodied slaves with them, abandoning the old, the very young, and the infirm; Frank Blair's notion that all of the canal-digging around Vicksburg might be done by sturdy contrabands was in error because so many refugees were not sturdy enough, and Grant said he was not letting any more Negroes come within his lines, adding tersely: "Humanity dictates this policy."[10]

15   But the tide kept rising. As a practical matter there was no way to keep the Negroes out, the container which had held them being in process of collapse. The camps multiplied, and the dictates of humanity were all but inaudible. A white woman sent to the Mississippi Valley by the Western Sanitary Commission to work with the refugees was appalled by what she saw in a camp near Helena, Arkansas. The hospital was "a wretched hovel," the streets were so deep with mud that army wagons stuck there, their mules dying in harness, the refugees themselves lived in quarters "void of comfort or decency," and conditions were so bad that the mere idea that there could ever be an improvement seemed to this woman to be impossible. Many of the refugees, she said, seemed to have come to the camp simply to die, "and they do die, very rapidly." Writing in February 1863, she noted that "the carcasses, filth and decay . . . will make the mortality fearful when warm weather comes."

16   To make matters worse, "the barbarities from our soldiers are unparallelled," and the refugees were often treated with incredible brutality. This woman cited one example: "One man came to Mr. Sawyer" (the army chaplain detailed to take charge of the camp) "and said that his wife had lived in a tent with soldiers, had been sick; they being ordered away pulled up the tent and left her on the ground, she had died, and now he wished her buried. Storming terribly as it was, the good chaplain started, but found her so far out that she could not be buried that night, for the teams could not get there and back, so they covered her as well as they could with a blanket and left her. In the morning they found her babe a few months old lying with her under the blanket, some person having become tired of it placed it there for the chaplain to see."

17   Her recital went on, a catalog of horrors. One group of twenty plantation hands came to camp, were robbed by the soldiers of the little they owned, and thirteen of them died of sickness and exposure. Their owner presently came to camp and asked the survivors if they did not want to go back to slavery. "They did not wish to go, faltered, changed their minds daily for a week, we encouraging them all we could, but as destitution, persecution and death stared them in the face the sad sufferers went back." A Federal gunboat brought in eighty-two Negroes, along with a load of cotton; the cotton, having good cash value, was promptly sent North for disposal, but the eighty-two Negroes were dumped at the Helena camp, and "one of the women, a cripple, came to me today, said they had been so abused and starved already that they wished themselves back." One surgeon ordered that contrabands suffering from diarrhea be tied up and flogged, on the theory that this would break them of the abominable habit of soiling their bedding; "it was often done, and to some that were dying."

18   People in the North sent clothing for the inmates, and here the Sanitary Commission agent found an unexpected problem. When a child died the Negroes who were all but naked would use the very best garments they had to clothe the dead child for burial. It was useless to try to explain that the clothing was desperately needed for the living. The parents could think only of the children who had died, who never in their brief lives had worn good clothing, and their answer invariably was: "We want them to look pretty."[11]

19   By slow degrees the worst abuses were corrected, and although many people died most of them after all lived; and the authorities tried to work out a system by which these fugitives could become self-supporting. Abandoned plantations were taken over, leased on one-year terms, and the contrabands were put to work for wages: $7 a month for able-bodied men, $5 for women, half-price for children. One investigator reported that "The plan would have answered a tolerable purpose had the lessees of the plantations been honest, upright, humane men; but with few exceptions they were adventurers and camp followers, who were

ready to turn their hands to any opportunity of getting gain by the oppression of the poor, the weak or the defenceless." The army appointed commissioners to supervise the business, but mostly the commissioners sided with the lessees rather than with the Negroes. The investigator noted that wages were based on the slave-hire rate that prevailed when cotton sold for 10 cents a pound; it sold for 70 cents now, $2 a head was deducted for medical care which often was not provided, and in many cases wages stopped on rainy days.

20   This exploitation was not confined to the Mississippi Valley. In the vicinity of Port Royal, South Carolina, the story was about the same. A number of plantations there were sold to Northerners who set up a share-crop system. One man acquired thirteen plantations, employing 400 former slaves, "not one of them able-bodied, all being old men, old or feeble women, or children." He raised sea island cotton, investing $40,000 altogether and clearing an $81,000 profit for his year's effort. On an average, his workers got $16.50 a month. In some instances small plantations were leased and operated by the Negroes themselves, and this seemed to work out fairly well except that the Negroes often feared to bring their crops to market because soldiers and civilian speculators either swindled them or took their produce by force.

21   A Federal officer said that he "found the prejudice of color and race here in full force, and the general feeling of the army of occupation was unfriendly to the blacks. It was manifested in various forms of personal insult and abuse, in depredations on their plantations, stealing and despoiling them of their crops and domestic animals and robbing them of their money." It was considered that the system set up by General Banks in Louisiana was the worst of all, labor being enforced by the army "often with great rigor" with everything arranged for the benefit of the planters. Here, as elsewhere, there was heavy mortality in the camps.[12]

22   Dawn was a long way off, and if there was a light in the sky the light was streaky, blood-red against the darkness. Yet the slaves kept on coming in, and on the whole what they came to seemed to matter less to them than what they were getting away from. After a few months of it General Grant told his friend and patron, Congressman Elihu B. Washburne of Illinois: "Slavery is already dead and cannot be resurrected. It would take a standing army to maintain slavery in the South if we were to make peace today guaranteeing to the South all their former Constitutional privileges." Grant went on to say that he himself had never been an abolitionist, "nor even what could be called anti-slavery"; he was simply telling what he saw.[13]

23   Grant was not overstating the case. The great change was taking place, and as the winter passed Negroes were not only coming into the army's lines: in increasing numbers they were coming into the army it-

self, the administration having at last made up its mind to put Negroes in uniform and make soldiers out of them.

24   Before the proclamation was issued this looked like too risky a step to take, and in the summer of 1862 President Lincoln had refused to take it. But after the proclamation came out he changed his mind, remarking to General John A. Dix at Fort Monroe that inasmuch as "we have it, and bear all the disadvantage of it (as we do bear some in certain quarters) we must also take some benefit from it, if practicable." He asked Dix if he could not raise Negro regiments, using them to garrison places in the rear areas so that the white troops there could be freed for field service. To Andrew Johnson, military governor of Tennessee, he wrote that the nation needed nothing so much as to have a man like Johnson—"an eminent citizen of a slave-state, and himself a slave-holder"—raise Negro troops. "The colored population," wrote Mr. Lincoln, "is the great *available* and yet *unavailed* of force for restoring the Union. The bare sight of 50,000 armed and drilled black soldiers on the banks of the Mississippi would end the rebellion at once. And who doubts that we can present that sight, if we but take hold in earnest?"

25   The hope that this spectacle would of itself end the rebellion turned out, of course, to be a wildly optimistic miscalculation, but a decision of immense importance had been made, and the administration pushed the program with energy. Authority to recruit and use Negro regiments had been granted by Congress much earlier and before the winter was out the War Department sent Adjutant General Lorenzo Thomas to the Mississippi Valley to see that such units were raised, officered, drilled and used. Halleck sent a private letter to Grant, remarking that he understood many of Grant's officers mistreated Negro refugees and tried to make them return to their masters and ordering him to "use your official and personal influences to remove prejudices on this subject and to fully and thoroughly carry out the policy now adopted and ordered by the government." This policy, in brief, was "to withdraw from the use of the enemy all the slaves you can, and to employ those so withdrawn to the best possible advantage against the enemy."

26   As Grant hardly needed to be told, this marked a significant change in the administration's attitude toward Secession, and Halleck underlined it:

27   "The character of the war has very much changed within the last year. There is now no possible hope of a reconciliation with the Rebels. The Union party in the South is virtually destroyed. There can be no peace but that which is enforced by the sword"—by the sword, the instrument which Mr. Vallandigham considered wholly impotent in this case.[14]

28   It was a long, painful process; a revolutionary change embraced reluctantly and from dire necessity. The nation had not been driven to war by its desire to free the slaves; instead it had been driven to free the

slaves by its desire to win the war. Now it had to change its thinking, and this was hard to do. Under the revolution involved in the act of changing slaves into free men, even into soldiers, there lay a profounder revolution involving the way individual men looked at their fellow human beings. Men of unquestioned goodwill found old habits of thought hard to break. Presidential Secretary John G. Nicolay this spring went to a Washington party where the Haitian Chargé d'Affairs was a guest, attended by his Secretary of Legation: two men of color, accepted on an equal footing in a roomful of whites. "They were quiet and well behaved, and said to be quite intelligent," wrote Nicolay. "'But on the whole it was rather difficult to dissociate them in one's mind from the other colored waiters in the room."[15]

29   It was difficult: even more so for men not conditioned as Nicolay had been conditioned. Colonel Edward S. Bragg of the 6th Wisconsin was a distinguished combat soldier, leader of one of the best regiments in the Army of the Potomac, and he found adjustment impossible. A few weeks before the Battle of Gettysburg he wrote thus to his wife:

30   "I understand there is a Negro regiment in town, but as I am confined to my room I have not had my nerves shocked by seeing 'a woolly head and black face' decked out in Uncle Sam's uniform. I wish a white man was as good as a Negro and elicited as much sympathy and attention. A man must be either 'a foreigner or a black' to receive early notice at the hands of our exceedingly discriminating public.

31   "A little nigger just came in my room, with 'our corps' badge on his hat which was given him by a Lieutenant—by the aid of a knife I soon destroyed the 'Cuffie's' plumage. What an ass a man must be to put his uniform on a dirty nigger that didn't belong to him."[16]

32   Something irrevocable was happening. A good many Cuffies were putting on the country's uniform this spring, and they had no illusions about the way they were regarded. One Federal officer intimately connected with the enlistment of Negro soldiers wrote frankly: "They were fully aware of the contempt, often times amounting to hatred, of their ostensible liberators. They felt the bitter derision, even from officers of high rank, with which the idea of their being transformed into available soldiers was met." But they had their own point of view, which was expressed bluntly by Frederick Douglass, the one-time slave who was the acknowledged spokesman for free Negroes in the North. He put it this way:

33   "Once let the black man get upon his person the brass letters *U.S.*; let him get an eagle on his button, and a musket on his shoulder, and bullets in his pocket, and there is no power on earth which can deny that he has earned the right to citizenship in the United States."[17]

34   For when the Negro put on his country's uniform it followed logically that at last he had a country.

Notes

[1]The Emancipation Proclamation, issued January 1, 1863, by President Abraham Lincoln (1809–1865), freed all slaves. [Eds.]

[2]Clement Laird Vallandigham (1820–1871), American legislator and representative from Ohio. [Eds.]

[3]Congressional Globe, 37th Congress, Third Session, Appendix, 55–56.

[4]Letter of T. J. Barnett to Barlow dated Nov. 30, 1862, detailing a conversation with President Lincoln, in the Barlow Papers, Huntington Library.

[5]Letter of Plumly to Lincoln dated Jan. 1, 1863, in the Robert Todd Lincoln Papers, Library of Congress.

[6]Appleton's *American Annual Cyclopaedia for 1863*, 428.

[7]John Eaton, *Grant, Lincoln and the Freedman*, cited in *Grant Moves South*, 357.

[8]Ulysses S. Grant (1822–1885), Union general and later (1869–1877) eighteenth president of the United States. [Eds.]

[9]Henry Wager Halleck (1790–1867), Union general. [Eds.]

[10]Letter of Grant to Halleck dated Feb. 18, 1863, in the *New York Historical Society*. There is an extensive discussion of the refugee camps in Appleton's *American Annual Cyclopaedia for 1863*, 428–429.

[11]Letters from Maria R. Mann at Helena, Ark., dated Feb 10 and April 19, 1863, in the Manuscript Division, Library of Congress.

[12]Many of these findings are from Appleton's *Cyclopaedia*, as noted in note 10; much of the material there apparently is based on a report by James E. Yeatman, president of the Western Sanitary Commission. See also a report to Secretary Stanton by Brig. Gen. R. Saxton in O.R., Series Three, Vol. IV, 1028–1029.

[13]Letter of Grant to Washburne dated Aug. 30, 1863, in the Illinois State Historical Library, Springfield.

[14]Letter of Halleck to Grant dated March 31, 1863, in the Lieber Collection, Huntington Library.

[15]Letter of Nicolay to his wife dated March 8, 1863, in the John G. Nicolay Papers, Library of Congress.

[16]Letter of Bragg to Mrs. Bragg dated June 13, 1863, in the Edward S. Bragg Papers, State Historical Society of Wisconsin Library.

[17]Saxton to Stanton, as in note 12 above. Frederick Douglass's statement is quoted in Benjamin Quarles, *The Negro in the Civil War*, p. 184.

Content Questions

1. Why didn't Lincoln follow his original plan to help blacks?
2. Why was the army forced to set up concentration camps during the Civil War?
3. What were the conditions for blacks immediately after the Emancipation Proclamation?
4. How were the conditions in the camps finally improved?
5. How did the Union benefit from the Emancipation Proclamation?

Questions on Presentation

1. How would you describe Catton's tone?
2. Bruce Catton is known as a popularizer of American history. What in this essay identifies it as a popular rather than a scholarly text?
3. Is the metaphor in paragraph 22 effective? Why or why not?
4. What makes the short final paragraph effective? Would a longer paragraph have greater or lesser impact?

Address to the Temperance Society

Elizabeth Cady Stanton

American suffrage activist Elizabeth Cady Stanton (1815–1902) was an advocate of many movements, including temperance and abolition, as well as women's rights. So strong were her feelings about women's rights that she insisted the word "obey" be omitted from her marriage ceremony. She was a student of Greek, Latin, and mathematics and graduated from Emma Willard's Troy Female Seminary in 1832. A friend of Susan B. Anthony and Lucretia Mott, both women's rights activists, Stanton campaigned strenuously for women's rights. She is the author of the controversial *Women's Bible* (1895–1898, two volumes) and was coeditor, with Anthony, of the first three volumes of the *History of Woman's Suffrage* (1881–1886). In this speech, delivered in 1853, she outlines and defends the women's rights movement.

1   A little more than one year ago, in this same hall, we formed the first Woman's State Temperance Society. We believed that the time had come for women to speak on this question, and to insist on her right to be heard in the councils of Church and State. It was proposed at that time that we, instead of forming a society, should go *en masse* into the Men's State Temperance Society. We were assured that in becoming members by paying the sum of $1, we should thereby secure the right to speak and vote in their meetings.

2   We who had watched the jealousy with which man had ever eyed the slow aggressions of woman, warned you against the insidious proposition made by agents from that Society. We told you they would no doubt gladly receive the dollar, but that you would never be allowed to speak or vote in their meetings. Many of you thought us suspicious and unjust toward the temperance men of the Empire State. The fact that

Abby Kelly had been permitted to speak in one of their public meetings, was brought up as an argument by some agent of that Society to prove our fears unfounded. We suggested that she spoke by favor and not right, and our right there as equals to speak and vote, we well knew would never be acknowledged. A long debate saved you from that false step, and our predictions have been fully realized in the treatment our delegates received at the annual meeting held at Syracuse last July, and at the recent Brick Church meeting in New York.

3   In forming our Society, the mass of us being radical and liberal, we left our platform free; we are no respecters of persons, all are alike welcome here without regard to sect, sex, color, or caste. There have been, however, many objections made to one feature in our Constitution, and that is, that although we admit men as members with equal right to speak in our meetings, we claim the offices for women alone. We felt, in starting, the necessity of throwing all the responsibility on woman, which we knew she never would take, if there were any men at hand to think, act, and plan for her. The result has shown the wisdom of what seemed so objectionable to many. It was, however, a temporary expedient, and as that seeming violation of man's rights prevents some true friends of the cause from becoming members of our Society, and as the officers are now well skilled in the practical business of getting up meetings, raising funds, etc., and have fairly learned how to stand and walk alone, it may perhaps be safe to raise man to an entire equality with ourselves, hoping, however, that he will modestly permit the women to continue the work they have so successfully begun. I would suggest, therefore, that after the business of the past year be disposed of, this objectionable feature of our Constitution be brought under consideration.

4   Our experience thus far as a Society has been most encouraging. We number over two thousand members. We have four agents who have traveled in various parts of the State, and I need not say what is well known to all present, that their labors thus far have given entire satisfaction to the Society and the public. I was surprised and rejoiced to find that women, without the least preparation or experience, who had never raised their voices in public one year ago, should with so much self-reliance, dignity, and force, enter at once such a field of labor, and so ably perform the work. In the metropolis of our country, in the capital of our State, before our Legislature, and in the country schoolhouse, they have been alike earnest and faithful to the truth. In behalf of our Society, I thank you for your unwearied labors during the past year. In the name of humanity, I bid you go on and devote yourselves humbly to the cause you have espoused. The noble of your sex everywhere rejoice in your success, and feel in themselves a new impulse to struggle upward and onward; and the deep, though silent gratitude that ascends to Heaven from the wretched outcast, the wives, the mothers, and the

daughters of brutal drunkards, is well known to all who have listened to their tales of woe, their bitter experience, the dark, sad passages of their tragic lives.

5   I hope this, our first year, is prophetic of a happy future of strong, united, and energetic action among the women of our State. If we are sincere and earnest in our love of this cause, in our devotion to truth, in our desire for the happiness of the race, we shall ever lose sight of self; each soul will, in a measure, forget its own individual interests in proclaiming great principles of justice and right. It is only a true, a deep, and abiding love of truth, that can swallow up all petty jealousies, envies, discords, and dissensions, and make us truly magnanimous and self-sacrificing. We have every reason to think, from reports we hear on all sides, that our Society has given this cause a new impulse, and if the condition of our treasury is a test, we have abundant reason to believe that in the hearts of the people we are approved, and that by their purses we shall be sustained.

6   It has been objected to our Society that we do not confine ourselves to the subject of temperance, but talk too much about woman's rights, divorce, and the Church. It could be easily shown how the consideration of this great question carries us legitimately into the discussion of these various subjects. One class of minds would deal with effects alone; another would inquire into causes; the work of the former is easily perceived and quickly done; that of the latter requires deep thought, great patience, much time, and a wise self-denial. Our physicians of the present day are a good type of the mass of our reformers. They take out cancers, cut off tonsils, drive the poison which nature has wisely thrown to the surface, back again, quiet unsteady nerves with valerian, and by means of ether infuse an artificial courage into a patient that he may bravely endure some painful operation. It requires but little thought to feel that the wise physician who shall trace out the true causes of suffering; who shall teach us the great, immutable laws of life and health; who shall show us how and where in our every-day life, we are violating these laws, and the true point to begin the reform, is doing a much higher, broader, and deeper work than he who shall bend all his energies to the temporary relief of suffering. Those temperance men or women whose whole work consists in denouncing rum-sellers, appealing to legislatures, eulogizing Neal Dow, and shouting Maine Law, are superficial reformers, mere surface-workers. True, this outside work is well, and must be done; let those who see no other do this, but let them lay no hindrances in the way of that class of mind, who, seeing in our present false social relations the causes of the moral deformities of the race, would fain declare the immutable laws that govern mind as well as matter, and point out the true causes of the evils we see about us, whether

lurking under the shadow of the altar, the sacredness of the marriage institution, or the assumed superiority of man.

7   We have been obliged to preach woman's rights, because many, instead of listening to what we had to say on temperance, have questioned the right of a woman to speak on any subject. In courts of justice and legislative assemblies, if the right of the speaker to be there is questioned, all business waits until that point is settled. Now, it is not settled in the mass of minds that woman has any rights on this footstool, and much less a right to stand on an even pedestal with man, look him in the face as an equal, and rebuke the sins of her day and generation. Let it be clearly understood, then, that we are a woman's rights Society; that we believe it is woman's duty to speak whenever she feels the impression to do so; that it is her right to be present in all the councils of Church and State. The fact that our agents are women, settles the question of our character on this point.

8   Again, in discussing the question of temperance, all lecturers, from the beginning, have made mention of the drunkards' wives and children, of widows' groans and orphans' tears; shall these classes of sufferers be introduced but as themes for rhetorical flourish, as pathetic touches of the speaker's eloquence; shall we passively shed tears over their condition, or by giving them their rights, bravely open to them the doors of escape from a wretched and degraded life? Is it not legitimate in this to discuss the social degradation, the legal disabilities of the drunkard's wife? If in showing her wrongs, we prove the right of all womankind to the elective franchise; to a fair representation in the government; to the right in criminal cases to be tried by peers of her own choosing, shall it be said that we transcend the bounds of our subject? If in pointing out her social degradation, we show you how the present laws outrage the sacredness of the marriage institution; if in proving to you that justice and mercy demand a legal separation from drunkards, we grasp the higher idea that a unity of soul alone constitutes and sanctifies true marriage, and that any law or public sentiment that forces two immortal, high-born souls to live together as husband and wife, unless held there by love, is false to God and humanity; who shall say that the discussion of this question does not lead us legitimately into the consideration of the important subject of divorce?

9   But why attack the Church? We do not attack the Church; we defend ourselves merely against its attacks. It is true that the Church and reformers have always been in an antagonistic position from the time of Luther down to our own day, and will continue to be until the devotional and practical types of Christianity shall be united in one harmonious whole. To those who see the philosophy of this position, there seems to be no cause for fearful forebodings or helpless regret. By the light of rea-

son and truth, in good time, all these seeming differences will pass away. I have no special fault to find with that part of humanity that gathers into our churches; to me, human nature seems to manifest itself in very much the same way in the Church and out of it. Go through any community you please—into the nursery, kitchen, the parlor, the places of merchandise, the market-place, and exchange, and who can tell the church member from the outsider? I see no reason why we should expect more of them that other men. Why, say you, they lay claim to greater holiness; to more rigid creeds; to a belief in a sterner God; to a closer observance of forms. The Bible, with them, is the rule of life, the foundation of faith, and why should we not look to them for patterns of purity, goodness, and truth above all other men? I deny the assumption. Reformers on all sides claim for themselves a higher position than the Church. Our God is a God of justice, mercy, and truth. Their God sanctions violence, oppression, and wine-bibbing, and winks at gross moral delinquencies. Our Bible commands us to love our enemies; to resist not evil; to break every yoke and let the oppressed go free; and makes a noble life of more importance than a stern faith. Their Bible permits war, slavery, capital punishment, and makes salvation depend on faith and ordinances. In their creed it is a sin to dance, to pick up sticks on the Sabbath day, to go to the theater, or large parties during Lent, to read a notice of any reform meeting from the altar, or permit a woman to speak in the church. In our creed it is a sin to hold a slave; to hang a man on the gallows; to make war on defenseless nations, or to sell rum to a weak brother, and rob the widow and the orphan of a protector and a home. Thus may we write out some of our differences, but from the similarity in the conduct of the human family, it is fair to infer that our differences are more intellectual than spiritual, and the great truths we hear so clearly uttered on all sides, have been incorporated as vital principles into the inner life of but few indeed.

10   We must not expect the Church to leap *en masse* to a higher position. She sends forth her missionaries of truth one by one. All of our reformers have, in a measure, been developed in the Church, and all our reforms have started there. The advocates and opposers of the reforms of our day, have grown up side by side, partaking of the same ordinances and officiating at the same altars; but one, by applying more fully his Christian principles to life, and pursuing an admitted truth to its legitimate results, has unwittingly found himself in antagonism with his brother.

11   Belief is not voluntary, and change is the natural result of growth and development. We would fain have all church members sons and daughters of temperance; but if the Church, in her wisdom, has made her platform so broad that wine-bibbers and rum-sellers may repose in ease

thereon, we who are always preaching liberality ought to be the last to complain.

Content Questions

1. Why did the women not want to join the Men's State Temperance Society? Was this the right response, according to Stanton?
2. Why were men not allowed to be officeholders in the Women's State Temperance Society?
3. Why did the Temperance Society have to discuss women's rights?
4. Why does Stanton believe the Women's Society will be successful?
5. Who does Stanton see as superficial reformers? Why?

Questions on Presentation

1. Is the comparison between reformers and physicians in paragraph 6 effective? Why or why not?
2. In paragraph 8 Stanton uses the same phrase ("If in . . .") several times. What is the effect of this usage?
3. Is Stanton's argument for divorce convincing? Why or why not?
4. Stanton makes frequent use of rhetorical questions. What effect does this have on the essay?
5. How would you characterize Stanton's audience?

Questions for Discussion and Writing

1. Some of the selections in this section argue for individualism. Their authors want readers to see that being unique is valuable. Rather than being a copy of someone else or trying to fulfill someone else's image of a type of person (e.g., worker, designer, football player, college student), people should be individuals. How do the writers make this point? Is the point valid? Is it reasonable?
2. The essays in this section discuss various concepts of political, religious, and personal dissent. Are there common themes among these essays? Is there a basis for dissent, regardless of the institution to which people object? Do dissenters have common goals? Do they see a purpose for their dissent, or are they objecting just to be heard?
3. Several of the essays in this section depend on examples, rather than reasoning, to make their points. For example, two of the writers, Clemens and Jefferson, have very different purposes but use a similar strategy—

exemplification—to support their ideas. Which essays in this section used examples most effectively? Which essays needed more examples or different types of examples? Do the types of examples differ with the various purposes of the authors?

4. Gaustad writes that "no society—ecclesiastical or political, military, or literary—can afford to be snared by its own slogans." A university or college, or education in general, is a type of society that could be subject to Gaustad's statement. Write an essay analyzing how a university or college could be trapped by slogans. Suggest in your essay how this society can avoid the trap.

Section 3

BUSINESS ETHICS

Is Corporate Executive Compensation Excessive?

Robert Thomas

Economist Robert Thomas teaches at the University of Washington. He wrote the following selection for Bruce Johnson's anthology *The Attack on Corporate America: The Corporate Issues Sourcebook* (1978). In this essay Thomas analyzes the justifications for high executive salaries, compensation many Americans feel is excessive.

1   Ralph Nader stands at the end of a long line of critics who assail the high incomes of top corporate executives. Nader and his associates suggest that "in the absence of judicial limitations, excessive remuneration has become the norm."[1] They observe that the average top executive in each of the fifty largest industrial corporations earns more salary in a year than many of the corporate employees earn in a lifetime. Salaries are only part (albeit the major part) of the compensation the top executives receive. Bonuses, lavish retirements, stock options, and stock ownership combine to swell the incomes of corporate chief executives by another 50 to 75 percent of the executives' direct remunerations. Nader and his associates conclude that the top corporate executives receive "staggeringly large salaries and stock options."[2]

The Attack on Executive Income

2   Those who criticize the level of compensation that corporate executives receive are critical of any persons who are, or who become rich. The top executives of our major corporations *do* become rich. *Fortune* magazine, in a survey of the chief executives of the 500 largest industrial corporations, discovered that the median income in 1976 was $209,000 a year and that when only the 100 largest corporations were considered, the median salary was $344,000 a year.[3]

3   Most Americans, however, do not consider becoming rich to be a crime. Indeed, the opposite is true. Achieving wealth reflects a high level of performance in providing through the market what the economy desires.

4   Nader and his coauthors recognize this admiration for performance and attack the level of executive compensation on other grounds. They suggest that the chief corporate executives are not entrepreneurs who risk their own capital in the search for profits, but functionaries who perform essentially the same tasks as government employees. The chief corporate executives "serve as the bureaucrats of private industry."[4]

5   The difference between industry and government is that the boards of directors of large corporations allegedly are more lax in discharging their responsibilities to their shareholders (by constraining excessive executive salaries) than the members of the Congress of the United States and the various elected officials of state and local governments who serve as the watchdogs for the public interest. The managements of large corporations take advantage of this laxness to request and receive excessive compensation. Moreover, this is not an isolated phenomenon confined to an occasional corporation. Nader reports that it "has become the norm."[5]

Why Executives Are Well Paid

6   In response, consider first who a chief corporate executive is, and examine the responsibilities a chief corporate executive must discharge. The typical top executive in each of the 500 largest industrial corporations is a white Protestant male aged sixty. He got his top position at age fifty-five; he averages between fifty-five and sixty-four hours a week on the job, takes three weeks of vacation each year, and earns a salary of $209,000 a year. He has attended graduate school, and he has worked for more than two companies during his business career. He owns less than $500,000 worth of stock in the company for which he works, and during the past decade he has seen his salary rise less rapidly, in percentage terms, than the salaries of his employees. In short, he is well prepared, experienced, hardworking, and beyond middle age.

7   Two things distinguish each of these 500 persons from several thousand others who have similar qualities. First, each is paid more. Second, each has been chosen as the person responsible for his company's present and future.

8   The Fortune 500 Company corporate executive directs a company whose sales in 1975 averaged almost $1.75 billion, whose assets totaled $1.33 billion, and which provided employment for almost 29,000 people.[6] This executive directs the firm in a manner that allows it to earn an 11.6 percent return on its total investment. Such a rate of return is not guaranteed simply because a corporation is large. The opportunities

to lose money are many; the managements of 28 of the 500 largest industrial corporations managed to show a loss in the recovery year of 1975. It is possible, moreover, to lose big: Singer reported a loss of $451.9 million in that year, and Chrysler $259.5 million. A chief executive who heads a management team that can avoid such losses and constantly succeed in earning a profit is obviously very valuable to the shareholders of a corporation. He is valuable not only to his employers but also to other corporations; thus his own firm pays him handsomely to retain his services.

9   Many pages of our national magazines devoted to business news— *Business Week, Forbes, Fortune*—report the movements of business executives from one firm to another. These shifts are induced by substantial increases in salary, often, according to one publication, of 30 percent or more.[7] Some excellently managed corporations, such as IBM, General Motors, Procter and Gamble, and Xerox, are known in industry as "executive breeders."[8] Xerox admitted in its 1976 proxy statement that its management was increasingly becoming "a target for other corporations seeking talented executives," and it proposed a new incentive plan for its executives.[9] This request for increased executive compensation was not self-serving on the part of Xerox's management; it stemmed in part from the prior move of twelve Xerox executives to a rival copier manufacturer.

10   The high salaries and fringe benefits that talented executives in large corporations receive stem not from laxness on the part of the boards of directors but, rather, from the boards' vigilance. Corporations must pay their executives, as well as any other employees, what they could earn by working for a rival firm, or lose them. Competition among corporations for the best people sets the level of executive compensation. If one person is to be placed in charge of a billion dollars in shareholder assets, which can easily be lost through mismanagement, even the $766,085 a year that the highest-paid corporate executive in the United States receives might not appear excessive to shareholders, especially if that salary is what it takes to get the services of the best available person.

11   There are many examples of corporations that are well rewarded for paying the price necessary to get the best person to remedy a bad situation. In one recent case, a firm that once tried to produce computers, and whose stock had sold for as high as $173 a share, fell on hard times; in 1973 it lost $119 million on sales of $177 million and had $300 million in long-term debts.[10] A new chief executive, who by 1976 had made the firm profitable once again, received $200,000 a year, performance incentives that earned him another $400,000, and stock options that made him a millionaire on paper. Clearly the compensation this executive received meets the Nader criterion for being "excessive." Yet, the Bank of America thought it was a worthwhile investment to guarantee his salary in an attempt, which proved successful, to ensure the eventual repay-

ment of the large loans it had made to the firm. Individual shareholders also applauded the move; as a result of the executive's efforts, the value of a share has increased from $2 to over $21. In this one instance, the efforts of the new chief executive succeeded in increasing the market value of the company ten times.

12   A talented executive is highly paid because he is very productive. He earns for his firm additional net revenue at least equal in value to his compensation. If he did not, his firm would let him go. If his firm does not pay him what he is worth to others, it will lose him to a rival. The same holds true for any other valuable input in our economy and accounts as well for the high incomes received by talented persons in other fields.

Salaries of Other Persons

13   Consider, for a moment, the salaries paid to entertainers. The fastest way to become a millionaire is not to become a corporate executive, but to become a big rock 'n' roll star or a superstar in professional sports. In 1973, for example, there were an estimated fifty music performers earning between $1 million and $6 million a year.[11] These thirty-five persons and fifteen groups made, annually, between three and seven times the salary paid to America's highest-paid executive. While the musicians performed, that highest-paid executive directed, and was responsible for, a company that employed 376,000 persons, had sales of over $11 billion and assets of over $10 billion, and earned almost $400 million in profits. Rock stars, moreover, earn their fortunes sooner than business executives; most start their careers as teenage idols; few have their best earning years after thirty. The average chief executive in each of the 500 largest industrial corporations does not attain that degree of success until the age of fifty-five.

14   Or, examine the compensation paid to the superstars in professional sports. The most interesting stories on sports pages now are not reports of games but stories about the fabulous salaries received by star athletes; $3 million to Julius Erving, $1.5 million each to O. J. Simpson and Pele, $500,000 to Kareem Abdul-Jabbar, $450,000 each to Tiny Archibald and Joe Namath, $400,000 to Catfish Hunter, $360,000 to Bob Lanier, $325,000 to Bill Bradley, $302,000 to Spencer Haywood, $250,000 to John Havlicek, $237,500 to Rick Barry, $230,000 to Tom Seaver, and $225,000 to Dick Allen.[12] More names from golf, hockey, and tennis could easily be added to the list. The reported incomes of these superstars are probably understated, since they exclude payments for endorsements and the like. These people, furthermore, work only part of the year, while the average chief executive has a forty-nine-week season.

15   When considered in the light of the compensation paid to extremely talented persons in other areas, the rewards earned by corporate execu-

tives do not appear excessive. A competitive economy ensures that highly productive persons command high rewards.

Notes

[1]Ralph Nader and Mark Green, Eds. *Corporate Power in America*. (New York: Grossman, 1973), p. 115.
[2]Nader and Green, p. 118.
[3]Charles G. Burck, "A Group Profile of the Fortune 500 Chief Executive," *Fortune*, May 1976, p. 172.
[4]Nader and Green, p. 118.
[5]Nader and Green, p. 115.
[6]Burck, p. 172.
[7]*Business Week*, October 4, 1971, p. 62.
[8]*Business Week*, p. 57.
[9]*Business Week*, p. 57.
[10]*Forbes*, October 15, 1976, p. 78.
[11]*Forbes*, April 15, 1973, p. 28.
[12]Burck, p. 170.

Content Questions

1. What is Nader's complaint about corporate executives?
2. Why are "executive breeders" important to corporations?
3. How can a top executive benefit a company?

Questions on Presentation

1. Thomas argues that top corporate executives are worth the seemingly excessive compensation they make. What are his main points supporting his position? How well does he prove those points?
2. Are the functions of paragraphs 3 and 8 different? What is the function of each?
3. Why does Thomas shift to the imperative voice in paragraph 13?

The Budget Masquerade

Robert J. Samuelson

Robert J. Samuelson is a contributing editor for *Newsweek* magazine and writes a weekly column on economic affairs for *The National Journal.* In the following essay, taken from *Newsweek,* Samuelson analyzes some of the reasons for the budget deficit and its impact on public and private credit. Samuelson criticizes political leaders for their unwillingness to address budget issues and warns us of the dangers of ignoring rising deficits.

1   The frightening thing about President Reagan's budget is not today's deficit, but tomorrow's. The Office of Management and Budget estimates the 1989 deficit (when unemployment is assumed to drop to 5.7 percent) at $193 billion under current tax and spending policies. Covering that with taxes requires personal and corporate income-tax increases of about a third. The Congressional Budget Office, with more pessimistic assumptions, estimates a comparable 1989 deficit of more than $300 billion; the necessary tax increases would exceed 50 percent.

2   Nothing better illustrates the blurring between economics and politics than this rapidly deteriorating budget outlook. It is a political stalemate masquerading as an economic dispute. For 20 years, we have regarded the budget as a tool to manipulate the economy while forgetting the traditional view that the budget represents what people want from government and what they are willing to pay for. Mushrooming deficits resulted because they became increasingly easy to rationalize: Democrats did so in the name of John Maynard Keynes, Ronald Reagan did so in the name of "supply-side economics."

3   Although everyone deplores them in the abstract, huge deficits actually reflect today's political mood and maneuvering. People do not want either higher taxes or lower spending. The deficits also serve both Democrats and the White House. As long as the economy expands and unemployment declines, large deficits remain the Democrats' only economic attacking point. For Reagan, closing the deficits might mean abandoning his 1981 tax cut.

4   This easy tolerance of deficits throws onto economic analysis the entire burden of arguing their evils. But economists cannot do this—though many have tried—because the deficits' effects are cumulative and invisible, not sudden and dramatic. As dire economic prophecies have failed to materialize, political pressures for cutting them have abated.

5   The need now is to separate the economics and politics of deficits. The common complaint holds that deficits raise interest rates and that this is bad. But neither of these assumptions—that low interest rates are always good or that deficits are the main cause of increases—is self-evidently true.

6   Recall that low interest rates in the late 1970s fueled inflation by encouraging excessive borrowing. Between 1975 and 1979, household and business borrowing more than tripled (from $94 billion to $328 billion). This credit explosion helped bid up the price of everything, from gold to

homes. And what propelled it was interest rates that were low or negative after taking inflation and taxes into account. In 1978, when inflation averaged 7.4 percent, conventional mortgage rates were only 9.6 percent. Because interest expenses are tax deductible, the after-tax mortgage rate for an individual in the 35 percent tax bracket was only 6.2 percent, lower than the inflation rate. Borrowing terms for top-rated corporations, which can deduct nearly half their interest costs, were even better.

7   The Federal Reserve exercises the most control over interest rates, and today's higher rates stem mostly from the Fed's apparent determination not to reignite inflation with cheap money. Because the tax laws are so complicated and future inflation so uncertain, no one can say how high today's effective interest rates are. But they did not, despite forecasts to the contrary, prevent a brisk recovery.

8   This does not mean that deficits don't also push up rates. Unless the laws of supply and demand have been repealed, the deficits—by raising the demand for credit—probably do increase rates. But this analysis does deny a simple prescription for high rates. Lowering deficits might help, but even more powerful medicine might be tax changes that limit the existing subsidies (i.e., interest deductibility) for borrowing.

9   And there's the rub. Without assured economic rewards, the political payoffs for treating deficits fade. To say that the budget cannot be cut is lunacy. In fiscal 1985, farm-price-support programs will cost an estimated $10.8 billion, Amtrak $700 million, maritime subsidies $400 million, general revenue sharing for states and localities $4.6 billion and the B-1 bomber $5.6 billion.

10   But each of these programs has its defenders and dependents. The same can be said for the byzantine tax code that, replete with deductions and credits, keeps tax rates up. Tax rates could be lowered and tax revenues increased by reducing deductions and credits, but trying that could also provoke a huge public backlash.

11   The trouble with this stalemate is not that it will automatically cause recession—though something ultimately is bound to cause a recession—but that it is inherently unstable. Large deficits and higher interest rates inflate interest payments as a share of spending. Since 1979 they have jumped from 9.6 to 14.5 percent of the total. As the debt burden grows, so do pressures for offsetting tax increases or spending cuts.

12   The longer choices are evaded, the worse they become—until they reach the sobering proportions of the 1989 projections. By forgetting the budget's basic political purpose, we have created enormous uncertainty over whose taxes will be raised or whose spending will be cut. This cannot but unsettle economic decision making and, when the issues are finally faced, deepen public suspicion of political leaders.

13   The choices are so unattractive that, privately, some Democrats won-

der whether the party might be better off losing the election. Budget director David Stockman argues that the administration hasn't been clearer about the choices because it's pointless to line up "all of these changes . . . so that every candidate running for office in the House and Senate . . . can pledge not to do them when we get back . . .''

14   But if elections aren't about choice, what are they about? Good question. Elections should inform, and deficits reflect misinformation: the illusion that choices can be avoided.

Content Questions

1. What consequences does the rapidly deteriorating budget outlook masquerade?
2. Why was it more economical to buy items on credit in the 1970s?
3. Why are congressional leaders fostering the illusion that budget choices can be avoided?

Questions on Presentation

1. The paragraphs in Samuelson's essay are generally short, implying that Samuelson hasn't developed his thesis completely. Does he provide sufficient information to make his points?
2. Samuelson uses emotionally charged language. Identify instances of this sort of language. What is its effect on the essay?
3. Who do you believe is Samuelson's audience? Is it the same as Thomas's audience?
4. How does Samuelson use words such as *dire* (4) and *byzantine* (10) to contribute to the tone of the essay?

Business Without Science
David Vogel

Born in New York City and educated at Queens College and Princeton University, David Vogel (b. 1947) is an associate professor in the School of Business Administration at the University of California at Berkeley. Vogel is the editor of *California Management Review* and has contributed essays to many scholarly and popular journals including *Nation, Polity, The New Republic, Daedalus,* and *The New York Times.* In addition Vogel has written several books such as *Ethics and Profits* (in 1976 with Leonard Silk), *Lobbying the Corporation: Citizen Challenges to Business Authority* (1978), and *Corporations and Their Critics* (1981). In *Lobbying the Corporation,* Vogel evaluates how various social and environmental groups have tried to influence companies like Du Pont and General Motors to change their social and environmental policies. His conclusion is sound and clearly stated: to influence others, there is no substitute for knowing your audience and for organizing your campaign. In the following essay, taken from the July 1981 issue of *Science Digest,* Vogel evaluates the U.S. position as a leader in world trade and the threats to that position that come not from our competitors but from our business practices.

1   American industry's growing inability to compete internationally has become a major source of public concern. Since 1970, the share of the world market claimed by U.S. manufactured goods has fallen by nearly one-quarter. Twenty-six percent of all the automobiles sold in the United States are now produced overseas, compared with only 15 percent in 1970. As a result of the inability of American companies to compete in world markets, the American economy lost a total of 2 million manufacturing jobs in less than 10 years. The manufacture of a wide array of products that an entire generation of American workers had come to depend upon as a stable source of employment now takes place in Western Europe, Japan and in the newly industrializing nations of Asia and Latin America.

2   Not only does this deterioration of the American economy show no signs of reversing itself—it appears to be getting worse. Since 1977, productivity in the United States has declined every year; we have the slowest growth in productivity of any nation except Great Britain.

3   A recent article in the *Wall Street Journal* reported that one of the most important obstacles confronting American companies trying to sell in Japan is the Japanese public's identification of the label "Made in the U.S.A." with shoddy workmanship. Even the American semiconductor industry, generally looked upon as the "modern citadel of American industrial prowess," may be heading toward a troubled future. A test conducted in 1980 reported that U.S.-made computer-memory chips were three times as likely to fail as those made in Japan. If Japanese companies succeed in winning a substantial share of the $1-billion-a-year market for that tiny bit of silicon upon which the microcomputer industry rests, the result will be an even more dramatic increase in the American trade deficit.

4   Clearly an important share of the responsibility for this state of affairs lies in the hands of the American government. The adversary role that has traditionally existed between business and government in the

United States has meant that American companies, particularly those at the cutting edge of technological innovation, have received considerably less financial support from their government than their counterparts in France, Japan and even in Third World nations such as Brazil and South Korea.

5   But the root of our problem has less to do with political decisions than with management priorities and practice. More and more, American companies are falling behind because the people who run them understand little and care less about how goods are actually produced. According to a survey recently published in the *Harvard Business Review*, between 1948 and 1977 the percentage of corporation presidents with backgrounds in finance and law increased by one-third, while those with technical training decreased by a similar percentage. Compared with both their foreign competitors and U.S. business executives of a generation ago, today's top corporate managers lack an adequate background in either science or engineering. As a result, they have become overly obsessed with short-term financial results and fail to appreciate the importance of "technological superiority as a competing weapon." Not surprisingly, U.S. corporate expenditures on research and development (R and D) have been declining since the mid-Sixties, while R and D spending by our major overseas competitors has been increasing.

6   Consider what has happened to two of our largest and most important companies, Du Pont and General Electric, over the past decade. Du Pont has a well-deserved reputation, going back more than 175 years, for being one of America's most innovative companies. Its long record of success was due almost entirely to the quality of its research in the basic sciences. But during the 1970s, Du Pont, for the first time in its history, appointed as chief executive officer (CEO) an attorney who lacked any scientific training. Under the leadership of Irving Shapiro, the company has cut back on its R and D budget rather than on shareholders' dividends. R and D expenditures as a percentage of sales declined from 6.6 percent in 1970 to a little over 3 percent in 1979. Because of these budget cuts, the company failed to develop new product lines to reduce their dependence on synthetic fibers. The result: the company was hit harder by the recession of the late 1970s than almost any other chemical company. While Shapiro's legal skills were an asset in Du Pont's dealings with the government, it now remains for Du Pont's new CEO, a chemist named Edward Jefferson, to see if he can restore the company to its leadership role in science and technology.

Bottom-Line Mentality

7   GE's experience over the past decade reveals a seemingly similar story. While Reginald Jones's financial skills did succeed in maintaining

GE's earnings throughout the period and while he was recently acclaimed the No. 1 CEO of the *Fortune* 500 companies, the price the company paid for its continued profitability has proved to be a high one. By strictly emphasizing bottom-line results, Jones pressured GE's profitable consumer divisions to reduce their costs. The consequence: a dramatic decline in the historically high quality of GE's consumer products. Moreover, by attempting to carefully quantify risks, GE discouraged its managers from experimenting with new product designs and production processes. Not coincidentally, GE's new CEO, John Welch, is a chemical engineer who, like Du Pont's Jefferson, appears committed to increasing the company's emphasis on innovation. A program is under way for training factory managers, executives and engineers in new technologies. Welch told *Business Week*, "I want to see high-level managers in the labs, shaking a chemist by the shirt."

8   Clearly, U.S. companies urgently need to review the standards they use for hiring and promoting managers. Training in finance and law is certainly important; companies need people who are able to interact with both Wall Street and Washington. But those skills can too easily become overemphasized; in the long run, they are not substitutes for training in engineering and science. As Robert Hayes, a professor at the Harvard Business School, put it, "A lot of U.S. companies are finding that people without a technological background are unskilled in understanding the nature of technological risk. They substitute a degree of caution and risk aversion because they can't stomach that risk." If American companies are to survive in an increasingly competitive world, they must hire and promote people who fully appreciate the importance of science and technology.

Content Questions

1. Why is American industry falling behind the industries of other countries?
2. What changes did Du Pont's CEO make that eroded the company's ability to compete?
3. Why is a "bottom-line mentality" hurting American industry?

Questions on Presentation

1. What is the effect of Vogel's use of statistics in the first paragraph?
2. Identify Vogel's thesis and his reasons for arguing it. Is his argument a compelling one? Why or why not?
3. Which of Vogel's supporting evidence is most effective? Why?

Why Not Call Up the Economists?

Adam Smith

The first Adam Smith to make his mark evaluating economic systems was an eighteenth-century Scotsman whose book *The Wealth of Nations* (1776) virtually inaugurated the study of economics. Today, economist George J. W. Goodman (b. 1930) uses the pseudonym Adam Smith when he evaluates economic trends and humorously debunks Wall Street pundits and everyday investors. Goodman was born in St. Louis, Missouri, and graduated magna cum laude from Harvard University in 1952. He completed further study as a Rhodes Scholar at Oxford University. His first published works were not treatises on economics but novels such a *The Bubble Makers* (1956), *A Time For Paris* (1957), *A Killing in the Market* (1958), and *The Wheeler Dealers* (1959) (his first book using the pen name Adam Smith). Smith was a reporter for *Collier's* and *Barron's* and wrote screenplays for *The Wheeler Dealers, The Americanization of Emily,* as well as other movies. His first work of nonfiction, *The Money Game* (1968), was the fastest selling book in its publisher's history. In *The Money Game* Smith combines his techniques as a novelist with his understanding of human nature and investment practices. The following essay, excerpted from Smith's satiric *Paper Money* (1981), analyzes what causes investors to be suspicious of economists and their predictions. "Why Not Call Up the Economists?" continues Smith's concern that people understand not only economics but also more about themselves.

1   The word *economics* derives from two Greek words: *oikos,* "household," and *nomia,* "management, arrangement, control." Thus economics is household management. I like that better than the dictionary definition, which says that economics is the science relating to the creation and distribution of wealth and the consumption of goods and services. I like it better because economics isn't quite a science, no matter what the dictionary says. If economics were a perfect science, we could call up the economists, give them the problems, and ask them to have the solutions back on Wednesday.

2   Experimental science, said James Bryant Conant in the marvelous little book *On Understanding Science,* is based on observations, then on an experiment that uses those observations; and anyone, anywhere, anytime, should be able to repeat the experiment if its basis is true. A "conceptual scheme" holds the related experiments together, produces further experiments, and science marches on. Time doesn't matter. A

magnet pulls today, and the same magnet pulls tomorrow. Alas, economics isn't so neat. A tax today might work differently from a tax next year. And the observations themselves are more suspect than watching a magnet pick up a tack.

3   The pure scientist has an advantage over the economist: he works in a laboratory, where he can control the factors he starts with. The economist has to use the actions of people, and people do not behave as consistently as magnets or laboratory mice. Nor do economists go out among the people, like the disguised prince in the fairy tale, to see what's going on; they call up government agencies and get the data from them.

4   "There are very few economic facts which we know with precision," wrote Sir John Hicks, an Oxford University Nobel Prize winner, in *Causality in Economics*. ". . . most of the 'macro' magnitudes which figure so largely in economic discussions are subject to errors and ambiguities which are far in excess of those which in most natural sciences would be regarded as tolerable. There are few economic 'laws' which can be regarded as at all firmly based."

5   It's natural for us to call up the economists and ask for the answers, and it's confusing when the answers come back all over the place.

6   "An economist," said Will Rogers, "is a man that can tell you anything about . . . well, he will tell you what can happen under any given condition, and his guess is liable to be as good as anybody else's, too."

7   There are two points to be made here. The second is strategic and has to do with the waning of a great theory. The first is tactical and can perhaps be illustrated by this little story.

"You Keep Bringing Up Exogenous Variables"

8   I have a friend called Arthur, who has a pleasant smile, a wife, two children, two sets of skis, and who has, in economics, what is called an ideal quantitative background. Practically from second grade, Arthur loved math. It was a mystery to him why some people had to chew their pencils in math exams; to him, math was as easy as watching television was to some of his contemporaries. And although excellent marks came showering upon him all through school, he was never a serious, innovative mathematician. Great mathematicians, like competitive swimmers, mature early. At sixteen they have solved Fermat's Last Theorem, and at twenty-six they had better be teaching somewhere, because they are burned out. Arthur knew, at eighteen, that he was not that kind of scholar-mathematician, so he looked around at college and found a congenial home in economics. Arthur's hardest course came in his freshman year; it was English, and he had to write a paper on two Joseph Conrad stories, *Heart of Darkness* and *The Secret Agent*. He had a

ghastly time with it. When he finished the Conrad paper, he says, he was very glad that he would never again have to do anything like that.

9   The graduate students who taught sections of the economics courses were very strong in econometrics, which is a mathematical and statistical form of economics, and Arthur was marvelously adept at that. After he got his Ph.D., Arthur thought about teaching. But one of his professors was a consultant to a commercial firm I will call Economics, Inc., which had built a computer model of the whole economy and which sold this service to various businesses. Economics, Inc., offered Arthur such a high starting salary that he went right to work there and has been very happy ever since.

10   At various times I visited Arthur, and we would sit at his computer console. His cuffs would shoot out of his sport jacket, and his fingers would be poised over the computer keyboard like those of E. Power Biggs at the organ.[1] The computer keyboard was like a typewriter keyboard, *q-w-e-r-t-y-u-i-o-p*, except that it had a lot of extra keys you had to press before you could ask it questions. Once, I had just come back from the Middle East and I was worried that the price of oil might go to $15 a barrel, or even $20 a barrel.

11   "Ask it what the inflation rate will be if oil goes to fifteen dollars a barrel," I would say, and Arthur would go tapety-tapety-tap on the keyboard. The answer—when the computer did not ask us for more information, or tell us to start over—would appear on the CRT screen. "Wow," said Arthur. "Inflation of nine percent, all other things being equal."

12   "Ask it what the mortgage rate will be with oil at fifteen dollars a barrel," I said. Tapety-tapety-tap. "Ten percent?" Arthur said. "That's awfully high. It can't be right. Maybe we have to have an assumption about housing starts, too." Tapety-tapety-tapety-tapety-*tap*.

13   I have called Arthur, periodically, over the years, but I have never had to act specifically on his information. In 1973, for example, Economics, Inc., missed the inflation rate by a wide margin. "Well, we did better than the Council of Economic Advisers," Arthur said, referring to the group appointed by the President, which sits in Washington. "They predicted inflation would be down to two and a half percent." Indeed they had, and Economics, Inc., had done better.

14   In order to have something as neat and symmetrical as an equation, you have to have assumptions, even if the assumption is very basic— let × equal the unknown, let Σ mean "the sum of." There is an old joke, used by economists at departmental dinners, in which three men are stranded on a desert island and all they have is one huge can of tuna, but the tuna is inside the can and they are starving. The first man, a physicist, suggests a way to make a fire hot enough to melt the can. The second is an engineer, who is thinking up a complicated slingshot that

will hurl the can against a rock with enough force to puncture it. The third is an economist. He has the answer. He says, "Assume a can opener." Then he proceeds with a theory.

15 Economics, Inc., had all kinds of assumptions and all kinds of assessments.

16 None of this, by the way, hurt Economics, Inc. Businessmen and institutions quested for certainty, and the computer at Economics, Inc., was very certain, even if it was not always right. The CRT screen would say ERROR if the processing was inconsistent, but not if the conclusions didn't match the brawling world outside.

17 As I said, I was worried about the Middle East. If the price of oil went high enough fast enough, we would have a depression because all that money for imports would get taken out of our economy, unless the oil countries reinvested the money productively, unless the Federal Reserve loosened the money to make up for the oil, unless the new price of oil brought up more oil . . . you see the process. So I was talking to Arthur about Saudi Arabia, and the health of King Khalid, and the Shiites of the eastern province who worked in the oil fields, and I could tell it all sounded to Arthur like Conrad's Congo in *Heart of Darkness*—unfathomable. Revolutionary Iran had thrown out the Shah, the price of oil was doubling, gold was going to new highs, and I had been saying how far off the great Economics, Inc., model was; it wasn't telling me what I so urgently needed to know. Arthur lost his temper.

18 *"You keep bringing up exogenous variables!"* he shouted.

19 Like *economist, exogenous* is another Greek-rooted word, from *exo,* "outside, coming from outside."

20 "Who the hell knew there was an ayatollah?" Arthur said. "Who knew the Russian wheat crop was going to bomb? Who cares about whoever it is in the eastern province?"

21 "But *life* is exogenous variables," I said. All I wanted was the answers. I was worried that if *one* ayatollah could, in a short time, cause oil to go up, the truckers then to go on strike, the airlines to flirt with bankruptcy, the defense budget to gather momentum, the Japanese to replace us as the buyers of Iranian oil—what if there was *another* fanatic Islamic cleric somewhere dictating into cassettes? What if there was a sorehead colonel in an oil country deciding that Allah wished the prime minister to meet with a nine-millimeter bullet?

22 But Arthur had hung up. And suddenly I knew one of the problems with economics. Arthur was brilliant. He had never sold a can of shoe polish, or bought a carload of lumber, or hired anybody, or fired anybody, or even worried about his checking account; in fact, he had never done anything but economics. In his own shop he could make lemmas dance around stochastic equilibria,[2] he could rip off multiple regressions, he could make equations whistle "Dixie." The trouble came from

that joke, "Assume a can opener." For deep, deep in the Economics, Inc., computer was a very tiny person upon whom the assumptions were based. Would the tiny person spend? Would the tiny person save? If you tapped the tiny person on the knee, his leg would jerk; if you tickled him, he would laugh. But the tiny, tiny person, upon whom all the vast panoply of computer modeling had been done, *was an economist.* If you asked him something, he would take a tiny sheet of yellow paper and ask, "What are the costs, and what are the benefits?" With a column for each, very coolly and rationally. He never threw an ashtray at his tiny wife, breaking a window and raising the gross national product by the price of the new window. Fear and greed and panic and emotion and nationalism and religious fervor, ayatollahs and Shiites and sinister Middle Eastern colonels were not part of his world.

23   This is *not* meant to be a trivial complaint about the limits of models. This is of interest to the people who use them, who naturally want to do the best possible job, and the subject has been well debated by such respected figures as Harvard's Hendrik Houthakker, an expert on econometric models and the varying relationships known as elasticities. I have another friend, Princeton's Geoffrey Watson, who, many years ago, with James Durbin, derived an equation that made them both famous in the field. The Durbin-Watson equation is one test for the mathematical work upon which the complex computer models are based. "Mathematics has so much prestige," Geoffrey says, "that people sometimes back away from their own intuitive judgments. What used to be called 'political economy' at Oxford and Cambridge has been overshadowed. I had a distinguished economics professor at Cambridge, Richard Stern, whose background was in classics."

24   There were once two kinds of economists, one might argue: the Smiths and the Ricardos. The Smith is the 1723 Adam Smith, and the Ricardo is David Ricardo,[3] his immediate successor. Both the Smiths and the Ricardos were concerned with human activity and with the institutions that produce, preserve, and distribute wealth. The Smiths observed; the Ricardos sought the universal and logical principles, using algebra and its succeeding languages. The Smiths looked for what is to be explained, the Ricardos for the principles that did the explaining. Until comparatively recently, economists could write in both languages; that is, they could describe human activity in some detail, using the detail in written analysis, and they could reason mathematically and abstractly about the governing principles.

25   Today the Ricardos are fashionable and the Smiths are not. Economists who write well in English—there may be eight of them—run the risk of being labeled with the pejorative term "literary." The Ricardos admire the elegance of perfect equations; the highest terms of their praise are "rigorous" and "scientific."

26   When the problem was contained enough, when the numbers were discrete enough, the mathematical descriptions of the Ricardos worked. Government economists who favored deregulation of the airline industry found that scenario unfolding much as they had planned. But too often the real world did not match the movements of that tiny economist inside the computer. All through the 1970s, the economists missed the impact of OPEC because, when they described it mathematically, they treated it as if it were a rational, profit-maximizing convention of economists. They did not know about *asibaya*, the Arab sense of community, nor could they quantify Third World indignation at past histories, or Middle East rivalries, or Western myopia, all of which became more important than the more easily quantified data. Some years ago the sociologist and pollster Daniel Yankelovich described a process he called the McNamara fallacy, after the Secretary of Defense who had so carefully quantified the Vietnam War.

27   "The first step," he said, "is to measure what can easily be measured. The second is to disregard what can't be measured, or give it an arbitrary quantitative value. This is artificial and misleading. The third step is to presume that what can't be measured easily isn't very important. This is blindness. The fourth step is to say that what can't be easily measured really doesn't exist." The philosopher A. N. Whitehead[4] called this tendency, in another form, "the fallacy of misplaced concreteness."

28   The Hopi language, an American Indian language, contains no words, grammatical forms, constructions, or expressions that refer to what we call "time," or to past, present, or future. The whole structure we base on "time"—wages, rent, credit, interest, depreciation, insurance—cannot be expressed in Hopi and is not part of that world view. The main Eskimo language has twenty-seven different words for snow, each connoting another nuance of texture, utility, and consistency, so the Eskimo's ability to communicate about snow is far greater than ours. The picture of the universe, of "reality," shifts from language to language. The economists whose counsel we seek—as do presidents and prime ministers—speak from a world within the world, just as the Hopi spoke from a world without time, credit, wages, and rent. That cold, neat, elegant world of mathematics views a different reality than blunt, ambiguous English.

29   Poets know they must use the slippery sibilances and jagged edges of language, as well as the meanings of the words, to communicate. Poets know that life throws up exogenous variables. I made a note that at the next meeting of the Advisory Council of the university Department of Economics on which I serve I would propose that we recruit some poets. I am sure the council will treat the suggestion as merely amusing, and I'm not totally sure it's a great idea; but I know it's aimed in the right direction. I sent Arthur the classic *Language, Thought, and Reality* by

Benjamin Whorf, from which I took the example of the Hopi, but I haven't heard back. Maybe it reminds him of *Heart of Darkness*, and maybe he's just too busy.

Notes

[1] Edgar Power Biggs (b. 1906), organist and recording artist whose records vary from classical to popular music. [Eds.]

[2] *Stochastic equilibria* is the probability that two elements, such as supply and demand, will at some point be in balance. [Eds.]

[3] David Ricardo (1772–1823), British businessman and writer whose treatise *Principles of Political Economy and Taxation* (1817) formulated "classic economics." [Eds.]

[4] Alfred North Whitehead (1861–1947), British philosopher and mathematician, proposed that mathematics could be deduced from the premises of formal logic. Whitehead's most interesting theories appear in *Principia Mathematica*, a book he coauthored with fellow philosopher Bertrand Russell. [Eds.]

Content Questions

1. How should a conceptual scheme work?
2. How does Will Rogers' definition of an economist match Smith's definition?
3. Why does Smith think life is exogenous?
4. Why does Arthur have difficulty including exogenous variables in his equations?
5. What do economists leave out of their calculations?
6. What is the McNamara fallacy?

Questions on Presentation

1. Smith begins his essay with a definition, a rhetorical tactic many writing teachers dislike, and uses this tactic throughout his essay. Despite this, has Smith written an interesting, informative essay? Why or why not?
2. While Smith's essay is essentially one of definition, his topic could be addressed through other rhetorical modes. How would such an essay differ from Smith's?
3. Smith distrusts "experts." How does he make this clear in the essay?
4. Is Smith's use of the anecdote beginning in paragraph 8 effective? What is its purpose?
5. Why does Smith make the references to language in paragraphs 28 and 29?

⚖

Assume a Need

Jonathan Briggs

In this essay, using Adam Smith's "Why Not Call Up the Economists?" as his inspiration, business and English major Jonathan Briggs analyzes the dangers of our over-reliance on technology and mathematical models, not only in business but in many sectors of our culture. Here Briggs shows us another way to use Smith's material.

1   In his essay "Why Not Call Up the Economists?" Adam Smith describes the dilemma of modern economists. As Smith explains it, during the nineteenth century the two prominent schools of economics were represented by the Smiths and the Ricardos. The Smiths used language to describe their economics, "looking for what is to be explained"; the Ricardos, in contrast, used mathematics and looked for the "principles to do the explaining." Since this division took place, the Ricardos and their mathematical method have become prominent and "prestigious," while the Smiths, including the current "Adam Smith," have been made to stand in the wings, hissing and jeering when the Ricardos' magical mathematical models failed to create economic paradise around the world. The public, especially in the United States, has consequently developed an attitude of hearty skepticism about economics as a science and about the people who call themselves economists. From presidential advisors to Wall Street wizards, economists are tolerated but seldom heeded by the general populace. After all, everyone knows economists seldom agree and are even less often correct.

2   For the modern Adam Smith, economists fail when they pursue the mathematical side of economics and disregard the language-oriented side. An important distinction Smith makes in his article is that economics is not a science like the natural, pure or experimental sciences such as biology or physics. Economics is a social science akin to sociology, pyschology, and political science. These disciplines use scientific methods where possible, but they cannot meet the rigorous scientific standards of the natural sciences. The social sciences deal with too many variables, and the laboratory is the human milieu, ever out of control. Even if a supercomputer could manipulate the huge quantities of variables to make an economic model reflect a real life situation, the unpredictability of human behavior cannot be programmed into the model,

so it cannot accurately reflect reality. Therefore, no computer can make empirically verifiable predictions. For all its mathematical precision, the computer can still only guess.

3   Thus is economics always going to be something people who can't find other work do, or can it have a meaningful place in the world? The same criticism that is made of economics, that it isn't an empirical science, has been made of the other social sciences. Sociology and psychology have managed to survive and even gain acceptance despite their nonempirical approaches. For instance, a recent *Wall Street Journal* article stated that in the last ten years the number of employees undergoing psychotherapy has increased from 7 to 47 percent. (As the article explains, this is due in part to the fact that many employers are providing health plans which cover some or all of the expense of treatment, but if the employees didn't think there was some value to the treatment they wouldn't use it.) There are several reasons psychology has become more accepted by the public and why economics could develop some credibility with the general public.

4   Recent world events have shaken people's confidence in the trustworthiness of the heretofore dependable empirical sciences. Despite all the advances made in medicine, new horrors such as AIDS still baffle the doctors; despite our success with the space program, catastrophes such as the destruction of the Space Shuttle cannot be prevented, and, despite President Reagan's unflagging support of it, SDI or Star Wars remains a controversial and problematic solution to the arms race, which even scientists cannot agree on. All this and more has people turning from the vision they had of technology and making them more receptive to less "scientific" solutions for their problems. All the solutions they choose are not new or in the social sciences, of course. Again, to cite a recent newspaper article, this one from the Albuquerque *Journal*, psychics, astrologers, and other practitioners of occult traditions are enjoying a resurgence of popularity. A very important similarity among all these alternatives to technology, including the social sciences, is their use of language rather than mathematics, words not numbers. Words are human, numbers are not. People use words, machines use numbers. And weren't there some economists who used and use words, one or two named Smith at least?

5   At the end of his article, today's Adam Smith says he might suggest putting some poets on the economists' team. He says, "Poets must use the slippery sibilances and jagged edges of language, as well as the meanings of words to communicate." He also says, " . . . I'm not sure it's a great idea; but I know it's aimed in the right direction." Doubt and intuition. Smith's statement is light years from the assured expressions of the empirical scientist, but it has appeal and it's in language we can identify with and therefore trust even if it doesn't give us a clear answer

we can just plug in. If economists want to survive, if they want to gain credibility with the public, and, most importantly, if they want to do more than just squabble among themselves about inaccurate predictions based on unreal data, they are going to have to listen to the Smiths of this world and start talking their language. Is that the phone I hear . . . ?

Analytic Ivory Towers

Thomas J. Peters and Robert H. Waterman

In the late 1970s, Thomas Peters, an engineer and consultant educated at Cornell and Stanford universities, and his coauthor, Robert Waterman, a mining engineer, were consultants for McKinsey & Company. While at McKinsey, Peters and Waterman investigated how the most successful companies in America gained and continued their successes. They evaluated sixty-two firms, ranging from hamburger franchisers to computer manufacturers, using for their evaluation criteria such factors as financial performance and innovativeness. Their optimistic report identified eight attributes that distinguish the most successful businesses in America. This report became the best-selling book *In Search of Excellence: Lessons from America's Best-Run Companies* (1982). The following selection, taken from their book, analyzes contemporary American business practices and, using numerous examples and anecdotes, shows how these practices can have shortcomings as well as potential.

1   The reason behind the absence of focus on product or people in so many American companies, it would seem, is the simple presence of a focus on something else. That something else is overreliance on analysis from corporate ivory towers and overreliance on financial sleight of hand, the tools that would appear to eliminate risk but also, unfortunately, eliminate action.

2   "A lot of companies overdo it," says Ed Wrapp. "They find planning more interesting than getting out a salable product. . . . Planning is a welcome respite from operating problems. It is intellectually more rewarding, and does not carry the pressures that operations entail. . . . Formal long-range planning almost always leads to overemphasis of technique." Fletcher Byrom of Koppers offers a suggestion. "As a regimen," he says, "as a discipline for a group of people, planning is very valuable. My position is, go ahead and plan, but once you've done your planning, put it on the shelf. Don't be bound by it. Don't use it as a ma-

jor input to the decision-making process. Use it mainly to recognize change as it takes place." In a similar vein, *Business Week* recently reported: "Significantly, neither Johnson & Johnson, nor TRW, nor 3M—all regarded as forward thinking—has anyone on board called a corporate planner."

3   David Ogilvy, founder of Ogilvy and Mather, states bluntly: "The majority of businessmen are incapable of original thought because they are unable to escape from the tyranny of reason." Harvard's renowned marketing professor Theodore Levitt said recently: "Modelers build intricate decision trees whose pretension to utility is exceeded only by the awe in which high-level line managers hold the technocrats who construct them." Finally, we have a recent account of a Standard Brands' new product strategy that was an abject failure. The reason, according to a *Business Week* cover story, was that Standard Brands hired a bevy of GE planners and then gave them something akin to operating responsibility. After letting most of them go, the chairman noted: "The guys were bright, [but they] were not the kind of people who could implement the programs."

4   Now, all of this is apparently bad news for many who have made a life's work of number crunching. But the problem is not that companies ought not to plan. They damn well should plan. The problem is that the planning becomes an end in itself. It goes far beyond Byrom's sensible dictum to use it to enhance mental preparedness. Instead, the plan becomes the truth, and data that don't fit the preconceived plan (e.g., real customer response to a pre-test market action) are denigrated or blithely ignored. Gamesmanship replaces pragmatic action. ("Have you polled the corporate staffs yet about the estimate?" was a common query in one corporate operating committee that we observed for years.)

5   Business performance in the United States has deteriorated badly, at least compared to that of Japan, and sometimes to other countries—and in many cases absolutely, in terms of productivity and quality standards. We no longer make the best or most reliable products and we seldom make them for less, especially in internationally competitive industries (e.g., autos, chips).

6   The first wave of attack on the causes of this problem focused on government regulators. That, however, seemed to be an incomplete answer. Then, in mid-1980, the quest for root causes took thoughtful executives, business reporters, and academics alike into the heartland of management practice, all trying to figure out what had gone wrong. Not surprisingly, America's recent dependence on overanalysis and a narrow form of rationality bore the brunt of the attack. Both seemed especially at odds with the Japanese approach to the work force and to quality—even allowing for cultural differences.

7   The inquiry ran into two formidable roadblocks. The first was inherent defensivensss. The businessman's intellect and soul were finally un-

der attack. Until then he had been encouraged by the press simply to increase his finger pointing at others, namely, the government. Second, the attack ran into a language problem. It wasn't seen as an attack on "a narrow form of rationality," what we have termed the "rational model," thereby calling for a broader form. It was seen as an attack on rationality and logical thought per se, thus implicitly encouraging escape into irrationality and mysticism. One was led to believe that the only solution was to move Ford board meetings to the local Zen center. And, obviously, that wasn't going to be the solution.

8   But let us stop for a moment and ask: What exactly do we mean by the fall of the rational model? We really are talking about what Thomas Kuhn, in his landmark book *The Structure of Scientific Revolutions*, calls a paradigm shift. Kuhn argues that scientists in any field and in any time possess a set of shared beliefs about the world, and for that time the set constitutes the dominant paradigm. What he terms "normal science" proceeds nicely under this set of shared beliefs. Experiments are carried out strictly within the boundaries of those beliefs and small steps toward progress are made. An old but excellent example is the Ptolemaic[1] view of the universe (which held until the sixteenth century) that the earth was at the center of the universe, and the moon, sun, planets, and stars were embedded in concentric spheres around it. Elaborate mathematical formulas and models were developed that would accurately predict astronomical events based on the Ptolemaic paradigm. Not until Copernicus and Kepler[2] found that the formula worked more easily when the sun replaced the earth as the center of it all did an instance of paradigm shift begin.

9   After a paradigm shift begins, progress is fast though fraught with tension. People get angry. New discoveries pour in to support the new belief system (e.g., those of Kepler and Galileo),[3] and scientific revolution occurs. Other familiar examples of paradigm shift and ensuing revolution in science include the shift to relativity in physics, and to plate tectonics in geology. The important point in each instance is that the old "rationality" is eventually replaced with a new, different, and more useful one.

10   We are urging something of this kind in business. The old rationality is, in our opinion, a direct descendant of Frederick Taylor's[4] school of scientific management and has ceased to be a useful discipline. Judging from the actions of managers who seem to operate under this paradigm, some of the shared beliefs include:

- Big is better because you can always get economies of scale. When in doubt, consolidate things; eliminate overlap, duplication, and waste. Incidentally, as you get big, make sure everything is carefully and formally coordinated.
- Low-cost producers are the only sure-fire winners. Customer utility

functions lead them to focus on cost in the final analysis. Survivors always make it cheaper.

- Analyze everything. We've learned that we can avoid big dumb decisions through good market research, discounted cash-flow analysis, and good budgeting. If a little is good, then more must be better, so apply things like discounted cash flow to risky investments like research and development. Use budgeting as a model for long-range planning. Make forecasts. Set hard numerical targets on the basis of those forecasts. Produce fat planning volumes whose main content is numbers. (Incidentally, forget the fact that most long-range forecasts are bound to be wrong the day they are made. Forget that the course of invention is, by definition, unpredictable.)

- Get rid of the disturbers of the peace—i.e., fanatical champions. After all, we've got a plan. We want one new product development activity to produce the needed breakthrough, and we'll put 500 engineers on it if necessary, because we've got a better idea.

- The manager's job is decision making. Make the right calls. Make the touch calls. Balance the portfolio. Buy into the attractive industries. Implementation, or execution, is of secondary importance. Replace the whole management team if you have to to get implementation right.

- Control everything. A manager's job is to keep things tidy and under control. Specify the organization structure in great detail. Write long job descriptions. Develop complicated matrix organizations to ensure that every possible contingency is accounted for. Issue orders. Make black and white decisions. Treat people as factors of production.

- Get the incentives right and productivity will follow. If we give people big, straightforward monetary incentives to do right and work smart, the productivity problem will go away. Over-reward the top performers. Weed out the 30 to 40 percent dead wood who don't want to work.

- Inspect to control quality. Quality is like everything else; order it done. Triple the quality control department if necessary (forget that the QC force per unit of production in Japanese auto companies is just a third the size of ours). Have it report to the president. We'll show them (i.e., workers) that we mean business.

- A business is a business is a business. If you can read the financial statements, you can manage anything. The people, the products, and the services are simply those resources you have to align to get good financial results.

- Top executives are smarter than the market. Carefully manage the cosmetics of the income statement and balance sheet, and you will look good to outsiders. Above all, don't let quarterly earnings stop growing.

- It's all over if we stop growing. When we run out of opportunity in our industry, buy into industries we don't understand. At least we can then continue growing.

11   Much as the conventional business rationality seems to drive the engine of business today, it simply does not explain most of what makes the excellent companies work. Why not? What are its shortcomings?

12   *For one, the numerative, analytical component has an in-built conservative bias. Cost reduction becomes priority number one and revenue enhancement takes a back seat.* This leads to obsession with cost,
not quality and value; to patching up old products rather than fooling
with untidy new product or business development; and to fixing productivity through investment rather than revitalization of the work force.
A buried weakness in the analytic approach to business decision making
is that people analyze what can be most readily analyzed, spend more
time on it, and more or less ignore the rest.

13   As Harvard's John Steinbruner observes, "If quantitative precision is
demanded, it is gained, in the current state of things, only by so reducing the scope of what is analyzed that most of the important problems
remain external to the analysis." This leads to fixation on the cost side
of the equation. The numbers are "hardest" there. The fix, moreover, is
mechanical and easy to picture—buy a new machine to replace nineteen
jobs, reduce paperwork by 25 percent, close down two lines and speed
up the remaining one.

14   Numerative analysis leads simultaneously to another unintended
devaluation of the revenue side. Analysis has no way of valuing the
extra oomph, the overkill, added by an IBM or Frito-Lay sales force. In
fact, according to a recent observer, every time the analysts got their
hands on Frito's "99.5 percent service level" (an "unreasonable" level of
service in a so-called commodity business) their eyes began to gleam
and they proceeded to show how much could be saved if only Frito
would reduce its commitment to service. The analysts are "right"; Frito
would immediately save money. But the analysts cannot possibly demonstrate the impact of a tiny degree of service unreliability on the heroic
10,000-person sales force—to say nothing of the Frito's retailers—and,
therefore, on eventual market share loss or margin decline. Viewed analytically, the overcommitment to reliability by Caterpillar ("Forty-eight-
hour parts service anywhere in the world—or Cat pays") or Maytag
("Ten years' trouble-free operation") makes no sense. Analytically, pur-
poseful duplication of effort by IBM and 3M on product development, or
cannibalization of one P&G brand by another P&G brand is, well, just
that, duplication. Delta's family feeling, IBM's respect for the individual,
and McDonald's and Disney's fetish for cleanliness make no sense in
quantitative terms.

15   *The exclusively analytic approach run wild leads to an abstract,
heartless philosophy.* Our obsession with body counts in Viet Nam and
our failure to understand the persistence and long-time horizon of the
Eastern mind culminated in America's most catastrophic misallocation
of resources—human, moral, and material. But McNamara's[5] fascination with numbers was just a sign of the times. One of his fellow whiz
kids at Ford, Roy Ash, fell victim to the same affliction. Says *Fortune* of

his Litton misadventures, "Utterly abstract in his view of business, [Ash] enjoyed to the hilt exercising his sharp mind in analyzing the most sophisticated accounting techniques. His brilliance led him to think in the most regal of ways: building new cities; creating a shipyard that would roll off the most technically advanced vessels the way Detroit builds automobiles." Sadly, *Fortune's* analysis speaks not only of Ash's Litton failure but also of the similar disaster ten years later that undid AM International under his leadership.

16   The rationalist approach takes the living element out of situations that should, above all, be alive. Lewis Lapham, the editor of *Harper's*, describes the fallacy of the numerative bias in an Easy Chair piece entitled "Gift of the Magi": "The magi inevitably talk about number and weight—barrels of oil, the money supply—always about material and seldom about human resources; about things; not about people. The prevailing bias conforms to the national prejudice in favor of institutions rather than individuals." John Steinbeck[6] made the same point about lifeless rationality:

> The Mexican Sierra has 17 plus 15 plus 9 spines in the dorsal fin. These can easily be counted. But if the sierra strikes hard on the line so that our hands are burned, if the fish sounds and nearly escapes and finally comes in over the rail, his colors pulsing and his tail beating the air, a whole new relational externality has come into being—an entity which is more than the sum of the fish plus the fisherman. The only way to count the spines of the sierra unaffected by this second relational reality is to sit in a laboratory, open an evil-smelling jar, remove a stiff colorless fish from the formalin solution, count the spines and write the truth. . . . There you have recorded a reality which cannot be assailed—probably the least important reality concerning either the fish or yourself. . . . It is good to know what you are doing. The man with this pickled fish has set down one truth and recorded in his experience many lies. The fish is not that color, that texture, that dead, nor does he smell that way.

17   *To be narrowly rational is often to be negative.* Peter Drucker gives a good description of the baleful influence of management's analytic bias: " 'Professional' management today sees itself often in the role of a judge who says 'yes' or 'no' to ideas as they come up. . . . A top management that believes its job is to sit in judgment will inevitably veto the new idea. It is always 'impractical.' " John Steinbruner makes a similar point commenting on the role of staffs in general: "It is inherently easier to develop a negative argument than to advance a constructive one." In his analysis of the MLF (NATO's proposed shared nuclear multi-lateral force) decision, Steinbruner recounts an exchange between a conservative academic and a real-world statesman. Secretary of State Dean Acheson said to the Harvard-trained presidential adviser Richard Neustadt, "You think Presidents should be warned. You're wrong. Presidents

should be given confidence." Steinbruner goes on to analyze the roles of "warners" versus "bolsterers." Notwithstanding his attempt to present a balanced case, it is clear that the weight of the neutrally applied analytic model falls on the side of the warning, not the bolstering.

18   Mobil's chief executive, Rawleigh Warner, Jr., echoed the theme in explaining why his company decided not to bid on the 1960 off-shore oil tracks in Prudhoe Bay: "The financial people in this company did a disservice to the exploration people. . . . The poor people in exploration were adversely impacted by people who knew nothing about oil and gas." Hayes and Abernathy, as usual, are eloquent on the subject: "We believe that during the past two decades American managers have increasingly relied on principles which prize analytical detachment and methodological elegance over insight . . . based on experience. Lacking hands-on experience, the analytic formulas of portfolio theory push managers even further toward an extreme of caution in allocating resources." Finally, George Gilder in *Wealth and Poverty* says, "Creative thought [the precursor to invention] requires an act of faith." He dissects example after example in support of his point, going back to the laying out of railroads, insisting that "when they were built they could hardly be justified in economic terms."

19   *Today's version of rationality does not value experimentation and abhors mistakes.* The conservatism that leads to inaction and years-long "study groups" frequently confronts businessmen with precisely what they were trying to avoid—having to make, eventually, one big bet. Giant product development groups analyze and analyze until years have gone by and they've designed themselves into one home-run product, with every bell and whistle attractive to every segment. Meanwhile, Digital, 3M, HP, and Wang, amid a hotbed of experimentation, have proceeded "irrationally" and chaotically, and introduced ten or more new products each during the same period. Advancement takes place only when we do something: try an early prototype on a customer or two, run a quick and dirty test market, stick a jury-rig device on an operating production line, test a new sales promotion on 50,000 subscribers.

20   The dominant culture in most big companies demands punishment for a mistake, no matter how useful, small, invisible. This is especially ironic because the most noble ancestor of today's business rationality was called *scientific* management. Experimentation is the fundamental tool of science: if we experiment successfully, by definition, we will make many mistakes. But overly rational businessmen are in pretty good company here, because even science doesn't own up to its messy road to progress. Robert Merton, a respected historian of science, describes the typical paper:

> [There is a] rockbound difference between scientific work as it appears in print and the actual course of inquiry. . . . The difference is a little like that

between textbooks of scientific method and the ways in which scientists actually think, feel, and go about their work. The books on methods present ideal patterns, but these tidy, normative patterns . . . do not reproduce the typically untidy, opportunistic adaptations that scientists really make. The scientific paper presents an immaculate appearance which reproduces little or nothing of the intuitive leaps, false starts, mistakes, loose ends, and happy accidents that actually cluttered up the inquiry.

Sir Peter Medawar, Nobel laureate in immunology, flatly declares, "It is no use looking to scientific 'papers,' for they do not merely conceal but actively misrepresent the reasoning which goes into the work they describe."

21   *Anti-experimentation leads us inevitably to overcomplexity and inflexibility.* The "home-run product" mentality is nowhere more evident than in the pursuit of the "superweapon" in defense. A *Village Voice* commentator notes:

> The quickest way to understand the dread evoked in the Pentagon by Spinney [senior analyst with the Program Analysis and Evaluation division of the Department of the Defense] is to quote his bottom line: "Our strategy of pursuing ever-increasing technical complexity and sophistication has made high-technology solutions and combat readiness mutually exclusive." That is, the more money the U.S. presently spends on defense, the less able it is to fight. . . . More money has produced fewer but more complex planes which do not work much of the time. Deployment of fewer planes means a more elaborate and delicate communication system which is not likely to survive in war conditions.

22   Caution and paralysis-induced-by-analysis lead to an anti-experimentation bias. That, in turn, ironically leads to an ultimately risky "big bet" or the "superweapon" mentality. The screw turns once more. To produce such superproducts, hopelessly complicated and ultimately unworkable management structures are required. The tendency reaches its ultimate expression in the formal matrix organizational structure. Interestingly, some fifteen years before the mid-seventies matrix heyday, the researcher Chris Argyris identified the key matrix pathologies:

> Why are these new administrative structures and strategies having trouble? . . . The assumption behind this [matrix] theory was that if objectives and critical paths to these objectives were defined clearly, people would tend to cooperate to achieve these objectives according to the best schedule they could devise. However, in practice, the theory was difficult to apply. . . . It was not long before the completion of the paperwork became an end in itself. Seventy-one percent of the middle managers reported that the maintenance of the product planning and program review paper flow became as crucial as accomplishing the line responsibility assigned to each group. . . .

Another mode of adaptation was to withdraw and let the upper levels become responsible for the successful administration of the program. "This is their baby—let them make it work." . . . Still another frequently reported problem was the immobilization of the group with countless small decisions.

23   One can beat the complexity syndrome, but it is not easy. The IBM 360 is one of the grand product success stories in American business history, yet its development was sloppy. Along the way, chairman Thomas Watson, Sr., asked vice-president Frank Cary to "design a system to ensure us against a repeat of this kind of problem." Cary did what he was told. Years later, when he became chairman himself, one of his first acts was to get rid of the laborious product development structure that he had created for Watson. "Mr. Watson was right," he conceded. "It [the product development structure] will prevent a repeat of the 360 development turmoil. Unfortunately, it will also ensure that we don't ever invent another product like the 360."

24   The excellent company response to complexity is fluidity, the administrative version of experimentation. Reorganizations take place all the time. "If you've got a problem, put the resources on it and get it fixed," says one Digital executive. "It's that simple." Koppers's Fletcher Byrom adds support: "Of all the things that I have observed in corporations, the most disturbing has been a tendency toward over-organization, producing a rigidity that is intolerable in an era of rapidly accelerating change." HP's David Packard notes, "You've got to avoid having too rigid an organization. . . . If an organization is to work effectively, the communication should be through the most effective channel regardless of the organization chart. That is what happens a lot around here. I've often thought that after you get organized, you ought to throw the chart away." Speaking on the subject of American organizational rationality, our Japanese colleague Ken Ohmae says: "Most Japanese companies don't even have a reasonable organization chart. Nobody knows how Honda is organized, except that it uses lots of project teams and is quite flexible. . . . Innovation typically occurs at the interface, requiring multiple disciplines. Thus, the flexible Japanese organization has now, especially, become an asset."

25   *The rationalist approach does not celebrate informality.* Analyze, plan, tell, specify, and check up are the verbs of the rational process. Interact, test, try, fail, stay in touch, learn, shift direction, adapt, modify, and see are some of the verbs of the informal managing processes. We hear the latter much more often in our interviews with top performers. Intel puts in extra conference rooms, simply to increase the likelihood of informal problem solving among different disciplines. 3M sponsors clubs of all sorts specifically to enhance interaction. HP and Digital

overspend on their own air and ground transportation systems just so people will visit one another. Product after product flows from Patrick Haggerty's bedrock principle of "tight coupling" at TI. It all means that people talk, solve problems and fix things rather than posture, debate, and delay.

26   Unfortunately, however, management by edict feels more comfortable to most American managers. They shake their heads in disbelief at 3M, Digital, HP, Bloomingdale's, or even IBM, companies whose core processes seem out of control. After all, who in his right mind would establish Management By Wandering Around as a pillar of philosophy, as HP does? It turns out that the informal control through regular, casual communication is actually much tighter than rule by numbers, which can be avoided or evaded. But you'd have a hard time selling that idea outside the excellent companies.

27   *The rational model causes us to denigrate the importance of values.* We have observed few, if any, bold new company directions that have come from goal precision or rational analysis. While it is true that the good companies have superb analytic skills, we believe that their major decisions are shaped more by their values than by their dexterity with numbers. The top performers create a broad, uplifting, shared culture, a coherent framework within which charged-up people search for appropriate adaptations. Their ability to extract extraordinary contributions from very large numbers of people turns on the ability to create a sense of highly valued purpose. Such purpose invariably emanates from love of product, providing top-quality services, and honoring innovation and contribution from all. Such high purpose is inherently at odds with 30 quarterly MBO objectives, 25 measures of cost containment, 100 demeaning rules for production-line workers, or an ever-changing, analytically derived strategy that stresses costs this year, innovation next, and heaven knows what the year after.

28   *There is little place in the rationalist world for internal competition.* A company is not supposed to compete with itself. But throughout the excellent companies research, we saw example after example of that phenomenon. Moreover, we saw peer pressure—rather than orders from the boss—as the main motivator. General Motors pioneered the idea of internal competition sixty years ago; 3M, P&G, IBM, HP, Bloomingdale's, and Tupperware are its masters today. Division overlap, product-line duplication, multiple new product development teams, and vast flows of information to spur productivity comparison—and improvements—are the watchwords. Why is it that so many have missed the message?

29   Again, the analyze-the-analyzable bias is ultimately fatal. It is true that costs of product-line duplication and nonuniformity of manufactur-

ing procedures can be measured precisely. But the incremental revenue benefits from a steady flow of new products developed by zealous champions and the increment of productivity gains that comes from continuous innovation by competing shop floor teams are much harder, if not impossible, to get a handle on.

Notes

[1]Ptolemy, second century A.D. Greek astronomer and geographer. [Eds.]
[2]Nicolaus Copernicus (1473–1543), Polish astronomer. Johannes Kepler (1571–1630), German astronomer and mathematician. [Eds.]
[3]Galileo Galilei (1564–1642), Italian astronomer and physicist. [Eds.]
[4]Frederick Winslow Taylor (1856–1915), American engineer and efficiency expert. [Eds.]
[5]Robert S. McNamara (b. 1916), American politician and public official, was the Secretary of Defense in the Kennedy administration. [Eds.]
[6]John Steinbeck (1902–1968), American author of books such as *The Grapes of Wrath* and *Of Mice and Men*. [Eds.]

Content Questions

1. Why do the corporate tools that eliminate risk also eliminate potential?
2. What are the dangers of planning in business?
3. How were the roadblocks to evaluating American businesses overcome?
4. How does a paradigm shift differ from a rational model?
5. How can businesses avoid the "analyze-the-analyzable bias"?

Questions on Presentation

1. To make their argument understandable, Peters and Waterman compare and contrast the rational model with an informal management process. Using the information they present, define these two models. Why do Peters and Waterman prefer one model to the other?
2. One of the analogies Peters and Waterman use is a comparison of approaches from business and science. How effective is Peters and Waterman's analogy as a means to support their argument?
3. How would you characterize the audience for this essay? On what do you base that characterization?
4. Why are the examples the authors use to support their answers to the rhetorical questions in paragraph 11 effective?

⚖

Reasons for Opposition to Payment of Salaries to the Executive Branch

Benjamin Franklin

American statesman, inventor, and writer Benjamin Franklin (1706–1790) was among the most outspoken of the American partisans during and after the Revolution. The fifteenth of seventeen children, Franklin grew up in Boston, and when he was thirteen he was apprenticed to his brother James, a printer. In 1723 Franklin left Boston for Philadelphia where he worked as a printer and eventually became the publisher of the *Pennsylvania Gazette*. In addition to his newspaper work, Franklin is known for his inventions, including the Franklin stove and bifocal glasses. During the American Revolution Franklin served as the American envoy to France and was one of the diplomats who concluded the peace treaty with Great Britain in 1781. Among his writings his best known is *Poor Richard's Almanac* (1732) and *Proposals Relating to the Education of Youth in Pennsylvania* (1749). In this speech, delivered before the Constitutional Convention in 1787, Franklin gives a perspective different from that offered by Robert Thomas regarding the salaries of CEOs, here the chief executive of the U.S. government.

1   Sir, it is with reluctance that I rise to express a disapprobation of any one article of the plan, for which we are so much obliged to the honorable gentleman who laid it before us. From its first reading, I have borne a good will to it, and in general, wished it success. In this particular of salaries to the executive branch, I happen to differ; and, as my opinion may appear new and chimerical, it is only from a persuasion that it is right, and from a sense of duty, that I hazard it. The Committee will judge of my reasons when they have heard them, and their judgment may possibly change mine. I think I see inconveniences in the appointment of salaries; I see none in refusing them, but on the contrary great advantages.

2   Sir, there are two passions which have a powerful influence in the affairs of men. These are *ambition* and *avarice:* the love of power and the love of money. Separately, each of these has great force in prompting men to action; but when united in view of the same object, they have in many minds the most violent effects. Place before the eyes of such men a post of *honor*, that shall at the same time be a place of *profit*, and they will move heaven and earth to obtain it. The vast number of such places it is that renders the British government so tempestuous. The

struggles for them are the true source of all those factions which are perpetually dividing the nation, distracting its councils, hurrying it sometimes into fruitless and mischievous wars, and often compelling a submission to dishonorable terms of peace.

3   And of what kind are the men that will strive for this profitable preeminence, through all the bustle of cabal, the heat of contention, the infinite mutual abuse of parties, tearing to pieces the best of characters? It will not be the wise and moderate, the lovers of peace and good order, the men fittest for the trust. It will be the bold and violent, the men of strong passions and indefatigable activity in their selfish pursuits. These will thrust themselves into your government, and be your rulers. And these, too, will be mistaken in the expected happiness of their situation; for their vanquished competitors, of the same spirit, and from the same motives, will perpetually be endeavoring to distress their administration, thwart their measures, and render them odious to the people.

4   Besides these evils, sir, though we may set out in the beginning with moderate salaries, we shall find that such will not be of long continuance. Reasons will never be wanting for proposed augmentations, and there will always be a party for giving more to the rulers, that the rulers may be able to return to give more to them. Hence, as all history informs us, there has been in every state and kingdom a constant kind of warfare between the governing and the governed; the one striving to obtain more for its support, and the other to pay less. And this alone has occasioned great convulsions, actual civil wars, ending either in dethroning of the princes or enslaving of the people.

5   Generally, indeed, the ruling power carries its point, and we see the revenues of princes constantly increasing, and we see that they are never satisfied, but always in want of more. The more the people are discontented with the oppression of taxes, the greater need the prince has of money to distribute among his partisans, and pay the troops that are to suppress all resistance and enable him to plunder at pleasure. There is scarce a king in a hundred, who would not, if he could, follow the example of Pharaoh—get first all the people's money, then all their lands, and then make them and their children servants forever.

6   It will be said that we do not propose to establish kings. I know it. But there is a natural inclination in mankind to kingly government. It sometimes relieves them from aristocratic domination. They had rather have one tyrant than five hundred. It gives more of the appearance of equality among citizens; and that they like. I am apprehensive, therefore—perhaps too apprehensive—that the government of these States may in future times end in a monarchy. But this catastrophe, I think, may be long delayed, if in our proposed system we do not sow the seeds of contention, faction, and tumult, by making our posts of honor places of profit. If we do, I fear that, though we employ at first a number and

not a single person, the number will in time be set aside; it will only nourish the foetus of a king (as the honorable gentleman from Virginia very aptly expressed it), and a king will the sooner be set over us.

7   It may be imagined by some that this is an utopian idea, and that we can never find men to serve us in the executive department, without paying them well for their services. I conceive this to be a mistake. Some existing facts present themselves to me, which incline me to a contrary opinion. The High Sheriff of a county in England is an honorable office, but it is not a profitable one. It is rather expensive, and therefore not sought for. But yet it is executed, and well executed, and usually by some of the principal gentlemen of the county. In France, the office of Counsellor, or member of their judiciary parliaments, is more honorable. It is therefore purchased at a high price; there are indeed fees on the law proceedings, which are divided among them, but these fees do not amount to more than three percent on the sum paid for the place. Therefore, as legal interest is there at five percent, they in fact pay two percent for being allowed to do the judiciary business of the nation, which is at the same time entirely exempt from the burden of paying them any salaries for their services. I do not, however, mean to recommend this as an eligible mode for our judiciary department. I only bring the instance to show that the pleasure of doing good and serving their country, and the respect such conduct entitles them to, are sufficient motives with some minds to give up a great portion of their time to the public, without the mean inducement of pecuniary satisfaction.

8   Another instance is that of a respectable society, who have made the experiment, and practiced it with success, now more than a hundred years. I mean the Quakers. It is an established rule with them that they are not to go to law, but in their controversies they must apply to their monthly, quarterly, and yearly meetings. Committees of these sit with patience to hear the parties, and spend much time in composing their differences. In doing this, they are supported by a sense of duty and the respect paid to usefulness. It is honorable to be so employed, but it was never made profitable by salaries, fees, or perquisites. And indeed, in all cases of public service, the less the profit the greater the honor.

9   To bring the matter nearer home, have we not seen the greatest and most important of our offices, that of General of our Armies, executed for eight years together, without the smallest salary, by a patriot whom I will not now offend by any other praise; and this, through fatigues and distresses, in common with the other brave men, his military friends and companions, and the constant anxieties peculiar to his station? And shall we doubt finding three or four men in all the United States, with public spirit enough to bear sitting in peaceful council, for perhaps an equal term, merely to preside over our civil concerns, and see that our

laws are duly executed? Sir, I have a better opinion of our country. I think we shall never be without a sufficient number of wise and good men to undertake, and execute well and faithfully, the office in question.

10   Sir, the saving of the salaries, that may at first be proposed, is not an object with me. The subsequent mischiefs of proposing them are what I apprehend. And therefore it is that I move the amendment. If it is not seconded or accepted, I must be contented with the satisfaction of having delivered my opinion frankly, and done my duty.

Content Questions

1. What, according to Franklin, influences men's actions?
2. Who will want positions that produce profit?
3. Why is there a "natural inclination . . . to kingly government"?
4. What are Franklin's examples of honorable, unpaid positions?

Questions on Presentation

1. What lets you know this is a speech?
2. Why does Franklin begin paragraph 3 with a rhetorical question?
3. Which of the examples of unpaid but honorable men would Franklin's audience find most effective? Why?

Questions for Discussion and Writing

1. Several of the writers in this section, as well as other sections, are critical of the influence business has on science and the arts. Yet many other people see the situation differently. Some would argue that science and any of the fine arts are businesses. Others feel that any scientific or artistic project would be better run if it were operated in a businesslike fashion. Is the influence of business in science or the arts a bad thing? Can business be beneficial to scientists or artists? If so, when and how? If not, why not?
2. This section presents several problems businesses face today. Identify one type of problem and write an essay in which you explain why that problem exists and how you would solve it.
3. Several of the essays in this section suggest that it is dangerous to trust "experts." Write an essay in which you discuss the need for experts in a field and explore reasons why they should or should not be trusted.

Section 4

GENDER AND CULTURE

The Achievement of Desire

Richard Rodriguez

California writer and lecturer Richard Rodriguez was born in 1944 in San Francisco to Spanish-speaking immigrant parents. Although more at ease speaking Spanish than English, his parents deliberately moved the family from a Chicano to a "gringo" neighborhood. Rodriguez entered Sacred Heart parochial school in Sacramento, fluent in Spanish but speaking almost no English. Because the sisters at Sacred Heart insisted that he learn English immediately, Rodriguez not only learned the language quickly but also became a voracious reader. The background and learning he gained from his reading helped Rodriguez win a scholarship to a private high school; he went on to attend Stanford, Columbia, London's Warburg Institute, and the University of California at Berkeley where he earned a Ph.D. in English literature.

Education distanced him from his parents and their culture, a separation discussed in the following selection from his controversial book *Hunger of Memory: The Education of Richard Rodriguez* (1982), a book considered a political memoir of a man growing up between two cultures. As a contributor to *The American Scholar, The Saturday Review, The New Republic,* and other magazines, Rodriguez often writes about his passion, language, bilingualism, and education. He supports a public language, one common to America as a country rather than individual to immigrants. For Rodriguez, teachers are responsible for public forms of language and their appropriate use; parents are responsible for teaching cultural values. These views place Rodriguez in the center of current controversies about English as an official language and bilingual education, a concept he does not support. His views also have forced him to explore, as he does in the following selection, what he feels he gained from school and how his attraction to learning changed his attitudes toward his family.

1   I stand in the ghetto classroom—"the guest speaker"—attempting to lecture on the mystery of the sounds of our words to rows of diffident

students. "Don't you hear it? Listen? The music of our words. *'Sumer is i-cumen in . . .'* And songs on the car radio. We need Aretha Franklin's voice to fill plain words with music—her life." In the face of their empty stare I try to create an enthusiasm. But the girls in the back row turn to watch some boy passing outside. There are flutters of smiles, waves. And someone's mouth elongates heavy, silent words through the barrier of glass. Silent words—the lips straining to shape each voiceless syllable: *"Meet meee late errr."* By the door, the instructor smiles at me, apparently hoping that I will be able to spark some enthusiasm in the class. But only one student seems to be listening. A girl, maybe four-teen. In this gray room her eyes shine with ambition. She keeps nodding and nodding at all that I say; she even takes notes. And each time I ask a question, she jerks up and down in her desk like a marionette, while her hand waves over the bowed heads of her classmates. It is myself (as a boy) I see as she faces now (a man in my thirties).

2 The boy who first entered a classroom barely able to speak English, twenty years later concluded his studies in the stately quiet of the read-ing room of the British Museum. Thus with one sentence I can summa-rize my academic career. It will be harder to summarize what sort of life connects the boy to the man.

3 With every award, each graduation from one level of education to the next, people I'd meet would congratulate me. Their refrain always the same: "Your parents must be very proud." Sometimes they'd ask me how I managed it—my "success." (How?) After a while, I had several quick answers to give in reply. I'd admit, for one thing, that I went to an excellent grammar school. (My earliest teachers, the nuns, made my success their ambition.) And my brother and both my sisters were very good students. (They often brought home the shiny school trophies I came to want.) And my mother and father always encouraged me. (At every graduation they were behind the stunning flash of the camera when I turned to look at the crowd.)

4 As important as these factors were, however, they account inade-quately for my academic advance. Nor do they suggest what an odd suc-cess I managed. For although I was a very good student, I was also a very bad student. I was a "scholarship boy," a certain kind of scholarship boy. Always successful, I was always unconfident. Exhilarated by my prog-ress. Sad. I became the prized student—an imitative and unoriginal pu-pil. My brother and two sisters enjoyed the advantages I did, and they grew to be as successful as I, but none of them ever seemed so anxious about their schooling. A second-grade student, I was the one who came home and corrected the "simple" grammatical mistakes of our parents. ("Two negatives make a positive.") Proudly I announced—to my fam-ily's startled silence—that a teacher had said I was losing all trace of a Spanish accent. I was oddly annoyed when I was unable to get parental

help with a homework assignment. The night my father tried to help me with an arithmetic exercise, he kept reading the instructions, each time more deliberately, until I pried the textbook out of his hands, saying, "I'll try to figure out some more by myself."

5   When I reached the third grade, I outgrew such behavior. I became more tactful, careful to keep separate the two very different worlds of my day. But then, with ever-increasing intensity, I devoted myself to my studies. I became bookish, puzzling to all my family. Ambition set me apart. When my brother saw me struggling home with stacks of library books, he would laugh, shouting: "Hey, Four Eyes!" My father opened a closet one day and was startled to find me inside, reading a novel. My mother would find me reading when I was supposed to be asleep or helping around the house or playing outside. In a voice angry or worried or just curious, she'd ask: "What do you see in your books?" It became the family's joke. When I was called and wouldn't reply, someone would say I must be hiding under my bed with a book.

6   (How did I manage my success?)

7   What I am about to say to you has taken me more than twenty years to admit: *A primary reason for my success in the classroom was that I couldn't forget that schooling was changing me and separating me from the life I enjoyed before becoming a student.* That simple realization! For years I never spoke to anyone about it. Never mentioned a thing to my family or my teachers or classmates. From a very early age, I understood enough, just enough about my classroom experiences to keep what I knew repressed, hidden beneath layers of embarrassment. Not until my last months as a graduate student, nearly thirty years old, was it possible for me to think much about the reasons for my academic success. Only then. At the end of my schooling, I needed to determine how far I had moved from my past. The adult finally confronted, and now must publicly say, what the child shuddered from knowing and could never admit to himself or those many faces that smiled at his every success. ("Your parents must be very proud. . . .")

8   From an early age I knew that my mother and father could read and write both Spanish and English. I had observed my father making his way through what, I now suppose, must have been income tax forms. On other occasions I waited apprehensively while my mother read onion-paper letters airmailed from Mexico with news of a relative's illness or death. For both my parents, however, reading was something done out of necessity and as quickly as possible. Never did I see either of them read an entire book. Nor did I see them read for pleasure. Their reading consisted of work manuals, prayer books, newspapers, recipes.

9   Richard Hoggart imagines how, at home,

... [The scholarship boy] sees strewn around, and reads regularly himself, magazines which are never mentioned at school, which seem not to belong to the world to which the school introduces him; at school he hears about and reads books never mentioned at home. When he brings those books into the house they do not take their place with other books which the family are reading, for often there are none or almost none; his books look, rather, like strange tools.[1]

In our house each school year would begin with my mother's careful instruction: "Don't write in your books so we can sell them at the end of the year." The remark was echoed in public by my teachers, but only in part: "Boys and girls, don't write in your books. You must learn to treat them with great care and respect."

10   OPEN THE DOORS OF YOUR MIND WITH BOOKS, read the red and white poster over the nun's desk in early September. It soon was apparent to me that reading was the classroom's central activity. Each course had its own book. And the information gathered from a book was unquestioned. READ TO LEARN, the sign on the wall advised in December. I privately wondered: What was the connection between reading and learning? Did one learn something only by reading it? Was an idea only an idea if it could be written down? In June, CONSIDER BOOKS YOUR BEST FRIENDS. Friends? Reading was, at best, only a chore. I needed to look up whole paragraphs of words in a dictionary. Lines of type were dizzying, the eye having to move slowly across the page, then down, and across. . . . The sentences of the first books I read were coolly impersonal. Toned hard. What most bothered me, however, was the isolation reading required. To console myself for the loneliness I'd feel when I read, I tried reading in a very soft voice. Until: "Who is doing all that talking to his neighbor?" Shortly after, remedial reading classes were arranged for me with a very old nun.

11   At the end of each school day, for nearly six months, I would meet with her in the tiny room that served as the school's library but was actually only a storeroom for used textbooks and a vast collection of *National Geographics*. Everything about our sessions pleased me: the smallness of the room; the noise of the janitor's broom hitting the edge of the long hallway outside the door; the green of the sun, lighting the wall; and the old woman's face blurred white with a beard. Most of the time we took turns. I began with my elementary text. Sentences of astonishing simplicity seemed to me lifeless and drab: "The boys ran from the rain . . . She wanted to sing . . . The kite rose in the blue." Then the old nun would read from her favorite books, usually biographies of early American presidents. Playfully she ran through complex sentences, calling the words alive with her voice, making it seem that the author

somehow was speaking directly to me. I smiled just to listen to her. I sat there and sensed for the very first time some possibility of fellowship between a reader and a writer, a communication, never *intimate* like what I heard spoken words at home convey, but one nonetheless *personal.*

12   One day the nun concluded a session by asking me why I was so reluctant to read by myself. I tried to explain; said something about the way written words made me feel all alone—almost, I wanted to add but didn't, as when I spoke to myself in a room just emptied of furniture. She studied my face as I spoke; she seemed to be watching more than listening. In an uneventful voice she replied that I had nothing to fear. Didn't I realize that reading would open up whole new worlds? A book could open doors for me. It could introduce me to people and show me places I never imagined existed. She gestured toward the bookshelves. (Bare-breasted African women danced, and the shiny hubcaps of automobiles on the back covers of the *Geographic* gleamed in my mind.) I listened with respect. But her words were not very influential. I was thinking then of another consequence of literacy, one I was too shy to admit but nonetheless trusted. Books were going to make me "educated." *That* confidence enabled me, several months later, to overcome my fear of the silence.

13   In fourth grade I embarked upon a grandiose reading program. "Give me the names of important books," I would say to startled teachers. They soon found out that I had in mind "adult books." I ignored their suggestion of anything I suspected was written for children. (Not until I was in college, as a result, did I read *Huckleberry Finn* or *Alice's Adventures in Wonderland.*) Instead, I read *The Scarlet Letter* and Franklin's *Autobiography.* And whatever I read I read for extra credit. Each time I finished a book, I reported the achievement to a teacher and basked in the praise my effort earned. Despite my best efforts, however, there seemed to be more and more books I needed to read. At the library I would literally tremble as I came upon whole shelves of books I hadn't read. So I read and I read and I read: *Great Expectations;* all the short stories of Kipling; *The Babe Ruth Story;* the entire first volume of the *Encyclopedia Britannica* (A–ANSTEY); the *Iliad; Moby Dick; Gone with the Wind; The Good Earth; Ramona; Forever Amber; The Lives of the Saints; Crime and Punishment; The Pearl* . . . Librarians who initially frowned when I checked out the maximum ten books at a time started saving books they thought I might like. Teachers would say to the rest of the class, "I only wish the rest of you took reading as seriously as Richard obviously does."

14   But at home I would hear my mother wondering, "What do you see in your books?" (Was reading a hobby like her knitting? Was so much read-

ing even healthy for a boy? Was it the sign of "brains"? Or was it just a convenient excuse for not helping around the house on Saturday mornings?) Always, "What do you see . . . ?"

15   What *did* I see in my books? I had the idea that they were crucial for my academic success, though I couldn't have said exactly how or why. In the sixth grade I simply concluded that what gave a book its value was some major idea or theme it contained. If that core essence could be mined and memorized, I would become learned like my teachers. I decided to record in a notebook the themes of the books that I read. After reading *Robinson Crusoe*, I wrote that its theme was "the value of learning to live by oneself." When I completed *Wuthering Heights*, I noted the danger of "letting emotions get out of control." Rereading these brief moralistic appraisals usually left me disheartened. I couldn't believe that they were really the source of reading's value. But for many more years, they constituted the only means I had of describing to myself the educational value of books.

16   In spite of my earnestness, I found reading a pleasurable activity. I came to enjoy the lonely good company of books. Early on weekday mornings, I'd read in my bed. I'd feel a mysterious comfort then, reading in the dawn quiet—the blue-gray silence interrupted by the occasional churning of the refrigerator motor a few rooms away or the more distant sounds of a city bus beginning its run. On weekdays I'd go to the public library to read, surrounded by old men and women. Or, if the weather was fine, I would take my books to the park and read in the shade of a tree. A warm summer evening was my favorite reading time. Neighbors would leave for vacation and I would water their lawns. I would sit through the twilight on the front porches or in backyards, reading to the cool, whirling sounds of the sprinklers.

17   I also had favorite writers. But often those writers I enjoyed most I was least able to value. When I read William Saroyan's *The Human Comedy*, I was immediately pleased by the narrator's warmth and the charm of his story. But as quickly I became suspicious. A book so enjoyable to read couldn't be very "important." Another summer I determined to read all the novels of Dickens. Reading his fat novels, I loved the feeling I got—after the first hundred pages—of being at home in a fictional world where I knew the names of the characters and cared about what was going to happen to them. And it bothered me that I was forced away at the conclusion, when the fiction closed tight, like a fortune-teller's fist—the futures of all the major characters neatly resolved. I never knew how to take such feelings seriously, however. Nor did I suspect that these experiences could be part of a novel's meaning. Still, there were pleasures to sustain me after I'd finish my books. Carrying a volume back to the library, I would be pleased by its weight. I'd run my

fingers along the edge of the pages and marvel at the breadth of my achievement. Around my room, growing stacks of paperback books reinforced my assurance.

18 I entered high school having read hundreds of books. My habit of reading made me a confident speaker and writer of English. Reading also enabled me to sense something of the shape, the major concerns, of Western thought. (I was able to say something about Dante and Descartes and Engels and James Baldwin in my high school term papers.) In these various ways, books brought me academic success as I hoped that they would. But I was not a good reader. Merely bookish, I lacked a point of view when I read. Rather, I read in order to acquire a point of view. I vacuumed books for epigrams, scraps of information, ideas, themes—anything to fill the hollow within me and make me feel educated. When one of my teachers suggested to his drowsy tenth-grade English class that a person could not have a "complicated idea" until he had read at least two thousand books, I heard the remark without detecting either its irony or its very complicated truth. I merely determined to compile a list of all the books I had ever read. Harsh with myself, I included only once a title I might have read several times. (How, after all, could one read a book more than once?) And I included only those books over a hundred pages in length. (Could anything shorter be a book?)

19 There was yet another high school list I compiled. One day I came across a newspaper article about the retirement of an English professor at a nearby state college. The article was accompanied by a list of the "hundred most important books of Western Civilization." "More than anything else in my life," the professor told the reporter with finality, "these books have made me all that I am." That was the kind of remark I couldn't ignore. I clipped out the list and kept it for the several months it took me to read all of the titles. Most books, of course, I barely understood. While reading Plato's *Republic*, for instance, I needed to keep looking at the book jacket comments to remind myself what the text was about. Nevertheless, with the special patience and superstition of a scholarship boy, I looked at every word of the text. And by the time I reached the last word, relieved, I convinced myself that I had read the *Republic*. In a ceremony of great pride, I solemnly crossed Plato off my list.

Notes

[1]Richard Hoggart (b. 1918) is a British writer and educator whose publications, such as *The Uses of Literacy* (1957) and *How and Why Do We Learn* (1965), influenced Rodriguez's thinking about education. [Eds.]

Content Questions

1. What terms does Rodriguez use to characterize his experience with scholarship?
2. Who is "the scholarship boy" and why is he important?
3. What does Rodriguez believe is the primary reason for his success in school?
4. How does Rodriguez define a "good reader"? Does he fit his own definition?

Questions on Presentation

1. What is the effect of the choppiness in the first paragraph?
2. How does Rodriguez present his reasons for not giving up his life as a student? Are his reasons sufficient justification for his decision?
3. Is Rodriguez's explanation of how he was both "a very good student [and] a very bad student" (4) clear?
4. How does Rodriguez present his argument in paragraph 14?

Omnilingual

H. Beam Piper

H. Beam Piper (1904–1964) was an engineer and science fiction writer who worked on the engineering staff of the Pennsylvania Railroad before his suicide in 1964. Many of Piper's science fiction stories form a "future history" series. "Omnilingual," first published in 1957, describes interstellar adventures that echo contemporary sounds.

1   Martha Dane paused, looking up at the purple-tinged copper sky. The wind had shifted since noon, while she had been inside, and the dust storm that was sweeping the high deserts to the east was now blowing out over Syrtis. The sun, magnified by the haze, was a gorgeous magenta ball, as large as the sun of Terra, at which she could look directly. Tonight, some of that dust would come shifting down from the upper at-

mosphere to add another film to what had been burying the city for the last fifty thousand years.

2   The red loess lay over everything, covering the streets and the open spaces of park and plaza, hiding the small houses that had been crushed and pressed flat under it and the rubble that had come down from the tall buildings when roofs had caved in and walls had toppled outward. Here where she stood, the ancient streets were a hundred to a hundred and fifty feet below the surface; the breach they had made in the wall of the building behind her had opened into the sixth story. She could look down on the cluster of prefabricated huts and sheds, on the brush-grown flat that had been the waterfront when this place had been a sea-port on the ocean that was now Syrtis Depression; already, the bright metal was thinly coated with red dust. She thought, again, of what clearing this city would mean, in terms of time and labor, of people and supplies and equipment brought across fifty million miles of space. They'd have to use machinery; there was no other way it could be done. Bull-dozers and power shovels and draglines; they were fast, but they were rough and indiscriminate. She remembered the digs around Harappa and Mohenjo-Daro, in the Indus Valley, and the careful, patient native labor-ers—the painstaking foremen, the pickmen and spademen, the long files of basketmen carrying away the earth. Slow and primitive as the civili-zation whose ruins they were uncovering, yes, but she could count on the fingers of one hand the times one of her pickmen had damaged a valuable object in the ground. If it hadn't been for the underpaid and un-complaining native laborer, archaeology would still be back where Winckelmann had found it. But on Mars there was no native labor; the last Martian had died five hundred centuries ago.

3   Something started banging like a machine gun, four or five hundred yards to her left. A solenoid jack-hammer; Tony Lattimer must have de-cided which building he wanted to break into next. She became con-scious, then, of the awkward weight of her equipment, and began redistributing it, shifting the straps of her oxy-tank pack, slinging the camera from one shoulder and the board and drafting tools from the other, gathering the notebooks and sketchbooks under her left arm. She started walking down the road, over hillocks of buried rubble, around snags of wall jutting up out of the loess, past buildings still standing, some of them already breached and explored, and across the brush-grown flat to the huts.

4   There were ten people in the main office room of Hut One when she entered. As soon as she had disposed of her oxygen equipment, she lit a cigarette, her first since noon, then looked from one to another of them. Old Selim von Ohlmhorst, the Turco-German, one of her two fellow ar-chaeologists, sitting at the end of the long table against the farther wall,

smoking his big curved pipe and going through a looseleaf notebook. The girl ordnance officer, Sachiko Koremitsu, between two droplights at the other end of the table, her head bent over her work. Colonel Hubert Penrose, the Space Force CO, and Captain Field, the intelligence officer, listening to the report of one of the airdyne pilots, returned from his afternoon survey flight. A couple of girl lieutenants from Signals, going over the script of the evening telecast, to be transmitted to the *Cyrano*, on orbit five thousand miles off planet and relayed from thence to Terra via Lunar. Sid Chamberlain, the Trans-Space News Service man, was with them. Like Selim and herself, he was a civilian; he was advertising the fact with a white shirt and a sleeveless blue sweater. And Major Lindemann, the engineer officer, and one of his assistants, arguing over some plans on a drafting board. She hoped, drawing a pint of hot water to wash her hands and sponge off her face, that they were doing something about the pipeline.

5   She started to carry the notebooks and sketchbooks over to where Selim von Ohlmhorst was sitting, and then, as she always did, she turned aside and stopped to watch Sachiko. The Japanese girl was restoring what had been a book, fifty thousand years ago; her eyes were masked by a binocular loup, the black headband invisible against her glossy black hair, and she was picking delicately at the crumbled page with a hair-fine wire set in a handle of copper tubing. Finally, loosening a particle as tiny as a snowflake, she grasped it with tweezers, placed it on the sheet of transparent plastic on which she was reconstructing the page, and set it with a mist of fixative from a little spraygun. It was a sheer joy to watch her; every movement was as graceful and precise as though done to music after being rehearsed a hundred times.

6   "Hello, Martha. It isn't cocktail-time yet, is it?" The girl at the table spoke without raising her head, almost without moving her lips, as though she were afraid that the slightest breath would disturb the flaky stuff in front of her.

7   "No, it's only fifteen-thirty. I finished my work, over there. I didn't find any more books, if that's good news for you."

8   Sachiko took off the loup and leaned back in her chair, her palms cupped over her eyes.

9   "No, I like doing this. I call it micro-jigsaw puzzles. This book, here, really is a mess. Selim found it lying open, with some heavy stuff on top of it; the pages were simply crushed." She hesitated briefly. "If only it would mean something, after I did it."

10   There could be a faintly critical overtone to that. As she replied, Martha realized that she was being defensive.

11   "It will, some day. Look how long it took to read Egyptian hieroglyphics, even after they had the Rosetta Stone."

12   Sachiko smiled. "Yes, I know. But they did have the Rosetta Stone."

13   "And we don't. There is no Rosetta Stone, not anywhere on Mars. A whole race, a whole species, died while the first Crô-Magnon cave-artist was daubing pictures of reindeer and bison, and across fifty thousand years and fifty million miles there was no bridge of understanding."

14   "We'll find one. There must be something, somewhere, that will give us the meaning of a few words, and we'll use them to pry meaning out of more words, and so on. We may not live to learn this language, but we'll make a start, and some day somebody will."

15   Sachiko took her hands from her eyes, being careful not to look toward the unshaded lights, and smiled again. This time Martha was sure that it was not the Japanese smile of politeness, but the universally human smile of friendship.

16   "I hope so, Martha; really I do. It would be wonderful for you to be the first to do it, and it woud be wonderful for all of us to be able to read what these people wrote. It would really bring this dead city to life again." The smile faded slowly. "But it seems so hopeless."

17   "You haven't found any more pictures?"

18   Sachiko shook her head. Not that it would have meant much if she had. They had found hundreds of pictures with captions; they had never been able to establish a positive relationship between any pictured object and any printed word. Neither of them said anything more, and after a moment Sachiko replaced the loup and bent her head forward over the book.

19   Selim von Ohlmhorst looked up from his notebook, taking his pipe out of his mouth.

20   "Everything finished, over there?" he asked, releasing a puff of smoke.

21   "Such as it was." She laid the notebooks and sketches on the table. "Captain Gicquel's started airsealing the building from the fifth floor down, with an entrance on the sixth; he'll start putting in oxygen generators as soon as that's done. I have everything cleared up where he'll be working."

22   Colonel Penrose looked up quickly, as though making a mental note to attend to something later. Then he returned his attention to the pilot, who was pointing something out on a map.

23   Von Ohlmhorst nodded. "There wasn't much to it, at that," he agreed. "Do you know which building Tony has decided to enter next?"

24   "The tall one with the conical thing like a candle extinguisher on top, I think. I heard him drilling for the blasting shots over that way."

25   "Well, I hope it turns out to be one that was occupied up to the end."

50   26   The last one hadn't. It had been stripped of its contents and fittings, a piece of this and a bit of that, haphazardly, apparently over a long period of time, until it had been almost gutted. For centuries, as it had

died, this city had been consuming itself by a process of autocannibalism. She said something to that effect.

27   "Yes. We always find that—except, of course, at places like Pompeii. Have you seen any of the other Roman cities in Italy?" he asked. "Minturnae, for instance? First the inhabitants tore down this to repair that, and then, after they had vacated the city, other people came along and tore down what was left, and burned the stones for lime, or crushed them to mend roads, till there was nothing left but the foundation traces. That's where we are fortunate; this is one of the places where the Martian race perished, and there were no barbarians to come later and destroy what they had left." He puffed slowly at his pipe. "Some of these days, Martha, we are going to break into one of these buildings and find that it was one in which the last of these people died. Then we will learn the story of the end of this civilization."

28   And if we learn to read their language, we'll learn the whole story, not just the obituary. She hesitated, not putting the thought into words. "We'll find that, sometime, Selim," she said, then looked at her watch. "I'm going to get some more work done on my lists, before dinner."

29   For an instant, the old man's face stiffened in disapproval; he started to say something, thought better of it, and put his pipe back into his mouth. The brief wrinkling around his mouth and the twitch of his white mustache had been enough, however; she knew what he was thinking. She was wasting time and effort, he believed; time and effort belonging not to herself but to the expedition. He could be right, too, she realized. But he had to be wrong; there had to be a way to do it. She turned from him silently and went to her own packing-case seat, at the middle of the table.

30   Photographs, and photostats of restored pages of books, and transcripts of inscriptions, were piled in front of her, and the notebooks in which she was compiling her lists. She sat down, lighting a fresh cigarette, and reached over to a stack of unexamined material, taking off the top sheet. It was a photostat of what looked like the title page and contents of some sort of a periodical. She remembered it; she had found it herself, two days before, in a closet in the basement of the building she had just finished examining.

31   She sat for a moment, looking at it. It was readable, in the sense that she had set up a purely arbitrary but consistently pronounceable system of phonetic values for the letters. The long vertical symbols were vowels. There were only ten of them; not too many, allowing separate characters for long and short sounds. There were twenty of the short horizontal letters, which meant that sounds like -ng or -ch or -sh were single letters. The odds were millions to one against her system being

anything like the original sound of the language, but she had listed several thousand Martian words, and she could pronounce all of them.

32   And that was as far as it went. She could pronounce between three and four thousand Martian words, and she couldn't assign a meaning to one of them. Selim von Ohlmhorst believed that she never would. So did Tony Lattimer, and he was a great deal less reticent about saying so. So, she was sure, did Sachiko Koremitsu. There were times, now and then, when she began to be afraid that they were right.

33   The letters on the page in front of her began squirming and dancing, slender vowels with fat little consonants. They did that, now, every night in her dreams. And there were other dreams, in which she read them as easily as English; waking, she would try desperately and vainly to remember. She blinked, and looked away from the photostated page; when she looked back, the letters were behaving themselves again. There were three words at the top of the page, over-and-underlined, which seemed to be the Martian method of capitalization. *Masthar-norvod Tadavas Sornhulva.* She pronounced them mentally, leafing through her notebooks to see if she had encountered them before, and in what contexts. All three were listed. In addition, *masthar* was a fairly common word, and so was *norvod*, and so was *nor*, but *-vod* was a suffix and nothing but a suffix. *Davas*, was a word, too, and *ta-* was a common prefix; *sorn* and *hulva* were both common words. This language, she had long ago decided, must be something like German; when the Martians had needed a new word, they had just pasted a couple of existing words together. It would probably turn out to be a grammatical horror. Well, they had published magazines, and one of them had been called *Mastharnorvod Tadavas Sornhulva.* She wondered if it had been something like the *Quarterly Archaeological Review,* or something more on the order of *Sexy Stories.*

34   A smaller line, under the title, was plainly the issue number and date; enough things had been found numbered in series to enable her to identify the numerals and determine that a decimal system of numeration had been used. This was the one thousand and seven hundred and fifty-fourth issue, for Doma, 14837; then Doma must be the name of one of the Martian months. The word had turned up several times before. She found herself puffing furiously on her cigarette as she leafed through notebooks and piles of already examined material.

35   Sachiko was speaking to somebody, and a chair scraped at the end of the table. She raised her head, to see a big man with red hair and a red face, in Space Force green, with the single star of a major on his shoulder, sitting down. Ivan Fitzgerald, the medic. He was lifting weights from a book similar to the one the girl ordnance officer was restoring.

36   "Haven't had time, lately," he was saying in reply to Sachiko's ques-

tion. "The Finchley girl's still down with whatever it is she has, and it's something I haven't been able to diagnose yet. And I've been checking on bacteria cultures, and in what spare time I have, I've been dissecting specimens for Bill Chandler. Bill's finally found a mammal. Looks like a lizard, and it's only four inches long, but it's a real warm-blooded, gamogenetic, placental, viviparous mammal. Burrows, and seems to live on what pass for insects here."

37 "Is there enough oxygen for anything like that?" Sachiko was asking.

38 "Seems to be, close to the ground." Fitzgerald got the headband of his loup adjusted, and pulled it down over his eyes. "He found this thing in a ravine down on the sea bottom—Ha, this page seems to be intact; now, if I can get it out all in one piece—"

39 He went on talking inaudibly to himself, lifting the page a little at a time and sliding one of the transparent plastic sheets under it, working with minute delicacy. Not the delicacy of the Japanese girl's small hands, moving like the paws of a cat washing her face, but like a steam-hammer cracking a peanut. Field archaeology requires a certain delicacy of touch, too, but Martha watched the pair of them with envious admiration. Then she turned back to her own work, finishing the table of contents.

40 The next page was the beginning of the first article listed; many of the words were unfamiliar. She had the impression that this must be some kind of scientific or technical journal; that could be because such publications made up the bulk of her own periodical reading. She doubted if it were fiction; the paragraphs had a solid, factual look.

41 At length, Ivan Fitzgerald gave a short, explosive grunt.

42 "Ha! Got it!"

43 She looked up. He had detached the page and was cementing another plastic sheet onto it.

44 "Any pictures?" she asked.

45 "None on this side. Wait a moment." He turned the sheet. "None on this side, either." He sprayed another sheet of plastic to sandwich the page, then picked up his pipe and relighted it.

46 "I get fun out of this, and it's good practice for my hands, so don't think I'm complaining," he said, "but, Martha, do you honestly think anybody's ever going to get anything out of this?"

47 Sachiko held up a scrap of the silicone plastic the Martians had used for paper with her tweezers. It was almost an inch square.

48 "Look; three whole words on this piece," she crowed. "Ivan, you took the easy book."

49 Fitzgerald wasn't being sidetracked. "This stuff's absolutely meaningless," he continued. "It had a meaning fifty thousand years ago, when it was written, but it has none at all now."

50 She shook her head. "Meaning isn't something that evaporates with

time," she argued. "It has just as much meaning now as it ever had. We just haven't learned how to decipher it."

51   "That seems like a pretty pointless distinction," Selim von Ohlmhorst joined the conversation. "There no longer exists a means of deciphering it."

52   "We'll find one." She was speaking, she realized, more in self-encouragement than in controversy.

53   "How? From pictures and captions? We've found captioned pictures, and what have they given us? A caption is intended to explain the picture, not the picture to explain the caption. Suppose some alien to our culture found a picture of a man with white beard and mustache sawing a billet from a log. He would think the caption meant, 'Man Sawing Wood.' How would he know that it was really 'Wilhelm II in Exile at Doorn'?"

54   Sachiko had taken off her loup and was lighting a cigarette.

55   "I can think of pictures intended to explain their captions," she said. "These picture-language books, the sort we use in the Service—little line drawings, with a word or phrase under them."

56   "Well, of course, if we found something like that," von Ohlmhorst began.

57   "Michael Ventris found something like that, back in the Fifties," Hubert Penrose's voice broke in from directly behind her.

58   She turned her head. The colonel was standing by the archaeologists' table; Captain Field and the airdyne pilot had gone out.

59   "He found a lot of Greek inventories of military stores," Penrose continued. "They were in Cretan Linear B script, and at the head of each list was a little picture, a sword or a helmet or a cooking tripod or a chariot wheel. That's what gave him the key to the script."

60   "Colonel's getting to be quite an archaeologist," Fitzgerald commented. "We're all learning each others' specialties, on this expedition."

61   "I heard about that long before this expedition was even contemplated." Penrose was tapping a cigarette on his gold case. "I heard about that back before the Thirty Days' War, at Intelligence School, when I was a lieutenant. As a feat of cryptanalysis, not an archaeological discovery."

62   "Yes, cryptanalysis," von Ohlmhorst pounced. "The reading of a known language in an unknown form of writing. Ventris' lists were in the known language, Greek. Neither he nor anybody else ever read a word of the Cretan language until the finding of the Greek-Cretan bilingual in 1963, because only with a bilingual text, one language already known, can an unknown ancient language be learned. And what hope, I ask you, have we of finding anything like that here? Martha, you've been working on these Martian texts ever since we landed here—for the

last six months. Tell me, have you found a single word to which you can positively assign a meaning?"

63 "Yes, I think I have one." She was trying hard not to sound too exultant. *"Doma.* It's the name of one of the months of the Martian calendar."

64 "Where did you find that?" von Ohlmhorst asked. "And how did you establish—?"

65 "Here." She picked up the photostat and handed it along the table to him. "I'd call this the title page of a magazine."

66 He was silent for a moment, looking at it. "Yes. I would say so, too. Have you any of the rest of it?"

67 "I'm working on the first page of the first article, listed there. Wait till I see; yes, here's all I found, together, here." She told him where she had gotten it. "I just gathered it up, at the time, and gave it to Geoffrey and Rosita to photostat; this is the first I've really examined it."

68 The old man got to his feet, brushing tobacco ashes from the front of his jacket, and came to where she was sitting, laying the title page on the table and leafing quickly through the stack of photostats.

69 "Yes, and here is the second article, on page eight, and here's the next one." He finished the pile of photostats. "A couple of pages missing at the end of the last article. This is remarkable; surprising that a thing like a magazine would have survived so long."

70 "Well, this silicone stuff the Martians used for paper is pretty durable," Hubert Penrose said. "There doesn't seem to have been any water or any other fluid in it originally, so it wouldn't dry out with time."

71 "Oh, it's not remarkable that the material would have survived. We've found a good many books and papers in excellent condition. But only a really vital culture, an organized culture, will publish magazines, and this civilization had been dying for hundreds of years before the end. It might have been a thousand years before the time they died out completely that such activities as publishing ended."

72 "Well, look where I found it; in a closet in a cellar. Tossed in there and forgotten, and then ignored when they were stripping the building. Things like that happen."

73 Penrose had picked up the title page and was looking at it.

74 "I don't think there's any doubt about this being a magazine, at all." He looked again at the title, his lips moving silently. *"Mastharnorvod Tadavas Sornhulva.* Wonder what it means. But you're right about the date—*Doma* seems to be the name of a month. Yes, you have a word, Dr. Dane."

75 Sid Chamberlain, seeing that something unusual was going on, had come over from the table at which he was working. After examining the

title page and some of the inside pages, he began whispering into the stenophone he had taken from his belt.

76 "Don't try to blow this up to anything big, Sid," she cautioned. "All we have is the name of a month, and Lord only knows how long it'll be till we even find out which month it was."

77 "Well, it's a start, isn't it?" Penrose argued. "Grotefend only had the word for 'king' when he started reading Persian cuneiform."

78 "But I don't have the word for month; just the name of a month. Everybody knew the names of the Persian kings, long before Grotefend."

79 "That's not the story," Chamberlain said. "What the public back on Terra will be interested in is finding out that the Martians published magazines, just like we do. Something familiar; make the Martians seem more real. More human."

80 Three men had come in, and were removing their masks and helmets and oxy-tanks, and peeling out of their quilted coveralls. Two were Space Force lieutenants; the third was a youngish civilian with close-cropped blond hair in a checked woolen shirt. Tony Lattimer and his helpers.

81 "Don't tell me Martha finally got something out of that stuff?" he asked, approaching the table. He might have been commenting on the antics of the village half-wit, from his tone.

82 "Yes; the name of one of the Martian months." Hubert Penrose went on to explain, showing the photostat.

83 Tony Lattimer took it, glanced at it, and dropped it on the table.

84 "Sounds plausible, of course, but just an assumption. That word may not be the name of a month, at all—could mean 'published' or 'authorized' or 'copyrighted' or anything like that. Fact is, I don't think it's more than a wild guess that that thing's anything like a periodical." He dismissed the subject and turned to Penrose. "I picked out the next building to enter; that tall one with the conical thing on top. It ought to be in pretty good shape inside; the conical top wouldn't allow dust to accumulate, and from the outside nothing seems to be caved in or crushed. Ground level's higher than the other one, about the seventh floor. I found a good place and drilled for the shots; tomorrow I'll blast a hole in it, and if you can spare some people to help, we can start exploring it right away."

85 "Yes, of course, Dr. Lattimer. I can spare about a dozen, and I suppose you can find a few civilian volunteers," Penrose told him. "What will you need in the way of equipment?"

86 "Oh, about six demolition-packets; they can all be shot together. And the usual thing in the way of lights, and breaking and digging tools, and climbing equipment in case we run into broken or doubtful stairways. We'll divide into two parties. Nothing ought to be entered for the first

time without a qualified archaeologist along. Three parties, if Martha can tear herself away from this catalogue of systematized incomprehensibilities she's making long enough to do some real work."

87　She felt her chest tighten and her face become stiff. She was pressing her lips together to lock in a furious retort when Hubert Penrose answered for her.

88　"Dr. Dane's been doing as much work, and as important work, as you have," he said brusquely. "More important work, I'd be inclined to say."

89　Von Ohlmhorst was visibly distressed; he glanced once toward Sid Chamberlain, then looked hastily away from him. Afraid of a story of dissension among archaeologists getting out.

90　"Working out a system of pronunciation by which the Martian language could be transliterated was a most important contribution," he said. "And Martha did that almost unassisted."

91　"Unassisted by Dr. Lattimer, anyway," Penrose added. "Captain Field and Lieutenant Koremitsu did some work, and I helped out a little, but nine-tenths of it she did herself."

92　"Purely arbitrary," Lattimer disdained. "Why, we don't even know that the Martians could make the same kind of vocal sounds we do."

93　"Oh, yes, we do," Ivan Fitzgerald contradicted, safe on his own ground. "I haven't seen any actual Martian skulls—these people seem to have been very tidy about disposing of their dead—but from statues and busts and pictures I've seen, I'd say that their vocal organs were identical with our own."

94　"Well, grant that. And grant that it's going to be impressive to rattle off the names of Martian notables whose statues we find, and that if we're ever able to attribute any place-names, they'll sound a lot better than this horse-doctors' Latin the old astronomers splashed all over the map of Mars," Lattimer said. "What I object to is her wasting time on this stuff, of which nobody will ever be able to read a word if she fiddles around with those lists till there's another hundred feet of loess on this city, when there's so much real work to be done and we're as short-handed as we are."

95　That was the first time that had come out in just so many words. She was glad Lattimer had said it and not Selim von Ohlmhorst.

96　"What you mean," she retorted, "is that it doesn't have the publicity value that digging up statues has."

97　For an instant, she could see that the shot had scored. Then Lattimer, with a side glance at Chamberlain, answered:

98　"What I mean is that you're trying to find something that any archaeologist, yourself included, should know doesn't exist. I don't object to your gambling your professional reputation and making a laughingstock of yourself; what I object to is that the blunders of one archaeologist discredit the whole subject in the eyes of the public."

99   That seemed to be what worried Lattimer most. She was framing a reply when the communication-outlet whistled shrilly, and then squawked: "Cocktail time! One hour to dinner; cocktails in the library, Hut Four!"

100   The library, which was also lounge, recreation room, and general gathering-place, was already crowded; most of the crowd was at the long table topped with sheets of glasslike plastic that had been wall panels out of one of the ruined buildings. She poured herself what passed, here, for a martini, and carried it over to where Selim von Ohlmhorst was sitting alone.

101   For a while, they talked about the building they had just finished exploring, then drifted into reminiscences of their work on Terra—von Ohlmhorst's in Asia Minor, with the Hittite Empire, and hers in Pakistan, excavating the cities of the Harappa civilization. They finished their drinks—the ingredients were plentiful; alcohol and flavoring extracts synthesized from Martian vegetation—and von Ohlmhorst took the two glasses to the table for refills.

102   "You know, Martha," he said, when he returned, "Tony was right about one thing. You are gambling your professional standing and reputation. It's against all archaeological experience that a language so completely dead as this one could be deciphered. There was a continuity between all the other ancient languages—by knowing Greek, Champollion learned to read Egyptian; by knowing Egyptian, Hittite was learned. That's why you and your colleagues have never been able to translate the Harappa hieroglyphics; no such continuity exists there. If you insist that this utterly dead language can be read, your reputation will suffer for it."

103   "I heard Colonel Penrose say, once, that an officer who's afraid to risk his military reputation seldom makes much of a reputation. It's the same with us. If we really want to find things out, we have to risk making mistakes. And I'm a lot more interested in finding things out than I am in my reputation."

104   She glanced across the room, to where Tony Lattimer was sitting with Gloria Standish, talking earnestly, while Gloria sipped one of the counterfeit martinis and listened. Gloria was the leading contender for the title of Miss Mars, 1996, if you liked big bosomy blondes, but Tony would have been just as attentive to her if she'd looked like the Wicked Witch in "The Wizard of Oz," because Gloria was the Pan-Federation Telecast System commentator with the expedition.

105   "I know you are," the old Turco-German was saying. "That's why, when they asked me to name another archaeologist for this expedition, I named you."

106   He hadn't named Tony Lattimer; Lattimer had been pushed onto the

expedition by his university. There'd been a lot of high-level string-pulling to that; she wished she knew the whole story. She'd managed to keep clear of universities and university politics; all her digs had been sponsored by nonacademic foundations or art museums.

107   "You have an excellent standing; much better than my own, at your age. That's why it disturbs me to see you jeopardizing it by this insistence that the Martian language can be translated. I can't, really, see how you can hope to succeed."

108   She shrugged and drank some more of her cocktail, then lit another cigarette. It was getting tiresome to try to verbalize something she only felt.

109   "Neither do I, now, but I will. Maybe I'll find something like the picture-books Sachiko was talking about. A child's primer, maybe; surely they had things like that. And if I don't, I'll find something else. We've only been here six months. I can wait the rest of my life, if I have to, but I'll do it sometime."

110   "I can't wait so long," von Ohlmhorst said. "The rest of my life will only be a few years, and when the *Schiaparelli* orbits in, I'll be going back to Terra on the *Cyrano*."

111   "I wish you wouldn't. This is a whole new world of archeology. Literally."

112   "Yes." He finished the cocktail and looked at his pipe as though wondering whether to re-light it so soon before dinner, then put it in his pocket. "A whole new world—but I've grown old, and it isn't for me. I've spent my life studying the Hittites. I can speak the Hittite language, though maybe King Muwatallis wouldn't be able to understand my modern Turkish accent. But the things I'd have to learn, here—chemistry, physics, engineering, how to run analytic tests on steel girders and beryllo-silver alloys and plastics and silicones. I'm more at home with a civilization that rode in chariots and fought with swords and was just learning how to work iron. Mars is for young people. This expedition is a cadre of leadership—not only the Space Force people, who'll be the commanders of the main expedition, but us scientists, too. And I'm just an old cavalry general who can't learn to command tanks and aircraft. You'll have time to learn about Mars. I won't."

113   His reputation as the dean of Hittitologists was solid and secure, too, she added mentally. Then she felt ashamed of the thought. He wasn't to be classed with Tony Lattimer.

114   "All I came for was to get the work started," he was continuing. "The Federation Government felt that an old hand should do that. Well, it's started, now; you and Tony and whoever come out on the *Schiaparelli* must carry it on. You said it, yourself; you have a whole new world. This is only one city, of the last Martian civilization. Behind this, you have the Late Upland Culture, and the Canal Builders, and all the civili-

zations and races and empires before them, clear back to the Martian Stone Age." He hesitated for a moment. "You have no idea what all you have to learn, Martha. This isn't the time to start specializing too narrowly."

115 They all got out of the truck and stretched their legs and looked up the road to the tall building with the queer conical cap askew on its top. The four little figures that had been busy against its wall climbed into the jeep and started back slowly, the smallest of them, Sachiko Koremitsu, paying out an electric cable behind. When it pulled up beside the truck, they climbed out; Sachiko attached the free end of the cable to a nuclear-electric battery. At once, dirty gray smoke and orange dust puffed out from the wall of the building, and, a second later, the multiple explosion banged.

116 She and Tony Lattimer and Major Lindemann climbed onto the truck, leaving the jeep stand by the road. When they reached the building, a satisfying wide breach had been blown in the wall. Lattimer had placed his shots between two of the windows; they were both blown out along with the wall between, and lay unbroken on the ground. Martha remembered the first building they had entered. A Space Force officer had picked up a stone and thrown it at one of the windows, thinking that would be all they'd need to do. It had bounced back. He had drawn his pistol—they'd all carried guns, then, on the principle that what they didn't know about Mars might easily hurt them—and fired four shots. The bullets had ricochetted, screaming thinly; there were four coppery smears of jacket-metal on the window, and a little surface spalling. Somebody tried a rifle; the 4000-f.s. bullet had cracked the glasslike pane without penetrating. An oxyacetylene torch had taken an hour to cut the window out; the lab crew, aboard the ship, were still trying to find out just what the stuff was.

117 Tony Lattimer had gone forward and was sweeping his flashlight back and forth, swearing petulantly, his voice harshened and amplified by his helmet-speaker.

118 "I thought I was blasting into a hallway; this lets us into a room. Careful; there's about a two-foot drop to the floor, and a lot of rubble from the blast just inside."

119 He stepped down through the breach; the others began dragging equipment out of the trucks—shovels and picks and crowbars and sledges, portable floodlights, cameras, sketching materials, an extension ladder, even Alpinists' ropes and crampons and pickaxes. Hubert Penrose was shouldering something that looked like a surrealist machine gun but which was really a nuclear-electric jack-hammer. Martha selected one of the spike-shod mountaineer's ice axes, with which she could dig or chop or poke or pry or help herself over rough footing.

120   The windows, grimed and crusted with fifty millennia of dust, filtered in a dim twilight; even the breach in the wall, in the morning shade, lighted only a small patch of floor. Somebody snapped on a floodlight, aiming it at the ceiling. The big room was empty and bare; dust lay thick on the floor and reddened the once-white walls. It could have been a large office, but there was nothing left in it to indicate its use.

121   "This one's been stripped up to the seventh floor!" Lattimer exclaimed. "Street level'll be cleaned out, completely."

122   "Do for living quarters and shops, then," Lindemann said. "Added to the others, this'll take care of everybody on the *Schiparelli*."

123   "Seem to have been a lot of electric or electronic apparatus over along this wall," one of the Space Force officers commented. "Ten or twelve electric outlets." He brushed the dusty wall with his glove, then scraped on the floor with his foot. "I can see where things were pried loose."

124   The door, one of the double sliding things the Martians had used, was closed. Selim von Ohlmhorst tried it, but it was stuck fast. The metal latch-parts had frozen together, molecule bonding itself to molecule, since the door had last been closed. Hubert Penrose came over with the jack-hammer, fitting a spear-point chisel into place. He set the chisel in the joint between the doors, braced the hammer against his hip, and squeezed the trigger-switch. The hammer banged briefly like the weapon it resembled, and the doors popped a few inches apart, then stuck. Enough dust had worked into the recesses into which it was supposed to slide to block it on both sides.

125   That was old stuff; they ran into that every time they had to force a door, and they were prepared for it. Somebody went outside and brought in a power-jack and finally one of the doors inched back to the door-jamb. That was enough to get the lights and equipment through; they all passed from the room to the hallway beyond. About half the other doors were open; each had a number and a single word, *Darfhulva*, over it.

126   One of the civilian volunteers, a woman professor of natural ecology from Penn State University, was looking up and down the hall.

127   "You know," she said, "I feel at home here. I think this was a college of some sort, and these were classrooms. That word, up there; that was the subject taught, or the department. And those electronic devices, all where the class would face them; audio-visual teaching aids."

128   "A twenty-five-story university?" Lattimer scoffed. "Why, a building like this would handle thirty thousand students."

129   "Maybe there were that many. This was a big city, in its prime," Martha said, moved chiefly by a desire to oppose Lattimer.

130   "Yes, but think of the snafu in the halls, every time they changed classes. It'd take half an hour to get everybody back and forth from one

floor to another." He turned to von Ohlmhorst. "I'm going up above this floor. This place has been looted clean up to here, but there's a chance there may be something above," he said.

131   "I'll stay on this floor, at present," the Turco-German replied. "There will be much coming and going, and dragging things in and out. We should get this completely examined and recorded first. Then Major Lindemann's people can do their worst, here."

132   "Well, if nobody else wants it, I'll take the downstairs," Martha said.

133   "I'll go along with you," Hubert Penrose told her. "If the lower floors have no archaeological value, we'll turn them into living quarters. I like this building; it'll give everybody room to keep out from under everybody else's feet." He looked down the hall. "We ought to find escalators at the middle."

134   The hallway, too, was thick underfoot with dust. Most of the open rooms were empty, but a few contained furniture, including small seat-desks. The original proponent of the university theory pointed these out as just what might be found in classrooms. There were escalators, up and down, on either side of the hall, and more on the intersecting passage to the right.

135   "That's how they handled the students, between classes," Martha commented. "And I'll bet there are more ahead, there."

136   They came to a stop where the hallway ended at a great square central hall. There were elevators, there, on two of the sides, and four escalators, still usable as stairways. But it was the walls, and the paintings on them, that brought them up short and staring.

137   They were clouded with dirt—she was trying to imagine what they must have looked like originally, and at the same time estimating the labor that would be involved in cleaning them—but they were still distinguishable, as was the word, *Darfhulva*, in golden letters above each of the four sides. It was a moment before she realized, from the murals, that she had at last found a meaningful Martian word. They were a vast historical panorama, clockwise around the room. A group of skin-clad savages squatting around a fire. Hunters with bows and spears, carrying the carcass of an animal slightly like a pig. Nomads riding long-legged, graceful mounts like hornless deer. Peasants sowing and reaping; mud-walled hut villages, and cities; processions of priests and warriors; battles with swords and bows, and with cannon and muskets; galleys, and ships with sails, and ships without visible means of propulsion, and aircraft. Changing costumes and weapons and machines and styles of architecture. A richly fertile landscape, gradually merging into barren deserts and bushlands—the time of the great planet-wide drought. The Canal Builders—men with machines recognizable as steam-shovels and

derricks, digging and quarrying and driving across the empty plains with aqueducts. More cities—seaports on the shrinking oceans; dwindling, half-deserted cities; an abandoned city, with four tiny humanoid figures and a thing like a combat-car in the middle of a brush-grown plaza, they and their vehicle dwarfed by the huge lifeless buildings around them. She had not the least doubt; *Darfhulva* was History.

138 "Wonderful!" von Ohlmhorst was saying. "The entire history of this race. Why, if the painter depicted appropriate costumes and weapons and machines for each period, and got the architecture right, we can break the history of this planet into eras and periods and civilizations."

139 "You can assume they're authentic. The faculty of this university would insist on authenticity in the *Darfhulva—History—Department*," she said.

140 "Yes! *Darfhulva*—History! And your magazine was a journal of *Sornhulva*!" Penrose exclaimed. "You have a word, Martha!" It took her an instant to realize that he had called her by her first name, and not Dr. Dane. She wasn't sure if that weren't a bigger triumph than learning a word of the Martian language. Or a more auspicious start. "Alone, I suppose that *hulva* means something like science or knowledge, or study; combined, it would be equivalent to our 'ology. And *darf* would mean something like past, or old times, or human events, or chronicles."

141 "That gives you three words, Martha!" Sachiko jubilated. "You did it."

142 "Let's don't go too fast," Lattimer said, for once not derisively. "I'll admit that *darfhulva* is the Martian word for history as a subject of study; I'll admit that *hulva* is the general word and *darf* modifies it and tells us which subject is meant. But as for assigning specific meanings, we can't do that because we don't know just how the Martians thought, scientifically or otherwise."

143 He stopped short, startled by the blue-white light that blazed as Sid Chamberlain's Kliegettes went on. When the whirring of the camera stopped, it was Chamberlain who was speaking:

144 "This is the biggest thing yet; the whole history of Mars, Stone Age to the end, all on four walls. I'm taking this with the fast shutter, but we'll telecast it in slow motion, from the beginning to the end. Tony, I want you to do the voice for it—running commentary, interpretation of each scene as it's shown. Would you do that?"

145 Would he do that! Martha thought. If he had a tail, he'd be wagging it at the very thought.

146 "Well, there ought to be more murals on the other floors," she said. "Who wants to come downstairs with us?"

147 Sachiko did; immediately, Ivan Fitzgerald volunteered. Sid decided to go upstairs with Tony Lattimer, and Gloria Standish decided to go up-

stairs, too. Most of the party would remain on the seventh floor, to help Selim von Ohlmhorst get it finished. After poking tentatively at the escalator with the spike of her ice axe, Martha led the way downward.

148   The sixth floor was *Darfhulva*, too; military and technological history, from the character of the murals. They looked around the central hall, and went down to the fifth; it was like the floors above except that the big quadrangle was stacked with dusty furniture and boxes. Ivan Fitzgerald, who was carrying the floodlight, swung it slowly around. Here the murals were of heroic-sized Martians, so human in appearance as to seem members of her own race, each holding some object—a book, or a test tube, or some bit of scientific apparatus, and behind them were scenes of laboratories and factories, flame and smoke, lightning-flashes. The word at the top of each of the four walls was one with which she was already familiar—*Sornhulva*.

149   "Hey, Martha; there's that word." Ivan Fitzgerald exclaimed. "The one in the title of your magazine." He looked at the paintings. "Chemistry, or physics."

150   "Both," Hubert Penrose considered. "I don't think the Martians made any sharp distinction between them. See, the old fellow with the scraggly whiskers must be the inventor of the spectroscope; he has one in his hands, and he has a rainbow behind him. And the woman in the blue smock, beside him, worked in organic chemistry; see the diagrams of long-chain molecules behind her. What word would convey the idea of chemistry and physics taken as one subject?"

151   "*Sornhulva*," Sachiko suggested. "If *hulva's* something like science, *sorn* must mean matter, or a substance, or physical object. You were right, all along, Martha. A civilization like this would certainly leave something like this, that would be self-explanatory."

152   "This'll wipe a little more of that superior grin off Tony Lattimer's face," Fitzgerald was saying, as they went down the motionless escalator to the floor below. "Tony wants to be a big shot. When you want to be a big shot, you can't bear the possibility of anybody else being a bigger big shot, and whoever makes a start on reading this language will be the biggest big shot archaeology ever saw."

153   That was true. She hadn't thought of it, in that way, before, and now she tried not to think about it. She didn't want to be a big shot. She wanted to be able to read the Martian language, and find things out about the Martians.

154   Two escalators down, they came out on a mezzanine around a wide central hall on the street level, the floor forty feet below them and the ceiling forty feet above. Their lights picked out object after object below—a huge group of sculptured figures in the middle; some kind of a motor vehicle jacked up on trestles for repairs; things that looked like

machine guns and auto-cannon; long tables, top littered with a dust-covered miscellany; machinery; boxes and crates and containers.

155 They made their way down and walked among the clutter, missing a hundred things for every one they saw, until they found an escalator to the basement. There were three basements, one under another, until at last they stood at the bottom of the last escalator, on a bare concrete floor, swinging the portable floodlight over stacks of boxes and barrels and drums, and heaps of powdery dust. The boxes were plastic—nobody had ever found anything made of wood in the city—and the barrels and drums were of metal or glass or some glasslike substance. They were outwardly intact. The powdery heaps might have been anything organic, or anything containing fluid. Down here, where wind and dust could not reach, evaporation had been the only force of destruction after the minute life that caused putrefaction had vanished.

156 They found refrigeration rooms, too, and using Martha's ice axe and the pistol-like vibratool Sachiko carried on her belt, they pounded and pried one open, to find desiccated piles of what had been vegetables, and leathery chunks of meat. Samples of that stuff, rocketed up to the ship, would give a reliable estimate, by radio-carbon dating, of how long ago this building had been occupied. The refrigeration unit, radically different from anything their own culture had produced, had been electrically powered. Sachiko and Penrose, poking into it, found the switches still on; the machine had only ceased to function when the power-source, whatever that had been, had failed.

157 The middle basement had also been used, at least toward the end, for storage; it was cut in half by a partition pierced by but one door. They took half an hour to force this, and were on the point of sending above for heavy equipment when it yielded enough for them to squeeze through. Fitzgerald, in the lead with the light, stopped short, looked around, and then gave a groan that came through his helmet-speaker like a foghorn.

158 "Oh, no! *No!*"

159 "What's the matter, Ivan?" Sachiko, entering behind him, asked anxiously.

160 He stepped aside. "Look at it, Sachi! Are we going to have to do all that?"

161 Martha crowded through behind her friend and looked around, then stood motionless, dizzy with excitement. Books. Case on case of books, half an acre of cases, fifteen feet to the ceiling. Fitzgerald, and Penrose, who had pushed in behind her, were talking in rapid excitement; she only heard the sound of their voices, not their words. This must be the main stacks of the university library—the entire literature of the vanished race of Mars. In the center, down an aisle between the cases, she

could see the hollow square of the librarian's desk, and stairs and dumb-waiter to the floor above.

162   She realized that she was walking forward, with the others, toward this. Sachiko was saying: "I'm the lightest; let me go first." She must be talking about the spidery metal stairs.

163   "I'd say they were safe," Penrose answered. "The trouble we've had with doors around here shows that the metal hasn't deteriorated."

164   In the end, the Japanese girl led the way, more catlike than ever in her caution. The stairs were quite sound, in spite of their fragile appearance, and they all followed her. The floor above was a duplicate of the room they had entered, and seemed to contain about as many books. Rather than waste time forcing the door here, they returned to the middle base-ment and came up by the escalator down which they had originally de-scended.

165   The upper basement contained kitchens—electric stoves, some with pots and pans still on them—and a big room that must have been, origi-nally, the students' dining room, though when last used it had been a workshop. As they expected, the library reading room was on the street-level floor, directly above the stacks. It seemed to have been converted into a sort of common living room for the building's last occupants. An adjoining auditorium had been made into a chemical works; there were vats and distillation apparatus, and a metal fractionating tower that ex-tended through a hole knocked in the ceiling seventy feet above. A good deal of plastic furniture of the sort they had been finding everywhere in the city was stacked about, some of it broken up, apparently for repro-cessing. The other rooms on the street floor seemed also to have been devoted to manufacturing and repair work; a considerable industry, along a number of lines, must have been carried on here for a long time after the university had ceased to function as such.

166   On the second floor, they found a museum; many of the exhibits re-mained, tantalizingly half-visible in grimed glass cases. There had been administrative offices there, too. The doors of most of them were closed, and they did not waste time trying to force them, but those that were open had been turned into living quarters. They made notes, and rough floor plans, to guide them in future more thorough examination; it was almost noon before they had worked their way back to the seventh floor.

167   Selim von Ohlmhorst was in a room on the north side of the building, sketching the position of things before examining them and collecting them for removal. He had the floor checkerboarded with a grid of chalked lines, each numbered.

168   "We have everything on this floor photographed," he said. "I have three gangs—all the floodlights I have—sketching and making measure-ments. At the rate we're going, with time out for lunch, we'll be finished by the middle of the afternoon."

169 "You're been working fast. Evidently you aren't being high-church about a 'qualified archaeologist' entering rooms first," Penrose commented.

170 "Ach, childishness!" the old man exclaimed impatiently. "These officers of yours aren't fools. All of them have been to Intelligence School and Criminal Investigation School. Some of the most careful amateur archaeologists I ever knew were retired soldiers or policemen. But there isn't much work to be done. Most of the rooms are either empty or like this one—a few bits of furniture and broken trash and scraps of paper. Did you find anything down on the lower floors?"

171 "Well, yes," Penrose said, a hint of mirth in his voice. "What would you say, Martha?"

172 She started to tell Selim. The others, unable to restrain their excitement, broke in with interruptions. Von Ohlmhorst was staring in incredulous amazement.

173 "But this floor was looted almost clean, and the buildings we've entered before were all looted from the street level up," he said, at length.

174 "The people who looted this one lived here," Penrose replied. "They had electric power to the last; we found refrigerators full of food, and stoves with the dinner still on them. They must have used the elevators to haul things down from the upper floor. The whole first floor was converted into workshops and laboratories. I think that this place must have been something like a monastery in the Dark Ages in Europe, or what such a monastery would have been like if the Dark Ages had followed the fall of a highly developed scientific civilization. For one thing, we found a lot of machine guns and light auto-cannon on the street level, and all the doors were barricaded. The people here were trying to keep a civilization running after the rest of the planet had gone back to barbarism; I suppose they'd have to fight off raids by the barbarians now and then."

175 "You're not going to insist on making this building into expedition quarters, I hope, colonel?" von Ohlmhorst asked anxiously.

176 "Oh, no! This place is an archaeological treasure-house. More than that; from what I saw, our technicians can learn a lot, here. But you'd better get this floor cleaned up as soon as you can, though. I'll have the subsurface part, from the sixth floor down, airsealed. Then we'll put in oxygen generators and power units, and get a couple of elevators into service. For the floors above, we can use temporary airsealing floor by floor, and portable equipment; when we have things atmosphered and lighted and heated, you and Martha and Tony Lattimer can go to work systematically and in comfort, and I'll give you all the help I can spare from the other work. This is one of the biggest things we've found yet."

177 Tony Lattimer and his companions came down to the seventh floor a little later.

178 "I don't get this, at all," he began, as soon as he joined them. "This building wasn't stripped the way the others were. Always, the procedure seems to have been to strip from the bottom up, but they seem to have stripped the top floors first, here. All but the very top. I found out what that conical thing is, by the way. It's a wind-rotor, and under it there's an electric generator. This building generated its own power."

179 "What sort of condition are the generators in?" Penrose asked.

180 "Well, everything's full of dust that blew in under the rotor, of course, but it looks to be in pretty good shape. Hey, I'll bet that's it! They had power, so they used the elevators to haul stuff down. That's just what they did. Some of the floors above here don't seem to have been touched, though." He paused momentarily; back of his oxy-mask, he seemed to be grinning. "I don't know that I ought to mention this in front of Martha, but two floors above we hit a room—it must have been the reference library for one of the departments—that had close to five hundred books in it."

181 The noise that interrupted him, like the squawking of a Brobdingnagian parrot, was only Ivan Fitzgerald laughing through his helmet-speaker.

182 Lunch at the huts was a hasty meal, with a gabble of full-mouthed and excited talking. Hubert Penrose and his chief subordinates snatched their food in a huddled consultation at one end of the table; in the afternoon, work was suspended on everything else and the fifty-odd men and women of the expedition concentrated their efforts on the university. By the middle of the afternoon, the seventh floor had been completely examined, photographed and sketched, and the murals in the square central hall covered with protective tarpaulins, and Laurent Gicquel and his airsealing crew had moved in and were at work. It had been decided to seal the central hall at the entrances. It took the French-Canadian engineer most of the afternoon to find all the ventilation-ducts and plug them. An elevator-shaft on the north side was found reaching clear to the twenty-fifth floor; this would give access to the top of the building; another shaft, from the center, would take care of the floors below. Nobody seemed willing to trust the ancient elevators, themselves; it was the next evening before a couple of cars and the necessary machinery could be fabricated in the machine shops aboard the ship and sent down by landing-rocket. By that time, the airsealing was finished, the nuclear-electric energy-converters were in place, and the oxygen generators set up.

183 Martha was in the lower basement, an hour or so before lunch the day after, when a couple of Space Force officers came out of the elevator, bringing extra lights with them. She was still using oxygen-equipment; it was a moment before she realized that the newcomers had no masks,

and that one of them was smoking. She took off her own helmet-speaker, throat-mike and mask and unslung her tank-pack, breathing cautiously. The air was chilly, and musty-acrid with the odor of antiquity—the first Martian odor she had smelled—but when she lit a cigarette, the lighter flamed clear and steady and the tobacco caught and burned evenly.

184   The archaeologists, many of the other civilian scientists, a few of the Space Force officers and the two news-correspondents, Sid Chamberlain and Gloria Standish, moved in that evening, setting up cots in vacant rooms. They installed electric stoves and a refrigerator in the old library reading room, and put in a bar and lunch counter. For a few days, the place was full of noise and activity, then, gradually, the Space Force people and all but a few of the civilians returned to their own work. There was still the business of airsealing the more habitable of the buildings already explored, and fitting them up in readiness for the arrival, in a year and a half, of the five hundred members of the main expedition. There was work to be done enlarging the landing field for the ship's rocket craft, and building new chemical-fuel tanks.

185   There was the work of getting the city's ancient reservoirs cleared of silt before the next spring thaw brought more water down the underground aqueducts everybody called canals in mistranslation of Schiaparelli's Italian word, though this was proving considerably easier than anticipated. The ancient Canal Builders must have anticipated a time when their descendants would no longer be capable of maintenance work, and had prepared against it. By the day after the university had been made completely habitable, the actual work there was being done by Selim, Tony Lattimer and herself, with half a dozen Space Force officers, mostly girls, and four or five civilians, helping.

186   They worked up from the bottom, dividing the floor-surfaces into numbered squares, measuring and listing and sketching and photographing. They packaged samples of organic matter and sent them up to the ship for carbon-14 dating and analysis; they opened cans and jars and bottles, and found that everything fluid in them had evaporated, through the porosity of glass and metal and plastic if there were no other way. Wherever they looked, they found evidence of activity suddenly suspended and never resumed. A vise with a bar of metal in it, half cut through and the hacksaw beside it. Pots and pans with hardened remains of food in them; a leathery cut of meat on a table, with the knife ready at hand. Toilet articles on washstands; unmade beds, the bedding ready to crumble at a touch but still retaining the impress of the sleeper's body; papers and writing materials on desks, as though the writer had gotten up, meaning to return and finish in a fifty-thousand-year-ago moment.

187   It worried her. Irrationally, she began to feel that the Martians had

never left this place; that they were still around her, watching disapprovingly every time she picked up something they had laid down. They haunted her dreams, now, instead of their enigmatic writing. At first, everybody who had moved into the university had taken a separate room, happy to escape the crowding and lack of privacy of the huts. After a few nights, she was glad when Gloria Standish moved in with her, and accepted the newswoman's excuse that she felt lonely without somebody to talk to before falling asleep. Sachiko Koremitsu joined them the next evening, and before going to bed, the girl officer cleaned and oiled her pistol, remarking that she was afraid some rust may have gotten into it.

188   The others felt it, too. Selim von Ohlmhorst developed the habit of turning quickly and looking behind him, as though trying to surprise somebody or something that was stalking him. Tony Lattimer, having a drink at the bar that had been improvised from the librarian's desk in the reading room, set down his glass and swore.

189   "You know what this place is? It's an archaeological *Marie Celeste!*" he declared. "It was occupied right up to the end—we've all seen the shifts these people used to keep a civilization going here—but what was the end? What happened to them? Where did they go?"

190   "You didn't expect them to be waiting out front, with a red carpet and a big banner, *Welcome Terrans,* did you, Tony?" Gloria Standish asked.

191   "No, of course not; they've all been dead for fifty thousand years. But if they were the last of the Martians, why haven't we found their bones, at least? Who buried them, after they were dead?" He looked at the glass, a bubble-thin goblet, found, with hundreds of others like it, in a closet above, as though debating with himself whether to have another drink. Then he voted in the affirmative and reached for the cocktail pitcher. "And every door on the old ground level is either barred or barricaded from the inside. How did they get out? And why did they leave?"

192   The next day, at lunch, Sachiko Koremitsu had the answer to the second question. Four or five electrical engineers had come down by rocket from the ship, and she had been spending the morning with them, in oxy-masks, at the top of the building.

193   "Tony, I thought you said those generators were in good shape," she began, catching sight of Lattimer. "They aren't. They're in the most unholy mess I ever saw. What happened, up there, was that the supports of the wind-rotor gave way, and weight snapped the main shaft, and smashed everything under it."

194   "Well, after fifty thousand years, you can expect something like that," Lattimer retorted. "When an archaeologist says something's in good shape, he doesn't necessarily mean it'll start as soon as you shove a switch in."

195   "You didn't notice that it happened when the power was on, did you," one of the engineers asked, nettled at Lattimer's tone. "Well, it was.

Everything's burned out or shorted or fused together; I saw one busbar eight inches across melted clean in two. It's a pity we didn't find things in good shape, even archaeologically speaking. I saw a lot of interesting things, things in advance of what we're using now. But it'll take a couple of years to get everything sorted out and figure what it looked like originally."

196 "Did it look as though anybody'd made any attempt to fix it?" Martha asked.

197 Sachiko shook her head. "They must have taken one look at it and given up. I don't believe there would have been any possible way to repair anything."

198 "Well, that explains why they left. They needed electricity for lighting, and heating, and all their industrial equipment was electrical. They had a good life, here, with power; without it, this place wouldn't have been habitable."

199 "Then why did they barricade everything from the inside, and how did they get out?" Lattimer wanted to know.

200 "To keep other people from breaking in and looting. Last man out probably barred the last door and slid down a rope from upstairs," von Ohlmhorst suggested. "This Houdini-trick doesn't worry me too much. We'll find out eventually."

201 "Yes, about the time Martha starts reading Martian," Lattimer scoffed.

202 "That may be just when we'll find out," von Ohlmhorst replied seriously. "It wouldn't surprise me if they left something in writing when they evacuated this place."

203 "Are you really beginning to treat this pipe dream of hers as a serious possibility, Selim?" Lattimer demanded. "I know, it would be a wonderful thing, but wonderful things don't happen just because they're wonderful. Only because they're possible, and this isn't. Let me quote that distinguished Hittitologist, Johannes Friedrich: 'Nothing can be translated out of nothing.' Or that later but not less distinguished Hittitologist, Selim von Ohlmhorst: 'Where are you going to get your bilingual?' "

204 "Friedrich lived to see the Hittite language deciphered and read," von Ohlmhorst reminded him.

205 "Yes, when they found Hittite-Assyrian bilinguals." Lattimer measured a spoonful of coffee-powder into his cup and added hot water. "Martha, you ought to know, better than anybody, how little chance you have. You've been working for years in the Indus Valley; how many words of Harappa have you or anybody else ever been able to read?"

206 "We never found a university, with a half-million-volume library, at Harappa or Mohenjo-Daro."

207 "And, the first day we entered this building, we established meaning for several words," Selim von Ohlmhorst added.

208 "And you've never found another meaningful word since," Lattimer added. "And you're only sure of general meaning, not specific meaning of word-elements, and you have a dozen different interpretations for each word."

209 "We made a start," von Ohlmhorst maintained. "We have Grotefend's word for 'king.' But I'm going to be able to read some of those books, over there, if it takes me the rest of my life here. It probably will, anyhow."

210 "You mean you've changed your mind about going home on the *Cyrano*?" Martha asked. "You'll stay on here?"

211 The old man nodded. "I can't leave this. There's too much to discover. The old dog will have to learn a lot of new tricks, but this is where my work will be, from now on."

212 Lattimer was shocked. "You're nuts!" he cried. "You mean you're going to throw away everything you've accomplished in Hittitology and start all over again here on Mars? Martha, if you've talked him into his crazy decision, you're a criminal!"

213 "Nobody talked me into anything," von Ohlmhorst said roughly. "And as for throwing away what I've accomplished in Hittitology, I don't know what the devil you're talking about. Everything I know about the Hittite Empire is published and available to anybody. Hittitology's like Egyptology; it's stopped being research and archaeology and become scholarship and history. And I'm not a scholar or a historian; I'm a pick-and-shovel field archaeologist—a highly skilled and specialized grave-robber and junk-picker—and there's more pick-and-shovel work on this planet than I could do in a hundred lifetimes. This is something new; I was a fool to think I could turn my back on it and go back to scribbling footnotes about Hittite kings."

214 "You could have anything you wanted, in Hittitology. There are a dozen universities that'd sooner have you than a winning football team. But no! You have to be the top man in Martiology, too. You can't leave that for anybody else—" Lattimer shoved his chair back and got to his feet, leaving the table with an oath that was almost a sob of exasperation.

215 Maybe his feelings were too much for him. Maybe he realized, as Martha did, what he had betrayed. She sat, avoiding the eyes of the others, looking at the ceiling, as embarrassed as though Lattimer had flung something dirty on the table in front of them. Tony Lattimer had, desperately, wanted Selim to go home on the *Cyrano*. Martiology was a new field; if Selim entered it, he would bring with him the reputation he had already built in Hittitology, automatically stepping into the leading role that Lattimer had coveted for himself. Ivan Fitzgerald's words echoed back to her—when you want to be a big shot, you can't bear the possibility of anybody else being a bigger big shot. His derision of her

own efforts became comprehensible, too. It wasn't that he was convinced that she would never learn to read the Martian language. He had
been afraid that she would.

216   Ivan Fitzgerald finally isolated the germ that had caused the Finchly
girl's undiagnosed illness. Shortly afterward, the malady turned into a
mild fever, from which she recovered. Nobody else seemed to have
caught it. Fitzgerald was still trying to find out how the germ had been
transmitted.

217   They found a globe of Mars, made when the city has been a seaport.
They located the city, and learned that its name had been Kukan—or
something with a similar vowel-consonant ratio. Immediately, Sid
Chamberlain and Gloria Standish began giving their telecasts a Kukan
dateline, and Hubert Penrose used the name in his official reports. They
also found a Martian calendar; the year had been divided into ten more
or less equal months, and one of them had been Doma. Another month
was Nor, and that was a part of the name of the scientific journal Martha had found.

218   Bill Chandler, the zoologist, had been going deeper and deeper into the
old sea bottom of Syrtis. Four hundred miles from Kukan, and at fifteen
thousand feet lower altitude, he shot a bird. At least, it was a something
with wings and what were almost but not quite feathers, though it was
more reptilian than avian in general characteristics. He and Ivan Fitzgerald skinned and mounted it, and then dissected the carcass almost tissue
by tissue. About seven-eighths of its body capacity was lungs; it certainly breathed air containing at least half enough oxygen to support human life, or five times as much as the air around Kukan.

219   That took the center of interest away from archaeology, and started a
new burst of activity. All the expedition's aircraft—four jetticopters and
three wingless airdyne reconnaissance fighters—were thrown into intensified exploration of the lower sea bottoms, and the bio-science boys
and girls were wild with excitement and making new discoveries on
each flight.

220   The university was left to Selim and Martha and Tony Lattimer, the
latter keeping to himself while she and the old Turco-German worked
together. The civilian specialists in other fields, and the Space Force
people who had been holding tape lines and making sketches and snap-
ping cameras, were all flying to lower Syrtis to find out how much oxygen there was and what kind of life it supported.

221   Sometimes Sachiko dropped in; most of the time she was busy helping Ivan Fitzgerald dissect specimens. They had four or five species of
what might loosely be called birds, and something that could easily be
classed as a reptile, and a carnivorous mammal the size of a cat with
birdlike claws, and a herbivore almost identical with the piglike thing

in the big *Darfhulva* mural, and another like a gazelle with a single horn in the middle of its forehead.

222 The high point came when one party, at thirty thousand feet below the level of Kukan, found breathable air. One of them had a mild attack of *sorroche* and had to be flown back for treatment in a hurry, but the others showed no ill effects.

223 The daily newscasts from Terra showed a corresponding shift in interest at home. The discovery of the university had focused attention on the dead past of Mars; now the public was interested in Mars as a possible home for humanity. It was Tony Lattimer who brought archaeology back into the activities of the expedition and the news at home.

224 Martha and Selim were working in the museum on the second floor, scrubbing the grime from the glass cases, noting contents, and grease-penciling numbers; Lattimer and a couple of Space Force officers were going through what had been the administrative offices on the other side. It was one of these, a young second lieutenant, who came hurrying in from the mezzanine, almost bursting with excitement.

225 "Hey, Martha! Dr. von Ohlmhorst!" he was shouting. "Where are you? Tony's found the Martians!"

226 Selim dropped his rag back in the bucket; she laid her clipboard on top of the case beside her.

227 "Where?" they asked together.

228 "Over on the north side." The lieutenant took hold of himself and spoke more deliberately. "Little room, back of one of the old faculty offices—conference room. It was locked from the inside, and we had to burn it down with a torch. That's where they are. Eighteen of them, around a long table—"

229 Gloria Standish, who had dropped in for lunch, was on the mezzanine, fairly screaming into a radio-phone extension:

230 ". . . Dozen and a half of them! Well, of course they're dead. What a question! They look like skeletons covered with leather. No, I do not know what they died of. Well, forget it; I don't care if Bill Chandler's found a three-headed hippopotamus. Sid, don't you get it? We've found the *Martians!*"

231 She slammed the phone back on its hook, rushing away ahead of them.

232 Martha remembered the closed door; on the first survey, they hadn't attempted opening it. Now it was burned away at both sides and lay, still hot along the edges, on the floor of the big office room in front. A floodlight was on in the room inside, and Lattimer was going around looking at things while a Space Force officer stood by the door. The center of the room was filled by a long table; in armchairs around it sat the eighteen men and women who had occupied the room for the last fifty

millennia. There were bottles and glasses on the table in front of them, and, had she seen them in a dimmer light, she would have thought that they were merely dozing over their drinks. One had a knee hooked over his chair-arm and was curled in foetus-like sleep. Another had fallen forward onto the table, arms extended, the emerald set of a ring twinkling dully on one finger. Skeletons covered with leather, Gloria Standish had called them, and so they were—faces like skulls, arms and legs like sticks, the flesh shrunken onto the bone under it.

233 "Isn't this something!" Lattimer was exulting. "Mass suicide, that's what it was. Notice what's in the corners?"

234 Braziers, made of perforated two-gallon-odd metal cans, the white walls smudged with smoke above them. Von Ohlmhorst had noticed them at once, and was poking into one of them with his flashlight.

235 "Yes, charcoal. I noticed a quantity of it around a couple of handforges in the shop on the first floor. That's why you had so much trouble breaking in; they'd sealed the room on the inside." He straightened and went around the room, until he found a ventilator, and peered into it. "Stuffed with rags. They must have been all that were left, here. Their power was gone, and they were old and tired, and all around them their world was dying. So they just came in here and lit the charcoal, and sat drinking together till they all fell asleep. Well, we know what became of them, now, anyhow."

236 Sid and Gloria made the most of it. The Terran public wanted to hear about Martians, and if live Martians couldn't be found, a room full of dead ones was the next best thing. Maybe an even better thing; it had been only sixty-odd years since the Orson Welles invasion-scare. Tony Lattimer, the discoverer, was beginning to cash in on his attentions to Gloria and his ingratiation with Sid; he was always either making voice-and-image talks for telecast or listening to the news from the home planet. Without question, he had become, overnight, the most widely known archaeologist in history.

237 "Not that I'm interested in all this, for myself," he disclaimed, after listening to the telecast from Terra two days after his discovery. "But this is going to be a big thing for Martian archaeology. Bring it to the public attention; dramatize it. Selim, can you remember when Lord Carnarvon and Howard Carter found the tomb of Tutankhamen?"

238 "In 1923? I was two years old, then," von Ohlmhorst chuckled. "I really don't know how much that publicity ever did for Egyptology. Oh, the museums did devote more space to Egyptian exhibits, and after a museum department head gets a few extra showcases, you know how hard it is to make him give them up. And, for a while, it was easier to get financial support for new excavations. But I don't know how much good all this public excitement really does, in the long run."

239 "Well, I think one of us should go back on the *Cyrano*, when the *Schi-*

aparelli orbits in," Lattimer said. "I'd hoped it would be you; your voice would carry the most weight. But I think it's important that one of us go back, to present the story of our work, and what we have accomplished and what we hope to accomplish, to the public and to the universities and the learned societies, and to the Federation Government. There will be a great deal of work that will have to be done. We must not allow the other scientific fields and the so-called practical interests to monopolize public and academic support. So, I believe I shall go back at least for a while, and see what I can do—"

240 Lectures. The organization of a Society of Martian Archaeology, with Anthony Lattimer, Ph.D., the logical candidate for the chair. Degrees, honors; the deference of the learned, and the adulation of the lay public. Positions, with impressive titles and salaries. Sweet are the uses of publicity.

241 She crushed out her cigarette and got to her feet. "Well, I still have the final lists of what we found in *Halvhulva*—Biology—Department to check over. I'm starting on *Sornhulva* tomorrow, and I want that stuff in shape for expert evaluation."

242 That was the sort of thing Tony Lattimer wanted to get away from, the detail-work and the drudgery. Let the infantry do the slogging through the mud; the brass-hats got the medals.

243 She was halfway through the fifth floor, a week later, and was having midday lunch in the reading room on the first floor when Hubert Penrose came over and sat down beside her, asking her what she was doing. She told him.

244 "I wonder if you could find me a couple of men, for an hour or so," she added. "I'm stopped by a couple of jammed doors at the central hall. Lecture room and library, if the layout of that floor's anything like the ones below it."

245 "Yes. I'm a pretty fair door-buster, myself." He looked around the room. "There's Jeff Miles; he isn't doing much of anything. And we'll put Sid Chamberlain to work, for a change, too. The four of us ought to get your doors open." He called to Chamberlain, who was carrying his tray over to the dishwasher. "Oh, Sid; you doing anything for the next hour or so?"

246 "I was going up to the fourth floor, to see what Tony's doing."

247 "Forget it. Tony's bagged his season limit of Martians. I'm going to help Martha bust in a couple of doors; we'll probably find a whole cemetery full of Martians."

248 Chamberlain shrugged. "Why not. A jammed door can have anything back of it, and I know what Tony's doing—just routine stuff."

249 Jeff Miles, the Space Force captain, came over, accompanied by one of the lab-crew from the ship who had come down on the rocket the day before.

250 "This ought to be up your alley, Mort," he was saying to his companion. "Chemistry and Physics Department. Want to come along?"

251 The lab man, Mort Tranter, was willing. Seeing the sights was what he'd come down from the ship for. She finished her coffee and cigarette, and they went out into the hall together, gathered equipment and rode the elevator to the fifth floor.

252 The lecture hall door was the nearest; they attacked it first. With proper equipment and help, it was no problem and in ten minutes they had it open wide enough to squeeze through with the floodlights. The room inside was quite empty, and, like most of the rooms behind closed doors, comparatively free from dust. The students, it appeared, had sat with their backs to the door, facing a low platform, but their seats and the lecturer's table and equipment had been removed. The two side walls bore inscriptions: on the right, a pattern of concentric circles which she recognized as a diagram of atomic structure, and on the left a complicated table of numbers and words, in two columns. Tranter was pointing at the diagram on the right.

253 "They got as far as the Bohr atom, anyhow," he said. "Well, not quite. They knew about electron shells, but they have the nucleus pictured as a solid mass. No indication of proton-and-neutron structure. I'll bet, when you come to translate their scientific books, you'll find that they taught that the atom was the ultimate and indivisible particle. That explains why you people never found any evidence that the Martians used nuclear energy."

254 "That's a uranium atom," Captain Miles mentioned.

255 "It is?" Sid Chamberlain asked, excitedly. "Then they did know about atomic energy. Just because we haven't found any pictures of A-bomb mushrooms doesn't mean—"

256 She turned to look at the other wall. Sid's signal reactions were getting away from him again; uranium meant nuclear power to him, and the two words were interchangeable. As she studied the arrangement of the numbers and words, she could hear Tranter saying:

257 "Nuts, Sid. We knew about uranium a long time before anybody found out what could be done with it. Uranium was discovered on Terra in 1789, by Klaproth."

258 There was something familiar about the table on the left wall. She tried to remember what she had been taught in school about physics, and what she had picked up by accident afterward. The second column was a continuation of the first: there were forty-six items in each, each item numbered consecutively—

259 "Probably used uranium because it's the largest of the natural atoms," Penrose was saying. "The fact that there's nothing beyond it there shows that they hadn't created any of the transuranics. A student could go to that thing and point out the outer electron of any of the ninety-two elements."

260   Ninety-two! That was it: there were ninety-two items in the table on the left wall! Hydrogen was Number One, she knew; One, *Sarfaldsorn*. Helium was Two; that was *Tirfaldsorn*. She couldn't remember which element came next, but in Martian it was *Sarfalddavas*. *Sorn* must mean matter, or substance, then. And *davas;* she was trying to think of what it could be. She turned quickly to the others, catching hold of Hubert Penrose's arm with one hand and waving her clipboard with the other.

261   "Look at this thing, over here," she was clamoring excitedly. "Tell me what you think it is. Could it be a table of the elements?"

262   They all turned to look. Mort Tranter stared at it for a moment.

263   "Could be. If I only knew what those squiggles meant—"

264   That was right; he'd spent his time aboard the ship.

265   "If you could read the numbers, would that help?" she asked, beginning to set down the Arabic digits and their Martian equivalents. "It's decimal system, the same as we use."

266   "Sure. If that's a table of elements, all I'd need would be the numbers. Thanks," he added as she tore off the sheet and gave it to him.

267   Penrose knew the numbers, and was ahead of him. "Ninety-two items, numbered consecutively. The first number would be the atomic number. Then a single word, the name of the element. Then the atomic weight—"

268   She began reading off the names of the elements. "I know hydrogen and helium; what's *tirfalddavas*, the third one?"

269   "Lithium," Tranter said. "The atomic weights aren't run out past the decimal point. Hydrogen's one plus, if that double-hook dingus is a plus sign; Helium's four-plus, that's right. And lithium's given as seven, that isn't right. It's six-point-nine-four-oh. Or is that thing a Martian minus sign?"

270   "Of course! Look! A plus sign is a hook, to hang things together; a minus sign is a knife, to cut something off from something—see, the little loop is the handle and the long pointed loop is the blade. Stylized, of course, but that's what it is. And the fourth element, *kiradavas;* what's that?"

271   "Beryllium. Atomic weight given as nine-and-a-hook; actually it's nine-point-oh-two."

272   Sid Chamberlain had been disgruntled because he couldn't get a story about the Martians having developed atomic energy. It took him a few minutes to understand the newest development, but finally it dawned on him.

273   "Hey! You're reading that!" he cried. "You're reading Martian!"

274   "That's right," Penrose told him. "Just reading it right off. I don't get the two items after the atomic weight, though. They look like months of the Martian calendar. What ought they to be, Mort?"

275 Tranter hesitated. "Well, the next information after the atomic weight ought to be the period and group numbers. But those are words."

276 "What would the numbers be for the first one, hydrogen?"

277 "Period One, Group One. One electron shell, one electron in the outer shell," Tranter told her. "Helium's period one, too, but it has the outer—only—electron shell full, so it's in the group of inert elements."

278 "*Trav, Trav. Trav*'s the first month of the year. And helium's *Trav, Yenth; Yenth* is the eighth month."

279 "The inert elements could be called Group Eight, yes. And the third element, lithium, is Period Two, Group One. That check?"

280 "It certainly does, *Sanv, Trav; Sanv*'s the second month. What's the first element in Period Three?"

281 "Sodium, Number Eleven."

282 "That's right; it's *Krav, Trav*. Why, the names of the months are simply numbers, one to ten, spelled out."

283 "*Doma*'s the fifth month. That was your first Martian word, Martha," Penrose told her. "The word for five. And if *davas* is the word for metal, and *sornhulva* is chemistry and/or physics, I'll bet *Tadavas Sornhulva* is literally translated as: 'Of-Metal Matter-Knowledge.' Metallurgy, in other words. I wonder what *Mastharnorvod* means." It surprised her that, after so long and with so much happening in the meantime, he could remember that. "Something like 'Journal,' or 'Review,' or maybe 'Quarterly.' "

284 "We'll work that out, too," she said confidently. After this, nothing seemed impossible. "Maybe we can find—" Then she stopped short. "You said 'Quarterly.' I think it was 'Monthly,' instead. It was dated for a specific month, the fifth one. And if *nor* is ten, *Mastharnorvod* could be 'Year-Tenth.' And I'll bet we'll find that *masthar* is the word for year." She looked at the table on the wall again. "Well, let's get all these words down, with translations for as many as we can."

285 "Let's take a break for a minute," Penrose suggested, getting out his cigarettes. "And then, let's do this in comfort. Jeff, suppose you and Sid go across the hall and see what you find in the other room in the way of a desk or something like that, and a few chairs. There'll be a lot of work to do on this."

286 Sid Chamberlain had been squirming as though he were afflicted with ants, trying to contain himself. Now he let go with an excited jabber.

287 "This is really it! *The* it, not just it-of-the-week, like finding the reservoirs or those statues or this building, or even the animals and the dead Martians! Wait till Selim and Tony see this! Wait till Tony sees it; I want to see his face! And when I get this on telecast, all Terra's going to go nuts about it!" He turned to Captain Miles. "Jeff, suppose you take a look at that other door, while I find somebody to send to tell Selim and Tony. And Gloria; wait till she sees this—"

288 "Take it easy, Sid," Martha cautioned. "You'd better let me have a look at your script, before you go too far overboard on the telecast. This is just a beginning; it'll take years and years before we're able to read any of those books downstairs."

289 "It'll go faster than you think, Martha," Hubert Penrose told her. "We'll all work on it, and we'll teleprint material to Terra, and people there will work on it. We'll send them everything we can . . . everything we work out, and copies of books, and copies of your word-lists—"

290 And there would be other tables—astronomical tables, tables in physics and mechanics, for instance—in which words and numbers were equivalent. The library stacks, below, would be full of them. Transliterate them into Roman alphabet spellings and Arabic numerals, and somewhere, somebody would spot each numerical significance, as Hubert Penrose and Mort Tranter and she had done with the table of elements. And pick out all the chemistry textbooks in the library; new words would take on meaning from contexts in which the names of elements appeared. She'd have to start studying chemistry and physics, herself—

291 Sachiko Koremitsu peeped in through the door, then stepped inside.

292 "Is there anything I can do—?" she began. "What's happened? Something important?"

293 "Important?" Sid Chamberlain exploded. "Look at that, Sachi! We're reading it! Martha's found out how to read Martian!" He grabbed Captain Miles by the arm. "Come on, Jeff; let's go. I want to call the others—" He was still babbling as he hurried from the room.

294 Sachi looked at the inscription. "Is it true?" she asked, and then, before Martha could more than begin to explain, flung her arms around her. "Oh, it really is! You are reading it! I'm so happy!"

295 She had to start explaining again when Selim von Ohlmhorst entered. This time, she was able to finish.

296 "But, Martha, can you be really sure? You know, by now, that learning to read this language is as important to me as it is to you, but how can you be so sure that those words really mean things like hydrogen and helium and boron and oxygen? How do you know that their table of elements was anything like ours?"

297 Tranter and Penrose and Sachiko all looked at him in amazement.

298 "That isn't just the Martian table of elements; that's *the* table of elements. It's the only one there is," Mort Tranter almost exploded. "Look, hydrogen has one proton and one electron. If it had more of either, it wouldn't be hydrogen, it'd be something else. And the same with all the rest of the elements. And hydrogen on Mars is the same as hydrogen on Terra, or on Alpha Centauri, or in the next galaxy—"

299 "You just set up those numbers, in that order, and any first-year chemistry student could tell you what elements they represented," Penrose said. "Could if he expected to make a passing grade, that is."

300　The old man shook his head slowly, smiling. "I'm afraid I wouldn't make a passing grade. I didn't know, or at least didn't realize, that. One of the things I'm going to place an order for, to be brought on the *Schiaparelli*, will be a set of primers in chemistry and physics, of the sort intended for a bright child of ten or twelve. It seems that a Martiologist has to learn a lot of things the Hittites and the Assyrians never heard about."

301　Tony Lattimer, coming in, caught the last part of the explanation. He looked quickly at the walls and, having found out just what had happened, advanced and caught Martha by the hand.

302　"You really did it, Martha! You found your bilingual! I never believed that it would be possible; let me congratulate you!"

303　He probably expected that to erase all the jibes and sneers of the past. If he did, he could have it that way. His friendship would mean as little to her as his derision—except that his friends had to watch their backs and his knife. But he was going home on the *Cyrano*, to be a big shot. Or had this changed his mind for him again?

304　"This is something we can show the world, to justify any expenditure of time and money on Martian archaeological work. When I get back to Terra, I'll see that you're given full credit for this achievement—"

305　On Terra, her back and his knife would be out of her watchfulness.

306　"We won't need to wait that long," Hubert Penrose told him dryly. "I'm sending off an official report, tomorrow; you can be sure Dr. Dane will be given full credit, not only for this but for her previous work, which made it possible to exploit this discovery."

307　"And you might add, work done in spite of the doubts and discouragements of her colleagues," Selim von Ohlmhorst said. "To which I am ashamed to have to confess my own share."

308　"You said we had to find a bilingual," she said. "You were right, too."

309　"This is better than a bilingual, Martha," Hubert Penrose said. "Physical science expresses universal facts; necessarily it is a universal language. Heretofore archaeologists have dealt only with pre-scientific cultures."

Content Questions

1. What are the problems Dr. Dane encounters trying to translate the Martian language?
2. How does Dr. Dane discover that *sornhulva* means *physical object/ science* or *physics*?
3. What kind of society did the Martians have? What were the last days of that society like?
4. Why do expedition members feel the Martians are "haunting" them when they're in the university building?
5. Why does Lattimer criticize Dr. Dane's investigations?

Questions on Presentation

1. How does Piper use the explorers' nervous habits to develop the story?
2. One of the themes of this story is the difficulty women may have in proving their professional worth. How does Piper develop this theme?
3. Piper takes the process of translating from one language into another—a process many people would consider tedious—and turns it into an interesting story. What techniques does Piper use to keep the reader's attention?
4. How does the reference in paragraph 189 enhance the story?
5. One of the problems of science fiction is creating a believable world. How does Piper make the setting of this story believable?

How Many Sheep Will It Hold?

Barre Toelken

Barre Toelken was born in 1935 in Ware, Massachusetts. Educated at Utah State University and the University of Oregon, Toelken is currently a professor, writer, and folklorist living in Eugene, Oregon. His special interests are traditional ballads and native American literature and religion, especially Navajo. In addition to numerous teaching awards including the Danforth Association Award (1973), Toeklen has published several articles on folklore, riddles, and ballads including his 1979 book *The Dynamics of Folklore*. In the following essay, taken from *Seeing With a Native Eye*, Toelken compares Anglo and native American cultures by tracing how people define and react to everyday events. He illustrates not only the differences between Anglo culture and native American culture but also the differences among Indian cultures.

1   There are some things that one knows already if he or she has read very much about the Native Americans. One of the most important is that there is almost nothing that can be said about "the Indians" as a whole. Every tribe is different from every other in some respects, and similar in other respects, so that nearly everything one says normally has to be qualified by footnotes. What I am about to say here does not admit room for that. I propose, therefore, to give a few examples from the Navajo culture and take some small glances at other Indian cultures that I know a little bit about; that is simply a device to keep my observations from appearing as though they were meant to be generally applicable to Indians of the whole country.

2   It is estimated that there were up to 2,000 separate cultures in the Northern hemisphere before the advent of the white man. Many of these groups spoke mutually unintelligible languages. Anthropologists estimate that there were as many as eighty such languages in the Pacific Northwest alone. In terms of language and traditions, these cultures were very much separated from each other; and although they have been lumped into one category by whites every since (and that is the source of some of their problems), any given Indian will have a few things in common with some other tribes and many things not in common with others. My generalizations are made with this in mind from the start. But one must start *somewhere* in an attempt to cope with the vast conceptual gulf which lies between Anglos in general and natives in general, for it is a chasm which has not often been bridged, especially in religious discussion.

3   I do not claim, either, to be one of those rare people who *have* succeeded in making the leap—an insider, a confidant, a friend of the Red Man's Council Fire—in short, one of those Tarzans even more rare in reality than one would conclude from their memoirs. But I did have the good fortune to be adopted by an old Navajo, Tsinaabaas Yazhi ("Little Wagon"), in southern Utah in the mid-fifties during the uranium rush. I moved in with his family, learned Navajo, and lived essentially a Navajo life for roughly two years. Of course I have gone back since then on every possible occasion to visit my family, although my adopted father is now dead, as is his wife and probably 50 percent of the people I knew in the fifties. If one has read the Navajo statistics he knows why. This is not intended to be a tale of woe, however; I simply want it understood that I was not a missionary among the Navajo. Nor was I an anthropologist, a teacher, a tourist, or any of the other things that sometimes cause people to come to know another group briefly and superficially. Although, indeed, at one time I had it in my mind to stay with them forever, it is probably because my culture did not train me to cope with almost daily confrontation with death that I was unable to do so. I learned much from them, and it is no exaggeration to say that a good part of my education was gained there. It was probably the most important part. "Culture shock" attended my return to the Anglo world even though I left the Navajos as "un-Navajo" as when I arrived.

4   With that for background, though, I think I can say something about how differently we see things, envision things, look at things, how dissimilarly different cultures try to process the world of reality, which, for many Native American tribes, includes the world of religion. In Western culture, religion seems to occupy a niche reserved for the unreal, the Otherworld, a reference point that is reached only upon death or through the agency of the priest. Many native American tribes see religious experience as something that surrounds man all the time. In fact, my friends the Navajos would say that there is probably *nothing* that

can be called nonreligious. To them, almost anything anyone is likely to do has some sort of religious significance, and many other tribes concur. Procedurally, then, our problem is to learn how to talk about religion, even in preliminary ways, knowing perfectly well that in one society what is considered art may in another be considered religion, or that what is considered as health in one culture may be religion in another. Before we can proceed, in other words, we need to reexamine our categories, our "pigeonholes," in order to "see" things through someone else's set of patterns. This is the reason for the odd title: "Seeing With a Native Eye."

5   Through our study of linguistics and anthropology we have learned that different groups of people not only think in different ways, but that they often "see" things in different ways. Good scientific experiments can be provided, for example, to prove that if certain ideas are offered to people in patterns which they have not been taught to recognize, not only will they not understand them, they often will not even see them. We see things in "programmed" ways. Of course Professor Whorf was interested in demonstrating the pervasiveness of this theory with respect to language, and many anthropologists and linguists have had reservations about his theories. But the experimentation continues, and there is some interesting and strong evidence that a person will look right through something that he or she is not trained to see, and that different cultures train people in different ways. I will not get into the Jungian possibilities that we may be born with particularized codes as well; this is beyond my area of expertise. But it is clear that when we want to talk about native American religion, we want to try to see it as much as possible (if it is possible) with the "native eye." That is to say, if we talk about native American religions using the categories of Western religions, we are simply going to see what *we* already know is there. We will recognize certain kinds of experiences as religious, and we will cancel out others. To us, for example, dance may be an art form, or it may be a certain kind of kinesis. With certain native American tribes, dance may be the most religious act a person can perform. These differences are very significant; on the basis of this kind of cultural blindness, for example, Kluckhohn classified the Navajo coyote tales as "secular" primarily because they are humorous.

6   The subtitle of this paper comes from my adopted Navajo father. My first significant educational experience came when I was trying to educate him to what the outside world looked like. Here was an eighty- or ninety-year-old man in the 1950s who had never seen a paved road or a train; he had seen airplanes flying overhead and was afraid of them. He had seen almost nothing of what you and I experience as the "modern, advanced world." I decided I would try to cushion the shock for him by showing him pictures, and then I would invite him into town with me

sometime when I went to Salt Lake City. I felt he needed some preparation for the kind of bombardment of the senses one experiences in the city after living out in the desert.

7   I showed him a two-page spread of the Empire State Building which appeared in *Life* that year. His question was, immediately, "How many sheep will it hold?" I had to admit that I didn't know, and that even if I did know, I couldn't count that high in Navajo; and I tried to show him how big a sheep might look if you held it up against one of those windows, but he was interested neither in my excuses nor in my intent to explain the size of the building. When I told him what it was for, he was shocked. The whole concept of so many people filed together in one big drawer—of course he would not have used those terms—was shocking to him. He felt that people who live so close together cannot live a very rich life, so he expected that whites would be found to be spiritually impoverished and personally very upset by living so close together. I tried to assure him that this was not so. Of course I was wrong. Little by little one learns.

8   The next episode in this stage of my learning occurred about six months later, when I was at the trading post and found a magazine with a picture of the latest jet bomber on it. I brought that to him to explain better what those things were that flew over all the time. He asked the same question in spite of the fact there were lots of little men standing around the plane and he could see very well how big it was. Again he said, "How many sheep will it carry?" I started to shrug him off as if he were simply plaguing me, when it became clear to me that what he was really asking was, "What is it good for in terms of something that I know to be valid and viable in the world?" (That, of course, is not his wording either.) In effect, he was saying that he was not willing even to try to understand the Empire State Building or the bomber unless I could give those particular sensations to him in some kind of patternings from which he could make some assessment. He was not really interested in how big they were, he was interested in what they were doing in the world. When I told him what the jet bomber was for, he became so outraged that he refused ever to go to town, and he died without ever having done so as far as I know. He said that he had heard many terrible things about the whites, but the idea of someone killing that many people by dropping the bomb and remaining so far out of reach that he was not in danger was just too much!

9   The only other thing that approached such outrage, by the way, was when I explained to him about the toilet facilities in white houses, and I mentioned indoor toilet functions. He could hardly believe that one. "They do that right in the house, right inside where everyone lives?" "No, no, you don't understand. There is a separate room for it." That was even worse—that there could be a special place for such things. A

world so neatly categorized and put in boxes really bothered him, and he steadfastly refused to go visit it. At the time I thought he was being what we call primitive, backward—he was dragging his feet, refusing to understand the march of science and culture. What I "see" now is that, as a whole, he was simply unable to—it did not "compute" in the way we might put it today; he did not "see" what I meant. In turn, he was trying to call my attention to that fact, and I was not receiving the impression.

10 I bring these matters up not because they are warm reminiscences, but because difficulties in communicating religious ideas are parallel to these examples. When my adopted father asked, "How many sheep will it hold?" he was asking, "What is it doing here, how does it function? Where does it go? Why do such things occur in the world?" We might consider the Pueblo view that in the springtime Mother Earth is pregnant, and one does not mistreat her any more than one might mistreat a pregnant woman. When our technologists go and try to get Pueblo farmers to use steel plows in the spring, they are usually rebuffed. For us it is a technical idea—"Why don't you just use plows? You plow, and you get 'x' results from doing so." For the Pueblos this is meddling with a formal religious idea (in Edward Hall's terms). Using a plow, to borrow the Navajo phrase, "doesn't hold any sheep." In other words, it does not make sense in the way the world operates. It is against the way things really go. Some Pueblo folks still take the heels off their shoes, and sometimes the shoes of their horses, during the spring. I once asked a Hopi whom I met in that country, "Do you mean to say, then, that if I kick the ground with my foot, it will botch everything up, so nothing will grow?" He said, "Well, I don't know whether that would happen or not, but it would just really show what kind of person you are."

11 One learns slowly that in many of these native religions, religion is viewed as embodying the reciprocal relationships between people and the sacred *processes* going on in the world. It may not involve a "god." It may not be signified by praying or asking for favors, or doing what may "look" religious to people in our culture. For the Navajo, for example, almost *everything* is related to health. For us health is a medical issue. We may have a few home remedies, but for most big things we go to a doctor. A Navajo goes to the equivalent of a priest to get well because one needs not only medicine, the Navajo would say, but one needs to reestablish his relationship with the rhythms of nature. It is the ritual as well as the medicine which gets one back "in shape." The medicine may cure the symptoms, but it won't cure you. It does not put you back in step with the things, back in the natural cycles—this is a job for the "singer." Considering the strong psychological and spiritual role of such a person, it should not come as a surprise that it is on spiritual (magic?) grounds, not medicinal, that some medicinal materials are *not* used. For

example, Pete Catches, a Sioux medicine man (who practices the Eagle "way" of the Sacred Pipe), knows about but will not employ abortion-producing plants, for such use would run counter to and thus impede the ritualistic function of the pipe ceremony, a good part of which is to help increase the live things in the world. In the reciprocative life pattern, death is not a proper ingredient.

12   I want to go a little further into this, because these patterns, these cycles, these reciprocations that we find so prominently in native American religions, are things which for our culture are not only puzzling but often considered absolutely insane. It is the conflict or incongruency in patterning that often impedes our understanding. Let me give a few examples of this patterning. In Western culture—I suppose in most of the technological cultures—there has been a tremendous stress on lineal patterning and lineal measurements, grid patterns, straight lines. I think one reason for this is that technological cultures have felt that it is not only desirable but even necessary to control nature. We know there are very few straight lines in nature. One of the ways people can tell if they are controlling nature is to see that it is put in straight lines—we have to put things "in order." And so we not only put our filing cases and our books in straight lines and alphabetical "order," we also put nature in straight lines and grid patterns—our streets, our houses, our acreage, our lives, our measurement of time and space, our preference for the shortest distance between two points, our extreme interest in being "on time."

13   Those who have read the works of Hall and other anthropologists on the anthropology of time and space are familiar with these ideas. Each culture has a kind of spatial system through which one knows by what he sees as he grows up how close he can stand to someone else, how he is to walk in public and in private, where his feet are supposed to fall, where things are supposed to go. These patterns show up in verbal expressions too—we have to "get things straightened out," "get things straight between us," make someone "toe the line." We also arranged classrooms and auditoriums in some sort of lineal order (other groups might want these to be arranged in a circle). To us, having things "in order" means lining things up, getting things in line. We talk about "getting straight with one another," looking straight into each other's eyes, being "straight shooters." We even talk about the "straight" people vs. the "groovy" people. Notice how we often depict someone who is crazy with a circular hand motion around the ear. Someone who does not speak clearly "talks in circles," or uses circuitous logic. We think of logic itself as being in straight lines: A plus B equals C. We look forward to the conclusion of things, we plan into the future, as though time were a sort of straight track along which we move toward certain predictable goals.

14   If one knows much about native Americans of almost any tribe, he realizes that I am choosing, intentionally, certain lineal and grid patterns which are virtually unmatched in native American patterns. We learn to find each other in the house or in the city by learning the intersection of straight lines—so many doors down the hallway is the kitchen, or the bathroom, and we are never to confuse them. We separate them. One does not cook in the bathroom—it is ludicrous to get them mixed up. We have it all neatly separated and categorized. For most native American groups, almost the reverse is true—things are brought together. Instead of separating into categories of this sort, family groups sit in circles, meetings are in circles, dances are often—not always—in circles, especially the dances intended to welcome and include people. With the exception of a few tribes such as the Pueblo peoples, who live in villages which have many straight lines, most of the tribes usually live (or lived) in round dwellings like the hogan of the Navajo, the tipi of the plains Indians, the igloo of the Eskimo. The Eastern Indians and some Northwestern tribes sometimes lived in long houses, but the families or clans sat in circles within.

15   There is, then, a "logical" tendency to recreate the pattern of the circle at every level of the culture, in religion as well as in social intercourse. I think the reason for it is that what makes sense, what "holds sheep" for many tribes, is the concept that reciprocation is at the heart of everything going on in the world. I have had Pueblo people tell me that what they are doing when they participate in the rain dances or fertility dances is not asking help from the sky; rather, they are doing something which they characterize as a hemisphere which is brought together in conjunction with another hemisphere. It is a participation in a kind of interaction which I can only characterize as sacred reciprocation. It is a sense that everything always goes this way. We are always interacting, and if we refuse to interact, or if some taboo action has caused a break in this interaction, then disease or calamity comes about. It is assumed that reciprocation is the order of things, and so we will expect it to keep appearing in all forms.

16   I think that it makes anthropological and linguistic sense to say that any culture will represent things religiously, artistically, and otherwise, the way its members "see" things operating in the world. But here is where the trick comes in. When we from one culture start looking at the patterns of another culture, we will often see what *our* culture has trained us to see. If we look at a Navajo rug, for example, we are inclined to say that Navajos use many straight lines in their rugs. And yet if we talk to Navajos about weaving, the *gesture* we often see is a four-way back-and-forth movement; and they talk about the interaction within the pattern—a reciprocation. Most often the Navajo rug reciprocates its pattern from side to side and from end to end, creating mirror images.

My adopted sister, who is a very fine weaver, always talks about this kind of balance. She says, "When I am thinking up these patterns, I am trying to spin something, and then I unspin it. It goes up this way and it comes down that way." And she uses circular hand gestures to illustrate. While we are trained to see the straight lines, and to think of the rug in terms of geometric patterns, she makes the geometrical necessities of weaving—up one, over one—fit a kind of circular logic about how nature works and about how man interacts with nature. If we are going to talk about her beliefs with respect to rugs, we need somehow to project ourselves into her circles.

17   Let me give a couple of other examples. These, by the way, are not intended to be representative, but are just some things that I have encountered. They are simply illustrative of the way a Navajo might explain things. There is a species of beads that one often finds in curio shops these days. They are called "ghost" beads by the whites, though I do not know any Navajos who call them that except when talking to whites (they feel they ought to phrase it the way the whites will understand it). The brown beads in these arrangements are the inside of the blue juniper berries, which the Navajo call literally "juniper's eyes." In the most preferred way of producing these necklaces, Navajos search to find where the small ground animals have hidden their supply of juniper seeds. Usually a small girl, sometimes a boy, will look for likely hiding places, scoop them all out when she finds them, and look for the seeds that have already been broken open, so as not to deprive the animals of food. She puts all the whole seeds back, and takes only the ones that have a hole in one end. She takes them home, cleans them, punches a hole in the other end with a needle, and strings them together. I do not know any Navajo in my family or among my acquaintances who ever goes without these beads on him somewhere, usually in his pocket.

18   My Navajo sister says that the reason these beads will prevent nightmares and keep one from getting lost in the dark is that they represent the partnership between the tree that gives its berries, the animals which gather them, and humans who pick them up (being careful not to deprive the animals of their food). It is a three-way partnership—plant, animal, and man. Thus, if you keep these beads on you and think about them, your mind, in its balance with nature, will tend to lead a healthy existence. If you are healthy by Navajo standards, you are participating properly in all the cycles of nature, and thus you will not have bad dreams. Bad dreams are a *sign* of being sick, and getting lost is a *sign* of being sick. So these beads are not warding off sickness itself; rather, they are reminders of a frame of mind which is essentially cyclic, in the proper relationship with the rest of nature—a frame of mind necessary to the maintenance of health.

19   Again, using the weaving of rugs as an example, I want to explain the

significance of the spindle and the yarn. The yarn comes from the sheep, of course. The Navajos explain the relationship there not in terms of the rug, the end product—which, of course, is what our culture is interested in—but in terms of the relationship with the yarn and with the sheep, and with the spinning of the yarn, which has to be done in a certain direction because it goes along with everything else that is spinning. Everything for the Navajos is moving; an arbitary term in English such as *east* is phrased in Navajo, "something round moves up regularly." When one spins the yarn, then, one does not just twist it to make string out of it; one twists it in the right direction (sunwise) with everything else (otherwise, the thread will ravel). Thus, the yarn itself becomes a further symbol of man's interaction with the animal on the one hand, and with the whole of the cosmos on the other. When one works with yarn one is working with something that remains a symbol of the cyclic or circular interaction with nature. Even the spindle can be seen as an agency of, or focal point in, a religious view of man and nature.

20   In a recent experiment by an anthropologist and a moviemaker, some young Navajos were given cameras and encouraged to make their own movies. One girl made a movie called "Navajo Weaving." It lasts, as I recall, almost forty-five minutes, but there are only a few pictures of rugs in it. Most of the film is about people riding horseback, wandering out through the sagebrush, feeding the sheep, sometimes shearing them, sometimes following them through the desert, sometimes picking and digging the roots from which the dyes are made. Almost the entire film is made up of the things that the Navajo find important about making rugs: human interaction with nature. That is what rugmaking is for the Navajos. Something which for us is a secular craft or a technique is for these people a part or extension of the reciprocations embodied in religion.

21   Religious reciprocity extends even into the creation of the rug's design. My Navajo sister wove a rug for me as a gift, the kind which the traders call *yei* (*yei* means something like "the holy people"). The pattern in this particular rug is supposed to represent five lizard people. The two on opposite ends are the same color, and the next two inward the same color, and the one in the middle a distinctly different color. The middle one is the dividing line, so that the pattern reciprocates from end to end of the rug. When my sister gave it to me, she said, "These represent your five children." Of course I was moved to inquire of her why she should represent my five children as lizards (I had private ideas about why she might). I wondered what her reasoning was, and I certainly knew children are not "holy people"—far from it. She pointed out, "Your oldest and youngest are girls, and they are represented by the two opposite figures on each end. Then you have twin boys—they are the two white ones, because they are alike. Then there is another boy,

who doesn't have a mate in your family, so he is the center point of the family, even though he isn't that in terms of age." She made the pattern reciprocate from one end to the other not only in terms of representing my family but in terms of color. All the dyes were from particular plants which were related in her mind to good health. Lizards represent longevity, and by making them congruent with the lizard people, she was making a statement of, an embodiment of, their health and longevity. This is a wish that any Navajo might want to express, because, as noted above, health and longevity are central to Navajo religious concerns. If I knew more about the symbolic function of certain colors in the rug, or the use of the dye-producing plants in Navajo medicine, I have no doubt that I would have still more to say about the religious expression intended therein.

22   Reciprocity is central to the production of many other Navajo items, especially so in the making of moccasins. My brother-in-law, Yellow-man, when he goes hunting for skins to put on the body, tries to produce what the Navajos call "sacred deerskin." It is supposed to be produced from a deer whose hide is not punctured in the killing. If one wants the deer for meat, it can be simply shot (Yellowman, though he is in his early sixties, still hunts with a bow and arrow). But when he hunts deer for moccasins, or for cradle boards for his family (the deerskin helps to surround the baby), then he wants skin of the sacred kind. To obtain sacred deerskin in the old fashion, one runs the deer down until it is exhausted, and then smothers it to death.

23   It is done in this manner: one first gathers pollen, which he carries with him in a small pouch. He then gets the deer out into open country and jogs along behind it, following until it is totally exhausted. Deer run very rapidly for awhile but soon get tired. The man who is good at jogging can keep it up for some distance. Still, it is no easy job, as you can imagine if you have ever visited the desert of the Monument Valley area. When the deer is finally caught, he is thrown to the ground as gently as possible, his mouth and nose are held shut, and covered with a handful of pollen so that he may die breathing the sacred substance. And then—I am not sure how widespread this is with the Navajos—one sings to the deer as it is dying, and apologizes ritually for taking its life, explaining that he needs the skin for his family. The animal is skinned in a ritual way, and the rest of the deer is disposed of in a ritual manner (I do not feel free to divulge the particulars here).

24   The deerhide is brought home and tanned in the traditional way. The coloration is taken from particular kinds of herbs and from parts of the deer (including its brains). Then the moccasins are made by sewing the deerhide uppers together with cowhide soles. In many cases they are buried in wet sand until the person for whom they are designed comes by. He puts them on and wears them until they are dry. In so doing, of

course, he wears his footprints into them. You can always tell when you have on someone else's moccasins, if that mistake should ever occur, because they hurt. Your own toe prints are in your own moccasins, for they have become part of you. It is no accident that the word for moccasin or shoe is *shi ke*, "my shoe," which is exactly the same word for "my foot." Religiously speaking, what happens is that the deerskin becomes part of us, and this puts us in an interactive relationship with the deer. The whole event is ritualized, carried out in "proper" ways, because it falls into a formal religious category, not a mere craft. The moccasin is more than something to keep the foot warm and dry; it is symbolic of that sacred relation and interaction with the plants and the animals that the Navajo see as so central to "reality."

25   Also central to Navajo religion is the restoration of health when it has been lost. The *hogan* is the round dwelling the Navajos live in. The fire is in the middle of the floor, and the door always faces east. One of the reasons for this, as my adopted father told me, was to make sure that people always live properly oriented to the world of nature. The door frames the rising sun at a certain time of the year. The only light that comes is either through the smokehole on the top, or through the door, if it happens to be open. Healing rituals involving "sandpainting" are usually enacted inside the hogan, and are oriented to the four directions. When the patient takes his or her place on the sandpainting, ritually they are taking their place within the world of the "holy people," related to all the cycling and reciprocation of the universe. It is partly that orientation which cures one.

26   Yellowman still hunts for meat with bow and arrow. His arrowheads are made out of ordinary carpenters' nails pounded out between rocks, although he has a whole deerskin bag of stone arrowheads that he has picked up on the desert. When I asked him why he did not use those nice stone points on his own arrows, he looked at me very strangely. (I knew that the Navajos put them in the bottom of medicine containers when they are making medicine, but I thought that perhaps he knew how to make them himself given the proper kind of rock.) I asked whether he knew how the oldtimers used to make them. He looked at me as if I were absolutely insane. He finally answered, "Men don't make them at all; lizards make arrowheads." For him, stone arrowheads, such as one might find, are sacred items, and they fall into the same category as lizards, lightning, and corn pollen. Lizards, as I mentioned earlier, are related to long life and good health. When one finds a lizard or an arrowhead, he picks it up and holds it against the side of his arm or over his heart, the same places where pollen is placed during a ceremony. Clearly, stone arrowheads are for curing, not killing; or, more properly, they are for killing *diseases*. Thus, even arrowheads have to do with special sacred medicinal categories, not with the kinds of practical catego-

ries our culture might see. In other words, learning about Navajo religion and daily life requires the learning of a whole new set of concepts, codes, patterns, and assumptions.

27   A student of mine paraphrased an old proverb this way: "If I hadn't believed it I never would have seen it." This is essentially what I am saying about viewing religion in other cultures. Our usual approach is in terms of pictures, patterns, gestures, and attitudes that we already know how to see. For example, when some dance specialists went to Tucson a couple of years ago to watch the Yaqui Easter ceremonies, all they saw were the dances. They did not see that on a couple of occasions, several people very prominent in the ritual were simply sitting next to the altar for extremely long periods of time. I talked to almost every person at that conference, and only a few of them had seen those people sitting there. There wasn't any dancing going on there, and so the dance people weren't "seeing." And yet it was probably a very important part of the dance. I do not pretend to have understood this part, but the point is that the strangers had not even seen it; they were watching for what they as Anglos and dance specialists could recognize as dance steps. I would not accuse them of stupidity, ignorance, or narrowmindedness. Rather, they had not been taught to "read," to see other kinds of patternings than their own.

28   To complicate matters further, many tribes feel the real world is not one that is most easily seen, while the Western technological culture thinks of *this* as the real world, the one that *can* be seen and touched easily. To many native Americans the world that is real is the one we reach through special, religious means, the one we are taught to "see" and experience *via* ritual and sacred patterning. Instead of demanding proof for the Otherworld, as the scientific mind does, many native Americans are likely to counter by demanding proof that *this* one exists in any real way, since, by itself, it is not ritualized.

29   What the different cultures are taught to see, and how they see it, are thus worlds apart (although not, I think, mutually exclusive). One culture looks for a meaning in the visible, one looks for a meaning beyond the visible. The "cues" are different because the referents and the connotations are different. Add to this basic incongruency the fact that the patterning of one is based on planning, manipulation, predictability, competition, and power, while the other is based in reciprocation, "flowering," response to situation, and cooperation—and who would be surprised to find the actual symbols and meanings of the two religious modes will be perceived and expressed in quite contrastive forms? We must seek to understand the metaphor of the native American, and we must be willing to witness to the validity of its sacred function, or else we should not pretend to be discussing this religion. Before we can see, we must learn how to look.

Content Questions

1. What makes Toelken qualified to assess and explain cultural values?
2. What is Toelken's reaction to the question "how many sheep will it hold?"
3. How does Toelken describe a native American's view of religion?
4. Why didn't the Navajo girl's movie about weaving show more about weaving?

Questions on Presentation

1. Toelken argues that "one culture [the Anglo] looks for a meaning in the visible, one [the Navajo] looks for a meaning beyond the visible . . . the patterning of one is based on planning, manipulation, predictability, competition, and power, while the other is based in reciprocation, 'flowering,' response to situation, and cooperation." Does his support for this conclusion seem sufficient?
2. Would Toelken's argument about what cultures "look for" be a sound way of exploring differences between other cultures?
3. What is the purpose and effect of the disclaimer that begins paragraph 3?
4. How does Toelken convey the outrage of the elderly Navajo man without being condescending?
5. How would you characterize Toelken's audience?

To See or Not to See

Larry Blanchard

Larry Blanchard is an engineering major who, before entering college, toured Greece with his wife, at the time his fiancée, by motorcycle. In this essay he explores some of the ways a person from one culture "looks for" things in a very different culture.

1   Most Americans are very narrow minded about cultural differences, even among themselves; Northerners differ from Southerners, Easterners differ from Westerners, and their comments about other cultural groups can, at times, be very degrading. Americans tend to draw, from

their own limited experiences, a pattern of how the whole world should be, and they fail to find any value in a culture, or lifestyle, that differs from their own. The effect of this intolerance is even more pronounced when they are in a foreign country. This fact became very evident to me during the year that I lived and worked in Greece. There the American was truly ugly.

2   Greece can trace its culture and heritage back thousands of years to the beginnings of recorded history, America, a scant two hundred years. Greece is a country filled with history and tradition, and its culture is based on traditional values. The large cities, such as Athens and the tourist centers, have, to some extent, become westernized, but the small villages, that the tourist rarely, if ever, sees, are very much ingrained in the old ways. Greece is basically a poor country. There are a few rich Greeks, but the majority of the people are poor. A middle class, as we know it, is only a recent phenomenon. Their culture is not based on monetary values, yet the American expects to be catered to because he has money.

3   The *taverna* (restaurant) menu, in the tourist centers, is printed in both Greek and English; their English translations leave much to be desired. The American, when he isn't understood or doesn't understand, begins to shout, and he becomes very indignant. He does not try to resolve the misunderstanding; he just raises the decibel level and then complains about the poor service.

4   Shortly after arriving, I was riding up the coast and stopped at a taverna in a small out of the way village. While motorcycles are not unknown, BMWs, because of their high cost, are in themselves novelties. I, with my cowboy boots and western shirt, was also a novelty and, unquestionably, a foreigner. There was no menu, let alone an English translation. I was, instead, taken into the kitchen to see the menu. The Greeks are a very proud people, and the cook was very proud to show me what he was cooking. No one in the taverna, or the village for that matter, spoke English, and I at that time did not speak any Greek, yet we understood each other, and I had a very enjoyable dinner. Upon returning there a few months later with my fiancée, because our first encounter was so pleasant and I had put forth an effort to understand, I was welcomed with open arms and made to feel like a member of the family.

5   The Greek conception of time is another cultural difference that is hard for Americans to accept. Americans are so rigidly fixed to schedules that they find any deviation intolerable. I think, that with the advent of digital watches that give the precise time right down to the second, they feel that everyone's life should be synchronized. *Avrio*, translated "tomorrow," is a favorite Greek expression that sums up their attitude toward time. A Greek will be an hour or two late for an appoint-

ment and think nothing of it. Life is going to continue regardless, so why get upset?

6   One of the hardest things our company had to do, in establishing a plant there, was to get the Greeks in the habit of punching a clock and abiding by a continuous eight-hour workday with fixed periods for break and lunch. The Greek day, as in most Mediterranean countries, is divided after noon by a siesta. The shops close and people go home to sleep during the hottest part of the day. No business is conducted and it is very discourteous to call during that time. As a consequence, the Greek dinner hour does not start until late evening. Most of the better tavernas don't even open until seven, and they have few customers before nine. After I had first arrived, I thought they must be going broke until I learned the cultural differences.

7   This difference of time concept was another problem for the Americans. When they set an appointment time, they expected it to be kept, and they became quite upset when the other party was late. Greek families would often carry their dinner hour late into the night, well past the time most Americans went to bed. Consequently, the noise from the neighbors would give rise to another American complaint—they couldn't get any sleep.

8   I have touched on only a few of the cultural differences between the Greeks and the Americans, and the Americans' intolerance of those differences. I am not saying that one is right and the other wrong, only that they are different. America is a wonderful country, and the freedoms she offers are found nowhere else in the world. The sad part is that Americans have an opportunity to act as goodwill ambassadors, but, instead, they foster a dislike for both themselves and America. What Americans fail to realize, after all, is that it is the Greek's country, their culture, and it has been in existence long before America was ever discovered.

American Character

Hector St. John de Crèvecoeur

Michel-Guillaume-Jean de Crèvecoeur (1735–1813) was born near Caen, France, and was educated in France and England. After serving under General Montcalm during the French and Indian War, he began a tour of the British colonies in North America in 1754. He became a British citizen in 1765 and settled as a farmer in Orange County, New York, in 1769. Returning to France in

1780, he served as French Counsel to the United States between 1783 and 1790. A number of essays he wrote, in English, under the name Hector St. John, were published as *Letters from an American Farmer* (1782), and it is from this collection the following selection comes. In this essay, as in his other writings, he explores the American character and life during the colonial period and early years of the United States.

1   Let us view the new colonist as possessed of property. This has a great weight and a mighty influence. From earliest infancy we are accustomed to a greater exchange of things, a greater transfer of property than the people of the same class in Europe. Whether it is occasioned by that perpetual and necessary emigrating genius which constantly sends the exuberancy of full societies to replenish new tracts; whether it proceeds from our being richer; whether it is that we are fonder of trade which is but an exchange,—I cannot ascertain. This man, thus bred, from a variety of reasons is determined to improve his fortune by removing to a new district, and resolves to purchase as much land as will afford substantial farms to every one of his children,—a pious thought which causes so many even wealthy people to sell their patrimonial estates to enlarge their sphere of action and leave a sufficient inheritance to their progeny.

2   No sooner he is resolved than he takes all the information he can with regard to the country he proposes to go to inhabit. He finds out all travellers who have been on the spot; he views maps; attentively weighs the benefits and disadvantages of climate, seasons, situation, etc.; he compares it with his own. A world of the most ponderous reflections must needs fill his mind. He at last goes to the capital and applies to some great land-holders. He wants to make a purchase. Each party sets forth the peculiar goodness of its tracts in all the various possible circumstances of health, soil, proximity of lakes, rivers, roads, etc. Maps are presented to him; various lots are spread before him as pieces of linen in the shop of a draper. What a sagacity must this common farmer have, first, to enable him to choose the province, the country, the peculiar tract most agreeable to his fortune; then to resist, to withstand the sophistry of these learned men armed with all the pomp of their city arguments! Yet he is a match for them all. These mathematical lines and sheets of paper would represent nothing to a man of his class in Europe, yet he understands their meaning, even the various courses by which the rivers and mountains are known. He remembers them while in the woods, and is not at a loss to trace them through the impervious forest, and to reason accurately upon the errors and mistakes which may have been made by the surveyor's neglect or ignorance in the representation of them. He receives proper directions and departs for the intended place, for he wants to view and examine ere he purchases.

3   When near the spot, he hires a man, perhaps a hunter, of which all the frontiers are full, and instead of being lost and amazed in the middle of these gloomy retreats, he finds the place of beginning on which the whole survey is founded. This is all the difficulty he was afraid of; he follows the ancient blazed trees with a sagacity and quickness of sight which have many times astonished me, though bred in the woods. Next he judges of the soil by the size and the appearance of the trees; next he judges of the goodness of the timber by that of the soil. The humble bush which delights in the shade, the wild ginseng, the spignet,[1] the weeds on which he treads teach him all he wants to know. He observes the springs, the moisture of the earth, the range of the mountains, the course of the brooks. He returns at last; he has formed his judgment as to his future buildings; their situation, future roads, cultivation, etc. He has properly combined the future mixture of conveniences and inconveniences which he expects to meet with. In short the complicated arrangement of a great machine would not do greater honour to the most skilful artist than the reduction and digesting of so many thoughts and calculations by this hitherto obscure man.

4   He meets once more the land-proprietors; a new scene ensues. He is startled at the price. He altercates with them, for now he has something to say, having well explored the country. Now he makes them an offer; now he seems to recede; now wholly indifferent about the bargain; now willing to fulfil it if the terms are reasonable. If not, he can't but stay where he is, or perhaps accept of better offers which have been made to him by another person. He relinquishes, he pursues his object—that is his advantage—through a more complex labyrinth than a European could well imagine. He is diffident; he is mistrustful as to the title; ancientness of patent, priority of claim, etc. The idea that would occur to an Englishman of his class would be that such great and good men would not deceive such a poor farmer as he is; he would feel an inward shame to doubt their assertions. You are wrong, my friends; these are not your country parish-squires who would by so gross a deceit defame their characters and lose your vote. Besides, the price of things is better ascertained there in all possible bargains than here. This is a land-merchant who, like all other merchants, has no other rule than to get what he can. This is the general standard except where there is some competition. The native sagacity of this American colonist carries him at last through the whole bargain. He purchases fifteen hundred acres at three dollars per acre to be paid in three equal yearly payments. He gives his bond for the same, and the whole tract is mortgaged as a security. On the other hand, he obtains bonds of indemnity to secure him against the miscarriages of the patent and other claims.

5   He departs with all his family, and great and many are the expenses and fatigues of this removal with cows, and cattle. He at last arrives on

the spot. He finds himself suddenly deprived of the assistance of friends, neighbours, tradesmen, and of all those inferior links which make a well-established society so beautiful and pleasing. He and his family are now alone. On their courage, perseverance, and skill their success depends. There is now no retreating; shame and ruin would infallibly overtake them. What is he to do in all possible cases of accidents, sickness, and other casualties which may befall his family, his cattle and horses, breaking of the implements of husbandry, etc.? A complicated scene presents itself to the contemplative mind, which does the Americans a superlative honour. Whence proceed that vigour and energy, those resources which they never fail to show on these trying occasions? From the singularity of their situation, from that locality of existence which is peculiar to themselves as a new people improving a new country?

6   I have purposely visited many who have spent the earliest part of their lives in this manner; now ploughmen, now mechanics, sometimes even physicians. They are and must be everything. Nay, who would believe it? This new man will commence as a hunter and learn in these woods how to pursue and overtake the game with which it abounds. He will in a short time become master of that necessary dexterity which this solitary life inspires. Husband, father, priest, principal governor,—he fills up all these stations, though in the humble vale of life. Are there any of his family taken sick, either he or his wife must recollect ancient directions received from aged people, from doctors, from a skilful grandmother, perhaps, who formerly learned of the Indians of her neighbourhood how to cure simple diseases by means of simple medicines. The swamps and woods are ransacked to find the plants, the bark, the roots prescribed. An ancient almanac, constituting perhaps all his library, with his Bible, may chance to direct him to some more learned ways.

7   Has he a cow or an ox sick, his anxiety is not less, for they constitute part of his riches. He applies what recipes he possesses; he bleeds, he foments; he has no farrier at hand to assist him. Does either his plough or his cart break, he runs to his tools; he repairs them as well as he can. Do they finally break down, with reluctance he undertakes to rebuild them, though he doubts of his success. This was an occupation committed before to the mechanic of his neighbourhood, but necessity gives him invention, teaches him to imitate, to recollect what he has seen. Somehow or another 'tis done, and happily there is no traveller, no inquisitive eye to grin and criticize his work. It answers the purposes for the present. Next time he arrives nearer perfection. Behold him henceforth a sort of intuitive carpenter! Happy man, thou hast nothing to demand of propitious heaven but a long life to enable thee to finish the most material part of thy labours, in order to leave each of thy children an improved inheritance. Thank God and thy fate, thy wife can weave.

This happy talent constitutes the most useful part of her portion. Then all is with thee as well as it can be. The yarn which thy daughters have spun will now be converted into coarse but substantial cloth. Thus his flax and the wool clothes all the family; most women are something of tailors. Thus if they are healthy, these settlers find within themselves a resource against all probable accidents.

8   His ingenuity in the fields is not less remarkable in executing his rural work in the most expeditious manner. He naturally understands the use of levers, handspikes, etc. He studies how to catch the most favourable seasons for each task. This great field of action deters him not. But what shall he do for shoes? Never before did he find himself so near going barefooted. Long wintry nights come on. It ought to be a time of inactivity and repose, considering the amazing fatigues of the summer. The great fire warms the whole house; cheers all the family; it makes them think less of the severity of the season. He hugs himself with an involuntary feeling; he is conscious of present ease and security. He hears the great snow-storm driving by his door; he hears the impotent wind roaring in his chimney. If he regrets his ancient connections, the mug of cider and other conveniences he enjoyed before, he finds himself amply remunerated by the plenty of fuel he now possesses, etc. The rosy children sitting around the hearth, sweat and sleep with their basins of samp on their laps; the industrious mother is rattling at her loom, avariciously improving every minute of her time. Shall the master, the example of so happy a family, smoke and sleep and be idle? No, he has heard the children complain of sores and chilblains for want of shoes; he has leather, but no shoemaker at hand. A secret wish arises, natural enough to a father's heart: he wants to see them all happy. So noble a motive can't but have a successful end. He has, perhaps, a few lasts and some old tools; he tries to mend an old pair. Heaven be praised! The child can walk with them, and boast to the others of his new acquisition. A second pair is attempted; he succeeds as well. He ventures at last to make a new one. They are coarse, heavy, ponderous, and clumsy, but they are tight and strong, and answer all the intended purposes. What more can he want? If his gears break, he can easily repair them. Every man here understands how to spin his own yarn and to make his own ropes. He is a universal fabricator like Crusoe. With bark and splinters the oldest of the children amuse themselves by making little baskets. The hint being praised by the father is further improved, and in a little time they are supplied with what baskets they want.

9   Casks require too much labour and particular ingenuity. He in vain attempts it; he cannot succeed, but indulgent Nature offers him a sufficient compensation. In the woods which surround him hollow trees present themselves to him; he can easily distinguish them by the sound they yield when struck with the ax. They have long served as winter

habitations to squirrels and other animals. Now they are cut into proper lengths, smoothed on the inside. They are placed on the floor and are ready to contain anything but liquids. Tight vessels are not wanted as yet, for he has no fermented liquor to preserve (save spruce beer), until his young orchard begins to bear, and by that time the natural improvement of the country will bring the necessary tradesmen into his neighbourhood.

10   Happy man, did'st thou but know the extent of thy good fortune! Permit me to hold for a minute the sketch of thy political felicity, that thou mayest never forget that share of gratitude which thou owest to the mild government under which thou livest. Thou hast no church-dues to pay derived from the most unaccountable donations, the pious offerings of rough ignorance or mistaken zeal; those ancient calamities are unknown to thy land. Thou mayest go to toil and exert the whole energy and circle of thy industry, and try the activity of human nature in all situations. Fear not that a clergyman whom thou never hearest, or any other, shall demand the tenth part of thy labour. Thy land, descended from its great Creator, holds not its precarious tenure either from a supercilious prince or a proud lord. Thou need'st not dread any contradictions in thy government and laws of thy country; they are simple and natural, and if they are sometimes burdensome in the execution, 'tis the fault of men. Thou need'st not fear those absurd ordinances alternately puzzling the understanding and the reason of subjects, and crushing all national industry. Thou need'st not tremble lest the most incomprehensible prohibitions shall rob thee of that sacred immunity with which the produce of thy farm may circulate from hand to hand until it reaches those of the final exporter. 'Tis all as free as the air which thou breathest. Thy land, thy canton is not claimed by any neighbouring monarch who, anxious for the new dominion, ravages, devastates, and despoils its peaceable inhabitants. Rest secure: no cruel militia-laws shall be enacted to ravish from thee thy son, and to make him serve an unknown master in his wars; to enrich a foreign land with his carcass, unrelieved in his pains and agonies, unpitied in his death. The produce of thy loins shall not feed foreign wolves and vultures.

11   No, undisturbed, this offspring of thine shall remain with thee to co-operate in that family partnership of which thou art the first director and manager. At a proper season thou shalt see him marry, perhaps thy neighbour's daughter. Thou then shalt have the pleasure of settling him on that land which he has helped thee to earn and to clear; henceforth he shall become also a new neighbour to thee, still remaining thy son and friend. Thy heart shall swell with inward exultation when thou shalt see him prosper and flourish, for his future prosperity will be a part of thine in the same proportion as thy family happiness is a part of that diffusive one which overspreads thy country's. In the future extensive

harvests thou shalt raise; and other laborious undertakings which the seasons and the elements bid thee execute quickly. The reunited aid of the combined family by a reciprocal assistance will often throughout the year combine together to accomplish the most painful tasks.

12   Humanity is not obliged here, as in the old world, to pass through the slow windings of the alembic. Here 'tis an abundant spring, running and dividing itself everywhere agreeable to the nature and declivity of the ground. Neither dams nor mounds nor any other obstructions restrain it; 'tis never artificially gathered as a turbid flood to exhale in the sun, nor sunken under ground for some sinister purposes. 'Tis a regular fecundating stream left to the laws of declivity and invariably pursuing its course.

13   Thus this man devoid of society learns more than ever to center every idea within that of his own welfare. To him all that appears good, just, equitable, has a necessary relation to himself and family. He has been so long alone that he has almost forgot the rest of mankind except it is when he carries his crops on the snow to some distant market.

14   The country, however, fills with new inhabitants. His granary is resorted to from all parts by other beginners who did not come so well prepared. How will he sell his grain to these people who are strangers to him? Shall he deduct the expense of carrying it to a distant mill? This would appear just, but where is the necessity of this justice? His neighbours absolutely want his supply; they can't go to other places. He, therefore, concludes upon having the full price. He remembers his former difficulties; no one assisted him then. Why should he assist others? They are all able to work for themselves. He has a large family, and it would be giving its lawful substance away; he cannot do it. How should he be charitable? He has scarcely seen a poor man in his life. How should he be merciful, except from native instinct? He has never heard that it was a necessary qualification, and he has never seen objects that required the benefits of his sympathy. He has had to struggle alone through numbers of difficult situations and inconveniences; he, therefore, deals hardly with his new neighbours. If they are not punctual in their payment, he prosecutes them at law, for by this time its benefits have reached him. 'Tis laid out into a new county, and divided into townships. Perhaps he takes a mortgage on his neighbour's land. But it may happen that it is already encumbered by anterior and more ponderous debts. He knows instinctively the coercive power of the laws: he impeaches the cattle; he has proper writings drawn; he gets bonds in judgment. He secures himself; and all this is done from native knowledge; he has neither counsellor nor advisor. Who can be wiser than himself in this half-cultivated country? The sagacity peculiar to the American never forsakes him; it may slumber sometimes, but upon the appearance of danger it arises again as vigorous as ever.

15   But behold him happily passed through the course of many laborious

years; his wealth and, therefore, his consequence increase with the progress of the settlement. If he is litigious, overbearing, purse-proud, which will very probably be the bent of his mind, he has a large field. Among so many beginners there need be many needy, inconsiderate, drunken, and lazy. He may bring the necessary severity of the law to flourish even in these wilds. Well may we be subjects to its lash, or else we would be too happy, for this is almost all the tribute we pay.

16   Now advanced in life and grown rich, he builds a good substantial stone or frame house, and the humble log one, under which he has so much prospered, becomes the kitchen. Several roads intersect and meet near this spot, which he has contrived on purpose. He becomes an inn-holder and a country-merchant. This introduces him into all the little mysteries of self-interest, clothed under the general name of profits and emoluments. He sells for good that which perhaps he knows to be indifferent, because he also knows that the ashes he has collected, the wheat he has taken in may not be so good or so clean as it was asserted. Fearful of fraud in all his dealings and transactions, he arms himself, therefore, with it. Strict integrity is not much wanted, as each is on his guard in his daily intercourse, and this mode of thinking and acting becomes habitual. If any one is detected in anything too glaring but without the reach of the law, where is the recollection of ancient principles, either civil or religious, that can raise the blush of conscious shame? No minister is at hand by his daily admonitions to put him in remembrance of a vindictive God punishing all frauds and bad intentions, rewarding rectitude and justice. Whatever ideas of this kind they might have imbibed when young; whatever conscience may say; these voices have been so long silent, that they are no longer heard. The law, therefore, and its plain meaning are the only forcible standards which strike and guide their senses and become their rule of action. 'Tis to them an armour serving as well for attack as for defence; 'tis all that seems useful and pervading. Its penalties and benefits are the only thing feared and remembered, and this fearful remembrance is what we might call in the closet a reverence for the law.

17   With such principles of conduct as these, follow him in all these situations which link men in society, in that vast variety of bargains, exchanges, barters, sales, etc.; and adduce the effects which must follow. If it is not "bellum omnium contra omnes," 'tis a general mass of keenness and sagacious acting against another mass of equal sagacity; 'tis caution against caution. Happy, when it does not degenerate into fraud against fraud! The law, which cannot pervade and direct every action, here leaves her children to themselves, and abandons those peccadilloes (which convulse not though they may [dim] some of the most beautiful colours of society) to the more invisible efficacy of religion.

18   But here this great resource fails in some measure, at least with a great many of them, from the weakness of their religious education, from a

long inattention, from the paucity of instructions received. Is it a wonder that new rules of action should arise? It must constitute a new set of opinions, the parent of manners. You have already observed this colonist is necessarily different from what he was in the more ancient settlements he originally came from; become such by his new local situation, his new industry, that share of cunning which was absolutely necessary in consequence of his intercourse with his new neighbours.

Note

[1] A corrupt spelling of "spikenard."

Content Questions

1. How is the American land buyer superior to his European counterpart?
2. Why must the frontier landowner "be everything"?
3. What are the political advantages under which the American landowner lives?
4. Why is the law so important in the developing frontier?

Questions on Presentation

1. What is the effect of Crèvecoeur's frequent use of rhetorical questions?
2. What style differences mark this as being other than a twentieth-century document?
3. How would you describe the tone of voice?
4. Is the metaphor of the stream in paragraph 12 effective? Why?
5. What audience does Crèvecoeur have in mind when he uses words such as exuberancy (1), progeny (1), sagacity (3), indemnity (4), foments (7), farrier (7), remunerated (8), samp (8), chilblains (8), felicity (10), supercilious (10), alembic (12), declivity (12), and litigious (15)?

America's Gunpowder Women

Pearl S. Buck

Pearl S. Buck (1892–1973) was the daughter of American missionaries. When she was three months old her parents took her to China, where she spent the major portion of her first forty years. In 1928, realizing that her daughter was mentally retarded, Buck turned to writing to earn money. Her most well known, and generally considered best work is *The Good Earth* (1931). In addition she is known for *East Wind, West Wind* (1930), *Pavilion of Women* (1946), *Peony* (1948), and *The Exile* and *Fighting Angel* (both 1936), biographies of her mother and father respectively. In 1938 she won the Nobel prize for literature, and by her death had published more than eighty-five novels and short story or essay collections.

Buck's lifelong love for China was matched by her concern for the position of women; many of her novels deal with this subject, as do many of her essays. In this essay, which first appeared in *Harper's* in 1937, she classifies American women and analyzes their position and desires.

1   Some months ago I had the temerity to write an article entitled "America's Medieval Women." These women have had their full revenge on me, not, as I had hoped they would, by much disagreement with me, but by the most dismaying agreement expressed in so many letters, so much talk, and—whenever I had to speak in public—such urgent requests that I go on about women that I wonder why I ever began it.

2   And yet now, completely aware of my own folly in pursuing a course which can lead to none of the peace which I love above all things, here I go on again, not with any hope of accomplishing anything by doing so, but merely because I find there is still something more I want to say about women.

3   I observe of course that American women are not born all alike, whatever they achieve in this direction afterward. By nature they seem indeed among other possible classifications, to fall into three congenital groups. The first one is the talented women, or women with a natural vocation. This group is, naturally, a small one; for the women who are in it must have beside their talent an unusual energy which drives them, in spite of shelter and privilege, to exercise their own powers. They are single-minded creatures and they cannot sink into idleness or fritter away life and time or endure discontent. They possess that rarest gift, integrity of purpose, and they can work, day upon day, mentally and spiritually, as well as physically, upon the one necessity. Such women sacrifice, without knowing they do, what many women hold dear—amusement, society, play of one kind or another—to choose solitude, and profound thinking and feeling, and at last final expression.

4   "To what end?" another woman may ask. To the end perhaps of science—science which has given us light and speed and health and comfort and lifted us out of physical savagery; to the end perhaps of art—art which has lifted us out of mental and spiritual savagery.

5   I remark, however, in passing that I observe also that it is notable in the United States when a woman, even of this small talented group,

chooses to spare herself nothing of the labor which a similarly talented man performs for the same ends. Why should this be unless perhaps it is because we are accustomed to expect so little from a woman?

6   The second group of women is, though far larger than this first one, yet like it in having a vocation; but here it is the vocation of the home. In this group is the woman who is really completely satisfied mentally and spiritually with the physical routine of motherhood and the activity of housekeeping. When her children grow up she begins again with her grandchildren. Her brain has been literally encompassed by the four walls of her home, and is engrossed and satisfied with its enclosed activities. As long as her four walls stand she is contented, busy, useful— a sweet, comforting, essential creature who perfectly fulfils her being and her function, who brings nothing but simple happiness to those about her, though only so long as she gives them freedom to come and go as they will and does not limit them by her own simplicity.

7   But both of these, the woman born talented and the woman born domestic, may be dismissed from mind for the moment. In the first place, important as they are, their combined number in proportion to the whole number of women is very small, and in the second place they are safe and stable citizens, since they know what they want to do and are doing it—in short, they are contented; and any contented person is safe and relatively sane.

8   There remains a third group, a very large one, and these are the ones I call the gunpowder women. Here are millions of America's women, all those whose families are not undergoing actual adversity, who are not compelled to earn money to keep from starvation, who have no definite talent or vocation, who have only a normal interest in home and children so that when these are adequately tended they still have surplus time, energy, and ability which they do not know how to use. To make conditions more difficult for them they have usually a fair or even an excellent education and brains good enough at least to be aware of discontent.

9   It is these gunpowder women who suffer most under the burden of privilege which American women have been given to bear.

10   I set this sentence alone, I throw it like a rock, though I am aware that thus unexplained it will hit some gunpowder woman and, if it does not hurt her, at least it will make her angry. But I take the risk because the very existence of these gunpowder women is a result of this heritage of privilege which so oppresses American women. The talented woman can ignore the oppression and go on doing what she was made to do, as a man does. And a born housekeeper, if her disposition be amiable, as, thank God, it more often is than not, is a comforting and comfortable soul who cannot be spoiled by privilege, since she is happy in her work. But here is this other and far more frequent woman, able, free, educated,

who really quite often wants to contribute something directly to her world and not merely through husband and children. She seldom can, however. Privilege denies it—she is so privileged that her world makes no demand upon her. More than that, no one even expects anything of her. Her very friends discourage her, though they be her fellows in discontent. If she tries tentatively to do something a little more serious than her fellows are doing they cry at her, "My dear, aren't you *wonderful!*"—meaning, "Why on earth do you do it?"—meaning, "Aren't you queer?"—meaning, "You think you're smart!"—meaning, indeed, all those things which discontented helpless women do mean when they see one of their number behaving as the rest of them do not and being, therefore, a reproach to those who do nothing.

II

11   For the vicious result of privilege is that the creature who receives it becomes incapacitated by it as by a disease. Privilege is a serious misfortune anywhere and the more serious because American women do not realize that the privilege they boast is really their handicap and not their blessing. I am sure they do not realize it, because in the agreement and disagreement I had with my former article nearly all the women said, reproachfully, if they disagreed, "You seem to forget that women in America are the most privileged on earth," and, apologetically, if they agreed, "Of course I know women in America are the most privileged on earth, but—"

12   And every time this was said, in either fashion, a certain bit of Chinese history came warningly into my mind. This is the history:

13   Centuries ago when astute China was about to be conquered by the naïve and childlike Manchus, the Chinese used a weapon which gave them the final and actual victory, though the Manchus never knew it. When they were conquered the Chinese said, in effect, to the Manchus, "You are our superiors. Therefore we will perform all unpleasant tasks for you. You shall live in palaces apart and there enjoy yourselves. Sums of money will be set aside for you. You need not labor or strive. We will do everything for you. We want you only to be happy and enjoy yourselves."

14   The Manchus were delighted with this. They laid aside their weapons, went joyfully to the fine palaces the Chinese gave them, and began to spend their lives in pleasure. In a short time the Chinese were ruling their own country again as they always had and the Manchus were as good as dead. Easy food and drink and plenty of leisure had reduced them to complete ineffectuality, just as the Chinese had planned it.

15   Now, therefore, whenever I hear an American woman begin brightly, "Well, anyway, we are the most privileged. . . ." I remember the Man-

chus and am troubled. There is something sinister in this matter of privilege.

16 And yet it is true—I cannot deny it, though I wish I could—the women of the United States are the most privileged in the world. We have never even had a very serious struggle to achieve our privileges, at least any struggle comparable to that of women in other enlightened countries. Privileges have been bestowed upon us, thanks largely to the inflated value which pioneer times gave to American women. That inflation still lasts, although happily it is decreasing. For the moment when American women hit what commercially is called an all-time low they will be forced to wake up, and then perhaps they will put an honest value on themselves, and thus the struggle which other women have made or are making will begin and the result ought to be valuable to everybody. But that moment has not yet arrived, and meanwhile women go on under the handicap of privilege.

17 Of course many women in other countries, not understanding any more than we do the effect of unearned privilege, envy American women.

18 I suppose thousands of Oriental women have said to me at one time or another, "How lucky you are to be an American woman! You have freedom and equality with man. Your parents do not groan when you are born and your brothers do not look down on you as less than they. You can go to school. You need not even marry if you do not wish to— at least, you need never marry someone you do not like."

19 I agreed to all of this and I still agree to it. I had rather be an American woman than a woman of any other country in the world because everything lies ahead of us still, as women. But if I had a chance now at those Oriental women, after these years spent among my own countrywomen, I'd answer something like this:

20 "You know, it's true we are very free. We can be anything we like, we American women—lawyers, doctors, artists, scientists, engineers, anything. But, somehow, we're not!"

21 "You're not!" the Oriental woman would say, astonished. "Why not? Do you mean the doors are open and you don't go out?"

22 "Well, we go out—" I would have to acknowledge. "I suppose most of us go out in some sort of work if we don't marry first; but we secretly hope to marry first, so that we need not, or we want to work just a year or two, and then come back into the home and shut the door and be secure in the old way."

23 "Don't you want to be independent, to be free to come and go as you like?" the Oriental woman cries. "Ah, if I could support myself, know I need not obey father, mother, husband, son all my life—"

24 "Oh, we American women don't obey anyone," I tell her quickly. "Our husbands support us in the home, but we don't obey them. We do come and go as we like. Of course we work in our own way at house

and children, and for a few years we are even quite busy. But we have a great many ways to save labor, and the schools take our children early and then we have a great deal of leisure—at least, *you* would think us very leisured."

25 "Then what do you do?" the Oriental woman asks blankly.

26 "We amuse ourselves somehow," I reply.

27 "You are fed and clothed for that?" she asks.

28 "Yes," I reply. "Many of us—and we all expect it."

29 She cannot understand this, and indeed it is difficult to understand and I cannot explain it to her. Why, in a country where everything is free to women and women are so privileged, is it remarkable when a woman is first-rate in anything? But it is. Thanks to our privileges which compel us to no effort, it is the truth that men excel us, numerically as well as actually, at everything except childbearing, and doubtless if men had to bear children they would soon find some better way of doing it. And women, seeing themselves outstripped without understanding why they are, and yet feeling themselves as able as men, grow discontented and join the crowded ranks of the gunpowder women.

30 The home of course has been the stronghold of this privilege. Behind its sheltering walls women have taken full advantage of every privilege—the privilege of security, the privilege of noncompetitive work, the privilege of privacy. Yes, of privileges women have had plenty, and yet most of them have been denied the one great blessing of man's life— the necessity to go out into the world and earn their bread directly. And this one blessing is worth all privileges put together; for by it man has been compelled to put forth his utmost effort, whetting his brain and sharpening his ambition, and so he has accomplished much.

31 For Nature is not unjust. She does not steal into the womb and like an evil fairy give her good gifts secretly to men and deny them to women. Men and women are born free and equal in ability and brain. The injustice begins after brith. The man is taught that he must develop himself and work, lest he and his woman starve. But the woman is taught merely to develop such things as will please the man, lest she starve because he does not want to feed her. Because of this one simple, overwhelming fact, men have been the producers, the rulers, and even the artists.

32 For necessity makes artists too. Many a talent is born without its mate, energy, and so comes to nothing unless energy is somehow created to develop the talent. Necessity is the magic of this creation for the man; for if he has talent he will, if driven desperately enough, apply his compelled energy to his talent and become at least a fair artist—for genius still remains the combination of highest natural talent and highest natural energy of a quality which functions without outside stimulus— and this combination is rare.

33 "But," a gunpowder woman retorted to this yesterday, "a man can

combine his talent with his bread-winning." She looked round on the walls of her comfortable prison. I could feel her thinking, "If I had been free I might have been a great painter."

34   To which I retorted, "How do you know it is not as easy to combine housekeeping and art as it is to make art a business? You have never tried it because you never had to."

35   No, the man is lucky. By compulsion of society and public opinion, if he has any ability and pride, he simply must work. Nothing excuses him. Home cannot be his escape. And in desperation he somehow begins to try to make a living by what he wants to do. And whether he succeeds or fails in it, he has no refuge from work, hard and endless, and full of insecurity. He bears, indeed, the brunt of that heaviest load of all—insecurity.

36   The curse of too many women has been that they have this privilege of refuge in the home. Behind closed doors they may or must work, it is true, but according to their own hours and ways. They escape all the discipline of concentration upon one task, often uncongenial, hour after hour, year after year, the mental discipline of hard creative thinking, the ruthless discipline of social organization. I have been both breadwinner and housekeeper, and I know that breadwinning is infinitely more tedious, more taxing, more nerve-racking, than housekeeping. Indeed, cooking, cleaning, caring for children, if you know necessary bills are pretty certainly going to be paid, is almost a soporific and as good as play after the insecurity of competition in business and the arts. For safe in the home a woman becomes used to flitting from one thing to another, and her mind forgets or never learns how to concentrate or perhaps to work at all. There, leaning upon another's efforts, she becomes lazy, if not physically lazy, lazy in that core of her being which is the source of life and development, so that when her children are grown—and in a few years they are—and her mechanical tasks are over, she is fit for nothing more. She has excused herself from a life of labor because of these short-lived tasks, which, necessary as they are for a time, should never have been considered adequate for her whole self.

III

37   The truth is that although women are needed to-day in every sort of life in the United States they do not even see they are needed. They have become so corrupted by privilege that they stare out on events and conditions around them with the same unseeing, lack-luster eyes with which women in India have looked out of the windows of their zenanas. The Indian woman was not educated and she could not pass out of her door uncovered, and this American woman is free to come and go and she has been given what education she wanted, and yet there is the

same look of defeat in her eyes that there is in the Indian woman's. Neither is fulfilling that for which she was born; but the American's discontent is keener because she knows it, whether she will acknowledge it or not, and the more clever she is, the more educated, the more of a gunpowder woman she is.

38   I do not in the least blame her for being a gunpowder woman. I can only sympathize with all her small daily explosions, her restlessness, her irritability, her silliness, her running after this and that in heroes, in art, in clothes, in love, in amusements, her secret cynicisms and her childish romanticism, her fears and her explosions too of daring which accomplish so little because they never go far enough. She is unpredictable, not from a calculated desire to charm, but because she really does not know what to do with her inner self.

39   And why should she know? Why should so much more be demanded of her, if she does anything, than is demanded of a man? A man is educated and turned out to work. But a woman is educated—and turned out to grass. The wonder is not that she is unpredictable but that she is not insane. Nothing is arranged for her as it is arranged for the man who under the rule of society, by a series of efforts combined with ability, has his life laid out for him. I say that if a gunpowder woman with no boss to tell her what to do, with no office to schedule her days and force her to activity, with no financial necessity compelling her, no creative demand driving her, no social approbation urging her, if this woman can be her own taskmaster and fulfil herself by some accomplishment, then she is a creature almost superhuman. It is too much to ask of her very often, and when she achieves something she ought to be greatly praised.

40   For consider, please, the advantge a man has in our country over a woman. I repeat, for it is the key to all his success, a man must work or he starves. If he does not actually starve, at least society looks down upon him and makes him ashamed. But a woman within her home may live an absolutely idle existence without starving and without being despised for it. Yet an idle woman ought to be despised as much as an idle man for the good and happiness of all women if nothing else. Anyone who takes food and clothing and shelter for granted, even though it is given by one who loves to give it, and makes no return except privately to an individual, ought to be despised. A woman owes something to the society which gives her husband a chance to earn for her, and social pressure should compel her to make that return.

41   And yet this woman has not even the help of that social pressure. Society pays no attention to her so long as she "behaves herself" and stays at home. She is that most unfortunate of persons, idle because nothing is demanded or expected of her, and yet unable to be happy because she is idle. No wonder discontent is her atmosphere, that "discontent of women" which a visitor from Europe once said struck him "like a hot

wind" when he landed in the United States. What is discontent but spiritual gunpowder of the fullest inflammability? Only the stupid woman can avoid it.

42 When I consider this handicap of privilege, then, which has produced these gunpowder women in my country, I cannot find a single word of blame for them. I know that men would never have risen to their present preeminence in all fields if they had had such a handicap—if, in short, they had not had the advantage of the compulsory discipline of work. I am sure that men would behave certainly no better than women if after the wife was off to office and the children to school, the man were left alone in the house. If he could sit down and read a mystery story at ten o'clock in the morning, he too would do so although a busy world hummed about him. He would curl his hair or waste an hour on his fingernails if there were no one to tell him it was not the time for that sort of thing. He would, it is true, have as she does a deadline to meet in the late afternoon, but with no one to check on him to see how time-wasting he was in getting there, he would waste as much time. He could even be as poor a housekeeper as she sometimes is and no one would blame him very much. His wife would merely work a little harder so as to be able to hire a cook. No, without the discipline of regular labor, of fixed hours, of competitive standards, the man would be where the woman is now.

43 If women excel in nothing it is at bottom as simple as this, and not because men's brains are better than women's. It is a pity, for these gunpowder women are as much a lost source of power in the nation as are the flood waters that rise and rush over the land to no useful purpose. Spoiled, petty, restless, idle, they are our nation's greatest unused resource—good brains going to waste in bridge and movies and lectures and dull gossip, instead of constructively applied to the nation's need of them.

IV

44 "What can we do about it," some of them cry at me, "if that's the way things are?" "Nothing," is my reply, "nothing at all, unless it happens you also want to do something. Nobody will make you do anything. It all depends on how much of a self-starter you are whether or not you can overcome your handicap. Nobody will help you to set about finding out what you want to be or help you to be it. For I don't want to stress doing something as much as *being* what you want to be. Mere activity is the occupation of monkeys and lunatics. Still, unfortunately, doing and being are very closely tied together and unless you are doing what you secretly want to do, you aren't able to be the sort of person you want to be."

45   Yet perhaps it is too much to demand of women that, without any help or encouragement, and indeed often with active discouragement and ridicule, they put aside privilege and take their place in the world's work as ordinary human beings. The Manchus could not do it. They too went on helplessly living in their palaces and houses, and then one day the Chinese realized there was no use in feeding them any more since they were no use to anybody, and so they put them all to death in a quiet, matter-of-fact way, and that was the end of the Manchus in China.

46   Of course exactly that will not happen to women anywhere unless some too enterprising male scientist succeeds in creating life without the help of the female. Women would then doubtless have a very hard time convincing the invincible male that there was any real reason for their further existence. But I hope that long before then the gunpowder women will have come to such a unified state of combustion out of sheer boredom that they will refuse to tolerate their condition of privilege any longer.

47   For the vital difference between the privileged Manchu and the privileged American woman is that the clever Chinese allowed the Manchu no modern education. He was born into his ivory tower and never left it. But the privileged American woman enters hers when she reaches her majority, and she takes with her the influences and the memories of a world in which she had a vital part in her youth and school years, and consequently she never becomes quite tame. If education improves enough, or if society suddenly develops a new need for women, the gunpowder may work more quickly than it is working now merely through the medium of individual discontent. The best thing of course that could happen to American women would be to have some real privation and suffering come upon us because we are women, instead of all this privilege. But we have had no such suffering and are not likely to have any. Everything has been too easy for us and is too easy now. We do not feel anybody's wrongs because we have never been severely wronged, except by all these privileges.

48   I am aware that at this point there are those who will insist that I am unrealistic when I say that the best thing that could happen to American women would be to lose their privileges—that, in the first place, when adversity comes upon a family the woman has plenty of work to do, and second, if women should go out in any large numbers to find jobs, men would promptly pass laws to prevent women holding jobs. To which I reply, first, if she can be occupied thoroughly at home, let her be, and second, laws discriminating against women on a large scale would be a splendid thing for women—especially for American women, spoiled and wilful, but high-spirited daughters of the same fathers as their men. If laws so discriminated on any large scale, then gunpowder

women would rise up against them, and this revolt would do them in-finite good. It would bring them out of their seclusion into the life of the nation. In demanding their rights as human beings they would realize at last that they had to *be* human beings as well as women to secure and hold that which they demand. And having fought for something, they might go on from there.

49   As things are, the only real hope for the progress of women generally is in those women who because of some personal necessity do work and take an active share in the life of the world, who are participants and not parasites. The working woman—may her numbers increase!—will not perhaps ever fight for women, but perhaps she will fight to right a wrong near her, and by her work, even now, all women are brought more actively into the life of the world.

50   For I am convinced there is no way of progress for women except the way men have gone—the way of work or starve, work or be disgraced. A good many women are plodding, willingly or unwillingly, along that way, learning to take what they get and do with it, to live with hazard and competition, to push past failure and begin again, to keep their mouths shut instead of spilling over into talk or a good childish cry—in other words, they are becoming mature individuals in their own right.

51   It is a hard road for long-privileged creatures, and one is alternately amused and angry to see many of them avoiding it and retreating again into the home. The newest generation of women, frightened by the real-ities of depression and economic struggle, are clamoring afresh for mar-riage and the home, and to-day marriage competition is keener than ever. Women's interest in work and a profession has not been lower since the pioneering fight for women's rights was won than it is now. Indeed, it seems that the newest generation of women, having seen a glimpse of reality in the depression years, are in definite, full retreat into the safety of femininity, into the easy old ways of living to please one man, and catching him and persuading him to do the work for two. That more women now than ever before take it as a matter of course that they must find jobs and earn their living is meaningless so long as so many of them secretly hope to give up these jobs as soon as they marry—"stop work" as they put it—and go back to the traditional place in the home. Mind you, there are ways and places and times when a woman can find a full job in her home. But to one such woman there are fifty who do not and cannot, and there is no use in pretending they are earning their keep as human beings.

52   "Why earn if I don't have to?" someone asks. Well, why, if not simply to see if women do not feel happier, as men do, in using all faculties and capabilities? I am always glad when I hear a woman has to earn her own living. I scorn the usual talk, "Poor thing, she has to go out and work after all these years of being provided for!" Who gave anyone the right

of being provided for all those years when everywhere in the world people have to work? Yet this is not the important thing. The real point upon which this woman is to be congratulated when she does have to work is that at last compulsion is upon her to exert her body and mind to its utmost, so that she may know what real fatigue is and honest exhaustion and the salutary fear that maybe she is not good enough for the job which brings her bread, and above all, know the final inexpressible joy of complete self-forgetfulness which comes only in soul-fulfilling work.

53 Work is the one supreme privilege which too many women in America with all their extraordinary unearned privileges never know. And yet it is the one privilege which will make them free.

V

54 I ought really to stop here. It is a good stopping place. But I am uncomfortably aware of women who will cry out when they read this, "Why don't you tell us what to do? It is easy enough to say something is wrong, but the useful thing is to say what will right it."

55 To which I answer, nothing will right it for everybody at once. The most tragic person in our civilization is the middle-aged woman whose duties in the home are finished, whose children are gone, and who is in her mental and physical prime and yet feels there is no more need for her. She should have begun years before to plan for this. Her mind at least should have been working toward it all the times when her hands were busy. It is as difficult for her to begin something now in middle life as it would be for a middle-aged man to change his profession. How can she re-educate herself at fifty?

56 And yet I do not know that she is more piteous than the many young women, educated for nothing in particular, who now out of school are trying to find out what they are for. For the most part of course they occupy themselves in the enormously competitive marriage business which they carry on, unaided, in spite of their inexperience. If they marry, they follow the path the fifty-year-old woman has gone and arrive at the same dead end. The gunpowder group is made up of all of them, young and old.

57 "But what can we do?" When they are pricked, thus they bleed.

58 Well, what can women do in the United States, women who do not have to do anything?

59 I wonder if they realize, in the first place, how the United States looks to someone coming here freshly for the first time? It has of course many aspects. But all of these blend into one general impression. It looks like a bachelor's house. One does not see the much-talked-of "woman's touch" anywhere. It looks what it is—a country men have made alone.

There are things and places of great beauty in it—and everywhere ugliness and untidiness and carelessness. It is a man's house, well furnished and with good pictures and rugs and considerable comfort, but there is dust and the rugs have not been swept under since they were put down, and things are lying about and there is disorder and lack of organization. I have driven through cities and towns and villages in many parts of the United States and thought to myself, "Can it be possible there are any women living here? How can they let this place be so hideous?" Billboards and tawdry stands, dirty streets and unpainted buildings, staring signs and dumps and filthy water—the much vaunted feminine instincts for beauty and organization and cleanliness seem not to extend beyond the four walls of immaculate individual homes. Women have the zenana outlook here too, it seems—these things outside the home are not their business.

60   I have not gone anywhere in the country without seeing something vitally necessary for women to do and which is not done—and without finding, too, these gunpowder women fuming with discontent because there was nothing to do. Can the American woman not see? It is simply foolish to list the things waiting for them to do. There is nothing they cannot do if they only would. They can make cleanliness and beauty in town and countryside in small ways and large, they can improve housing, plan houses and build them, go seriously after government positions, get better laws made and kept, improve conditions locally and nationally for children, investigate and change obsolete education in schools and text-books—work for women is everywhere. Who said men's brains were better at politics and government than women's? Yet only yesterday an able woman, working for her political party, sat in my office and told me disconsolately that women were given only petty offices in the party, assistant something-or-other, vice-presidencies on small committees, where their only duty was to obey the man above them. And why should obstetricians be men, or dentists or scientists or architects? I heard a famous gynecologist say last week that gynecology could never be perfected until women entered the field seriously, for no man could ever understand completely what child-bearing was or a woman's needs at that time. Business has been built almost entirely without the practical, constructive hands of women. If women had not been so hidden in the home we might never have had this accursed relation between capital and labor, not because women's influence would "exalt" a work-a-day world in the ridiculous sentimental sense in which some women like to think it would, but merely because women are more practical about human relations than men are, more sensitive to justice in diverse claims, and above all, far more experienced in adjustment and compromise. They should be better bargainers than men.

61   But all this sort of thing is obvious and every member of a woman's

club must be familiar with it. Modern young women of energy are indeed fairly sick of hearing of such work and damn it as "uplift," without, however, I observe, having done anything about it. Then let their interest, if they have any, be expressed in individual competence and achievement, too personal to allow of general suggestion here. Such individuals should take a good aptitude test and find out their own capabilities. My point still stands—to the newcomer, the United States presents the aspects of a bachelor's house. Woman's influence has everywhere been lacking. Whatever has developed in the life of the nation has developed without her brains and her effort. I do not put any stock in this matter of her inspiration of man in his home. It seems not to have had much actual effect. He has done as he wanted to do, with or without it. I suspect woman's inspiration of man has been a good deal of what men call "kidding the little woman along." How can one inspire when one does not understand through ordinary participation?

62   Of course if women's work in the nation has scarcely begun, I am too much of a realist to believe that were it all done the nation would be completely changed for the better. Some things would be much better and some might be worse. The great change would not be in what women accomplished. It would be in the women themselves—that is, the gunpowder women. The talented women of the first group and the homemakers of the second group would be about as they are. Nothing will change them much. But the gunpowder women would be no longer fussing and fretting. Their energies would be happily released elsewhere than on harassed husbands and overwrought children.

63   But I refuse to be too cynical. I do believe the whole nation would be better off if women would do the work waiting to be done, and not only because these women themselves would be happier and their relations with men more satisfying than they now are. I believe that by using the energy now idle and the brains now disintegrating in that idleness women could immeasurably improve all conditions in our country, if they would. And, I repeat, it is perfect nonsense for any woman to ask what there is for her to do. There is everything for her to do. If she wants a small job, let her look around her village or her neighborhood. If she wants a big job, let her look around her State, or think as largely as her nation or even realize there is a world beyond. Let her remember she can do anything she wills to do. Not to see the infinite number of things to be done is to prove the damage that privilege does to the perceptions; not to do after she sees, is to prove the damage already done to the will.

64   Is it hopeless? For the women resigned to privilege, it is hopeless—for these women give up even discontent and pass into nothing. It is not necessary to give them a group to themselves. Having died, they simply await burial.

65   But for the gunpowder women there is every hope. I listen to their dis-

content with all the excitement and delight that a doctor knows when he hears the murmur and feels the beat of an uncertain heart, however fluttering and unstable, beneath his instrument. I know this, at least— as long as a woman complains, she is a gunpowder woman—and still alive.

Content Questions

1. What are the three groups into which Buck classifies women?
2. What is the result of privilege?
3. Why does Buck use the term "gunpowder women"? What are they?
4. What is the only way women may progress?
5. Who is the most tragic person in "our civilization"? Why?

Questions on Presentation

1. Why does Buck chose the first person in which to present her essay? How is the effect different from what the effect would have been had she used the third person?
2. Buck's essay is divided into five parts. How does each division advance the overall argument?
3. Why does Buck set the sentence in paragraph 9 alone, as she says, "throw it like a rock"?
4. Is the dialogue Buck presents in paragraphs 20–28 an effective way of making her point? Why?
5. Is Buck's comparison of American women with the Manchus effective? Why?

Whispers from a Dead World

Joseph Little

Joseph Little grew up on the Mescalero Apache reservation in New Mexico, close to the mountains he loves and frequently writes about. He graduated from the University of New Mexico and entered law school to study Indian law. While in school, Little feels he learned much about the Anglo race and came to see how justice and human prejudice are entwined. He writes that it saddens him to see "that a race that can produce such noble ideals cannot live by them. I am caught between mixed blood, mixed cultures, mixed hopes." In the following story, taken from *The Man to Send Rain Clouds* (1974), Little dramatizes the conflicts he feels.

1   *Aquinas,[1] as a philosopher of being, says a creature exercises its most basic act by simply being, but in existing it tends to perfect its being.*

2   The sun was already well on its daily ramble when Walter stepped out of the house, the ripped screen door slamming behind him. He adjusted his black cowboy hat as he walked across the dirt road that took up where his short front yard left off. He ducked through the large hole in a barbed-wire fence where the strands had been stretched apart, and threaded his way down the side of the hill toward the main highway.

3   *Augustine's[2] ethics are based on love and the use of the will. His ethical outlook establishes a search for earthly well-being leading to a preparation of the soul for eternal salvation. It is theocentric eudaimonism.*

4   It wasn't quite noon when Walter stepped into the dimly lit recesses of the tribal bar. Little spots danced in front of his eyes, miniature copies of the sun that glared outside. His eyes quickly adjusted, and he could make out three figures sitting on bar stools by the time he reached the counter. The bartender stood behind the counter wiping a glass, the glass resting on his stomach which his T-shirt strained to contain. Walter blinked and asked him, "Have you seen my wife?"

5   "Not since you two were in here together, and that was two days ago."

6   "Oh, well give me a Coors, will ya."

7   Walter was about halfway through his second drink when he felt a hand clutch his shoulder. He turned and was hit by a wave of wine-sweet breath. He looked into a pair of bloodshot eyes.

8   "How about a drink?"

9   "I'm broke."

10   "Don't give me that shit. How about a drink?"

11   "I'm broke, I told you. Go find someone else to bother."

12   The hand left his shoulder, and the sickly sweet wine odor dissipated, smothering a string of garbled curses.

13   *The promptings of an informed reason and moral conscience represent an inherent tendency in the nature of man, and conformity to this nature fulfills both the cosmic plan of the creator and the direct commands of God as revealed by Scripture.*

14   The sun was resting on the mountains when Walter finally stumbled out of the bar. Arm in arm he and a friend weaved their way down a dirt path edged by a wall of weeds. They reached the creek and flopped down on its grassy bank. They both dropped their heads into the icy water and came up shaking them. They pulled their shirt tails out of their pants and wiped their faces almost dry. On their knees, with streams of water dribbling down their chests, they burst out laughing. Slowly subsiding into fits of choking, they dragged themselves to some nearby trees, and sat leaning against the cottonwood trunks. It was almost dark now, and the crickets could be heard all around. A cool breeze swept through the limbs of the creaking cottonwoods, and the sweet smell of grass filled their nostrils.

15   "Hey, Paul, I thought you were working."

16   "I got laid off last week. Laid a bunch of us off."

17   "Hand me that bottle of wine."

18   "Hey, saw your wife last night. She was over at your brother's house."

19   *. . . it is not sufficient for our conscience to be aware of the law; our will must be rectified so that it will yield to it and put it into practice. This rectification of the will is brought about by the illuminating action of the divine virtues.*

20   The dogs were barking wildly when Walter staggered the last few steps to the porch and wrapped his arms around one of its pole supports. He closed his eyes and his head became a black, swirling abyss. He opened them quickly and tried to focus them on the front door. He remained staring at it for a couple of minutes before he pulled himself together and attacked it. Leaning on it for support, he banged on the door with both fists and tried to curse as best his thick tongue would allow.

21   The door finally opened, and his brother stood facing him, hair rumpled, his face distorted by sleep, and clad only in his underwear. Walter stood rocking back and forth, trying to enunciate, "Where is my wife?" Finally he fell against his brother, making a clumsy attempt to grasp his throat. Then his head snapped back as a fist slammed into his mouth. He sailed backward off the porch and rolled to a stop in a clump of bushes. As he got to his hands and knees, he could make out the outlines of his wife's face bobbing over his brother's shoulder, and caught her curses. Then the door slammed.

22   *. . . the nature of man is determined by the eternal law, one is in accord with the eternal law by doing what is in accord with nature. When one acts contrary to nature, one is in the wrong.*

23   Walter had washed himself clean in the creek in the early purple light

of dawn. The early morning wind whipped his hair and stirred the branches of the piñon trees into life. He had just started to trace one of the many deer trails that zigzagged along the side of the mountain slope, when he stopped and looked back down into the valley below him. Thousands of clustered sunflowers were raising their heads toward the sun as it grew over the mountain rim. Farther down, the sheen of the sinuous creek disappeared into a forest of willows. Above him the slope of the mountain swept steeply upward. Yucca plants and mesquite bushes clung tenaciously to its side, their roots lost in rocks. Way above, the demarcation of the timber line stretched like a hairline along the top of the mountain. Walter's ears caught the sound of the bluejays and robins as he started his ascent.

24   *Man's greatest virtue is "authenticity," a kind of honesty and courage to see the world in its absurdity and to face the necessity of decisions, the recognition of their moral aspects, and the acceptance of responsibility for it.*

25   Walter stood on a high ledge and looked down into the valley. The pines whispered about him, and his mind rode on the wave of those whispers. The sun caressed his back. And, now stripped to the waist, his body soaked in the warmth. From below, an eagle rose upward in ever-increasing circles. It stretched out its wings and rose toward the sun. Walter stretched out his arms and gave his body to the wind. And for an instant he, too, soared free. And then he traced the upward path of the eagle.

Notes

[1]St. Thomas Aquinas (c. 1224–1274), a Catholic theologian and philosopher, sought compromise for many questions. He argues, for example, that faith falls between opinion and scientific truth and that man, by an act of will, accepts faith. [Eds.]

[2]St. Augustine (354–430), author of the *Confessions*, was an important figure in the transition from Roman paganism to Christianity in the Middle Ages. [Eds.]

Content Questions

1.   What whispers do the characters hear from a dead world?
2.   Why do Walter and Paul laugh when they get out of the icy water?
3.   Why are the philosophical quotations important to the story?

Questions on Presentation

1. Why does Little insert the quotations where he does, rather than grouping them together at the beginning of the story?
2. In any short story, the setting is important because it can establish the mood and can foreshadow how the story will end. How does Little use setting to help readers understand Walter's character and his suicide?

Good Souls
Dorothy Parker

Poet, short story writer, and critic Dorothy Parker (1893–1968) was born in New Jersey and educated in New York City at the Blessed Sacrament Convent. In 1917 she became the drama critic for *Vanity Fair*, the magazine that first published "Good Souls." Parker was also a regular contributor to *The New Yorker* magazine from its beginnings in 1925. She published several books of short stories including *Laments for the Living* (1930) and *Here Lies* (1939). In her books of poetry, such as *Enough Rope* (1927), *Death and Taxes* (1931), and *Not So Deep As a Well* (1936), Parker dissects people's frailties and blunderings with caustic wit and sardonic humor. In her poetry as well as in her essays, Parker turned her attention to "middle-class pretenses," actions such as those of the well-meaning but infuriating good soul.

1   All about us, living in our very families, it may be, there exists a race of curious creatures. Outwardly, they possess no marked peculiarities; in fact, at a hasty glance, they may be readily mistaken for regular human beings. They are built after the popular design; they have the usual number of features, arranged in the conventional manner; they offer no variations on the general run of things in their habits of dressing, eating, and carrying on their business.

2   Yet, between them and the rest of the civilized world, there stretches an impassable barrier. Though they live in the very thick of the human race, they are forever isolated from it. They are fated to go through life, congenital pariahs. They live out their little lives, mingling with the world, yet never a part of it.

3   They are, in short, Good Souls.

4   And the piteous thing about them is that they are wholly unconscious of their condition. A Good Soul thinks he is just like anyone else. Nothing could convince him otherwise. It is heartrending to see him, going cheerfully about, even whistling or humming as he goes, all unconscious of his terrible plight. The utmost he can receive from the world is an attitude of good-humored patience, a perfunctory word of approbation, a praising with faint damn's, so to speak,—yet he firmly believes that everything is all right with him.

5   There is no accounting for Good Souls.

6   They spring up anywhere. They will suddenly appear in families which, for generations, have had no slightest stigma attached to them. Possibly they are throw-backs. There is scarcely a family without at least one Good Soul somewhere in it at the present moment—maybe in the form of an elderly aunt, an unmarried sister, an unsuccessful brother, an indigent cousin. No household is complete without one.

7   The Good Soul begins early; he will show signs of his condition in extreme youth. Go now to the nearest window, and look out on the little children playing so happily below. Any group of youngsters that you may happen to see will do perfectly. Do you observe the child whom all the other little dears make "it" in their merry games? Do you follow the child from whom the other little ones snatch the cherished candy, to consume it before his streaming eyes? Can you get a good look at the child whose precious toys are borrowed for indefinite periods by the other playful youngsters, and are returned to him in fragments? Do you see the child upon whom all the other kiddies play their complete repertory of childhood's winsome pranks—throwing bags of water on him, running away and hiding from him, shouting his name in quaint rhymes, chalking coarse legends on his unsuspecting back?

8   Mark that child well. He is going to be a Good Soul when he grows up.

9   Thus does the doomed child go through early youth and adolescence. So does he progress towards the fulfilment of his destiny. And then, some day, when he is under discussion, someone will say of him, "Well, he means well, anyway." That settles it. For him, that is the end. Those words have branded him with the indelible mark of his pariahdom. He has come into his majority; he is a full-fledged Good Soul.

10   The activities of the adult of the species are familiar to us all. When you are ill, who is it that hastens to your bedside bearing moulds of blanc-mange,[1] which, from infancy, you have hated with unspeakable loathing? As usual, you are way ahead of me, gentle reader,—it is indeed the Good Soul. It is the Good Souls who efficiently smooth out your pillow when you have just worked it into the comfortable shape, who creak about the room on noisy tiptoe, who tenderly lay on your fevered

brow damp cloths which drip ceaselessly down your neck. It is they who ask, every other minute, if there isn't something that they can do for you. It is they who, at great personal sacrifice, spend long hours sitting beside your bed, reading aloud the continued stories in the *Woman's Home Companion*, or chatting cozily on the increase in the city's death rate.

11   In health, as in illness, they are always right there, ready to befriend you. No sooner do you sit down, than they exclaim that they can see you aren't comfortable in that chair, and insist on your changing places with them. It is the Good Souls who just *know* that you don't like your tea that way, and who bear it masterfully away from you to alter it with cream and sugar until it is a complete stranger to you. At the table, it is they who always feel that their grapefruit is better than yours and who have to be restrained almost forcibly from exchanging with you. In a restaurant, the waiter invariably makes a mistake and brings them something which they did not order—and which they refuse to have changed, choking it down with a wistful smile. It is they who cause traffic blocks, by standing in subway entrances arguing altruistically as to who is to pay the fare.

12   At the theatre, should they be members of a box-party, it is the Good Souls who insist on occupying the rear chairs; if the seats are in the orchestra, they worry audibly, all through the performance, about their being able to see better than you, until finally in desperation you grant their plea and change seats with them. If, by so doing, they can bring a little discomfort on themselves—sit in a draught, say, or behind a pillar—then their happiness is complete. To feel the genial glow of martyrdom—that is all that they ask of life.

13   Good Souls are punctilious in their observation of correct little ceremonies. If, for example, they borrow a postage stamp, they immediately offer two pennies in return for it—they insist upon this business transaction. They never fail to remember birthdays—their little gift always brings with it a sharp stab of remembrance that you have blissfully ignored their own natal day. At the last moment, on Christmas Eve, comes a present from some Good Soul whose existence, in the rush of holiday shopping you have completely overlooked. When they go away, be it only for an overnight stay, they never neglect to send postcards bearing views of the principal buildings of the place to all their acquaintances; to their intimates, they always bring back some local souvenir— a tiny dish, featuring the gold-lettered name of the town; a thimble in an appropriate case, both bearing the name of their native city; a tie-rack with the name of its place of residence burned decoratively on its wood; or some such useful novelty.

14   The lives of Good Souls are crowded with Occasions, each with its own ritual which must be solemnly followed. On Mothers' Day, Good

Souls conscientiously wear carnations; on St. Patrick's Day, they faithfully don boutonnieres of shamrocks; on Columbus Day, they carefully pin on miniature Italian flags. Every feast must be celebrated by the sending out of cards—Valentine's Day, Arbor Day, Groundhog Day, and all the other important festivals, each is duly observed. They have a perfect genius for discovering appropriate cards of greeting for the event. It must take hours of research.

15   If it's too long a time between holidays, then the Good Soul will send little cards or little mementoes, just by way of surprises. He is strong on surprises, anyway. It delights him to drop in unexpectedly on his friends. Who has not known the joy of those evenings when some Good Soul just runs in, as a surprise? It is particularly effective when a chosen company of other guests happens to be present—enough for two tables of bridge, say. This means that the Good Soul must sit wistfully by, patiently watching the progress of the rubber, or else must cut in at intervals, volubly voicing his desolation at causing so much inconvenience, and apologizing constantly during the evening.

16   His conversation, admirable though it is, never receives its just due of attention and appreciation. He is one of those who believe and frequently quote the exemplary precept that there is good in everybody; hanging in his bedchamber is the whimsically phrased, yet vital, statement, done in burned leather—"There is so much good in the worst of us and so much bad in the best of us that it hardly behooves any of us to talk about the rest of us." This, too, he archly quotes on appropriate occasions. Two or three may be gathered together, intimately discussing some mutual acquaintance. It is just getting really absorbing, when comes the Good Soul, to utter his dutiful, "We mustn't judge harshly— after all, we must always remember that many times our own actions may be misconstrued." Somehow, after several of these little reminders, there seems to be a general waning of interest; the little gathering breaks up, inventing quaint excuses to get away and discuss the thing more fully, adding a few really good details, some place where the Good Soul will not follow. While the Good Soul, pitifully ignorant of their evil purpose, glows with the warmth of conscious virtue, and settles himself to read the Contributors' Club, in the *Atlantic Monthly*, with a sense of duty well done.

17   Yet it must not be thought that their virtue lifts Good Souls above the enjoyment of popular pastimes. Indeed, it does not; they are enthusiasts on the subject of good, wholesome fun. They lavishly patronize the drama, in its cleaner forms. They flock to the plays of Miss Rachel Crothers, Miss Eleanor Porter, and Mr. Edward Childs Carpenter. They are passionate admirers of the art of Mr. William Hodge. In literature, they worship at the chaste shrines of Harold Bell Wright, Gene Stratton-

Porter, Eleanor Hallowell Abbott, Alice Hegan Rice, and the other triple-named apostles of optimism. They have never felt the same towards Arnold Bennett since he sprung "The Pretty Lady" on them; they no longer give "The Human Machine" and "How to Live on Twenty-four Hours a Day" as birthday offerings to their friends. In poetry, though Tennyson, Whittier, and Longfellow stand for the highest, of course, they have marked leaning toward the later works of Mrs. Ella Wheeler Wilcox. They are continually meeting people who know her, encounters of which they proudly relate. Among humorists, they prefer Mr. Ellis Parker Butler.

18   Good Souls, themselves, are no mean humorists. They have a time-honored formula of fun-making, which must be faithfully followed. Certain words or phrases must be whimsically distorted every time they are used. "Over the river," they dutifully say, whenever they take their leave. "Don't you cast any asparagus on me," they warn, archly; and they never fail to speak of "three times in concussion." According to their ritual, these screaming phrases must be repeated several times, for the most telling effect, and are invariably followed by hearty laughter from the speaker, to whom they seem eternally new.

19   Perhaps the most congenial rôle of the Good Soul is that of advice-giver. He loves to take people aside and have serious little personal talks, all for their own good. He thinks it only right to point out faults or bad habits which are, perhaps unconsciously, growing on them. He goes home and laboriously writes long, intricate letters, invariably beginning, "Although you may feel that this is no affair of mine, I think that you really ought to know," and so on, indefinitely. In his desire to help, he reminds one irresistibly of Marcelline, who used to try so pathetically and so fruitlessly to be of some assistance in arranging the circus arena, and who brought such misfortunes on his own innocent person thereby.

20   The Good Souls will, doubtless, gain their reward in Heaven; on this earth, certainly, theirs is what is technically known as a rough deal. The most hideous outrages are perpetrated on them. "Oh, he won't mind," people say. "He's a Good Soul." And then they proceed to heap the rankest impositions upon him. When Good Souls give a party, people who have accepted weeks in advance call up at the last second and refuse, without the shadow of an excuse save that of a subsequent engagement. Other people are invited to all sorts of entertaining affairs; the Good Soul, unasked, waves them a cherry good-bye and hopes wistfully that they will have a good time. His is the uncomfortable seat in the motor; he is the one to ride backwards in the train; he is the one who is always chosen to solicit subscriptions and make up deficits. People borrow his

money, steal his servants, lose his golf balls, use him as a sort of errand boy, leave him flat whenever something more attractive offers—and carry it all off with their cheerful slogan, "Oh, he won't mind—he's a Good Soul."

21   And that's just it—Good Souls never do mind. After each fresh atrocity they are more cheerful, forgiving and virtuous, if possible, than they were before. There is simply no keeping them down—back they come, with their little gifts, and their little words of advice, and their little endeavors to be of service, always anxious for more.

22   Yes, there can be no doubt about it—their reward will come to them in the next world.

23   Would that they were even now enjoying it!

Note

[1]A type of sweetened milk pudding made with cornstarch. [Eds.]

Content Questions

1.   What traits characterize Good Souls?
2.   If they have so many good traits, why are Good Souls detestable?
3.   Why are Good Souls "wholly unconscious to their condition"?
4.   What should happen to Good Souls?

Questions on Presentation

1.   What is Parker's tone?
2.   Rather than give readers generalities about Good Souls, Parker details certain actions shared by all Good Souls. Does Parker create a convincing character portrait by using details rather than generalities?
3.   Whenever we read, we ask ourselves what a writer's purpose is and what actions a writer wants readers to take based on an essay. How well does Parker make her purpose and intentions known to readers?
4.   Which of Parker's examples of Good Souls is most effective? Why?
5.   What is the purpose of the very short paragraphs 3, 5, and 8?

⚖

Movimientos de rebeldía
y las culturas que traicionan

Gloria Anzaldúa

Poet and essayist Gloria Anzaldúa (b. 1942) grew up in the Chicano community of the Texas-Mexican border where her father was a sharecropper. In her book *Borderlands/La Frontera* (1987), from which this essay is taken, she examines her life of growing up caught between cultures: Chicano and Anglo, male and female, traditional and modern. She runs the gamut of emotions in her text, but finally her work is about the joy, the exuberance of life.

1   *Esos movimientos de rebeldía que tenemos en la sangre nosotros los mexicanos surgen como ríos desbocanados en mis venas. Y como mi raza que cada en cuando deja caer esa esclavitud de obedecer, de callarse y aceptar, en mi está la rebeldía encimita de mi carne. Debajo de mi humillada mirada está una cara insolente lista para explotar. Me costó muy caro mi rebeldía—acalambrada con desvelos y dudas, sintiendome inútil, estúpida, e impotente.*

2   *Me entra una rabia cuando alguien—sea mi mamá, la Iglesia, la cultura de los anglos—me dice haz esto, haz eso sin considerar mis deseos.*

3   *Repele. Hable pa' 'tras. Fuí muy hocicona. Era indiferente a muchos valores de mi cultura. No me deje de los hombres. No fuí buena ni obediente.*

4   *Pero he crecido. Ya no soló paso toda mi vida botando las costumbres y los valores de mi cultura que me traicionan. También recojo las costumbres que por el tiempo se han provado y las costumbres de respeto a las mujeres.* But despite my growing tolerance, for this Chicana *la guerra de independencia* is a constant.*

The Strength of My Rebellion

5   I have a vivid memory of an old photograph: I am six years old. I stand between my father and mother, head cocked to the right, the toes of my flat feet gripping the ground. I hold my mother's hand.

6   To this day I'm not sure where I found the strength to leave the source, the mother, disengage from my family, *mi tierra, mi gente,* and all that picture stood for. I had to leave home so I could find myself, find my own intrinsic nature buried under the personality that had been imposed on me.

7   I was the first in six generations to leave the Valley, the only one in

my family to ever leave home. But I didn't leave all the parts of me: I kept the ground of my own being. On it I walked away, taking with me the land, the Valley, Texas. *Gané mi camino y me largué, Muy anda-riega mi hija.* Because I left of my own accord *me dicen, "¿Cómo te gusta la mala vida?"*

8   At a very early age I had a strong sense of who I was and what I was about and what was fair. I had a stubborn will. It tried constantly to mobilize my soul under my own regime, to live life on my own terms no matter how unsuitable to others they were. *Terca.* Even as a child I would not obey. I was "lazy." Instead of ironing my younger brothers' shirts or cleaning the cupboards, I would pass many hours studying, reading, painting, writing. Every bit of self-faith I'd painstakingly gathered took a beating daily. Nothing in my culture approved of me. *Había agarrado malos pasos.* Something was "wrong" with me. *Estabá más allá de la tradición.*

9   There is a rebel in me—the Shadow-Beast. It is a part of me that refuses to take orders from outside authorities. It refuses to take orders from my conscious will, it threatens the sovereignty of my rulership. It is that part of me that hates constraints of any kind, even those self-imposed. At the least hint of limitations on my time or space by others, it kicks out with both feet. Bolts.

Cultural Tyranny

10   Culture forms our beliefs. We perceive the version of reality that it communicates. Dominant paradigms, predefined concepts that exist as unquestionable, unchallengeable, are transmitted to us through the culture. Culture is made by those in power—men. Males make the rules

---

*Those movements of rebellion that we Mexicans have in our blood surge like raging rivers in my veins. And like my "raza" that every once in a while lets go of the slavery of obedience, of keeping quiet in acceptance, this rebellion within me lies at the very surface of my flesh. Beneath the look of humiliation in my eyes, there is a face insolent and ready to explode. My rebellion has been costly—seized by sleeplessness and doubt. I've often felt useless, stupid, and impotent.

A rabid anger takes me over when someone—be it my mother, the Church, Anglo culture—tells me to do something, without ever considering what I want.

I turned against that. I talked back. I was a loudmouth. I was indifferent to many of my own cultural values. I would not let men take advantage of me. I was neither good nor obedient.

But I have grown. Nowadays I don't just pass my time throwing off the costumes and values of my culture, even though they betray me. I also embrace the costumes that are time-tested as well as those that respect women. But despite my growing tolerance, for this Chicana the war of independence is a constant. [Eds.]

and laws; women transmit them. How many times have I heard mothers and mothers-in-law tell their sons to beat their wives for not obeying them, for being *hociconas* (big mouths), for being *callajeras* (going to visit and gossip with neighbors), for expecting their husbands to help with the rearing of children and the housework, for wanting to be something other than housewives?

11   The culture expects women to show greater acceptance of, and commitment to, the value system than men. The culture and the Church insist that women are subservient to males. If a woman rebels she is a *mujer mala*. If a woman doesn't renounce herself in favor of the male, she is selfish. If a woman remains a *virgen* until she marries, she is a good woman. For a woman of my culture there used to be only three directions she could turn: to the Church as a nun, to the streets as a prostitute, or to the home as a mother. Today some of us have a fourth choice: entering the world by way of education and career and becoming self-autonomous persons. A very few of us. As a working class people our chief activity is to put food in our mouths, a roof over our heads and clothes on our backs. Educating our children is out of reach for most of us. Educated or not, the onus is still on woman to be a wife/mother— only the nun can escape motherhood. Women are made to feel total failures if they don't marry and have children. "*¿Y cuándo te casas, Gloria? Se te va a pasar el tren.*" Y yo les digo, "*Pos si me caso, no va ser con un hombre.*" Se quedan calladitas. Sí, soy hija de la Chingada. I've always been her daughter. *No 'tés chingando.*

12   Humans fear the supernatural, both the undivine (the animal impulses such as sexuality, the unconscious, the unknown, the alien) and the divine (the superhuman, the god in us). Culture and religion seek to protect us from these two forces. The female, by virtue of creating entities of flesh and blood in her stomach (she bleeds every month but does not die), by virtue of being in tune with nature's cycles, is feared. Because, according to Christianity and most other major religions, woman is carnal, animal, and closer to the undivine, she must be protected. Protected from herself. Woman is the stranger, the other. She is man's recognized nightmarish pieces, his Shadow-Beast. The sight of her sends him into a frenzy of anger and fear.

13   *La gorra, el rebozo, la mantilla* are symbols of my culture's "protection" of women. Culture (read males) professes to protect women. Actually it keeps women in rigidly defined roles. It keeps the girlchild from other men—don't poach on my preserves, only I can touch my child's body. Our mothers taught us well, "*Los hombres nomás quieren una cosa*"; men aren't to be trusted, they are selfish and are like children. Mothers made sure we didn't walk into a room of brothers or fathers or uncles in nightgowns or shorts. We were never alone with men, not even those of our own family.

14   Through our mothers, the culture gave us mixed messages: *No voy a dejar que ningún pelado desgraciado maltrate a mis hijos.* And in the next breath it would say, *La mujer tiene que hacer lo que le diga el hombre.* Which was it to be—strong, or submissive, rebellious or conforming?

15   Tribal rights over those of the individual insured the survival of the tribe and were necessary then, and, as in the case of all indigenous peoples in the world who are still fighting off intentional, premeditated murder (genocide), they are still necessary.

16   Much of what the culture condemns focuses on kinship relationships. The welfare of the family, the community, and the tribe is more important than the welfare of the individual. The individual exists first as kin—as sister, as father, as *padrino*—and last as self.

17   In my culture, selfishness is condemned, especially in women; humility and selflessness, the absence of selfishness, is considered a virtue. In the past, acting humble with members outside the family ensured that you would make no one *envidioso* (envious); therefore he or she would not use witchcraft against you. If you get above yourself, you're an *envidiosa*. If you don't behave like everyone else, *la gente* will say that you think you're better than others, *que te crees grande*. With ambition (condemned in the Mexican culture and valued in the Anglo) comes envy. *Respeto* carries with it a set of rules so that social categories and hierarchies will be kept in order: respect is reserved for *la abuela, papá, el patrón*, those with power in the community. Women are at the bottom of the ladder one rung above the deviants. The Chicano, *mexicano,* and some Indian cultures have no tolerance for deviance. Deviance is whatever is condemned by the community. Most societies try to get rid of their deviants. Most cultures have burned and beaten their homosexuals and others who deviate from the sexual common.[1] The queer are the mirror reflecting the heterosexual tribe's fear: being different, being other and therefore lesser, therefore sub-human, inhuman, non-human.

Half and Half

18   There was a *muchacha* who lived near my house. *La gente del pueblo* talked about her being *una de las otras*, "of the Others." They said that for six months she was a woman who had a vagina that bled once a month, and that for the other six months she was a man, had a penis and she peed standing up. They called her half and half, *mita' y mita'*, neither one nor the other but a strange doubling, a deviation of nature that horrified, a work of nature inverted. But there is a magic aspect in abnormality and so-called deformity. Maimed, mad, and sexually different people were believed to possess supernatural powers by primal cultures' magico-religious thinking. For them, abnormality was the price a person had to pay for her or his inborn extraordinary gift.

19   There is something compelling about being both male and female, about having an entry into both worlds. Contrary to some psychiatric tenets, half and halfs are not suffering from a confusion of sexual identity, or even from a confusion of gender. What we are suffering from is an absolute despot duality that says we are able to be only one or the other. It claims that human nature is limited and cannot evolve into something better. But I, like other queer people, am two in one body, both male and female. I am the embodiment of the *hieros gamos*: the coming together of opposite qualities within.

Fear of Going Home: Homophobia

20   For the lesbian of color, the ultimate rebellion she can make against her native culture is through her sexual behavior. She goes against two moral prohibitions: sexuality and homosexuality. Being lesbian and raised Catholic, indoctrinated as straight, I *made the choice to be queer* (for some it is genetically inherent). It's an interesting path, one that continually slips in and out of the white, the Catholic, the Mexican, the indigenous, the instincts. In and out of my head. It makes for *loquería*, the crazies. It is a path of knowledge—one of knowing (and of learning) the history of oppression of our *raza*. It is a way of balancing, of mitigating duality.

21   In a New England college where I taught, the presence of a few lesbians threw the more conservative heterosexual students and faculty into a panic. The two lesbian students and we two lesbian instructors met with them to discuss their fears. One of the students said, "I thought homophobia meant fear of going home after a residency."

22   And I thought, how apt. Fear of going home. And of not being taken in. We're afraid of being abandoned by the mother, the culture, *la Raza*, for being unacceptable, faulty, damaged. Most of us unconsciously believe that if we reveal this unacceptable aspect of the self our mother/culture/race will totally reject us. To avoid rejection, some of us conform to the values of the culture, push the unacceptable parts into the shadows. Which leaves only one fear—that we will be found out and that the Shadow-Beast will break out of its cage. Some of us take another route. We try to make ourselves conscious of the Shadow-Beast, stare at the sexual lust and lust for power and destruction we see on its face, discern among its features the undershadow that the reigning order of heterosexual males project on our Beast. Yet still others of us take it another step: we try to waken the Shadow-Beast inside us. Not many jump at the chance to confront the Shadow-Beast in the mirror without flinching at her lidless serpent eyes, her cold clammy moist hand dragging us underground, fangs barred and hissing. How does one put feathers on this particular serpent? But a few of us have been lucky—on the

face of the Shadow-Beast we have seen not lust but tenderness; on its face we have uncovered the lie.

Intimate Terrorism: Life in the Borderlands

23   The world is not a safe place to live in. We shiver in separate cells in enclosed cities, shoulders hunched, barely keeping the panic below the surface of the skin, daily drinking shock along with our morning coffee, fearing the torches being set to our buildings, the attacks in the streets. Shutting down. Woman does not feel safe when her own culture, and white culture, are critical of her; when the males of all races hunt her as prey.

24   Alienated from her mother culture, "alien" in the dominant culture, the woman of color does not feel safe within the inner life of her Self. Petrified, she can't respond, her face caught between *los intersticios*, the spaces between the different worlds she inhabits.

25   The ability to respond is what is meant by responsibility, yet our cultures take away our ability to act—shackle us in the name of protection. Blocked, immobilized, we can't move forward, can't move backwards. That writhing serpent movement, the very movement of life, swifter than lightning, frozen.

26   We do not engage fully. We do not make full use of our faculties. We abnegate. And there in front of us is the crossroads and choice: to feel a victim where someone else is in control and therefore responsible and to blame (being a victim and transferring the blame on culture, mother, father, ex-lover, friend, absolves me of responsibility), or to feel strong, and, for the most part, in control.

27   My Chicana identity is grounded in the Indian woman's history of resistance. The Aztec female rites of mourning were rites of defiance protesting the cultural changes which disrupted the equality and balance between female and male, and protesting their demotion to a lesser status, their denigration. Like *la Llorona*, the Indian woman's only means of protest was wailing.

28   So *mamá, Raza*, how wonderful, *no tener que rendir cuentas a nadie*. I feel perfectly free to rebel and to rail against my culture. I fear no betrayal on my part because, unlike Chicanas and other women of color who grew up white or who have only recently returned to their native cultural roots, I was totally immersed in mine. It wasn't until I went to high school that I "saw" whites. Until I worked on my master's degree I had not gotten within an arm's distance of them. I was totally immersed *en lo mexicano*, a rural, peasant, isolated, *mexicanismo*. To separate from my culture (as from my family) I had to feel competent enough on the outside and secure enough inside to live life on my own. Yet in leaving home I did not lose touch with my origins because *lo*

mexicano is in my system. I am a turtle, wherever I go I carry "home" on my back.

29   Not me sold out my people but they me. So yes, though "home" permeates every sinew and cartilage in my body, I too am afraid of going home. Though I'll defend my race and culture when they are attacked by non-*mexicanos, conosco el malestar de mi cultura.* I abhor some of my culture's ways, how it cripples its women, *como burras,* our strengths used against us, lowly *burras* bearing humility with dignity. The ability to serve, claim the males, is our highest virtue. I abhor how my culture makes *macho* caricatures of its men. No, I do not buy all the myths of the tribe into which I was born. I can understand why the more tinged with Anglo blood, the more adamantly my colored and colorless sisters glorify their colored culture's values—to offset the extreme devaluation of it by the white culture. It's a legitimate reaction. But I will not glorify those aspects of my culture which have injured me and which have injured me in the name of protecting me.

30   So, don't give me your tenets and your laws. Don't give me your lukewarm gods. What I want is an accounting with all three cultures— white, Mexican, Indian. I want the freedom to carve and chisel my own face, to staunch the bleeding with ashes, to fashion my own gods out of my entrails. And if going home is denied me then I will have to stand and claim my space, making a new culture—*una cultura mestiza*— with my own lumber, my own bricks and mortar and my own feminist architecture.

The Wounding of the india-Mestiza

31   *Estas carnes indias que despreciamos nosotros los mexicanos asi como despreciamos y condenamos a nuestra madre, Malinali. Nos condenamos a nosotros mismos. Esta raza vencida, enemigo cuerpo.*

32   Not me sold out my people but they me. *Malinali Tenepat,* or *Malintzin,* has become known as *la Chingada*—the fucked one. She has become the bad word that passes a dozen times a day from the lips of Chicanos. Whore, prostitute, the woman who sold out her people to the Spaniards are epithets Chicanos spit out with contempt.

33   The worst kind of betrayal lies in making us believe that the Indian woman in us is the betrayer. We, *indias y mestizas,* police the Indian in us, brutalize and condemn her. Male culture has done a good job on us. *Son los costumbres que traicionan. La india en mí es la sombra: La Chingada, Tlazolteotl, Coatlicue. Son ellas que oyemos lamentando a sus hijas perdidas.*

34   Not me sold out my people but they me. Because of the color of my skin they betrayed me. The dark-skinned woman has been silenced,

gagged, caged, bound into servitude with marriage, bludgeoned for 300 years, sterilized and castrated in the twentieth century. For 300 years she has been a slave, a force of cheap labor, colonized by the Spaniard, the Anglo, by her own people (and in Mesoamerica her lot under the Indian patriarchs was not free of wounding). For 300 years she was invisible, she was not heard. Many times she wished to speak, to act, to protest, to challenge. The odds were heavily against her. She hid her feelings; she hid her truths; she concealed her fire; but she kept stoking the inner flame. She remained faceless and voiceless, but a light shone through her veil of silence. And though she was unable to spread her limbs and though for her right now the sun has sunk under the earth and there is no moon, she continues to tend the flame. The spirit of the fire spurs her to fight for her own skin and a piece of ground to stand on, a ground from which to view the world—a perspective, a home-ground where she can plumb the rich ancestral roots into her own ample *mestiza* heart. She waits till the waters are not so turbulent and the mountains not so slippery with sleet. Battered and bruised she waits, her bruises throwing her back upon herself and the rhythmic pulse of the feminine. *Coatlalopeuh* waits with her.

Aquí en la soledad prospera su rebeldía.
En la soledad Ella prospera.

Note

[1]Francisco Guerra, *The Pre-Columbian Mind: A study into the aberrant nature of sexual drives, drugs affecting behaviour, and the attitude towards life and death, with a survey of psychotherapy in pre-Columbian America* (New York, NY: Seminar Press, 1971).

Content Questions

1. What is the Shadow-Beast?
2. How does culture form an individual's beliefs?
3. How does Chicano culture define men? Women?
4. Why does Anzaldúa reject her "culture"?
5. According to Anzaldúa, what is the worst betrayal?

Questions on Presentation

1. What is the effect of interspersing the English text with Spanish words, phrases, or passages?

2. Why does Anzaldúa use so many references to the supernatural?
3. Is the definition of culture in paragraphs 10 and 11 effective? How does it direct the rest of the essay?
4. Why does Anzaldúa refer, near the beginning of the essay, to the photograph?
5. Paragraphs 29, 32, and 34 begin with the same statement. Why has the author done this?

Questions for Discussion and Writing

1. Many of the essays in Section 4 discuss the confrontations between one culture and another. Analyze the ways in which such a confrontation is developed in one of the essays. Is the confrontation understandable and/or believable? If so, what did the writer do to make it realistic? If not, why isn't the situation believable?
2. Compare and contrast the ways in which two authors in this section reveal the confrontation with another culture. Are both writers equally effective? What makes one writer's approach more effective than the other's? If they are both good writers, why? Do they use similar techniques or ideas? If so, what are they? Do these ideas help the authors create effective essays?
3. Several of the essays in this section deal with how we learn about ourselves. The authors present various insights into what we know about intelligence, how we classify types of individuals, and how we come to understand who we are. Based on the essays in Section 4, what are the general approaches to understanding ourselves and our culture? Which approaches seem most useful to you and why? Which approaches will never work and why?
4. Some of the selections in this section identify clashes between two cultures, a theme repeated throughout this textbook. How is the clash between cultures, depicted in a work such as "The Bride Comes to Yellow Sky," similar to or different from the clash depicted in a work such as "How Many Sheep Will It Hold?" or "Whispers from a Dead World"?
5. Stereotyping is a common technique writers use to highlight differences between people or groups. Frequently, for example, writers point out the differences between men and women by stereotyping both. There are certain expected roles for men and women, certain ways they may or may not respond to situations. These stereotypes, in turn, are parodied either explicitly or, as you have seen in some of the selections in this section, implicitly. What is the contemporary stereotype for men? How do you see it in the readings in this section? Is it a reasonable image? Is it one that contemporary men can accept? Why or why not?

Section 5

LITERARY ANALYSIS

Fenimore Cooper's Literary Offenses

Samuel L. Clemens

In his essays, as in his best-known novels *The Adventures of Tom Sawyer* (1876) and *The Adventures of Huckleberry Finn* (1884), Clemens enriched American literature by using humor, enduring characterizations, and the cadence of American speech. As a critic and humorist, Clemens delighted in satirizing social evils, pretentious puritans and conservatives, and in debunking the claims of politicians and fundamentalists. He was distressed by language that was pretentious, obscure, or difficult, believing that the plain speech of the American people was the most effective means of communication. In this essay he attacks what he sees as the overblown, romantic, and unconvincing language used by Fenimore Cooper in *The Deerslayer* (1841), one of Cooper's most popular books.

1   *The Pathfinder* and *The Deerslayer* stand at the head of Cooper's novels as artistic creations. There are others of his works which contain parts as perfect as are to be found in these, and scenes even more thrilling. Not one can be compared with either of them as a finished whole.

2   The defects in both of these tales are comparatively slight. They were pure works of art.—*Prof. Lounsbury.*

3   The five tales reveal an extraordinary fulness of invention.

4   . . . One of the very greatest characters in fiction, Natty Bumppo. . . .

5   The craft of the woodsman, the tricks of the trapper, all the delicate art of the forest, were familiar to Cooper from his youth up.—*Prof. Brander Matthews.*

6   Cooper is the greatest artist in the domain of romantic fiction yet produced by America.—*Wilkie Collins.*

7   It seems to me that it was far from right for the Professor of English Literature in Yale, the Professor of English Literature in Columbia, and Wilkie Collins to deliver opinions on Cooper's literature without having read some of it. It would have been much more decorous to keep silent and let persons talk who have read Cooper.

8   Cooper's art has some defects. In one place in *Deerslayer,* and in the restricted space of two-thirds of a page, Cooper has scored 114 offences against literary art out of a possible 115. It breaks the record.

9   There are nineteen rules governing literary art in the domain of romantic fiction—some say twenty-two. In *Deerslayer* Cooper violated eighteen of them. These eighteen require:

10   1. That a tale shall accomplish something and arrive somewhere. But the *Deerslayer* tale accomplishes nothing and arrives in the air.

11   2. They require that the episodes of a tale shall be necessary parts of the tale, and shall help to develop it. But as the *Deerslayer* tale is not a tale, and accomplishes nothing and arrives nowhere, the episodes have no rightful place in the work, since there was nothing for them to develop.

12   3. They require that the personages in a tale shall be alive, except in the case of corpses, and that always the reader shall be able to tell the corpses from the others. But this detail has often been overlooked in the *Deerslayer* tale.

13   4. They require that the personages in a tale, both dead and alive, shall exhibit a sufficient excuse for being there. But this detail also has been overlooked in the *Deerslayer* tale.

14   5. They require that when the personages of a tale deal in conversation, the talk shall sound like human talk, and be talk such as human beings would be likely to talk in the given circumstances, and have a discoverable meaning, also a discoverable purpose, and a show of relevancy, and remain in the neighborhood of the subject in hand, and be interesting to the reader, and help out the tale, and stop when the people cannot think of anything more to say. But this requirement has been ignored from the beginning of the *Deerslayer* tale to the end of it.

15   6. They require that when the author describes the character of a personage in his tale, the conduct and conversation of that personage shall justify said description. But this law gets little or no attention in the *Deerslayer* tale, as Natty Bumppo's case will amply prove.

16   7. They require that when a personage talks like an illustrated, gilt-edged, tree-calf, hand-tooled, seven-dollar Friendship's Offering in the beginning of a paragraph, he shall not talk like a negro minstrel in the end of it. But this rule is flung down and danced upon in the *Deerslayer* tale.

17   8. They require that crass stupidities shall not be played upon the reader as "the craft of the woodsman, the delicate art of the forest," by

either the author or the people in the tale. But this rule is persistently violated in the *Deerslayer* tale.

18   9. They require that the personages of a tale shall confine themselves to possibilities and let miracles alone; or, if they venture a miracle, the author must so plausibly set it forth as to make it look possible and reasonable. But these rules are not respected in the *Deerslayer* tale.

19   10. They require that the author shall make the reader feel a deep interest in the personages of his tale and in their fate; and that he shall make the reader love the good people in the tale and hate the bad ones. But the reader of the *Deerslayer* tale dislikes the good people in it, is indifferent to the others, and wishes they would all get drowned together.

20   11. They require that the characters in a tale shall be so clearly defined that the reader can tell beforehand what each will do in a given emergency. But in the *Deerslayer* tale this rule is vacated.

21   In addition to these large rules there are some little ones. These require that the author shall

22   12. *Say* what he is proposing to say, not merely come near it.

23   13. Use the right word, not its second cousin.

24   14. Eschew surplusage.

25   15. Not omit necessary details.

26   16. Avoid slovenliness of form.

27   17. Use good grammar.

28   18. Employ a simple and straightforward style.

29   Even these seven are coldly and persistently violated in the *Deerslayer* tale.

30   Cooper's gift in the way of invention was not a rich endowment; but such as it was he liked to work it, he was pleased with the effects, and indeed he did some quite sweet things with it. In his little box of stage properties he kept six or eight cunning devices, tricks, artifices for his savages and woodsmen to deceive and circumvent each other with, and he was never so happy as when he was working these innocent things and seeing them go. A favorite one was to make a moccasined person tread in the tracks of the moccasined enemy, and thus hide his own trail. Cooper wore out barrels and barrels of moccasins in working that trick. Another stage-property that he pulled out of his box pretty frequently was his broken twig. He prized his broken twig above all the rest of his effects, and worked it the hardest. It is a restful chapter in any book of his when somebody doesn't step on a dry twig and alarm all the reds and whites for two hundred yards around. Every time a Cooper person is in peril, and absolute silence is worth four dollars a minute, he is sure to step on a dry twig. There may be a hundred handier things to step on, but that wouldn't satisfy Cooper. Cooper requires him to turn out and find a dry twig; and if he can't do it, go and borrow one. In fact,

the Leather Stocking Series ought to have been called the Broken Twig Series.

31   I am sorry there is not room to put in a few dozen instances of the delicate art of the forest, as practised by Natty Bumppo and some of the other Cooperian experts. Perhaps we may venture two or three samples. Cooper was a sailor—a naval officer; yet he gravely tells us how a vessel, driving towards a lee shore in a gale, is steered for a particular spot by her skipper because he knows of an *undertow* there which will hold her back against the gale and save her. For just pure woodcraft, or sailor-craft, or whatever it is, isn't that neat? For several years Cooper was daily in the society of artillery, and he ought to have noticed that when a cannon-ball strikes the ground it either buries itself or skips a hundred feet or so; skips again a hundred feet or so—and so on, till it finally gets tired and rolls. Now in one place he loses some "females"—as he always calls women—in the edge of a wood near a plain at night in a fog, on purpose to give Bumppo a chance to show off the delicate art of the forest before the reader. These mislaid people are hunting for a fort. They hear a cannon-blast, and a cannon-ball presently comes rolling into the wood and stops at their feet. To the females this suggests nothing. The case is very different with the admirable Bumppo. I wish I may never know peace again if he doesn't strike out promptly and *follow the track* of that cannon-ball across the plain through the dense fog and find the fort. Isn't it a daisy? If Cooper had any real knowledge of Nature's ways of doing things, he had a most delicate art in concealing the fact. For instance: one of his acute Indian experts, Chingachgook (pronounced Chicago, I think), has lost the trail of a person he is tracking through the forest. Apparently that trail is hopelessly lost. Neither you nor I could ever have guessed out the way to find it. It was very different with Chicago. Chicago was not stumped for long. He turned a running stream out of its course, and there, in the slush in its old bed, were that person's moccasin-tracks. The current did not wash them away, as it would have done in all other like cases—no, even the eternal laws of Nature have to vacate when Cooper wants to put up a delicate job of woodcraft on the reader.

32   We must be a little wary when Brander Matthews tells us that Cooper's books "reveal an extraordinary fulness of invention." As a rule, I am quite willing to accept Brander Matthews's literary judgments and applaud his lucid and graceful phrasing of them; but that particular statement needs to be taken with a few tons of salt. Bless your heart, Cooper hadn't any more invention than a horse; and I don't mean a high-class horse, either; I mean a clothes-horse. It would be very difficult to find a really clever "situation" in Cooper's books, and still more difficult to find one of any kind which he has failed to render absurd by his handling of it. Look at the episodes of "the caves"; and at the celebrated

scuffle between Maqua and those others on the table-land a few days later; and at Hurry Harry's queer water-transit from the castle to the ark; and at Deerslayer's half-hour with his first corpse; and at the quarrel between Hurry Harry and Deerslayer later; and at—but choose for yourself; you can't go amiss.

33 If Cooper had been an observer his inventive faculty would have worked better; not more interestingly, but more rationally, more plausibly. Cooper's proudest creations in the way of "situations" suffer noticeably from the absence of the observer's protecting gift. Cooper's eye was splendidly inaccurate. Cooper seldom saw anything correctly. He saw nearly all things as through a glass eye, darkly. Of course a man who cannot see the commonest little every-day matters accurately is working at a disadvantage when he is constructing a "situation." In the *Deerslayer* tale Cooper has a stream which is fifty feet wide where it flows out of a lake; it presently narrows to twenty as it meanders along for no given reason, and yet when a stream acts like that it ought to be required to explain itself. Fourteen pages later the width of the brook's outlet from the lake has suddenly shrunk thirty feet, and become "the narrowest part of the stream." This shrinkage is not accounted for. The stream has bends in it, a sure indication that it has alluvial banks and cuts them; yet these bends are only thirty and fifty feet long. If Cooper had been a nice and punctilious observer he would have noticed that the bends were oftener nine hundred feet long than short of it.

34 Cooper made the exit of that stream fifty feet wide, in the first place, for no particular reason; in the second place, he narrowed it to less than twenty to accommodate some Indians. He bends a "sapling" to the form of an arch over this narrow passage, and conceals six Indians in its foliage. They are "laying" for a settler's scow or ark which is coming up the stream on its way to the lake; it is being hauled against the stiff current by a rope whose stationary end is anchored in the lake; its rate of progress cannot be more than a mile an hour. Cooper describes the ark, but pretty obscurely. In the matter of dimensions "it was little more than a modern canal-boat." Let us guess, then, that it was about one hundred and forty feet long. It was of "greater breadth than common." Let us guess, then, that it was about sixteen feet wide. This leviathan had been prowling down bends which were but a third as long as itself, and scraping between banks where it had only two feet of space to spare on each side. We cannot too much admire this miracle. A low-roofed log dwelling occupies "two-thirds of the ark's length"—a dwelling ninety feet long and sixteen feet wide, let us say—a kind of vestibule train. The dwelling has two rooms—each forty-five feet long and sixteen feet wide, let us guess. One of them is the bedroom of the Hutter girls, Judith and Hetty; the other is the parlor in the daytime, at night it is papa's bedchamber. The ark is arriving at the stream's exit now, whose width has

been reduced to less than twenty feet to accommodate the Indians—say to eighteen. There is a foot to spare on each side of the boat. Did the Indians notice that there was going to be a tight squeeze there? Did they notice that they could make money by climbing down out of that arched sapling and just stepping aboard when the ark scraped by? No; other Indians would have noticed these things, but Cooper's Indians never notice anything. Cooper thinks they are marvellous creatures for noticing, but he was almost always in error about his Indians. There was seldom a sane one among them.

35   The ark is one hundred and forty feet long; the dwelling is ninety feet long. The idea of the Indians is to drop softly and secretly from the arched sapling to the dwelling as the ark creeps along under it at the rate of a mile an hour, and butcher the family. It will take the ark a minute and a half to pass under. It will take the ninety foot dwelling a minute to pass under. Now, then, what did the six Indians do? It would take you thirty years to guess, and even then you would have to give it up, I believe. Therefore, I will tell you what the Indians did. Their chief, a person of quite extraordinary intellect for a Cooper Indian, warily watched the canal-boat as it squeezed along under him, and when he had got his calculations fined down to exactly the right shade, as he judged, he let go and dropped. And *missed the house!* That is actually what he did. He missed the house, and landed in the stern of the scow. It was not much of a fall, yet it knocked him silly. He lay there unconscious. If the house had been ninety-seven feet long he would have made the trip. The fault was Cooper's, not his. The error lay in the construction of the house. Cooper was no architect.

36   There still remained in the roost five Indians. The boat has passed under and is now out of their reach. Let me explain what the five did— you would not be able to reason it out for yourself. No. 1 jumped for the boat, but fell in the water astern of it. Then No. 2 jumped for the boat, but fell in the water still farther astern of it. Then No. 3 jumped for the boat, and fell a good way astern of it. Then No. 4 jumped for the boat, and fell in the water *away* astern. Then even No. 5 made a jump for the boat—for he was a Cooper Indian. In the matter of intellect, the difference between a Cooper Indian and the Indian that stands in front of the cigar-shop is not spacious. The scow episode is really a sublime burst of invention; but it does not thrill, because the inaccuracy of the details throws a sort of air of fictitiousness and general improbability over it. This comes of Cooper's inadequacy as an observer.

37   The reader will find some examples of Cooper's high talent for inaccurate observation in the account of the shooting-match in *The Pathfinder*.

A common wrought nail was driven lightly into the target, its head having been first touched with paint.

38   The color of the paint is not stated—an important omission, but Cooper deals freely in important omissions. No, after all, it was not an important omission; for this nail-head is *a hundred yards* from the marksmen, and could not be seen by them at that distance, no matter what its color might be. How far can the best eyes see a common house-fly? A hundred yards? It is quite impossible. Very well; eyes that cannot see a house-fly that is a hundred yards away cannot see an ordinary nail-head at that distance, for the size of the two objects is the same. It takes a keen eye to see a fly or a nail-head at fifty yards—one hundred and fifty feet. Can the reader do it?

39   The nail was lightly driven, its head painted, and game called. Then the Cooper miracles began. The bullet of the first marksman clipped an edge of the nail-head; the next man's bullet drove the nail a little way into the target—and removed all the paint. Haven't the miracles gone far enough now? Not to suit Cooper; for the purpose of this whole scheme is to show off his prodigy, Deerslayer-Hawkeye-Long-Rifle-Leather-Stocking-Pathfinder-Bumppo before the ladies.

> "Be all ready to clench it, boys!" cried out Pathfinder, stepping into his friend's tracks the instant they were vacant. "Never mind a new nail; I can see that, though the paint is gone, and what I can see I can hit at a hundred yards, though it were only a mosquito's eye. Be ready to clench!"
>
> The rifle cracked, the bullet sped its way, and the head of the nail was buried in the wood, covered by the piece of flattened lead.

40   There, you see, is a man who could hunt flies with a rifle, and command a ducal salary in a Wild West show to-day if we had him back with us.

41   The recorded feat is certainly surprising just as it stands; but it is not surprising enough for Cooper. Cooper adds a touch. He has made Pathfinder do this miracle with another man's rifle; and not only that, but Pathfinder did not have even the advantage of loading it himself. He had everything against him, and yet he made that impossible shot; and not only made it, but did it with absolute confidence, saying, "Be ready to clench." Now a person like that would have undertaken that same feat with a brickbat, and with Cooper to help he would have achieved it, too.

Pathfinder showed off handsomely that day before the ladies. His very first feat was a thing which no Wild West show can touch. He was standing with the group of marksmen, observing—a hundred yards from the target, mind; one Jasper raised his rifle and drove the centre of the bull's-eye. Then the Quartermaster fired. The target exhibited no result this time. There was a laugh. "It's a dead miss," said Major Lundie. Pathfinder waited an impressive moment or two; then said, in that calm, indifferent, know-it-all way of his, "No, Major, he has covered Jasper's bullet, as will be seen if any one will take the trouble to examine the target."

42   Wasn't it remarkable! How *could* he see that little pellet fly through the air and enter that distant bullet-hole? Yet that is what he did; for nothing is impossible to a Cooper person. Did any of those people have any deep-seated doubts about this thing? No; for that would imply sanity, and these were all Cooper people.

> The respect for Pathfinder's skill and for his *quickness and accuracy of sight* [the italics are mine] was so profound and general, that the instant he made this declaration the spectators began to distrust their own opinions; and a dozen rushed to the target in order to ascertain the fact. There, sure enough, it was found that the Quartermaster's bullet had gone through the hole made by Jasper's, and that, too, so accurately as to require a minute examination to be certain of the circumstance, which, however, was soon clearly established by discovering one bullet over the other in the stump against which the target was placed.

43   They made a "minute" examination; but never mind, how could they know that there were two bullets in that hole without digging the latest one out? for neither probe nor eyesight could prove the presence of any more than one bullet. Did they dig? No; as we shall see. It is the Pathfinder's turn now; he steps out before the ladies, takes aim, and fires.

44   But, alas! here is a disappointment; an incredible, an unimaginable disappointment —for the target's aspect is unchanged; there is nothing there but that same old bullet-hole!

> "If one dared to hint at such a thing," cried Major Duncan, "I should say that the Pathfinder has also missed the target."

45   As nobody had missed it yet, the "also" was not necessary; but never mind about that, for the Pathfinder is going to speak.

> "No, no, Major," said he, confidently, "that *would* be a risky declaration. I didn't load the piece, and can't say what was in it; but if it was lead, you will find the bullet driving down those of the Quartermaster and Jasper, else is not my name Pathfinder."
>
> A shout from the target announced the truth of this assertion.

46   Is the miracle sufficient as it stands? Not for Cooper. The Pathfinder speaks again, as he "now slowly advances towards the stage occupied by the females":

> "That's not all, boys, that's not all; if you find the target touched at all, I'll own to a miss. The Quartermaster cut the wood, but you'll find no wood cut by that last messenger."

47   The miracle is at last complete. He knew—doubtless *saw*—at the distance of a hundred yards—that his bullet had passed into the hole *without fraying the edges*. There were now three bullets in that one hole—three bullets embedded processionally in the body of the stump back of the target. Everybody knew this—somehow or other—and yet nobody had dug any of them out to make sure. Cooper is not a close observer, but he is interesting. He is certainly always that, no matter what happens. And he is more interesting when he is not noticing what he is about than when he is. This is a considerable merit.

48   The conversations in the Cooper books have a curious sound in our modern ears. To believe that such talk really ever came out of people's mouths would be to believe that there was a time when time was of no value to a person who thought he had something to say; when it was the custom to spread a two-minute remark out to ten; when a man's mouth was a rolling-mill, and busied itself all day long in turning four-foot pigs of thought into thirty-foot bars of conversational railroad iron by attenuation; when subjects were seldom faithfully stuck to, but the talk wandered all around and arrived nowhere; when conversations consisted mainly of irrelevances, with here and there a relevancy, a relevancy with an embarrassed look, as not being able to explain how it got there.

49   Cooper was certainly not a master in the construction of dialogue. Inaccurate observation defeated him here as it defeated him in so many other enterprises of his. He even failed to notice that the man who talks corrupt English six days in the week must and will talk it on the seventh, and can't help himself. In the *Deerslayer* story he lets Deerslayer talk the showiest kind of book talk sometimes, and at other times the basest of base dialects. For instance, when some one asks him if he has a sweetheart, and if so, where she abides, this is his majestic answer:

> "She's in the forest—hanging from the boughs of the trees, in a soft rain—in the dew on the open grass—the clouds that float about in the blue heavens—the birds that sing in the woods—the sweet springs where I slake my thirst—and in all the other glorious gifts that come from God's Providence!"

50   And he preceded that, a little before, with this:

> "It consarns me as all things that touches a fri'nd consarns a fri'nd."

51   And this is another of his remarks:

> "If I was Injin born, now, I might tell of this, or carry in the scalp and boast of the expl'ite afore the whole tribe; or if my inimy had only been a bear"—and so on.

52   We cannot imagine such a thing as a veteran Scotch Commander-in-Chief comporting himself in the field like a windy melodramatic actor, but Cooper could. On one occasion Alice and Cora were being chased by the French through a fog in the neighborhood of their father's fort:

> "*Point de quartier aux coquins!*" cried an eager pursuer, who seemed to direct the operations of the enemy.
>
> "Stand firm and be ready, my gallant 60ths!" suddenly exclaimed a voice above them; "wait to see the enemy; fire low, and sweep the glacis."
>
> "Father! father!" exclaimed a piercing cry from out the mist; "it is I! Alice! thy own Elsie! spare, O! save your daughters!"
>
> "Hold!" shouted the former speaker, in the awful tones of parental agony, the sound reaching even to the woods, and rolling back in solemn echo. " 'Tis she! God has restored me my children! Throw open the sally-port; to the field, 60ths, to the field; pull not a trigger, lest ye kill my lambs! Drive off these dogs of France with your steel."

53   Cooper's word-sense was singularly dull. When a person has a poor ear for music he will flat and sharp right along without knowing it. He keeps near the tune, but it is *not* the tune. When a person has a poor ear for words, the result is a literary flatting and sharping; you perceive what he is intending to say, but you also perceive that he doesn't *say* it. This is Cooper. He was not a word-musician. His ear was satisfied with the *approximate* word. I will furnish some circumstantial evidence in support of this charge. My instances are gathered from half a dozen pages of the tale called *Deerslayer*. He uses "verbal," for "oral"; "precision," for "facility"; "phenomena," for "marvels"; "necessary," for "predetermined"; "unsophisticated," for "primitive"; "preparation," for "expectancy"; "rebuked," for "subdued"; "dependant on," for "resulting from"; "fact," for "condition"; "fact," for "conjecture"; "precaution," for "caution"; "explain," for "determine"; "mortified," for "disappointed"; "meretricious," for "factitious"; "materially," for "considerably"; "decreasing," for "deepening"; "increasing," for "disappearing"; "embedded," for "enclosed"; "treacherous," for "hostile"; "stood," for "stooped"; "softened," for "replaced"; "rejoined," for "remarked"; "situation," for "condition"; "different," for "differing"; "insensible," for "unsentient"; "brevity," for "celerity"; "distrusted," for "suspicious"; "mental imbecility," for "imbecility"; "eyes," for "sight"; "counteracting," for "opposing"; "funeral obsequies," for "obsequies."

54   There have been daring people in the world who claimed that Cooper could write English, but they are all dead now—all dead but Lounsbury. I don't remember that Lounsbury makes the claim in so many words, still he makes it, for he says that *Deerslayer* is a "pure work of art." Pure, in that connection, means faultless—faultless in all details—and language is a detail. If Mr. Lounsbury had only compared Cooper's En-

glish with the English which he writes himself—but it is plain that he didn't; and so it is likely that he imagines until this day that Cooper's is as clean and compact as his own. Now I feel sure, deep down in my heart, that Cooper wrote about the poorest English that exists in our language, and that the English of *Deerslayer* is the very worst that even Cooper ever wrote.

55   I may be mistaken, but it does seem to me that *Deerslayer* is not a work of art in any sense; it does seem to me that it is destitute of every detail that goes to the making of a work of art; in truth, it seems to me that *Deerslayer* is just simply a literary *delirium tremens*.

56   A work of art? It has no invention; it has no order, system, sequence, or result; it has no lifelikeness, no thrill, no stir, no seeming of reality; its characters are confusedly drawn, and by their acts and words they prove that they are not the sort of people the author claims that they are; its humor is pathetic; its pathos is funny; its conversations are— oh! indescribable; its love-scenes odious; its English a crime against the language.

57   Counting these out, what is left is Art. I think we must all admit that.

Content Questions

1. What are the rules "governing literary art in the domain of romantic fiction"?
2. What is the one offense out of 115 which Cooper has not committed?
3. Why must we be "a little wary when Brander Matthews tells us that Cooper's books 'reveal an extraordinary fulness of invention' "?
4. Why does Clemens feel Cooper's eye was "splendidly inaccurate"?
5. Why does Clemens attack Cooper's "word-sense"? Do you feel the attack is justified?

Questions on Presentation

1. Why does Clemens begin his essay with quotations from critics?
2. Clemens' strongest tool in this essay is sarcasm. Where do you find instances of it? What is its effect on the argument?
3. Do you feel Clemens' use of plot summary is effective? Why or why not?
4. In paragraph 53 Clemens provides a long list of words he maintains Cooper misused and what he feels should be the proper word. What effect does this have on the reader?
5. Without having read *The Deerslayer*, how accurate do you believe Clemens' criticism is? How convincing is it?

⚖️

The Eighty-Yard Run

Irwin Shaw

American playwright, novelist, and short story writer Irwin Shaw (1913–1984) began his writing career as a radio scriptwriter for the "Andy Gump" and "Dick Tracy" programs. Born in New York City, Shaw began writing professionally immediately upon graduating from Brooklyn College. He was the drama critic for *The New Republic* and a creative writing teacher at New York University. He was also a warrant officer during the Second World War. Shaw blended these experiences into a commercially successful career. He first gained critical notice for his antiwar play *Bury the Dead,* but it was his short stories, many of which appeared in *The New Yorker,* that increased his popularity and his reputation as a skilled creator of credible, familiar characters. His short story "Walking Wounded" won the O'Henry Memorial Award in 1944 when Shaw was at the height of his career. Several of Shaw's novels were adapted for the screen including *The Young Lions* (1948) and *Rich Man, Poor Man* (1970), a novel that inspired the television craze for miniseries.

Taken from his collection *Mixed Company* (1942), "The Eighty-Yard Run" is typical of Shaw's fiction. The story chronicles an episode in a college football player's life when he ran for an eighty-yard touchdown in practice; tragically, he cannot equal this achievement.

1   The pass was high and wide and he jumped for it, feeling it slap flatly against his hands, as he shook his hips to throw off the halfback who was diving at him. The center floated by, his hands desperately brushing Darling's knee as Darling picked his feet up high and delicately ran over a blocker and an opposing linesman in a jumble on the ground near the scrimmage line. He had ten yards in the clear and picked up speed, breathing easily, feeling his thigh pads rising and falling against his legs, listening to the sound of cleats behind him, pulling away from them, watching the other backs heading him off toward the sideline, the whole picture, the men closing in on him, the blockers fighting for position, the ground he had to cross, all suddenly clear in his head, for the first time in his life not a meaningless confusion of men, sounds, speed. He smiled a little to himself as he ran, holding the ball lightly in front of him with his two hands, his knees pumping high, his hips twisting in the almost girlish run of a back in a broken field. The first halfback came at him and he fed him his leg, then swung at the last moment, took the shock of the man's shoulder without breaking stride, ran right

through him, his cleats biting securely into the turf. There was only the safety man now, coming warily at him, his arms crooked, hands spread. Darling tucked the ball in, spurted at him, driving hard, hurling himself along, his legs pounding, knees high, all two hundred pounds bunched into controlled attack. He was sure he was going to get past the safety man. Without thought, his arms and legs working beautifully together, he headed right for the safety man, stiff-armed him, feeling blood spurt instantaneously from the man's nose onto his hand, seeing his face go awry, head turned, mouth pulled to one side. He pivoted away, keeping the arm locked, dropping the safety man as he ran easily toward the goal line, with the drumming of cleats diminishing behind him.

2   How long ago? It was autumn then, and the ground was getting hard because the nights were cold and leaves from the maples around the stadium blew across the practice fields in gusts of wind, and the girls were beginning to put polo coats over their sweaters when they came to watch practice in the afternoons.... Fifteen years. Darling walked slowly over the same ground in the spring twilight, in his neat shoes, a man of thirty-five dressed in a double-breasted suit, ten pounds heavier in the fifteen years, but not fat, with the years between 1925 and 1940 showing in his face.

3   The coach was smiling quietly to himself and the assistant coaches were looking at each other with pleasure the way they always did when one of the second stringers suddenly did something fine, bringing credit to them, making their $2,000 a year a tiny bit more secure.

4   Darling trotted back, smiling, breathing deeply but easily, feeling wonderful, not tired, though this was the tail end of practice and he'd run eighty yards. The sweat poured off his face and soaked his jersey and he liked the feeling, the warm moistness lubricating his skin like oil. Off in a corner of the field some players were punting and the smack of leather against the ball came pleasantly through the afternoon air. The freshmen were running signals on the next field and the quarterback's sharp voice, the pound of the eleven pairs of cleats, the "Dig, now *dig!*" of the coaches, the laughter of the players all somehow made him feel happy as he trotted back to midfield, listening to the applause and shouts of the students along the sidelines, knowing that after that run the coach would have to start him Saturday against Illinois.

5   Fifteen years, Darling thought, remembering the shower after the workout, the hot water steaming off his skin and the deep soapsuds and all the young voices singing with the water streaming down and towels going and managers running in and out and the sharp sweet smell of oil of wintergreen and everybody clapping him on the back as he dressed and Packard, the captain, who took being captain very seriously, coming over to him and shaking his hand and saying, "Darling, you're going to go places in the next two years."

6   The assistant manager fussed over him, wiping a cut on his leg with alcohol and iodine, the little sting making him realize suddenly how fresh and whole and solid his body felt. The manager slapped a piece of adhesive tape over the cut, and Darling noticed the sharp clean white of the tape against the ruddiness of the skin, fresh from the shower.

7   He dressed slowly, the softness of his shirt and the soft warmth of his wool socks and his flannel trousers a reward against his skin after the harsh pressure of the shoulder harness and thigh and hip pads. He drank three glasses of cold water, the liquid reaching down coldly inside of him, smoothing the harsh dry places in his throat and belly left by the sweat and running and shouting of practice.

8   Fifteen years.

9   The sun had gone down and the sky was green behind the stadium and he laughed quietly to himself as he looked at the stadium, rearing above the trees, and knew that on Saturday when the 70,000 voices roared as the team came running out onto the field, part of that enormous salute would be for him. He walked slowly, listening to the gravel crunch satisfactorily under his shoes in the still twilight, feeling his clothes swing lightly against his skin, breathing the thin evening air, feeling the wind move softly in his damp hair, wonderfully cool behind his ears and at the nape of his neck.

10   Louise was waiting for him at the road, in her car. The top was down and he noticed all over again, as he always did when he saw her, how pretty she was, the rough blonde hair and the large, inquiring eyes and the bright mouth, smiling now.

11   She threw the door open. "Were you good today?" she asked.

12   "Pretty good," he said. He climbed in, sank luxuriously into the soft leather, stretched his legs far out. He smiled, thinking of the eighty yards. "Pretty damn good."

13   She looked at him seriously for a moment, then scrambled around, like a little girl, kneeling on the seat next to him, grabbed him, her hands along his ears, and kissed him as he sprawled, head back, on the seat cushion. She let go of him, but kept her head close to his, over his. Darling reached up slowly and rubbed the back of his hand against her cheek, lit softly by a street lamp a hundred feet away. They looked at each other, smiling.

14   Louise drove down to the lake and they sat there silently, watching the moon rise behind the hills on the other side. Finally he reached over, pulled her gently to him, kissed her. Her lips grew soft, her body sank into his, tears formed slowly in her eyes. He knew, for the first time, that he could do whatever he wanted with her.

15   "Tonight," he said. "I'll call for you at seven-thirty. Can you get out?"

16   She looked at him. She was smiling, but the tears were still full in her eyes. "All right," she said. "I'll get out. How about you? Won't the coach raise hell?"

17   Darling grinned. "I got the coach in the palm of my hand," he said. "Can you wait till seven-thirty?"

18   She grinned back at him. "No," she said.

19   They kissed and she started the car and they went back to town for dinner. He sang on the way home.

20   Christian Darling, thirty-five years old, sat on the frail spring grass, greener now than it ever would be again on the practice field, looked thoughtfully up at the stadium, a deserted ruin in the twilight. He had started on the first team that Saturday and every Saturday after that for the next two years, but it had never been as satisfactory as it should have been. He never had broken away, the longest run he'd ever made was thirty-five yards, and that in a game that was already won, and then that kid had come up from the third team, Diederich, a blank-faced German kid from Wisconsin, who ran like a bull, ripping lines to pieces Saturday after Saturday, plowing through, never getting hurt, never changing his expression, scoring more points, gaining more ground than all the rest of the team put together, making everybody's All-American, carrying the ball three times out of four, keeping everybody else out of the headlines. Darling was a good blocker and he spent his Saturday afternoons working on the big Swedes and Polacks who played tackle and end for Michigan, Illinois, Purdue, hurling into huge pile-ups, bobbing his head wildly to elude the great raw hands swinging like meat-cleavers at him as he went charging in to open up holes for Diederich coming through like a locomotive behind him. Still, it wasn't so bad. Everybody liked him and he did his job and he was pointed out on the campus and boys always felt important when they introduced their girls to him at their proms, and Louise loved him and watched him faithfully in the games, even in the mud, when your own mother wouldn't know you, and drove him around in her car keeping the top down because she was proud of him and wanted to show everybody that she was Christian Darling's girl. She bought him crazy presents because her father was rich, watches, pipes, humidors, an icebox for beer for his room, curtains, wallets, a fifty-dollar dictionary.

21   "You'll spend every cent your old man owns," Darling protested once when she showed up at his rooms with seven different packages in her arms and tossed them onto the couch.

22   "Kiss me," Louise said, "and shut up."

23   "Do you want to break your poor old man?"

24   "I don't mind. I want to buy you presents."

25   "Why?"

26   "It makes me feel good. Kiss me. I don't know why. Did you know that you're an important figure?"

27   "Yes," Darling said gravely.

28   "When I was waiting for you at the library yesterday two girls saw you

coming and one of them said to the other, 'That's Christian Darling. He's an important figure.' "

29   "You're a liar."

30   "I'm in love with an important figure."

31   "Still, why the hell did you have to give me a forty-pound dictionary?"

32   "I wanted to make sure," Louise said, "that you had a token of my esteem. I want to smother you in tokens of my esteem."

33   Fifteen years ago.

34   They'd married when they got out of college. There'd been other women for him, but all casual and secret, more for curiosity's sake, and vanity, women who'd thrown themselves at him and flattered him, a pretty mother at a summer camp for boys, an old girl from his home town who'd suddenly blossomed into a coquette, a friend of Louise's who had dogged him grimly for six months and had taken advantage of the two weeks that Louise went home when her mother died. Perhaps Louise had known, but she'd kept quiet, loving him completely, filling his rooms with presents, religiously watching him battling with the big Swedes and Polacks on the line of scrimmage on Saturday afternoons, making plans for marrying him and living with him in New York and going with him there to the night clubs, the theaters, the good restaurants, being proud of him in advance, tall, white-teethed, smiling, large, yet moving lightly, with an athlete's grace, dressed in evening clothes, approvingly eyed by magnificently dressed and famous women in theater lobbies, with Louise adoringly at his side.

35   Her father, who manufactured inks, set up a New York office for Darling to manage and presented him with three hundred accounts, and they lived on Beekman Place with a view of the river with fifteen thousand dollars a year between them, because everybody was buying everything in those days, including ink. They saw all the shows and went to all the speakeasies and spent their fifteen thousand dollars a year and in the afternoons Louise went to the art galleries and the matinees of the more serious plays that Darling didn't like to sit through and Darling slept with a girl who danced in the chorus of *Rosalie* and with the wife of a man who owned three copper mines. Darling played squash three times a week and remained as solid as a stone barn and Louise never took her eyes off him when they were in the same room together, watching him with a secret, miser's smile, with a trick of coming over to him in the middle of a crowded room and saying gravely, in a low voice, "You're the handsomest man I've ever seen in my whole life. Want a drink?"

36   Nineteen twenty-nine came to Darling and to his wife and father-in-law, the maker of inks, just as it came to everyone else. The father-in-law waited until 1933 and then blew his brains out and when Darling

went to Chicago to see what the books of the firm looked like he found out all that was left were debts and three or four gallons of unbought ink.

37   "Please, Christian," Louise said, sitting in their neat Beekman Place apartment, with a view of the river and prints of paintings by Dufy and Braque and Picasso on the wall, "please, why do you want to start drinking at two o'clock in the afternoon?"

38   "I have nothing else to do," Darling said, putting down his glass, emptied of its fourth drink. "Please pass the whisky."

39   Louise filled his glass. "Come take a walk with me," she said. "We'll walk along the river."

40   "I don't want to walk along the river," Darling said, squinting intensely at the prints of paintings by Dufy, Braque and Picasso.

41   "We'll walk along Fifth Avenue."

42   "I don't want to walk along Fifth Avenue."

43   "Maybe," Louise said gently, "you'd like to come with me to some art galleries. There's an exhibition by a man named Klee. . . ."

44   "I don't want to go to any art galleries. I want to sit here and drink Scotch whisky," Darling said. "Who the hell hung those goddam pictures up on the wall?"

45   "I did," Louise said.

46   "I hate them."

47   "I'll take them down," Louise said.

48   "Leave them there. It gives me something to do in the afternoon. I can hate them." Darling took a long swallow. "Is that the way people paint these days?"

49   "Yes, Christian. Please don't drink any more."

50   "Do you like painting like that?"

51   "Yes, dear."

52   "Really?"

53   "Really."

54   Darling looked carefully at the prints once more. "Little Louise Tucker. The middle-western beauty. I like pictures with horses in them. Why should you like pictures like that?"

55   "I just happen to have gone to a lot of galleries in the last few years . . ."

56   "Is that what you do in the afternoon?"

57   "That's what I do in the afternoon," Louise said.

58   "I drink in the afternoon."

59   Louise kissed him lightly on the top of his head as he sat there squinting at the pictures on the wall, the glass of whiskey held firmly in his hand. She put on her coat and went out without saying another word. When she came back in the early evening, she had a job on a woman's fashion magazine.

60   They moved downtown and Louise went out to work every morning and Darling sat home and drank and Louise paid the bills as they came up. She made believe she was going to quit work as soon as Darling found a job, even though she was taking over more responsibility day by day at the magazine, interviewing authors, picking painters for the illustrations and covers, getting actresses to pose for pictures, going out for drinks with the right people, making a thousand new friends whom she loyally introduced to Darling.

61   "I don't like your hat," Darling said, once, when she came in in the evening and kissed him, her breath rich with Martinis.

62   "What's the matter with my hat, Baby?" she asked, running her fingers through his hair. "Everybody says it's very smart."

63   "It's too damned smart," he said. "It's not for you. It's for a rich, sophisticated woman of thirty-five with admirers."

64   Louise laughed. "I'm practicing to be a rich, sophisticated woman of thirty-five with admirers," she said. He stared soberly at her. "Now, don't look so grim, Baby. It's still the same simple little wife under the hat." She took the hat off, threw it into a corner, sat on his lap. "See? Homebody Number One."

65   "Your breath could run a train," Darling said, not wanting to be mean, but talking out of boredom, and sudden shock at seeing his wife curiously a stranger in a new hat, with a new expression in her eyes under the little brim, secret, confident, knowing.

66   Louise tucked her head under his chin so he couldn't smell her breath. "I had to take an author out for cocktails," she said. "He's a boy from the Ozark Mountains and he drinks like a fish. He's a Communist."

67   "What the hell is a Communist from the Ozarks doing writing for a woman's fashion magazine?"

68   Louise chuckled. "The magazine business is getting all mixed up these days. The publishers want to have a foot in every camp. And anyway, you can't find an author under seventy these days who isn't a Communist."

69   "I don't think I like you to associate with all those people, Louise," Darling said. "Drinking with them."

70   "He's a very nice, gentle boy," Louise said. "He reads Ernest Dowson."[1]

71   "Who's Ernest Dowson?"

72   Louise patted his arm, stood up, fixed her hair. "He's an English poet."

73   Darling felt that somehow he had disappointed her. "Am I supposed to know who Ernest Dowson is?"

74   "No, dear. I'd better go in and take a bath."

75   After she had gone, Darling went over to the corner where the hat was lying and picked it up. It was nothing, a scrap of straw, a red flower, a

veil, meaningless on his big hand, but on his wife's head a signal of something . . . big city, smart and knowing women drinking and dining with men other than their husbands, conversation about things a normal man wouldn't know much about, Frenchmen who painted as though they used their elbows instead of brushes, composers who wrote whole symphonies without a single melody in them, writers who knew all about politics and women who knew all about writers, the movement of the proletariat, Marx, somehow mixed up with five-dollar dinners and the best-looking women in America and fairies who made them laugh and half-sentences immediately understood and secretly hilarious and wives who called their husbands "Baby." He put the hat down, a scrap of straw and a red flower, and a little veil. He drank some whisky straight and went into the bathroom where his wife was lying deep in her bath, singing to herself and smiling from time to time like a little girl, paddling the water gently with her hands, sending up a slight spicy fragrance from the bath salts she used.

76   He stood over her, looking down at her. She smiled up at him, her eyes half closed, her body pink and shimmering in the warm, scented water. All over again, with all the old suddenness, he was hit deep inside him with the knowledge of how beautiful she was, how much he needed her.

77   "I came in here," he said, "to tell you I wish you wouldn't call me 'Baby.' "

78   She looked up at him from the bath, her eyes quickly full of sorrow, half-understanding what he meant. He knelt and put his arms around her, his sleeves plunged heedlessly in the water, his shirt and jacket soaking wet as he clutched her wordlessly, holding her crazily tight, crushing her breath from her, kissing her desperately, searchingly, regretfully.

79   He got jobs after that, selling real estate and automobiles, but somehow, although he had a desk with his name on a wooden wedge on it, and he went to the office religiously at nine each morning, he never managed to sell anything and he never made any money.

80   Louise was made assistant editor, and the house was always full of strange men and women who talked fast and got angry on abstract subjects like mural painting, novelists, labor unions. Negro short-story writers drank Louise's liquor, and a lot of Jews, and big solemn men with scarred faces and knotted hands who talked slowly but clearly about picket lines and battles with guns and leadpipe at mine-shaft-heads and in front of factory gates. And Louise moved among them all, confidently, knowing what they were talking about, with opinions that they listened to and argued about just as though she were a man. She knew everybody, condescended to no one, devoured books that Darling had

never heard of, walked along the streets of the city, excited, at home, soaking in all the million tides of New York without fear, with constant wonder.

81   Her friends liked Darling and sometimes he found a man who wanted to get off in the corner and talk about the new boy who played fullback for Princeton, and the decline of the double wing-back, or even the state of the stock market, but for the most part he sat on the edge of things, solid and quiet in the high storm of words. "The dialectics of the situation . . . The theater has been given over to expert jugglers . . . Picasso? What man has a right to paint old bones and collect ten thousand dollars for them? . . . I stand firmly behind Trotsky[2] . . . Poe[3] was the last American critic. When he died they put lilies on the grave of American criticism. I don't say this because they panned my last book, but . . ."

82   Once in a while he caught Louise looking soberly and consideringly at him through the cigarette smoke and the noise and he avoided her eyes and found an excuse to get up and go into the kitchen for more ice or to open another bottle.

83   "Come on," Cathal Flaherty was saying, standing at the door with a girl, "you've got to come down and see this. It's down on Fourteenth Street, in the old Civic Repertory, and you can only see it on Sunday nights and I guarantee you'll come out of the theater singing." Flaherty was a big young Irishman with a broken nose who was the lawyer for a longshoreman's union, and he had been hanging around the house for six months on and off, roaring and shutting everybody else up when he got in an argument. "It's a new play, *Waiting for Lefty*; it's about taxi-drivers."

84   "Odets," the girl with Flaherty said. "It's by a guy named Odets."

85   "I never heard of him," Darling said.

86   "He's a new one," the girl said.

87   "It's like watching a bombardment," Flaherty said. "I saw it last Sunday night. You've got to see it."

88   "Come on, Baby," Louise said to Darling, excitement in her eyes already. "We've been sitting in the Sunday *Times* all day, this'll be a great change."

89   "I see enough taxi-drivers every day," Darling said, not because he meant that, but because he didn't like to be around Flaherty, who said things that made Louise laugh a lot and whose judgment she accepted on almost every subject. "Let's go to the movies."

90   "You've never seen anything like this before," Flaherty said. "He wrote this play with a baseball bat."

91   "Come on," Louise coaxed, "I bet it's wonderful."

92   "He has long hair," the girl with Flaherty said. "Odets. I met him at a party. He's an actor. He didn't say a goddam thing all night."

93   "I don't feel like going down to Fourteenth Street," Darling said, wishing Flaherty and his girl would get out. "It's gloomy."

94   "Oh, hell!" Louise said loudly. She looked coolly at Darling, as though she'd just been introduced to him and was making up her mind about him, and not very favorably. He saw her looking at him, knowing there was something new and dangerous in her face and he wanted to say something, but Flaherty was there and his damned girl, and anyway, he didn't know what to say.

95   "I'm going," Louise said, getting her coat. "I don't think Fourteenth Street is gloomy."

96   "I'm telling you," Flaherty was saying, helping her on with her coat, "it's the Battle of Gettysburg, in Brooklynese."

97   "Nobody could get a word out of him," Flaherty's girl was saying as they went through the door. "He just sat there all night."

98   The door closed. Louise hadn't said good night to him. Darling walked around the room four times, then sprawled out on the sofa, on top of the Sunday *Times*. He lay there for five minutes looking at the ceiling, thinking of Flaherty walking down the street talking in that booming voice, between the girls, holding their arms.

99   Louise had looked wonderful. She'd washed her hair in the afternoon and it had been very soft and light and clung close to her head as she stood there angrily putting her coat on. Louise was getting prettier every year, partly because she knew by now how pretty she was, and made the most of it.

100   "Nuts," Darling said, standing up. "Oh, nuts."

101   He put on his coat and went down to the nearest bar and had five drinks off by himself in a corner before his money ran out.

102   The years since then had been foggy and downhill. Louise had been nice to him, and in a way, loving and kind, and they'd fought only once, when he said he was going to vote for Landon.[4] ("Oh, Christ," she'd said, "doesn't *anything* happen inside your head? Don't you read the papers? The penniless Republican!") She'd been sorry later and apologized for hurting him, but apologized as she might to a child. He'd tried hard, had gone grimly to the art galleries, the concert halls, the bookshops, trying to gain on the trail of his wife, but it was no use. He was bored, and none of what he saw or heard or dutifully read made much sense to him and finally he gave it up. He had thought, many nights as he ate dinner alone, knowing that Louise would come home late and drop silently into bed without explanation, of getting a divorce, but he knew the loneliness, the hopelessness, of not seeing her again would be too much to take. So he was good, completely devoted, ready at all times to go any place with her, do anything she wanted. He even got a small job, in a broker's office and paid his own way, bought his own liquor.

103   Then he'd been offered the job of going from college to college as a tailor's representative. "We want a man," Mr. Rosenberg had said, "who as soon as you look at him, you say, 'There's a university man.' " Rosenberg had looked approvingly at Darling's broad shoulders and well-kept waist, at his carefully brushed hair and his honest, wrinkle-less face. "Frankly, Mr. Darling, I am willing to make you a proposition. I have inquired about you, you are favorably known on your old campus, I understand you were in the backfield with Alfred Diederich."

104   Darling nodded. "Whatever happened to him?"

105   "He is walking around in a cast for seven years now. An iron brace. He played professional football and they broke his neck for him."

106   Darling smiled. That, at least, had turned out well.

107   "Our suits are an easy product to sell, Mr. Darling," Rosenberg said. "We have a handsome, custom-made garment. What has Brooks Brothers got that we haven't got? A name. No more."

108   "I can make fifty, sixty dollars a week," Darling said to Louise that night. "And expenses. I can save some money and then come back to New York and really get started here."

109   "Yes, Baby," Louise said.

110   "As it is," Darling said carefully, "I can make it back here once a month, and holidays and the summer. We can see each other often."

111   "Yes, Baby." He looked at her face, lovelier now at thirty-five than it had ever been before, but fogged over now as it had been for five years with a kind of patient, kindly, remote boredom.

112   "What do you say?" he asked. "Should I take it?" Deep within him he hoped fiercely, longingly, for her to say, "No, Baby, you stay right here," but she said, as he knew she'd say, "I think you'd better take it."

113   He nodded. He had to get up and stand with his back to her, looking out the window, because there were things plain on his face that she had never seen in the fifteen years she'd known him. "Fifty dollars is a lot of money," he said. "I never thought I'd ever see fifty dollars again." He laughed. Louise laughed, too.

114   Christian Darling sat on the frail green grass of the practice field. The shadow of the stadium had reached out and covered him. In the distance the lights of the university shone a little mistily in the light haze of evening. Fifteen years. Flaherty even now was calling for his wife, buying her a drink, filling whatever bar they were in with that voice of his and that easy laugh. Darling half-closed his eyes, almost saw the boy fifteen years ago reach for the pass, slip the halfback, go skittering lightly down the field, his knees high and fast and graceful, smiling to himself because he knew he was going to get past the safety man. That was the high point, Darling thought, fifteen years ago, on an autumn afternoon, twenty years old and far from death, with the air coming easily into his lungs, and a deep feeling inside him that he could do anything, knock

over anybody, outrun whatever had to be outrun. And the shower after and the three glasses of water and the cool night air on his damp head and Louise sitting hatless in the open car with a smile and the first kiss she ever really meant. The high point, an eighty-yard run in the practice, and a girl's kiss and everything after that a decline. Darling laughed. He had practiced the wrong thing, perhaps. He hadn't practiced for 1929 and New York City and a girl who would turn into a woman. Somewhere, he thought, there must have been a point where she moved up to me, was even with me for a moment, when I could have held her hand, if I'd known, held tight, gone with her. Well, he'd never known. Here he was on a playing field that was fifteen years away and his wife was in another city having dinner with another and better man, speaking with him a different, new language, a language nobody had ever taught him.

115   Darling stood up, smiled a little, because if he didn't smile he knew the tears would come. He looked around him. This was the spot. O'Connor's pass had come sliding out just to here . . . the high point. Darling put up his hands, felt all over again the flat slap of the ball. He shook his hips to throw off the halfback, cut back inside the center, picked his knees high as he ran gracefully over two men jumbled on the ground at the line of scrimmage, ran easily, gaining speed, for ten yards, holding the ball lightly in his two hands, swung away from the halfback diving at him, ran, swinging his hips in the almost girlish manner of a back in a broken field, tore into the safety man, his shoes drumming heavily on the turf, stiff-armed, elbow locked, pivoted, raced lightly and exultantly for the goal line.

116   It was only after he had sped over the goal line and slowed to a trot that he saw the boy and girl sitting together on the turf, looking at him wonderingly.

117   He stopped short, dropping his arms. "I . . ." he said, gasping a little, though his condition was fine and the run hadn't winded him. "I—once I played here."

118   The boy and the girl said nothing. Darling laughed embarrassedly, looked hard at them sitting there, close to each other, shrugged, turned and went toward his hotel, the sweat breaking out on his face and running down into his collar.

Notes

1Ernest Dowson (1867–1900), Victorian poet known for his translations of French poets and his graceful, lyrical poetry. [Eds.]

2Leon Trotsky (1879–1940), Russian revolutionary and statesman. [Eds.]

3Edgar Allan Poe (1809–1849), American writer and critic who believed that American fiction suffered from writers' emphases on materialism. [Eds.]

4Alfred Mossman Landon (1887–1987), Republican governor of Kansas (1933–37) and unsuccessful nominee for president (1936). [Eds.]

Content Questions

1. How old is Christian when the story begins?
2. What happens to Christian's competitor, Diederich?
3. Who was Louise's father? What happens to him?
4. What was Louise like when she first met Christian? How did she change? What caused the change?
5. Why does Christian object to Louise's hat?
6. Why isn't Christian successful as a salesman? What does he try to sell?
7. Why does Louise continue to call Christian "Baby" after he asks her to stop?
8. Was there ever a time when Louise was "even with [Christian] for a moment"?

Questions on Presentation

1. How would you characterize Shaw's audience?
2. Why does Shaw begin his story from the point of view of a player?
3. What is the effect of Shaw's narrator shifting between past and present in the opening nine paragraphs? Is the effect the same as that of the reminiscence of paragraph 20?

Il Plœ:r Dã Mõ Kœ:r

Hortense Calisher

The older child of an upper-middle-class family, Hortense Calisher (b. 1911) is a New York writer who began publishing short stories in 1948. Calisher was educated at Barnard College and worked as a social worker in New York City. Her first collection of short stories, *In the Absence of Angels* (1951), like her subsequent collections, *Tale for the Mirror* (1962) and *Extreme Magic* (1963), includes stories of the Elkins, a family roughly based on Calisher's own family. In many of these stories Calisher affirms the importance of viewing oneself and others fairly, of the self-trust and acceptance individuals must develop, and of the loneliness of individual consciousness. Calisher uses her short stories and novels to depict the independence individuals seek and the cost that independence may extract.

Calisher's novels continue her themes of individualism: in *Queenie* (1971) she lightheartedly chronicles the heroine's sexual coming of age; *Standard*

Dreaming (1972) retells a father's painful journey to understanding and acceptance of his own son; *Eagle Eye* (1973) explores the hero's reevaluation and restructuring of his own life; and *On Keeping Women* (1977) traces the breakup of a family as an act of liberation. In "Il Plœ:r Dã Mõ Kœ:r" Calisher weaves a somewhat different tale of the frustrations of learning and the satisfactions of knowledge.

1 I was taught to speak French *with* tears. It was not I who wept, or the other girls in my high-school class, but the poet Verlaine—the one who wrote "Il plœ:r dã mõ kœ:r." Inside forty slack American mouths, he wept phonetically for almost a semester. During this time, we were not taught a word of French grammar or meaning—only the International Phonetic Alphabet, the sounds the symbols stood for, and Verlaine translated into them. We could not even pick up the celebrated pen of our aunt. But by the time Verlaine and our teacher Mlle. Girard had finished with us, we were indeed ready to pick it up, and in the most classically passionate accents this side of the Comédie Française.

2 Mlle. Girard achieved her feat in this way. On the very first morning, she explained to us that French could never be spoken properly by us Anglo-Saxons unless we learned to reanimate those muscles of the face, throat, *poitrine* that we possessed—even as the French—but did not use. Ours, she said, was a speech almost without lilt, spoken on a dead level of intonation, "like a sobway train."

3 "Like this," she said, letting her jaw loll idiotically and choosing the most American subject she could find: "Ay wahnt sahm ay-iss cream." French, on the other hand, was a language *passionné* and *spirituel*, of vowels struck without pedal, of "l's" made with a sprightly tongue tip—a sound altogether unlike our "l," which we made with our tongues plopping in our mouths. By her manner, she implied that all sorts of national differences might be assumed from this, although she could not take the time to puruse them.

4 She placed a wiry thumb and forefinger, gray with chalk dust, on either side of her mouth. "It is these muscles 'ere I shall teach you to use," she said. (If that early we had been trained to think in phonetic symbols, we would have known that what she had actually said was "moeslz.") When she removed her hand, we saw that she had two little, active, wrinkling pouches, one on either side of her mouth. In the ensuing weeks I often wondered whether all French people had them, and we would get them, too. Perhaps only youthful body tone saved us, as, morning after morning, she went among us pinching and poking our lips into grimaces and compelling sudden ventriloquisms from our astonished sinuses.

5 As a final coup, she taught us the classic "r." "Demoiselles," she said,

"this is an *élégance* almost impossible for Americans, but you are a special class—I think you may do it." By this time, I think she had almost convinced herself that she had effected somatic changes in our Anglo-Saxonism. *"C'est produit,"* she said, imparting the knowledge to us in a whisper, "by vibr-rating the uvula!"

6   During the next week, we sat there, like forty purring Renaults, vibrating our uvulas.

7   *Enfin* came Verlaine, with his tears. As a supreme exercise, we were to learn to declaim a poem by one of the famous harmonists of France, and we were to do it entirely by ear. (At this time, we knew the meaning of not one word except *"ici!"* with which, carefully admonished to chirp "oep, not down!" we had been taught to answer the roll.) Years later, when I could *read* French, I came upon the poem in its natural state. To my surprise, it looked like this:

Il pleure dans mon coeur
Comme il pleut sur la ville.
Quelle est cette langueur
Qui pénètre mon coeur?

O bruit doux de la pluie
Par terre . . .

And so on. But the way it is engraved on my heart, my ear, and my uvula is something else again. As hour after hour, palm to breast, wrist to brow, we moaned like a bevy of Ulalumes, making the exquisite distinction between *"pleure"* and *"pleut,"* sounding our "r" like cat women, and dropping "l"s liquid as bulbuls, what we saw in our mind's eye was this:

il plœ:rə dã mõ kœ:r
kɔm il plø syr la vij
kɛl ɛ sɛtə lãgœ:r
ki penɛtrə mõ kœ:r

o bryi du də la plyi
par te:r . . .

And so on.

8   Late in the term, Mme. Cécile Sorel paid New York a visit, and Mlle. Girard took us to see her in *La Dame aux Camélias.* Sorel's tea gowns and our own romantic sensibilities helped us to get some of her phthisic story. But what we marvelled at most was that she sounded exactly like us.

9   *L'envoi* comes somewhat late—twenty years later—but, like the

tragic flaw of the Greeks, what Mlle. G. had planted so irrevocably was bound to show up in a last act somewhere. I went to France.

10 During the interim, I had resigned myself to the fact that although I had "had" French so intensively—for Mlle. G. had continued to be just as exacting all the way through grammar, *dictée*, and the rest of it—I still did not seem to "have" it. In college, my accent had earned me a brief eminence, but, of course, we did not spend much time *speaking* French, this being regarded as a frivolous addiction, the pursuit of which had best be left to the Berlitz people, or to tacky parlor groups presided over by stranded foreign widows in need of funds. As for vocabulary or idiom, I stood with Racine on my right hand and Rimbaud on my left— a *cordon-bleu* cook who had never been taught how to boil an egg. Across the water, there was presumably a nation, *obscurcie de miasmes humains*, that used its own speech for purposes of asking the way to the bathroom, paying off porters, and going shopping, but for me the language remained the vehicle of de Vigny, Lamartine, and Hugo, and France a murmurous orchestral country where the *cieux* were full of *clarté*, the oceans sunk in *ombres profondes*, and where the most useful verbs were *souffler* and *gémir*.

11 On my occasional encounters with French visitors, I would apologize, in a few choicely carved phrases that always brought compliments, for being out of practice, after which I retired—into English if *they* had *it*, into the next room if they hadn't. Still, when I sailed, it was with hope—based on the famous accent—that in France I would somehow speak French. If I had only known, it would have been far better to go, as an underprivileged friend of mine did, armed with the one phrase her husband had taught her—*"Au secours!"*

12 Arriving at my small hotel in Paris, I was met by the owner, M. Lampacher, who addressed me in arrogantly correct English. When we finished our arrangements in that language, I took the plunge. *"Merci!"* I said. It came out just lovely, the "r" like treacle, the "ci" not down but oep.

13 "Ah, Madame!" he said. "You speak French."

14 I gave him the visitor's routine.

15 "You mock, Madame. You have the accent *absolument pur*."

16 The next morning, I left the hotel early for a walk around Paris. I had not been able to understand the boy who brought me breakfast, but no doubt he was from the provinces. Hoping that I would not encounter too many people from the provinces, I set out. I tramped for miles, afloat upon the first beatific daze of tourism. One by one, to sounds as of northern lights popping and sunken cathedrals emerging, all the postcards were coming true, and it was not until I was returning on the bus from Chaillot that, blinking, I listened for the first time that day.

17 Two women opposite me were talking; from their glances, directed at

my plastic rain boots, they were talking about me. I was piqued at their apparent assumption that I would not understand them. A moment later, listening with closed eyes, I was glad that they could not be aware of the very odd way in which I was not understanding them. For what I was hearing went something like this: "rəgard lamerikɛn se kautʃu sɛkõvnabl sa nɛspa purlãsã bl õ pøvwarlesulje"

18   "a ɛl nəsõpavremã ʃik lezamerikɛn ʃakynrəsãblalotr"

19   a wi [Pause] tykonɛ mari la fijœl də mõ dəmi frɛr ãdre səlwi [or sɛl] avɛk lɛbuk tylarãkõtre ʃemwa alo:r lœdi swa:r ɛl [or il] a fɛt yn foskuʃ"

20   Hours later, in my room, with the help of a dictionary and Mlle. G.'s training in *dictée*, I pieced together what they had said. It seemed to have been roughly this: "*Regarde, l'Américaine, ses caoutchoucs. C'est convenable, ça, n'est-ce pas, pour l'ensemble. On peut voir les souliers.*"

21   "*Ah, elles ne sont pas vraiment chics, les Américaines. Chacune ressemble à l'autre.*"

22   "*Ah, oui.* [Pause] *Tu connais Marie, la filleule de mon demi-frère André—celui* [or *celle*] *avec le bouc. Tu l'as rencontré chez moi. Alors, lundi soir, elle* [or *il*] *a fait une fausse couche!*"

23   One of them, then, had thought my boots convenient for the ensemble, since one could see the shoes; the other had commented on the lack of real chic among American women, who all resembled one another. Digressing, they had gone on to speak of Marie, the goddaughter of a stepbrother, the one with the *bouc*. "You have met him [or her, since one could not tell from the construction] at my house." Either he or Marie had made a false couch, whatever that was.

24   The latter I could not find in the dictionary at all. "*Bouc*" I at first recalled as "*banc*"—either André or Marie had some kind of bench, then, or pew. I had just about decided that André had a seat in the Chamber of Deputies and had made some kind of political mistake, when it occurred to me that the word had been "*bouc*"—goatee—which almost certainly meant André. What had he done? Or Marie? What the hell did it mean "to make a false couch"?

25   I sat for the good part of an hour, freely associating—really, now, the goddaughter of a stepbrother! When I could bear it no longer, I rang up an American friend who had lived in Paris for some years, with whom I was to lunch the next day.

26   "Oh, yes, how are you?" said Ann.

27   "Dead tired, actually," I said, "and I've had a slight shock. Listen, it seems I can't speak French after all. Will you translate something?"

28   "Sure."

29   "What does to '*faire une fausse couche*' mean?"

30   "Honey!" said Ann.

31   "What?"

32   "Where are you, dear?" she said, in a low voice. "At a doctor's?"

33   "No, for God's sake, I'm at the hotel. What's the matter with you? You're as bad as the dictionary."

34   "Nothing's the matter with *me*," said Ann. "The phrase just means 'to have a miscarriage,' that 's all."

35   "Ohhh," I said. "Then it was Marie after all. Poor Marie."

36   "*Are* you all right?"

37   "Oh, I'm fine," I said. "Just fine. And thanks. I'll see you tomorrow."

38   I went to bed early, assuring myself that what I had was merely disembarkation jitters (what would the psychologists call it—transliteration syndrome?), which would disappear overnight. Otherwise it was going to be very troublesome having to retire from every conversation to work it out in symbols.

39   A month went by, and the syndrome had not disappeared. Now and then, it was true, the more familiar nouns and verbs did make their way straight to my brain, bypassing the tangled intermediaries of my ear and the International Phonetic Alphabet. Occasionally, I was able to pick up an unpoetically useful phrase: to buy a brassiere you asked for "something to hold up the gorge with"; the French said "Couci-couça" (never "*Comme ci, comme ça*") and, when they wanted to say "I don't know," turned up their palms and said "Schpuh." But meanwhile, my accent, fed by the lilt of true French, altogether outsoared the shadow of my night. When I did dare the phrases prepared carefully in my room for the eventualities of the day, they fell so superbly that any French vis-à-vis immediately dropped all thought of giving me a handicap and addressed me in the native argot, at the native rate—leaving me struck dumb.

40   New Year's Eve was my last night in Paris. I had planned to fly to London to start the new year with telephones, parties, the wireless, conversation, in a wild blaze of unrestricted communication. But the airport had informed me that no planes were flying the Channel, or perhaps anywhere, for the next twenty-four hours, New Year's Eve being the one night on which the pilots were traditionally "allowed" to get drunk. At least, it *seemed* to me that I had been so informed, but perhaps I libel, for by now my passion for accurately understanding what was said to me was dead. All my pockets and purses were full of paper scraps of decoding, set down in vowel-hallucinated corners while my lips moved grotesquely, and it seemed to me that, if left alone here any longer, I would end by having composed at random a phonetic variorum for France.

41   In a small, family-run cafe around the corner from my hotel, where I had often eaten alone, I ordered dinner, successive *cafés filtres*, and repeated doses of marc. Tonight, at the elegiac opening of the new year, it was "allowed"—for pilots and the warped failures of educational

snobbism—to get drunk. Outside, it was raining, or weeping; in my heart, it was doing both.

42   Presently, I was the only customer at any of the zinc tables. Opposite, in a corner, the *grand-père* of the family of owners lit a Gauloise and regarded me with the privileged stare of the elderly. He was the only one there who seemed aware that I existed; for the others I had the invisibility of the foreigner who cannot "speak"—next door to that of a child, I mused, except for the adult password of money in the pocket. The old man's daughter, or daughter-in-law, a dark woman with a gall-bladder complexion and temperament, had served me obliquely and retired to the kitchen, from which she emerged now and then to speak sourly to her husband, a capped man, better-looking than she, who ignored her, lounging at the bar like a customer. I should have liked to know whether her sourness was in her words as well as her manner, and whether his lordliness was something personal between them or only the authority of the French male, but their harsh gutturals, so far from sugarplum sounds I had been trained to that they did not even dissolve into phonetics, went by me like the crude blue smoke of the Gauloise. A girl of about fourteen—their daughter, I thought—was tending bar and deflecting the remarks of the customers with a petted, precocious insouciance. Now and then, her parents addressed remarks, either to her or to the men at the bar, that seemed to have the sharpness of reprimand, but I could not be sure; to my eye the gaiety of the men toward the young girl had a certain avuncular decorum that made the scene pleasant and tender to watch. In my own country, I loved to listen at bars, where the human scene was often arrested as it is in those genre paintings whose deceptively simple contours must be approached with all one's knowledge of the period, and it saddened me not to be able to savor those nuances here.

43   I lit a Gauloise, too, with a flourish that the old man, who nodded stiffly, must have taken for a salute. And why not? Pantomime was all that was left to me. Or money. To hell with my perfectionist urge to understand; I must resign myself to being no different from those summer thousands who jammed the ocean every June, to whom Europe was merely a montage of their own sensations, a glamorous old phoenix that rose seasonally, just for them. On impulse, I mimed an invitation to the old man to join me in a marc. On second thought, I signaled for marc for everybody in the house.

44   "To the new year!" I said, in French, waving my glass at the old man. Inside my brain, my monitor tapped his worried finger—did *"nouvelle"* come before or after *"année"* in such cases, and wasn't the accent a little "ice cream"? I drowned him, in another marc.

45   Across the room from me, the old man's smile faded in and out like the Cheshire cat's; I was not at all surprised when it spoke, in words I

seemed to understand, inquiring politely as to my purpose in Paris. I was here on a scholarship, I replied. I was a writer. ("*Ecrivain? Romancier?*" asked my monitor faintly.)

46 "Ah," said the old man. "I am familiar with one of your writers. Père Le Buc."

47 "Père Le Buc?" I shook my head sadly. "I regret, but it is not known to me, the work of the Father Le Buc."

48 "*Pas un homme!*" he said. "*Une femme! Une femme qui s'appelle Père Le Buc!*"

49 My monitor raised his head for one last time. "Pɛrləbyk!" he chirped desperately. "Pɛrləbyk!"

50 I listened. "Oh, my God," I said then. "Of course. That is how it would be. Pearl Buck!"

51 "*Mais oui,*" said the old man, beaming and raising his glass. "Pɛrləbyk!"

52 At the bar, the loungers, thinking we were exchanging some toast, raised their own glasses in courteous imitation. "Pɛrləbyk!" they said, politely. "Pɛrləbyk!"

53 I raised mine. "*Il pleure,*" I began, "*il pleure dans mon coeur comme il pleut . . .*"

54 Before the evening was over, I had given them quite a selection: from Verlaine, from Heredia's "Les Trophées," from Baudelaire's poem on a painting by Delacroix, from de Musset's "R-r-ra-ppelle-toi!" As a final tribute, I gave them certain stanzas from Hugo's "L'Expiation"—the ones that begin "*Waterloo! Waterloo! Waterloo! Morne plaine!*" And in between, raised or lowered by a new faith that was not all brandy, into an air freed of cuneiform at last—I spoke French.

55 Making my way home afterward, along the dark stretches of the Rue du Bac, I reflected that to learn a language outside its native habitat you really must believe that the other country exists—in its humdrum, its winter self. Could I remember to stay there now—down in that lower-case world in which stairs creaked, cops yelled, in which women bought brassières and sometimes made the false couch?

56 The door of my hotel was locked. I rang, and M. Lampacher admitted me. He snapped on the stair light, economically timed to go out again in a matter of seconds, and watched me as I mounted the stairs with the aid of the banister.

57 "Off bright and early, hmm?" he said sleepily, in French. "Well, good night, Madame. Hope you had a good time here."

58 I turned, wanting to answer him properly, to answer them all. At that moment, the light went off, perhaps to reinforce forever my faith in the mundanity of France.

59 "*Ah, ça va, ça va!*" I said strongly, into the dark. "Couci-couça. Schpuh."

Content Questions

1. Why did the narrator learn French?
2. Why did the students marvel that the French actress sounded "exactly" like them?
3. Why does the narrator have difficulty when she visits France?
4. Is the person that the narrator calls to help her understand the women on the bus helpful or not?
5. Why does the narrator leave France?
6. What sort of relationship develops between the narrator and the man in the bar?

Questions on Presentation

1. Calisher's story has a humorous side to it. What are the techniques Calisher uses to create humor in the story? Are they obvious or subtle techniques? How does Calisher's use of humor help develop the theme of the story?
2. Is it important that the reader understand the French words and phrases in the story?
3. How does Calisher make the narrator's frustration understandable?
4. Is the scene in which the narrator is "freed of cuneiform at last" convincing? Why or why not?
5. What is the effect of Calisher's use of words such as somatic (5), Ulalumes (7), bulbuls (7), insouciance (42), and avuncular (42)?

The Possibility of Evil

Shirley Jackson

California author Shirley Jackson (1916–1965) is best known for her chilling short stories such as "The Lottery," from her collection *The Lottery* (1949), and her novels such as *The Haunting of Hill House* (1959) and *We Have Always Lived in the Castle* (1962). Jackson entered Syracuse University in 1937 where she and her future husband, Stanley Edgar Hyman, and others created *Spectre*, a controversial literary magazine noted for its liberalism and criticism. Jackson and her husband moved to New York City where they both began their careers as professional writers. Hyman was a staff writer at *The New Republic* when the magazine published Jackson's first work "My Life with R. H. Macy" (1941). Jackson regarded herself as a professional writer as well as a wife and mother. In *Life Among the Savages* (1953) and *Raising Demons* (1957), her highly fictionalized autobiographies, Jackson humorously retells her experiences from college to raising her four children. She omits, however, her disciplined approach to writing. Years later, Hyman expressed amusement at the surprise many people felt when they found that the writer of comic yet horrifying stories was a gentle woman with a keen sense of humor.

In her stories and novels, Jackson often blends commonplace, civilized people with seemingly ordinary, unthreatening surroundings and events to reveal twisted behavior and horror. Like Hawthorne, Jackson explores human reactions to the haunting fear of the unknown in her fiction. In this story, taken from the December 1965 issue of *The Saturday Evening Post*, Jackson presents with little commentary Miss Strangeworth, the town's seemingly harmless, fussy old maid.

1   Miss Adela Strangeworth came daintily along Main Street on her way to the grocery. The sun was shining, the air was fresh and clear after the night's heavy rain, and everything in Miss Strangeworth's little town looked washed and bright. Miss Strangeworth took deep breaths and thought that there was nothing in the world like a fragrant summer day.

2   She knew everyone in town, of course; she was fond of telling strangers—tourists who sometimes passed through the town and stopped to admire Miss Strangeworth's roses—that she had never spent more than a day outside this town in all her long life. She was seventy-one, Miss Strangeworth told the tourists, with a pretty little dimple showing by her lip, and she sometimes found herself thinking that the town belonged to her. "My grandfather built the first house on Pleasant Street," she would say, opening her blue eyes wide with the wonder of it. "This house, right here. My family has lived here for better than a hundred years. My grandmother planted these roses, and my mother tended them, just as I do. I've watched my town grow; I can remember when Mr. Lewis, Senior, opened the grocery store, and the year the river flooded out the shanties on the low road, and the excitement when some young folks wanted to move the park over to the space in front of where the new post office is today. They wanted to put up a statue of Ethan Allen"—Miss Strangeworth would frown a little and sound stern—"but it should have been a statue of my grandfather. There wouldn't have been a town here at all if it hadn't been for my grandfather and the lumber mill."

3   Miss Strangeworth never gave away any of her roses, although the tourists often asked her. The roses belonged on Pleasant Street, and it bothered Miss Strangeworth to think of people wanting to carry them

away, to take them into strange towns and down strange streets. When the new minister came, and the ladies were gathering flowers to decorate the church, Miss Strangeworth sent over a great basket of gladioli; when she picked the roses at all, she set them in bowls and vases around the inside of the house her grandfather had built.

4   Walking down Main Street on a summer morning, Miss Strangeworth had to stop every minute or so to say good morning to someone or to ask after someone's health. When she came into the grocery, half a dozen people turned away from the shelves and the counters to wave at her or call out good morning.

5   "And good morning to you, too, Mr. Lewis," Miss Strangeworth said at last. The Lewis family had been in the town almost as long as the Strangeworths; but the day young Lewis left high school and went to work in the grocery, Miss Strangeworth had stopped calling him Tommy and started calling him Mr. Lewis, and he had stopped calling her Addie and started calling her Miss Strangeworth. They had been in high school together, and had gone to picnics together, and to high-school dances and basketball games; but now Mr. Lewis was behind the counter in the grocery, and Miss Strangeworth was living alone in the Strangeworth house on Pleasant Street.

6   "Good morning," Mr. Lewis said, and added politely, "Lovely day."

7   "It is a very nice day," Miss Strangeworth said, as though she had only just decided that it would do after all. "I would like a chop, please, Mr. Lewis, a small, lean veal chop. Are those strawberries from Arthur Parker's garden? They're early this year."

8   "He brought them in this morning," Mr. Lewis said.

9   "I shall have a box," Miss Strangeworth said. Mr. Lewis looked worried, she thought, and for a minute she hesitated, but then she decided that he surely could not be worried over the strawberries. He looked very tired indeed. He was usually so chipper, Miss Strangeworth thought, and almost commented, but it was far too personal a subject to be introduced to Mr. Lewis, the grocer, so she only said, "And a can of cat food and, I think, a tomato."

10   Silently, Mr. Lewis assembled her order on the counter, and waited. Miss Strangeworth looked at him curiously and then said, "It's Tuesday, Mr. Lewis. You forgot to remind me."

11   "Did I? Sorry."

12   "Imagine your forgetting that I always buy my tea on Tuesday," Miss Strangeworth said gently. "A quarter pound of tea, please, Mr. Lewis."

13   "Is that all, Miss Strangeworth?"

14   "Yes, thank you, Mr. Lewis. Such a lovely day, isn't it?"

15   "Lovely," Mr. Lewis said.

16   Miss Strangeworth moved slightly to make room for Mrs. Harper at

the counter. "Morning, Adela," Mrs. Harper said, and Miss Strangeworth said, "Good morning, Martha."

17 "Lovely day," Mrs. Harper said, and Miss Strangeworth said, "Yes, lovely," and Mr. Lewis, under Mrs. Harper's glance, nodded.

18 "Ran out of sugar for my cake frosting," Mrs. Harper explained. Her hand shook slightly as she opened her pocketbook. Miss Strangeworth wondered, glancing at her quickly, if she had been taking proper care of herself. Martha Harper was not as young as she used to be, Miss Strangeworth thought. She probably could use a good strong tonic.

19 "Martha," she said, "you don't look well."

20 "I'm perfectly all right," Mrs. Harper said shortly. She handed her money to Mr. Lewis, took her change and her sugar, and went out without speaking again. Looking after her, Miss Strangeworth shook her head slightly. Martha definitely did *not* look well.

21 Carrying her little bag of groceries, Miss Strangeworth came out of the store into the bright sunlight and stopped to smile down on the Crane baby. Don and Helen Crane were really the two most infatuated young parents she had ever known, she thought indulgently, looking at the delicately embroidered baby cap and the lace-edged carriage cover.

22 "That little girl is going to grow up expecting luxury all her life," she said to Helen Crane.

23 Helen laughed. "That's the way we want her to feel," she said. "Like a princess."

24 "A princess can see a lot of trouble sometimes," Miss Strangeworth said dryly. "How old is Her Highness now?"

25 "Six months next Tuesday," Helen Crane said, looking down with rapt wonder at her child. "I've been worrying, though, about her. Don't you think she ought to move around more? Try to sit up, for instance?"

26 "For plain and fancy worrying," Miss Strangeworth said, amused, "give me a new mother every time."

27 "She just seems—slow," Helen Crane said.

28 "Nonsense. All babies are different. Some of them develop much more quickly than others."

29 "That's what my mother says." Helen Crane laughed, looking a little bit ashamed.

30 "I suppose you've got young Don all upset about the fact that his daughter is already six months old and hasn't yet begun to learn to dance?"

31 "I haven't mentioned it to him. I suppose she's just so precious that I worry about her all the time."

32 "Well, apologize to her right now," Miss Strangeworth said. "*She* is probably worrying about why you keep jumping around all the time." Smiling to herself and shaking her old head, she went on down the

sunny street, stopping once to ask little Billy Moore why he wasn't out riding in his daddy's shiny new car, and talking for a few minutes outside the library with Miss Chandler, the librarian, about the new novels to be ordered and paid for by the annual library appropriation. Miss Chandler seemed absent-minded and very much as though she were thinking about something else. Miss Strangeworth noticed that Miss Chandler had not taken much trouble with her hair that morning, and sighed. Miss Strangeworth hated sloppiness.

33   Many people seemed disturbed recently, Miss Strangeworth thought. Only yesterday the Stewarts' fifteen-year-old Linda had run crying down her own front walk and all the way to school, not caring who saw her. People around town thought she might have had a fight with the Harris boy, but they showed up together at the soda shop after school as usual, both of them looking grim and bleak: Trouble at home, people concluded, and sighed over the problem of trying to raise kids right these days.

34   From halfway down the block Miss Strangeworth could catch the heavy scent of her roses, and she moved a little more quickly. The perfume of roses meant home, and home meant the Strangeworth House on Pleasant Street. Miss Strangeworth stopped at her own front gate, as she always did, and looked with deep pleasure at her house, with the red and pink and white roses massed along the narrow lawn, and the rambler going up along the porch; and the neat, the unbelievably trim lines of the house itself, with its slimness and its washed white look. Every window sparkled, every curtain hung stiff and straight, and even the stones of the front walk were swept and clear. People around town wondered how old Miss Strangeworth managed to keep the house looking the way it did, and there was a legend about a tourist once mistaking it for the local museum and going all through the place without finding out about his mistake. But the town was proud of Miss Strangeworth and her roses and her house. They had all grown together.

35   Miss Strangeworth went up her front steps, unlocked her front door with her key, and went into the kitchen to put away her groceries. She debated about having a cup of tea and then decided that it was too close to midday dinnertime; she would not have the appetite for her little chop if she had tea now. Instead she went into the light, lovely sitting room, which still glowed from the hands of her mother and her grandmother, who had covered the chairs with bright chintz and hung the curtains. All the furniture was spare and shining, and the round hooked rugs on the floor had been the work of Miss Strangeworth's grandmother and her mother. Miss Strangeworth had put a bowl of her red roses on the low table before the window, and the room was full of their scent.

36   Miss Strangeworth went to the narrow desk in the corner and unlocked it with her key. She never knew when she might feel like writing

letters, so she kept her notepaper inside and the desk locked. Miss Strangeworth's usual stationery was heavy and cream-colored, with STRANGEWORTH HOUSE engraved across the top, but, when she felt like writing her other letters, Miss Strangeworth used a pad of various-colored paper bought from the local newspaper shop. It was almost a town joke, that colored paper, layered in pink and green and blue and yellow; everyone in town bought it and used it for odd, informal notes and shopping lists. It was usual to remark, upon receiving a note written on a blue page, that so-and-so would be needing a new pad soon—here she was, down to the blue already. Everyone used the matching envelopes for tucking away recipes, or keeping odd little things in, or even to hold cookies in the school lunchboxes. Mr. Lewis sometimes gave them to the children for carrying home penny candy.

37 Although Miss Strangeworth's desk held a trimmed quill pen which had belonged to her grandfather, and a gold-frosted fountain pen which had belonged to her father, Miss Strangeworth always used a dull stub of pencil when she wrote her letters, and she printed them in a childish block print. After thinking for a minute, although she had been phrasing the letter in the back of her mind all the way home, she wrote on a pink sheet: DIDN'T YOU EVER SEE AN IDIOT CHILD BEFORE? SOME PEOPLE JUST SHOULDN'T HAVE CHILDREN SHOULD THEY?

38 She was pleased with the letter. She was fond of doing things exactly right. When she made a mistake, as she sometimes did, or when the letters were not spaced nicely on the page, she had to take the discarded page to the kitchen stove and burn it at once. Miss Strangeworth never delayed when things had to be done.

39 After thinking for a minute, she decided that she would like to write another letter, perhaps to go to Mrs. Harper, to follow up the ones she had already mailed. She selected a green sheet this time and wrote quickly: HAVE YOU FOUND OUT YET WHAT THEY WERE ALL LAUGHING ABOUT AFTER YOU LEFT THE BRIDGE CLUB ON THURSDAY? OR IS THE WIFE REALLY ALWAYS THE LAST ONE TO KNOW?

40 Miss Strangeworth never concerned herself with facts; her letters all dealt with the more negotiable stuff of suspicion. Mr. Lewis would never have imagined for a minute that his grandson might be lifting petty cash from the store register if he had not had one of Miss Strangeworth's letters. Miss Chandler, the librarian, and Linda Stewart's parents would have gone unsuspectingly ahead with their lives, never aware of possible evil lurking nearby, if Miss Strangeworth had not sent letters opening their eyes. Miss Strangeworth would have been genuinely shocked if there *had* been anything between Linda Stewart and the Harris boy, but, as long as evil existed unchecked in the world, it was Miss Strangeworth's duty to keep her town alert to it. It was far more sensible for Miss Chandler to wonder what Mr. Shelley's first wife had

really died of than to take a chance on not knowing. There were so many wicked people in the world and only one Strangeworth left in the town. Besides, Miss Strangeworth liked writing her letters.

41   She addressed an envelope to Don Crane after a moment's thought, wondering curiously if he would show the letter to his wife, and using a pink envelope to match the pink paper. Then she addressed a second envelope, green, to Mrs. Harper. Then an idea came to her and she selected a blue sheet and wrote: YOU NEVER KNOW ABOUT DOCTORS. REMEMBER THEY'RE ONLY HUMAN AND NEED MONEY LIKE THE REST OF US. SUPPOSE THE KNIFE SLIPPED ACCIDENTALLY. WOULD DR. BURNS GET HIS FEE AND A LITTLE EXTRA FROM THAT NEPHEW OF YOURS?

42   She addressed the blue envelope to old Mrs. Foster, who was having an operation next month. She had thought of writing one more letter, to the head of the school board, asking how a chemistry teacher like Billy Moore's father could afford a new convertible, but, all at once, she was tired of writing letters. The three she had done would do for one day. She could write more tomorrow; it was not as though they all had to be done at once.

43   She had been writing her letters—sometimes two or three every day for a week, sometimes no more than one in a month—for the past year. She never got any answers, of course, because she never signed her name. If she had been asked, she would have said that her name, Adela Strangeworth, a name honored in the town for so many years, did not belong on such trash. The town where she lived had to be kept clean and sweet, but people everywhere were lustful and evil and degraded, and needed to be watched; the world was so large, and there was only one Strangeworth left in it. Miss Strangeworth sighed, locked her desk, and put the letters into her big black leather pocketbook, to be mailed when she took her evening walk.

44   She broiled her little chop nicely, and had a sliced tomato and a good cup of tea ready when she sat down to her midday dinner at the table in her dining room, which could be opened to seat twenty-two, with a second table, if necessary, in the hall. Sitting in the warm sunlight that came through the tall windows of the dining room, seeing her roses massed outside, handling the heavy, old silverware and the fine, translucent china, Miss Strangeworth was pleased; she would not have cared to be doing anything else. People must live graciously, after all, she thought, and sipped her tea. Afterward, when her plate and cup and saucer were washed and dried and put back onto the shelves where they belonged, and her silverware was back in the mahogany silver chest, Miss Strangeworth went up the graceful staircase and into her bedroom, which was the front room overlooking the roses, and had been her mother's and her grandmother's. Their Crown Derby dresser set and furs had been kept here, their fans and silver-backed brushes and their own

bowls of roses; Miss Strangeworth kept a bowl of white roses on the bed table.

45   She drew her shades, took the rose satin spread from the bed, slipped out of her dress and her shoes, and lay down tiredly. She knew that no doorbell or phone would ring; no one in town would dare to disturb Miss Strangeworth during her afternoon nap. She slept, deep in the rich smell of roses.

46   After her nap she worked in her garden for a little while, sparing herself because of the heat; then she came in to her supper. She ate asparagus from her own garden, with sweet-butter sauce and a soft-boiled egg, and, while she had her supper, she listened to a late-evening news broadcast and then to a program of classical music on her small radio. After her dishes were done and her kitchen set in order, she took up her hat— Miss Strangeworth's hats were proverbial in the town; people believed that she had inherited them from her mother and her grandmother— and, locking the front door of her house behind her, set off on her evening walk, pocketbook under her arm. She nodded to Linda Stewart's father, who was washing his car in the pleasantly cool evening. She thought that he looked troubled.

47   There was only one place in town where she could mail her letters, and that was the new post office, shiny with red brick and silver letters. Although Miss Strangeworth had never given the matter any particular thought, she had always made a point of mailing her letters very secretly; it would, of course, not have been wise to let anyone see her mail them. Consequently, she timed her walk so she could reach the post office just as darkness was starting to dim the outlines of the trees and the shapes of people's faces, although no one could ever mistake Miss Strangeworth, with her dainty walk and her rustling skirts.

48   There was always a group of young people around the post office, the very youngest roller-skating upon its driveway, which went all the way around the building and was the only smooth road in town; and the slightly older ones already knowing how to gather in small groups and chatter and laugh and make great, excited plans for going across the street to the soda shop in a minute or two. Miss Strangeworth had never had any self-consciousness before the children. She did not feel that any of them were staring at her unduly or longing to laugh at her; it would have been most reprehensible for their parents to permit their children to mock Miss Strangeworth of Pleasant Street. Most of the children stood back respectfully as Miss Strangeworth passed, silenced briefly in her presence, and some of the older children greeted her, saying soberly, "Hello, Miss Strangeworth."

49   Miss Strangeworth smiled at them and quickly went on. It had been a long time since she had known the name of every child in town. The mail slot was in the door of the post office. The children stood away as

Miss Strangeworth approached it, seemingly surprised that anyone should want to use the post office after it had been officially closed up for the night and turned over to the children. Miss Strangeworth stood by the door, opening her black pocketbook to take out the letters, and heard a voice which she knew at once to be Linda Stewart's. Poor little Linda was crying again, and Miss Strangeworth listened carefully. This was, after all, her town, and these were her people; if one of them was in trouble she ought to know about it.

50 "I can't tell you, Dave," Linda was saying—so she *was* talking to the Harris boy, as Miss Strangeworth had supposed—"I just *can't*. It's just *nasty*."

51 "But why won't your father let me come around any more? What on earth did I do?"

52 "I can't tell you. I just wouldn't tell you for *anything*. You've got to have a dirty, dirty mind for things like that."

53 "But something's happened. You've been crying and crying, and your father is all upset. Why can't *I* know about it, too? Aren't I like one of the family?"

54 "Not any more, Dave, not any more. You're not to come near our house again; my father said so. He said he'd horsewhip you. That's all I can tell you: You're not to come near our house any more."

55 "But I didn't *do* anything."

56 "Just the same, my father said . . . "

57 Miss Strangeworth sighed and turned away. There was so much evil in people. Even in a charming little town like this one, there was still so much evil in people.

58 She slipped her letters into the slot, and two of them fell inside. The third caught on the edge and fell outside, onto the ground at Miss Strangeworth's feet. She did not notice it because she was wondering whether a letter to the Harris boy's father might not be of some service in wiping out this potential badness. Wearily Miss Strangeworth turned to go home to her quiet bed in her lovely house, and never heard the Harris boy calling to her to say that she had dropped something.

59 "Old lady Strangeworth's getting deaf," he said, looking after her and holding in his hand the letter he had picked up.

60 "Well, who cares?" Linda said. "Who cares any more, anyway?"

61 "It's for Don Crane," the Harris boy said, "this letter. She dropped a letter addressed to Don Crane. Might as well take it on over. We pass his house anyway." He laughed. "Maybe it's got a check or something in it and he'd be just as glad to get it tonight instead of tomorrow."

62 "Catch old lady Strangeworth sending anybody a check," Linda said.

63 "Throw it in the post office. Why do anyone a favor?" She sniffled.

64 "Doesn't seem to me anybody around here cares about us," she said.

65 "Why should we care about them?"

66 "I'll take it over anyway," the Harris boy said. "Maybe it's good news for them. Maybe they need something happy tonight, too. Like us."

67 Sadly, holding hands, they wandered off down the dark street, the Harris boy carrying Miss Strangeworth's pink envelope in his hand.

68 Miss Strangeworth awakened the next morning with a feeling of intense happiness and, for a minute wondered why, and then remembered that this morning three people would open her letters. Harsh, perhaps, at first, but wickedness was never easily banished, and a clean heart was a scoured heart. She washed her soft old face and brushed her teeth, still sound in spite of her seventy-one years, and dressed herself carefully in her sweet, soft clothes and buttoned shoes. Then, coming downstairs and reflecting that perhaps a little waffle would be agreeable for breakfast in the sunny dining room, she found the mail on the hall floor and bent to pick it up. A bill, the morning paper, a letter in a green envelope that looked oddly familiar. Miss Strangeworth stood perfectly still for a minute, looking down at the green envelope with the penciled printing, and thought: It looks like one of my letters. Was one of my letters sent back? No, because no one would know where to send it. How did this get here?

69 Miss Strangeworth was a Strangeworth of Pleasant Street. Her hand did not shake as she opened the envelope and unfolded the sheet of green paper inside. She began to cry silently for the wickedness of the world when she read the words: LOOK OUT AT WHAT USED TO BE YOUR ROSES.

Content Questions

1. How did Miss Strangeworth's most prized possession become so prized?
2. Why doesn't Miss Strangeworth send letters to everyone?
3. Why are the items that Miss Strangeworth, her grandmother, and mother made for their house important?
4. Why doesn't Miss Strangeworth sign all her letters?

Questions on Presentation

1. How does the title of the story indicate Jackson's thesis?
2. Jackson's story is a type of detective story where the reader is the detective. Evaluate whether Jackson's story is an effective mystery story for all audiences.

3. The introduction to a story (or essay) is always important to understanding the theme. What is the effect of the first paragraph of this story on the reader? On the theme?

4. What is the effect of Mr. Lewis and Mrs. Harper acting so strangely? Do you see any connection between their actions and Miss Strangeworth's?

5. Jackson frequently uses understatement to emphasize the horror or shame of a situation. Where does she use this technique in this story?

⚖⚖

The Uses of Understatement

Terrence Padilla

An English major, Terrence Padilla enjoys the analysis of literature. In this essay he explores Shirley Jackson's ability to create tension in a story.

1   Shirley Jackson spins an extremely effective tale in "The Possibility of Evil," a tale especially effective on an emotional level. Jackson's use of understatement is especially good in creating an atmosphere of tension and unease throughout the story.

2   Jackson begins her story by painting a particularly bright picture of the little town her main character (Miss Strangeworth) lives in. She uses words and phrases that give the reader a sense of familiarity, which, in turn, allows the reader to "drop his defenses." The title of the story alerts the reader to the possibility of a disturbing story, but when Jackson begins with, "The sun was shining, the air was fresh and clear after the night's heavy rain, and everything in Miss Strangeworth's little town looked washed and bright," the reader's guard slackens, may even drop completely. Just when the reader thinks he is safe in another sweet tale of life in suburbia, Jackson slips in a few understated passages that begin to chip away at that feeling of security, and eventually demolish it completely, exposing the sheer insanity and evil that pass for Miss Strangeworth's thinking process. These few words, that Jackson uses so well, serve to heighten and drive along the horror of the story.

3   Jackson starts to take down the "safety net" when her character Mr. Lewis, the grocer and long-time friend, forgets Miss Strangeworth's tea. In itself, this is an innocent mistake, but the reader is told that Miss Strangeworth has purchased tea weekly for years. When he forgets, it is

an indicator that everything is not right in the town. This is a good example of how Jackson uses understatement to set the tone for her story. The little incident with Mr. Lewis is not a clear indication of how badly the town is affected below the surface, only a suggestion of problems. But when Mrs. Harper, another long-time friend, comes into the story, the reader is given more insight into the underlying current of unease that is so important to the tension Jackson builds. Mrs. Harper's shaking hand, "as she opened her pocketbook," suggests nervous tension which must have as its cause one of the people present; since she knew Mr. Lewis would be in his store, the cause must be Miss Strangeworth. That lady, however, only observes the fact, and attributes it to illness.

4   It is these little observations, made by Miss Strangeworth throughout the story, that build its tension. It is with this same sort of understatement that Jackson shows Miss Strangeworth's truly evil personality. In paragraph 37 Miss Strangeworth innocently sits down to write a letter, but the reader is not fully prepared for what she writes. Earlier in the story Miss Strangeworth meets a young mother with her infant daughter. The mother (Helen Crane) expresses her concern with her daughter's lack of interest in trying to sit up. Miss Strangeworth assures her that all children are different and to give the baby time. Understandably, it is a shock when the reader learns what the kindly, well-liked Miss Strangeworth has written in her letter: "Didn't you ever see an idiot child before? Some people shouldn't have children should they?" Yet the alert reader will not be totally surprised since the responses of other characters, Miss Strangeworth's awareness that "many people seemed disturbed lately," even her hatred of sloppiness should suggest that something is wrong. And the seemingly matter-of-fact way she writes the letter serves to heighten the horror the reader feels.

5   The understated, even serene, tone of the beginning of the story is in sharp contrast to the latter part of the story (paragraph 37 to the end). The reader can only marvel at the sheer evil Miss Strangeworth embodies as she writes another letter, this one implying that a woman's husband is commiting adultery while the whole town laughs behind the wife's back. The ease with which she writes these destructive letters is frightening and is another example of Jackson's use of understatement.

6   Jackson does an excellent job with her use of understatement in "The Possibility of Evil." She uses it so well that the reader is often unaware of its use, recognizing it only in retrospect, sensing at first only a general feeling of unease. Her use of this literary technique serves to move the story to its conclusion, a conclusion in marked contrast to the understatement of the rest of the story. Jackson delivers everything her title offers and more. From Miss Strangeworth's understated observations of the troubled characters to the ease with which she writes her "letters," she is a study in understatement. Jackson's controlled use of understate-

ment is so vital to this story that without it the story would not achieve the tone it needs to be effective.

Paul's Case
Willa Cather

American novelist and short story writer Willa Cather (1873–1947) was born in Virginia but grew up in Nebraska. During her college days she edited the student literary magazine and wrote for a newspaper in Lincoln, Nebraska. After college, she took a job as editor of the *Home Monthly* in Pittsburgh, Pennsylvania, and later taught English in a Pennsylvania high school. In 1906 she worked at *McClure's Magazine* and eventually became the managing editor. By 1912 she had published her first novel, *Alexander's Bridge*, which, though it brought her little recognition, convinced her she should quit journalism and devote her time to writing fiction.

Cather's subsequent novels were better received by both critics and the public. For *O Pioneers!* (1913) Cather created Alexandra Bergson, a woman whose creative spirit is stifled by her unresourceful neighbors. Bergson is only one of Cather's protagonists who escape from the small town mentality of their homes to pursue their fascination with an aesthetic, cultured life. She followed this novel with several others including *My Antonia* (1918), considered by many her best novel and *Death Comes to the Archbishop* (1927), which documents how the divided interests of southwestern American culture converge and separate. In her Pultizer Prize winning novel *One of Ours* (1922), Cather introduces her favorite character Claude Wheeler. Wheeler lives a confining life in Gopher Prairie, Nebraska. He escapes by joining the army but dies in battle before he can explore the new life offered him in Europe. Wheeler's conflict is central to Cather's fiction. In many of her novels she uses a classical style to present the conflict between European perceptions and the pragmatism of the New World.

Cather's short fiction continues her major themes and her preference for a restrained rather than sweeping portrait of one character or idea. In the collection *Youth and the Bright Medusa* (1920), from which "Paul's Case" is taken, Cather uses the Medusa as an image of the alluring ideal of art, an ideal that attracts youth to the Medusa, often with fatal consequences.

1   It was Paul's afternoon to appear before the faculty of the Pittsburgh High School to account for his various misdemeanours. He had been suspended a week ago, and his father had called at the Principal's office and confessed his perplexity about his son. Paul entered the faculty

room suave and smiling. His clothes were a trifle out-grown and the tan velvet on the collar of his open overcoat was frayed and worn; but for all that there was something of the dandy about him, and he wore an opal pin in his neatly knotted black four-in-hand, and a red carnation in his button-hole. This latter adornment the faculty somehow felt was not properly significant of the contrite spirit befitting a boy under the ban of suspension.

2   Paul was tall for his age and very thin, with high, cramped shoulders and a narrow chest. His eyes were remarkable for a certain hysterical brilliancy, and he continually used them in a conscious, theatrical sort of way, peculiarly offensive in a boy. The pupils were abnormally large, as though he were addicted to belladonna, but there was a glassy glitter about them which that drug does not produce.

3   When questioned by the Principal as to why he was there, Paul stated, politely enough, that he wanted to come back to school. This was a lie, but Paul was quite accustomed to lying; found it, indeed, indispensable for overcoming friction. His teachers were asked to state their respective charges against him, which they did with such a rancour and aggrieved-ness as evinced that this was not a usual case. Disorder and imperti-nence were among the offences named, yet each of his instructors felt that it was scarcely possible to put into words the real cause of the trou-ble, which lay in a sort of hysterically defiant manner of the boy's; in the contempt which they all knew he felt for them, and which he seem-ingly made not the least effort to conceal. Once, when he had been mak-ing a synopsis of a paragraph at the blackboard, his English teacher had stepped to his side and attempted to guide his hand. Paul had started back with a shudder and thrust his hands violently behind him. The as-tonished woman could scarcely have been more hurt and embarrassed had he struck at her. The insult was so involuntary and definitely per-sonal as to be unforgettable. In one way and another, he had made all his teachers, men and women alike, conscious of the same feeling of physical aversion. In one class he habitually sat with his hand shading his eyes; in another he always looked out of the window during the reci-tation; in another he made a running commentary on the lecture, with humorous intention.

4   His teachers felt this afternoon that his whole attitude was symbol-ized by his shrug and his flippantly red carnation flower, and they fell upon him without mercy, his English teacher leading the pack. He stood through it smiling, his pale lips parted over his white teeth. (His lips were continually twitching, and he had a habit of raising his eyebrows that was contemptuous and irritating to the last degree.) Older boys than Paul had broken down and shed tears under that baptism of fire, but his set smile did not once desert him, and his only sign of discom-fort was the nervous trembling of the fingers that toyed with the but-

tons of his overcoat, and an occasional jerking of the other hand that held his hat. Paul was always smiling, always glancing about him, seeming to feel that people might be watching him and trying to detect something. This conscious expression, since it was as far as possible from boyish mirthfulness, was usually attributed to insolence or "smartness."

5 As the inquisition proceeded, one of his instructors repeated an impertinent remark of the boy's, and the Principal asked him whether he thought that a courteous speech to have made to a woman. Paul shrugged his shoulders slightly and his eyebrows twitched.

6 "I don't know," he replied. "I didn't mean to be polite or impolite, either. I guess it's a sort of way I have of saying things regardless."

7 The Principal, who was a sympathetic man, asked him whether he didn't think that a way it would be well to get rid of. Paul grinned and said he guessed so. When he was told that he could go, he bowed gracefully and went out. His bow was but a repetition of the scandalous red carnation.

8 His teachers were in despair, and his drawing master voiced the feeling of them all when he declared there was something about the boy which none of them understood. He added: "I don't really believe that smile of his comes altogether from insolence; there's something sort of haunted about it. The boy is not strong, for one thing. I happen to know that he was born in Colorado, only a few months before his mother died out there of a long illness. There is something wrong about the fellow."

9 The drawing master had come to realize that, in looking at Paul, one saw only his white teeth and the forced animation of his eyes. One warm afternoon the boy had gone to sleep at his drawing-board, and his master had noted with amazement what a white, blue-veined face it was; drawn and wrinkled like an old man's about the eyes, the lips twitching even in his sleep, and stiff with a nervous tension that drew them back from his teeth.

10 His teachers left the building dissatisfied and unhappy; humiliated to have felt so vindictive toward a mere boy, to have uttered this feeling in cutting terms, and to have set each other on, as it were, in the grewsome game of intemperate reproach. Some of them remembered having seen a miserable street cat set at bay by a ring of tormentors.

11 As for Paul, he ran down the hill whistling the Soldiers' Chorus from *Faust* looking wildly behind him now and then to see whether some of his teachers were not there to writhe under his lightheartedness. As it was now late in the afternoon and Paul was on duty that evening as usher at Carnegie Hall, he decided that he would not go home to supper. When he reached the concert hall the doors were not yet open and, as it was chilly outside, he decided to go up into the picture gallery—always deserted at this hour—where there were some of Raffaelli's gay studies of Paris streets and an airy blue Venetian scene or two that always exhil-

arated him. He was delighted to find no one in the gallery but the old guard, who sat in one corner, a newspaper on his knee, a black patch over one eye and the other closed. Paul possessed himself of the place and walked confidently up and down, whistling under his breath. After a while he sat down before a blue Rico and lost himself. When he bethought him to look at his watch, it was after seven o'clock, and he rose with a start and ran downstairs, making a face at Augustus, peering out from the cast-room, and an evil gesture at the Venus of Milo as he passed her on the stairway.

12   When Paul reached the ushers' dressing-room half-a-dozen boys were there already, and he began excitedly to tumble into his uniform. It was one of the few that at all approached fitting, and Paul thought it very becoming—though he knew that the tight, straight coat accentuated his narrow chest, about which he was exceedingly sensitive. He was always considerably excited while he dressed, twanging all over to the tuning of the strings and the preliminary flourishes of the horns in the music-room; but to-night he seemed quite beside himself, and he teased and plagued the boys until, telling him that he was crazy, they put him down on the floor and sat on him.

13   Somewhat calmed by his suppression, Paul dashed out to the front of the house to seat the early comers. He was a model usher; gracious and smiling he ran up and down the aisles; nothing was too much trouble for him; he carried messages and brought programmes as though it were his greatest pleasure in life, and all the people in his section thought him a charming boy, feeling that he remembered and admired them. As the house filled, he grew more and more vivacious and animated, and the colour came to his cheeks and lips. It was very much as though this were a great reception and Paul were the host. Just as the musicians came out to take their places, his English teacher arrived with checks for the seats which a prominent manufacturer had taken for the season. She betrayed some embarrassment when she handed Paul the tickets, and a *hauteur* which subsequently made her feel very foolish. Paul was startled for a moment, and had the feeling of wanting to put her out; what business had she here among all these fine people and gay colours? He looked her over and decided that she was not appropriately dressed and must be a fool to sit downstairs in such togs. The tickets had probably been sent her out of kindness, he reflected as he put down a seat for her, and she had about as much right to sit there as he had.

14   When the symphony began Paul sank into one of the rear seats with a long sigh of relief, and lost himself as he had done before the Rico. It was not that symphonies, as such, meant anything in particular to Paul, but the first sigh of the instruments seemed to free some hilarious and potent spirit within him; something that struggled there like the Genius in the bottle found by the Arab fisherman. He felt a sudden zest of life;

the lights danced before his eyes and the concert hall blazed into unimaginable splendour. When the soprano soloist came on, Paul forgot
even the nastiness of his teacher's being there and gave himself up to
the peculiar stimulus such personages always had for him. The soloist
chanced to be a German woman, by no means in her first youth, and the
mother of many children; but she wore an elaborate gown and a tiara,
and above all she had that indefinable air of achievement, that world-
shine upon her, which, in Paul's eyes, made her a veritable queen of
Romance.

15   After a concert was over Paul was always irritable and wretched until
he got to sleep, and to-night he was even more than usually restless. He
had the feeling of not being able to let down, of its being impossible to
give up this delicious excitement which was the only thing that could
be called living at all. During the last number he withdrew and, after
hastily changing his clothes in the dressing-room, slipped out to the side
door where the soprano's carriage stood. Here he began pacing rapidly
up and down the walk, waiting to see her come out.

16   Over yonder the Schenley, in its vacant stretch, loomed big and square
through the fine rain, the windows of its twelve stories glowing like
those of a lighted card-board house under a Christmas tree. All the actors and singers of the better class stayed there when they were in the
city, and a number of the big manufacturers of the place lived there in
the winter. Paul had often hung about the hotel, watching the people go
in and out, longing to enter and leave school-masters and dull care behind him forever.

17   At last the singer came out, accompanied by the conductor, who
helped her into her carriage and closed the door with a cordial *auf wie-
dersehen*, which set Paul to wondering whether she were not an old
sweetheart of his. Paul followed the carriage over to the hotel, walking
so rapidly as not to be far from the entrance when the singer alighted
and disappeared behind the swinging glass doors that were opened by a
negro in a tall hat and a long coat. In the moment that the door was ajar,
it seemed to Paul that he, too, entered. He seemed to feel himself go
after her up the steps, into the warm, lighted building, into an exotic, a
tropical world of shiny, glistening surfaces and basking ease. He reflected upon the mysterious dishes that were brought into the dining-
room, the green bottles in buckets of ice, as he had seen them in the
supper party pictures of the *Sunday World* supplement. A quick gust of
wind brought the rain down with sudden vehemence, and Paul was startled to find that he was still outside in the slush of the gravel driveway;
that his boots were letting in the water and his scanty overcoat was
clinging wet about him; that the lights in front of the concert hall were
out, and that the rain was driving in sheets between him and the orange
glow of the windows above him. There it was, what he wanted—tangi-

bly before him, like the fairy world of a Christmas pantomime, but mocking spirits stood guard at the doors, and, as the rain beat in his face, Paul wondered whether he were destined always to shiver in the black night outside, looking up at it.

18 He turned and walked reluctantly toward the car tracks. The end had to come sometime; his father in his night-clothes at the top of the stairs, explanations that did not explain, hastily improvised fictions that were forever tripping him up, his upstairs room and its horrible yellow wall-paper, the creaking bureau with the greasy plush collar-box, and over his painted wooden bed the pictures of George Washington and John Calvin, and the framed motto, "Feed my Lambs," which had been worked in red worsted by his mother.

19 Half an hour later, Paul alighted from his car and went slowly down one of the side streets off the main thoroughfare. It was a highly respectable street, where all the houses were exactly alike, and where business men of moderate means begot and reared large families of children, all of whom went to Sabbath-school and learned the shorter catechism, and were interested in arithmetic; all of whom were as exactly alike as their homes, and of a piece with the monotony in which they lived. Paul never went up Cordelia Street without a shudder of loathing. His home was next to the house of the Cumberland minister. He approached it to-night with the nerveless sense of defeat, the hopeless feeling of sinking back forever into ugliness and commonness that he had always had when he came home. The moment he turned into Cordelia Street he felt the waters close above his head. After each of these orgies of living, he experienced all the physical depression which follows a debauch; the loathing of respectable beds, of common food, of a house permeated by kitchen odours; a shuddering repulsion for the flavourless, colourless mass of every-day existence; a morbid desire for cool things and soft lights and fresh flowers.

20 The nearer he approached the house, the more absolutely unequal Paul felt to the sight of it all; his ugly sleeping chamber; the cold bathroom with the grimy zinc tub, the cracked mirror, the dripping spiggots; his father, at the top of the stairs, his hairy legs sticking out from his night-shirt, his feet thrust into carpet slippers. He was so much later than usual that there would certainly be inquiries and reproaches. Paul stopped short before the door. He felt that he could not be accosted by his father to-night; that he could not toss again on that miserable bed. He would not go in. He would tell his father that he had no car fare, and it was raining so hard he had gone home with one of the boys and stayed all night.

21 Meanwhile, he was wet and cold. He went around to the back of the house and tried one of the basement windows, found it open, raised it cautiously, and scrambled down the cellar wall to the floor. There he

stood, holding his breath, terrified by the noise he had made, but the floor above him was silent, and there was no creak on the stairs. He found a soap-box, and carried it over to the soft ring of light that streamed from the furnace door, and sat down. He was horribly afraid of rats, so he did not try to sleep, but sat looking distrustfully at the dark, still terrified lest he might have awakened his father. In such reactions, after one of the experiences which made days and nights out of the dreary blanks of the calendar, when his senses were deadened, Paul's head was always singularly clear. Suppose his father had heard him getting in at the window and had come down and shot him for a burglar? Then, again, suppose his father had come down, pistol in hand, and he had cried out in time to save himself, and his father had been horrified to think how nearly he had killed him? Then, again, suppose a day should come when his father would remember that night, and wish there had been no warning cry to stay his hand? With this last supposition Paul entertained himself until daybreak.

22   The following Sunday was fine; the sodden November chill was broken by the last flash of autumnal summer. In the morning Paul had to go to church and Sabbath-school, as always. On seasonable Sunday afternoons the burghers of Cordelia Street always sat out on their front "stoops," and talked to their neighbors on the next stoop, or called to those across the street in neighbourly fashion. The men usually sat on gay cushions placed upon the steps that led down to the sidewalk, while the women, in their Sunday "waists," sat in rockers on the cramped porches, pretending to be greatly at their ease. The children played in the streets; there were so many of them that the place resembled the recreation grounds of a kindergarten. The men on the steps—all in their shirt sleeves, their vests unbuttoned—sat with their legs well apart, their stomachs comfortably protruding, and talked of the prices of things, or told anecdotes of the sagacity of their various chiefs and overlords. They occasionally looked over the multitude of squabbling children, listened affectionately to their high-pitched, nasal voices, smiling to see their own proclivities reproduced in their offspring, and interspersed their legends of the iron kings with remarks about their sons' progress at school, their grades in arithmetic, and the amounts they had saved in their toy banks.

23   On this last Sunday of November, Paul sat all the afternoon on the lowest step of his "stoop," staring into the street, while his sisters, in their rockers, were talking to the minister's daughters next door about how many shirt-waists they had made in the last week, and how many waffles some one had eaten at the last church supper. When the weather was warm, and his father was in a particularly jovial frame of mind, the girls made lemonade, which was always brought out in a red-glass pitcher, ornamented with forget-me-nots in blue enamel. This the girls

thought very fine, and the neighbors always joked about the suspicious colour of the pitcher.

24   To-day Paul's father sat on the top step, talking to a young man who shifted a restless baby from knee to knee. He happened to be the young man who was daily held up to Paul as a model, and after whom it was his father's dearest hope that he would pattern. This young man was of a ruddy complexion, with a compressed, red mouth, and faded, near-sighted eyes, over which he wore thick spectacles, with gold bows that curved about his ears. He was clerk to one of the magnates of a great steel corporation, and was looked upon in Cordelia Street as a young man with a future. There was a story that, some five years ago—he was now barely twenty-six—he had been a trifle dissipated, but in order to curb his appetites and save the loss of time and strength that a sowing of wild oats might have entailed, he had taken his chief's advice, oft reit-erated to his employees, and at twenty-one had married the first woman whom he could persuade to share his fortunes. She happened to be an angular school-mistress, much older than he, who also wore thick glasses, and who had now borne him four children, all near-sighted, like herself.

25   The young man was relating how his chief, now cruising in the Medi-terranean, kept in touch with all the details of the business, arranging his office hours on his yacht just as though he were at home, and "knocking off work enough to keep two stenographers busy." His father told, in turn, the plan his corporation was considering, of putting in an electric railway plant at Cairo. Paul snapped his teeth; he had an awful apprehension that they might spoil it all before he got there. Yet he rather liked to hear these legends of the iron kings, that were told and retold on Sundays and holidays; these stories of palaces in Venice, yachts on the Mediterranean, and high play at Monte Carlo appealed to his fancy, and he was interested in the triumphs of these cash boys who had become famous, though he had no mind for the cash-boy stage.

26   After supper was over, and he had helped to dry the dishes, Paul ner-vously asked his father whether he could go to George's to get some help in his geometry, and still more nervously asked for car fare. This latter request he had to repeat, as his father, on principle, did not like to hear requests for money, whether much or little. He asked Paul whether he could not go to some boy who lived nearer, and told him that he ought not to leave his school work until Sunday; but he gave him the dime. He was not a poor man, but he had a worthy ambition to come up in the world. His only reason for allowing Paul to usher was, that he thought a boy ought to be earning a little.

27   Paul bounded upstairs, scrubbed the greasy odour of the dish-water from his hands with the ill-smelling soap he hated, and then shook over his fingers a few drops of violet water from the bottle he kept hidden in

his drawer. He left the house with his geometry conspicuously under his arm, and the moment he got out of Cordelia Street and boarded a downtown car, he shook off the lethargy of two deadening days, and began to live again.

28 The leading juvenile of the permanent stock company which played at one of the downtown theatres was an acquaintance of Paul's, and the boy had been invited to drop in at the Sunday-night rehearsals whenever he could. For more than a year Paul had spent every available moment loitering about Charley Edwards's dressing-room. He had won a place among Edwards's following not only because the young actor, who could not afford to employ a dresser, often found him useful, but because he recognized in Paul something akin to what churchmen term "vocation."

29 It was at the theatre and at Carnegie Hall that Paul really lived; the rest was but a sleep and a forgetting. This was Paul's fairy tale, and it had for him all the allurement of a secret love. The moment he inhaled the gassy, painty, dusty odour behind the scenes, he breathed like a prisoner set free, and felt within him the possibility of doing or saying splendid, brilliant, poetic things. The moment the cracked orchestra beat out the overture from *Martha*, or jerked at the serenade from *Rigoletto*, all stupid and ugly things slid from him, and his senses were deliciously, yet delicately fired.

30 Perhaps it was because, in Paul's world, the natural nearly always wore the guise of ugliness, that a certain element of artificiality seemed to him necessary in beauty. Perhaps it was because his experience of life elsewhere was so full of Sabbath-school picnics, petty economies, wholesome advice as to how to succeed in life, and the unescapable odours of cooking, that he found this existence so alluring, these smartly-clad men and women so attractive, that he was so moved by these starry apple orchards that bloomed perennially under the limelight.

31 It would be difficult to put it strongly enough how convincingly the stage entrance of that theatre was for Paul the actual portal of Romance. Certainly none of the company ever suspected it, least of all Charley Edwards. It was very like the old stories that used to float about London of fabulously rich Jews, who had subterranean halls there, with palms, and fountains, and soft lamps and richly apparelled women who never saw the disenchanting light of London day. So, in the midst of that smoke-palled city, enamoured of figures and grimy toil, Paul had his secret temple, his wishing carpet, his bit of blue-and-white Mediterranean shore bathed in perpetual sunshine.

32 Several of Paul's teachers had a theory that his imagination had been perverted by garish fiction, but the truth was that he scarcely ever read at all. The books at home were not such as would either tempt or corrupt a youthful mind, and as for reading the novels that some of his friends urged upon him—well, he got what he wanted much more

quickly from music; any sort of music, from an orchestra to a barrel organ. He needed only the spark, the indescribable thrill that made his imagination master of his senses, and he could make plots and pictures enough of his own. It was equally true that he was not stage-struck— not, at any rate, in the usual acceptation of that expression. He had no desire to become an actor, any more than he had to become a musician. He felt no necessity to do any of these things; what he wanted was to see, to be in the atmosphere, float on the wave of it, to be carried out, blue league after blue league, away from everything.

33   After a night behind the scenes, Paul found the school-room more than ever repulsive; the bare floors and naked walls; the prosy men who never wore frock coats, or violets in their button-holes; the women with their dull gowns, shrill voices, and pitiful seriousness about prepositions that govern the dative. He could not bear to have the other pupils think, for a moment, that he took these people seriously; he must convey to them that he considered it all trivial, and was there only by way of a jest, anyway. He had autograph pictures of all the members of the stock company which he showed his classmates, telling them the most incredible stories of his familiarity with these people, of his acquaintance with the soloists who came to Carnegie Hall, his suppers with them and the flowers he sent them. When these stories lost their effect, and his audience grew listless, he became desperate and would bid all the boys good-bye, announcing that he was going to travel for awhile; going to Naples, to Venice, to Egypt. Then, next Monday, he would slip back, conscious and nervously smiling; his sister was ill, and he should have to defer his voyage until spring.

34   Matters went steadily worse with Paul at school. In the itch to let his instructors know how heartily he despised them and their homilies, and how thoroughly he was appreciated elsewhere, he mentioned once or twice that he had no time to fool with theorems; adding—with a twitch of the eyebrows and a touch of that nervous bravado which so perplexed them—that he was helping the people down at the stock company; they were old friends of his.

35   The upshot of the matter was, that the Principal went to Paul's father, and Paul was taken out of school and put to work. The manager at Carnegie Hall was told to get another usher in his stead; the doorkeeper at the theatre was warned not to admit him to the house; and Charley Edwards remorsefully promised the boy's father not to see him again.

36   The members of the stock company were vastly amused when some of Paul's stories reached them—especially the women. They were hard-working women, most of them supporting indigent husbands or brothers, and they laughed rather bitterly at having stirred the boy to such fervid and florid inventions. They agreed with the faculty and with his father that Paul's was a bad case.

37   The east-bound train was ploughing through a January snow-storm; the dull dawn was beginning to show grey when the engine whistled a mile out of Newark. Paul started up from the seat where he had lain curled in uneasy slumber, rubbed the breath-misted window glass with his hand, and peered out. The snow was whirling in curling eddies above the white bottom lands, and the drifts lay already deep in the fields and along the fences, while here and there the long dead grass and dried weed stalks protruded black above it. Lights shone from the scattered houses, and a gang of labourers who stood beside the track waved their lanterns.

38   Paul had slept very little, and he felt grimy and uncomfortable. He had made the all-night journey in a day coach, partly because he was ashamed, dressed as he was, to go into a Pullman, and partly because he was afraid of being seen there by some Pittsburgh business man, who might have noticed him in Denny & Carson's office. When the whistle awoke him, he clutched quickly at his breast pocket, glancing about him with an uncertain smile. But the little, clay-bespattered Italians were still sleeping, the slatternly women across the aisle were in open-mouthed oblivion, and even the crumby, crying babies were for the nonce stilled. Paul settled back to struggle with his impatience as best he could.

39   When he arrived at the Jersey City station, he hurried through his breakfast, manifestly ill at ease and keeping a sharp eye about him. After he reached the Twenty-third Street station, he consulted a cabman, and had himself driven to a men's furnishing establishment that was just opening for the day. He spent upward of two hours there, buying with endless reconsidering and great care. His new street suit he put on in the fitting-room; the frock coat and dress clothes he had bundled into the cab with his linen. Then he drove to a hatter's and a shoe house. His next errand was at Tiffany's, where he selected his silver and a new scarf-pin. He would not wait to have his silver marked, he said. Lastly, he stopped at a trunk shop on Broadway, and had his purchases packed into various traveling bags.

40   It was a little after one o'clock when he drove up to the Waldorf, and after settling with the cabman, went into the office. He registered from Washington; said his mother and father had been abroad, and that he had come down to await the arrival of their steamer. He told his story plausibly and had no trouble, since he volunteered to pay for them in advance, in engaging his rooms; a sleeping-room, sitting-room and bath.

41   Not once, but a hundred times Paul had planned this entry into New York. He had gone over every detail of it with Charley Edwards, and in his scrap book at home there were pages of description about New York hotels, cut from the Sunday papers. When he was shown to his sitting-room on the eighth floor, he saw at a glance that everything was as it should be; there was but one detail in his mental picture that the place

did not realize, so he rang for the bell boy and sent him down for flowers. He moved about nervously until the boy returned, putting away his new linen and fingering it delightedly as he did so. When the flowers came, he put them hastily into water, and then tumbled into a hot bath. Presently he came out of his white bathroom, resplendent in his new silk underwear, and playing with the tassels of his red robe. The snow was whirling so fiercely outside his windows that he could scarcely see across the street, but within the air was deliciously soft and fragrant. He put the violets and jonquils on the taboret beside the couch, and threw himself down, with a long sigh, covering himself with a Roman blanket. He was thoroughly tired; he had been in such haste, he had stood up to such a strain, covered so much ground in the last twenty-four hours, that he wanted to think how it had all come about. Lulled by the sound of the wind, the warm air, and the cool fragrance of the flowers, he sank into deep, drowsy retrospection.

42   It had been wonderfully simple; when they had shut him out of the theatre and concert hall, when they had taken away his bone, the whole thing was virtually determined. The rest was a mere matter of opportunity. The only thing that at all surprised him was his own courage—for he realized well enough that he had always been tormented by fear, a sort of apprehensive dread that, of late years, as the meshes of the lies he had told closed about him, had been pulling the muscles of his body tighter and tighter. Until now, he could not remember the time when he had not been dreading something. Even when he was a little boy, it was always there—behind him, or before, or on either side. There had always been the shadowed corner, the dark place into which he dared not look, but from which something seemed always to be watching him—and Paul had done things that were not pretty to watch, he knew.

43   But now he had a curious sense of relief, as though he had at last thrown down the gauntlet to the thing in the corner.

44   Yet it was but a day since he had been sulking in the traces; but yesterday afternoon that he had been sent to the bank with Denny & Carson's deposit, as usual—but this time he was instructed to leave the book to be balanced. There was above two thousand dollars in checks, and nearly a thousand in the bank notes which he had taken from the book and quietly transferred to his pocket. At the bank he had made out a new deposit slip. His nerves had been steady enough to permit of his returning to the office, where he had finished his work and asked for a full day's holiday to-morrow, Saturday, giving a perfectly reasonable pretext. The bank book, he knew, would not be returned before Monday or Tuesday, and his father would be out of town for the next week. From the time he slipped the bank notes into his pocket until he boarded the night train for New York, he had not known a moment's hesitation. It was not the first time Paul had steered through treacherous waters.

45   How astonishingly easy it had all been; here he was, the thing done;

and this time there would be no awakening, no figure at the top of the stairs. He watched the snow flakes whirling by his window until he fell alseep.

46   When he awoke, it was three o'clock in the afternoon. He bounded up with a start; half of one of his precious days gone already! He spent more than an hour in dressing, watching every stage of his toilet carefully in the mirror. Everything was quite perfect; he was exactly the kind of boy he had always wanted to be.

47   When he went downstairs, Paul took a carriage and drove up Fifth Avenue toward the Park. The snow had somewhat abated; carriages and tradesmen's wagons were hurrying soundlessly to and fro in the winter twilight; boys in woolen mufflers were shovelling off the doorsteps; the avenue stages made fine spots of colour against the white street. Here and there on the corners were stands, with whole flower gardens blooming under glass cases, against the sides of which the snow flakes stuck and melted; violets, roses, carnations, lilies of the valley—somehow vastly more lovely and alluring that they blossomed thus unnaturally in the snow. The Park itself was a wonderful stage winter-piece.

48   When he returned, the pause of the twilight had ceased, and the tune of the streets had changed. The snow was falling faster, lights streamed from the hotels that reared their dozen stories fearlessly up into the storm, defying the raging Atlantic winds. A long, black stream of carriages poured down the avenue, intersected here and there by other streams, tending horizontally. There were a score of cabs about the entrance of his hotel, and his driver had to wait. Boys in livery were running in and out of the awning stretched across the sidewalk, up and down the red velvet carpet laid from the door to the street. Above, about, within it all was the rumble and roar, the hurry and toss of thousands of human beings as hot for pleasure as himself, and on every side of him towered the glaring affirmation of the omnipotence of wealth.

49   The boy set his teeth and drew his shoulders together in a spasm of realization; the plot of all dramas, the text of all romances, the nerve-stuff of all sensations was whirling about him like the snow flakes. He burnt like a faggot in a tempest.

50   When Paul went down to dinner, the music of the orchestra came floating up the elevator shaft to greet him. His head whirled as he stepped into the thronged corridor, and he sank back into one of the chairs against the wall to get his breath. The lights, the chatter, the perfumes, the bewildering medley of colour—he had, for a moment, the feeling of not being able to stand it. But only for a moment; these were his own people, he told himself. He went slowly about the corridors, through the writing-rooms, smoking-rooms, reception-rooms, as though he were exploring the chambers of an enchanted palace, built and peopled for him alone.

51   When he reached the dining-room he sat down at a table near a window. The flowers, the white linen, the many-coloured wine glasses, the gay toilettes of the women, the low popping of corks, the undulating repetitions of the *Blue Danube* from the orchestra, all flooded Paul's dream with bewildering radiance. When the roseate tinge of his champagne was added—that cold, precious bubbling stuff that creamed and foamed in his glass—Paul wondered that there were honest men in the world at all. This was what all the world was fighting for, he reflected; this was what all the struggle was about. He doubted the reality of his past. Had he ever known a place called Cordelia Street, a place where fagged-looking business men got on the early car; mere rivets in a machine they seemed to Paul,—sickening men, with combings of children's hair always hanging to their coats, and the smell of cooking in their clothes. Cordelia Street—Ah! that belonged to another time and country; had he not always been thus, had he not sat here night after night, from as far back as he could remember, looking pensively over just such shimmering textures, and slowly twirling the stem of a glass like this one between his thumb and middle finger? He rather thought he had.

52   He was not in the least abashed or lonely. He had no especial desire to meet or to know any of these people; all he demanded was the right to look on and conjecture, to watch the pageant. The mere stage properties were all he contended for. Nor was he lonely later in the evening, in his loge at the Metropolitan. He was now entirely rid of his nervous misgivings, of his forced aggressiveness, of the imperative desire to show himself different from his surroundings. He felt now that his surroundings explained him. Nobody questioned the purple; he had only to wear it passively. He had only to glance down at his attire to reassure himself that here it would be impossible for any one to humiliate him.

53   He found it hard to leave his beautiful sitting-room to go to bed that night, and sat long watching the raging storm from his turret window. When he went to sleep, it was with the lights turned on in his bedroom; partly because of his old timidity, and partly so that, if he should wake in the night, there would be no wretched moment of doubt, no horrible suspicion of yellow wall-paper, or of Washington and Calvin above his bed.

54   Sunday morning the city was practically snow-bound. Paul breakfasted late, and in the afternoon he fell in with a wild San Francisco boy, a freshman at Yale, who said he had run down for a "little flyer" over Sunday. The young man offered to show Paul the night side of the town, and the two boys went out together after dinner, not returning to the hotel until seven o'clock the next morning. They had started out in the confiding warmth of a champagne friendship, but their parting in the elevator was singularly cool. The freshman pulled himself together to

make his train, and Paul went to bed. He awoke at two o'clock in the afternoon, very thirsty and dizzy, and rang for ice-water, coffee, and the Pittsburgh papers.

55 On the part of the hotel management, Paul excited no suspicion. There was this to be said for him, that he wore his spoils with dignity and in no way made himself conspicuous. Even under the glow of his wine he was never boisterous, though he found the stuff like a magician's wand for wonder-building. His chief greediness lay in his ears and eyes, and his excesses were not offensive ones. His dearest pleasures were the grey winter twilights in his sitting-room; his quiet enjoyment of his flowers, his clothes, his wide divan, his cigarette and his sense of power. He could not remember a time when he had felt so at peace with himself. The mere release from the necessity of petty lying, lying every day and every day, restored his self-respect. He had never lied for pleasure, even at school; but to be noticed and admired, to assert his difference from other Cordelia Street boys; and he felt a good deal more manly, more honest, even, now that he had no need for boastful pretensions, now that he could, as his actor friends used to say, "dress the part." It was characteristic that remorse did not occur to him. His golden days went by without a shadow, and he made each as perfect as he could.

56 On the eighth day after his arrival in New York, he found the whole affair exploited in the Pittsburgh papers, exploited with a wealth of detail which indicated that local news of a sensational nature was at a low ebb. The firm of Denny & Carson announced that the boy's father had refunded the full amount of the theft, and that they had no intention of prosecuting. The Cumberland minister had been interviewed, and expressed his hope of yet reclaiming the motherless lad, and his Sabbath-school teacher declared that she would spare no effort to that end. The rumour had reached Pittsburgh that the boy had been seen in a New York hotel, and his father had gone East to find him and bring him home.

57 Paul had just come in to dress for dinner; he sank into a chair, weak to the knees, and clasped his head in his hands. It was to be worse than jail, even; the tepid waters of Cordelia Street were to close over him finally and forever. The grey monotony stretched before him in hopeless, unrelieved years; Sabbath-school, Young People's Meeting, the yellow-papered room, the damp dish-towels; it all rushed back upon him with a sickening vividness. He had the old feeling that the orchestra had suddenly stopped, the sinking sensation that the play was over. The sweat broke out on his face, and he sprang to his feet, looked about him with his white, conscious smile, and winked at himself in the mirror. With something of the old childish belief in miracles with which he had so

often gone to class, all his lessons unlearned, Paul dressed and dashed whistling down the corridor to the elevator.

58 He had no sooner entered the dining-room and caught the measure of the music than his remembrance was lightened by his old elastic power of claiming the moment, mounting with it, and finding it all sufficient. The glare and glitter about him, the mere scenic accessories had again, and for the last time, their old potency. He would show himself that he was game, he would finish the thing splendidly. He doubted, more than ever, the existence of Cordelia Street, and for the first time he drank his wine recklessly. Was he not, after all, one of those fortunate beings born to the purple, was he not still himself and in his own place? He drummed a nervous accompaniment to the Pagliacci music and looked about him, telling himself over and over that it had paid.

59 He reflected drowsily, to the swell of the music and the chill sweetness of his wine, that he might have done it more wisely. He might have caught an outbound steamer and been well out of their clutches before now. But the other side of the world had seemed too far away and too uncertain then; he could not have waited for it; his need had been too sharp. If he had to choose over again, he would do the same thing tomorrow. He looked affectionately about the dining-room, now gilded with a soft mist. Ah, it had paid indeed!

60 Paul was awakened next morning by a painful throbbing in his head and feet. He had thrown himself across the bed without undressing, and had slept with his shoes on. His limbs and hands were lead heavy, and his tongue and throat were parched and burnt. There came upon him one of those fateful attacks of clear-headedness that never occurred except when he was physically exhausted and his nerves hung loose. He lay still and closed his eyes and let the tide of things wash over him.

61 His father was in New York; "stopping at some joint or other," he told himself. The memory of successive summers on the front stoop fell upon him like a weight of black water. He had not a hundred dollars left; and he knew now, more than ever, that money was everything, the wall that stood between all he loathed and all he wanted. The thing was winding itself up; he had thought of that on his first glorious day in New York, and had even provided a way to snap the thread. It lay on his dressing-table now; he had got it out last night when he came blindly up from dinner, but the shiny metal hurt his eyes, and he disliked the looks of it.

62 He rose and moved about with a painful effort, succumbing now and again to attacks of nausea. It was the old depression exaggerated; all the world had become Cordelia Street. Yet somehow he was not afraid of anything, was absolutely calm; perhaps because he had looked into the dark corner at last and knew. It was bad enough, what he saw there, but

somehow not so bad as his long fear of it had been. He saw everything clearly now. He had a feeling that he had made the best of it, that he had lived the sort of life he was meant to live, and for half an hour he sat staring at the revolver. But he told himself that was not the way, so he went downstairs and took a cab to the ferry.

63   When Paul arrived at Newark, he got off the train and took another cab, directing the driver to follow the Pennsylvania tracks out of the town. The snow lay heavy on the roadways and had drifted deep in the open fields. Only here and there the dead grass or dried weed stalks projected, singularly black, above it. Once well into the country, Paul dismissed the carriage and walked, floundering along the tracks, his mind a medley of irrelevant things. He seemed to hold in his brain an actual picture of everything he had seen that morning. He remembered every feature of both his drivers, of the toothless old woman from whom he had bought the red flowers in his coat, the agent from whom he had got his ticket, and all of his fellow-passengers on the ferry. His mind, unable to cope with vital matters near at hand, worked feverishly and deftly at sorting and grouping these images. They made for him a part of the ugliness of the world, of the ache in his head, and the bitter burning on his tongue. He stooped and put a handful of snow into his mouth as he walked, but that, too, seemed hot. When he reached a little hillside, where the tracks ran through a cut some twenty feet below him, he stopped and sat down.

64   The carnations in his coat were drooping with the cold, he noticed; their red glory all over. It occurred to him that all the flowers he had seen in the glass cases that first night must have gone the same way, long before this. It was only one splendid breath they had, in spite of their brave mockery at the winter outside the glass; and it was a losing game in the end, it seemed, this revolt against the homilies by which the world is run. Paul took one of the blossoms carefully from his coat and scooped a little hole in the snow, where he covered it up. Then he dozed a while, from his weak condition, seeming insensible to the cold.

65   The sound of an approaching train awoke him, and he started to his feet, remembering only his resolution, and afraid lest he should be too late. He stood watching the approaching locomotive, his teeth chattering, his lips drawn away from them in a frightened smile; once or twice he glanced nervously sidewise, as though he were being watched. When the right moment came, he jumped. As he fell, the folly of his haste occurred to him with merciless clearness, the vastness of what he had left undone. There flashed through his brain, clearer than ever before, the blue of Adriatic water, the yellow of Algerian sands.

66   He felt something strike his chest, and that his body was being thrown swiftly through the air, on and on, immeasurably far and fast, while his limbs were gently relaxed. Then, because the picture making

mechanism was crushed, the disturbing visions flashed into black, and Paul dropped back into the immense design of things.

Content Questions

1. Why do Paul's teachers want his suspension from school to continue?
2. Why does Paul resent his English teacher's presence at the theater? Why is his English teacher embarrassed?
3. What is Paul's relationship to his father?
4. How does Paul's vision of the stock company's members differ from their actual lives?
5. Where does Paul get the money for his trip to New York?
6. Why does Paul wear a carnation?

Questions on Presentation

1. Cather's title for this short story has intrigued many readers because there could be more than one type of case implied by the title. Why did Cather select this title? What is Paul's case?
2. How does Cather first make Paul seem an unsavory character?
3. Why is paragraph 41 important to the story?
4. Do you anticipate Paul's suicide? Why or why not?
5. Define evinced (3), debauch (19), sagacity (22), garish (32), and florid (36).
6. How do Cather's descriptions of cities, buildings, and even people contribute to the tone of impending disaster in the story? What do the descriptions tell us about the world Paul lives in and the world he wishes he lived in?

The Emperor of the Air

Ethan Canin

Ethan Canin (b. 1960) grew up in Ohio, Pennsylvania, and San Francisco. He graduated from Stanford University and was the fiction editor of *The Iowa Review* before entering Harvard Medical School in Boston, Massachusetts. He has published stories in magazines such as *The Atlantic Monthly, Ploughshares,* and *Redbook* and has won the Henfield Foundation/Transatlantic Review award for fiction and the Houghton Mifflin Literary Fellowship for a collection of short stories, tentatively entitled *Emperor of the Air.* Canin draws on both his scientific background and his analysis of human nature for the following story, "The Emperor of the Air."

1   Let me tell you who I am. I'm sixty-nine years old, live in the same house I was raised in, and have been the high school biology and astronomy teacher in this town so long that I have taught the grandson of one of my former students. I wear my father's wristwatch, which tells me it is past four-thirty in the morning, and though I have thought otherwise, I now think hope is the essence of all good men.

2   My wife, Vera, and I have no children, and this has enabled us to do a great many things in our lives: we have stood on the Great Wall of China, toured the Pyramid of Cheops, sunned in Lapland at midnight. Vera, who is near my age, is off on the Appalachian Trail. She has been gone two weeks and expects to be gone one more, on a trip on which a group of men and women, some of them half her age, are walking all the way through three states. Age, it seems, has left my wife alone. She ice-skates and hikes and will swim nude in a mountain lake. She does these things without me, however, for now my life has slowed. Last fall, as I pushed a lawnmower around our yard, I felt a squeezing in my chest and a burst of pain in my shoulder, and I spent a week in a semi-private hospital room. A heart attack. Myocardial infarction, minor. I will no longer run for a train, and in my shirt pocket I keep a small vial of nitroglycerine pills. In slow supermarket lines or traffic snarls I tell myself that impatience is not worth dying over, and last week, as I stood at the window and watched my neighbor, Mr. Pike, cross the yard toward our front door carrying a chain saw, I told myself that he was nothing but a doomed and hopeless man.

3   I had found the insects in my elm a couple of days before, the slim red line running from the ground up the long trunk and vanishing into the lower boughs. I brought out a magnifying glass to examine them—their shiny arthroderms, torsos elongated like drops of red liquid; their tiny legs, jointed and wiry, climbing the fissured bark. The morning I found them, Mr. Pike came over from next door and stood on our porch. "There's vermin in your elm," he said.

4   "I know," I said. "Come in."

5   "It's a shame, but I'll be frank: there's other trees on this block. I've got my own three elms to think of."

6   Mr. Pike is a builder, a thick and unpleasant man with whom I have rarely spoken. Though I had seen him at high school athletic events, the judgmental tilt to his jaw always suggested to me that he was merely

watching for the players' mistakes. He is short, with thick arms and a thick neck and a son, Kurt, in whose bellicose shouts I can already begin to hear the thickness of his father. Mr. Pike owns or partly owns a construction company that erected a line of low prefabricated houses on the outskirts of town, on a plot I remember from my youth as having been razed by fire. Once, a plumber who was working on our basement pipes told me that Mr. Pike was a poor craftsman, a man who valued money over quality. The plumber, a man my age who kept his tools in a wooden chest, shook his head when he told me that Mr. Pike used plastic pipes in the houses he had built. "They'll last ten years," the plumber told me. "Then the seams will go and the walls and ceilings will start to fill with water." I myself had had little to do with Mr. Pike until he told me he wanted my elm cut down to protect the three saplings in his yard. Our houses are separated by a tall stand of rhododendron and ivy, so we don't see each other's private lives as most neighbors do. When we talked on the street, we spoke only about a football score or the incessant rain, and I had not been on his property since shortly after he moved in, when I had gone over to introduce myself and he had shown me the spot where, underneath his rolling back lawn, he planned to build a bomb shelter.

7   Last week he stood on my porch with the chain saw in his hands. "I've got young elms," he said. "I can't let them be infested."

8   "My tree is over two hundred years old."

9   "It's a shame," he said, showing me the saw, "but I'll be frank. I just wanted you to know I could have it cut down as soon as you gave the word."

10   All week I had a hard time sleeping. I read Dickens in bed, heated cups of milk, but nothing worked. The elm was dying. Vera was gone, and I lay in bed thinking of the insects, of their minature jaws carrying away heartwood. It was late summer, the nights were still warm, and sometimes I went outside in my nightclothes and looked up at the sky. I teach astronomy, as I have said, and though sometimes I try to see the stars as milky dots or pearls, they are forever arranged in my eye according to the astronomic charts. I stood by the elm and looked up at Ursa Minor and Lyra, at Cygnus and Corona Borealis. I went back inside, read, peeled an orange. I sat at the window and thought about the insects, and every morning at five a boy who had once taken my astronomy class rode by on his bicycle, whistling the national anthem, and threw the newspaper onto our porch.

11   Sometimes I heard them, chewing the heart of my splendid elm.

12   The day after I first found the insects I called a man at the tree nursery. He described them for me, the bodies like red droplets, the wiry legs; he told me their genus and species.

13   "Will they kill the tree?"

14   "They could."

15   "We can poison them, can't we?"

16   "Probably not," he said. He told me that once they were visible outside the bark they had already invaded the tree too thoroughly for pesticide. "To kill them," he said, "we would end up killing the tree."

17   "Does that mean the tree is dead?"

18   "No," he said. "It depends on the colony of insects. Sometimes they invade a tree but don't kill it, don't even weaken it. They eat the wood, but sometimes they eat it so slowly that the tree can replace it."

19   When Mr. Pike came over the next day, I told him this. "You're asking me to kill a two-hundred-and-fifty-year-old tree that otherwise wouldn't die for a long time."

20   "The tree's over eighty feet tall," he said.

21   "So?"

22   "It stands fifty-two feet from my house."

23   "Mr. Pike, it's older than the Liberty Bell."

24   "I don't want to be unpleasant," he said, "but a storm could blow twenty-eight feet of that tree through the wall of my house."

25   "How long have you lived in that house?"

26   He looked at me, picked at his tooth. "You know."

27   "Four years," I said. "I was living here when a czar ruled Russia. An elm grows one quarter inch in width each year, when it's still growing. That tree is four feet thick, and it has yet to chip the paint on either your house or mine."

28   "It's sick," he said. "It's a sick tree. It could fall."

29   "Could," I said. "It *could* fall."

30   "It very well *might* fall."

31   We looked at each other for a moment. Then he averted his eyes, and with his right hand adjusted something on his watch. I looked at his wrist. The watch had a shiny metal band, with the hours, minutes, seconds, blinking in the display.

32   The next day he was back on my porch.

33   "We can plant another one," he said.

34   "What?"

35   "We can plant another tree. After we cut the elm, we can plant a new one."

36   "Do you have any idea how long it would take to grow a tree like that one?"

37   "You can buy trees half-grown. They bring them in on a truck and replant them."

38   "Even a half-grown tree would take a century to reach the size of the elm. A century."

39   He looked at me. Then he shrugged, turned around, and went back down the steps. I sat down in the open doorway. A century. What would

be left of the earth in a century? I didn't think I was a sentimental man, and I don't weep at plays or movies, but certain moments have always been peculiarly moving for me, and the mention of a century was one. There have been others. Standing out of the way on a fall evening, as couples and families converge on the concert hall from the radiating footpaths, has always filled me with a longing, though I don't know for what. I have taught the life of the simple hydra that is drawn, for no reasons it could ever understand, toward the bright surface of the water, and the spectacle of a thousand human beings organizing themselves into a single room to hear the quartets of Beethoven is as moving to me as birth or death. I feel the same way during the passage in an automobile across a cantilever span above the Mississippi, mother of rivers. These moments overwhelm me, and sitting on the porch that day as Mr. Pike retreated up the footpath, paused at the elm, and then went back into his house, I felt my life open up and present itself to me.

40   When he had gone back into his house I went out to the elm and studied the insects, which emerged from a spot in the grass and disappeared above my sight, in the lowest branches. Their line was dense and unbroken. I went inside and found yesterday's newspaper, which I rolled up and brought back out. With it I slapped up and down the trunk until the line was in chaos. I slapped until the newspaper was wet and tearing; with my fingernails I squashed stragglers between the narrow crags of bark. I stamped the sod where they emerged, dug my shoe tip into their underground tunnels. When my breathing became painful, I stopped and sat on the ground. I closed my eyes until the pulse in my neck was calm, and I sat there, mildly triumphant, master at last. After a while I looked up again at the tree and found the line perfectly restored.

41   That afternoon I mixed a strong insect poison, which I brought outside and painted around the bottom of the trunk. Mr. Pike came out onto his steps to watch. He walked down, stood on the sidewalk behind me, made little chuckling noises. "There's no poison that'll work," he whispered.

42   But that evening, when I came outside, the insects were gone. The trunk was bare. I ran my finger around the circumference. I rang Mr. Pike's doorbell and we went out and stood by the tree together. He felt in the notches of the bark, scratched bits of earth from the base. "I'll be damned," he said.

43   When I was a boy in this town, the summers were hot and the forest to the north and east often dried to the point where the undergrowth, not fit to compete with the deciduous trees for groundwater, turned crackling brown. The shrubbery became as fragile as straw, and the summer I was sixteen the forest ignited. A sheet of flame raced and bellowed

day and night as loud as a fleet of propeller planes. Whole families gathered in the street and evacuation plans were made, street routes drawn out beneath the night sky, which, despite the ten miles' distance to the fire, shone with orange light. My father had a wireless with which he communicated to the fire lines. He stayed up all night and promised that he would wake the neighbors if the wind changed or the fire otherwise turned toward town. That night the wind held, and by morning a firebreak the width of a street had been cut. My father took me down to see it the next day, a ribbon of cleared land as bare as if it had been drawn with a razor. Trees had been felled, the underbrush sickled down and removed. We stood at the edge of the cleared land, the town behind us, and watched the fire. Then we got into my father's Plymouth and drove as close as we were allowed. A fireman near the flames had been asphyxiated, someone said, when the cone of fire had turned abruptly and sucked up all the oxygen in the air. My father explained to me how a flame breathed oxygen like a man. We got out of the car. The heat curled the hair on our arms and turned the ends of our eyelashes white.

44   My father was a pharmacist and had taken me to the fire out of curiosity. Anything scientific interested him. He kept tide tables, and collected the details of nature—butterflies and moths, seeds, wildflowers—and stored them in glass-fronted cases, which he leaned against the stone wall of our cellar. One summer he taught me the constellations of the Northern Hemisphere. We went outside at night, and as the summer progressed he showed me how to find Perseus and Arcturus and Andromeda, how some of the brightest stars illuminated Lyra and Aquila, how, though the constellations proceed with the seasons, Polaris remains most fixed and is thus the set point of a mariner's navigation. He taught me the night sky, and I find now that this is rare knowledge. Later, when I taught astronomy, my students rarely cared about the silicon or iron on the sun, but when I spoke of Cepheus or Lacerta, they were silent and attended my words. At a party now I can always find a drinking husband who will come outside with me and sip cognac while I point out the stars and say their names.

45   That day, as I stood and watched the fire, I thought the flames were as loud and powerful as the sea, and that evening, when we were home, I went out to the front yard and climbed the elm to watch the forest burn. Climbing the elm was forbidden me, because the lowest limbs even then were well above my reach and because my father believed that anybody lucky enough to make it up into the lower boughs would almost certainly fall on the way down. But I knew how to climb it anyway. I had done it before, when my parents were gone. I had never made it as far as the first limbs, but I had learned the knobs and handholds on which, with balance and strength, I could climb to within a single jump of the boughs. The jump frightened me, however, and I had never at-

tempted it. To reach the boughs one had to gather strength and leap upward into the air, propelled only by the purchase of feet and hands on
the small juttings of bark. It was a terrible risk. I could no more imagine
myself making this leap than I could imagine diving headlong from a
coastal cliff into the sea. I was an adventurous youth, as I was later an
adventurous man, but all my adventures had a quality about them of
safety and planned success. This is still true. In Ethiopia I have photographed a lioness with her cubs; along the Barrier Reef I have dived
among barracuda and scorpion fish—but these things have never frightened me. In my life I have done few things that have frightened me.

46   That night, though, I made the leap into the lower boughs of the elm.
My parents were inside the house, and I made my way upward until I
crawled out of the leaves onto a narrow top branch and looked around
me at a world that on two sides was entirely red and orange with flame.
After a time I came back down and went inside to sleep, but that night
the wind changed. My father woke us, and we gathered outside on the
street with all the other families on our block. People carried blankets
filled with the treasures of their lives. One woman wore a fur coat,
though the air was suffused with ash and was as warm as an afternoon.
My father stood on the hood of a car and spoke. He had heard through
the radio that the fire had leaped the break, that a house on the eastern
edge of town was in full flame, and, as we all could feel, that the wind
was strong and blowing straight west. He told the families to finish loading their cars and leave as soon as possible. Though the fire was still
across town, he said, the air was filling with smoke so rapidly that
breathing would soon be difficult. He got down off the car and we went
inside to gather things together. We had an RCA radio in our living
room and a set of Swiss china in my mother's cupboard, but my father
instead loaded a box with the *Encyclopaedia Britannica* and carried up
from the basement the heavy glass cases that contained his species chart
of the North American butterflies. We carried these things outside to
the Plymouth. When we returned, my mother was standing in the
doorway.

47   "This is my home," she said.

48   "We're in a hurry," my father said.

49   "This is my home, this is my children's home. I'm not leaving."

50   My father stood on the porch looking at her. "Stay here," he said to
me. Then he took my mother's arm and they went into the house. I
stood on the steps outside, and when my father came out again in a few
minutes, he was alone, just as when we drove west that night and slept
with the rest of our neighborhood on Army cots in the high school gym
in the next town, we were alone. My mother had stayed behind.

51   Nothing important came of this. That night the wind calmed and the
burning house was extinguished; the next day a heavy rain wet the fire

and it was put out. Everybody came home, and the settled ash was swept from the houses and walkways into black piles in the street. I mention the incident now only because it points out, I think, what I have always lacked: I inherited none of my mother's moral stubbornness. In spite of my age, still, arriving on foot at a crosswalk where the light is red but no cars are in sight, I'm thrown into confusion. My decisions never seem to engage the certainty that I had hoped to enjoy late in my life. But I was adamant and angry when Mr. Pike came to my door. The elm was ancient and exquisite: we could not let it die.

52   Now, though, the tree was safe. I examined it in the morning, in the afternoon, in the evening, and with a lantern at night. The bark was clear. I slept.

53   The next morning Mr. Pike was at my door.

54   "Good morning, neighbor," I said.

55   "They're back."

56   "They can't be."

57   "They are. Look," he said, and walked out to the tree. He pointed up to the first bough.

58   "You probably can't see them," he said, "but I can. They're up there, a whole line of them."

59   "They couldn't be."

60   "They sure are. Listen," he said, "I don't want to be unpleasant, but I'll be frank."

61   That evening he left a note in our mail slot. It said that he had contacted the authorities, who had agreed to enforce the cutting of the tree if I didn't do it myself. I read the note in the kitchen. Vera had been cooking some Indian chicken before she left for the Appalachian Trail, and on the counter was a big jar filled with flour and spices that she shook pieces of chicken in. I read Mr. Pike's note again. Then I got a fishing knife and a flashlight from the closet, emptied Vera's jar, and went outside with these things to the elm. The street was quiet. I made a few calculations, and then with the knife cut the bark. Nothing. I had to do it only a couple more times, however, before I hit the mark and, sure enough, the tree sprouted insects. Tiny red bugs shot crazily from the slit in the bark. I touched my finger there and they spread in an instant all over my hand and up my arm. I had to shake them off. Then I opened the jar, laid the fishing knife out from the opening like a bridge, and touched the blade to the slit in the tree. They scrambled up the knife and began to fill the jar as fast as a trickling spring. After a few minutes I pulled out the knife, closed the lid, and went back into the house.

62   Mr. Pike is my neighbor, and so I felt a certain remorse. What I contemplated, however, was not going to kill the elms. It was going to save them. If Mr. Pike's trees were infested, they would still more than likely live, and he would no longer want mine chopped down. This is the na-

ture of the world. In the dark house, feeling half like a criminal and half like a man of mercy, my heart arrhythmic in anticipation, I went upstairs to prepare. I put on black pants and a black shirt. I dabbed shoe polish on my cheeks, my neck, my wrists, the backs of my hands. Over my white hair I stretched a tight black cap. Then I walked downstairs. I picked up the jar and the flashlight and went outside into the night.

63   I have always enjoyed gestures—never failing to bow, for example, when I finished dancing with a woman—but one attribute I have acquired with age is the ability to predict when I am about to act foolishly. As I slid calmly into the shadowy cavern behind our side-yard rhododendron and paused to catch my breath, I thought that perhaps I had better go back inside and get into my bed. But then I decided to go through with it. As I stood there in the shadow of the swaying rhododendron, waiting to pass into the backyard of my neighbor, I thought of Hannibal and Napoleon and MacArthur. I tested my flashlight and shook the jar, which made a soft colliding sound as if it were filled with rice. A light was on in the Pikes' living room, but the alley between our houses was dark. I passed through.

64   The Pikes' yard is large, larger than ours, and slopes twice within its length, so that the lawn that night seemed like a dark, furrowed flag stretching back to the three elms. I paused at the border of the driveway, where the grass began, and looked out at the young trees outlined by the lighted houses behind them. In what strange ways, I thought, do our lives turn. Then I got down on my hands and knees. Staying along the fence that separates our yards, I crawled toward the back of the Pikes' lawn. In my life I have not crawled a lot. With Vera I have gone spelunking in the limestone caves of southern Minnesota, but there the crawling was obligate, and as we made our way along the narrow, wet channel into the heart of the rock, I felt a strange grace in my knees and elbows. The channel was hideously narrow, and my life depended on the sureness of my limbs. Now, in the Pikes' yard, my knees felt arthritic and torn. I made my way along the driveway toward the young elms against the back fence. The grass was wet and the water dampened my trousers. I was hurrying as best I could across the open lawn, the insect-filled jar in my hand, the flashlight in my pocket, when I put my palm on something cement. I stopped and looked down. In the dim light I saw what looked like the hatch door on a submarine. Round, the size of a manhole, marked with a fluorescent cross—oh, Mr. Pike, I didn't think you'd do it. I put down the jar and felt for the handle in the dark, and when I found it I braced myself and turned. I certainly didn't expect it to give, but it did, circling once, twice, around in my grasp and loosening like the lid of a bottle. I pulled the hatch and up it came. Then I picked up the insects, felt with my feet for the ladder inside, and went down, closing the hatch behind me.

65   I still planned to deposit the insects on his trees, but something about

crime is contagious. I knew that what I was doing was foolish and that it increased the risk of being caught, but as I descended the ladder into Mr. Pike's bomb shelter, I could barely distinguish fear from elation. At the bottom of the ladder I switched on the flashlight. The room was round, the ceiling and floor were concrete, and against the wall stood a cabinet of metal shelves filled with canned foods. On one shelf were a dictionary and some magazines. Oh, Mr. Pike. I thought of his sapling elms, of the roots making their steady, blind way through the earth; I thought of his houses ten years from now, when the pipes cracked and the ceilings began to pool with water. What a hopeless man he seemed to me then, how small and afraid.

66   I stood thinking about him, and after a moment I heard a door close in the house. I climbed the ladder and peeked out under the hatch. There on the porch stood Kurt and Mr. Pike. As I watched, they came down off the steps and walked over and stood on the grass near me. I could see the watch blinking on Mr. Pike's wrist. I lowered my head. They were silent, and I wondered what Mr. Pike would do if he found me in his bomb shelter. He was thickly built, as I have said, but I didn't think he was a violent man. One afternoon I had watched as Kurt slammed the front door of their house and ran down the steps onto the lawn, where he stopped and threw an object—an ashtray, I think it was—right through the front window of the house. When the glass shattered, he ran, and Mr. Pike soon appeared on the front steps. The reason I say that he is not a violent man is that I saw something beyond anger, perhaps a certain doom, in his posture as he went back inside that afternoon and began cleaning up the glass with a broom. I watched him through the broken front window of their house.

67   How would I explain to him, though, the bottle of mad insects I now held? I could have run then, I suppose, made a break up and out of the shelter while their backs were turned. I could have been out the driveway and across the street without their recognizing me. But there was, of course, my heart. I moved back down the ladder. As I descended and began to think about a place to hide my insects, I heard Mr. Pike speak. I climbed back up the ladder. When I looked out under the hatch, I saw the two of them, backs toward me, pointing at the sky. Mr. Pike was sighting something with his finger, and Kurt followed. Then I realized that he was pointing out the constellations, but that he didn't know what they were and was making up their names as he spoke. His voice was not fanciful. It was direct and scientific, and he was lying to his son about what he knew. "These," he said, "these are the Mermaid's Tail, and south you can see the three peaks of Mount Olympus, and then the sword that belongs to the Emperor of the Air." I looked where he was pointing. It was late summer, near midnight, and what he had described was actually Cygnus's bright tail and the outstretched neck of Pegasus.

68   Presently he ceased speaking, and after a time they walked back across the lawn and went into the house. The light in the kitchen went on, then off. I stepped from my hiding place. I suppose I could have continued with my mission, but the air was calm, it was a perfect and still night, and my plan, I felt, had been interrupted. In my hand the jar felt large and dangerous. I crept back across the lawn, staying in the shadows of the ivy and rhododendron along the fence, until I was in the driveway between our two houses. In the side window of the Pikes' house a light was on. I paused at a point where the angle allowed me a view through the glass, down the hallway, and through an open door into the living room. Mr. Pike and Kurt were sitting together on a brown couch against the far wall of the room, watching television. I came up close to the window and peered through. Though I knew this was foolish, that any neighbor, any man walking his dog at night, would have thought me a burglar in my black clothing, I stayed and watched. The light was on inside, it was dark around me, and I knew I could look in without being seen. Mr. Pike had his hand on Kurt's shoulder. Every so often when they laughed at something on the screen, he moved his hand up and tousled Kurt's hair. The sight of this suddenly made me feel the way I do on the bridge across the Mississippi River. When he put his hand on Kurt's hair again, I moved out of the shadows and went back to my own house.

69   I wanted to run, or kick a ball, or shout a soliloquy into the night. I could have stepped up on a car hood then and lured the Pikes, the paper boy, all the neighbors, out into the night. I could have spoken about the laboratory of a biology teacher, about the rows of specimen jars. How could one not hope here? At three weeks the human embryo has gill arches on its neck, like a fish; at six weeks, amphibians' webs still connect its blunt fingers. Miracles. This is true everywhere in nature. The evolution of 500 million years is mimicked in each gestation: birds that in the egg look like fish; fish that emerge like their spineless, leaflike ancestors. What it is to study life! Anybody who had seen a cell divide could have invented religion.

70   I sat down on the porch steps and looked at the elm. After a while I stood up and went inside. With turpentine I cleaned the shoe polish from my face, and then I went upstairs. I got into bed. For an hour or two I lay there, sleepless, hot, my thoughts racing, before I gave up and went to the bedroom window. The jar, which I had brought up with me, stood on the sill, and I saw that the insects were either asleep or dead. I opened the window then and emptied them down onto the lawn, and at that moment, as they rained away into the night, glinting and cascading, I thought of asking Vera for a child. I knew it was not possible, but I considered it anyway. Standing there at the window, I thought of Vera, ageless, in forest boots and shorts, perspiring through a flannel blouse as

she dipped drinking water from an Appalachian stream. What had we, she and I? The night was calm, dark. Above me Polaris blinked.

71   I tried going to sleep again. I lay in bed for a time, and then gave up and went downstairs. I ate some crackers. I drank two glasses of bourbon. I sat at the window and looked out at the front yard. Then I got up and went outside and looked up at the stars, and I tried to see them for their beauty and mystery. I thought of billions of tons of exploding gases, hydrogen and helium, red giants, supernovas. In places they were as dense as clouds. I thought of magnesium and silicon and iron. I tried to see them out of their constellatory order, but it was like trying to look at a word without reading it, and I stood there in the night unable to scramble the patterns. Some clouds had blown in and begun to cover Auriga and Taurus. I was watching them begin to spread and refract moonlight when I heard the paper boy whistling the national anthem. When he reached me, I was standing by the elm, still in my nightclothes, unshaven, a little drunk.

72   "I want you to do something for me," I said.

73   "Sir?"

74   "I'm an old man and I want you to do something for me. Put down your bicycle," I said. "Put down your bicycle and look up at the stars."

Content Questions

1. Who is the Emperor of the Air and how did he get his name?
2. Why doesn't the narrator cut down the elm tree?
3. Why does the narrator remember the fire?
4. Who benefits from looking at the stars?

Questions on Presentation

1. Every story has at least one main theme or major idea that the author wants readers to understand. Canin's theme has to do with why people behave the way they do. To explain that theme, Canin suggests an analogy and draws it out to its fullest. Identify the major analogy Canin uses, and explain whether you believe the analogy is reasonable.
2. Canin has the narrator retell his father's history so that readers will see the similarities between the father and the narrator. What do you believe readers should learn about the narrator from his description of his father?
3. Why does Canin introduce the narrator in the first paragraph with what amounts to a list of qualities?

4. How does Canin maintain the reader's sympathy for the narrator?
5. Define arthroderms (3), incessant (6), deciduous (43) and asphyxiated (43).
6. The elm tree is obviously important for the plot of Canin's story. What does the tree tell readers about the characters and the way they react to one another?

The Bride Comes to Yellow Sky

Stephen Crane

American poet, novelist, and short story writer Stephen Townley Crane (1871–1900) was the fourteenth child of the Methodist minister Jonathan T. Crane. Born in Newark, New Jersey, Crane was writing stories by the time he was eight years old. Early in his life he rejected his background, cultivating "vices" such as baseball, the theater, and writing. Crane spent several years in New York as a reporter before becoming a traveling correspondent. He traveled the world for various publishers, reporting on news stories such as the wars in Cuba and Turkey. When not reporting the news, Crane wrote several novels and short stories. The following story, published in *The Open Boat and Other Tales of Adventure*, is a somewhat comic episode in the passing of the Old West.

1   The great Pullman was whirling onward with such dignity of motion that a glance from the window seemed simply to prove that the plains of Texas were pouring eastward. Vast flats of green grass, dull-hued spaces of mesquit and cactus, little groups of frame houses, woods of light and tender trees, all were sweeping into the east, sweeping over the horizon, a precipice.

2   A newly married pair had boarded this coach at San Antonio. The man's face was reddened from many days in the wind and sun, and a direct result of his new black clothes was that his brick-colored hands were constantly performing in a most conscious fashion. From time to time he looked down respectfully at his attire. He sat with a hand on each knee, like a man waiting in a barber's shop. The glances he devoted to other passengers were furtive and shy.

3   The bride was not pretty, nor was she very young. She wore a dress of blue cashmere, with small reservations of velvet here and there, and with steel buttons abounding. She continually twisted her head to re-

gard her puff sleeves, very stiff, straight, and high. They embarrassed her. It was quite apparent that she had cooked, and that she expected to cook, dutifully. The blushes caused by the careless scrutiny of some passengers as she had entered the car were strange to see upon this plain, under-class countenance, which was drawn in placid, almost emotionless lines.

4 They were evidently very happy. "Ever been in a parlor-car before?" he asked, smiling with delight.

5 "No," she answered, "I never was. It's fine, ain't it?"

6 "Great! And then after a while we'll go forward to the diner, and get a big lay-out. Finest meal in the world. Charge a dollar."

7 "Oh, do they?" cried the bride. "Charge a dollar? Why, that's too much—for us—ain't it, Jack?"

8 "Not this trip, anyhow," he answered bravely. "We're going to go the whole thing."

9 Later he explained to her about the trains. "You see, it's a thousand miles from one end of Texas to the other; and this train runs right across it, and never stops but four times." He had the pride of an owner. He pointed out to her the dazzling fittings of the coach; and in truth her eyes opened wider as she contemplated the sea-green figured velvet, the shining brass, silver, and glass, the wood that gleamed as darkly brilliant as the surface of a pool of oil. At one end a bronze figure sturdily held a support for a separated chamber, and at convenient places on the ceiling were frescos in olive and silver.

10 To the minds of the pair, their surroundings reflected the glory of their marriage that morning in San Antonio; this was the environment of their new estate; and the man's face in particular beamed with an elation that made him appear ridiculous to the negro porter. This individual at times surveyed them from afar with an amused and superior grin. On other occasions he bullied them with skill in ways that did not make it exactly plain to them that they were being bullied. He subtly used all the manners of the most unconquerable kind of snobbery. He oppressed them; but of this oppression they had small knowledge, and they speedily forgot that infrequently a number of travelers covered them with stares of derisive enjoyment. Historically there was supposed to be something infinitely humorous in their situation.

11 "We are due in Yellow Sky at 3:42," he said, looking tenderly into her eyes.

12 "Oh, are we?" she said, as if she had not been aware of it. To evince surprise at her husband's statement was part of her wifely amiability. She took from a pocket a little silver watch; and as she held it before her, and stared at it with a frown of attention, the new husband's face shone.

13   "I bought it in San Anton' from a friend of mine," he told her gleefully.

14   "It's seventeen minutes past twelve," she said, looking up at him with a kind of shy and clumsy coquetry. A passenger, noting this play, grew excessively sardonic, and winked at himself in one of the numerous mirrors.

15   At last they went to the dining-car. Two rows of negro waiters, in glowing white suits, surveyed their entrance with the interest, and also the equanimity, of men who had been forewarned. The pair fell to the lot of a waiter who happened to feel pleasure in steering them through their meal. He viewed them with the manner of a fatherly pilot, his countenance radiant with benevolence. The patronage, entwined with the ordinary deference, was not plain to them. And yet, as they returned to their coach, they showed in their faces a sense of escape.

16   To the left, miles down a long purple slope, was a little ribbon of mist where moved the keening Rio Grande. The train was approaching it at an angle, and the apex was Yellow Sky. Presently it was apparent that, as the distance from Yellow Sky grew shorter, the husband became commensurately restless. His brick-red hands were more insistent in their prominence. Occasionally he was even rather absent-minded and far-away when the bride leaned forward and addressed him.

17   As a matter of truth, Jack Potter was beginning to find the shadow of a deed weigh upon him like a leaden slab. He, the town marshal of Yellow Sky, a man known, liked, and feared in his corner, a prominent person, had gone to San Antonio to meet a girl he believed he loved, and there, after the usual prayers, had actually induced her to marry him, without consulting Yellow Sky for any part of the transaction. He was now bringing his bride before an innocent and unsuspecting community.

18   Of course people in Yellow Sky married as it pleased them, in accordance with a general custom; but such was Potter's thought of his duty to his friends, or of their idea of his duty, or of an unspoken form which does not control men in these matters, that he felt he was heinous. He had committed an extraordinary crime. Face to face with this girl in San Antonio, and spurred by his sharp impulse, he had gone headlong over all the social hedges. At San Antonio he was like a man hidden in the dark. A knife to sever any friendly duty, any form, was easy to his hand in that remote city. But the hour of Yellow Sky—the hour of daylight— was approaching.

19   He knew full well that his marriage was an important thing to his town. It could only be exceeded by the burning of the new hotel. His friends could not forgive him. Frequently he had reflected on the advisability of telling them by telegraph, but a new cowardice had been upon him. He feared to do it. And now the train was hurrying him toward a

scene of amazement, glee, and reproach. He glanced out of the window at the line of haze swinging slowly in toward the train.

20 Yellow Sky had a kind of brass band, which played painfully, to the delight of the populace. He laughed without heart as he thought of it. If the citizens could dream of his prospective arrival with his bride, they would parade the band at the station and escort them, amid cheers and laughing congratulations, to his adobe home.

21 He resolved that he would use all the devices of speed and plains-craft in making the journey from the station to his house. Once within that safe citadel, he could issue some sort of a vocal bulletin, and then not go among the citizens until they had time to wear off a little of their enthusiasm.

22 The bride looked anxiously at him. "What's worrying you, Jack?"

23 He laughed again. "I'm not worrying, girl; I'm only thinking of Yellow Sky."

24 She flushed in comprehension.

25 A sense of mutual guilt invaded their minds and developed a finer tenderness. They looked at each other with eyes softly aglow. But Potter often laughed the same nervous laugh; the flush upon the bride's face seemed quite permanent.

26 The traitor to the feelings of Yellow Sky narrowly watched the speeding landscape. "We're nearly there," he said.

27 Presently the porter came and announced the proximity of Potter's home. He held a brush in his hand, and, with all his airy superiority gone, he brushed Potter's new clothes as the latter slowly turned this way and that way. Potter fumbled out a coin and gave it to the porter, as he had seen others do. It was a heavy and muscle-bound business, as that of a man shoeing his first horse.

28 The porter took their bag, and as the train began to slow they moved forward to the hooded platform of the car. Presently the two engines and their long string of coaches rushed into the station of Yellow Sky.

29 "They have to take water here," said Potter, from a constricted throat and in mournful cadence, as one announcing death. Before the train stopped his eye had swept the length of the platform, and he was glad and astonished to see there was none upon it but the station-agent, who, with a slightly hurried and anxious air, was walking toward the water-tanks. When the train had halted, the porter alighted first, and placed in position a little temporary step.

30 "Come on, girl," said Potter, hoarsely. As he helped her down they each laughed on a false note. He took the bag from the negro, and bade his wife cling to his arm. As they slunk rapidly away, his hang-dog glance perceived that they were unloading the two trunks, and also that the station-agent, far ahead near the baggage-car, had turned and was running toward him, making gestures. He laughed, and groaned as he

laughed, when he noted the first effect of his marital bliss upon Yellow Sky. He gripped his wife's arm firmly to his side, and they fled. Behind them the porter stood, chuckling fatuously.

31   The California express on the Southern Railway was due at Yellow Sky in twenty-one minutes. There were six men at the bar of the Weary Gentleman Saloon. One was a drummer,[1] who talked a great deal and rapidly; three were Texans, who did not care to talk at that time; and two were Mexican sheepherders, who did not talk as a general practice in the Weary Gentleman Saloon. The barkeeper's dog lay on the board walk that crossed in front of the door. His head was on his paws, and he glanced drowsily here and there with the constant vigilance of a dog that is kicked on occasion. Across the sandy street were some vivid green grass-plots, so wonderful in appearance, amid the sands that burned near them in a blazing sun, that they caused a doubt in the mind. They exactly resembled the grass mats used to represent lawns on the stage. At the cooler end of the railway station, a man without a coat sat in a tilted chair and smoked his pipe. The fresh-cut bank of the Rio Grande circled near the town, and there could be seen beyond it a great plum-colored plain of mesquit.

32   Save for the busy drummer and his companions in the saloon, Yellow Sky was dozing. The new-comer leaned gracefully upon the bar, and recited many tales with the confidence of a bard who has come upon a new field.

33   "—and at the moment that the old man fell down-stairs with the bureau in his arms, the old woman was coming up with two scuttles of coal, and of course—"

34   The drummer's tale was interrupted by a young man who suddenly appeared in the open door. He cried: "Scratchy Wilson's drunk, and has turned loose with both hands." The two Mexicans at once set down their glasses and faded out of the rear entrance of the saloon.

35   The drummer, innocent and jocular, answered: "All right, old man. S'pose he has? Come in and have a drink, anyhow."

36   But the information had made such an obvious cleft in every skull in the room that the drummer was obliged to see its importance. All had become instantly solemn. "Say," said he, mystified, "what is this?" His three companions made the introductory gesture of eloquent speech; but the young man at the door forestalled them.

37   "It means, my friend," he answered, as he came into the saloon, "that for the next two hours this town won't be a health resort."

38   The barkeeper went to the door, and locked and barred it; reaching out of the window, he pulled in heavy wooden shutters, and barred them. Immediately a solemn, chapel-like gloom was upon the place. The drummer was looking from one to another.

39   "But say," he cried, "what is this, anyhow? You don't mean there is going to be a gun-fight?"

40   "Don't know whether there'll be a fight or not," answered one man, grimly; "but there'll be some shootin'—some good shootin'."

41   The young man who had warned them waved his hand. "Oh, there'll be a fight fast enough, if any one wants it. Anybody can get a fight out there in the street. There's a fight just waiting."

42   The drummer seemed to be swayed between the interest of a foreigner and a perception of personal danger.

43   "What did you say his name was?" he asked.

44   "Scratchy Wilson," they answered in chorus.

45   "And will he kill anybody? What are you going to do? Does this happen often? Does he rampage around like this once a week or so? Can he break in that door?"

46   "No; he can't break down that door," replied the barkeeper. "He's tried it three times. But when he comes you'd better lay down on the floor, stranger. He's dead sure to shoot at it, and a bullet may come through."

47   Thereafter the drummer kept a strict eye upon the door. The time had not yet been called for him to hug the floor, but, as a minor precaution, he sidled near to the wall. "Will he kill anybody?" he said again.

48   The man laughed low and scornfully at the question.

49   "He's out to shoot, and he's out for trouble. Don't see any good in experimentin' with him."

50   "But what do you do in a case like this? What do you do?"

51   A man responded: "Why, he and Jack Potter—"

52   "But," in chorus the other men interrupted, "Jack Potter's in San Anton'."

53   "Well, who is he? What's he got to do with it?"

54   "Oh, he's the town marshal. He goes out and fights Scratchy when he gets on one of these tears."

55   "Wow!" said the drummer, mopping his brow. "Nice job he's got."

56   The voices had toned away to mere whisperings. The drummer wished to ask further questions, which were born of an increasing anxiety and bewilderment; but when he attempted them, the men merely looked at him in irritation and motioned him to remain silent. A tense waiting hush was upon them. In the deep shadows of the room their eyes shone as they listened for sounds from the street. One man made three gestures at the barkeeper; and the latter, moving like a ghost, handed him a glass and a bottle. The man poured a full glass of whiskey, and set down the bottle noiselessly. He gulped the whiskey in a swallow, and turned again toward the door in immovable silence. The drummer saw that the barkeeper, without a sound, had taken a Winchester from beneath the bar. Later he saw this individual beckoning to him, so he tiptoed across the room.

57   "You better come with me back of the bar."

58   "No, thanks," said the drummer, perspiring; "I'd rather be where I can make a break for the back door."

59   Whereupon the man of bottles made a kindly but peremptory gesture. The drummer obeyed it, and, finding himself seated on a box with his head below the level of the bar, balm was laid upon his soul at sight of various zinc and copper fittings that bore a resemblance to armor-plate. The barkeeper took a seat comfortably upon an adjacent box.

60   "You see," he whispered, "this here Scratchy Wilson is a wonder with a gun—a perfect wonder; and when he goes on the war-trail, we hunt our holes—naturally. He's about the last one of the old gang that used to hang out along the river here. He's a terror when he's drunk. When he's sober he's all right—kind of simple—wouldn't hurt a fly—nicest fellow in town. But when he's drunk—whoo!"

61   There were periods of stillness. "I wish Jack Potter was back from San Anton'," said the barkeeper. "He shot Wilson up once,—in the leg,—and he would sail in and pull out the kinks in this thing."

62   Presently they heard from a distance the sound of a shot, followed by three wild yowls. It instantly removed a bond from the men in the darkened saloon. There was a shuffling of feet. They looked at each other. "Here he comes," they said.

63   A man in a maroon-colored flannel shirt, which had been purchased for purposes of decoration, and made principally by some Jewish women on the East Side of New York, rounded a corner and walked into the middle of the main street of Yellow Sky. In either hand the man held a long, heavy, blue-black revolver. Often he yelled, and these cries rang through a semblance of a deserted village, shrilly flying over the roofs in a volume that seemed to have no relation to the ordinary vocal strength of a man. It was as if the surrounding stillness formed the arch of a tomb over him. These cries of ferocious challenge rang against walls of silence. And his boots had red tops with gilded imprints, of the kind beloved in winter by little sledding boys on the hillsides of New England.

64   The man's face flamed in a rage begot of whisky. His eyes, rolling, and yet keen for ambush, hunted the still doorways and windows. He walked with the creeping movement of the midnight cat. As it occurred to him, he roared menacing information. The long revolvers in his hands were as easy as straws; they were moved with an electric swiftness. The little fingers of each hand played sometimes in a musician's way. Plain from the low collar of the shirt, the cords of his neck straightened and sank, straightened and sank, as passion moved him. The only sounds were his terrible invitations. The calm adobes preserved their demeanor at the passing of this small thing in the middle of the street.

65   There was no offer of fight—no offer of fight. The man called to the sky. There were no attractions. He bellowed and fumed and swayed his revolvers here and everywhere.

66   The dog of the barkeeper of the Weary Gentleman Saloon had not appreciated the advance of events. He yet lay dozing in front of his master's door. At sight of the dog, the man paused and raised his revolver humorously. At sight of the man, the dog sprang up and walked diagonally away, with a sullen head, and growling. The man yelled, and the dog broke into a gallop. As it was about to enter an alley, there was a loud noise, a whistling, and something spat the ground directly before it. The dog screamed, and, wheeling in terror, galloped headlong in a new direction. Again there was a noise, a whistling, and sand was kicked viciously before it. Fear-stricken, the dog turned and flurried like an animal in a pen. The man stood laughing, his weapons at his hips.

67   Ultimately the man was attracted by the closed door of the Weary Gentleman Saloon. He went to it, and, hammering with a revolver, demanded drink.

68   The door remaining imperturbable, he picked a bit of paper from the walk, and nailed it to the framework with a knife. He then turned his back contemptuously upon this popular resort, and, walking to the opposite side of the street, and spinning there on his heel quickly and lithely, fired at the bit of paper. He missed it by a half-inch. He swore at himself, and went away. Later he comfortably fusilladed the windows of his most intimate friend. The man was playing with this town; it was a toy for him.

69   But still there was no offer of fight. The name of Jack Potter, his ancient antagonist, entered his mind, and he concluded that it would be a glad thing if he should go to Potter's house, and by bombardment induce him to come out and fight. He moved in the direction of his desire, chanting Apache scalp-music.

70   When he arrived at it, Potter's house presented the same still front as had the other adobes. Taking up a strategic position, the man howled a challenge. But this house regarded him as might a great stone god. It gave no sign. After a decent wait, the man howled further challenges, mingling with them wonderful epithets.

71   Presently there came the spectacle of a man churning himself into deepest rage over the immobility of a house. He fumed at it as the winter wind attacks a prairie cabin in the North. To the distance there should have gone the sound of a tumult like the fighting of two hundred Mexicans. As necessity bade him, he paused for breath or to reload his revolvers.

72   Potter and his bride walked sheepishly and with speed. Sometimes they laughed together shamefacedly and low.

73   "Next corner, dear," he said finally.

74   They both put forth the efforts of a pair walking bowed against a strong wind. Potter was about to raise a finger to point the first appear-

ance of the new home when, as they circled the corner, they came face to face with a man in a maroon-colored shirt, who was feverishly pushing cartridges into a large revolver. Upon the instant the man dropped his revolver to the ground, and, like lightning, whipped another from his holster. The second weapon was aimed at the bridegroom's chest.

75   There was a silence. Potter's mouth seemed to be merely a grave for his tongue. He exhibited an instinct to at once loosen his arm from the woman's grip, and he dropped the bag to the sand. As for the bride, her face had gone as yellow as old cloth. She was a slave to hideous rites, gazing at the apparitional snake.

76   The two men faced each other at a distance of three paces. He of the revolver smiled and with a new and quiet ferocity.

77   "Tried to sneak up on me," he said. "Tried to sneak up on me!" His eyes grew more baleful. As Potter made a slight movement, the man thrust his revolver venomously forward. "No; don't you do it, Jack Potter. Don't you move a finger toward a gun just yet. Don't you move an eyelash. The time has come for me to settle with you, and I'm goin' to do it my own way, and loaf along with no interferin'. So if you don't want a gun bent on you, just mind what I tell you."

78   Potter looked at his enemy. "I ain't got a gun on me, Scratchy," he said. "Honest, I ain't." He was stiffening and steadying, but yet somewhere at the back of his mind a vision of the Pullman floated: the sea-green figured velvet, the shining brass, silver, and glass, the wood that gleamed as darkly brilliant as the surface of a pool of oil—all the glory of the marriage, the environment of the new estate. "You know I fight when it comes to fighting, Scratchy Wilson; but I ain't got a gun on me. You'll have to do all the shootin' yourself."

79   His enemy's face went livid. He stepped forward, and lashed his weapon to and fro before Potter's chest. "Don't you tell me you ain't got no gun on you, you whelp. Don't tell me no lie like that. There ain't a man in Texas ever seen you without no gun. Don't take me for no kid." His eyes blazed with light, and his throat worked like a pump.

80   "I ain't takin' you for no kid," answered Potter. His heels had not moved an inch backward. "I'm takin' you for a——fool. I tell you I ain't got a gun, and I ain't. If you're goin' to shoot me up, you better begin now; you'll never get a chance like this again."

81   So much enforced reasoning had told on Wilson's rage; he was calmer. "If you ain't got a gun, why ain't you got a gun?" he sneered. "Been to Sunday-school?"

82   "I ain't got a gun because I've just come from San Anton' with my wife. I'm married," said Potter. "And if I'd thought there was going to be any galoots like you prowling around when I brought my wife home, I'd had a gun, and don't you forget it."

83   "Married!" said Scratchy, not at all comprehending.

84   "Yes, married. I'm married," said Potter, distinctly.

85   "Married?" said Scratchy. Seemingly for the first time, he saw the drooping, drowning woman at the other man's side. "No!" he said. He was like a creature allowed a glimpse of another world. He moved a pace backward, and his arm, with the revolver, dropped to his side. "Is this the lady?" he asked.

86   "Yes; this is the lady," answered Potter.

87   There was another period of silence.

88   "Well," said Wilson at last, slowly, "I s'pose it's all off now."

89   "It's all off if you say so, Scratchy. You know I didn't make the trouble." Potter lifted his valise.

90   "Well, I 'low it's off, Jack," said Wilson. He was looking at the ground. "Married!" He was not a student of chivalry; it was merely that in the presence of this foreign condition he was a simple child of the earlier plains. He picked up his starboard revolver, and, placing both weapons in their holsters, he went away. His feet made funnel-shaped tracks in the heavy sand.

Note

[1]A traveling salesman. [Eds.]

Content Questions

1. What attitudes do Jack Potter and Scratchy Wilson share?
2. Why is Jack Potter nervous about his return to Yellow Sky?
3. Why aren't the men in the Weary Gentleman Saloon frightened of Scratchy Wilson?
4. What is the purpose of the drummer in the story?

Questions on Presentation

1. Crane's story is set in the West and, therefore, might be considered a "western." Does the story fit Miller's definition of a "western" (in "The 'Western'—A Theological Note," Section 8: Controversy in the Arts)? If it is a western, how does it fit the formula? If it isn't a western, why isn't it?
2. Many readers feel that the characters in this story are in many ways caricatures, deliberate exaggerations or distortions for comic effect. How does Crane create caricatures rather than believable characters? What peculiarities of character is Crane distorting? Why is the distortion comic?

3. Why are the newlyweds first introduced to the reader so distantly, almost as a part of the landscape, as if they are not the subjects of the story?
4. Crane's writing is highly imagistic. How does his use of color imagery enhance the story?
5. Is Scratchy Wilson's reaction to the news of Jack Potter's marriage justified by what appears in the rest of the story?

Questions for Discussion and Writing

1. Fiction writers use a variety of techniques (imagery or dialogue, for example) to create characters. Which of the authors in this section creates the most believable character? What techniques does that author use to accomplish this?
2. Using the materials in this section, write an essay in which you discuss the importance of setting in fiction.
3. Compare the narrators of two of these stories. How trustworthy is each? How did you determine that?
4. Symbolism is an important aspect of some pieces of literature. Write an essay in which you discuss the use of symbolism in any of these stories. How important is that symbolism in your understanding of the theme?
5. A common theme in these stories is "appearance and reality." Write an essay in which you discuss the development of this theme in one of the stories.

Section 6

ENVIRONMENTAL ISSUES

The Nuclear Winter

Carl Sagan

Essayist, science writer, and critic Carl Sagan (b. 1934) is the David Duncan Professor of Astronomy and Space Sciences and director of the Laboratory for Planetary Studies at Cornell University. When he was sixteen years old, Sagan entered the University of Chicago; ten years later he completed his Ph.D. in astronomy and astrophysics. Sagan received the NASA medals for Exceptional Scientific Achievement and for Distinguished Public Service, and the International Astronautics prize, the Prix Galabert, for his work on the Mariner, Viking, and Voyager expeditions. In addition to his other honors, Sagan has served as chair of the division of planetary sciences of the American Astronomical Society and as president of the planetology section of the American Geophysical Union.

Sagan's first publication, *Intelligent Life in the Universe* (1963), was an expanded translation of a Russian manuscript. Sagan has also written popular books on science including *The Cosmic Connection* (1973), *The Dragons of Eden* (1977), *Murmurs of the Earth* (1978), and *Broca's Brain: Reflections on the Romance of Science* (1978). To date Sagan has written over four hundred scientific and popular articles and has authored, coauthored, or edited more than a dozen books. His belief that everyone is interested in science led him to create the television show "Cosmos" for the Public Broadcasting Service. Winner of the 1978 Pulitzer Prize for *The Dragons of Eden*, Sagan is an outspoken and controversial critic whose essays question topics from evolution to human intelligence to cosmic time to the destructive potential of the arms race. Sagan has recently written several articles and appeared on many televised interviews advocating nuclear disarmament. In this essay, reprinted from *Parade* magazine, Sagan outlines for a general audience one of his arguments for disarmament, his concern about nuclear winter or the aftermath of a nuclear war.

"Into the eternal darkness, into fire, into ice.

Dante, *The Inferno*

1   Except for fools and madmen, everyone knows that nuclear war would be an unprecedented human catastrophe. A more or less typical strategic warhead has a yield of 2 megatons, the explosive equivalent of 2 million tons of TNT. But 2 million tons of TNT is about the same as all the bombs exploded in World War II—a single bomb with the explosive power of the entire Second World War but compressed into a few seconds of time and an area 30 or 40 miles across. . . .

2   In a 2-megaton explosion over a fairly large city, buildings would be vaporized, people reduced to atoms and shadows, outlying structures blown down like matchsticks and raging fires ignited. And if the bomb were exploded on the ground, an enormous crater, like those that can be seen through a telescope on the surface of the Moon, would be all that remained where midtown once had been. There are now more than 50,000 nuclear weapons, more than 13,000 megatons of yield, deployed in the arsenals of the United States and the Soviet Union—enough to obliterate a million Hiroshimas.

3   But there are fewer than 3000 cities on the Earth with populations of 100,000 or more. You cannot find anything like a million Hiroshimas to obliterate. Prime military and industrial targets that are far from cities are comparatively rare. Thus, there are vastly more nuclear weapons than are needed for any plausible deterrence of a potential adversary.

4   Nobody knows, of course, how many megatons would be exploded in a real nuclear war. There are some who think that a nuclear war can be "contained," bottled up before it runs away to involve much of the world's arsenals. But a number of detailed analyses, war games run by the U.S. Department of Defense, and official Soviet pronouncements all indicate that this containment may be too much to hope for. Once the bombs begin exploding, communications failures, disorganization, fear, the necessity of making in minutes decisions affecting the fates of millions, and the immense psychological burden of knowing that your own loved ones may already have been destroyed are likely to result in a nuclear paroxysm. Many investigations, including a number of studies for the U.S. government, envision the explosion of 5000 to 10,000 megatons—the detonation of tens of thousands of nuclear weapons that now sit quietly, inconspicuously, in missile silos, submarines and long-range bombers, faithful servants awaiting orders.

5   The World Health Organization, in a recent detailed study chaired by Sune K. Bergstrom (the 1982 Nobel laureate in physiology and medicine), concludes that 1.1 billion people would be killed outright in such a nuclear war, mainly in the United States, the Soviet Union, Europe, China and Japan. An additional 1.1 billion people would suffer serious

injuries and radiation sickness, for which medical help would be un-available. It thus seems possible that more than 2 billion people—almost half of all the humans on Earth—would be destroyed in the immediate aftermath of a global thermonuclear war. This would represent by far the greatest disaster in the history of the human species and, with no other adverse effects, would probably be enough to reduce at least the Northern Hemisphere to a state of prolonged agony and barbarism. Unfortunately, the real situation would be much worse.

6   In technical studies of the consequences of nuclear weapons explosions, there has been a dangerous tendency to underestimate the results. This is partly due to a tradition of conservatism which generally works well in science but which is of more dubious applicability when the lives of billions of people are at stake. In the Bravo test of March 1, 1954, a 15-megaton thermonuclear bomb was exploded on Bikini Atoll. It had about double the yield expected, and there was an unanticipated last-minute shift in the wind direction. As a result, deadly radioactive fallout came down on Rongelap in the Marshall Islands, more than 200 kilometers away. Almost all the children on Rongelap subsequently developed thyroid nodules and lesions, and other long-term medical problems, due to the radioactive fallout.

7   Likewise, in 1973, it was discovered that high-yield airbursts will chemically burn the nitrogen in the upper air, converting it into oxides of nitrogen; these, in turn, combine with and destroy the protective ozone in the Earth's stratosphere. The surface of the Earth is shielded from deadly solar ultraviolet radiation by a layer of ozone so tenuous that, were it brought down to sea level, it would be only 3 millimeters thick. Partial destruction of this ozone layer can have serious consequences for the biology of the entire planet.

8   These discoveries, and others like them, were made by chance. They were largely unexpected. And now another consequence—by far the most dire—has been uncovered, again more or less by accident.

9   The U.S. Mariner 9 spacecraft, the first vehicle to orbit another planet, arrived at Mars in late 1971. The planet was enveloped in a global dust storm. As the fine particles slowly fell out, we were able to measure temperature changes in the atmosphere and on the surface. Soon it became clear what had happened:

The dust, lofted by high winds off the desert into the upper Martian atmosphere, had absorbed the incoming sunlight and prevented much of it from reaching the ground. Heated by the sunlight, the dust warmed the adjacent air. But the surface, enveloped in partial darkness, became much chillier than usual. Months later, after the dust fell out of the atmosphere, the upper air cooled and the surface warmed, both returning to their normal conditions. We were able to calculate accurately, from how much dust there was in the atmosphere, how cool the Martian surface ought to have been.

10   Afterwards, I and my colleagues, James B. Pollack and Brian Toon of NASA's Ames Research Center, were eager to apply these insights to the Earth. In a volcanic explosion, dust aerosols are lofted into the high atmosphere. We calculated by how much the Earth's global temperature should decline after a major volcanic explosion and found that our results (generally a fraction of a degree) were in good accord with actual measurements. Joining forces with Richard Turco, who has studied the effects of nuclear weapons for many years, we then began to turn our attention to the climatic effects of nuclear war. [The scientific paper, "Global Atmospheric Consequences of Nuclear War," is written by R. P. Turco, O.B. Toon, T.P. Ackerman, J.B. Pollack and Carl Sagan. From the last names of the authors, this work is generally referred to as "TTAPS."]

11   We knew that nuclear explosions, particularly groundbursts, would lift an enormous quantity of fine soil particles into the atmosphere (more than 100,000 tons of fine dust for every megaton exploded in a surface burst). Our work was further spurred by Paul Crutzen of the Max Planck Institute for Chemistry in Mainz, West Germany, and by John Birks of the University of Colorado, who pointed out that huge quantities of smoke would be generated in the burning of cities and forests following a nuclear war.

12   Groundbursts—at hardened missile silos, for example—generate fine dust. Airbursts—over cities and unhardened military installations—make fires and therefore smoke. The amount of dust and soot generated depends on the conduct of the war, the yields of the weapons employed and the ratio of groundbursts to airbursts. So we ran computer models for several dozen different nuclear war scenarios. Our baseline case, as in many other studies, was a 5000-megaton war with only a modest fraction of the yield (20 percent) expended on urban or industrial targets. Our job, for each case, was to follow the dust and smoke generated, see how much sunlight was absorbed and by how much the temperatures changed, figure out how the particles spread in longitude and latitude, and calculate how long before it all fell out of the air back onto the surface. Since the radioactivity would be attached to these same fine particles, our calculations also revealed the extent and timing of the subsequent radioactive fallout.

13   Some of what I am about to describe is horrifying. I know, because it horrifies me. There is a tendency—psychiatrists call it "denial"—to put it out of our minds, not to think about it. But if we are to deal intelligently, wisely, with the nuclear arms race, then we must steel ourselves to contemplate the horrors of nuclear war.

14   The results of our calculations astonished us. In the baseline case, the

amount of sunlight at the ground was reduced to a few percent of normal—much darker, in daylight, than in a heavy overcast and too dark for plants to make a living from photosynthesis. At least in the Northern Hemisphere, where the great preponderance of strategic targets lies, an unbroken and deadly gloom would persist for weeks.

15   Even more unexpected were the temperatures calculated. In the baseline case, land temperatures, except for narrow strips of coastline, dropped to minus 25° Celsius (minus 13° Fahrenheit) and stayed below freezing for months—even for a summer war. (Because the atmospheric structure becomes much more stable as the upper atmosphere is heated and the lower air is cooled, we may have severely *under*estimated how long the cold and the dark would last.) The oceans, a significant heat reservoir, would not freeze, however, and a major ice age would probably not be triggered. But because the temperatures would drop so catastrophically, virtually all crops and farm animals, at least in the Northern Hemisphere, would be destroyed, as would most varieties of uncultivated or undomesticated food supplies. Most of the human survivors would starve.

16   In addition, the amount of radioactive fallout is much more than expected. Many previous calculations simply ignored the intermediate time-scale fallout. That is, calculations were made for the prompt fallout—the plumes of radioactive debris blown downwind from each target—and for the long-term fallout, the fine radioactive particles lofted into the stratosphere that would descend about a year later, after most of the radioactivity had decayed. However, the radioactivity carried into the upper atmosphere (but not as high as the stratosphere) seems to have been largely forgotten. We found for the baseline case that roughly 30 percent of the land at northern midlatitudes could receive a radioactive dose greater than 250 rads, and that about 50 percent of northern midlatitudes could receive a dose greater than 100 rads. A 100-rad dose is the equivalent of about 1000 medical X-rays. A 400-rad dose will, more likely than not, kill you.

17   The cold, the dark and the intense radioactivity, together lasting for months, represent a severe assault on our civilization and our species. Civil and sanitary services would be wiped out. Medical facilities, drugs, the most rudimentary means for relieving the vast human suffering, would be unavailable. Any but the most elaborate shelters would be useless, quite apart from the question of what good it might be to emerge a few months later. Synthetics burned in the destruction of the cities would produce a wide variety of toxic gases, including carbon monoxide, cyanides, dioxins and furans. After the dust and soot settled out, the solar ultraviolet flux would be much larger than its present value. Immunity to disease would decline. Epidemics and pandemics would be

rampant, especially after the billion or so unburied bodies began to thaw. Moreover, the combined influence of these severe and simultaneous stresses on life are likely to produce even more adverse consequences—biologists call them synergisms—that we are not yet wise enough to foresee.

18   So far, we have talked only of the Northern Hemisphere. But it now seems—unlike the case of a single nuclear weapons test—that in a real nuclear war, the heating of the vast quantities of atmospheric dust and soot in northern midlatitudes will transport these fine particles toward and across the Equator. We see just this happening in Martian dust storms. The Southern Hemisphere would experience effects that, while less severe than in the Northern Hemisphere, are nevertheless extremely ominous. The illusion with which some people in the Northern Hemisphere reassure themselves—catching an Air New Zealand flight in a time of serious international crisis, or the like—is now much less tenable, even on the narrow issue of personal survival for those with the price of a ticket.

19   But what if nuclear wars *can* be contained, and much less than 5000 megatons is detonated? Perhaps the greatest surprise in our work was that even small nuclear wars can have devastating climatic effects. We considered a war in which a mere 100 megatons were exploded, less than one percent of the world arsenals, and only in low-yield airbursts over cities. This scenario, we found, would ignite thousands of fires, and the smoke from these fires alone would be enough to generate an epoch of cold and dark almost as severe as in the 5000-megaton case. The threshold for what Richard Turco has called The Nuclear Winter is very low.

20   Could we have overlooked some important effect? The carrying of dust and soot from the Northern to the Southern Hemisphere (as well as more local atmospheric circulation) will certainly thin the clouds out over the Northern Hemisphere. But, in many cases, this thinning would be insufficient to render the climatic consequences tolerable—and every time it got better in the Northern Hemisphere, it would get worse in the Southern.

21   Our results have been carefully scrutinized by more than 100 scientists in the United States, Europe and the Soviet Union. There are still arguments on points of detail. But the overall conclusion seems to be agreed upon: There are severe and previously unanticipated global consequences of nuclear war—subfreezing temperatures in a twilit radioactive gloom lasting for months or longer.

22   Scientists initially underestimated the effects of fallout, were amazed that nuclear explosions in space disabled distant satellites, had no idea

that the fireballs from high-yield thermonuclear explosions could deplete the ozone layer and missed altogether the possible climatic effects of nuclear dust and smoke. What else have we overlooked?

23   Nuclear war is a problem that can be treated only theoretically. It is not amenable to experimentation. Conceivably, we have left something important out of our analysis, and the effects are more modest than we calculate. On the other hand, it is also possible—and, from previous experience, even likely—that there are further adverse effects that no one has yet been wise enough to recognize. With billions of lives at stake, where does conservatism lie—in assuming that the results will be better than we calculate, or worse?

24   Many biologists, considering the nuclear winter that these calculations describe, believe they carry somber implications for life on Earth. Many species of plants and animals would become extinct. Vast numbers of surviving humans would starve to death. The delicate ecological relations that bind together organisms on Earth in a fabric of mutual dependency would be torn, perhaps irreparably. There is little question that our global civilization would be destroyed. The human population would be reduced to prehistoric levels, or less. Life for any survivors would be extremely hard. And there seems to be a real possibility of the extinction of the human species.

25   It is now almost 40 years since the invention of nuclear weapons. We have not yet experienced a global thermonuclear war—although on more than one occasion we have come tremulously close. I do not think our luck can hold forever. Men and machines are fallible, as recent events remind us. Fools and madmen do exist, and sometimes rise to power. Concentrating always on the near future, we have ignored the long-term consequences of our actions. We have placed our civilization and our species in jeopardy.

26   Fortunately, it is not yet too late. We can safeguard the planetary civilization and the human family if we so choose. There is no more important or more urgent issue.

Something You Can Do

1   A few hundred megatons is more than adequate to destroy a few hundred cities, constituting a death blow to either the United States or the Soviet Union. In the 1950s, when there were only a few hundred deliverable strategic weapons in the world, each nation announced that this was enough to deter the other from initiating a nuclear war. A few hundred strategic weapons is also somewhere around the threshold for triggering a nuclear winter. So is it really prudent to have more than 13,000 megatons and more than 50,000 nuclear weapons on the planet?

2   Several serious proposals have been made to moderate or reverse the nuclear arms race—all bilateral, verifiable by treaty and not compromising the security of the United States or the Soviet Union:

• **Build-down.** An agreement under which each nation would destroy some number (two or three, say) of its nuclear warheads for every new one that it deploys. It has been advocated by Sens. Sam Nunn (D., Ga.), William Cohen (R., Maine) and Charles Percy (R., Ill.) and has received encouragement from the White House. There is concern, however, that the new systems might be more devastating than the old ones they replace.

• **Deep cuts.** An agreement under which each nation would turn in, to a bilateral or multilateral commission, equal numbers or equal yields of the plutonium "triggers" that ignite the H-bombs. The triggers would then be consumed in nuclear power plants. It is advocated by Adm. Noel Gayler (ret.), former director of the National Security Agency, and former ambassador George Kennan, author of the U.S. policy of "containment" of the Soviet Union, both of whom are associated with the American Committee on East-West Accord, 109 11th St., S.E., Washington, D.C. 20003.

• **Nuclear freeze.** This proposal has the more modest aim of preventing, mutually and verifiably, at least any further growth in the strategic arsenals. It was overwhelmingly supported by voters in the 1982 elections and was originated by Randall Forsberg. She is at the Institute for Defense and Disarmament Studies, 2001 Beacon St., Brookline, Mass. 02146.

3   These three proposals are not mutually exclusive. The Soviet Union has several times, including in addresses by its late President Brezhnev, indicated its support for massive cutbacks in the global strategic arsenals. I believe that a major bilateral reduction in nuclear armaments might be carried out safely—particularly if the ingenuity and dedication that went into developing strategic weapons systems in the first place were devoted to finding a way out of the deadly trap we have set for ourselves.

• **You can start doing something about it** by writing *two* letters, one to U.S. President Ronald Reagan and the other to Soviet President Yuri Andropov, both c/o PARADE, P.O. Box 4281, Grand Central Station, New York, N.Y. 10163. PARADE will see that your letters are delivered and will report on the results in a later issue.

—Carl Sagan

Content Questions

1. Why are fools and madmen people we must watch?
2. Why are the secondary effects of nuclear winter important?

3. Why is the U.S. Mariner 9 spacecraft mission of importance to scientists studying nuclear winter?
4. What will happen if people fail to recognize the "horrors" of nuclear winter?
5. What is the importance of the nuclear test at Bikini Atoll?

Questions on Presentation

1. Why does Sagan begin the essay with a quotation from Dante's *Inferno*?
2. In paragraph 4, Sagan juxtaposes emotional language and ideas with calm, but threatening language describing nuclear weapons. What is the effect of this combination of language?
3. What techniques does Sagan use to make a general audience, one not familiar with the scientific thought behind theories of nuclear winter, understand and believe his argument?
4. Sagan makes careful use of rhetorical questions. What is the effect of these? How do they advance the argument?
5. Is Sagan's presentation of possible solutions effective? How could they be made more effective?

Ways of Disarmament

Laura Arnold

Seeking a major in professional writing with a minor in environmental studies, Laura Arnold intends to work in environmental protection after graduation. Understandably, she is concerned about one of the major potential threats to the environment. In this essay she explores the issues Carl Sagan raises in "Nuclear Winter."

1   In the 1950s, the United States and the Soviet Union agreed that the few hundred deliverable strategic weapons in the world were enough to deter the initiation of a nuclear war. As of 1983, there were 50,000 weapons with far greater force than those of the 1950s. And we're building more. A small exchange of these weapons could render the planet unlivable, destroying the ozone layer, wiping out plant and animal life, and probably extinguishing mankind. We continue, though, to build more

weapons using money and resources that could be used to improve life rather than end it. We've entered an arms race that seemingly has no finish line but the destruction of the world. There is no winner when that finish line is crossed. There is incredible danger in continuing this race: the more weapons we build the greater the tension between the superpowers, and the closer the finish line comes. Historically, arms races have never been known to end in peace. We must act now to moderate this race, either by stopping it before the finish is reached or by reversing it.

2   In his article, "Nuclear Winter" (*Parade*, Oct. 30, 1983), Carl Sagan briefly outlines three plans to moderate the arms race. The first is a build-down. A build-down would replace two or three old weapons with one new one, thus reducing the total number of weapons. This is a conservative approach to a desperate problem. The new weapons produced are likely, as weaponry technology improves, to be more deadly than those they replace. A build-down would do little to moderate the arms race except to make it more efficient by reducing the number of weapons, but not their destructive potential.

3   A slightly less conservative approach is to simply freeze the production of weapons. This is a beneficial plan in that no more resources would be used, nor would the tension of the arms race continue to grow. Additionally, unlike a build-down, a freeze would not increase the destructive and lethal potential of nuclear weapons. A freeze, however, is like a build-down in that it too is a conservative approach. We must ask ourselves if it is really necessary to have enough weapons to destroy the planet several times over. A freeze may be a good step toward ending the arms race, allowing a stringent, radical plan to be developed, but it should not be considered a solution in itself.

4   A freeze would stop the insanity of the arms race, but it would not reduce the insanity that leads to such a race. As Sagan points out, even a limited exchange of 100 megatons (leaving 12,900 megatons at 1983 weapons levels) could trigger a nuclear winter. So why should we have more than a limited number of weapons? If a small number of weapons is enough to destroy large portions of the planet and kill millions, there is simply no need for more weapons. What we need to end the arms race is drastic cuts in the number of weapons. A verifiable bilateral treaty between the United States and the Soviet Union would allow a large cutback without danger to national security to either side. As Sagan stated:

> I believe that a major bilateral reduction in nuclear armaments might be carried out safely—particularly if the ingenuity and dedication that went into developing strategic weapons systems in the first place were devoted to finding a way out of the deadly trap we have set for ourselves.

Once such a treaty and the means of verification are in place it might become possible to work for the ideal of the eradication of nuclear weapons.

5   The threat of nuclear war is a very real threat; we have come close to it before and may again. Protecting our country need not be done at the cost of annihilation. Sagan's predictions of nuclear winter are conservative; once the bombs have exploded there is no going back. It is time to focus our energy on working for peace. Building shelters for the homeless, working toward cures for diseases, and feeding the hungry of the world are meaningless if we continue to find deadlier, more efficient ways of killing through nuclear force. We must stop the insanity now if we are to survive.

⚖⚖

The Climatic Effects of Nuclear Winter

Richard P. Turco, Owen B. Toon, Thomas P. Ackerman, James B. Pollack, and Carl Sagan

For years scientists have debated the consequences of a full-scale nuclear war. Late in 1983 a group of scientists predicted that a nuclear war would cause a nuclear winter, a period when dense clouds of smoke and dust generated by nuclear explosions would block out the sun. Temperatures on earth would drop an average of 20 to 35 degrees and a maximum of 55 degrees; these freezing conditions would easily cause crop failures over large areas. In addition to the temperature drop and famine, survivors would face radioactive fallout, atmospheric pollution, ozone depletion, and difficulty in distributing food and in obtaining medical care. Although the specifics of this group's prediction have been challenged, the basic theory remains unchanged.

The group of scientists called itself TTAPS, an acronym of the last names of the authors Richard P. Turco, Owen B. Toon, Thomas P. Ackerman, James B. Pollack, and Carl Sagan. Richard Turco, an electrical engineer and physicist, is a visiting professor at UCLA. Owen Toon, Thomas Ackerman, and James Pollack are NASA research scientists at the Ames Research Center. Carl Sagan, an astronomer, writer, and frequent critic of the arms race, is the director of the Laboratory for Planetary Studies at Cornell University. Since their first publication, the authors have collaborated on several articles, incuding the following excerpt from *Scientific American* that discusses the climatic effects of nuclear winter and outlines their proposals for avoiding this catastrophe.

1   Since the beginning of the nuclear arms race four decades ago it has been generally assumed that the most devastating consequence of a major nuclear war between the U.S. and the U.S.S.R. would be a gigantic number of human casualties in the principal target zones of the Northern Hemisphere. Although in the wake of such a war the social and economic structure of the combatant nations would presumably collapse, it has been argued that most of the noncombatant nations—and hence the majority of the human population—would not be endangered, either directly or indirectly. Over the years questions have been raised about the possible global extent of various indirect, long-term effects of nuclear war, such as delayed radioactive fallout, depletion of the protective ozone layer in the upper atmosphere and adverse changes in the climate. Until recently, however, the few authoritative studies available on these added threats have tended to play down their significance, in some cases emphasizing the uncertainty inherent in any attempt to predict the combined effects of multiple nuclear explosions.

2   This comparatively optimistic view of the potential global impact of nuclear war may now have to be revised. Recent findings by our group, confirmed by workers in Europe, the U.S. and the U.S.S.R., suggest that the long-term climatic effects of a major nuclear war are likely to be much severer and farther-reaching than had been supposed. In the aftermath of such a war vast areas of the earth could be subjected to prolonged darkness, abnormally low temperatures, violent windstorms, toxic smog and persistent radioactive fallout—in short, the combination of conditions that has come to be known as "nuclear winter." The physical effects of nuclear war would be compounded by the widespread breakdown of transportation systems, power grids, agricultural production, food processing, medical care, sanitation, civil services and central government. Even in regions far from the conflict the survivors would be imperiled by starvation, hypothermia, radiation sickness, weakening of the human immune system, epidemics and other dire consequences. Under some circumstances, a number of biologists and ecologists contend, the extinction of many species of organisms—including the human species—is a real possibility.

3   Our own involvement in the reassessment of the global effects of nuclear war originated in a confluence of several lines of inquiry. Before joining forces we had separately and collectively been engaged in research on such phenomena as dust storms on Mars and the climatic effects of explosive volcanic eruptions on the earth; more recently we all became interested in the hypothesis that one or more of the mass extinctions of species evident in the geologic record were caused by immense clouds of dust raised by the impact of an asteroid or a comet. In 1982 a committee of the National Academy of Sciences, recognizing the parallels between the dust raised by nuclear explosions and that raised

by other cataclysmic events, such as volcanic eruptions and meteorite impacts, asked us to look into the possible climatic effects of the dust likely to result from a nuclear war. We had already been considering the question, and to address it further we had at our disposal sophisticated computer models of both large- and small-scale atmospheric phenomena; the models had been developed over the preceding decade primarily to study the origins, properties and effects of particles in the atmosphere.

4   At about the same time another important aspect of the question came to our attention. An article in the Swedish environmental journal *Ambio*, coauthored by Paul J. Crutzen of the Max Planck Institute for Chemistry at Mainz in West Germany and John W. Birks of the University of Colorado at Boulder, pointed out that fires ignited by nuclear explosions could generate massive amounts of smoke, severely attenuating the sunlight reaching the ground. Accordingly we added smoke to dust as a likely perturbing influence of nuclear war on the climate.

5   In brief, our initial results, published in *Science* in December, 1983, showed that "the potential global atmospheric and climatic consequences of nuclear war . . . are serious. Significant hemispherical attenuation of the solar radiation flux and subfreezing land temperatures may be caused by fine dust raised in high-yield nuclear surface bursts and by smoke from city and forest fires ignited by airbursts of all yields." Moreover, we found that long-term exposure to nuclear radiation from the radioactive fallout of a nuclear war in the Northern Hemisphere could be an order of magnitude greater than previous studies had indicated; the radioactivity, like the other nuclear-winter effects, could even extend deep into the Southern Hemisphere. "When combined with the prompt destruction from nuclear blast, fires and fallout and the later enhancement of solar ultraviolet radiation due to ozone depletion," we concluded, "long-term exposure to cold, dark and radioactivity could pose a serious threat to human survivors and to other species." Subsequent studies, based on more powerful models of the general circulation of the earth's atmosphere, have tended to continue both the validity of our investigative approach and the main thrust of our findings.

6   Before one can understand the climatic effects of nuclear war one must first understand how the earth's radiation budget is normally balanced. The amount of sunlight absorbed by the atmosphere and the surface of the earth, averaged over time, is equal to the amount of thermal radiation emitted back into space. Because the intensity of the thermal radiation varies as the fourth power of the temperature, both the surface temperature and the atmospheric temperature can adjust fairly quickly to maintain the overall energy balance between the solar energy gained and the thermal energy lost.

7   If the earth were an airless body like the moon, its surface would radi-

ate the absorbed solar energy directly into space. In this case the globally averaged temperature of the earth would be well below the freezing point of water, and life as we know it could not exist on our planet. Fortunately the earth has an atmosphere, which absorbs and traps some of the heat emitted by the surface, thereby raising the average ground-level temperature to well above freezing and providing a favorable environment for forms of life, such as ours, that are based on liquid water.

8   The thermal insulation of the earth's surface by the atmosphere—the "greenhouse effect"—arises from the fact that sunlight passes through the atmosphere more readily than thermal radiation does. The radiation emitted by the sun is mainly in the visible part of the electromagnetic spectrum, whereas the thermal radiation emitted by the earth's surface is concentrated in the infrared part. The main infrared-absorbing components of the atmosphere are water (in the form of ice crystals, liquid droplets and vapor) and carbon dioxide gas, both of which are essentially transparent to visible light. Hence the atmosphere generally acts as a window for sunlight but as a blanket for heat.

9   Under normal conditions the temperature of the troposphere, or lower atmosphere, decreases gradually with increasing altitude up to a height of about 12 kilometers, the boundary called the tropopause. Heat from the earth's surface is transferred upward through the atmosphere by several mechanisms: thermal radiation, small-scale turbulence, large-scale convection and the release of latent heat through the condensation of ascending water vapor. In a purely radiative atmosphere (that is, one in which the air does not move vertically and all the energy is transferred by radiation) the lower layers of air, where most of the solar energy is absorbed, would be warmer than the higher layers; in this situation the upward thermal radiation would exceed the downward thermal radiation, allowing the excess heat to escape into space. If the opacity of the atmosphere to infrared radiation were to increase (with no change in the opacity to visible light), the temperature would increase. For example, if carbon dioxide, a good infrared absorber, were added to the atmosphere in sufficient quantities, it would warm the surface.

10   Conversely, if some component of the atmosphere were to reduce the amount of sunlight reaching the surface without significantly increasing the infrared opacity, the ground temperature would decrease. For example, if all the sunlight were absorbed high in the atmosphere and none reached the ground, and if the surface could radiate energy to space without hindrance, the surface temperature would fall to that of an airless planet. If the absorption of solar energy were to take place above most of the atmosphere, the earth's radiation budget would be balanced without the greenhouse effect. (Accordingly we refer to this condition as the "anti-greenhouse effect.") Below the layer where the sunlight was absorbed the temperature of the atmosphere would not vary with alti-

tude: at each lower level the upward infrared flux would equal the downward infrared flux and the net energy transfer would be negligible.

11   Particles in the atmosphere can affect the earth's radiation balance in several ways: by absorbing sunlight, by reflecting sunlight back into space and by absorbing or emitting infrared radiation. In general a cloud of fine particles—an aerosol—tends to warm the atmospheric layer it occupies, but it can either warm or cool the underlying layers and the surface, depending on whether the particles absorb infrared radiation more readily than they reflect and/or absorb visible light.

12   The anti-greenhouse effect of an aerosol is maximized for particles that are highly absorbing at visible wavelengths. Thus much less sunlight reaches the surface when an aerosol consists of dark particles such as soot, which strongly absorb visible light, than when an aerosol consists of bright particles such as soil dust, which mainly scatter the light. Consequently in evaluating the possible climatic effects of a nuclear war particular concern should be focused on the soot particles that are generated by fires, since soot is one of the few common particulate materials that absorb visible light much more strongly than they absorb infrared radiation.

13   How much an aerosol will cool the surface (by blocking sunlight) or warm the surface (by enhancing the greenhouse effect) depends on the size of the particles. If the average diameter of the particles is less than a typical infrared wavelength (about 10 micrometers), the infrared opacity of the aerosol will be less than its visible opacity. Accordingly an aerosol of very fine particles that even weakly absorb sunlight should have a visible effect greater than its infrared effect, giving rise to a significant cooling of the lower atmospheric layers and the surface. In the case of soot this is true even for somewhat larger particles.

14   The visible and infrared radiation effects associated with particle layers also depend on the thickness and density of the aerosol. The intensity of the sunlight reaching the ground decreases exponentially with the quantity of fine, absorbing particulate matter in the atmosphere. The infrared radiation reaching the ground, however, depends more on the air temperature than it does on the quantity of aerosol. Hence when a large amount of aerosol is present, the dominant climatic consequence tends to be strong surface cooling.

15   The "optical depth" of an aerosol (a measure of opacity equal to the negative natural logarithm of the attenuation of an incident light beam by absorption and scattering) serves as a convenient indicator of the aerosol's potential climatic effects. For example, a cloud with an optical depth of much less than 1 would cause only minor perturbations, since most of the light would reach the surface, whereas a cloud with an optical depth of 1 or more would cause a major disturbance, since most of

the light would be absorbed in the atmosphere and/or scattered away into space. Although volcanic particles happen to have an optimal size for enhancing visible effects over infrared effects, the magnitude of the induced surface cooling is limited by the modest optical depth of volcanic aerosols (less than about .3) and by their very weak intrinsic absorption at visible wavelengths. Nevertheless, the largest volcanic clouds may disturb the earth's radiation balance enough to cause anomalous weather. Much more significant climatic disturbances could result from the huge clouds of dust that would be thrown into the atmosphere by the impact of an asteroid or a comet with a diameter of several kilometers or more. These dust clouds could have a very large optical depth, perhaps initially as high as 1,000.

16   The radiative effects of an aerosol on the temperature of a planet depend not only on the aerosol's optical depth, its visible absorptivity and the average size of its particles but also on the variation of these properties with time. The longer a significant optical depth can be sustained, the closer the surface temperature and the atmospheric temperature will move toward a new state of equilibrium. Normally it takes the surface of the ocean several years to respond to changes in the global radiation balance, because of the great heat capacity of the mixed uppermost layer of the ocean, which extends to a depth of about 100 meters. In contrast, the air temperature and the continental land temperature approach new equilibrium values in only a few months. In fact, when the atmosphere is strongly cooled, convection above the surface ceases and the ground temperature falls rapidly by radiative cooling, reaching equilibrium in a few days or weeks. This happens naturally every night, although equilibrium is not reached in such a short period.

17   Particles are removed from the atmosphere by several processes: falling under the influence of gravity, sticking to the ground and other surfaces and scavenging by water clouds, rain and snow. The lifetime of particles against "wet" removal depends on the frequency of cloud formation and precipitation at various altitudes. In the first few kilometers of altitude in the normal atmosphere particles may in some places be washed out in a matter of days. In the upper troposphere (above five kilometers) the average lifetime of the particles increases to several weeks or more. Still higher, in the stratosphere (above 12 kilometers), water clouds rarely form and so the lifetime of small particles is typically a year or more. Stratospheric removal is primarily by gravitational settling and the large-scale convective transport of the particles. The deposition of particles on surfaces is very inefficient for average-size smoke and dust particles, requiring several months for significant depletion.

18   Clearly the height at which particles are injected into the atmosphere affects their residence time. In general, the higher the initial altitude,

the longer the residence time in the normal atmosphere. Massive injections of soot and dust, however, may profoundly alter both the structure of the atmosphere and the rate of particle removal.

19   In our analysis of the climatic effects of nuclear war we have adopted a number of specific scenarios, based on what is publicly known about the effects of individual nuclear explosions, the size and deployment of the world's present nuclear arsenals and the nuclear-war-fighting plans of the U.S. and the U.S.S.R. Among the several dozen cases we have analyzed are a 100-megaton "countervalue" attack directed strictly against cities, a 3,000-megaton "counterforce" attack directed strictly against missile silos and a 10,000-megaton "full-scale exchange" directed against an assortment of targets on both sides. Our "base line" case is a 5,000-megaton nuclear exchange, with about 20 percent of the total explosive yield detonated over urban, suburban and industrial areas. All the postulated attack scenarios are well within the present capabilities of the two nuclear superpowers.

20   A nuclear explosion can readily ignite fires in either an urban or a rural setting. The flash of thermal radiation from the nuclear explosion, which has a spectrum similar to that of sunlight, accounts for about a third of the total energy yield of the explosion. The flash is so intense that a variety of combustible materials are ignited spontaneously at ranges of 10 kilometers or more from a one-megaton air burst detonated at a nominal altitude of a kilometer. The blast wave from the explosion would extinguish many of the initial fires, but it would also start numerous secondary fires by disrupting open flames, rupturing gas lines and fuel storage tanks and causing electrical and mechanical sparks. The destruction resulting from the blast wave would also hamper effective fire fighting and so promote the spread of both the primary and the secondary fires. Based on the known incendiary effects of the nuclear explosions over Hiroshima and Nagasaki in 1945 it can be projected that the fires likely to be caused by just one of the far more powerful strategic nuclear weapons available today would extend over an area of from tens to hundreds of square kilometers. . . .

21   During the World War II bombing of Hamburg the center of the city was gutted by an intense firestorm, with heat-generated winds of hurricane force sweeping inward from all directions at ground level. Rapid heat release over a large area can create fire vortexes, heat tornadoes and cyclones with towering convective columns. The sheer intensity of such fires might act to reduce the smoke emission considerably through two processes: the oxidation of carbonaceous smoke particles at the extremely high temperatures generated in the fire zone and the washout of smoke particles by precipitation formed in the convective columns. Both effects were taken into account in our estimates of the total smoke emission from a nuclear war.

22   The climatic impact of smoke depends on its optical properties, which in turn are sensitive to the size, shape and composition of the smoke particles. The most effective light-screening smoke consists of particles with a radius of about .1 micrometer and a very sooty composition rich in graphite. The least effective smoke in attenuating sunlight consists of particles larger than .5 micrometer with a predominantly oily composition. The smoke from a forest fire is typically composed of extremely fine oily particles, whereas the smoke from an urban fire consists of larger agglomerations of sooty particles. Smoke from fierce fires usually contains large particles of ash, char, dust and other debris, which is swept up by the heat-generated winds. The largest of these particles fall out of the smoke clouds just downwind of the fire. Although very intense fires produce less smoke, they lift more fine dust and may burn metals such as aluminum and chromium, which efficiently generate fine aerosols.

23   The release of toxic compounds in urban fires has not been adequately studied. It is well known that many people who have died in accidental fires have been poisoned by toxic gases. In addition to carbon monoxide, which is produced copiously in many fires, hydrogen cyanide and hydrogen chloride are generated when the synthetic compounds in modern building materials and furnishings burn. If large stores of organic chemicals are released and burned in a nuclear conflict, additional airborne toxins would be generated. The possibility that vast areas could be contaminated by such pyrotoxins, absorbed on the surface of smoke, ash and dust particles and carried great distances by winds, needs further investigation.

24   Nuclear explosions at or near ground level throw up huge amounts of dust. The principal dust-forming mechanisms include the ejection and disaggregation of soil particles from the crater formed by the explosion; the vaporization and subsequent renucleation of soil and rock, and the lifting of surface dust and smoke. A one-megaton explosion on land can excavate a crater hundreds of meters in diameter, eject several million tons of debris, lift between 100,000 and 600,000 tons of soil to a high altitude and inject between 10,000 and 30,000 tons of submicrometer dust particles into the stratosphere. The height at which the dust is injected depends on the yield of the explosion: the dust clouds produced by explosions with a yield of less than about 100 kilotons will generally not penetrate into the stratosphere, whereas those from explosions with a yield of more than about a megaton will stabilize mainly within the stratosphere. Explosions above the ground can also raise large quantities of dust, which is vacuumed off the surface by the rising fireball. The combined effects of multiple explosions could enhance the total amount of dust raised to high altitudes.

25   The quantity of dust produced in a nuclear war would depend sensi-

tively on the way the weapons were used. Ground bursts would be directed at hard targets, such as missile silos and underground command posts. Soft targets could be attacked by air bursts as well as ground bursts. There are more than 1,000 missile silos in the continental U.S. alone, and at least two Russian warheads are probably committed to each of them. Some 1,400 missile silos in the U.S.S.R. are similarly targeted by U.S. warheads. Air bases and secondary airfields, submarine pens and command and control facilities are among the many other strategic targets to which ground bursts might be assigned. In short, it seems quite possible that at least 4,000 megatons of high-yield weapons might be detonated at or near ground level even in a war in which cities were not targeted, and that roughly 120 million tons of submicrometer soil particles could be injected into the stratosphere in the North Temperate Zone. This is many times greater than all the submicrometer dust lifted into the stratosphere by the eruption of the volcano El Chichón in Mexico in 1982 and is comparable to the global submicrometer dust injections of much larger volcanic eruptions such as that of Tambora in 1815 and Krakatau in 1833. . . .

26   Our study also considered a number of secondary climatic effects of nuclear war. Changes in the albedo, or reflectivity, of the earth's surface can be caused by widespread fires, by the deposition of soot on snow and ice and by regional modifications of vegetation. Short-term changes in albedo were evaluated and found to be unimportant compared with the screening of sunlight. If significant semipermanent albedo changes were to occur, long-term climatic shifts could ensue. On the other hand, the vast oceanic heat source would act to force the climate toward contemporary norms following any major disturbance. Accordingly we have tentatively concluded that a nuclear war is not likely to be followed by an ice age.

27   We have also analyzed the climatic effects caused by changes in the gaseous composition of the atmosphere. The maximum hemispheric temperature perturbation associated with the production of oxides of nitrogen and the accompanying depletion of ozone is a cooling of no more than a few degrees C. The concentrations of greenhouse-effect gases would also be modified by a nuclear war; such gases might produce a surface warming of several degrees after the smoke and dust had cleared. These mutually offsetting temperature perturbations are uncertain, however, because the chemical and physical changes in the atmosphere caused by a nuclear war would be coupled through processes that are not adequately treated in existing models. Further analysis is clearly needed on this point.

28   Of course, the actual consequences of a nuclear war can never be precisely foreseen. Synergistic interactions among individual physical stresses might compound the problem of survival for many organisms. The long-term destruction of the environment and the disruption of the

global ecosystem might in the end prove even more devastating for the human species than the awesome short-term destructive effects of nuclear explosions and their radioactive fallout. The strategic policies of both superpowers and their respective military alliances should be reassessed in this new light.

Content Questions

1. How did TTAPS become involved in assessing the probable effects of nuclear war?
2. How do the authors explain "the earth's radiation budget"?
3. How is the earth's radiation budget balanced?
4. What is the optimistic view of nuclear winter?
5. What effect does the optical depth of particles have on the amount of sunlight reaching the earth?
6. What did scientists learn from the bombings at Hiroshima, Nagasaki, and Hamburg?
7. Why do the authors think the question of nuclear winter and its aftermath is an important question?
8. How have the United States and the U.S.S.R. targeted each others' strategic locations?
9. Why is the anti-greenhouse effect noteworthy?

Questions on Presentation

1. Why do the authors begin the essay with a history of early studies of nuclear winter?
2. This essay is written for a less general audience than Sagan's essay. What evidence is there for this in the essay?
3. Define hypothermia (2), attenuating (4), troposphere (9), opacity (13), anomalous (15), vortexes (21), and albedo (26).

Design as Revision

Henry Petroski

Engineer Henry Petroski (b. 1942) received his doctorate in mechanical engineering from the University of Illinois in 1968. In the late 1960s, Petroski taught theoretical and applied mechanical engineering at Illinois and, later, aerospace engineering at the University of Texas. In 1975 he joined the Reactor Analysis and Safety Division of Argonne National Laboratory as a mechanical engineer. Currently, Petroski is a professor in the civil and environmental engineering department at Duke University.

Petroski's interests have taken him beyond mechanical engineering to speculations about technology and society. A frequent contributor to journals such as *Technology Review* and *Technology and Culture*, Petroski has written essays such as "Reflections on a Slide Rule," "When Cracks Become Breakthroughs," "The Amazing Crystal Palace," and "The Details, Oh, the Details." In his writing Petroski argues that the ideas of engineering, the concepts that allow people to create something that never before existed, are mainstays of human intelligence and experience. Even failures, experiences engineers seek to eliminate, teach all of us valuable lessons. In the following essay, taken from his first book *To Engineer Is Human* (1982), Petroski sets up an analogy comparing engineering and its requirements to writing and its numerous demands.

1   There is a familiar image of the writer staring at a blank sheet of paper in his typewriter beside a wastebasket overflowing with crumpled false starts at his story. This image is true figuratively if not literally, and it represents the frustrations of the creative process in engineering as well as in art. The archetypal writer may be thought to be trying to put together a new arrangement of words to achieve a certain end—trying to put a pineapple together, as Wallace Stevens[1] said. The writer wants the words to take the reader from here to there in a way that is both original and familiar so that the reader may be able to picture in his own mind the scenes and the action of the story or the examples and arguments of the essay. The crumpled pages in the wastebasket and on the floor represent attempts that either did not work or worked in a way unsatisfying to the writer's artistic or commercial sense. Sometimes the discarded attempts represent single sentences, sometimes whole chapters or even whole books.

2   Why the writer discards this and keeps that can often be attributed to his explicit or implicit judgment of what works and what does not. Judging what works is always trickier than what does not, and very often the writer fools himself into thinking this or that is brilliant because he does not subject it to objective criticism. Thus manuscripts full of flaws can be thought by their authors to be masterpieces. The obviously flawed manuscripts are usually caught by the editor and sent back to the author, often with reasons why they do not succeed. Manuscripts that come to be published are judged by critics and the general reader. Sometimes critic and reader agree in their judgment of a book; sometimes they do not. Positive judgments tend to be effusive and full of references to and comparisons with other successful books; negative judgments

tend to be full of examples demonstrating why the book does not work. Critics often point out inconsistencies or infelicities of plot, unconvincing or undeveloped characters, and in general give counter-examples to the thesis of author, editor, and publisher that this book works. In short, the critic points out how the book *fails*.

3   The point was made quite explicitly in a recent review of *The Man Who Could See Through Time*, a play by Terri Wagener in which a physics professor and a young sculptor debate science and art. Reviewing the play in *The New York Times*, Frank Rich wrote:

> The best two-character plays look so effortless that we tend to forget how much craft goes into them. . . . To see a two-character play that fails, however, is to appreciate just how difficult the form really is.

4   And so it is with engineering structures. The great suspension bridges look so simple in line and principle, yet the history of failures of the genre has demonstrated that their design takes a touch of genius. And geniuses like Washington Roebling[2] and Othmar Ammann[3] can arguably be said to have learned more what not to do from the great failures of their forgotten predecessors than today's designers can be expected to learn about how to design the next suspended masterpiece from either the Brooklyn or the Verrazano Narrows Bridge.

5   Some writers, even if they do not try to publish them, do not crumple up their false starts or their failed drafts. They save every scrap of paper as if they recognize that they will never reach perfection and will eventually have to choose the least imperfect from among all of their tries. These documents of the creative process are invaluable when they represent the successive drafts of a successful book or any work of a successful writer. What other authors tend to learn from the manuscripts and drafts of the masters that cannot be learned from the final published version of a work is that creating a book can be seen as a succession of choices and real or imagined improvements. An opening sentence or even a word may evolve to its final form only after going through dozens of rejected alternatives. Sometimes the final version is closer to the first than any of the intervening versions, and sometimes a word will be crossed out only to have a ladder of synonyms, near synonyms, remote synonyms, and even antonyms leading like Jack's beanstalk through the clouds of imagined riches, ultimately to have the author fall back on the very word with which he began. These creative iterations suggest that the author's choice of even a single word is more easily understood in terms of rejection than acceptance, in terms of failure rather than success, in terms of *no* rather than *yes*. The fair manuscript gives little if any hint as to why exactly the author put down what he did in his first draft. But the word changed, the sentence deleted, and other alterations

that may be traced through successive drafts show clearly that the author did not believe what he had originally written had been right. It failed in some way to contribute to the end that the author was working toward. This is not to say that something unchanged from first to last was deemed perfect by the author; it simply indicates that, rightly or wrongly, he detected no unacceptable fault with it or could see no alternative. The unchanged part of his book's structure might teach the student nothing about its composition, however.

6   Some of the acknowledged masters of the written word were seemingly never completely satisfied with their work. James Joyce[4] was apparently notorious for making voluminous changes even as his major works *Ulysses* and *Finnegans Wake* were being set in type by the printer. And what was set in type was revised by Joyce in the proofs. In 1984, after volumes of criticism were published based on the original 1922 version of *Ulysses*, a new edition appeared, reportedly correcting over five thousand errors that crept into the first edition. The book was claimed by one critic to be so changed by the restoration of a few dropped lines that a whole new interpretation of the novel was in order.

7   Other recognized masters often express the thought that they *abandon* a work rather than complete it. What they mean is that they come to realize that for all their drafts and revisions, a manuscript will never be perfect, and they must simply decide when they have caught all its major flaws and when it is as close to perfect as they can make it without working beyond reasonable limits. Even the twenty-odd-years Joyce spent on *Finnegans Wake* was apparently not enough for him to believe he gave a perfect manuscript to the printer, and all authors acknowledge implicitly that revisions to manuscripts reach a point of diminishing returns.

8   The work of the engineer is not unlike that of the writer. How the original design for a new bridge comes to be may involve as great a leap of the imagination as the first draft of a novel. The designer may already have rejected many alternatives, perhaps because he could see immediately upon their conception that they would not work for this or that reason. Thus he could see immediately that his work would fail. What the engineer eventually puts down on paper may even have some obvious flaws, but none that he believes could not be worked out in time. But sometimes even in the act of sketching a design on paper the engineer will see that the approach will not work, and he crumples up the failed bridge much as the writer will crumple up his abortive character sketch.

9   Some designs survive longer than others on paper. Eventually one evolves as *the* design, and it will be checked part by part for soundness, much as the writer checks his manuscript word by word. When a part is discovered that fails to perform the function it is supposed to, it is

replaced with another member from the mind's catalog, much as the writer searches the thesaurus in his own mind to locate a word that will not fail as he imagines the former choice has. Eventually the engineer, like the writer, will reach a version of his design that he believes to be as free of flaws as he thinks he can make it, and the design is submitted to other engineers who serve much as editors in assessing the success or failure of the design.

10   As few, if any, things in life are perfect, neither is the analogy between books and engineering structures. A book is much more likely to be an individual effort than is a building, bridge, or other engineering structure, though the preparation of a dictionary or an encyclopedia might be said to resemble the design of a modern nuclear power plant in that no individual knows everything about every detail of the project. Furthermore, the failure of a book may be arguable whereas the failure of a building collapsed into a heap of rubble is not. Yet the process of successive revision is as common to both writing and engineering as it is to music composition and science, and it is a fair representation of the creative process in writing and in engineering to see the evolution of a book or a design as involving the successive elimination of faults and error. It is this aspect of the analogy that is most helpful in understanding how the celebrated writers and engineers alike learn more from the errors of their predecessors and contemporaries than they do from all the successes in the world.

11   While engineers who play it safe and copy designs that have stood the test of time may be well paid (though perhaps not nearly as well paid as the authors of mass market paperbacks who use more formulas in their genre fiction than are available to any engineer), there is no more professional distinction in being such an engineer than there is literary recognition in being such an author. When we speak of creative engineers we are talking about as select a few as there are great writers. And just as the great writers are those who have given us unique and daring experiments that have worked, so it is that the great engineers are those who have given us their daring and unique structural experiments that have stood the test of time.

12   It is not capricious to compare engineers with artists on the one hand and with scientists on the other. Engineering does share traits with both art and science, for engineering is a human endeavor that is both creative and analytical. Being creative pursuits, the innovative works of engineering test the vocabulary of the critics, whoever they may be, and it is not always clear-cut whether a daring new structure will stand or fall, even in the make-believe world of hypothesis testing. The problem with the new structure lies in the very humanness of its origins and of the world in which it will function. Whether an engineering structure succeeds as a work of art may not be a question of life and death, but

whether it will stand or collapse beneath the weight of those attending the dedication ceremonies is indeed a question to be reckoned with.

13   The very newness of an engineering creation makes the question of its soundness problematical. What appears to work so well on paper may do so only because the designer has not imagined that the structure will be subjected to unanticipated traumas or because he has overlooked a detail that is indeed the structure's weakest link. Certainly no designer who remembers the ill-fated Tacoma Narrows Bridge will design another bridge like it, but a new bridge that is unique aesthetically or analytically may hold surprises even for the designer. To be safe the engineer should try to imagine the structure in every conceivable situation and check each case to be sure that not even the slightest part is liable to break. But to imagine and check *every* conceivable situation might take forever, and the engineer must make judgments as to which situations are the most severe and which are insignificant. The former are analyzed, while the latter are ignored.

14   But as the literary critic can discover meanings and symbols an author denies having been aware of in a piece of creative writing, so the analytical critic of a new engineering design can find interactions among the parts of a structure that surprise the designer. And just as a literary reevaluation can come years after a book has achieved critical acclaim, so an engineering structure can stand, though precariously, for years before it is reanalyzed, perhaps because it or a structure not unlike it has recently failed. In lucky cases the faulty structure will be caught before it collapses; in many cases it is catastrophe that prompts the postmortem exposé.

15   The engineering task of designing a bridge shares qualities with the tasks of both poetry and science. Like poetry, the exact bridge one designer conceives to span a given space during a given technological era may never exist in the mind of any other engineer at any other time. Yet, like discoveries in science, if the theoretical and motivational foundations for a bridge are laid, then a bridge will be built, and it will be *the* bridge for that place and time no matter who designs it. No poetic license is allowed in the design of the details of the bridge, for an erratic line on the blueprint or an eccentric number in a calculation can be the downfall of the structure, no matter how much like a sound bridge it looks on paper. And today, if a computer is used, even so small an error as an inadvertent slip of a punctuation mark, decimal point, or sign in an equation can lead to a bridge that fails even if the computer model works.

16   The bridges of Robert Maillart have been praised as works of art that are one with the Alps. In flights of innovation the Swiss engineer may be thought to have spanned the intricacy of contour lines on maps over which his mind floated like an eagle, light to the eye but strong to the

touch. Like the pensive man in Wallace Stevens' "Connoisseur of Chaos":

> . . . He sees that eagle float
> For which the intricate Alps are a single nest.

17   Maillart's use of concrete reinforced with steel put poetry in place of prosaic bulk, whose ease of understanding may have made a more conventional bridge clearly safe but did not distinguish it. Maillart's bridges were not conceived fully justified line by line upon the page, for they work as entities as spare as poems. And as with poems, in the end, they work simply because they work. Upon their completion on paper, Maillart's plans could be analyzed after a fashion, and they could be somewhat revised here and there to redistribute stresses or smooth the lines. Their proof was in the putting the plans into place, however. And when the concrete had set about the steel, then the falsework supporting the bridge a-building (as the platen supports the poem a-typing) was removed, and each bridge withstood its first test as the poem its first reading. As each new bridge endured the seasons of use and re-use, as the poem the readings and re-readings, each bridge became a success. But Maillart also saw in many of his masterpieces extra weight or an unnecessary line that he removed in the next. His practice of self-criticism and revision was not unlike the writer's.

18   The engineer no less than the poet sees the faults in his creations, and he learns more from his mistakes and those of others than he does from all the masterpieces created by himself and his peers. While Maillart mastered the steel-in-concrete bridge, he did not originate the form. In the closing years of the nineteenth century François Hennebique, whose French construction firm restored Gothic cathedrals among its other activities, carried out research on the use of steel embedded in concrete to resist the cracking that invariably occurs when concrete is tensed rather than compressed, as it is in all-masonry structures. Hennebique's firm gained experience in reinforced concrete structures by completing thousands of projects, but these were not all without flaws. The bridge crossing the Vienne River at Chatellerault, France, in particular, developed a number of cracks. This was the longest Hennebique arch bridge, and its pattern of cracking showed to all who would observe it that there was room for improvement in the design. As David Billington has argued in his award-winning monograph on Robert Maillart's bridges, Maillart, in particular, learned from such experiences, as he learned from the cracking of his own designs, such as his early bridge at Zuoz, Switzerland.

19   Small cracks in reinforced concrete do not necessarily pose any danger of structural collapse, for the steel will resist any further opening of the cracks. But cracks do signify a failure on the designer's part to under-

stand his design completely when it was only on paper, since the cracks incontrovertibly disprove the implicit hypothesis that stresses high enough to cause cracks to develop would not exist anywhere in the structure. Discovering cracks in a completed structure thus enables the designer to learn the weaknesses of his knowledge and thereby to improve upon future designs, if only to beef them up where the stresses are less precisely predictable. In this way an engineer's designs can evolve from early works that show promise to the mature works that are brilliant and develop no cracks, much as a poet's juvenilia evolve into masterpieces that appear to be seamless.

20   Engineering, like poetry, is an attempt to approach perfection. And engineers, like poets, are seldom completely satisfied with their creations. They notice, even if no one else does, the word that is not quite *le mot juste*[5] or the hairline crack that blemishes the structure. However, while poets can go back to a particular poem hundreds of times between its first publication and its final version in their collected works, engineers can seldom make major revisions in a completed structure. But an engineer can certainly learn from his mistakes.

21   Anton Tedesko, designer of such significant concrete shell structures as the sports arena in Hershey, Pennsylvania, and the airport terminal in St. Louis, relates the story of inspecting fine hairline cracks that developed in a hyperbolic paraboloidal shell in Denver that he designed for I. M. Pei.[6] The concrete shell does not possess the stiffening ribs that have been criticized as architectural blemishes on the St. Louis airport shell, but Tedesko believes the hypar shell's cracks, which he suspects most people are not even aware of, could have been avoided and he has inspected them for over two decades, whenever he stops in Denver. It is not that an engineer admires his own or gloats over others' mistakes, it is that he recognizes, unfortunate though they may be, that defects are unplanned experiments that can teach one how to make the next design better. As Tedesko has written in a retrospective article on concrete shell structures that interweaves stories of collapses with stories of triumph: "I have mentioned examples of unfortunate experiences because it is easier to draw lessons from examples of poor performance than from good performance." Art and literary criticism serve the same purpose, and it is not surprising that artists and writers, like engineers, are often their own severest critics.

22   Engineering students understand early on that there is a great deal to be learned from a mistake. In a recent engineering class at Duke, students participated in the design of an experiment to produce metals through a foaming process aboard the space shuttle to test the feasibility of manufacturing new lightweight structural materials in a weightless environment. One student in the course admitted that "real engineering is a lot harder than we thought," but he also recognized that the class was "learning a lot from failing and screwing up." These students were

coming to the realization that T. H. Huxley[7] expressed in his book *On Medical Education:* "There is the greatest practical benefit in making a few mistakes early in life."

Notes

[1]Wallace Stevens (1879–1955), American poet and critic. [Eds.]
[2]Washington Augustus Roebling (1837–1936), American engineer who designed the Brooklyn Bridge. [Eds.]
[3]Othmar Ammann (1879–1965), foremost American bridge builder of the 20th century. [Eds.]
[4]James Joyce (1882–1941), Irish novelist, author of *Ulysses* and *Dubliners.* [Eds.]
[5]Exact. [Eds.]
[6]Ieoh Ming Pei (b. 1917), Chinese-born American architect. [Eds.]
[7]Thomas Henry Huxley (1825–1895), British biologist and author. [Eds.]

Content Questions

1. In what ways can engineering be considered an art?
2. In what ways can engineering be considered a science?
3. Why must an engineer analyze some situations and ignore others?
4. What are engineers searching for when they reevaluate their designs?

Questions on Presentation

1. Is Petroski's analogy of engineering to writing effective?
2. Petroski directly quotes a poet, a drama critic, a biologist, and an engineering student, but no professional engineers. Why do you believe he does this?
3. Define infelicities (2), iterations (5), and capricious (12).

Defensible Space

Oscar Newman

Oscar Newman is the director of the Institute of Planning and Housing at New York University and a consultant for the U.S. Department of Housing and Urban

Development and the New York City Housing Authority. "Defensible Space" is Newman's recent assessment of how architecture and urban planning that promotes crime can be redesigned to reduce criminal activity.

1   Living in contemporary cities is living in a very shared environment, of rich and poor, of black and white, of old residents and new. In cities where a strongly defined societal structure exists, in which common goals and values are shared, and where the class lines are clearly defined and accepted, the close living proximity of rich and poor is possible and even convenient. Witness the structure of southern cities in the U.S. of as little as thirty years ago, or of Western European cities of the prewar era. But in contemporary Western urban society, social lines and boundaries are not well defined, understood, or respected. There is also little in the physical structure of our cities that reflects social stratification. In these circumstances, the close physical proximity of different income or ethnic groups may become intolerable. The flight of the middle class to the suburbs for the purpose of creating both economically and socially exclusive enclaves bears witness to this phenomenon. City planners, for idealistic motives not always fully thought through or formulated, advocate economic mixes in their housing developments. But their values and notions are little more than utopian and may not be shared by either their rich or poor clients.

2   Paradoxically, at a time when we are all just learning to open up—to question the value of the individual pursuit of wealth at the expense of society—the idea of a defensible space environment may be interpreted by some as a methodology for restriction and closing down. At a time when the Western world seems to have approached acceptance of the notion of an open society with accompanying open institutions, it is strange to find many of its proponents advocating what may appear as a retrenchment tactic. It is sad to have to conclude that the free and fertile soil of the liberalized imagination may also have nurtured the seeds of its own restriction. The challenge to the establishment's rights, methods, and motives may be being used by some in our society who, unlike the questioning liberal, have no constructive objectives to achieve— they are content simply with using the new opportunities to "rip-off" who and what they can.

3   It is strange, then, to find the enlightened middle class fleeing to the ghettoes of suburbia, fleeing from the liberalized atmosphere they have worked at creating in the cities; stranger still to observe their flight and apparent content with leaving behind an immobile population far more vulnerable to the ravages of criminals, addicts, and abusive agents of authority. For the middle class, criminal assault is a survivable nuisance; for the poor and working class, it may mean a total wipe-out: a life's

work gone, a psychological disaster. For our low-income population, security in their residential environment—security from the natural elements, from criminals, and from authority—is the first essential step to liberation.

4   The problem is that the opening up and change in our cities may have occurred too quickly for beneficiary and recipient alike. Too much has been created to cope with too soon. The decision to opt out is an easy one—the pastures of suburbia alluring and becoming—but for those who remember the rich advantages of city life, and who have experienced the "poverty" of suburbia, the city is not so easily relinquished, nor are the motivations behind the work put into the opening up of society. However, to be able to retain the purpose and carry out the goal beyond the heady moment of liberation may now require a restructuring of our cities. Defensible space may be the last stand of the urban man committed to an open society.

5   It is probably premature to come to this conclusion, but it is possible than an inadvertent result of a socially mobile and open society is its required segregation into physically separate, subclusters which are inviolable and uniform, both socially and economically. The residential portion of the urban environment, devoted to family life and the raising of children, may have to take place within small exclusive homogeneous clusters. The interaction necessary to business, education, and the pursuit of recreation, on the other hand, will involve intermingling of economic groups, but within a framework in which roles and behavior norms are very defined.

6   If this is to be the required format for future cities, the question is, at what level is such segregation to occur? Is it to be a core city isolated from the suburb, or is to take place at the scale where collections of defensible residential enclaves share a city, and where mutual association is of mutual benefit?

7   Within the present atmosphere of pervasive crime and ineffectual authority, the only effective measure for assuring a safe living environment is community control. We are advocating a program for the restructuring of residential developments in our cities to facilitate their control by the people who inhabit them. We see this as the only long-term measure of consequence in the battle for the maintenance of a sane urban society. Short-term measures involving flights to suburbia or additional police manpower and equipment are only palliatives.

8   The essential ingredient of our proposal is territorial definition coupled with improvements to the capacity of the territorial occupants to survey their newly defined realm. Territorial definition may appear to be the antithesis of the open society, and surveillance a further restriction on its freedom. Territory and surveillance have after all traditionally been understood as the devices of the propertied classes and their

agents or police authority. We, however, are advocating territorial definition and the creation of surveillance opportunities to allow the *citizen* of the open society to achieve control of his environment for the activities he wishes to pursue within it—to make him instrumental in curtailing others from destroying his habitat, whether the others are criminals or a reactionary authority.

9   The functioning of authority in crime prevention has been greatly curtailed by the new format of our evolving residential areas. The policeman's fear of entering projects minimizes his effectiveness—perhaps entirely nullifying it. If police are to be a final resort in dealing with (apprehending) criminals, then community self-assurance is an essential ingredient to intelligent demand and use of police. The difficulty lies in the fact that unlike a middle-class community, low-income neighborhoods hold various attitudes towards police. Where some may view them positively, others react with negative or hostile feelings. It becomes essential, therefore, for residents and police to create a situation in which the residents will assume responsibility for a summoned policeman's safety, just as they will, in turn, be able to require that the policeman perform in accord with a defined set of rules.

10   If territorial redefinition, as advocated in the "defensible space" program, proves to reinforce certain groups in taking over and controlling previous public space adjacent to their dwelling units, are we not, through these actions, removing much territory in the form of parks and open space from the public domain? Are we not by this exclusion placing further restriction on the already narrowing and limited resources of our cities? Some of our findings suggest that just the opposite may be true. Studies of the use of grounds of housing projects in many different cities—New York, Cleveland, San Francisco—indicate that the grounds of projects which were intentionally left open for public use (as a contribution to the open-space needs of the surrounding city) end up unused and neglected, by housing residents as well as members of the surrounding community. Each group, by experience, had found their activities easily disrupted by other groups and found that their claim to the use of the space for recreation difficult to enforce. By contrast, recreation space located within the interior of a housing project, clearly defined by surrounding dwellings, was found to be used more frequently by both groups. Project residents had clearly laid claim to these play spaces and set up an unwritten, but understood, set of rules for their use. These rules were enforced by parents and other children. Project residents had first claim to this use, followed by surrounding neighborhood children, who came both spontaneously and by invitation. Disputes almost always resulted in the expulsion of the visitors. Since visiting children really had nowhere else to go or to retreat to, the proprietary rights of

project children soon became understood and accepted, and further conflict was avoided by mutual desire, whenever possible.

11   In the course of our work, we have received expressions of concern from members of communities adjacent to the projects we have been working in. Their concern is that our endeavors would only succeed in displacing crime from one area to another. There is some evidence to support their hypothesis. Captain Arnold Berkman, of the New York City Housing Authority Police, keeps careful tabulations of variations in crime rates in all areas of his jurisdiction and has found that as a vigorous police effort is concentrated in one project, criminals respond by moving into adjacent projects. Displacement, however, is seldom a full 100 percent.

12   The nature of criminal acts is sometimes distinguished by the intent and motivation of the criminal. Much crime is crime of opportunity rather than premeditated. Since a sizable percentage of crimes in housing projects is estimated to be crime of opportunity, the reduction of opportunity may, therefore, result in less crime rather than in displacement.

13   If, for the sake of argument, one accepts as a proposition that the total amount of crime cannot be diminished, only displaced, this then offers a new question: is a pattern of uniformly distributed crime preferable to one in which crime is concentrated in particular areas? It is our contention that the second situation is more desirable. The home and its environs must be felt secure or the very fabric of society comes under threat. From our interviewing, we have been led to believe that people accept the fact that certain areas of a city are unsafe and, therefore, take steps to avoid, or minimize, the risk of using them. But they all find this an intolerable condition for their own residential environment. People can limit the use of dangerous areas to necessary occasions and, if too frightened, will find ways of collectively using these areas so as to add to their safety. (This often happens when women meet together to go shopping or to use the project laundry room.) In the home and its environs, no one wishes to feel so restricted. The family spends most of its time there. It is where future generations are raised, and where the most susceptible members of society live. It is also the shelter to which we all return from our forays. For these reasons, it must be made secure, even at the expense, if necessary, of making other nonresidential areas more dangerous. In many ways it would be a significant accomplishment to achieve this end alone: allowing displacement of crime to shopping, institutional, and business areas. The argument can be made that these other areas are inherently more easily served by formal police protection.

14   In spite of these justifications, there are serious moral implications to the question of displacement, and they are not as easily dismissed as

might be suggested. In the ensuing years of our study we will be examining the changing patterns of crime in the areas surrounding the projects we have altered, just as we observe the changes in the projects themselves. The full extent of the displacement problem is yet to be understood and a means for coping with it developed.

Content Questions

1. Why may the proximity of different ethnic or income groups become intolerable?
2. Why may it seem strange in the 1980s to find proponents who favor "closing down" neighborhoods?
3. What problems result from middle-class residents "fleeing" to the suburbs?
4. What are the benefits and disadvantages of opening up American cities?
5. What do people in different living areas feel about the police?

Questions on Presentation

1. To what audience is this essay directed?
2. Throughout this essay, Newman balances notions of what is with what should be, and uses language such as "paradoxically" and "strange." What does this approach tell you about the theme?
3. This is an essay of definition. What does Newman do to convince you that his definition of "defensible space" is the correct one?

The Road Back

Michael Brown

Reporter Michael Brown (b. 1952) gained notoriety when in a series of over one hundred articles he broke the story on the hazardous dump site at Love Canal. For his writing Brown received three Pulitzer Prize nominations and an award from the Environmental Protection Agency. The following selection, taken from *Laying Waste: The Poisoning of America*, warns readers of the price for indifference and greed.

1   During the summer of 1979, the New York State government took a startling new tack in its dealings with toxic waste problems, one that dramatically bared the inner thoughts of bureaucrats responding to environmental threats. In a sterile tower that looks down upon the gargantuan Albany Mall complex, researchers worked on a draft study for the Department of Health concerning contaminated groundwater in general and the probability of chemical substances causing cancer in particular. There was a well-founded apprehension within the department over how the public would respond to the study if it was released, for it was, in essence, an attempt to estimate and to articulate the financial value of saving people from exposure to toxic wastes. The state, having just witnessed the tragedy of Love Canal, and faced now with dozens of widespread well-contamination cases, had decided it was time to determine the cash value of salvaging human life and health from toxic waste jeopardy.

2   A key section of the 130-page draft, subtitled "The Benefit of Reducing Risk," contained six empirical estimates of what a life means financially to society. "Estimates range from $49,226 to $1 million with most values between $200,000 and $300,000," it said coolly. "These estimates will be used later to describe the benefit of reducing the risk of death." The department researchers took into consideration such factors as an individual's income, his productivity, and what it would cost to treat his ailment in order to determine whether the state's monies would be wisely invested in reducing the possibility of cancer. "Despite justifiable moral and philosophical objections," it noted, "this dilemma must be confronted if economic assessments are to be made."

3   With that, the state scientists analyzed various models of determining an individual's worth and the cost of installing water purification systems to reduce health hazards. They arrived at two formulas: $B = r_1/70 \times v$, where B stands for the per capita benefit in dollars a year, v is the assumed economic value of saving a life, r_1 is the per capita lifetime risk estimate, and 70 the average life expectancy; and $r_1 = .95\ C \times V \times r$, where C is the amount of contamination, V the per capita daily water intake, and r the lifetime risk for an oral dose. The value of preventing one death, as determined in these formulas, ranged from $100,000 to $1 million. As a basis for making these estimates, it was suggested that the researcher should "assess the worth of an invidivdual's present production. Further production is discounted because it is generally believed that future production is less than present production." A weakness of the specific methodology, admitted the report, was that it would "undervalue lives of housewives, elderly, unemployed, and underemployed," and provide "no allowance . . . for social values or the utility of life to an individual." On a more sensitive side, the report noted that while it was unlikely that one or two dozen extra deaths from toxic ex-

posure in the entire state would cause public concern, "these events certainly would be noticed by [those persons] directly affected, their friends, relatives, and business associates." That burst of warmth aside, the report went on to conclude that whenever trichloroethylene was greater than 50 parts per billion in drinking water, based on a risk of one extra death in a population of 100,000 and an assumed economic life value of $500,000, it would be worthwhile to install aeration treatment to decrease contaminant levels in a system serving 10 million gallons a day, but that "treatment of smaller systems cannot be justified based on these data." Therefore individuals who owned their own wells or who were attached to small municipal systems would not, based on economic considerations, be provided the proper protection.

4   The state's calculations were flawed in many respects. On technical grounds alone, the study had serious shortcomings. There were no numerical expressions to indicate possible teratogenic, mutagenic, central nervous system, liver, or blood effects, nor did it assess noncancerous diseases. The study was based on the probability of cancer alone and even in this it was deficient. By the draft's own admission, "the exact mechanism of carcinogenesis is unknown. The existence or nonexistence of a threshold level has never been proven. If one cellular change can lead to a malignant transformation and a lethal cancer, there will be no threshold level." And certainly no safe, or "acceptable," one. Whether a resident is drinking 1 part per billion of carbon tetrachloride, or 1 part per million, is immaterial. Both may produce cancer. Because there can be no experiments with human subjects, a chemical's toxicity can be gauged only by its observed effects on a laboratory animal. Such a method is not always accurate. There are indications, said the state, "that a substance will be less toxic in smaller animals than in man." Indeed, thalidomide had caused birth defects in women at one-hundredth the dose observed in a scientist's rats, and certain of the aromatic amines induced cancer in humans but not in treated mice. Moreover, the state's calculations did not take into account the reactions different chemicals have on each other when blended in a common soup. Often such an intermingling, as I have stressed, greatly increases the toxic effects. When certain organic phosphate pesticides and chlorinated hydrocarbons enter the body at the same time, the damage they wreak is ten times what they would inflict individually, for the chlorinated hydrocarbons damage the liver in a way that prevents the enzyme cholinesterase from properly protecting the nerve tissues, leaving them open for attack by those organophosphates that specialize in causing damage.

5   But New York's intriguing report is best criticized on its moral and philosophical grounds. Is one life truly worth more than another, and can a monetary figure be attached to the difference? Does the Constitution not provide for equal protection under the law?

6   Whatever its merits, such thinking had long been common in the chemical industry. Spokesmen there charged that a "chemophobia" was pervading the nation, and that the risk of chemical exposure is a necessary one, comparable to that of driving a car or riding a plane. They neglected to mention that those latter risks are voluntarily undertaken, while an individual does not have the same choice in drinking water or breathing air. Unembarrassed by hyperbole, the chemical manufacturers, in slick advertising campaigns, implied that life itself would not be possible without the finer medicines, more hardened plastics, and more potent pesticides that come forth from their steaming vats.

7   For years the industry had shielded the true dangers of its chemical processes and wastes from public purview and actively pressured politicians from full inquiry. All the while it was fighting stricter regulations, it knew that more cautious handling of its waste materials would not destroy the industry but only cut into its often exorbitant profits. The manufacturers not only downplayed the dangers but on occasion actively covered them up or kept them from entering the newspapers. The Manufacturing Chemists Association once maintained silence about its knowledge of the dangers associated with vinyl chloride; the Allied Chemical Company for years reportedly kept from public scrutiny the knowledge that its pesticide Kepone caused liver and central nervous system disorders. Even the august Stanford Research Institute had been accused of falsifying tumor studies for the sake of the Shell Chemical Company. In 1978 it was alleged that Stanford had cut tumors out of test animals and had not mentioned them in certification reports to the government, a charge it denies.

8   Industry's blind obsession with economics has often been abetted by government. In February 1979, a controversy developed between certain officials at the Environmental Protection Agency and White House economic advisers Alfred Kahn and Charles L. Schultze: the administration, despite President Carter's generous campaign pledges to protect the environment, pressed for relaxation of water pollution regulations, with the goal of reducing control costs to industry. When reports grew of resistance within the EPA to this policy, the president's press secretary, Jody Powell, informed news reporters that those dissatisfied "should be aware that their resignations will be gladly accepted at the earliest opportunity and should not be hesitant at all in offering them." That arrogant message provoked a counterattack by Senator Edmund Muskie, who, unlike those at the White House, had spoken with victims of Love Canal. Quite accurately, he accused White House "inflation fighters" of "treating public health as inflationary" and acting contrary to the intent of Congress in its passing the regulations to begin with. In August came another salvo at public officials in the form of a seventy-eight-page report issued by a Rockland County grand jury which, having investigated

cases of indiscriminate dumping, felt the need to sharply criticize government "at all levels" for the fashion in which it has dealt with "flagrant and widespread" hazardous waste practices; this has fostered "actual and potential criminality and profiteering," the report said, adding, "The evidence indicates the response of federal, state, and local governments to the problems posed by hazardous waste has been characterized by ignorance, neglect, laxity, and fractionalization of responsibility."

9 In such a milieu, it is not surprising that the United States finds itself today in the throes of what can only be termed a cancer epidemic. Cancer now accounts for nearly 20 percent of the deaths each year, second only to heart disease. About 55 million people now alive have contracted or eventually will contract cancer. Nor can increased longevity alone explain why more people are cancer victims, since so many children suddenly are succumbing to the disease. It seems too coincidental that the increase in cancer rates has so closely paralleled the increase in rates of chemical waste production, especially those of the solvents and halogenated hydrocarbons.

10 We can, as a society persist in our self-destruction. Or, we can begin now to reduce the slaughter. But for it to have an effect, we must do it soon. Some of the measures necessary to halt the contamination of our land will be relatively painless to achieve, and some are already mandated, in varying degrees, in laws such as the Resource Conservation and Recovery Act of 1976. Some will be more drastic and will infringe on the extravagant life-styles we have nurtured. But all are vital.

11 The immediate steps to be taken are not dramatic ones. They include keeping landfills away from major aquifers, rivers, and lakes, and especially from residential clusters. It would be prudent to set a standard location at fifteen miles or more from a central source of drinking water to ensure against long-term leaching. Ideally, landfills should be situated in regions where evaporation exceeds precipitation. Their construction should include thick, solid clay bases; improved synthetic liners on the sides and bottom; leachate withdrawal stations that run the length of the landfill; interception trenches; and on top, another coating of plastic, itself covered by a clay cap planted over with grass. Chemical drums must be well marked and carefully placed, and they should be implanted in grid fashion so that various types of chemicals do not intermix (and may even one day be excavated for recycling when the technology arrives). Those who operate landfills should be required to attend training sessions on the toxicity of chemicals and to pass a written examination. Operating firms must be forced to set aside large sums of money in performance bonds and trusts so that if they go bankrupt or simply abandon their pits, there will be the money to close the site and monitor it for

leachate. Chemical manifests recording wastes from the time they leave the factory to their ultimate disposal should be required and monitored by newly created state agencies with the manpower to make regular random checks that toxicants are disposed of only in secured landfills. Finally, serious criminal and civil sanctions should be imposed on those who violate these regulations, and landfill operators should be required to install air-monitoring devices so that governmental agencies can check for evaporation into the already chemically overburdened atmosphere.

12   But these are temporary measures. No landfill can be considered forever safe, so in the long run their very existence is not acceptable. The next step would be to ban the discharge of any chemicals into the ground except in unusual cases. If such a policy, however startling and unreasonable it may now seem, is not effected before the beginning of the next century, an intolerable number of acres will be rendered both useless and dangerous. In a nation that depends so heavily on the productive utilization of its soil, the dwindling of such a resource is intolerable. Should we continue burying our wastes, too many more fields will be despoiled, creeks barricaded, and homes boarded up and deserted.

13   In the years to come, the amount of toxic wastes destined for ground disposal will increase significantly. More chemicals are being manufactured, and waste sludges amounting to nearly 8 million dry tons annually are arriving from our new wastewater treatment plants. Other wastes once dumped into the ocean off barges but now restricted from that disposal method are being sent to the land. Because it is nearly impossible to remove a landfill once it is there, disposal provides no solution; the answer is disassemblage or direct destruction of waste products. Glimmerings of the next generation of sophisticated waste disposal systems have already appeared: a few firms have begun to separate waste materials through sedimentation, flocculation, filtration, and membrane osmosis; to collect and concentrate them through a process known as ion exchange; to reduce their toxicity by oxidation or by nurturing micro-organisms to feed on the wastes; and to render them into coke or activated charcoal by heating them in an oxygen-free atmosphere, the process known as pyrolysis. Even these advanced procedures do not totally eliminate toxic residues. A major research effort must be instituted, by government and industry, so that in the end toxicants will have been pulled apart and returned to the environment as simple, benign molecules. By the use of ozone or oxygen, or ultraviolet light and other as yet unseen forms of irradiation or chemical reactants, the chemicals might be completely dismantled. Small amounts of residue that remain could be solidified in rocklike form and set in secured landfills so that they do not leach. One way of doing that, suggested by a Pennsylvania waste firm, might be to add cement and aluminum silicate

to these ultimate dregs, trapping the chemicals in a polymer lattice as impermeable as clay.

14   While such research efforts are proceeding, there is a current need to reduce landfill-destined wastes by constructing effective regional incineration centers. For some compounds, high-temperature incineration is the only acceptable method of destruction. If properly managed and stringently monitored, and kept out of the hands of irresponsible corporations, such processes minimize the potential of adverse chronic exposure. For years, waste incineration has been employed by companies such as 3M Corporation, Dow Chemical Company, and the Kodak Company. While expensive to operate, they have been quite successful. Most use a combination of rotary kilns (horizontal brick-lined furnaces that turn as heat is directed at the inflowing chemicals) and secondary combustion chambers. Both liquid and solid waste can be burned in the units at temperatures ranging from 1,100 to 2,400 degrees Fahrenheit, and the residues deposited in a quenching chamber to be cooled to the point where vapors condense. A water scrubber cleans flue gases of fly ash and the precipitated vapors, and the solution is sent off to a wastewater treatment plant while the ash heads for a landfill. At a facility in Van Nuys, California, an experimental incinerator set at 1,348 degrees Centigrade destroyed the dense, dark brown fluid of C-56 and other organic compounds with 99.97 percent efficiency. While the cost was high—$487.59 per metric ton—no evidence of C-56 was found in the residues. Much of the incineration ash was composed of inert chemicals, salts, and heavy metals (which can still create land pollution problems) and the air emissions contained hydrochloric acid as well as carbon dioxide and water. These heating units should be placed a good distance from residences and monitored constantly. Perhaps they would best be operated on barges out at sea, for one puff of a potent organochlorine compound escaping by error from the stack would cause more serious contamination than the leakiest landfill. Wherever they are located, incinerators should be regarded only as interim solutions to waste disposal.

15   Those waste pits already in the ground, if their contents cannot be safely incinerated or otherwise treated, must be contained and their environs thoroughly investigated for contamination. Special attention must also be paid to those thousands of nasty open waste lagoons on back plant properties. All should be inventoried, catalogued, monitored, and publicly listed. Aerial surveys using infrared or ultraviolet filters have been found to be effective in detecting migration of leachate; if the dump is escaping its bounds, a drainage program must be implemented to capture the liquids before they reach a major aquifer, and persons living nearby should be tested for liver or pancreatic disease.

16   In the meantime, we need more research on ways to remove toxic substances from human bodies once they have lodged in the cells. For example, some success has been achieved in extracting metals from the

body by giving the victim dosages of what are termed "mixed ligand chelate agents," which combine with the metals and carry them to excretion. In the same way, a cholesterol-reducing drug, cholestyramine, has been found to speed the removal of Kepone from human bodies.

17   Rather than developing increasingly elaborate procedures for the destruction of toxic wastes, we can minimize production of such substances in the first place. This alternative is one that would include the curtailment of certain chemical processes and, if necessary, an outright ban on the manufacture of highly dangerous substances until industry, so slow to protect our needs, has demonstrated ways of destroying their wastes, or of making them innocuous to all segments of the ecology.

18   Certainly this is not to suggest that we demolish the chemical industry. That is a ridiculous proposal, and assuredly an unwanted one. It is after all the chemical manufacturers who provide 6 percent of our gross national product, whose labor force runs into the hundreds of thousands of workers, and whose products are essential in many aspects of our lives. Nevertheless, there is need for decreased production of many compounds. The technology could be made available, if industry were to be pressed for replacement of many of the pernicious chemicals—used in such things as pesticides, plastics, and synthetic wear—by other less malign ingredients.

19   There is in the end one fundamental thought: our lives are dependent upon an earth which can, fortunately, absorb considerable abuse but whose limits of resilience have been exceeded in numerous places. Our arrogance and our science have implanted in the life-sustaining soils and waters toxic substances with which they, and we, cannot contend. Only when we acknowledge our folly and temper our greed will our society begin to conform to the needs of the nature outside and inside ourselves. And only then will we be sure that what rises from the ground or what is in our air and rivers will be, as it ought, the source of life and good health—and not the agents of an untimely death.

Content Questions

1. What were the flaws in New York State's formulas to assess human worth?
2. Why is the New York report "best criticized on its moral and philosophical grounds"?
3. What economic factors interfere with political decisions about hazardous chemicals?
4. How valuable are the alternatives to chemical waste dumps?
5. How has industry been abetted by the government in perpetuating chemical dumps?

Questions on Presentation

1. Identify the primary examples Brown uses to support his argument. Is there a pattern to the examples or their presentation? If so, what is it?
2. Brown uses causal analysis as his rhetorical method here. Is this the most effective approach or would some other approach (definition, comparison/contrast, etc.) be at least as effective or perhaps more so?
3. Why does Brown discuss the effects of toxic waste (4) in such clinical terms? What would be the effect if more emotional descriptions had been used?
4. Why does Brown in paragraph 18 include the statement that abolishing the chemical industry is a "ridiculous proposal"?
5. Define teratogenic (4), mutagenic (4), hyperbole (6), milieu (9), leachate (11), and flocculation (13).

The Importance of Dust

Alfred Russel Wallace

Almost unknown to most contemporary readers, Alfred Russel Wallace (1823–1913) was an English naturalist whose theories of evolution paralleled those of his contemporary Charles Darwin. Like Darwin, Wallace was influenced by English economist Thomas R. Malthus and English geologist Sir Charles Lyell and based his theories not on speculation but on careful observation. He systematized the science of biogeography and wrote *The Geographical Distribution of Animals* (1876), *Island Life* (1880), *Darwinism* (1889), and *The Wonderful Century*, from which this selection is taken.

1   The majority of persons, if asked what were the uses of dust, would reply that they did not know it had any, but they were sure it was a great nuisance. It is true that dust, in our towns and in our houses, is often not only a nuisance but a serious source of disease: while in many countries it produces ophthalmia, often resulting in total blindness. Dust, however, as it is usually perceived by us, is, like dirt, only matter in the wrong place, and whatever injurious or disagreeable effects it produces are largely due to our own dealings with nature. So soon as we dispense with horsepower and adopt purely mechanical means of traction and conveyance, we can almost wholly abolish disease-bearing dust

from our streets, and ultimately from all our highways; while another kind of dust, that caused by the imperfect combustion of coal, may be got rid of with equal facility so soon as we consider pure air, sunlight, and natural beauty to be of more importance to the population as a whole than are the prejudices or the vested interests of those who produce the smoke.

2   But though we can thus minimize the dangers and the inconveniences arising from the grosser forms of dust, we cannot wholly abolish it; and it is, indeed, fortunate we cannot do so, since it has now been discovered that it is to the presence of dust we owe much of the beauty, and perhaps even the very habitability of the earth we live upon. Few of the fairy tales of science are more marvelous than these recent discoveries as to the varied effects and important uses of dust in the economy of nature.

3   The question why the sky and the deep ocean are both blue did not much concern the earlier physicists. It was thought to be the natural color of pure air and water, so pale as not to be visible when small quantities were seen, and only exhibiting its true tint when we looked through great depth of atmosphere or of organic water. But this theory did not explain the familiar facts of the gorgeous tints seen at sunset and sunrise, not only in the atmosphere and on the clouds near the horizon, but also in equally resplendent hues when the invisible sun shines upon Alpine peaks and snowfields. A true theory should explain all these colors, which comprise almost every tint of the rainbow.

4   The explanation was found through experiments on the visibility or non-visibility of air, which were made by the late Professor Tyndall about the year 1868. Everyone has seen the floating dust in a sunbeam when sunshine enters a partially darkened room; but it is not generally known that if there was absolutely no dust in the air the path of the sunbeam would be totally black and invisible, while if only very little dust was present in very minute particles the air would be as blue as the summer sky.

5   This was proved by passing a ray of electric light lengthways through a long glass cylinder filled with air of varying degrees of purity as regards dust. In the air of an ordinary room, however clean and well ventilated, the interior of the cylinder appears brilliantly illuminated. But if the cylinder is exhausted and then filled with air which is passed slowly through a fine gauze of intensely heated platinum wire, so as to burn up all the floating dust particles, which are mainly organic, the light will pass through the cylinder without illuminating the interior, which, viewed laterally, will appear as if filled with a dense black cloud. If, now, more air is passed into the cylinder through the heated gauze, but so rapidly that the dust particles are not wholly consumed, a slight blue haze will begin to appear, which will gradually become a pure blue, equal to

that of a summer sky. If more and more dust particles are allowed to enter, the blue becomes paler, and gradually changes to the colourless illumination of the ordinary air.

6   The explanation of these phenomena is that the number of dust particles in ordinary air is so great that they reflect abundance of light of all wave-lengths, and thus cause the interior of the vessel containing them to appear illuminated with white light. The air which is passed slowly over white-hot platinum has had the dust particles destroyed, thus showing that they were almost wholly of organic origin, which is also indicated by their extreme lightness, causing them to float permanently in the atmosphere. The dust being thus got rid of, and pure air being entirely transparent, there is nothing in the cylinder to reflect the light, which is sent through its centre in a beam of parallel rays so that none of it strikes against the sides; hence the inside of the cylinder appears absolutely dark. But when the larger dust particles are wholly or partially burnt, so that only the very smallest fragments remain, a blue light appears, because these are so minute as to reflect chiefly the more refrangible rays, which are of shorter wave-length—those at the blue end of the spectrum—and which are thus scattered in all directions, while the red and yellow rays pass straight on as before.

7   We have seen that the air near the earth's surface is full of rather coarse particles which reflect all the rays, and which therefore produce no one colour. But higher up the particles necessarily become smaller and smaller, since the comparatively rare atmosphere will support only the very smallest and lightest. These exist throughout a great thickness of air, perhaps from one mile to ten miles high or even more, and blue or violet rays being reflected from the innumerable particles in this great mass of air, which is nearly uniform in all parts of the world as regards the presence of minute dust particles, produces the constant and nearly uniform tint we call sky-blue. A certain amount of white or yellow light is no doubt reflected from the coarser dust in the lower atmosphere, and slightly dilutes the blue and renders it not quite so deep and pure as it otherwise would be. This is shown by the increasing depth of the sky-colour when seen from the tops of lofty mountains, while from the still greater heights attained in balloons the sky appears of a blue-black colour, the blue reflected from the comparatively small amount of dust particles being seen against the intense black of stellar space. It is for the same reason that the "Italian skies" are of so rich a blue, because the Mediterranean Sea on one side and the snowy Alps on the other do not furnish so large a quantity of atmospheric dust in the lower strata of air as in less favorably situated countries, thus leaving the blue reflected by the more uniformly distributed fine dust of the higher strata undiluted. But these Mediterranean skies are surpassed by those of the central Pacific ocean, where, owing to the small area of land, the lower atmo-

sphere is more free from coarse dust than in any other part of the world.

8   If we look at the sky on a perfectly fine summer's day, we shall find that the blue colour is the most pure and intense overhead, and when looking high up in a direction opposite to the sun. Near the horizon it is always less bright, while in the region immediately around the sun it is more or less yellow. The reason of this is that near the horizon we look through a very great thickness of the lower atmosphere, which is full of the larger dust particles reflecting white light, and this dilutes the pure blue of the higher atmosphere seen beyond. And in the vicinity of the sun a good deal of the blue light is reflected back into space by the finer dust, thus giving a yellowish tinge to that which reaches us reflected chiefly from the coarse dust of the lower atmosphere. At sunset and sunrise, however, this last effect is greatly intensified, owing to the great thickness of the strata of air through which the light reaches us. The enormous amount of this dust is well shown by the fact that, then only, we can look full at the sun, even when the whole sky is free from clouds and there is no apparent mist. But the sun's rays then reach us after having passed, first, through an enormous thickness of the higher strata of the air, the minute dust of which reflects most of the blue rays away from us, leaving the complementary yellow light to pass on. Then, the somewhat coarser dust reflects the green rays, leaving a more orange coloured light to pass on; and finally some of the yellow is reflected, leaving almost pure red. But owing to the constant presence of air currents, arranging both the dust and vapour in strata of varying extent and density, and of high or low clouds, which both absorb and reflect the light in varying degrees, we see produced all those wondrous combinations of tints and those gorgeous everchanging colours, which are a constant source of admiration and delight to all who have the advantage of an uninterrupted view to the west, and who are accustomed to watch for these not unfrequent exhibitions of nature's kaleidoscopic colour-painting. With every change in the altitude of the sun the display changes its character; and most of all when it has sunk below the horizon, and, owing to the more favourable angles, a larger quantity of the coloured light is reflected toward us. Especially is this the case when there is a certain amount of cloud. The clouds, so long as the sun is above the horizon, intercept much of the light and colour; but, when the great luminary has passed away from our direct vision, his light shines more directly on the under sides of all the clouds and air strata of different densities; a new and more brilliant light flushes the western sky, and a display of gorgeous ever-changing tints occurs which are at once the delight of the beholder and the despair of the artist. And all this unsurpassable glory we owe to—dust!

9   A remarkable confirmation of this theory was given during the two or three years after the great eruption of Krakatoa, near Java. The volcanic

débris was shot up from the crater many miles high, and the heavier portion of it fell upon the sea for several hundred miles around, and was found to be mainly composed of very thin flakes of volcanic glass. Much of this was of course ground to impalpable dust by the violence of the discharge, and was carried up to a height of many miles. Here it was caught by the return currents of air continually flowing northward and southward above the equatorial zone; and since, when these currents reach the temperate zone, where the surface rotation of the earth is less rapid, they continually flow eastward, the fine dust was thus carried at a great altitude completely around the earth. Its effects were traced some months after the eruption in the appearance of brilliant sunset glows of an exceptional character, often flushing with crimson the whole western half of the visible sky. These glows continued in diminishing splendour for about three years; they were seen all over the temperate zone; and it was calculated that, before they finally disappeared, some of this fine dust must have travelled three times around the globe.

10   The same principle is thought to explain the exquisite blue colour of the deep seas and oceans and of many lakes and springs. Absolutely pure water, like pure air, is colourless, but all seas and lakes, however clear and translucent, contain abundance of very finely divided matter, organic or inorganic, which, as in the atmosphere, reflects the blue rays in such quantity as to overpower the white or coloured light reflected from the fewer and more rapidly sinking particles of larger size. The oceanic dust is derived from many sources. Minute organisms are constantly dying near the surface, and their skeletons, or fragments of them, fall slowly to the bottom. The mud brought down by rivers, though it cannot be traced on the ocean floor more than about 150 miles from land, yet no doubt furnishes many particles of organic matter which are carried by surface currents to enormous distances and are ultimately dissolved before they reach the bottom. A more important source of finely divided matter is to be found in volcanic dust which, as in the case of Krakatoa, may remain for years in the atmosphere, but which must ultimately fall upon the surface of the earth and ocean. This can be traced in all the deep-sea oozes. Finally there is meteoric dust, which is continually falling to the surface of the earth, but in such minute quantities and in such a finely-divided state that it can be detected only in the oozes of the deepest oceans, where both inorganic and organic débris is almost absent.

11   The blue of the ocean varies in different parts from a pure blue somewhat lighter than that of the sky, as seen about the northern tropic in the Atlantic, to a deep indigo tint, as seen in the north temperate portions of the same ocean: owing, probably to differences in the nature, quantity, and distribution of the solid matter which causes the colour. The Mediterranean, and the deeper Swiss lakes, are also a blue of vari-

ous tints, due also to the presence of suspended matter, which Professor Tyndall thought might be so fine that it would require ages of quiet subsidence to reach the bottom. All the evidence goes to show, therefore, that the exquisite blue tints of sky and ocean, as well as all the sunset hues of sky and cloud, of mountain peak and Alpine snows, are due to the finer particles of that very dust which, in its coarser forms, we find so annoying and even dangerous.

12 But if this production of colour and beauty were the only useful function of dust, some persons might be disposed to dispense with it in order to escape its less agreeable effects. It has, however, been recently discovered that dust has another part to play in nature; a part so important that it is doubtful whether we could even live without it. To the presence of dust in the higher atmosphere we owe the formation of mists, clouds, and gentle beneficial rains, instead of water spouts and destructive torrents.

13 It is barely twenty years ago since the discovery was made, first in France by Coulier and Mascart, but more thoroughly worked out by Mr. John Aitken in 1880. He found that if a jet of steam is admitted into two large glass receivers,—one filled with ordinary air, the other with air which has been filtered through cotton wool so as to keep back all particles of solid matter,—the first will be instantly filled with condensed vapour in the usual cloudy form, while the other vessel will remain quite transparent. Another experiment was made, more nearly reproducing what occurs in nature. Some water was placed in the two vessels prepared as before. When the water had evaporated sufficiently to saturate the air the vessels were slightly cooled; a dense cloud was at once formed in the one while the other remained quite clear. These experiments, and many others, show that the mere cooling of vapour in air will not condense it into mist clouds or rain, unless *particles of solid matter* are present to form *nuclei* upon which condensation can begin. The density of the cloud is proportionate to the number of the particles; hence the fact that the steam issuing from the safety-valve or the chimney of a locomotive forms a dense white cloud, shows that the air is really full of dust particles, most of which are microscopic but none the less serving as centres of condensation for the vapour. Hence, if there were no dust in the air, escaping steam would remain invisible; there would be no cloud in the sky; and the vapour in the atmosphere, constantly accumulating through evaporation from seas and oceans and from the earth's surface, would have to find some other means of returning to its source.

14 One of these modes would be the deposition of dew, which is itself an illustration of the principle that vapour requires solid or liquid surfaces to condense upon; dew forms most readily and abundantly on grass, on account of the numerous centres of condensation this affords. Dew,

however, is now formed only on clear cold nights after warm or moist days. The air near the surface is warm and contains much vapour, though below the point of saturation. But the innumerable points and extensive surfaces of grass radiate heat quickly, and becoming cool, lower the temperature of the adjacent air, which then reaches saturation point and condenses the contained atmosphere on the grass. Hence, if the atmosphere at the earth's surface became supersaturated with aqueous vapour, dew would be continuously deposited, especially on every form of vegetation, the result being that everything, including our clothing, would be constantly dripping wet. If there were absolutely no particles of solid matter in the upper atmosphere, all the moisture would be returned to the earth in the form of dense mists, and frequent and copious dews, which in forests would form torrents of rain by the rapid condensation on the leaves. But if we suppose that solid particles were occasionally carried higher up through violent winds or tornadoes, then on those occasions the super-saturated atmosphere would condense rapidly upon them, and while falling would gather almost all the moisture in the atmosphere in that locality, resulting in masses or sheets of water, which would be so ruinously destructive by the mere weight and impetus of their fall that it is doubtful whether they would not render the earth almost wholly uninhabitable.

15   The chief mode of discharging the atmospheric vapour in the absence of dust would, however, be by contact with the higher slopes of all mountain ranges. Atmospheric vapour, being lighter than air, would accumulate in enormous quantities in the upper strata of the atmosphere, which would be always super-saturated and ready to condense upon any solid or liquid surfaces. But the quantity of land comprised in the upper half of all the mountains of the world is a very small fraction of the total surface of the globe, and this would lead to very disastrous results. The air in contact with the higher mountain slopes would rapidly discharge its water, which would run down the mountain sides in torrents. This condensation on every side of the mountains would leave a partial vacuum which would set up currents from every direction to restore the equilibrium, thus bringing in more super-saturated air to suffer condensation and add its supply of water, again increasing the in-draught of more air. The result would be that winds would be constantly blowing toward every mountain range from all directions, keeping up the condensation and discharging, day and night and from one year's end to another, an amount of water equal to that which falls during the heaviest tropical rains. All of the rain that now falls over the whole surface of the earth and ocean, with the exception of a few desert areas, would then fall only on rather high mountains or steep isolated hills, tearing down their sides in huge torrents, cutting deep ravines, and rendering all growth of vegetation impossible. The mountains would therefore be so

devasted as to be uninhabitable, and would be equally incapable of supporting either vegetable or animal life.

16   But this constant condensation on the mountains would probably check the deposit on the lowlands in the form of dew, because the continual up-draught toward the higher slopes would withdraw almost the whole of the vapour as it arose from the oceans, and other water-surfaces, and thus leave the lower strata over the plains almost or quite dry. And if this were the case there would be no vegetation, and therefore no animal life, on the plains and lowlands, which would thus be all arid deserts cut through by the great rivers formed by the meeting together of the innumerable torrents from the mountains.

17   Now, although it may not be possible to determine with perfect accuracy what would happen under the supposed condition of the atmosphere, it is certain that the total absence of dust would so fundamentally change the meteorology of our globe as, not improbably, to render it uninhabitable by man, and equally unsuitable for the larger portion of its existing animal and vegetable life.

18   Let us now briefly summarise what we owe to the universality of dust, and especially to that most finely divided portion of it which is constantly present in the atmosphere up to the height of many miles. First of all it gives us the pure blue of the sky, one of the most exquisitely beautiful colours in nature. It gives us also the glories of the sunset and the sunrise, and all those brilliant hues seen in high mountain regions. Half the beauty of the world would vanish with the absence of dust. But, what is far more important than the colour of sky and beauty of sunset, dust gives us also diffused daylight, or skylight, that most equable, and soothing, and useful, of all illuminating agencies. Without dust the sky would appear absolutely black, and the stars would be visible even at noonday. The sky itself would therefore give us no light. We should have bright glaring sunlight or intensely dark shadows, with hardly any half-tones. From this cause alone the world would be so totally different from what it is that all vegetable and animal life would probably have developed into very different forms, and even our own organisation would have been modified in order that we might enjoy life in a world of such harsh and violent contrasts.

19   In our houses we should have little light except when the sun shone directly into them, and even then every spot out of its direct rays would be completely dark, except for light reflected from the walls. It would be necessary to have windows all around and the walls all white; and on the north side of every house a high white wall would have to be built to reflect the light and prevent that side from being in total darkness. Even then we should have to live in a perpetual glare, or shut out the sun altogether and use artificial light as being a far superior article.

20   Much more important would be the effects of a dust-free atmosphere

in banishing clouds, or mist, or the "gentle rain of heaven," and in giving us in their place perpetual sunshine, desert lowlands, and mountains devastated by unceasing floods and raging torrents, so as, apparently, to render all life on the earth impossible.

21   There are a few other phenomena, apparently due to the same general causes, which may here be referred to. Everyone must have noticed the difference in the atmospheric effects and general character of the light in spring and autumn, at times when the days are of the same length, and consequently when the sun has the same altitude at corresponding hours. In spring we have a bluer sky and greater transparency of the atmosphere; in autumn, even on very fine days, there is always a kind of yellowish haze, resulting in a want of clearness in the air and purity of colour in the sky. These phenomena are quite intelligible when we consider that during winter less dust is formed, and more is brought down to the earth by rain and snow, resulting in the transparent atmosphere of spring, while exactly opposite conditions during summer bring about the mellow autumnal light. Again, the well-known beneficial effects of rain on vegetation, as compared with any amount of artificial watering, though, no doubt, largely due to the minute quantity of ammonia which the rain brings down with it from the air, must yet be partly derived from the organic or mineral particles which serve as the nuclei of every raindrop, and which, being so minute, are the more readily dissolved in the soil and appropriated as nourishment by the roots of plants.

22   It will be observed that all these beneficial effects of dust are due to its presence in such quantities as are produced by natural causes, since both gentle showers as well as ample rains and deep blue skies are present throughout the vast equatorial forest districts, where dust-forming agencies seem to be at a minimum. But in all densely-populated countries there is an enormous artificial production of dust—from our ploughed fields, from our roads and streets, where dust is continually formed by the iron-shod hoofs of innumerable horses, but chiefly from our enormous combustion of fuel pouring into the air volumes of smoke charged with unconsumed particles of carbon. This superabundance of dust, probably many times greater than that which would be produced under the more natural conditions which prevailed when our country was more thinly populated, must almost certainly produce some effect on our climate; and the particular effect it seems calculated to produce is the increase of cloud and fog, but not necessarily any increase of rain. Rain depends on the supply of aqueous vapour by evaporation; on temperature, which determines the dew point; and on changes in barometric pressure, which determine the winds. There is probably always and everywhere enough atmospheric dust to serve as centres of condensation at considerable altitudes, and thus to initiate rainfall when the other conditions are favourable; but the presence of increased quantities of

dust at the lower levels must lead to the formation of denser clouds, although the minute water-vesicles cannot descend as rain, because, as they pass down into warmer and dryer strata of air, they are again evaporated.

23   Now, there is much evidence to show that there has been a considerable increase in the amount of cloud, and consequent decrease in the amount of sunshine, in all parts of our country. It is an undoubted fact that in the Middle Ages England was a wine-producing country, and this implies more sunshine than we have now. Sunshine has a double effect, in heating the surface soil and thus causing more rapid growth, besides its direct effect in ripening the fruit. This is well seen in Canada, where, notwithstanding a six months' winter of extreme severity, vines are grown as bushes in the open ground, and produce fruit equal to that of our ordinary greenhouses. Some years back one of our gardening periodicals obtained from gardeners of forty or fifty years' experience a body of facts clearly indicating a comparatively recent change of climate. It was stated that in many parts of the country, especially in the north, fruits were formerly grown successfully and of good quality in gardens where they cannot be grown now; and this occurred in places sufficiently removed from manufacturing centres to be unaffected by any direct deleterious influence of smoke. But an increase of cloud, and consequent diminution of sunshine, would produce just such a result; and this increase is almost certain to have occurred owing to the enormously increased amount of dust thrown into the atmosphere as our country has become more densely populated, and especially owing to the vast increase of our smoke-producing manufactories. It seems highly probable, therefore, that to increase the wealth of our capitalist-manufacturers we are allowing the climate of our whole country to be greatly deteriorated in a way which diminishes both its productiveness and its beauty, thus injuriously affecting the enjoyment and the health of the whole population, since sunshine is itself an essential condition of healthy life. When this fact is thoroughly realised we shall surely put a stop to such a reckless and wholly unnecessary production of injurious smoke and dust.

24   In conclusion, we find that the much-abused and all-pervading dust, which, when too freely produced, deteriorates our climate and brings us dirt, discomfort, and even disease, is, nevertheless, under natural conditions, an essential portion of the economy of nature. It gives us much of the beauty of natural scenery, as due to varying atmospheric effects of sky, and cloud, and sunset tints, and thus renders life more enjoyable; while, as an essential condition of diffused daylight and of moderate rainfalls combined with a dry atmosphere, it appears to be absolutely necessary for our existence upon the earth, perhaps even for the very development of terrestrial, as opposed to aquatic life. The overwhelming importance of the small things, and even of the despised things, of our

world has never, perhaps, been so strikingly brought home to us as in these recent investigations into the wide-spread and far-reaching beneficial influences of Atmospheric Dust.

Content Questions

1. What contribution did Professor Tyndall make to the study of dust?
2. What are "Italian skies"?
3. Why is pure water clear?
4. What is dust's most important contribution? Who discovered this contribution? How does dust make this contribution?

Questions on Presentation

1. Why does Wallace summarize his argument in paragraph 18?
2. This essay was written nearly a century ago and is different in style from modern essays. What marks this as a nineteenth-century essay?
3. Keeping in mind that this is a nineteenth-century essay, how would you characterize Wallace's audience? Is it similar to the one for whom Asimov or Baskin writes? Or for whom the Goulds write? (See Section 7 for these essays.)

The Bird and the Machine

Loren Eiseley

Naturalist Loren C. Eiseley (1907–1977), a midwesterner, was born in Lincoln, Nebraska. In 1947 he joined the University of Pennsylvania as a professor of anthropology. Eiseley's interests, however, went far beyond anthropology. His works include *The Immense Journey, Darwin's Century, The Firmament of Time,* and *The Mind of Nature.* In this selection Eiseley retells a seemingly inconsequential incident and, in the retelling, connects that isolated event to the issue of modern values.

1   I suppose their little bones have years ago been lost among the stones and winds of those high glacial pastures. I suppose their feathers blew eventually into the piles of tumbleweed beneath the straggling cattle fences and rotted there in the mountain snows, along with dead steers and all the other things that drift to an end in the corners of the wire. I do not quite know why I should be thinking of birds over the *New York Times* at breakfast, particularly the birds of my youth half a continent away. It is a funny thing what the brain will do with memories and how it will treasure them and finally bring them into odd juxtapositions with other things, as though it wanted to make a design, or get some meaning out of them, whether you want it or not, or even see it.

2   It used to seem marvelous to me, but I read now that there are machines that can do these things in a small way, machines that can crawl about like animals, and that it may not be long now until they do more things—maybe even make themselves—I saw that piece in the *Times* just now. And then they will, maybe—well, who knows—but you read about it more and more with no one making any protest, and already they can add better than we and reach up and hear things through the dark and finger the guns over the night sky.

3   This is the new world that I read about at breakfast. This is the world that confronts me in my biological books and journals, until there are times when I sit quietly in my chair and try to hear the little purr of the cogs in my head and the tubes flaring and dying as the messages go through them and the circuits snap shut or open. This is the great age, make no mistake about it; the robot has been born somewhat appropriately along with the atom bomb, and the brain they say now is just another type of more complicated feedback system. The engineers have its basic principles worked out; it's mechanical, you know; nothing to get superstitious about; and man can always improve on nature once he gets the idea. Well, he's got it all right and that's why, I guess, that I sit here in my chair, with the article crunched in my hand, remembering those two birds and that blue mountain sunlight. There is another magazine article on my desk that reads "Machines Are Getting Smarter Every Day." I don't deny it, but I'll still stick with the birds. It's life I believe in, not machines.

4   Maybe you don't believe there is any difference. A skeleton is all joints and pulleys, I'll admit. And when man was in his simpler stages of machine building in the eighteenth century, he quickly saw the resemblances. "What," wrote Hobbes, "is the heart but a spring, and the nerves but so many strings, and the joints but so many wheels, giving motion to the whole body?" Tinkering about in their shops it was inevitable in the end that men would see the world as a huge machine "subdivided into an infinite number of lesser machines."

5   The idea took on with a vengeance. Little automatons toured the

country—dolls controlled by clockwork. Clocks described as little worlds were taken on tours by their designers. They were made up of moving figures, shifting scenes and other remarkable devices. The life of the cell was unknown. Man, whether he was conceived as possessing a soul or not, moved and jerked about like these tiny puppets. A human being thought of himself in terms of his own tools and implements. He had been fashioned like the puppets he produced and was only a more clever model made by a greater designer.

6   Then in the nineteenth century, the cell was discovered, and the single machine in its turn was found to be the product of millions of infinitesimal machines—the cells. Now, finally, the cell itself dissolves away into an abstract chemical machine—and that into some intangible, inexpressible flow of energy. The secret seems to lurk all about, the wheels get smaller and smaller, and they turn more rapidly, but when you try to seize it the life is gone—and so, by popular definition, some would say that life was never there in the first place. The wheels and the cogs are the secret and we can make them better in time—machines that will run faster and more accurately than real mice to real cheese.

7   I have no doubt it can be done, though a mouse harvesting seeds on an autumn thistle is to me a fine sight and more complicated, I think, in his multiform activity, than a machine "mouse" running a maze. Also, I like to think of the possible shape of the future brooding in mice, just as it brooded once in a rather ordinary mousy insectivore who became a man. It leaves a nice fine indeterminate sense of wonder that even an electronic brain hasn't got, because you know perfectly well that if the electronic brain changes, it will be because of something man has done to it. But what man will do to himself he doesn't really know. A certain scale of time and a ghostly intangible thing called change are ticking in him. Powers and potentialities like the oak in the seed, or a red and awful ruin. Either way, it's impressive; and the mouse has it, too. Or those birds, I'll never forget those birds—yet before I measured their significance, I learned the lesson of time first of all. I was young then and left alone in a great desert—part of an expedition that had scattered its men over several hundred miles in order to carry on research more effectively. I learned there that time is a series of planes existing superficially in the same universe. The tempo is a human illusion, a subjective clock ticking in our own kind of protoplasm.

8   As the long months passed, I began to live on the slower planes and to observe more readily what passed for life there. I sauntered, I passed more and more slowly up and down the canyons in the dry baking heat of midsummer. I slumbered for long hours in the shade of huge brown boulders that had gathered in tilted companies out on the flats. I had forgotten the world of men and the world had forgotten me. Now and

then I found a skull in the canyons, and these justified my remaining there. I took a serene cold interest in these discoveries. I had come, like many a naturalist before me, to view life with a wary and subdued attention. I had grown to take pleasure in the divested bone.

9   I sat once on a high ridge that fell away before me into a waste of sand dunes. I sat through hours of a long afternoon. Finally, as I glanced beside my boot an indistinct configuration caught my eye. It was a coiled rattlesnake, a big one. How long he had sat with me I do not know. I had not frightened him. We were both locked in the sleep-walking tempo of the earlier world, baking in the same high air and sunshine. Perhaps he had been there when I came. He slept on as I left, his coils, so ill discerned by me, dissolving once more among the stones and gravel from which I had barely made him out.

10   Another time I got on a higher ridge, among some tough little wind-warped pines half covered over with sand in a basin-like depression that caught everything carried by the air up to those heights. There were a few thin bones of birds, some cracked shells of indeterminable age, and the knotty fingers of pine roots bulged out of shape from their long and agonizing grasp upon the crevices of the rock. I lay under the pines in the sparse shade and went to sleep once more.

11   It grew cold finally, for autumn was in the air by then, and the few things that lived thereabouts were sinking down into an even chillier scale of time. In the moments between sleeping and waking I saw the roots about me and slowly, slowly, a foot in what seemed many centuries, I moved my sleep-stiffened hands over the scaling bark and lifted my numbed face after the vanishing sun. I was a great awkward thing of knots and aching limbs, trapped up there in some long, patient endurance that involved the necessity of putting living fingers into rock and by slow, aching expansion bursting those rocks asunder. I suppose, so thin and slow was the time of my pulse by then, that I might have stayed on to drift still deeper into the lower cadences of the frost, or the crystalline life that glistens pebbles, or shines in a snowflake, or dreams in the meteoric iron between the worlds.

12   It was a dim descent, but time was present in it. Somewhere far down in that scale the notion struck me that one might come the other way. Not many months thereafter I joined some colleagues heading higher into a remote windy tableland where huge bones were reputed to protrude like boulders from the turf. I had drowsed with reptiles and moved with the century-long pulse of trees; now, lethargically, I was climbing back up some invisible ladder of quickening hours. There had been talk of birds in connection with my duties. Birds are intense, fast-living creatures—reptiles, I suppose one might say, that have escaped out of the heavy sleep of time, transformed fairy creatures dancing over sunlit meadows. It is a youthful fancy, no doubt, but because of something

that happened up there among the escarpments of that range, it remains with me a lifelong impression. I can never bear to see a bird imprisoned.

13   We came into that valley through the trailing mists of a spring night. It was a place that looked as though it might never have known the foot of man, but our scouts had been ahead of us and we knew all about the abandoned cabin of stone that lay far up on one hillside. It had been built in the land rush of the last century and then lost to the cattlemen again as the marginal soils failed to take to the plow.

14   There were spots like this all over that country. Lost graves marked by unlettered stones and old corroding rim-fire cartridge cases lying where somebody had made a stand among the boulders that rimmed the valley. They are all that remain of the range wars; the men are under the stones now. I could see our cavalcade winding in and out through the mist below us: torches, the reflection of the truck lights on our collecting tins, and the far-off bumping of a loose dinosaur thigh bone in the bottom of a trailer. I stood on a rock a moment looking down and thinking what it cost in money and equipment to capture the past.

15   We had, in addition, instructions to lay hands on the present. The word had come through to get them alive—birds, reptiles, anything. A zoo somewhere abroad needed restocking. It was one of those reciprocal matters in which science involves itself. Maybe our museum needed a stray ostrich egg and this was the payoff. Anyhow, my job was to help capture some birds and that was why I was there before the trucks.

16   The cabin had not been occupied for years. We intended to clean it out and live in it, but there were holes in the roof and the birds had come in and were roosting in the rafters. You could depend on it in a place like this where everything blew away, and even a bird needed some place out of the weather and away from coyotes. A cabin going back to nature in a wild place draws them till they come in, listening at the eaves, I imagine, peeking softly among the shingles till they find a hole and then suddenly the place is theirs and man is forgotten.

17   Sometimes of late years I find myself thinking the most beautiful sight in the world might be the birds taking over New York after the last man has run away to the hills. I will never live to see it, of course, but I know just how it will sound because I've lived up high and I know the sort of watch birds keep on us. I've listened to sparrows tapping tentatively on the outside of air conditioners when they thought no one was listening, and I know how other birds test the vibrations that come up to them through the television aerials.

18   "Is he gone?" they ask, and the vibrations come up from below, "Not yet, not yet."

19   Well, to come back, I got the door open softly and I had the spotlight all ready to turn on and blind whatever birds there were so they couldn't see to get out through the roof. I had a short piece of ladder to put

against the far wall where there was a shelf on which I expected to make the biggest haul. I had all the information I needed just like any skilled assassin. I pushed the door open, the hinges squeaking only a little. A bird or two stirred—I could hear them—but nothing flew and there was a faint starlight through the holes in the roof.

20   I padded across the floor, got the ladder up and the light ready, and slithered up the ladder till my head and arms were over the shelf. Everything was dark as pitch except for the starlight at the little place back of the shelf near the eaves. With the light to blind them, they'd never make it. I had them. I reached my arm carefully over in order to be ready to seize whatever was there and I put the flash on the edge of the shelf where it would stand by itself when I turned it on. That way I'd be able to use both hands.

21   Everything worked perfectly except for one detail—I didn't know what kind of birds were there. I never thought about it at all, and it wouldn't have mattered if I had. My orders were to get something interesting. I snapped on the flash and sure enough there was a great beating and feathers flying, but instead of my having them, they, or rather he, had me. He had my hand, that is, and for a small hawk not much bigger than my fist he was doing all right. I heard him give one short metallic cry when the light went on and my hand descended on the bird beside him; after that he was busy with his claws and his beak was sunk in my thumb. In the struggle I knocked the lamp over on the shelf, and his mate got her sight back and whisked neatly through the hole in the roof and off among the stars outside. It all happened in fifteen seconds and you might think I would have fallen down the ladder, but no, I had a professional assassin's reputation to keep up, and the bird, of course, made the mistake of thinking the hand was the enemy and not the eyes behind it. He chewed my thumb up pretty effectively and lacerated my hand with his claws, but in the end I got him, having two hands to work with.

22   He was a sparrow hawk and a fine young male in the prime of life. I was sorry not to catch the pair of them, but as I dripped blood and folded his wings carefully, holding him by the back so that he couldn't strike again, I had to admit the two of them might have been more than I could have handled under the circumstances. The little fellow had saved his mate by diverting me, and that was that. He was born to it, and made no outcry now, resting in my hand hopelessly, but peering toward me in the shadows behind the lamp with a fierce, almost indifferent glance. He neither gave nor expected mercy and something out of the high air passed from him to me, stirring a faint embarrassment.

23   I quit looking into that eye and managed to get my huge carcass with its fist full of prey back down the ladder. I put the bird in a box too small to allow him to injure himself by struggle and walked out to welcome

the arriving trucks. It had been a long day, and camp still to make in the
darkness. In the morning that bird would be just another episode. He
would go back with the bones in the truck to a small cage in a city
where he would spend the rest of his life. And a good thing, too. I sucked
my aching thumb and spat out some blood. An assassin has to get used
to these things. I had a professional reputation to keep up.

24   In the morning, with the change that comes on suddenly in that high
country, the mist that had hovered below us in the valley was gone. The
sky was a deep blue, and one could see for miles over the high outcrop-
pings of stone. I was up early and brought the box in which the little
hawk was imprisoned out onto the grass where I was building a cage. A
wind as cool as a mountain spring ran over the grass and stirred my hair.
It was a fine day to be alive. I looked up and all around and at the hole
in the cabin roof out of which the other little hawk had fled. There was
no sign of her anywhere that I could see.

25   "Probably in the next county by now," I thought cynically, but before
beginning work I decided I'd have a look at my last night's capture.

26   Secretively, I looked again all around the camp and up and down and
opened the box. I got him right out in my hand with his wings folded
properly and I was careful not to startle him. He lay limp in my grasp
and I could feel his heart pound under the feathers but he only looked
beyond me and up.

27   I saw him look that last look away beyond me into a sky so full of
light that I could not follow his gaze. The little breeze flowed over me
again, and nearby a mountain aspen shook all its tiny leaves. I suppose
I must have had an idea then of what I was going to do, but I never let
it come up into consciousness. I just reached over and laid the hawk on
the grass.

28   He lay there a long minute without hope, unmoving, his eyes still
fixed on that blue vault above him. It must have been that he was already so far away in heart that he never felt the release from my hand.
He never even stood. He just lay with his breast against the grass.

29   In the next second after that long minute he was gone. Like a flicker
of light, he had vanished with my eyes full on him, but without actually
seeing even a premonitory wing beat. He was gone straight into that
towering emptiness of light and crystal that my eyes could scarcely bear
to penetrate. For another long moment there was silence. I could not see
him. The light was too intense. Then from far up somewhere a cry came
ringing down.

30   I was young then and had seen little of the world, but when I heard
that cry my heart turned over. It was not the cry of the hawk I had captured; for, by shifting my position against the sun, I was now seeing further up. Straight out of the sun's eye, where she must have been soaring
restlessly above us for untold hours, hurtled his mate. And from far up,

ringing from peak to peak of the summits over us, came a cry of such unutterable and ecstatic joy that it sounds down across the years and tingles among the cups on my quiet breakfast table.

31   I saw them both now. He was rising fast to meet her. They met in a great soaring gyre that turned to a whirling circle and a dance of wings. Once more, just once, their two voices, joined in a harsh wild medley of question and response, struck and echoed against the pinnacles of the valley. Then they were gone forever somewhere into those upper regions beyond the eyes of men.

32   I am older now, and sleep less, and have seen most of what there is to see and am not very much impressed any more, I suppose, by anything. "What Next in the Attributes of Machines?" my morning headline runs. "It Might Be the Power to Reproduce Themselves."

33   I lay the paper down and across my mind a phrase floats insinuatingly: "It does not seem that there is anything in the construction, constituents, or behavior of the human being which it is essentially impossible for science to duplicate and synthesize. On the other hand . . . "

34   All over the city the cogs in the hard, bright mechanisms have begun to turn. Figures move through computers, names are spelled out, a thoughtful machine selects the fingerprints of a wanted criminal from an array of thousands. In the laboratory an electronic mouse runs swiftly through a maze toward the cheese it can neither taste nor enjoy. On the second run it does better than a living mouse.

35   "On the other hand . . . " Ah, my mind takes up, on the other hand the machine does not bleed, ache, hang for hours in the empty sky in a torment of hope to learn the fate of another machine, nor does it cry out with joy nor dance in the air with the fierce passion of a bird. Far off, over a distance greater than space, that remote cry from the heart of heaven makes a faint buzzing among my breakfast dishes and passes on and away.

Content Questions

1. Why does Eiseley believe in life rather than machines?
2. Why does Eiseley refer to himself as an assassin with "a professional reputation to keep up"?
3. What does the hawk represent?

Questions on Presentation

1. Why does Eiseley begin his essay with speculative statements?
2. What is Eiseley's tone of voice when writing about machines? About birds? How do you recognize the difference?

3.   How would you characterize his audience?
4.   In paragraph 7 Eiseley discusses changes made by man in electronic brains and in his own. Is this discussion clear?
5.   Eiseley shifts his approach between analysis and narrative. Is this an effective technique? Why or why not?

Questions for Discussion and Writing

1.   Several of the essays in Section 6 are intended for an audience that has a general interest but not a specialized background in the topics. Others are for audiences with technical, scientific, or literary backgrounds. Which essays are aimed at a general audience and which at a specialized one? How can you identify essays intended for general audiences? What structures (e.g., sentence structures, choice of words, choice of details, paragraph structures) did the authors use that helped you make this identification? Do several authors use the same techniques?

2.   The importance of human beings is a common theme of several of the essays in this section. Despite technological advances, changes in the ways we live our lives, our fears of one another, and differences between cultures, the importance for the need of human beings to help and understand one another is reaffirmed. Which essays in this section seem to stress this theme the most? How do the writers treat this theme? Is it always a positive presentation of this idea, or do some writers present the negative side of it?

3.   Several of the authors in the section remark on our problem-solving abilities. They imply that we perceive a situation, identify a problem, propose a solution, and, finally, analyze the proposed solution in light of the problem. Sometimes this procedure is beneficial; other times, it's harmful. Does this pattern apply to all types of problems we encounter? Are there some types of problems that can be resolved by this procedure and others that cannot? What types? Is there one particular problem (such as writing an essay, registering for classes, balancing your checkbook, completing a research project) that would be easier to solve if we used this procedure?

4.   Several of the essays in this section use statistics or facts and figures to support their theses. Which essay is the most effective in providing such support? Does this support make the essay reasonable, or does the writer have to use other techniques to strengthen the argument?

5.   Many of these essays are directly or indirectly concerned with the impact of politics in our world. Write an essay in which you contrast the ways in which two of the essays in this section use political issues as a part of development.

Section 7

CONTROVERSIES IN SCIENCE

Were Dinosaurs Dumb?

Stephen Jay Gould

Harvard geology professor Stephen Jay Gould was born in 1941 in New York City. Educated at Antioch College and Columbia University, Gould joined the geology department at Harvard in 1966. The author of more than one hundred scientific articles, Gould is coauthor of *The Evolutionary Synthesis* (with Salvador E. Luria and Sam Singer), general editor of the "History of Paleontology" series, and author of "This View of Life," a monthly column in *Natural History* magazine. Gould's special quality as a writer is his ability to interpret scientific concepts into understandable language without trivializing the concepts. In books such as *Ever Since Darwin* (1977), *The Panda's Thumb* (1980), *The Mismeasure of Man* (1981), *The Flamingo's Smile* (1985), and *Hen's Teeth and Horse's Toes* (1983), Gould avoids telling tales of nature for their own sake; he uses these tales to represent general principles of evolution and how cultural factors influence scientific study. For Gould, science is not an objective search for information but a very human, creative activity. *The Panda's Thumb*, for example, illustrates Gould's theory that evolution is not a steady process but one that occurs in leaps. Rather than changing gradually, species evolve because of rapid changes in small numbers of them, interspersed throughout their history. Gould believes that misunderstandings about evolution stem from prejudices of the time, prejudices that may bias people unnecessarily. In the following selection, taken originally from his column in *Nature* magazine, Gould tries to dispel one type of bias by reflecting on our perceptions and misinformation about intelligence.

1   When Muhammad Ali flunked his army intelligence test, he quipped (with a wit that belied his performance on the exam): "I only said I was

the greatest; I never said I was the smartest." In our metaphors and fairy tales, size and power are almost always balanced by a want of intelligence. Cunning is the refuge of the little guy. Think of Br'er Rabbit and Br'er Bear; David smiting Goliath with a slingshot; Jack chopping down the beanstalk. Slow wit is the tragic flaw of a giant.

2   The discovery of dinosaurs in the nineteenth century provided, or so it appeared, a quintessential case for the negative correlation of size and smarts. With their pea brains and giant bodies, dinosaurs became a symbol of lumbering stupidity. Their extinction seemed only to confirm their flawed design.

3   Dinosaurs were not even granted the usual solace of a giant—great physical prowess. God maintained a discreet silence about the brains of behemoth, but he certainly marveled at its strength: "Lo, now, his strength is in his loins, and his force is in the navel of his belly. He moveth his tail like a cedar. . . . His bones are as strong pieces of brass; his bones are like bars of iron [Job 40:16–18]." Dinosaurs, on the other hand, have usually been reconstructed as slow and clumsy. In the standard illustration, *Brontosaurus* wades in a murky pond because he cannot hold up his own weight on land.

4   Popularizations for grade school curricula provide a good illustration of prevailing orthodoxy. I still have my third grade copy (1948 edition) of Bertha Morris Parker's *Animals of Yesterday*, stolen, I am forced to suppose, from P.S. 26, Queens (sorry Mrs. McInerney). In it, boy (teleported back to the Jurassic) meets brontosaur:

> It is huge, and you can tell from the size of its head that it must be stupid. . . . This giant animal moves about very slowly as it eats. No wonder it moves slowly! Its huge feet are very heavy, and its great tail is not easy to pull around. You are not surprised that the thunder lizard likes to stay in the water so that the water will help it hold up its huge body. . . . Giant dinosaurs were once the lords of the earth. Why did they disappear? You can probably guess part of the answer—their bodies were too large for their brains. If their bodies had been smaller, and their brains larger, they might have lived on.

5   Dinosaurs have been making a strong comeback of late, in this age of "I'm OK, you're OK." Most paleontologists are now willing to view them as energetic, active, and capable animals. The *Brontosaurus* that wallowed in its pond a generation ago is now running on land, while pairs of males have been seen twining their necks about each other in elaborate sexual combat for access to females (much like the neck wrestling of giraffes). Modern anatomical reconstructions indicate strength and agility, and many paleontologists now believe that dinosaurs were warmblooded.

6   The idea of warmblooded dinosaurs has captured the public imagina-tion and received a torrent of press coverage. Yet another vindication of dinosaurian capability has received very little attention, although I re-gard it as equally significant. I refer to the issue of stupidity and its cor-relation with size. The revisionist interpretation, which I support in this column, does not enshrine dinosaurs as paragons of intellect, but it does maintain that they were not small brained after all. They had the "right-sized" brains for reptiles of their body size.

7   I don't wish to deny that the flattened, minuscule head of largebodied *Stegosaurus* houses little brain from our subjective, top-heavy perspec-tive, but I do wish to assert that we should not expect more of the beast. First of all, large animals have relatively smaller brains than related, small animals. The correlation of brain size with body size among kin-dred animals (all reptiles, all mammals, for example) is remarkably regu-lar. As we move from small to large animals, from mice to elephants or small lizards to Komodo dragons, brain size increases, but not so fast as body size. In other words, bodies grow faster than brains, and large ani-mals have low ratios of brain weight to body weight. In fact, brains grow only about two-thirds as fast as bodies. Since we have no reason to be-lieve that large animals are consistently stupider than their smaller rela-tives, we must conclude that large animals require relatively less brain to do as well as smaller animals. If we do not recognize this relationship, we are likely to underestimate the mental power of very large animals, dinosaurs in particular.

8   Second, the relationship between brain and body size is not identical in all groups of vertebrates. All share the same rate of relative decrease in brain size, but small mammals have much larger brains than small reptiles of the same body weight. This discrepancy is maintained at all larger body weights, since brain size increases at the same rate in both groups—two-thirds as fast as body size.

9   Put these two facts together—all large animals have relatively small brains, and reptiles have much smaller brains than mammals at any common body weight—and what should we expect from a normal, large reptile? The answer, of course, is a brain of very modest size. No living reptile even approaches a middle-size dinosaur in bulk, so we have no modern standard to serve as a model for dinosaurs.

10   Fortunately, our imperfect fossil record has, for once, not severely dis-appointed us in providing data about fossil brains. Superbly preserved skulls have been found for many species of dinosaurs, and cranial capac-ities can be measured. (Since brains do not fill craniums in reptiles, some creative, although not unreasonable, manipulation must be ap-plied to estimate brain size from the hole within a skull.) With these data, we have a clear test for the conventional hypothesis of dinosaurian stupidity. We should agree, at the outset, that a reptilian standard is the

only proper one—it is surely irrelevant that dinosaurs had smaller brains than people or whales. We have abundant data on the relationship of brain and body size in modern reptiles. Since we know that brains increase two-thirds as fast as bodies as we move from small to large living species, we can extrapolate this rate to dinosaurian sizes and ask whether dinosaur brains match what we would expect of living reptiles if they grew so large.

11   Harry Jerison studied the brain sizes of ten dinosaurs and found that they fell right on the extrapolated reptilian curve. Dinosaurs did not have small brains; they maintained just the right-sized brains for reptiles of their dimensions. So much for Ms. Parker's explanation of their demise.

12   Jerison made no attempt to distinguish among various kinds of dinosaurs; ten species distributed over six major groups scarcely provide a proper basis for comparison. Recently, James A. Hopson of the University of Chicago gathered more data and made a remarkable and satisfying discovery.

13   Hopson needed a common scale for all dinosaurs. He therefore compared each dinosaur brain with the average reptilian brain we would expect at its body weight. If the dinosaur falls on the standard reptilian curve, its brain receives a value of 1.0 (called an encephalization quotient, or EQ—the ratio of actual brain to expected brain for a standard reptile of the same body weight). Dinosaurs lying above the curve (more brain than expected in a standard reptile of the same body weight) receive values in excess of 1.0, while those below the curve measure less than 1.0.

14   Hopson found that the major groups of dinosaurs can be ranked by increasing values of average EQ. This ranking corresponds perfectly with inferred speed, agility and behavioral complexity in feeding (or avoiding the prospect of becoming a meal). The giant sauropods, *Brontosaurus* and its allies, have the lowest EQ's—0.20 to 0.35. They must have moved fairly slowly and without great maneuverability. They probably escaped predation by virtue of their bulk alone, much as elephants do today. The armored ankylosaurs and stegosaurs come next with EQ's of 0.52 to 0.56. These animals, with their heavy armor, probably relied largely upon passive defense, but the clubbed tail of ankylosaurs and the spiked tail of stegosaurs imply some active fighting and increased behavioral complexity.

15   The ceratopsians rank next at about 0.7 to 0.9. Hopson remarks: "The larger ceratopsians, with their great horned heads, relied on active defensive strategies and presumably required somewhat greater agility than the tail-weaponed forms, both in fending off predators and in intraspecific combat bouts. The smaller ceratopsians, lacking true horns, would have relied on sensory acuity and speed to escape from predators." The

ornithopods (duckbills and their allies) were the brainiest herbivores, with EQ's from 0.85 to 1.5. They relied on "acute senses and relatively fast speeds" to elude carnivores. Flight seems to require more acuity and agility than standing defense. Among ceratopsians, small, hornless, and presumably fleeing *Protoceratops* had a higher EQ than great three-horned *Triceratops*.

16   Carnivores have higher EQ's than herbivores, as in modern vertebrates. Catching a rapidly moving or stoutly fighting prey demands a good deal more upstairs than plucking the right kind of plant. The giant theropods (*Tyrannosaurus* and its allies) vary from 1.0 to nearly 2.0. Atop the heap, quite appropriately at its small size, rests the little coelurosaur *Stenonychosaurus* with an EQ well above 5.0. Its actively moving quarry, small mammals and birds perhaps, probably posed a greater challenge in discovery and capture than *Triceratops* afforded *Tyrannosaurus*.

17   I do not wish to make a naive claim that brain size equals intelligence or, in this case, behavioral range and agility (I don't know what intelligence means in humans, much less in a group of extinct reptiles). Variation in brain size within a species has precious little to do with brain power (humans do equally well with 900 or 2,500 cubic centimeters of brain). But comparison across species, when the differences are large, seems reasonable. I do not regard it as irrelevant to our achievements that we so greatly exceed koala bears—much as I love them—in EQ. The sensible ordering among dinosaurs also indicates that even so coarse a measure as brain size counts for something.

18   If behavioral complexity is one consequence of mental power, then we might expect to uncover among dinosaurs some signs of social behavior that demand coordination, cohesiveness, and recognition. Indeed we do, and it cannot be accidental that these signs were overlooked when dinosaurs labored under the burden of a falsely imposed obtuseness. Multiple trackways have been uncovered, with evidence for more than twenty animals traveling together in parallel movement. Did some dinosaurs live in herds? At the Davenport Ranch sauropod trackway, small footprints lie in the center and larger ones at the periphery. Could it be that some dinosars traveled much as some advanced herbivorous mammals do today, with large adults at the borders sheltering juveniles in the center?

19   In addition, the very structures that seemed most bizarre and useless to older paleontologists—the elaborate crests of hadrosaurs, the frills and horns of ceratopsians, and the nine inches of solid bone above the brain of *Pachycephalosaurus*—now appear to gain a coordinated explanation as devices for sexual display and combat. Pachycephalosaurs may have engaged in head-butting contests much as mountain sheep do today. The crests of some hadrosaurs are well designed as resonating chambers; did they engage in bellowing matches? The ceratopsian horn

and frill may have acted as sword and shield in the battle for mates. Since such behavior is not only intrinsically complex, but also implies an elaborate social system, we would scarcely expect to find it in a group of animals barely muddling through at a moronic level.

20   But the best illustration of dinosaurian capability may well be the fact most often cited against them—their demise. Extinction, for most people, carries many of the connotations attributed to sex not so long ago— a rather disreputable business, frequent in occurrence, but not to anyone's credit, and certainly not to be discussed in proper circles. But, like sex, extinction is an ineluctable part of life. It is the ultimate fate of all species, not the lot of unfortunate and ill-designed creatures. It is no sign of failure.

21   The remarkable thing about dinosaurs is not that they became extinct, but that they dominated the earth for so long. Dinosaurs held sway for 100 million years while mammals, all the while, lived as small animals in the interstices of their world. After 70 million years on top, we mammals have an excellent track record and good prospects for the future, but we have yet to display the staying power of dinosaurs.

22   People, on this criterion, are scarcely worth mentioning—5 million years perhaps since *Australopithecus*, a mere 50,000 for our own species, *Homo sapiens*. Try the ultimate test within our system of values: Do you know anyone who would wager a substantial sum, even at favorable odds, on the proposition that *Homo sapiens* will last longer than *Brontosaurus*?

Content Questions

1.   Why are dinosaurs the "quintessential case for the negative correlation of size and smarts"?
2.   Why are people amazed to find that dinosaurs were warm blooded?
3.   Why is there no reason to believe that larger animals are consistently dumber than smaller animals?
4.   What is the Hopson's Scale used for?

Questions on Presentation

1.   How would you describe the tone of this essay?
2.   Why does Gould begin with the anecdote about Muhammad Ali?
3.   What is the effect of Gould's use of rhetorical questions in paragraph 18?
4.   Why does Gould give such a relatively lengthy discussion of Hopson's EQ scale?

The Way We Act

Yvonne Baskin

Yvonne Baskin is currently an Alicia Patterson Foundation Fellow researching her next work, "The Release of Genetically Engineered Organisms into the Environment." A frequent contributor to such magazines as *Omni, Science Digest, Technical Review*, and *Science*, Baskin graduated magna cum laude from Baylor University with a degree in journalism. She has been a medical writer and science reporter for various newspapers in Texas and California and a staff writer for The Associated Press. She followed her first book, *The Gene Doctors: Medical Genetics at the Frontier* (1984) with an even more successful one, *Woman of Tomorrow* (with Kathy Keeton, president of *Omni* magazine). Baskin frequently shares her interest in genetic engineering with gifted students in the California public school systems. She encourages young scientists to become fluent in English as well as Pascal. This essay, originally published in *Science 85*, illustrates Baskin's dual interest in science and effective writing. "The Way We Act" explains scientists' recent discoveries on how biochemistry influences our behavior.

1   Imagine you've been strolling along a tropical beach all morning, your thoughts wandering. You haven't a want in the world. In just a few minutes, however, a rather singleminded goal is going to drive you indoors.

2   Deep in your brain, in a tiny cluster of cells called the subfornical organ, blood-borne molecules of the hormone angiotensin are arriving, sounding an alert as they latch onto receptors on the surface of nerve cells. Inside each cell a gene, perhaps newly aroused by the arriving hormone, launches into production. Chemical messengers pour into the tiny junctions between nerves. Ions flow in and out of membrane pores as signals are fired along to the hypothalamus, to a tiny cell cluster there called the paraventicular nucleus. From this cluster of cells deep in the brain, the chemical cascade fans out to rouse your body's stress response by way of your autonomic nervous system. Your adrenal glands begin churning out steroid hormones. Your blood vessels constrict. Your kidneys stop producing urine. The silent message is clear: You're dehydrated. Conserve fluids.

3   But conservation alone won't solve this problem. It's time to get the organism motivated. So the juices of subfornical cells also speed their message along other pathways to the limbic system and the cerebral cortex, centers of emotion and thought, where neuronal bureaucracies filter

and interpret the signals. Suddenly you realize, "I'm terribly thirsty! I'd die for a glass of water." And you head straight across the sand toward the nearest cantina.

4   Armed with a flood of newly discovered chemicals and the techniques of cellular and molecular biology, brain scientists are beginning to track the origins of some of our most basic emotions, drives, and behaviors from the level of genes and molecules to specific nerve circuits and brain systems. What they're finding are the biological underpinnings not only of thirst but also of hunger, pleasure, pain, stress, sexual arousal, and even learning.

5   "I think that behavior is much more hardwired, much less flexible than people thought," says Candace Pert, chief of the Section on Brain Biochemistry of the National Institute of Mental Health. We carry in our genes, she believes, in the coded instructions for making proteins, an innate personality substrate that influences the way we perceive the world and the way we think, feel, and act in it.

6   Just a few decades ago, the chemistry of the brain looked too simple and predictable to play such a role. Only three or four neurotransmitters were known, including acetylcholine and adrenaline. Their job, so it seemed, was simply to assist the electrical signals, the one-way flow of information, across the gaps, or synapses, between nerve endings.

7   But the newly revealed complexity of brain chemistry has completely revised our concept of what nerves can say and do to one another. The action at synapses now looks more like a committee meeting than a simple one-way relay of orders.

8   The nerve terminal that is doing the transmitting has receptors listening to its own messages and to chemical back talk from the receiving nerve terminal. At the same time the transmitting terminal may be intercepting chemical messages drifting into the area from the bloodstream or from neighboring nerve endings. All this feedback can change the activity of the transmitting cell as well as that of the receiving one.

9   Today we know that a nerve cell may also release two or more different transmitters at a single synapse. Or a neuron may switch transmitters. Thus a single neuron can send different messages at different times, depending on what's going on in various parts of the body.

10   To add to this complexity, the number of known neurotransmitters has jumped to more than 60, and there is no end in sight. Among these is a newly discovered class of protein messengers called peptides, first spotted serving as hormones in the gut, the pituitary, and other parts of the body.

11   A neurotransmitter may act in classic fashion to encourage or discourage the recipient cell's firing, then disappear in a matter of milliseconds. Or, in contrast, the neurotransmitter may order a long-lasting metabolic

change in the receiving cell, perhaps switching on genes that order the production of new transmitters or receptors.

12 The impact goes well beyond the single nerve cell. For instance, opiate peptides such as the endorphins can sedate, cause euphoria, or kill pain depending on which type of receptor in what brain circuit they reach. Thus no wiring diagram alone is going to tell us how nerve networks that can recognize metaphors or fall in love differ from those that can orchestrate a mean moonwalk or remember your 16th birthday. For that we also need to know what's being said and done at the chemical level.

13 Major efforts in Pert's and many other labs are directed to mapping the distribution of peptides in the brain and the location of receptors that recognize and respond to them. Neuropeptide receptors are turning out to be especially dense in the limbic system, the emotion-mediating area of our brains, and in structures that filter information from our senses or set thresholds for sexual arousal or pain.

14 Pert says there is clear evidence that most, if not all, neuropeptides can alter our behavior or our mood. The strongest case for these mood-altering effects can be made for neuropeptides that are the brain's own versions of psychoactive drugs such as morphine, Valium, and PCP.

15 In fact, all drugs now used to treat mental illness function either by mimicking or blocking the action of natural transmitters. Working to define the transmitter and receptor systems that underlie specific mood states and drives should help in designing new drugs to treat disorders like depression, schizophrenia, drug addiction, and obesity. To Pert, the research also suggests that we have within us the capacity to alter our own physiology without drugs. "The study of emotions," she says, "is very ambitious and exciting. If we figure them out, we figure ourselves out."

16 Pert and immunologist Michael Ruff, also at the NIMH, recently reported finding receptors for Valium on cells of the human immune system, which defends against infectious disease and cancer. They speculate that this link between an antianxiety substance in the brain and the immune system will provide clues to psychosomatic illness and the way our moods affect our physical health.

17 Such disclosures are tantalizing, but the crucial next step is to find out just how neuropeptides interact in specific nerve networks to evoke distinct moods or behaviors. That's a tough order because the human brain is a dense thicket of hundreds of billions of nerve cells, each capable of forming anywhere from 1,000 to 500,000 synapses. At any given time, a neuron is talking with dozens to thousands of other neurons at synapses along its vast network of branches. It must compile and average out all the incoming signals before it decides whether to fire and at what rate and what neurotransmitter to release.

18   But before researchers can begin to work out circuitry and chemistry in useful detail, they must have some idea where to look in the vast black box of the brain. The search for the molecular origins of behavior in creatures with simpler nervous systems is yielding some tantalizing results. Molecular biologists working with the sea snail *Aplysia*, for example, have already succeeded in linking certain features of the animal's reproductive behavior directly to the activities of specific genes and the peptides they encode.

19   The life of this undistinguished slug is largely devoted to eating and reproducing. The latter behavior is a fixed-action pattern, an innate ritual that's not open to change or learning. Scientists had already isolated a peptide called egg-laying hormone, ELH, that when injected, triggers parts of this ritual. Their next goal was to use genetic engineering techniques to isolate the gene that encodes this behavior-provoking substance, then find out exactly what nerve circuits ELH activates to evoke behavior.

20   Richard Axel at Columbia University College of Physicians and Surgeons cloned the ELH gene and got a surprise. The gene's DNA sequence actually codes not just for the single peptide he was seeking but for a much larger polypeptide, which can be chopped into smaller segments—ELH and at least five other peptides. (Many peptides in the human body seem to be cut in the same way from polypeptides.)

21   This raised a fascinating possibility. Perhaps all the behaviors in the innate egg-laying ritual, not just the few triggered by ELH, are orchestrated by the peptide products of a single gene. Axel's group and researchers at Stanford and the University of California, San Francisco, have found three active peptides made by this gene and have tied them directly to two pieces of the ritual.

22   The polypeptide containing ELH is produced in the bag cells, two clusters of nerve cells that sit atop one of the snail's major nerve bundles. When the bag cells fire, they release at least three peptides cut from the polypeptide: One, ELH, travels via the bloodstream to excite the muscles of the animal's reproductive duct, making them contract and extrude the egg string. A second peptide stimulates the bag cell that produced it, keeping it excited so that it continues to fire and release peptides. Both ELH and the third active peptide identified so far also excite other nearby nerve cells, causing them to pour out a different array of peptides.

23   So the complexity continues. Cloning of the DNA from this newest set of neurons in the chain has turned up even more polypeptide genes that seem to code for this secondary cascade of neuropeptides.

24   These peptides may be responsible for completing the ritual: *Aplysia* stops walking and eating, its heart and respiratory rates rise, it grabs the egg string in its mouth and begins waving its head back and forth; it pulls the string out of its duct and winds it up; finally it sticks the whole thing to a rock.

25   "Our next task is to figure out, as we did in ELH, which of the peptides are indeed released and what their biological activity is," Axel says. "We're not there yet." To find out what each peptide does, he must stick microscopic electrodes into the neurons in *Aplysia's* well-mapped neural circuits, drop a peptide on the neuron, and record whether the cell fires or ceases firing. Working on live animals, he hopes to discover whether the peptide causes the head to wave, for example, or the heart to race.

26   Few of our behaviors are likely to be as closely orchestrated by our genes, as inaccessible to learning and conscious control, as *Aplysia's* egg-laying ritual. And yet humans in every culture share a repertoire of innate and stereotyped emotional expressions—smiles, frowns, tears, laughter (although the provocations shift with culture and learning). Psychologists such as Paul Ekman at the University of California, San Francisco, are exploring the possibility that these largely involuntary facial movements actually spark changes in neurons that alter our moods, heart rate, and other body operations.

27   We also know of at least one example in mammals where the injection of a substance triggers a stereotyped response, just as the injection of ELH provokes a snail. That substance, as we saw in the opening scenario, is angiotensin. "If you inject angiotensin, people actually get the sensation of thirst," says Larry Swanson, a neurobiologist at the Salk Institute. "I think it's really the first example of a real behavior with cognitive parts where we know what triggers it. We've actually got a hormone."

28   Researchers in England discovered in the 1960s that in a dehydrated animal the liver releases into the bloodstream a polypeptide that's cut up to produce the peptide hormone angiotensin. That hormone constricts blood vessels to keep fluid loss from lowering blood pressure. It halts urine production. It causes thirst. To cause this sensation, of course, it must act on the brain.

29   "So the next question was, Exactly where does it act in the brain?" Swanson says. His lab and others recently answered that question by tracking it to the subfornical organ (SFO) above the hypothalamus. Blood vessels in this tiny cluster lack the special membrane qualities that keep neuropeptides from entering most brain cells. When you infuse angiotensin directly into the SFO, the brain responds just as it would to actual fluid loss. "I think it's the best example of getting a foothold on some actual circuits in the brain that underlie the coordination of the visceral response and the behavioral response," Swanson says.

30   One of those circuits, a particularly interesting one, involves the stress response centered in the paraventricular nucleus (PVN) of the hypothalamus. There a cluster of cells produces corticotropin-releasing factor (CRF), the peptide the brain uses to launch the classic hormone cascade of stress—the release of pituitary hormones that cause the adre-

nal gland to pour out steroid hormones. Your heart races, you breathe harder, your stomach tightens, you are infused with nervous energy. When the steroid hormones reach a certain level in the blood, they tell the brain to stop the chain of command that's releasing them—a classic negative-feedback regulatory system.

31   When Swanson's team removed the adrenal glands from rats, eliminating the steroid hormones and thus the negative-feedback response, the PVN did as expected. It stepped up the stress alert to make the pituitary increase hormone release. But it did this in an unexpected way: It not only stepped up CRF production but also began making two new peptide hormones, vasopressin and angiotensin, both already known to stimulate pituitary hormone release. Swanson believes the steroid hormones act directly on the genes in the paraventricular nucleus nerve cells to speed the production of pituitary hormones.

32   Molecular biologists collaborating with Swanson, Michael Rosenfeld of the University of California, San Diego, and Ronald Evans of Salk, are transplanting synthetic genes into mice to study how peptides and steroid hormones influence the genes inside the nuclei of nerve cells.

33   The most intriguing possibility opened up by this work is that the brain systems underlying some of our most basic moods, drives, and behaviors don't always respond the same way to the same situation. Their response—and perhaps your anxiety level or blood pressure—will depend on your hormonal state. The innate underpinnings of personality remain, but the thresholds for triggering pain, pleasure, depression, anger, or even memory are reset by chemistry.

34   "Instead of thinking of nerve circuits as fixed anatomical circuits that always do pretty much the same thing, there's a metabolic or biochemical plasticity, a real chemical dynamic in brain circuits that is probably different to some extent in different people," Swanson says. "There are CRF cells in other parts of the brain, like the cortex and the limbic system that are thought to be involved with cognition and motivation and to affect feelings and moods." The emotional centers of the brain have circuits that talk directly to the PVN, providing a way for anxiety, worry, and thought to provoke changes in blood pressure and other body systems.

35   "So now, if you take chronic stress—putting someone under stress for weeks or months where there are chronically high levels of steroid hormones in the blood—the person may be exposed to the same stimuli as before, but now since the biochemistry of this circuitry has changed somewhat, they're going to start at least physiologically responding differently," Swanson says. And they begin to pour out more or less of various neurotransmitters.

36   "Now the big question is, you take two groups of people and subject them to the same chronic stress, and some people thrive and some peo-

ple can't take it," Swanson says. "We really would like to know if there's something different about the biochemistry in the limbic and the hypothalamic circuits in people that can't handle stress."

37   Perhaps some individuals are born with genetic quirks that affect the biochemistry of these circuits and leave them innately predisposed to depression, severe anxiety, ulcers, and hypertension when they encounter pressures or setbacks. By defining the links between genes, brain chemistry, and behavior, we may learn ways to intervene and protect ourselves from stress.

38   This research has also yielded clues to the long-suspected link between stress and the biochemical events in the brain that underlie learning and memory. The steroid hormones that come into play when we encounter stress can also alter the activities of nerve cells in the hippocampus, a brain region known to play an important part in learning and memory, says Bruce McEwen of Rockefeller University. These cells are loaded with steroid hormone receptors, and prolonged stress exposes the receptors to steroids, actually killing some of those cells and destroying a feedback circuit that normally helps turn off the stress system.

39   But stress may in fact enhance some types of learning. It's well known that we learn best when we're alert and attentive and somewhat aroused by the experience or lesson. And when we're severely aroused—horrified, frightened, grief-stricken—the experiences are often carved indelibly into our brains.

40   "If you stop and think about what you really remember—when your mother died, for instance—it's associated with just a tremendous emotional response at the same time," Swanson says. "That's something that only happens to you once, but you'll remember it forever. And there's a lot of people who think this tremendous surge of steroid hormones feeds back on the hippocampus and in this way jacks up the memory formation process."

41   Exactly how this might happen, no one knows. But several stress-related peptides do seem to be candidates for a part in the system. In rats, infusions of the pituitary hormone adrenocorticotropic hormone (ACTH) will enhance certain types of learning. In humans, Dutch researchers determined years ago that a nasal spray of vasopressin seems to improve performance on long-term memory tests.

42   These are tantalizing leads to follow. But before the molecular mechanisms of learning and memory can be worked out in detail, researchers must known if there are different kinds of learning and memory and where to look for their traces in the vast circuitry of the brain.

43   Working separately, Mortimer Mishkin of the National Institute of Mental Health and Larry Squire of the University of California, San Diego and the Veterans Administration Medical Center have already identified two distinct types of memory: Skill or procedural memory

stores habits or "how to" functions and conditioned reflexes. Fact or declarative memory stores faces, dates, numbers, and the sorts of things you usually say after, "I remember. . . ." (It's this second type that fuels our thought, colors our world view, and contributes to our sense of self.)

44   Skill or reflex memory has been easier to track to the molecular level since virtually all organisms share some capacity for it. In several instances stored memory traces in rabbits have been tracked to a speck of tissue in the cerebellum, a brain region that controls motor functions. The memories are conditioned responses, such as an eyeblink reflex. When Stanford neurophysiologist Richard Thompson destroys that tiny bit of brain matter, his trained rabbits no longer respond on cue, even though they're still perfectly able to blink their eyes.

45   Two research teams working on conditioned reflexes in the marine snails *Aplysia* and *Hermissenda* have already proposed cellular mechanisms that might explain this type of memory. While *Aplysia* can't change its egg-laying ritual, it can learn to alter some of its other behaviors. In both snails, researchers have found that, after training, there are membrane changes in nerve cells that leave the neurons more excitable or primed to fire with less provocation the next time around.

46   Such mechanisms may explain the short-term storage of conditioned responses, even in humans, but they're not likely to explain our unique ability for long-term factual memory: how you remember your favorite teacher's face and cheery voice and the multiplication tables she taught you 40 years ago.

47   Eric Kandel and James Schwartz at Columbia have suggested that this second type of memory may require the enhancement or repression of the activity of specific genes, which can make new proteins that change the functioning of the cell.

48   But other scientists believe that if, as we suspect, each cell with its perhaps 500,000 synapses participates in the storage of many memories, a genetic change is too global and crude a way to store all the bits of factual information we pack into our cortex in a lifetime.

49   "How can you change synapse number 9,742 and at the same time synapse number 62,121 without changing any of the others if you're turning on genes?" asks Gary Lynch of the University of California, Irvine.

50   Without waiting for someone to pinpoint the trace of a stored factual memory in the brain, Lynch has proposed a mechanism for permanent changes at the synaptic level that he believes could underlie this type of learning.

51   Bursts of high-frequency electrical stimulation can cause some nerve cells in the cortex and hippocampus to remain more responsive to this stimulation for weeks or even months. The phenomenon is called long-term potentiation (LTP), and its involvement in memory has long been

suspected. Lynch theorizes that during LTP, an enzyme called calpain is activated at the excited synapse. Calpain attacks the protein skeleton that shapes the nerve cell membrane, exposing hidden receptors at the synapse, reshaping the branches of the cell, and even creating new synapses.

52   The mechanism could explain the findings of University of Illinois neurobiologist William Greenough, who's shown that when rats learn, their nerve cells sprout more branches and form new synapses. Lynch has tested his mechanism by perfusing the brains of rats with a substance that blocks calpain. Just as he predicted, this impairs the rodents' ability to learn cognitive tasks. The rats are still able to learn new conditioned reflexes, however.

53   "The next stage for the field is to say, 'Okay, now you've got this [possible mechanism]. Put it in a circuit and let's see what kind of memory comes out,' " Lynch says. "Let's go now to the next level of analysis, which is the circuits and the systems level.

54   "In the next 20 years we will no longer be dodging human cognitive operations," Lynch predicts. "We went into classical conditioning because that's what we could study. Okay. But the moment is on us now, I think, where we will no longer be avoiding the properties like human associative memory."

55   He's not alone in his prediction. "I think the biggest area of challenge in neuroscience in general is to integrate the behavioral and psychological with these incredible new discoveries in the biochemical area," Pert says. "I'm no longer interested in studying merely the brain. I'm now ready to study the mind. And I think it's now possible to do."

Content Questions

1. Why is a neurotransmitter's function important?
2. What limits the search for the molecular origins of behavior?
3. What insights into human behavior has the sea snail *Aplysia* shown researchers?
4. Why do some scientists believe that brain systems don't always respond to the same situation in the same way?
5. What proof do researchers present that typical human behaviors can be triggered by genes?

Questions on Presentation

1. Why does Baskin begin the essay by asking the reader to imagine a pleasant situation?

2. Gould generally summarizes the ideas of others while Baskin frequently quotes scientists directly. Where does Baskin use these quotes? Why?
3. How would you characterize Baskin's audience? Why?
4. Is Baskin's use of the committee meeting simile in paragraph 7 effective? Why?
5. Define hypothalamus (2), substrate (5), neurotransmitter (10), limbic (13), evoke (19), and infuse (29).

Can a Bee Behave Intelligently?

James L. Gould and Carol G. Gould

Yale Professor James L. Gould (b. 1931) received his degrees from the California Institute of Technology and Rockefeller University in ethology (the scientific study of animal behavior). He and his coauthor, research associate Carol G. Gould, are biologists at Princeton University where their research on animal behavior includes investigations of how honeybees communicate and learn. The Goulds see similarities between animal learning and orientation behavior and the same phenomena in humans. The following essay, first published in *The New Scientist*, describes the governing principles of bees' behavior, discriminates between behavior and learning, and proposes a definition for intelligence.

1   When a foraging honey bee finds a new source of nectar or pollen, she returns to the hive to recruit help. She performs a ritualised dance that tells the other bees the distance, direction, and quality of the food. They "memorise" the information she supplies, process it somehow, and then, compensating for crosswinds and the movement of the Sun, fly out on their own directly to the flower patch. This behaviour looks on the surface like a complex communication system, and the participants seem to be acting at least intelligently, even rationally. The more we learn about bees' capabilities, though, the more glaring their limitations become, and the question of what constitutes intelligence emerges as a central issue in understanding behaviour.

2   Largely as a result of Donald Griffin's book *The Question of Animal Awareness* (Rockefeller UP, 2nd ed 1981), ethologists have begun to re-examine the issue of animal intellect and to ask whether the organisms they study are, as we presume ourselves to be, something more than mere mindless circuitry. But the mind is, by nature, a private organ. How are we to judge from an animal's overt behaviour whether we are

observing a well-oiled machine or a creature with some degree of intelligence and creativity? Particularly with insects, whose chitinous exoskeletons make it difficult to consider them in anthropomorphic terms, how are we to discover the extent to which they might be acting intelligently?

3   Several lines of evidence for insect intelligence have come to the fore, but a little careful thinking, observation, and experimentation indicate that most of these criteria are untrustworthy. One intuitively powerful argument, for instance, is that since animals regularly face problems and solve them in sensible ways, they must have some intellectual grasp of the problem. When a honey bee, for instance, encounters a dead bee in the hive, it very properly tosses it out of the colony. But experience tells us that adaptive behaviour most often reflects the intelligence of evolution rather than that of the animals it has so carefully programmed. Bees recognise their dead colleagues by means of a "sign stimulus"—a single key feature of an object which is taken to represent the entire object. In this case a special "death odour", possibly oleic acid, releases the act of removal. So mindless is the wiring of this sensible hygienic behaviour that a drop of oleic acid on an otherwise innocuous piece of wood or even on a live bee results in the removal of the offending object. The sight of one bee carrying out a struggling sister or even the queen should convince us that behaviour can seem intelligent in its normal context without any need for the intellectual participation of the actors.

4   A second criterion frequently suggested is that the very regularity and invariability of such robot-like behaviour may be a guide to what behaviour is performed automatically and without the need for thinking. As we all know from personal experience, intellect will often come up with two very different solutions to the same problem in two different individuals, or even in the same individual on two different occasions. An automatic computer would come up with one "best" answer. When the 19th-century French naturalist Jean Henri Fabre interfered with the prey-capture ritual of a cricket-hunting wasp by moving its paralysed victim, he stumbled upon some of the wiring that runs the wasp's routine. The wasp, whose behaviour appears eccentric but intelligent, invariably leaves the cricket she has caught lying on its back, its antennae just touching the tunnel entrance, while she inspects her burrow. Each time Fabre moved it even slightly away from the entrance, the re-emerging wasp insisted on repositioning the cricket precisely, and inspecting the tunnel again. Fabre continued this trivial alteration 40 times and the wasp, locked in a behavioural "do-loop", never thought to skip an obviously pointless step in her program. Clearly the wasp is a machine in this context, entirely inflexible in her behaviour.

5   The remarkable persistence of the wasp's performance serves also to remind us that most other animals have contingency plans to extricate

them from such behavioural *culs-de-sac*. By far the most common escape mechanism for organisms ranging from bacteria to human beings is "habituation", a kind of behavioural boredom by which an animal becomes less responsive as it encounters the same stimulus repeatedly. But habituation and other such escape strategies are not the result of any active intellect. They are merely sophisticated programming ploys, and in the sea slug *Aplysia*, the neural and biochemical bases of the machinery are pretty well understood. The mindlessness of this acquired behavioural numbness is illustrated by the contrary phenomenon of sensitisation: almost any irrelevant but novel stimulus can instantly destroy habitation's insensitivity.

6   Other sorts of seemingly intelligent behavioural variability, though, cannot be accounted for either by "noise" in the computer or by habituation. Honey bees, for example, show spontaneous preferences for certain colours and shapes of artificial flowers, with many-petalled purple flowers being the most attractive to the apian mind. This display of aesthetic preference is not absolute, but probabilistic: given a choice between two colours that we know from learning experiments they can distinguish reliably—purple and blue, for example—the bees will choose their favourite, purple, only 70 per cent of the time rather than 100 per cent. Similarly, in a conflict an animal will sometimes fight and sometimes flee. Even in experiments in which care has been taken to factor out the role of immediate past experience, this sort of predictable variability persists.

7   Can the perplexing unreliability of animal behaviour be taken as evidence for something more (or perhaps less) than machinery making decisions? Probably not. Game theory demonstrates that it is usually most adaptive to be variable or unpredictable, so long as evolution or personal experience takes care to set the odds appropriately. Though flowers may more often be purple than blue, it makes sense to try blue-coloured objects from time to time rather than to concentrate exclusively on purple. Even this sort of quasi-aesthetic "decision" makes enough evolutionary sense that there is a good chance that it results from programming rather than intelligence; and in most carefully studied cases it is clear that variability *is* innate.

8   But though a great deal may be programmed into animals, there must surely be a limit to the complexity possible. There must be a point beyond which no set of built-in computer-like elements can suffice to account for an animal's apparent grasp of its situation, particularly in the face of variable or unpredictable environmental contingencies. The difficulty in drawing this intellectual line, however, is daunting. Some of the most impressively complex examples of behaviour we see are known to be wholly innate. The intricate knot-tying nest building of weaver birds is a case in point, but given the undoubtedly limited intellectual ability of the performer surely the construction of orb webs is

even more impressive. In total darkness, without prior experience, and with the location of potential anchor points for the support structure unpredictable, a mere spider sets about constructing a precise and complex network of several different kinds of threads held together with hundreds of precisely placed "welds". It automatically repairs even damage that occurs during construction. All this is accomplished through one master program and several subroutines, and requires no conscious grasp of the problem.

9   The use of subroutines to deal with the unpredictable is especially obvious in navigation. Honey bees, for example, regularly use the Sun as their compass, compensating for its changing azimuth as it moves from east to west. This is a formidable task even for a human navigator, but as we have found out in the past few years, the bees' trigonometric adjustments are perfectly mindless, depending only on a memory of the Sun's azimuth relative to the bee's goal on the previous trip (or day) and an extrapolation of the Sun's current rate of azimuth movement. The strategy is innate, though the program must include steps for measuring the relevant variables when necessary. Bees recognise the Sun by an equally innate criterion—its low ratio of ultraviolet to visible light—so that a dim, 10 degree, triangular, highly polarised, green object against a dark background is just as acceptable as the actual, intensely bright ½ degree, circular, unpolarised white Sun which the bees see almost every day in the normal sky.

10   When the Sun is invisible (obscured perhaps by a cloud, a landmark, or the horizon) the bee's whole Sun-centred system is discarded in favour of a backup system—a separate navigational subroutine—based on the patterns of polarised light generated in the sky by the scattering of sunlight. This analysis itself is composed of a primary and backup system, and uses sign stimuli and very simple processing. When the polarisation is unavailable as well (as on overcast days, for example), bees fall back on yet a third system, based on landmarks, and there is no reason to suppose we have exhausted the set of fail-safe plans built into bees. The apparent complexity of the formidable navigational behaviour that many insects display is, in fact, based on the interplay of groups of subroutines which are themselves quite simple. They depend as a rule on the same sorts of schematic stimulus-recognition systems and simple processing seen in less elaborate behaviour. Since a staggering degree of behavioural complexity can be generated by a set of individually simple subroutines, mere complexity of behaviour cannot be in itself a trustworthy guide to intelligence.

Does Learning Involve Intelligence?

11   Another commonly accepted indication of intelligence is the way animals deal with the unpredictable contingencies of their world through

learning; and it is here that our intuition tells us that we must be dealing with something very like intellect. After all, learning suggests to most of us some degree of understanding, some conscious comprehension of the problem to be solved. Alas, headless flies can learn to hold their legs in a particular position to avoid a shock, and even solve the problem faster than those still encumbered with brains.

12   Learning theory has traditionally recognised two general sorts of learning: associative learning (also known as classical or Pavlovian conditioning) and trial-and-error learning (also known as operant or Skinnerian conditioning). Associative learning is the process by which an animal comes to replace an innately recognised cue—the sign stimulus—with another cue or set of cues. It is nature's version of inductive reasoning: animals learn only cues which tend to *predict* the imminent arrival of something desirable, like food, and the reliability of the new cue does not need to be by any means perfect. Trial-and-error learning involves learning to perform a novel motor behaviour, which is used to solve a problem posed by nature. Animals discover by experimentation what works and what does not, and so experience shapes the behaviour. This process is in many ways analogous to deductive reasoning.

13   To understand the role of inductive and deductive learning in the lives of animals and how these processes relate to the issue of intelligence, let us look at how they work in honey bees. As we shall see, there is much in the organisation of bee learning that suggests the gears and wheels of an automatic pilot rather than any aware intelligence. When a honey bee discovers a flower, for example, she sets in motion a learning sequence which seems utterly mechanical in nature. A forager learns many things about a food source that aid her in the future, including its colour, shape, odour, location, nearby landmarks, time of nectar production, how to approach, land, enter, and reach the nectar, and so on. Colour learning, for instance, has all the marks of associative learning: bees have an innate program which recognises flowers by their dark centres and light petals (as seen in ultraviolet light—these markings are usually invisible to our eyes). After it has served its purpose, though, this sign stimulus is replaced by associative learning with a far more detailed picture of the flower. Bees learn colour only in the final three seconds as they land: the colour visible to the bee before the landing sequence, the colours it sees while standing on the flower to feed and while circling the blossom before flying off, simply never register. Experimenters can change them at will and the bee will never be fooled. A naive bee *carried* to the feeder from the hive and placed on the food source will circle repeatedly after taking on a load of sugar water as if "studying" the source, and yet when she returns a few minutes later she will be unable to choose the correct feeder colour. And yet, so mechanical is this learning routine that if we interrupt such a bee while she is feeding so she must take off and land again of her own accord, that landing permits her

to choose the correct feeder colour on her next visit. Similarly, bees learn landmarks after taking off: a recruit who arrived and fed at the feeder, but was transported back to the hive while feeding, returned without the slightest memory of the landmarks she must certainly have seen on her arrival.

Desirable Imperfection

14   Other aspects of the associative component of flower learning seem equally curious. Although a bee learns a flower's odour almost perfectly in one visit, she must make several trips to learn its colour with precision; and even then a bee never chooses the correct colour 100 per cent of the time. It learns shape less quickly, and time of day more slowly still. It is as though perfection, clearly possible in other contexts, is not in this case desirable. It appears, in fact, that the speed and reliability of a bee's flower memory at least roughly corresponds to the degree of variability it is likely to encounter among flowers of the same species in nature (including variation from day to day of an individual blossom). In fact, the rate at which a bee learns each component differs dramatically between various geographic races of honey bee, strongly implicating a genetic basis for the different learning curves.

15   Once a bee has learned how to recognise a particular kind of flower and when and where to find it, it is as though the information is stored in the manner of an appointment book. As a result, changing any component of the set—the odour, say, which is learned to virtual perfection after one visit—forces the bees to relearn painstakingly all the other pieces of information at their characteristic (slower) rates even though they have not changed. So, logical and impressive as the associate flower learning of honey bees seems, these hard-working insects appear simply to be well-programmed learning machines, attending only to the cues deemed salient by evolution (and then only in well-defined contexts and often during precise critical periods)—and then filing the information thus obtained in pre-existing arrays. Nothing in this behaviour, wonderful as it is, suggests any true flexibility or awareness. Nor is the situation any different when we look at the trial-and-error component of the behaviour by which bees learn to harvest flower species efficiently.

16   We can see that the widespread strategy of programmed learning is the means by which the genes tell their dim-witted couriers when and what to learn (how else could an insect reason it out?) and then what to do with the knowledge thus obtained. There are, however, cases of apparently self-directed learning that may admit of another explanation. Indeed, one of the main factors leading to the demise of classical behaviourism was the discovery that animals can learn a motor behaviour—which way to run in a maze to get some food—without the need for either associative learning or overt trial-and-error experimentation.

A rat, for instance, carried passively to each of two "goal boxes" at opposite ends of a runway and shown that one contains food and the other does not will, when released, run unerringly to the box with food. This phenomenon, which we call "cognitive trial-and-error", requires a deductive process to go on inside the mind of the animal without its actually *trying* different behaviours. The animal, be it the rat in its maze or a chimpanzee gazing from a group of boxes to a clump of bananas hung just out of reach overhead, must reason out a course of action in its *mind*. Here is something that seems very like intelligence, and we must ask whether it is really that, or merely another clever but mechanical programming finesse that we do not yet see.

17   There are among honey bees three reported examples that appear at first glance to qualify as cognitive trial-and-error. One instance revolves around their avoidance of alfalfa (lucerne). These flowers possess spring-loaded anthers that give honey bees a rough blow when they enter. Although bumble bees (which evolved pollinating alfalfa) do not seem to mind, honey bees, once so treated, avoid alfalfa religiously. Placed in the middle of a field of alfalfa, foraging bees will fly tremendous distances to find alternative sources of food. Modern agricultural practices and the finite flight range of honey bees, however, often bring bees to a grim choice between foraging on alfalfa or starving.

18   In the face of potential starvation, honey bees finally begin foraging on alfalfa, but they learn to avoid being clubbed. Some bees come to recognise tripped from untripped flowers and frequent only the former, while others learn to chew a hole in the side of the flower so as to rob untripped blossoms without ever venturing inside. Who has analysed and solved this problem—evolution, or the bees themselves? It may be that both cases are standard, pre-wired back-up ploys: differentiating tripped from untripped flowers could simply be a far more precise use of the associative learning program, while chewing through may be a strategy normally held in reserve for robbing flowers too small to enter.

Buzzing with Anticipation

19   Another slightly eerie case is not easy to dismiss. During training to an artificial food source, there comes a point at which at least some of the bees begin to "catch on" that the experimenter is systematically moving the food further and further away. The pioneer of bee research Karl von Frisch recalls (and we have observed) instances in which the trained foragers began to *anticipate* subsequent moves and to wait for the feeder at the presumptive new location. This seems an impressive intellectual feat. It is not easy to imagine anything in the behaviour of natural flowers for which evolution could conceivably have needed to program bees to anticipate regular changes in distance.

20   Along the same lines, we have on several occasions during experi-

ments on bee navigation seen behaviour that appears to reflect an ability to form what experimental psychologists refer to as a "cognitive map". The classic example of this phenomenon is the ability of a rat in an eight-arm maze to explore each arm in a random order without inspecting any arm twice. This ability to form a mental map and then formulate behaviour (perhaps by imagining various alternatives scenarios) seems very like the ability of chimpanzees to imagine the solution to the hanging-banana problem by stacking the boxes in their minds before performing the behaviour for real, and of course the same process goes on in our own minds all the time.

21   The first hint of such an ability in bees came years ago when von Frisch discovered that bees that had flown an indirect route to a food source were nevertheless able to indicate by their famous communication dances the straightline direction to the food. By itself, it is easy to interpret this ability as some sort of mindless, automatic exercise in trigonometry. Three years ago we trained foragers along a lake and tricked them into dancing to indicate to potential recruit bees in the hive that the food was in the middle of the lake. Recruits refused to search for these food sources, even when we put a food source in a boat in the lake at the indicated spot. At first we thought that the foragers might simply be suffering from some sort of apian hydrophobia, but when we increased the distance of the feeding station so that the dances indicated the far side of the lake, recruits turned up in great numbers. Apparently they "knew" how wide the lake was, and so were able to distinguish between sources allegedly in the lake and sources on the shore. We see no way to account for this behaviour on the basis of either associative or trial-and-error learning. This ability is accounted for most simply if we assume that the recruits have mental maps of the surroundings on which they somehow "place" the spots indicated by the dances.

22   This interpretation is further reinforced by another observation. While exploring the question of whether bees can use information about direction gathered on the flight back from the food, we transported foragers caught as they were leaving the hive for natural resources to an artificial feeder in the middle of a large car park hundreds of metres from the hive. After being allowed to feed, the majority of foragers circled the feeder and, in many cases, departed directly for the hive, which was out of sight. Many of the young bees, however, circled helplessly and never got home. When the successful foragers arrived at the hive, many danced to indicate the car park. Now for a bee to know the location of a barren car park which had certainly not been on their list of flower sites, it seems most reasonable to suppose that they were able to "place" it on some sort of internal map and then work out the direction home. That only older (and presumably more experienced) bees were successful at this task is consistent with this interpretation.

23   Taking these cases at face value, does the apparent ability to make and use maps provide convincing evidence of active intelligence? And if so, why are bees so thoroughly mindless in other contexts? The second question is easier to speculate on than the first. Intuitively it seems reasonable to suppose that if we were designing an animal, we would "hard-wire" as much of the behaviour as possible. Where there is a best way of doing something, or finding out how to do something, there seems little point in forcing an animal into the time-consuming, error-prone, and potentially fatal route of trial-and-error learning. But where explicit programming will not serve, it seems equally reasonable to direct an organism to fall back on "thinking", particularly when the solution to a problem can then, as in the case of imprinting, be wired into the system for later service.

24   It must be said that much of human behaviour seems to fall into this neurologically economical pattern: we work hard to master a problem, then turn the solution into a mindless, rote unit of behaviour. Difficult problems like learning to type, ride a bicycle, tie shoes, or knit seem almost impossible at first, but once learned become as matter-of-fact as breathing or walking.

Are Humans Machines Too?

25   But whether cognitive trial-and-error qualifies as intelligence is more difficult. On the one hand we can imagine how we might go about pre-wiring a Cartesian map, and how we could then encode the instructions by which the information to fill the map should be gathered, stored, and used. On the other hand, there is increasing evidence that many of the intellectual feats of our own species—language acquisition, Aristotelian logic, categorisation, pattern recognition, and the like—are themselves based on pre-existing wiring and storage. The more we learn about the brain, the more clearly we see how its specialised wiring affects what we are. It may be that the question is one of degree: to what extent is a pocket calculator "intelligent"? Does a TI-59 with its hardwired navigation module installed—a good approximation to a small part of a honey bee brain—qualify? What about a chess-playing machine, programmed to examine the board and then "imagine" thousands of possible moves and evaluate them in relation to each other? Or is it the provision for automatic self-programming such as we see when a flower trains a bee to exploit it that is intelligence?

26   The more we look at the behaviour of insects, birds, mammals, and man, the more we see a continuum of complexity rather than any difference in kind that might separate the intellectual Valhalla of our species from the apparently mindless computations of insects. We see the same biochemical processes, the same use of sign stimuli and programmed learning, identical strategies of information processing and storage, the

same potential for well-defined cognitive thinking, but very different storage and sorting capacities and, most of all, very different intellectual needs imposed by each species' niche. In short, the intelligence of insects, like that of our species, seems to be more than anything else the intelligence of evolutionary necessity.

Content Questions

1. Why do the authors feel that there must be some intelligent behavior in animals?
2. What are the Goulds' criteria for intelligence?
3. What difference is there between intelligence and the intelligence of evolution?
4. What types of behavior define habituation?
5. What is the difference between associative learning and trial-and-error learning?
6. What evidence do the authors present for "cognitive maps"?

Questions on Presentation

1. How successful are the Goulds in demonstrating the untrustworthiness of various "lines of evidence for insect intelligence"? What accounts for that success or lack of success?
2. The Goulds compare some insect behavior to a computer program. Is this comparison convincing?
3. Is the audience the Goulds address the same as Baskin's?
4. Why do the authors use the allusion to Valhalla in paragraph 26?
5. Most of the paragraphs in this essay are long and detailed and contain a great deal of information. Is this appropriate to the subject matter? To the audience?

What Science Can Learn from Science Frauds

Nicolas Wade

Nicholas Wade (b. 1942) was born in England but has lived in the United States since 1970. He was educated at King's College, Cambridge, and later became the deputy editor and Washington correspondent for *Nature* magazine. He then left *Nature* to become a staff writer for *Science* and an editorial writer for *The New York Times*. In books such as *The Nobel Duel* (1981) and *Betrayers of the Truth: Fraud and Deceit in the Halls of Science* (1983 with William Broad), Wade exposes the human fallibility of scientists, and chronicles the competition among scientists that may not be beneficial. Wade presents often unflattering descriptions of scientists and criticizes scientists for allowing ego, competitiveness, and the search for professional prestige to take priority over science. In this selection, adapted from one that appeared in *The New Scientist,* Wade turns his attention to science frauds, showing how they are unearthed and why they are of value to both science and the general public.

1   The scientific enterprise in Europe and the United States has been shaken by several spectacular cases of scientific fraud. During the first half of this year,[1] cases have been bubbling up at the rate of about one a month. Harvard and Yale seem as well represented as lesser institutions. Does this spate of fraud matter?

2   The response of some scientific spokesmen is generally no; a sensible answer is yes. Even if all fraud were of negligible importance, which is not the case, any public relations consultant can explain why one case a month is a disaster for the public image of science.

3   The public believes what it has so often been told, that science is a "self-correcting system." Since any fraud is bound to be detected, goes this comforting thesis, only a madman would attempt it. Therefore, by definition, any fraud that does occur is the work of unhinged minds, and explanation must be sought in individual psychopathology, not in the institutions of science.

4   When my colleague William Broad and I were both reporters on *Science* magazine, the organ of the American Association for the Advancement of Science, we investigated several cases of scientific fraud. At first we took the conventional explanation for granted. But as we looked at the details of each case, we began to notice a surprising and consistent pattern.

5   In none of the cases we examined had the "self-correcting mechanisms" of science brought the fraud to light. It was the envy or suspicions of close colleagues, often combined with egregious carelessness or arrogance on the part of the forger, that led to the detection of fraud. The vaunted self-correcting mechanisms came into play only in confirming the fraud already detected.

6   The failure of the checking mechanisms to detect fraud raises issues that go far beyond the problem of fraud itself. The checking mechanisms, after all, are reponsible for maintaining the intellectual integrity of science. It is they that reject shoddy and careless articles, and place the seal of approval on work that is the certified product of a community of scholars. But if the checking mechanisms cannot detect deliber-

ate error, how can they be relied upon to pick up the common but insidious pitfalls of self-deception and unconscious error? And if they regularly fail to detect even gross error, whether knowingly or unconsciously committed, how well do they perform their main task of quality control?

7   Fraud thus raises questions that go beyond mere trickery, to the philosophy and sociology of science. Just as physiologists have learned about the normal working of the body from study of its pathology, so fraud reveals much about the nature of science. In our book *Betrayers of the Truth* (Century Press, London, 1983), William Broad and I have tried to explore these wider issues from the perspective of scientific fraud.

8   The self-correcting system of science has three components. First is peer review, the committees of outside scientists that advise the government on the merit of their colleagues' applications for research funds. Next come the referees, consulted by the journal editor to whom a researcher sends his results for publication. The third, and theoretically most thorough, test is replication: once an experiment is published, other scientists may try to replicate it.

9   The case of John Long, a researcher who resigned from the Massachusetts General Hospital in 1980, exhibits the specific failure of all three mechanisms to detect gross error. Long's research career was based on studying test-tube cultures of cells taken from patients with Hodgkin's disease, an endeavour for which he was awarded $759,000 of public monies. To tell the end of the story first, a suspicious colleague discovered fraud by inspecting Long's laboratory notebooks, and another associate then established to general amazement that the test-tube cultures were not of Hodgkin's disease. Indeed, the owner of the cells was not even human, but a northern Colombian brown-footed owl monkey.

10   Probably without Long's knowledge, his cultures of Hodgkin's disease cells were at some stage contaminated and overgrown by the monkey cells. Cell contamination is a widely feared and advertised problem in biological research. Yet peer review committees twice ignored the warning signal and awarded him large research grants.

11   The referee system was equally helpless at spotting the problem. Long and his senior professor had articles published in leading scientific journals showing the chromosome set of their alleged Hodgkin's cells. "It is immediately obvious that this is not a human cell line," a cell culture expert remarked in retrospect. But the monkey cells made monkeys of everyone. As for that most acid of tests, replication, many researchers have tried and failed to grow Hodgkin's cells in culture. But no one for that reason dreamed of imputing fraud to Long. Replication in practice plays a very different role to that imputed to it by philosophers of the scientific method.

12   A scientist rarely attempts an exact replication of another's experi-

ment. The reason is that prizes in science go for originality, and replication is by definition unoriginal. When researchers repeat their colleagues' experiments, it is generally with the idea of improving or refining on them so as to be able to claim some advance on the original finding. The failure to confirm the colleague's result is no basis for accusing him of fraud. The second researcher may have performed the experiment incorrectly, or done it with the wrong ingredients or at a different phase of the Moon. Of all the reasons that can cause the same experiment to come out differently in two laboratories, fraud is the last that a prudent researcher will suggest.

"No Misleading Results"

13   Some cases of fraud occur in obscure subjects at less than eminent institutions. But consider by contrast the remarkable career of John Darsee, once described as "clearly one of the most remarkable young men in American medicine." Darsee's 13-year career of successful fakery was spent in two of the United States's leading centres of heart research.

14   Both at Emory University and at Harvard, Darsee produced copious quantities of forged data, which he published under his own name and those of his colleagues. The colleagues included Eugene Braunwald of Harvard and Willis Hurst of Emory, leading cardiologists who are authors of rival textbooks about the heart.

15   Darsee's fabrications were exposed because his colleagues became suspicious of his enormous productivity. Surreptitiously observing one day, they saw him generate in a few hours data that he later presented as having been gathered over several days. Even with this massive hint of something wrong, the Harvard authorities were strangely incapable of getting to the bottom of the affair.

16   Darsee's laboratory chiefs, Braunwald and Robert Kloner, spent five months auditing his previous research, which formed the basis of articles published by the three of them, and informed the dean of the medical school that "No misleading results have been released from our laboratory." The dean, Daniel Tosteson, appointed a blue ribbon committee, chaired by the dean of the Johns Hopkins School of Medicine, which also concluded that "the previously published work . . . is accurate."

17   Only through the inquiry of a genuinely independent panel appointed by the National Institutes of Health did it emerge that there were statistical implausibilities in Darsee's work that rendered all of it highly suspect. Braunwald and Kloner have now retracted the five scientific papers under their names that were based on Darsee's data. A belated investigation of Darsee's earlier career at Emory University revealed that Darsee

had faked eight scientific articles and 43 research abstracts during his time there.

18 What kind of checks were applied to Darsee's work during his long career? If his work was important, why didn't others try to replicate it? Why did his colleagues happily co-author scientific papers with him if they were not close enough to the experiments to know that they were being forged? Darsee's 13-year career sheds a dismal light on the values of the system that harboured him. As for the checking mechanisms of science, their impotence was complete. But for documentary proof of fraud retrieved by Darsee's associates from a waste paper basket, his fraud would perhaps never have been investigated.

19 But why should a scientist even contemplate faking data when he has undergone a lengthy training for the sole purpose of learning to uncover the truth about nature? Modern science is a career. In addition to the disinterested pursuit of truth, scientists necessarily have another goal—the pursuit of glory, of due credit for their ideas, of the rewards and prestige that will assist in the next step up the career ladder. For the most part the two goals are complementary and reinforce each other. But competitive pressures and the opportunism of certain scientific arrangements seem sometimes to force a disjunction between the scientist's two purposes.

20 Under the peer review system, particularly in the United States, senior scientists receive large government grants with which they can employ doctoral and postgraduate students. At its best, the relationship between a professor and his students is a vital bond through which a research tradition is inculcated and handed on. But some heads of department pursue credit at their students' expense. To build up their list of publications, they sign their names to work of their junior colleagues even if they have contributed little to the work in question. Though happy to share the glory, the same heads of department are quick to distance themselves when fraud comes to light.

21 The younger researchers go along with the system, in part because they hope to become heads of department in their turn, in part because they have little recourse for complaint. For some heads of department, maximising production of scientific articles becomes a goal in itself. It is scarcely surprising that in such an environment younger researchers should be tempted to shade their results, to tidy up the data so as to give the chief what he wants, and eventually even to invent data.

Defenceless against Burt

22 Several of the recent cases of fraud have occurred in laboratories with a heavy emphasis on paper production. Fraud may well be a sign of stresses in the contemporary scientific enterprise, stresses that include

excessive competitive pressures and inequities in the accepted distribution of resources and credit. Fairer arrangements for crediting scientific work would help reduce cynicism and the propensities of senior investigators to exploit graduate labour for their own ends.

23   Another recent fraud case, that involving the writings on IQ and heredity of Sir Cyril Burt, affords a pertinent insight into the role of non-logical factors in science. Burt, an educational psychologist, worked his way to the top of his academic profession in Britain, and was the first foreigner to receive the American Psychological Association's prestigious Thorndike prize in 1971. His strong belief in the overriding importance of heredity in determining IQ was backed by extensive batteries of psychological test reports, all presented in a lucid expository style and with an unusual mastery of statistical technique. Burt's results occupied centre stage of a fierce debate for many years, yet it took an outsider, Leon Kamin of Princeton, to spot the glaring statistical implausibilities in Burt's data. These turned out to be the sign of a wholesale invention of data. "It reflects on all of us that these figures should have been in the literature of a highly contentious and important area for more than a decade before anyone went back to examine them as Kamin did . . . That is not the way that a community of scholars should be working," a chastened psychologist remarked in retrospect.

24   Burt gained a commanding position in his field because he used the scientific method as a purely rhetorical tool to beat down opponents and advocate his own dogmatic ideas. Against such a weapon, the scientific community that harboured him proved defenceless.

25   Burt's success provides an important clue to that most important of scientific processes, the manner in which new ideas are accepted. The public, and indeed many scientists, still hold the view propounded by the Logical Empiricist school of philosophers, that science is a strictly logical process, that the scientific method compels objectivity, and that logic alone determines the survival or collapse of theories. By deliberately ignoring the historical context of science, and psychological factors such as imagination and intuition, the Logical Empiricists inevitably painted a picture of science that would exist only in an ideal, logical empirical world.

26   A central insight of Thomas Kuhn's brilliant essay of 1962, "The Structure of Scientific Revolutions," is that scientists are influenced by non-rational as well as logical factors in choosing between competing theories. Others before Kuhn have remarked on the surprising resistance that is sometimes shown in science to original ideas. "An important scientific innovation," said the quantum physicist Max Planck, "rarely makes its way by gradually winning over and converting its opponents . . . What does happen is that its opponents gradually die out and that the growing generation is familiarised with the idea from the beginning."

27   The resistance to new ideas, and the acceptance by scientists of plausibly presented fraud, are two sides of the same coin. Rhetoric and appearance, despite researchers' vehement claims to the contrary, can play influential roles in science.

28   How common is fraud in science? The question cannot be answered because no one knows the number of frauds that escape detection. The outright fabrication of data is probably rare, if only because of the difficulty of inventing a whole experiment with verisimilitude. It is much easier to do some of the work and shade the details to give a sufficiently impressive answer. Minor fraud, such as tidying up data or selective reporting, could be relatively common in science, particularly as the chances of detection by the standard checks are so small.

29   Most scientific articles, whether true or false, have no lasting influence on the forward march of science. Fraudulent papers disappear in the marshy wastes of the scientific literature and just like most others are quickly forgotten; in general, fraud almost certainly has little lasting importance. But there are notable exceptions: Cyril Burt's fraudulent data on IQ and heredity had far reaching consequences for educational and public policy both in Britain and the United States. There could well be other instances in which fraudulent academic research distorts public policy.

Decay of Bad Ideas

30   Fraud is important in another way. Because statements by scientists are assumed to have been rigorously tested by the checking mechanisms of science, we accord them more weight than other expressions of expert opinion, such as an art connoisseur or theatre critic may give. But if the checking system cannot even detect gross fraud, why should it be assumed capable of detecting mere errors of scientific judgment? Fraud in science underscores the reason for what we always knew—never trust experts.

31   Contrary to the textbooks and philosophers of the scientific method, bad ideas are rarely proved wrong in science: they are simply forgotten. The true test of scientific ideas is not the checking mechanisms but a much more objective judge: time. Over time, the good ideas are corroborated by being used as the basis for further advances, the bad and fraudulent ideas, which are the vast majority, fall by the wayside and are forgotten.

32   Several critics of our book have complained that it does not explain why science is successful. We were remiss in neglecting to foresee and answer this objection. Science is successful, over the long run, because time winnows the wheat from the chaff. By the time a scientific truth reaches the textbooks, say, it is pretty well established. But the checking mechanisms do not suffice to certify the material in today's scientific

literature. The implication of our book is that there is no instant science. Take this week's copy of *Nature,* at present the world's best scientific journal; half the papers in it will probably make no lasting contribution to science. But no one can tell you which half.

33   What should be done about fraud? We definitely do not advocate instituting stiff measures to crack down on fraud, because that would bring research to a grinding halt. More important than detecting every petty case of data-fudging is to reduce the temptations to fraud. Protection of graduate students, more honest distribution of credit, reducing the number of vanity press journals, and raising research standards, are all steps worth taking in their own right, as well as for their effect in reversing the erosion of the academic ethos.

34   Fraud is tempting for that small minority in science, as in any other profession, who see advantage in cutting corners. The rewards can presumably be worthwhile, and the chance of apprehension is small. Spengler cited fraud by scholars as one of the signs of a decadent civilization. The present cases can be less ominously interpreted. Yet they are not so trivial that they can be dismissed as the work of "bad apples." Fraud in science has something to do with the barrel.

Note

[1] 1983. [Eds.]

Content Questions

1. What thesis does Wade attempt to debunk?
2. What consistent pattern exists with scientific frauds?
3. How are the components of the self-correcting system of science related to one another?
4. In what way is modern science a career?
5. What nonlogical factors influence scientific investigations?
6. In what ways is fraud important and beneficial to science?
7. Why is time the true test of scientific ideas?

Questions on Presentation

1. Why does Wade end paragraph 1 with a question?
2. Is the discussion of John Long's case effective? Why? Which of Wade's examples of fraud do you believe is most effective?
3. What audience do you believe Wade is addressing?

The Hazards of Science

Lewis Thomas

Physician, researcher, teacher, and writer Lewis Thomas (b. 1913) was born in Flushing, New York, and received his medical degree from Harvard University in 1937. As a research pathologist, Thomas wrote numerous scholarly essays and taught at several schools including the University of Minnesota Medical School, New York University, and Yale University Medical School. From 1973 to 1983 Thomas was the chancellor of Memorial Sloan-Kettering Cancer Center and in 1971 he began a regular column on medicine, biology, and chemistry in the prestigious *New England Journal of Medicine*. His books include the collected essays from the column, published in 1974 in *The Lives of a Cell*, winner of the National Book Award, and in 1979 in *The Medusa and the Snail*. Thomas's most recent publications are *The Youngest Science: Notes of a Medicine Watcher* (1983), his memoirs as a physician, and *Late Night Thoughts on Listening to Mahler's Ninth Symphony* (1984). The following selection, taken from *The Medusa and the Snail*, attempts to define *hubris* as an influence in scientific research.

1   The code word for criticism of science and scientists these days is "hubris." Once you've said that word, you've said it all; it sums up, in a word, all of today's apprehensions and misgivings in the public mind—not just about what is perceived as the insufferable attitude of the scientists themselves but, enclosed in the same word, what science and technology are perceived to be doing to make this century, this near to its ending, turn out so wrong.

2   "Hubris" is a powerful word, containing layers of powerful meaning, derived from a very old word, but with a new life of its own, growing way beyond the limits of its original meaning. Today, it is strong enough to carry the full weight of disapproval for the cast of mind that thought up atomic fusion and fission as ways of first blowing up and later heating cities as well as the attitudes which led to strip-mining, offshore oil wells, Kepone, food additives, SSTs, and the tiny spherical particles of plastic recently discovered clogging the waters of the Sargasso Sea.

3   The biomedical sciences are now caught up with physical science and technology in the same kind of critical judgment, with the same pejorative word. Hubris is responsible, it is said, for the whole biological revolution. It is hubris that has given us the prospects of behavioral control,

psychosurgery, fetal research, heart transplants, the cloning of prominent politicians from bits of their own eminent tissue, iatrogenic disease, overpopulation, and recombinant DNA. This last, the new
technology that permits the stitching of one creature's genes into the
DNA of another, to make hybrids, is currently cited as the ultimate example of hubris. It is hubris for man to manufacture a hybrid of his own.

4   So now we are back to the first word again, from "hybrid" to "hubris,"
and the hidden meaning of two beings joined unnaturally together by
man is somehow retained. Today's joining is straight out of Greek mythology: it is the combining of man's capacity with the special prerogative of the gods, and it is really in this sense of outrage that the word
"hubris" is being used today. This is what the word has grown into, a
warning, a code word, a shorthand signal from the language itself: if
man starts doing things reserved for the gods, deifying himself, the outcome will be something worse for him, symbolically, than the litters of
wild boars and domestic sows were for the ancient Romans.

5   To be charged with hubris is therefore an extremely serious matter,
and not to be dealt with by murmuring things about antiscience and
antiintellectualism, which is what many of us engaged in science tend
to do these days. The doubts about our enterprise have their origin in
the most profound kind of human anxiety. If we are right and the critics
are wrong, then it has to be that the word "hubris" is being mistakenly
employed, that this is not what we are up to, that there is, for the time
being anyway, a fundamental misunderstanding of science.

6   I suppose there is one central question to be dealt with, and I am not
at all sure how to deal with it, although I am quite certain about my
own answer to it. It is this: are there some kinds of information leading
to some sorts of knowledge that human beings are really better off not
having? Is there a limit to scientific inquiry not set by what is knowable
but by what we *ought* to be knowing? Should we stop short of learning
about some things, for fear of what we, or someone, will do with the
knowledge? My own answer is a flat no, but I must confess that this is
an intuitive response and I am neither inclined nor trained to reason my
way through it.

7   There has been some effort, in and out of scientific quarters, to make
recombinant DNA into the issue on which to settle this argument. Proponents of this line of research are accused of pure hubris, of assuming
the rights of gods, of arrogance and outrage; what is more, they confess
themselves to be in the business of making live hybrids with their own
hands. The mayor of Cambridge and the attorney general of New York
have both been advised to put a stop to it, forthwith.

8   It is not quite the same sort of argument, however, as the one about
limiting knowledge, although this is surely part of it. The knowledge is
already here, and the rage of the argument is about its application in

technology. Should DNA for making certain useful or interesting proteins be incorporated into *E. coli* plasmids or not? Is there a risk of inserting the wrong sort of toxins or hazardous viruses, and then having the new hybrid organisms spread beyond the laboratory? Is this a technology for creating new varieties of pathogens, and should it be stopped because of this?

9   If the argument is held to this level, I can see no reason why it cannot be settled, by reasonable people. We have learned a great deal about the handling of dangerous microbes in the last century, although I must say that the opponents of recombinant-DNA research tend to downgrade this huge body of information. At one time or another, agents as hazardous as those of rabies, psittacosis, plague, and typhus have been dealt with by investigators in secure laboratories, with only rare instances of self-infection of the investigators themselves, and no instances at all of epidemics. It takes some high imagining to postulate the creation of brand-new pathogens so wild and voracious as to spread from equally secure laboratories to endanger human life at large, as some of the arguers are now maintaining.

10   But this is precisely the trouble with the recombinant-DNA problem: it has become an emotional issue, with too many irretrievably lost tempers on both sides. It has lost the sound of a discussion of technological safety, and begins now to sound like something else, almost like a religious controversy, and here it is moving toward the central issue: are there some things in science we should not be learning about?

11   There is an inevitably long list of hard questions to follow this one, beginning with the one which asks whether the mayor of Cambridge should be the one to decide, first off.

12   Maybe we'd be wiser, all of us, to back off before the recombinant-DNA issue becomes too large to cope with. If we're going to have a fight about it, let it be confined to the immediate issue of safety and security, of the recombinants now under consideration, and let us by all means have regulations and guidelines to assure the public safety wherever these are indicated or even suggested. But if it is possible let us stay off that question about limiting human knowledge. It is too loaded, and we'll simply not be able to cope with it.

13   By this time it will have become clear that I have already taken sides in the matter, and my point of view is entirely prejudiced. This is true, but with a qualification. I am not so much in favor of recombinant-DNA research as I am opposed to the opposition to this line of inquiry. As a longtime student of infectious-disease agents I do not take kindly the declarations that we do not know how to keep from catching things in laboratories, much less how to keep them from spreading beyond the laboratory walls. I believe we learned a lot about this sort of thing, long ago. Moreover, I regard it as a form of hubris-in-reverse to claim that

man can make deadly pathogenic microorganisms so easily. In my view, it takes a long time and a great deal of interliving before a microbe can become a successful pathogen. Pathogenicity is, in a sense, a highly skilled trade, and only a tiny minority of all the numberless tons of microbes on the earth has ever been involved itself in it; most bacteria are busy with their own business, browsing and recycling the rest of life. Indeed, pathogenicity often seems to me a sort of biological accident in which signals are misdirected by the microbe or misinterpreted by the host, as in the case of endotoxin, or in which the intimacy between host and microbe is of such long standing that a form of molecular mimicry becomes possible, as in the case of diphtheria toxin. I do not believe that by simply putting together new combinations of genes one can create creatures as highly skilled and adapted for dependence as a pathogen must be, any more than I have ever believed that microbial life from the moon or Mars could possibly make a living on this planet.

14   But, as I said, I'm not at all sure this is what the argument is really about. Behind it is that other discussion, which I wish we would not have to become enmeshed in.

15   I cannot speak for the physical sciences, which have moved an immense distance in this century by any standard, but it does seem to me that in the biological and medical sciences we are still far too ignorant to begin making judgments about what sorts of things we should be learning or not learning. To the contrary, we ought to be grateful for whatever snatches we can get hold of, and we ought to be out there on a much larger scale than today's, looking for more.

16   We should be very careful with that word "hubris," and make sure it is not used when not warranted. There is a great danger in applying it to the search for knowledge. The application of knowledge is another matter, and there is hubris in plenty of our technology, but I do not believe that looking for new information about nature, at whatever level, can possibly be called unnatural. Indeed, if there is any single attribute of human beings, apart from language, which distinguishes them from all other creatures on earth, it is their insatiable, uncontrollable drive to learn things and then to exchange the information with others of the species. Learning is what we do, when you think about it. I cannot think of a human impulse more difficult to govern.

17   But I can imagine lots of reasons for trying to govern it. New information about nature is very likely, at the outset, to be upsetting to someone or other. The recombinant-DNA line of research is already upsetting, not because of the dangers now being argued about but because it is disturbing, in a fundamental way, to face the fact that the genetic machinery in control of the planet's life can be fooled around with so easily. We do not like the idea that anything so fixed and stable

as a species line can be changed. The notion that genes can be taken out of one genome and inserted in another is unnerving. Classical mythology is peopled with mixed beings—part man, part animal or plant—and most of them are associated with tragic stories. Recombinant DNA is a reminder of bad dreams.

18   The easiest decision for society to make in matters of this kind is to appoint an agency, or a commission, or a subcommittee within an agency to look into the problem and provide advice. And the easiest course for a committee to take, when confronted by any process that appears to be disturbing people or making them uncomfortable, is to recommend that it be stopped, at least for the time being.

19   I can easily imagine such a committee, composed of unimpeachable public figures, arriving at the decision that the time is not quite ripe for further exploration of the transplantation of genes, that we should put this off for a while, maybe until next century, and get on with other affairs that make us less discomfited. Why not do science on something more popular, say, how to get solar energy more cheaply? Or mental health?

20   The trouble is, it would be very hard to stop once this line was begun. There are, after all, all sorts of scientific inquiry that are not much liked by one constituency or another, and we might soon find ourselves with crowded rosters, panels, standing committees, set up in Washington for the appraisal, and then the regulation, of research. Not on grounds of the possible value and usefulness of the new knowledge, mind you, but for guarding society against scientific hubris, against the kinds of knowledge we're better off without.

21   It would be absolutely irresistible as a way of spending time, and people would form long queues for membership. Almost anything would be fair game, certainly anything to do with genetics, anything relating to population control, or, on the other side, research on aging. Very few fields would get by, except perhaps for some, like mental health, in which nobody really expects anything much to happen, surely nothing new or disturbing.

22   The research areas in the greatest trouble would be those already containing a sense of bewilderment and surprise, with discernible prospects of upheaving present dogmas.

23   It is hard to predict how science is going to turn out, and if it is really good science it is impossible to predict. This is in the nature of the enterprise. If the things to be found are actually new, they are by definition unknown in advance, and there is no way of telling in advance where a really new line of inquiry will lead. You cannot make choices in this matter, selecting things you think you're going to like and shutting off the lines that make for discomfort. You either have science or you don't,

and if you have it you are obliged to accept the surprising and disturbing pieces of information, even the overwhelming and upheaving ones, along with the neat and promptly useful bits. It is like that.

24   The only solid piece of scientific truth about which I feel totally confident is that we are profoundly ignorant about nature. Indeed, I regard this as the major discovery of the past hundred years of biology. It is, in its way, an illuminating piece of news. It would have amazed the brightest minds of the eighteenth-century Enlightenment to be told by any of us how little we know, and how bewildering seems the way ahead. It is this sudden confrontation with the depth and scope of ignorance that represents the most significant contribution of twentieth-century science to the human intellect. We are, at last, facing up to it. In earlier times, we either pretended to understand how things worked or ignored the problem, or simply made up stories to fill the gaps. Now that we have begun exploring in earnest, doing serious science, we are getting glimpses of how huge the questions are, and how far from being answered. Because of this, these are hard times for the human intellect, and it is no wonder that we are depressed. It is not so bad being ignorant if you are totally ignorant; the hard thing is knowing in some detail the reality of ignorance, the worst spots and here and there the not-so-bad spots, but no true light at the end of any tunnel nor even any tunnels that can yet be trusted. Hard times, indeed.

25   But we are making a beginning, and there ought to be some satisfaction, even exhilaration, in that. The method works. There are probably no questions we can think up that can't be answered, sooner or later, including even the matter of consciousness. To be sure, there may well be questions we can't think up, ever, and therefore limits to the reach of human intellect which we will never know about, but that is another matter. Within our limits, we should be able to work our way through to all our answers, if we keep at it long enough, and pay attention.

26   I am putting it this way, with all the presumption and confidence that I can summon, in order to raise another, last question. Is this hubris? Is there something fundamentally unnatural, or intrinsically wrong, or hazardous for the species in the ambition that drives us all to reach a comprehensive understanding of nature, including ourselves? I cannot believe it. It would seem to me a more unnatural thing, and more of an offense against nature, for us to come on the same scene endowed as we are with curiosity, filled to overbrimming as we are with questions, and naturally talented as we are for the asking of clear questions, and then for us to do nothing about it or, worse, to try to suppress the questions. This is the greater danger for our species, to try to pretend that we are another kind of animal, that we do not need to satisfy our curiosity, that we can get along somehow without inquiry and exploration and experimentation, and that the human mind can rise above its ignorance by

simply asserting that there are things it has no need to know. This, to my way of thinking, is the real hubris, and it carries danger for us all.

Content Questions

1. Why is Thomas's definition of *hubris* important to his thesis?
2. Why should scientists avoid the hazards of science?
3. Why should politicians not help science face these hazards?

Questions on Presentation

1. In the opening paragraphs Thomas develops his definition of *hubris* by playing on words. Is this effective? How does he present the discussion in paragraph 4?
2. What are the functions of paragraphs 11, 14, and 22?
3. Why does Thomas point out the limitations in his training?
4. How does Thomas distinguish between the issues surrounding recombinant DNA and the argument about limiting knowledge?
5. Define plasmids (8), pathogens (8), endotoxin (13), insatiable (15), discomfited (19), and intrinsically (26).

Arachne and Daedelus

Peter Steinbach

A philosophy major, Peter Steinbach is interested in the history of ideas. In this essay he uses that interest as a means of criticizing and explaining Lewis Thomas's essay.

1   Lewis Thomas anchors his essay "The Hazards of Science" to the concept of hubris, while assuming that his readers are familiar with the voluminous background of its rich and subtle meaning. As a result, his application of the term to modern feelings about science is less than effective.

2   Hubris is a kind of pride, but it is better translated as insolence, as a rude departure from accepted customs. Among the ancient Greeks, no

custom was more solid than the worldview that separated men from gods absolutely. Insolence in the face of the gods spelled certain disaster. Arachne, the greatest of weavers, boasted that she could, in a contest, beat the goddess of weaving, Minerva. For her arrogance, she was turned into a spider by Minerva herself. Daedelus, the great designer and inventor, murdered a young rival who was soon to outdo his own feats, and for his pride and jealousy Daedelus lost his only son through the imperfections of one of his devices: a flying machine. In this story no particular god is implicated in the revenge taken on Daedelus.

3   The story of Arachne clearly illustrates Lewis Thomas's use of hubris as excessive pride encroaching on "the special prerogative of the gods." But Daedelus illustrates a distinction not pointed out by Thomas: the distinction between technical skill and wisdom. Skill without wisdom is incomplete knowledge. In the Tarot, the Tower is always shown on fire and crumbling. The Tower represents skill, the fire the disaster that befalls incomplete knowledge. This is the basis of the first definition because, although humans can be immensely skillful, wisdom is "the prerogative of the gods." No human may truly know right from wrong, and to boast such knowledge is to invite disaster.

4   Thomas's discussion of the arguments for and against limiting research amounts to three points. Foremost is this statement: "There is great danger in applying it [hubris] to the search for knowledge." Thomas claims that "learning is what we do," that it would be unnatural to limit learning on the grounds that some kinds of knowledge are unnatural. Secondly, he says "we are still far too ignorant to begin making judgments about what sort of things we should be learning or not learning," implying that charges of hubris are unfounded since we know we're ignorant and cannot be proud. Thomas's third point is that any practical and official attempts to curb research would blossom into a shooting gallery that would kill nearly all research by basing the value of research upon how little offense it presents to the lay mind. This, he says, would be due in part to a hubris-in-reverse—the mistaken faith the layman has in the scientist's expertise.

5   These three points correspond precisely to Thomas's definition of hubris as insolence in the face of the gods. But Daedelus has another point. Thomas suggests that "the application of knowledge is another matter, and there is hubris in plenty of our technology" but offers no plan for the use of the knowledge he brings to the world. It is not his job. He takes the position of most of the original nuclear physicists who said that their work was an achievement of pure science and that they had no responsibility in its application. By ignoring Daedelus, Thomas is ignoring the assertion that our skill is greater than our wisdom. This is what sums up "all of today's apprehensions and misgivings."

6   The craving for learning will always be with us. So will Icarus's com-

plaint. And Lewis Thomas is in a position to answer the complaint for himself and to ask advice from outside his expertise.

The Familiar Faces of Change

Michael Guillen

Californian Michael Guillen (b. 1949) received his doctorate in mathematical physics from Cornell University in 1981. He has contributed articles to *Science Digest* and *Psychology Today* as well as other magazines. In the following essay, taken from his 1983 book *Bridges to Infinity,* Guillen discusses the way mathematicians create catastrophe theories to account for and cope with change.

> Not Chaos-like, together crushed and bruised,
> But, as the world harmoniously confused:
> Where order in variety we see,
> And where, though all things differ, all agree.
>
> Alexander Pope

1   The only certainty in this world, as the saying goes, is change, and everything we learn from science bears this out. The contents of the universe and the universe itself are in an implacable state of flux. Things that appear constant—mountains, the atmosphere, the sun—are in fact constantly sustaining enormous changes of being; they are in an active state of balance. Even the cells in our own bodies are completely (and invisibly) replaced by new ones every seven years or so.

2   Our attitude toward change, especially abrupt change, has itself changed in the last several decades. In the past, things that happened suddenly, such as accidental deaths and natural disasters, were associated with some inscrutable agent such as a capricious god. The faces, the patterns, of abrupt change were mostly enigmatic to us and were therefore threatening. In the seventeenth century, during the Enlightenment, Isaac Newton did recognize that many instances of gradual change—population growth, for example—follow predictable patterns that can be represented by a few mathematical figures. But even then, and for decades thereafter, sudden changes appeared to be unsusceptible to such a mathematical categorization or to any satisfactory rational depiction at all.

3   About twenty years ago, the French mathematician René Thom did successfully categorize abrupt changes, or catastrophes, as he called them. He discovered that most catastrophes follow orderly patterns that are describable qualitatively in terms of seven mathematical figures. Though his discovery does not help us explain the origins of abrupt changes, it does indicate that these changes are not as irrational, as undisciplined, as they were previously believed to be.

4   It also indicates that the abrupt changes that affect us personally, such as nervous breakdowns and fits of spontaneous anger, are of the same qualitative variety as those sustained by the far-flung cosmic landscape. In this sense, Thom's theory enables us to recognize as never before the faces of catastrophic change that constantly transfigure the natural world.

5   In a dynamic world such as ours, it is inevitable that scientists require a mathematical means with which to study change, and it was mainly in response to this scientific need for a quantitative language of change that Newton invented the calculus. He designed it to describe changes that proceed in small, continuous steps—gradual changes, in other words—and so scientists use it for calculating such things as the motion of a planet around the sun, the growth of a population, or the constantly increasing speed of a falling object.

6   Just as significantly, however, they have learned in the process of using the calculus that gradually changing phenomena that appear to be unalike are actually related mathematically. For instance, the exponential-growth equation in calculus that describes the growth in value of a normal savings account is exactly the same one that describes the growth of bacteria in a petri dish, the growth in number of a chain letter, or the normal growth of an animal population.

7   Most notably, the calculus has enabled us to relate and to categorize all the possible motions of an object moving freely in a gravitational field. According to the calculus, such an object will follow one of only three archetypal trajectories, depending solely on the speed at which it is launched. Nothing about the projectile itself matters—not its shape, weight, density, or chemical composition. Irrespective of how different looking two projectiles may be, they will follow identical trajectories as long as they are launched at the same speed.

8   If a projectile is launched with a speed less than orbital speed (which for the earth's gravitational field is about 17,000 miles per hour), then its path will always resemble a parabola, the slowly curving arch usually followed by an arrow, a bullet, or a thrown rock. If, however, the object is launched with a speed between orbital speed and escape speed (which for the earth's gravitational field is about 25,000 miles per hour), then its path will always be an ellipse or a circle. Such is the case with all the planets orbiting the sun and with all the satellites circling the earth.

And, finally, if an object is launched with a speed equal to or greater than escape speed, then its path will be a hyperbola, which looks like a parabola with its arch more severely bent. This is the path that was followed by American astronauts to the moon and by spacecraft traveling to other planets. The discovery of these categories was considered as revolutionary in its day as Thom's categorization of abrupt change is today.

9   For all its merits, however, the calculus still left scientists with no comparable mathematical means to describe and relate abrupt changes. For want of such means, biologists were hampered in their theoretical studies of cell division, one of the most basic phenomena in biology, since cells tend to divide suddenly rather than gradually. Apparently, Thom was not only aware of this problem in biology, he was in part motivated by it to develop his catastrophe theory; some of his earliest explications of the theory were published, in 1968, as part of a series of books entitled *Toward a Theoretical Biology*.

10   Scientifically and mathematically, catastrophe theory complements the calculus. Whereas the calculus is a quantitative theory of gradual change, catastrophe theory is a largely qualitative theory of abrupt change. Specifically, catastrophe theory is elaborated in the language of topology, the qualitative mathematical study of shapes. Topology itself is a branch of geometry that was founded in the eighteenth century by the Swiss mathematician Leonhard Euler.

11   One key notion of topology that is particularly evident in Thom's mathematical approach to abrupt change is the notion of topological equivalence. Two objects are said to be topologically equivalent if they share certain essential attributes, regardless of their other dissimilarities. For instance, a doughnut and a coffee cup are topologically equivalent because each has a hole in it. The hole is an essential feature in the sense that if we imagine transfiguring a doughnut into a cup or vice versa, almost everything else about the object will have changed in the process except for the hole; *it* persists. Topological equivalence is always judged on the basis of such immutable (qualitative) attributes only, not mutable (quantitative) details such as the size of the doughnut or the specific shape of the cup. For this reason, it is possible, and even common, for two very different looking objects to be topologically equivalent.

12   In developing catastrophe theory, Thom set out to find an analogous way of qualitatively relating catastrophes, even ones that might be as outwardly dissimilar as cups and doughnuts. For this reason, he sought an analogy to the hole, some essential attribute of catastrophes that might be used to mathematically describe and classify them.

13   Such an attribute, he discovered, is the number of factors that control the dynamics of a catastrophe. By a control factor, Thom meant any ele-

ment of a situation undergoing sudden change that can actually affect the progress and direction of that change. For instance, the essential factor controlling the inflation (and, ultimately, the catastrophic rupturing) of a balloon is air pressure. By reducing or increasing this one factor alone, the progress and direction of the balloon's changing status is affected.

14   This single discovery—that the number of control factors is as essential an attribute of a catastrophe as the hole is to a doughnut—is the basis of Thom's definition of catastrophic equivalence. According to the definition, two or more instances of abrupt change are catastrophically equivalent if each one's behavior is controlled by the same number of factors; the bursting balloon is thus catastrophically equivalent to any and every other abruptly changing phenomenon whose behavior is controlled by a single factor of some sort. Similarly, other catastrophes are grouped by Thom according to whether their behavior is controlled by two, three, or more factors.

15   This definition, Thom's analogy to topological equivalence, is the nub of catastrophe theory. Conceptually, it decrees that if two phenomena are controlled by the same number of factors, then they will follow the same qualitative pattern of change, even if they don't match quantitatively and in other details. Following this definition, therefore, Thom is able to recognize qualitative family resemblances among apparently unrelated catastrophes.

16   In a sense, Thom's discovery that the essential attribute of a catastrophe is the number of factors controlling its behavior is comparable to Newton's discovery that the essential attribute of a trajectory in a gravitational field is the projectile's launch speed. In both these domains, all other attributes of a changing situation except for the essential attribute are mathematically inconsequential. They are masks disguising faces of change that are, in some sense, fundamentally similar.

17   There are, however, differences between Thom's and Newton's findings. Whereas three categories alone cover the gravitational situation, no fewer than seven cover all of the more widely known instances of abrupt change in the natural world. Also, whereas the three representative trajectories exist in real space and are therefore easily visualized, the concrete representations of the seven archetypal catastrophes exist in an abstract, mathematical space and are not as easy to picture.

18   Perhaps the easiest way to visualize them is to imagine, as Thom did, that experiencing a catastrophic change is qualitatively like sustaining a precipitous fall while traveling on some hazardous geometrical surface—that is, in falling precipitously, as in changing abruptly, we suddenly end up in a place very different from that in which we were just before we fell. Technically, this analogy means that the mathematics of

catastrophe theory is similar in some respects to the mathematics of geometrical surfaces, an established subject that is familiar to most mathematicians.

19 The factors that control the direction and progress of a catastrophe are imagined to control the direction and progress of our movements upon the corresponding abstract surface. This is why the surface is called the control surface, and the catastrophe is compared to falling off one part of the control surface and landing upon another. Also, it follows that there are as many dimensions to a catastrophe's control surface as there are control factors to the actual catastrophe: each factor controls movement along a single dimension.

20 If we do think of the faces of abrupt change as being like hazardous geometrical landscapes, then Thom's main discovery is that most of the landscapes we observe in nature and in ourselves involve only seven basic and distinct hazards. These are the seven familiar faces of change, and in an effort to help visualize them, Thom gave them names that are evocative of their shapes. In order of increasing complexity, the archetypal catastrophes are the fold, the cusp, the swallowtail, and the butterfly; there are three varieties of swallowtail and two of butterfly, thus bringing the total number to seven.

21 The fold catastrophe, which is controlled by a single factor, has the simplest face of all. Its control surface is technically not even a surface at all; it is a one-dimensional horizontal line that curves downward at one end to form the edge of a vertical cliff. According to catastrophe theory, this is the abstract mathematical visualization of an inflating balloon.

22 An increase in the balloon's air pressure corresponds graphically to movement along the line toward the cliff's edge, and a decrease corresponds to movement away from the cliff. Naturally, if we continue to inflate the balloon, a point is reached at which just one more molecule of air will be enough to blow the whole thing up. That point corresponds to being at the very edge of the cliff, and rupturing the balloon corresponds to falling off the edge. With a fold catastrophe, there is typically no bottom to the cliff, which means that once we've gone over the edge, there is no way back up. For our example, this signifies that once a balloon pops, it cannot be unpopped.

23 The normal aging process is also represented by a fold catastrophe, with the single control factor being time. Moving away from the cliff represents getting younger, and moving toward the cliff represents the normal situation, getting older. Our very last moment of being alive corresponds to standing on the cliff's brink; dying corresponds to falling off the cliff. According to catastrophe theory, therefore, a life follows the same mathematical pattern of change as an inflating balloon, and dying

is qualitatively similar to a bursting balloon in the sense that once a life has been destroyed, it cannot be revivified.

24   This irreversibility is not true of a cusp catastrophe, which by definition is an instance of sudden change that is controlled by two factors. According to Thom's theory, a cusp catastrophe is distinguished by the way it can recover—either partially or fully—from the catastrophic change.

25   What he is referring to here can easily be seen from looking at the mathematical face of a cusp catastrophe. The central region of its two-dimensional control surface is dominated by an overhang whose shadow on the surface beneath it has a roughly triangular shape, like a cusp. Most notably, the overall layout is such that after one falls off the overhang, it is always possible to hike back up to the edge (all the while staying on the control surface).

26   The working of one of those little toy metal "clickers," or frogs, is a cusp catastrophe, because the behavior of a frog is controlled by two factors—in this case, finger pressure and the elasticity of its metal tongue. Graphically, the frog's tongue in the relaxed position corresponds to being in a region atop the cusp's overhang, far from the edge. Pressing on the tongue with increasing pressure corresponds to moving closer to the edge. At some point, the pressure is great enough that the metal tongue suddenly buckles, with a click; this corresponds to falling off the edge of the overhang, onto the control surface below. There it stays, in fact, as long as we hold the frog's tongue in its bent position. Letting go corresponds graphically to the frog's wending its way back up to the overhang.

27   Of the seven catastrophes, the cusp is the one whose face, whose mathematical pattern of change, we see most often in the world. Catastrophe theory was not designed to explain why this might be, but certainly any explanation would refer to the prevalence of opposites in reality and the episodes of reversible sudden change that relate them.

28   We recognize cusp catastrophes in some patterns of waking and sleeping, for instance. Normally, we fall asleep gradually, in stages, but sometimes the transition is more abrupt, such as after a hard workout. In such a case, it is always possible to recover—to wake up—from the catastrophic change, and this is the hallmark of a cusp catastrophe.

29   The cusp catastrophe is also a familiar face in the moody behavior of a manic-depressive, in the spasmodic episodes of war and peace between irreconcilably hostile nations, and in the erratic highs and lows of the stock market. Like the metal frog, each of these examples of a cusp catastrophe involves a sudden swing from one extreme to another, followed by the possibility of returning to the original extreme. For this reason, unrelated though they may appear superficially, these phenomena can all be described with the same mathematical formulas and pic-

tured in terms of the same catastrophic landscape. With catastrophe theory, therefore, we are able to see fewer differences in the world than we would without it.

30   The five remaining catastrophes are not as widely applicable as the cusp catastrophe; neither are their control surfaces as easily visualized. The problem with visualizing these surfaces is that they are all more than two-dimensional, in keeping with the greater number of control factors for these catastrophes, which makes them unlike what we would normally picture to be a surface. All we can do is imagine what their two-dimensional shadows must look like; in fact, the swallowtail and butterfly surfaces got their names from the imagined appearance of their 2-D silhouettes. (To show that the pictures are largely a matter of imagination, Thom was wont to point out that the swallowtail catastrophe was named by a blind colleague of his, the French mathematician Bernard Morin.)

31   Of the butterfly and swallowtail catastrophes, we see the face of the former more often in nature. Mathematically, the control surface of a butterfly catastrophe (or, more precisely, its 2-D silhouette) is distinguished by not one but two centrally located overhangs. Their relative arrangement is hierarchical, so that it is possible to fall off the topmost one and land either on the intermediate one or on the surface beneath them both. In either case, as with the cusp landscape, it is always possible to hike back up to the topmost overhang.

32   In most examples of butterfly catastrophes, the intermediate overhang represents a compromise between whatever is represented by the top and bottom levels of the control surface. For instance, two hostile nations that behave qualitatively like a butterfly catastrophe always have the option of negotiating rather than going directly from peace to war.

33   One of the few examples of butterfly catastrophes in which the intermediate overhang represents something more unusual than a compromise involves the affliction of mostly young women known as anorexia nervosa. Untreated anorexics behave like cusp catastrophes, flipping between episodes of fasting and gorging. Recently, however, the British mathematician E. C. Zeeman reasoned that if catastrophe theory is correct, the phenomenon of anorexia nervosa could be transformed from a cusp to a butterfly catastrophe by bringing additional control factors to bear.

34   Zeeman collaborated with a British psychotherapist, who devised a therapy for anorexics based on this hypothesis. The therapy involves putting the patient in a trance. Being put in a trance is a sudden change that corresponds to jumping from either the lower level (fasting) or the upper one (gorging) to the intermediate level of the butterfly catastrophe. It is at this median level that anorexics appear to be most receptive

to psychological counseling. "When the patient is fasting," Zeeman ventures to explain, "she views the outer world with anxiety, and when she is gorging, she is overwhelmed by that world." However, he says, "during the trance [the patient] is isolated, her mind free both of food and of scheming to avoid food."

35   Although examples like this illustrate the scientific potential of catastrophe theory, there is presently a debate among scientists and mathematicians about how scientifically useful it will be in the long run. The pessimists generally argue that the scientific utility of the theory is limited by the qualitative nature of its founding notion, catastrophic equivalence. As we have seen, catastrophes controlled by the same number of factors are assumed in this theory to be equivalent, regardless of their detailed dissimilarities. Those mathematicians who are skeptical about the theory's scientific value point out that the very details that are ignored by the theory are those that science is liable to be interested in.

36   In the case of anorexia nervosa, for example, scientists undoubtedly wish to probe beyond the qualitative observations that the disorder follows an archetypal pattern of behavior that can be altered to follow another, different archetype; at some point scientists will also presumably wish to identify whatever detailed variations there might be to the archetypal pattern, in the hope of discovering which specific traits make a person more or less susceptible to becoming an anorexic.

37   However true such an argument might be, the qualitative character of Thom's theory is a welcome addition to mathematics and also to our culture's and age's accustomed way of looking at things. For one thing, the theory enriches the language of mathematics so that we can now express things about abrupt change that we were heretofore unable to express. In addition, Thom's theory and its qualitative foundation are also refreshing counterpoints to the reductionist's largely unchallenged reign of detailed, quantitative analysis. As the German physicist Bernhard Bavink once said, it allows us a rare opportunity to use mathematics "to place the concept of measurable and countable quantity in second place, and the basic biological concept of form, or gestalt, in first place."

38   To the extent that it *is* scientifically useful, Thom's theory bears out the vitalist's twin notions that the whole is greater than the sum of its parts and that looking at the whole can often be more enlightening than scrutinizing its parts. In defense of these notions, Thom lectures biologists and physicists at some length in his book *Structural Stability and Morphogenesis* on the dangers of looking at something too closely. He challenges the common reductionist belief "that the interaction of a small number of elementary particles embraces all macroscopic phenomena when, in fact, the finer the investigation is, the more complicated the events are, leading eventually to a new world to be explained in which one cannot discern among the relevant factors for macroscopic order."

39   At the very least, catastrophe theory does enable us to recognize that, in cataloging change, there *is* some order in the multifarious changes that are constantly transfiguring the universe and its contents. Three hundred years ago, Newton found that a round, gold object in flight behaves basically no differently from, say, a square, silver one; the only factor that determines the trajectory of each through a gravitational field is the speed at which it is launched. Similarly, Thom has found that the sudden change experienced by a mother awakened by her child's cry follows the same mathematical pattern among all mothers, no matter what nationality or race they may be part of.

40   In Newton's case, the presence of a gravitational field accounted for the fact that all kinds of gradual motion belong to one of only three categories. Thom discusses the possible existence of a *champ vital* (life field) to account for the fact that sudden changes, too, appear to boil down to a few categories. He speculates, in fact, that the *champ vital* might be just like a "gravitational or electromagnetic field" in which all "living beings would then be particles . . . of this field."

41   Speculation of a more modest kind can lead us to see in Thom's theory an eloquent mathematical elaboration of a basis for our empathy with the natural world. By merely cataloging disparate phenomena, they become less mysterious and more familiar to us. I wonder whether the evidence of the presence here on earth of Thom's seven catastrophes extends outward from our solar system to other worlds, perhaps inhabited by other beings. If mathematics is the universal language many of us believe it to be, then sudden change anywhere else should have faces just as familiar as those on earth, though the possibility does exist for some queer juxtapositions. . . . Imagine a world where balloons click and frogs pop.

Content Questions

1. Why did Newton invent calculus? What are its uses?
2. What does catastrophe theory seek to explain?
3. How do the faces of change differ?
4. Why are all other attributes "mathematically inconsequential" in both trajectory studies and catastrophe theory?
5. Why are some scientists skeptical about catastrophe theory?

Questions on Presentation

1. Why does Guillen begin his essay with a quotation from Alexander Pope? Is this similar to Petroski's use of quotation?
2. Are the examples used in paragraph 8 effective? Why?

3. Guillen must define a number of terms in this essay. Which definitions are most successful? Why?

4. Why is the parenthetical statement in paragraph 30 important? If it is important why is it parenthetical?

5. Why does Guillen end his essay with an invitation to imagine an impossibility?

The Shape of Things

Isaac Asimov

Born in the Soviet Union, Isaac Asimov (b. 1920) emigrated to the United States—he says stowed in his parents' baggage—when he was three years old. He grew up in Brooklyn, received his doctorate in biochemistry from Columbia University, and later became a professor at Boston University, distinguished for his scientific publications. Asimov started writing fiction at age eleven; at eighteen, he submitted his first story—which was quickly rejected. Four short months later, he was a published writer. In the early 1940s, Asimov began writing his robot stories; shortly afterward, he won public acclaim for his first major work of fiction, *I, Robot* (1950), a science fiction novel that presents provocative ideas about humans' relationships with machines and with themselves. Asimov's popularity grew when he published the *Foundation* trilogy, novels that won the Hugo Award for science fiction. Asimov jokes about his career that his books can be found in any major division of the Dewey library classification system: he has published countless science fiction and mystery stories and over 260 books on topics from Shakespeare to mathematics to the Bible. In addition Asimov has won numerous awards including the Edison Foundation Award for *Building Blocks of the Universe* (1957), the Blakeslee Award of the American Heart Association for *The Living River* (1960), and the Grady Award for science writing from the American Chemical Society (1965). In this essay, taken from *Adding a Dimension* (1964), Asimov blends history, science, and humor to give readers a sense of adventure.

1   Every child comes staggering out of grammar school with a load of misstatements of fact firmly planted in his head. He may forget, for instance, as the years drift by, that the Battle of Waterloo was fought in 1815 or that seven times six is forty-two; but he will never, never forget, while he draws breath, that Columbus proved the world was round.

2   And, of course, Columbus proved no such thing. What Columbus did prove was that it doesn't matter how wrong you are, as long as you're lucky.

3   The fact that the earth is spherical in shape was first suggested in the sixth century B.C. by various Greek philosophers. Some believed it out of sheer mysticism, the reasoning being that the sphere was the perfect solid and that therefore the earth was a sphere. To us, the premise is dubious and the conclusion a *non sequitur,* but to the Greek it carried weight.

4   However, not all Greek philosophers were mystics and there were rational reasons for believing the earth to be spherical. These were capably summarized by Aristotle in the fourth century B.C. and turned out to be three in number:

5   1. If the earth were flat, then all the stars visible from one point on the earth's surface would be visible from all other points (barring minor distortions due to perspective and, of course, the obscuring of parts of the horizon by mountains). However, as travelers went southward, some stars disappeared beyond the northern horizon, while new stars appeared above the southern horizon. This proved the earth was not flat but had some sort of curved shape. Once that was allowed, one could reason further that all things fell toward earth's center and got as close to it as they could. That solid shape in which the total distance of all parts from the center is a minimum is a sphere, Q.E.D.

6   2. Ships on leaving harbor and sailing off into the open sea seemed to sink lower and lower into the water, until at the horizon only the tops were visible. The most reasonable conclusion was that the water surface, though it seemed flat, was a gently curving hill behind which the ships disappeared. Furthermore, since this effect was equally intense whatever the direction in which the ship sailed, the gently curving hill of the ocean seemed to curve equally in all directions. The only solid shape that curves equally in all directions is a sphere, Q.E.D.

7   3. It was accepted by the Greek philosophers that the moon is eclipsed when it enters the earth's shadow. As darkness crossed over the face of the moon, the encroaching shadow marked off a projection of the shape of the earth, and that shadow was always the segment of a circle. It didn't matter whether the moon were high in the sky or at either horizon. The shadow was always circular. The only solid for which all projections are circular is a sphere, Q.E.D.

8   Now, Aristotle's reasoning carried conviction. All learned men throughout history who had access to Aristotle's books, accepted the sphericity of the earth. Even in the eighth century A.D., in the very depth of the Dark Ages, St. Bede (usually called "the Venerable Bede"), collecting what scraps of physical science were still remembered from Greek days, plainly stated the earth was a sphere. In the fourteenth century Dante's *Divine Comedy,* which advanced a detailed view of the orthodox astronomy of the day, presented the earth as spherical.

9   Consequently, there is no doubt that Columbus knew the earth was a sphere. But so did all other educated men in Europe.

10   In that case, what was Columbus's difficulty? He wanted to sail west
from Europe and cross the Atlantic to Asia. If the earth were spherical,
this was theoretically possible, and if educated men all agreed with the
premise and, therefore, with the conclusion, why the resistance to Columbus's scheme?

11   Well, to say the earth is a sphere is not enough? The question is—
how large is a sphere?

12   The first person to measure the circumference of the earth was a
Greek astronomer, named Eratosthenes of Cyrene, and he did it without
ever leaving home.

13   If the earth were a sphere, as Eratosthenes was certain it was, then the
sun's rays should, at any one instant of time, strike different parts of the
earth's surface at different angles. For instance, on June 21, the sun was
just overhead at noon in the city of Syene, Egypt. In Alexandria, Egypt
(where Eratosthenes lived), the sun was not quite overhead at that moment but made a small angle with the zenith.

14   Eratosthenes knew the distance between Alexandria and Syene, and it
was simple geometry to calculate the curvature of the earth's surface
that would account for the displacement of the sun. From that one could
further calculate the radius and the circumference of the earth.

15   Eratosthenes worked out this circumference to be 25,000 miles in our
modern units of length (or perhaps a little higher—the exact length in
miles of the unit he used is uncertain) and this is just about right!

16   About 100 B.C., however, a Greek geographer named Posidonius of
Apamea checked Eratosthenes' work and came out with a lower figure—a circumference of 18,000 miles.

17   This smaller figure may have seemed more comfortable to some
Greeks, for it reduced the area of the unknown. If the larger figure were
accepted, then the known world made up only about one sixth of the
earth's surface area. If the smaller figure were accepted, the earth's surface area was reduced by half and the known world made up a third of
the earth's surface area.

18   Now the Greek thinkers were much concerned with the unknown
portions of the earth (which seemed as unattainable and mysterious to
them as, until recently, the other side of the moon seemed to us) and
they filled in with imaginary continents. To have less of it to worry
about must have seemed a relief, and the Greek astronomer Claudius
Ptolemy, who lived about A.D. 150, was one of those who accepted Posidonius's figure.

19   It so happened that in the latter centuries of the Middle Ages, Ptolemy's books were as influential as Aristotle's, and if the fifteenth-
century geographers accepted Aristotle's reasoning as to the sphericity
of the earth, many of them also accepted Ptolemy's figure for its circumference.

20 An Italian geographer named Paolo Toscanelli was one of them. Since the extreme distance across Europe and Asia is some 13,000 miles (a piece of knowledge geographers had become acquainted with thanks to Marco Polo's voyages in the thirteenth century) and the total circumference was 18,000 miles or less, then one would have to travel westward from Spain no more than 5000 miles to reach "the Indies." In fact, since there were islands off the eastern coast of Asia, such as the Zipangu (Japan) spoken of by Marco Polo, the distance might be only 4000 miles or even less. Toscanelli drew a map in the 1470s showing this, picturing the Atlantic Ocean with Europe and Africa on one side and Asia, with its offshore islands, on the other.

21 Columbus obtained a copy of the map and some personal encouragement from Toscanelli and was an enthusiastic convert to the notion of reaching Asia by the westward route. All he needed now was government financing.

22 The most logical place to go for such financing was Portugal. In the fifteenth century many of Europe's luxuries (including spices, sugar, and silk) were available only by overland routes from the Far East, and the Turks who straddled the route charged all the traffic could bear in the way of middleman fees. Some alternate route was most desirable, and the Portuguese, who were at the extreme southeastern edge of Europe, conceived the notion of sailing around Africa and reaching the Far East by sea, outflanking the Turks altogether. Throughout the fourteenth century, then, the Portuguese had been sending out expedition after expedition, farther and farther down the African coast. (The Portuguese "African effort" was as difficult for those days as our "space effort" is for ours.)

23 In 1484, when Columbus appealed to John II of Portugal for financing, Portuguese expeditions had all but reached the southern tip of Africa (and in 1487 they were to do so).

24 The Portuguese, at the time, were the most experienced navigators in Europe, and King John's geographers viewed with distrust the low figure for the circumference of the earth. If it turned out that the high figure, 25,000 miles, were correct, and if the total east-west stretch of Europe and Asia were 13,000—then it followed, as the night the day, that a ship would have to sail 12,000 miles west from Portugal to reach Asia. No ship of that day could possibly make such an uninterrupted ocean voyage.

25 The Portuguese decision, therefore, was that the westward voyage was theoretically possible but, given the technology of the day, completely impractical. The geographers advised King John to continue work on Project Africa and to turn down the Italian dreamer. This was done.

26 Now, mind you, the Portuguese geographers were perfectly right. It *is* 12,000 miles from Portugal west to Asia, and no ship of the day could

possibly have made such a voyage. The fact is that Columbus never did reach Asia by the western route, whereas the Portuguese voyagers succeeded, within thirteen years, in reaching Asia by the African route. As a result, tiny Portugal built a rich and far-flung empire, becoming the first of the great European colonialists. Enough of that empire has survived into the 1960s to permit them to be the last as well.

27   And what is the reward of the Portuguese geographers for proving to be right in every last particular? Why, schoolchildren are taught to sneer at them.

28   Columbus obtained the necessary financing from Spain in 1492. Spain had just taken the last Moslem strongholds on the Iberian Peninsula and, in the flush of victory, was reaching for some daring feat of navigation that would match the deeds of the Portuguese. (In the language of today, they needed an "ocean spectacular" to improve their "world image.") So they gave Columbus three foundering hulks and let him have his pick of the prison population for crewmen and sent him off.

29   It would have meant absolutely certain death for Columbus and his men, thanks to his wrongness, were it not for his incredible luck. The Greek dreamers had been right. The unoccupied wastes of the earth did indeed possess other continents and Columbus ran aground on them after only 3000 miles. (As it was, he barely made it; another thousand miles and he would have been gone.)

30   The Portuguese geographers had not counted on what are now known as the American continents (they would have been fools to do so), but neither had Columbus. In fact, Columbus never admitted he had reached anything but Asia. He died in 1506 still convinced the earth was 18,000 miles in circumference—stubbornly wrong to the end.

31   So Columbus had not proved the earth was round; that was already known. In fact, since he had expected to reach Asia and had failed, his voyage was an argument *against* the sphericity of the earth.

32   In 1519, however, five ships set sail from Spain under Ferdinand Magellan (a Portuguese navigator in the pay of Spain), with the intention of completing Columbus's job and reaching Asia, and then continuing on back to Spain. Such an expedition was as difficult for its day as orbiting a man is for ours. The expedition took three years and made it by an inch. An uninterrupted 10,000-mile trip across the Pacific all but finished them (and they were far better prepared than Columbus had been). Magellan himself died en route. However, the one ship that returned brought back a large enough cargo of spices to pay for the entire expedition with plenty left over.

33   This first circumnavigation of the earth was experimental confirmation, in a way, of the sphericity of the planet, but that was scarcely needed. More important, it proved two other things. It proved the ocean was continuous; that there was one great sea in which the continents

were set as large islands. This meant that any seacoast could be reached from any other seacoast, which was vital knowledge (and good news) for merchantmen. Secondly, it proved once and for all that Eratosthenes was right and that the circumference of the earth was 25,000 miles.

34   And yet, after all, though the earth is round, it turned out, despite all Aristotle's arguments, that it wasn't a sphere after all.

35   Again we go back to the Greeks. The stars wheel about the earth in a stately and smooth twenty-four-hour cycle. The Greek philosophers realized that this could be explained in either of two ways. It was possible that the earth stood still and the heavens rotated about it in a twenty-four-hour period. Or the heavens might stand still while the earth rotated about itself in twenty-four hours.

36   A few Greeks (notably Aristarchus of Samos) maintained, in the third century B.C., that it was the earth that rotated. The majority, however, held for a stationary earth, and it was the latter who won out. After all, the earth is large and massive, while the heavens are light and airy; surely it is more logical to suppose the latter turned.

37   The notion of the stationary earth was accepted by Ptolemy and therefore by the medieval scholars and by the Church. It was not until 1543, a generation after Magellan's voyage, that a major onslaught was made against the view.

38   In that year Nicolaus Copernicus, a Polish astronomer, published his views of the universe and died at once, ducking all controversy. According to his views (which were like those of Aristarchus) the sun was the center of the universe, and the earth revolved about it as one planet among many. If the earth were only a minor body circling the sun, it seemed completely illogical to suppose that the stars revolved about our planet. Copernicus therefore maintained that the earth rotated on its axis.

39   The Copernican view was not, of course, accepted at once, and the world of scholarship argued the matter for a century. As late as 1633, Galileo was forced by the Inquisition to abjure his belief that the earth moved and to affirm that it was motionless. However, that was the dying gasp of the motionless-earth view, and there has been no scientific opposition to earth's rotation since. (Nevertheless, it was not until 1851 that the earth's rotation was actually confirmed by experiment, but that is another story.)

40   Now if the earth rotated, the theory that it was spherical in shape suddenly became untenable. The man who first pointed this out was Isaac Newton, in the 1680s.

41   If the earth were stationary, gravitational forces would force it into spherical shape (minimum total distance from the center) even if it were not spherical to begin with. If the earth rotated, however, the possession

of inertia by every particle on the planet would produce a centrifugal effect, which would act as though to counter gravity and move particles *away* from the center of the earth.

42   But the surface of a rotating sphere moves at varying velocities depending upon its distance from the axis of rotation. At the point where the axis of rotation intersects the surface (as at the North and South Poles) the surface is motionless. As distance from the Poles increases, the surface velocity increases; it is at its maximum at the Equator, which is equidistant from the Poles.

43   Whereas the gravitational force is constant (just about) at all points on the earth's surface, the centrifugal effect increases rapidly with surface velocity. As a result the surface of the earth lifts up slightly away from the center and the lifting is at its maximum at the Equator where the surface velocity is highest. In other words, said Newton, the earth should have an equatorial bulge. (Or, to put it another way, it should be flattened at the Poles.)

44   This means that if an east-west cross-section of the earth were taken at the Equator, that cross-section would have a circular boundary. If, however, a cross-section were taken north-south through the Poles, that cross-section would have an elliptical boundary and the shortest diameter of the ellipse would run from Pole to Pole. Such a solid body is not a sphere but an "oblate spheroid."

45   To be sure, the ellipticity of the north-south cross-section is so small that it is invisible to the naked eye and, viewed from space, the earth would seem a sphere. Nevertheless, the deviation from perfect sphericity is important, as I shall explain shortly.

46   Newton was arguing entirely from theory, of course, but it seemed to him he had experimental evidence as well. In 1673 a French scientific expedition in French Guiana found that the pendulum of their clock, which beat out perfect seconds in Paris, was moving slightly slower in their tropical headquarters—as compared with the steady motion of the stars. This could only mean that the force of gravity (which was what powered the swinging pendulum) was slightly weaker in French Guiana than in Paris.

47   This would be understandable if the scientific expedition were on a high mountain where the distance from the center of the earth were greater than at sea level and the gravitational force consequently weakened—but the expedition *was* at sea level. Newton, however, maintained that, in a manner of speaking, the expedition was not truly at sea level, but was high up on the equatorial bulge and that that accounted for the slowing of the pendulum.

48   In this, Newton found himself in conflict with an Italian-born French astronomer named Jean Dominique Cassini. The latter tackled the prob-

lem from another direction. If the earth were not a true sphere, then the curvature of its surface ought to vary from point to point. (A sphere is the only solid that has equal curvature everywhere on its surface.) By triangulation methods, measuring the lengths of the sides and the size of the angles of triangles drawn over large areas of earth's surface, one could determine the gentle curvature of that surface. If the earth were truly an oblate spheroid, then this curvature ought to decrease as one approached either Pole.

49   Cassini had conducted triangulation measurements in the north and south of France and decided that the surface curvature was less, not in the north, but in the south. Therefore, he maintained, the earth bulged at the Poles and was flattened at the Equator. If one took a cross-section of the earth through the Poles, it would have an elliptical boundary indeed, but the longest (and not the shortest) diameter would be through the Poles. Such a solid is a "prolate spheroid."

50   For a generation, the argument raged. It was not just a matter of pure science either. I said the deviation of the earth's shape from the spherical was important, despite the smallness of the deviation, and that was because ocean voyages had become commonplace in the eighteenth century. European nations were squabbling over vast chunks of overseas real estate, and victory could go to the nation whose ships got less badly lost en route. To avoid getting lost one had to have accurate charts and such charts could not be drawn unless the exact deviation of the earth's shape from the spherical were known.

51   It was decided that the difference in curvature between northern and southern France was too small to decide the matter safely either way. Something more extreme was needed. In 1735, therefore, two French expeditions set out. One went to Peru, near the Equator. The other went to Lapland, near the North Pole. Both expeditions took years to make their measurements (and out of their difficulties arose a strong demand for a reform in standards of measurement that led, eventually, to the establishment of the metric system a half century later). When the expeditions returned, the matter was settled. Cassini was wrong, and Newton was right. The equatorial bulge is thirteen miles high, which means that a point at sea level on the Equator is thirteen miles farther from the center of the earth than is sea level at either Pole.

52   The existence of this equatorial bulge neatly explained one particular astronomic mystery. The heavens seemed to rotate about an axis of which one end (the North Celestial Pole) is near the North Star. An ancient Greek astronomer, Hipparchus of Nicaea, was able to show about 150 B.C. that this celestial axis is not fixed. It marks out a circle in the heavens and takes some 25,800 years to complete one turn of the circle. This is called "the precession of the equinoxes."

53   To Hipparchus, it seemed that the heavenly sphere simply rotated slowly in that fashion. He didn't know why. When Copernicus advanced his theory, he had to say that the earth's axis wobbled in that fashion. He didn't know why, either.

54   Newton, however, pointed out that the moon traveled in an orbit that was not in the plane of the earth's Equator. During half of its revolution about the earth, it was well to the north of the Equator and during the other half it was well to the south. If the earth was perfectly spherical, the moon would attract it in an all-one-piece fashion from any point. As it was, the moon gave a special unsymmetrical yank at the equatorial bulge. Newton showed that this pull at the bulge produced the precession of the equinoxes. This could be shown experimentally by hanging a weight on the rim of a spinning gyroscope. The axis of the gyroscope then precesses.

55   And thus the moon itself came to the aid of scientists interested in the shape of things.

56   An artificial moon was to do the same, two and a half centuries after Newton's time.

57   The hero of the latest chapter in the drama of the earth's shape is Vanguard I, which was launched by the United States on March 17, 1958. It was the fourth satellite placed in orbit and is currently the oldest satellite still orbiting and emitting signals. Its path carried it so high above earth's surface that in the absence of atmospheric interference it will stay in orbit for a couple of centuries. Furthermore, it has a solar battery which will keep it delivering signals for years.

58   The orbit of Vanguard I, like that of the moon itself, is not in the plane of the earth's Equator, so Vanguard I pulls on the equatorial bulge and is pulled by it, just as the moon does. Vanguard I isn't large enough to affect the earth's motion, of course, but it is itself affected by the pull of the bulge, much more than the moon is.

59   For one thing, Vanguard I is nearer to the bulge and is therefore affected more strongly. For another, what counts in some ways is the total number of revolutions made by a satellite. Vanguard I revolves about the earth in two and a quarter hours, which means that in a period of fourteen months, it has completed about 4500 revolutions. This is equal to the total number of revolutions that the moon has completed since the invention of the telescope. It follows that the motions of Vanguard I better reveal the fine structure of the bulge than the motions of the moon do.

60   Sure enough, John A. O'Keefe, by studying the orbital irregularities of Vanguard I, was able to show that the earth's equatorial bulge is not symmetrical. The satellite is yanked just a little harder when it is south of the Equator, so that the bulge must be a little bulgier there. It has

been calculated that the southern half of the equatorial bulge is up to fifty feet (not miles but *feet*) farther from the earth's center than the northern half is. To balance this, the South Pole (calculating from sea level) is one hundred feet closer to the center of the earth than the North Pole is.

61 So the earth is not an exact oblate spheroid, either. It is very, very, very slightly egg-shaped, with a bulging southern half and a narrow northern half; with a flattened southern tip and a pointy northern tip.

62 *Nevertheless, to the naked eye, the earth is still a sphere, and don't you forget it.*

63 This final tiny correction is important in a grisly way. Nowadays the national insanity of war requires that missiles not get lost en route, and missiles must be aimed far more accurately than ever a sailing vessel had to be. The exact shape of the earth is more than ever important.

64 Moreover, this final correction even has theoretical implications. To allow such an asymmetry in the bulge against the symmetrical pull of gravity and the push of centrifugal force, O'Keefe maintains, the interior of the earth must be considerably more rigid than geophysicists had thought.

65 One final word: O'Keefe's descriptive adjective for the shape of the earth, as revealed by Vanguard I, is "pear-shaped," and the newspapers took that up at once. The result is that readers of headlines must have the notion that the earth is shaped like a Bartlett pear, or a Bosc pear, which is ridiculous. There are some varieties of pears that are closer to the egg-shaped, but the best-known varieties are far off. However, "pear-shaped" will last, I am sure, and will do untold damage to the popular conception of the shape of the earth. Undoubtedly the next generation of kids will gain the firm conviction that Columbus proved the earth is shaped like a Bartlett pear.

66 But it is an ill wind that blows no good, and I am breathlessly awaiting a certain opportunity. You see, in 1960 a book of mine entitled *The Double Planet* was published. It is about the earth and moon, which are more nearly alike in size than any other planet-satellite combination in the solar system, so that the two may rightly be referred to as a "double planet."

67 Now someday, someone is going to pick up a copy of the book in my presence (I have my books strategically scattered about my house), and leaf through it and say, "Is this about the earth?"

68 With frantically beating heart, I will say, "Yes."

69 And he will say (I hope, I hope), "Why do you call the earth a double planet?"

70 And then I will say (get this now), *"Because it is pair-shaped!!!"*

71 —Why am I the only one laughing?

Content Questions

1. The Greeks used three points to argue for a spherical earth. How did Columbus use these points?
2. Why were the Greeks "happy" with Posidonius's estimation of the circumference of the earth?
3. Who made the correct estimation of the earth's circumference and how did he make that estimation?
4. Why did Columbus die "stubbornly wrong to the end"?
5. What were Newton's and Cassini's arguments about how the earth is shaped?

Questions on Presentation

1. Why does Asimov begin his essay with the statement that a person will never forget certain false information: that Columbus proved the world was round?
2. Asimov uses a number of short, choppy paragraphs. Is this an effective style for presenting this material? Why?
3. How would you describe Asimov's tone of voice?
4. Asimov traces a line of his analysis from the Greeks forward, then returns to the Greeks to trace another line of analysis. Why is this particularly useful in structuring the essay?
5. Asimov presents some fairly sophisticated scientific theories in an easily understandable way. What about his presentation makes it so understandable?

Questions for Discussion and Writing

1. Several of the selections in this section talk about the ways science influences how we live our lives. In some ways science has improved the quality of life for all people. It has provided inventions, medications, and processes that help us; however, scientific discoveries have also cost us. How has science improved our lives? What has it contributed? How has science lessened the quality of our lives? Have the improvements been worth the cost?
2. Although it presents a complex theory, one that is still debated by scientists, Guillen's essay is understandable because he uses common examples to illustrate his generalizations. Readers faced with complex ideas expect a writer to provide several examples because readers expect writers to do the work—to make understanding ideas easier. Which selections in this section illustrate their generalizations most effectively? Why?

Do these same essays present their causal discussions most effectively? Why or why not? What suggestions would you make to one of the writers in this section that would improve that writer's essay?

3. Wade suggests that fraud does not exist in other disciplines, such as art or literature, the way it exists in science. Assume that you are writing an essay for your college's art or literary magazine. Explain how fraud exists in one of these fields and what you believe the students of that field should do to expose fraud.

4. Many of these essays are concerned with what Wade calls surprising "resistence to new ideas [in science], and the acceptance by scientists of plausibly presented fraud." Actually, few of us are surprised when people resist new ideas of any sort, and most of us tend to believe a person who argues logically for a position. By using an argument based on either ideas or facts, explain why you believe people studying a subject might resist new ideas.

Section 8

THE ARTS

Rock as Folk Art
Carl Belz

Born in 1937 in Camden, New Jersey, artist Carl Belz received his bachelor's degree in 1952, Master of Fine Arts degree in 1962, and doctorate in 1963 from Princeton University. After graduation, Belz taught art and art history at the University of Massachusetts, Mills College, and Brandeis University before accepting the directorship of the Rose Art Museum in 1974. A regular contributor to *Artforum*, Belz has written two books, *The Story of Rock* (1969; 1972), an evaluation of folk art, and *Cézanne* (1974), a critical evaluation of the painter's influence on modern art. In the following essay, taken from the 1969 edition of *The Story of Rock*, Belz distinguishes fine art from folk art and argues that rock music is a contemporary form of folk art.

1   The underlying contention of this study is that rock[1] is a part of the long tradition of folk art in the United States and throughout the world. However simple or obvious this thesis may seem at first, it nevertheless involves a number of complicated issues concerning the history of art, the relationship between folk art and fine art, and our notions about the creative act in either domain of expression. The fact that rock first emerged, and has since developed, within the area of popular art only complicates its relationship to the folk and fine art traditions. It is to this general question—of the distinction between folk art, fine art, and popular art—that I wish to address these introductory remarks in order to clarify the position of rock in the larger history of art.

2   Distinguishing between folk, fine, and popular art has become extremely difficult in the 1960's. We live in a culture which is determined to question the validity of such distinctions and in which such questioning has provoked some of the best artistic statements since World War

II. The complexity of this situation is partly due to the phenomenon of Pop Art, a fine art style which has been directly stimulated by popular or mass culture. Pop paintings and sculptures draw their inspiration from billboards, comic strips, advertising, and supermarkets, and sometimes look deceptively like the original objects in our predominantly man-made environment. Similarly, certain developments of theater— particularly the "living theater," "happenings," and "environments"— encourage the notion that the entire panorama of life can be viewed as a work of art. In the face of all this, drawing lines between art objects and non-art objects, or even distingishing between different *classes* of art objects, might seem a less important task than describing a seemingly delightful situation in which anything can be art and maybe everything is. For the critic-historian, however, these distinctions are fundamental. Rock has been considered as popular art, folk art, fine art, and even non-art. Which, in fact, is it?

3   The vast and current interest in rock might be viewed as a feedback from such phenomena as Pop Art. Taking a hint from the fine arts, the adult public has begun to appreciate material which was previously alien and embarrassing to the critics of modern American civilization. Such appreciation, however, is a development of the 1960's. The development of rock particularly during the first decade of its history, took place in the absence of such appreciation. The music emerged in response to a series of changing values and vital needs—not as the result of a sophistication gleaned from art galleries, museums, or periodicals. Its history, moreover, must be seen as a youth movement and as the reflection of a way of life radically different from the one which prevailed before the 1950's. When rock emerged, it spoke to these new values, to this youth, and to this changed way of life. But it did so in its capacity as a voice *of* the people rather than an art which talked *about* them from a detached and self-determined vantage point. On an immediate level as well as in its ultimate significance, the music has been a confrontation with reality rather than a confrontation with art. This distinctiveness of function marks rock as folk art rather than fine art.

4   The difference between the functions of folk art and fine art cannot be regarded as absolute or necessarily clear-cut. All art, it can be argued, arises in response to vital needs and reflects a changing way of life from generation to generation. Further, all art is admittedly concerned with reality. At this level of generalization, folk art and fine art become alike. But folk art and fine art are not so similar when we consider which elements are more or less important in the creation and appeal of each.

5   In the modern period the most advanced media of the fine arts have become increasingly conscious of their respective and unique identities. Painting, for instance, has consistently involved itself with questions of the intrinsic nature of its expression: its flatness, its shape, its optical-

ity, and so forth. Furthermore, these questions have evolved into an explicit *content*. In other words, the most successful expressions in the medium have tended to force the viewer to recognize that he is looking at a painting, a work of art. Moreover, by recognizing its particular medium in this way, the individual work compels its viewer to recognize that the object of his experience—in this case, the painting—is also distinct from other kinds of realities and from life in general. To put it another way, fine art declares itself as being different in kind from life. This is not to say that fine art ignores life or is irrelevant to the concerns of reality. Rather, any fine art expression confronts life, and has meaning in terms of it, only by engaging in an immediate confrontation with itself. In this sense, fine art is conscious of its own being, and, more generally, conscious of art.

6   In folk art, "art-consciousness" does not occupy the primary role that it does in fine art. A folk idiom's immediate concern is with issues of life and reality and with an overt expression of those issues. It is not aware of the identities of the separate media that it may employ. In the sense I am trying to define, a folk idiom employs different media unknowingly; it regards the identities of these media as being passive, like entities that need not be confronted in themselves. More simply, the difference between folk art and fine art can be stated in the following way: The work of folk art says of itself, as it were, "this is reality," while the work of fine art says "this is a picture of reality." In no way, of course, does this distinction imply that one type of expression is of a higher quality than the other.

7   The distinction I have just made must be cautiously applied. It might very well be rejected by the artists themselves. But, however fascinating and enlightening an artist's remarks may be, they constitute a different area of concern, that of autobiography. A given artist—someone, say, whom I consider the producer of fine art objects—may contend that he never thinks about "art" when he is making a picture. Similarly, the Beatles have frequently commented that they do not *intend* all the meanings the critics find in their songs. Such statements are perplexing unless we understand that they belong to the domain of autobiography. The emphasis in the present study is upon neither autobiography nor biography, but upon the works of art themselves and upon their inherent character as experienced objects. Such an emphasis is not simply capricious, nor is it meant to undermine the significance of other types of studies. It merely represents a method for relating works of art in an historical context, and, more important, for understanding the meanings those works compel in our experience of them.

8   The ways in which rock relates to the fine art–folk art distinction are apparent in various aspects of the music itself, in the fabric of media which has surrounded it, and in the responses it elicits. In the early days

of the *American Bandstand* television show, for instance, a panel of three or four teenagers periodically reviewed newly released records. The record was played, the audience danced, and a discussion of the song's merits followed. This discussion invariably contained remarks such as, "It's got a great beat. . . . I'll give it an 80," or, "You can really dance to it. . . . I'll give it an 85." The panelists never talked about the artistic properties of the record: the way the song was structured, the relation between its structure and meaning, its manipulations of the medium, the implications of its content, or any of the kinds of issues that are central to a meaningful statement about a work of fine art.

9   No one who appreciated or understood the music ever expected such questions to be discussed, for they are not part of the folk response. That response is spontaneous, and it is directed to the thing-as-reality. In other words, the connection between listener and song is an immediate one; no aesthetic distance separates the two, no gap that would provoke art-consciousness. With rock, as with any folk idiom, a consciousness of art is unnecessary for grasping the full impact of a particular work. This fact probably explains why the *Bandstand* panelists, however "uncritical" they may have appeared, were usually accurate in naming the best—that is, the most folk-like—of the new records.

10   The adult audiences and the popular press who condemned rock in the 1950's did so because they did not understand the identity of the music they heard. They failed to grasp the essential difference between folk art and fine art, a difference teenagers unconsciously took for granted. Adverse critics of the music complained that it was crude and primitive, that it used poor grammar and improper enunciation, and that its lyrics were literary nonsense. Even in the 1960's, on his *Open End* show, David Susskind[2] continued the effort to embarrass the music by reading the lyrics of some typical rock songs as if they were examples of fine art poetry. This sort of criticism was as futile and irrelevant as an art historian's criticism that a painting by Henri Rousseau[3] had awkward perspective or that its human figures were out of scale with the landscape.

11   Folk art is neither aware of, nor concerned about, the kinds of manipulations that constitute "proper" effects in the fine arts. The rock artist's "crude" enunciation sprang naturally from his spontaneous effort to express something real. Yet, the grammar of "Doncha jus know it" or "I got a girl named Rama Lama Ding Dong" does not alone transform a song into folk material. Artists in the fine arts have used unconventional or slang expressions for centuries, from Shakespeare to the present day. What distinguishes the folk artist is that he uses such expressions unconsciously rather than for a desired artistic effect. Unaware of the option at his disposal—between art and reality—the folk artist plunges naturally, though unknowingly, into the latter.

12   Just as rock does not "become" folk music simply because it includes certain kinds of grammar or sentence structures, its folk character is not assured by the use of particular musical instruments or by a devotion to specific subject matters. A common misunderstanding concerning these questions arose during the latter 1950's and continued into the 1960's. Groups like the Kingston Trio and individual singers like Joan Baez inspired a popular movement which seemed to equate folk music with songs telling a story or conveying a moralistic point and accompanied by the acoustic or solo guitar. To its enthusiastic audience, this type of music was pure, eschewing the so-called falsifications of recording-room manipulations. As such, it appeared to offer an alternative to the crude and primitive style of rock. The artists and audiences of this new trend failed to realize, however, that folk styles change. The acoustic guitar may have been all that was available to the folk artist of the 1930's, but his counterpart in the 1950's and the 1960's could work with electronics, with echo chambers, and with complicated recording techniques. Folk music could change its cloak—just as folk art changed its materials between the stone carvings of Cycladic culture, the bark paintings of Australia, and the oils of Rousseau.

13   A dramatic reflection of rock's essentially folk character is apparent in the large number of one-shot successes in the history of the music. A group or individual produces a high quality record on its first effort but fails to repeat that success. Although the group or individual artist generally issues a second or a third record, these follow-ups rarely achieve the special blend of ingredients that gave the initial song its impact. The explanation for this phenomenon—for the fact that the follow-ups are so often artistic failures—is directly connected with folk art's lack of art-consciousness. When the rock group produces its first record, it is not concerned with style or structure, but, rather, with a sense of immediate impact, with what the *Bandstand* panelists call "the great beat." With the second or third record, however, the group seems to become aware of *art*—that is, with the artistic character of the first record. The group tries to duplicate the elements of the first record with only minor or barely perceptible variations. Yet, as they try for artistic consistency, their folk orientation generally betrays them: Not really understanding art, or the complex blend of aesthetic decisions which produced the original sound, they produce an object bearing only superficial resemblance to the first record. In this instance, the folk artist's lack of art-consciousness plays an ironic role in his creative life: At a time when he consciously believes he is making art, he is merely producing reproductions of his own original and unconsciously creative gesture.

14   Rock history substantiates the notion that the realities in a particular song carry greater significance than the art of that song. This further suggests that the realities exist and are felt on a day-to-day basis. That

is, rock's past is generally experienced as being part of the present rather than a part of history. Its history, in other words, is not usually pursued as an end in itself. While many songs may be remembered from the early or middle 1950's, their artists are usually forgotten. In such cases, the very term "artist" has a radically different meaning from the way it is used in the fine arts. In the latter, the artist is regarded as an individual whose significance and responsibility are linked with the production of a number of objects which are vital to our understanding of art. But with folk art, the relevance of the object-as-reality assumes greater importance than the artist who was responsible for its production—as if that artist only *happened* to have created the record. Hence, we cherish and recognize numerous songs in the folk music tradition, but we do not feel compelled to connect them with particular artists. In the fine arts, such a connection is demanded by the works, and scholars labor for years to discover the names of the masters whose art has survived without evidence of authorship.

15   That the relevance of rock songs is experienced in terms of day-to-day realities is shown by the numerous polls of "all-time favorites" conducted by local radio stations across the country. These polls usually list 300 songs; of that number, however, more than half are examples from the same year as the poll or from the year preceding it. Contrary to what many disk jockeys say, these figures do not prove that rock has improved over the years. Rather, the polls demonstrate that the current songs are simply more *real* than the older ones. The lists of "all-time favorites" reflect only today's memories of realities which existed when the various songs were originally experienced. The albums of "Oldies But Goodies" are similarly folk-like in their stress upon experienced realities: They thrive because they enable listeners to relive the past in the present, not because they inform their audiences about the art of the past.

16   I have suggested that folk artists, in contrast to their fine art counterparts, tend to be anonymous in relation to the works they produce. Yet, rock has a distinctive style of anonymity. While the artists of still remembered songs are frequently forgotten, the writers of these songs are even more generally nameless. Rock has only recently granted significance to these figures. Through most of its history their names have merely appeared parenthetically beneath the song titles. Moreover, even the groups who are currently most popular remain tinged with folk anonymity. Most listeners know the Rascals, the Hermits, the Doors, and other groups, but I wonder how many listeners know the names of the individuals who compose those groups. Teenage newspapers and magazines seek to combat our ignorance with their feature stories on one or another group and its members. But, as time passes, even these efforts seem futile in the face of the relentless thrust of folk anonymity; and

they *are* futile because the experience of a folk music reality is ultimately more pressing and immediate than the name of the artist who
produced it.

17   This anonymity is one of the differences between rock and jazz. Jazz
is a music of great individualists. Further, its roots reach far back into
the beginnings of the twentieth century, and its stylistic manifestations
have been more varied than those of rock: New Orleans jazz, Chicago
jazz, swing, be-bop, and modern jazz *each* represent a whole movement,
one that is more expansive than the development so far of any of rock's
sub-styles. Finally, improvisation has always been far more important in
jazz than in rock. Nevertheless, they share a common ancestry in the
blues tradition of America, and they share a folk delight in spontaneity
of expression.

18   Perhaps the greatest difficulty in distinguishing rock as a folk idiom
lies in the fact that the music is so closely linked to the enormous and
complicated commercial music business, whereas generally works of art
in the larger folk tradition are not at all closely related to popular art.
This has caused the adverse critics of rock to say that the music has
been forced upon a gullible public by some mercenary wholesalers of
bad taste. In addition, these critics feel that the artists themselves are
exclusively interested in financial rewards and are unconcerned about
the quality of their music.

19   Suspicions like these are based on the fallacious assumption that the
quality of art and the salability of art are mutually exclusive. Such a
point, however, does not immediately dispel the suspicions themselves.
Admittedly, many rock artists have earned fortunes through the sales of
their records. My question, at the same time, is whether such evidence
provides any meaningful explanation of why rock came into being in the
first place, or why it has continued to exist. Rock artists have won and
lost commercially, but the experience of the music itself has continued
to possess vitality. I cannot imagine any artist who would not *enjoy* the
benefits of commercial success, but both folk art and fine art can be
originated and can survive without it. On the other hand, popular art
does depend on commercial success in order to exist. That is, popular
art *must* be popular, whereas folk art and fine art need not be, although
they *may* be at any given moment. This demand for popularity is linked
to the fact that popular art invariably has a product to sell: The product
may be a bottle of shampoo or a new automobile, but it may also be
non-material, such as diversion or escape, the "look" of reality or even
of art. Popular art has many guises, but unlike either folk art or fine art,
it is not self-sustaining.

20   Popular music, the Tin Pan Alley tradition, or *kitsch* music, has the
appearance of fine art but fails to engage in the creative or artistic prob-

lems of fine art. *Kitsch* feeds parasitically upon fine art, but only after the latter has passed through its experimental and innovative stages. *Kitsch* represents an institutionalizing of the fine arts, and its product is therefore only the "look" of art. These products may be pleasant, enjoyable, and entertaining—the records of Frank Sinatra, Perry Como, and Andy Williams, and other leading exponents of *kitsch* frequently are—but they are not fundamentally concerned with artistic creation. Rather, they adopt the style of a work of art after it has come into being elsewhere, and they refine it and make it palatable for audiences who could not understand it in its original form.

21   Popular art avoids an encounter with reality just as it avoids an encounter with art. It succeeds by selling the "look" of reality. So although rock emerged in the same domain as popular music, it cannot be classified simply as popular music. Admittedly, the task of separating the two types of music is occasionally problematic, particularly at those points in rock history where an artist's work, Elvis Presley's for instance, undergoes a transformation from folk art to popular art. But generally the distinction is clear.

22   I have tried to outline some of the qualities of rock which show that it is folk music. In doing so, I am aware of the risks in generalizing about so large a body of material: Many exceptions can no doubt be offered to my central thesis. More important than the exceptions, however, is the undeniable fact that the music has changed considerably since its beginnings in the mid-1950's. Its history reveals dramatic changes in its attitude both to subject matter and to technique. And developments in the late 1960's further suggest that the music may be changing in its relation to the folk art–fine art distinction. It has been folk music through the greater part of its history; but to say that it is folk music today is more difficult. A separate chapter must be devoted to this issue and to its implications; but that discussion must take place at the conclusion of this study, after a fuller examination of the development of the music itself.

Notes

[1]"Rock and Roll" is sometimes used generically to describe the whole movement studied in this book and sometimes to describe a particular type of music within the movement. I have avoided the term and use the accepted generic term "rock" throughout.

[2]David Susskind (1920–1987), American television producer and popular talk-show host during the 1960s. [Eds.]

[3]Henri Rousseau (1844–1910), French painter and critic. [Eds.]

Content Questions

1. What distinguishes folk art, fine art, and popular art?
2. Why does the relationship between contemporary art and American culture confuse a definition of rock as an art form?
3. Why didn't the teenage critics on "American Bandstand" evaluate the artistic merits of the music?
4. How do "one-song" successes confirm Belz's thesis?
5. What is rock's distinctive style of anonymity?

Questions on Presentation

1. What issues does Belz's seemingly obvious thesis introduce? Why is the thesis more complicated than it seems? What is his true thesis?
2. Belz asserts that "we live in a culture which is determined to question the validity" of distinctions in art (2). How does he support this assertion? How effective is that support?
3. In paragraphs 5 and 6 Belz makes distinctions between fine art and folk. How clear are those distinctions to you? Could they be made clearer?
4. How do you believe Belz perceives his audience? How do you determine that?

How We Listen

Aaron Copland

Born in Brooklyn, New York, composer Aaron Copland (b. 1900) not only wrote musical scores such as "Rodeo" and "Appalachian Spring," he is also the author of several discussions of music including *What to Listen for in Music* (1939), *Music and Imagination* (1952), *Connotations for Orchestra* (1962), and the more recent *Emblems for a Band* (1965). Copland studied piano under pianists Leopold Wolfson and Richardo Vines and composition with Rubin Goldmark. He began his career composing for orchestra and ballet as well as for the stage and films. A lecturer on contemporary music for the New School of Social Research, Copland has taught music at both Harvard University and the Berkshire Music Center. In the following essay, taken from *What to Listen for in Music*, Copland outlines a contemporary figure, the listener, and explains the various ways a listener experiences music.

1   We all listen to music according to our separate capacities. But, for the sake of analysis, the whole listening process may become clearer if we break it up into its component parts, so to speak. In a certain sense we all listen to music on three separate planes. For lack of a better terminology, one might name these: (1) the sensuous plane, (2) the expressive plane, (3) the sheerly musical plane. The only advantage to be gained from mechanically splitting up the listening process into these hypothetical planes is the clearer view to be had of the way in which we listen.

2   The simplest way of listening to music is to listen for the sheer pleasure of the musical sound itself. That is the sensuous plane. It is the plane on which we hear music without thinking, without considering it in any way. One turns on the radio while doing something else and absent-mindedly bathes in the sound. A kind of brainless but attractive state of mind is engendered by the mere sound appeal of the music.

3   You may be sitting in a room reading this book. Imagine one note struck on the piano. Immediately that one note is enough to change the atmosphere of the room—proving that the sound element in music is a powerful and mysterious agent, which it would be foolish to deride or belittle.

4   The surprising thing is that many people who consider themselves qualified music lovers abuse that plane in listening. They go to concerts in order to lose themselves. They use music as a consolation or an escape. They enter an ideal world where one doesn't have to think of the realities of everyday life. Of course they aren't thinking about the music either. Music allows them to leave it, and they go off to a place to dream, dreaming because of and apropos of the music yet never quite listening to it.

5   Yes, the sound appeal of music is a potent and primitive force, but you must not allow it to usurp a disproportionate share of your interest. The sensuous plane is an important one in music, a very important one, but it does not constitute the whole story.

6   There is no need to digress further on the sensuous plane. Its appeal to every normal human being is self-evident. There is, however, such a thing as becoming more sensitive to the different kinds of sound stuff as used by various composers. For all composers do not use that sound stuff in the same way. Don't get the idea that the value of music is commensurate with its sensuous appeal or that the loveliest sounding music is made by the greatest composer. If that were so, Ravel would be a greater creator than Beethoven. The point is that the sound element varies with each composer, that his usage of sound forms an integral part of his style and must be taken into account when listening. The reader can see, therefore, that a more conscious approach is valuable even on this primary plane of music listening.

7   The second plane on which music exists is what I have called the expressive one. Here, immediately, we tread on controversial ground. Composers have a way of shying away from any discussion of music's expressive side. Did not Stravinsky himself proclaim that his music was an "object," a "thing," with a life of its own, and with no other meaning than its own purely musical existence? This intransigent attitude of Stravinsky's may be due to the fact that so many people have tried to read different meanings into so many pieces. Heaven knows it is difficult enough to say precisely what it is that a piece of music means, to say it definitely, to say it finally so that everyone is satisfied with your explanation. But that should not lead one to the other extreme of denying to music the right to be "expressive."

8   My own belief is that all music has an expressive power, some more and some less, but that all music has a certain meaning behind the notes and that that meaning behind the notes constitutes, after all, what the piece is saying, what the piece is about. This whole problem can be stated quite simply by asking, "Is there a meaning to music?" My answer to that would be, "Yes." And "Can you state in so many words what the meaning is?" My answer to that would be, "No." Therein lies the difficulty.

9   Simple-minded souls will never be satisfied with the answer to the second of these questions. They always want music to have a meaning, and the more concrete it is the better they like it. The more the music reminds them of a train, a storm, a funeral, or any other familiar conception the more expressive it appears to be to them. This popular idea of music's meaning—stimulated and abetted by the usual run of musical commentator—should be discouraged wherever and whenever it is met. One timid lady once confessed to me that she suspected something seriously lacking in her appreciation of music because of her inability to connect it with anything definite. That is getting the whole thing backward, of course.

10   Still, the question remains, How close should the intelligent music lover wish to come to pinning a definite meaning to any particular work? No closer than a general concept, I should say. Music expresses, at different moments, serenity or exuberance, regret or triumph, fury or delight. It expresses each of these moods, and many others, in a numberless variety of subtle shadings and differences. It may even express a state of meaning for which there exists no adequate word in any language. In that case, musicians often like to say that it has only a purely musical meaning. They sometimes go farther and say that *all* music has only a purely musical meaning. What they really mean is that no appropriate word can be found to express the music's meaning and that, even if it could, they do not feel the need of finding it.

11   But whatever the professional musician may hold, most musical novices still search for specific words with which to pin down their musical reactions. That is why they always find Tschaikovsky easier to "understand" than Beethoven. In the first place, it is easier to pin a meaning-word on a Tschaikovsky piece than on a Beethoven one. Much easier. Moreover, with the Russian composer, every time you come back to a piece of his it almost always says the same thing to you, whereas with Beethoven it is often quite difficult to put your finger right on what he is saying. And any musician will tell you that this is why Beethoven is the greater composer. Because music which always says the same thing to you will necessarily soon become dull music, but music whose meaning is slightly different with each hearing has a greater chance of remaining alive.

12   Listen, if you can, to the forty-eight fugue themes of Bach's *Well Tempered Clavichord*. Listen to each theme, one after another. You will soon realize that each theme mirrors a different world of feeling. You will also soon realize that the more beautiful a theme seems to you the harder it is to find any word that will describe it to your complete satisfaction. Yes, you will certainly know whether it is a gay theme or a sad one. You will be able, in other words, in your own mind, to draw a frame of emotional feeling around your theme. Now study the sad one a little closer. Try to pin down the exact quality of its sadness. Is it pessimistically sad or resignedly sad; is it fatefully sad or smilingly sad?

13   Let us suppose that you are fortunate and can describe to your own satisfaction in so many words the exact meaning of your chosen theme. There is still no guarantee that anyone else will be satisfied. Nor need they be. The important thing is that each one feel for himself the specific expressive quality of a theme or, similarly, an entire piece of music. And if it is a great work of art, don't expect it to mean exactly the same thing to you each time you return to it.

14   Themes or pieces need not express only one emotion, of course. Take such a theme as the first main one of the *Ninth Symphony*, for example. It is clearly made up of different elements. It does not say only one thing. Yet anyone hearing it immediately gets a feeling of strength, a feeling of power. It isn't a power that comes simply because the theme is played loudly. It is a power inherent in the theme itself. The extraordinary strength and vigor of the theme results in the listener's receiving an impression that a forceful statement has been made. But one should never try to boil it down to "the fateful hammer of life," etc. That is where the trouble begins. The musician, in his exasperation, says it means nothing but the notes themselves, whereas the nonprofessional is only too anxious to hang on to any explanation that gives him the illusion of getting closer to the music's meaning.

15   Now, perhaps, the reader will know better what I mean when I say that music does have an expressive meaning but that we cannot say in so many words what that meaning is.

16   The third plane on which music exists is the sheerly musical plane. Besides the pleasurable sound of music and the expressive feeling that it gives off, music does exist in terms of the notes themselves and of their manipulation. Most listeners are not sufficiently conscious of this third plane. . . .

17   Professional musicians, on the other hand, are, if anything, too conscious of the mere notes themselves. They often fall into the error of becoming so engrossed with their arpeggios and staccatos that they forget the deeper aspects of the music they are performing. But from the layman's standpoint, it is not so much a matter of getting over bad habits on the sheerly musical plane as of increasing one's awareness of what is going on, in so far as the notes are concerned.

18   When the man in the street listens to the "notes themselves" with any degree of concentration, he is most likely to make some mention of the melody. Either he hears a pretty melody or he does not, and he generally lets it go at that. Rhythm is likely to gain his attention next, particularly if it seems exciting. But harmony and tone color are generally taken for granted, if they are thought of consciously at all. As for music's having a definite form of some kind, that idea seems never to have occurred to him.

19   It is very important for all of us to become more alive to music on its sheerly musical plane. After all, an actual musical material is being used. The intelligent listener must be prepared to increase his awareness of the musical material and what happens to it. He must hear the melodies, the rhythms, the harmonies, the tone colors in a more conscious fashion. But above all he must, in order to follow the line of the composer's thought, know something of the principles of musical form. Listening to all of these elements is listening on the sheerly musical plane.

20   Let us repeat that I have split up mechanically the three separate planes on which we listen merely for the sake of greater clarity. Actually, we never listen on one or the other of these planes. What we do is to correlate them—listening in all three ways at the same time. It takes no mental effort, for we do it instinctively.

21   Perhaps an analogy with what happens to us when we visit the theater will make this instinctive correlation clearer. In the theater, you are aware of the actors and actresses, costumes and sets, sounds and movements. All these give one the sense that the theater is a pleasant place to be in. They constitute the sensuous plane in our theatrical reactions.

22   The expressive plane in the theater would be derived from the feeling that you get from what is happening on the stage. You are moved to

pity, excitement, or gayety. It is this general feeling, generated aside from the particular words being spoken, a certain emotional something which exists on the stage, that is analogous to the expressive quality in music.

23   The plot and plot development is equivalent to our sheerly musical plane. The playwright creates and develops a character in just the same way that a composer creates and develops a theme. According to the degree of your awareness of the way in which the artist in either field handles his material will you become a more intelligent listener.

Content Questions

1. Why can't the process of listening to music be conveniently broken into phases?
2. Why are the sensuous plane, the expressive plane, and the sheerly musical plane individually important?
3. How does Beethoven's music fit in each of Copland's planes?
4. How does Copland feel most people should listen to music?

Questions on Presentation

1. Copland's paragraphs are much shorter than those in Miller's essay on the western (pages 521–526). What does this say about Copland's understanding of his audience?
2. Are Copland's explanations of the planes of listening understandable? Why?
3. Must the audience be familiar with the music of Stravinsky and the other composers Copland mentions in order to understand the essay? How do these references enhance the essay?
4. Is the analogy with which Copland ends the essay an effective one? Why?

The "Ideal" Listener

Ricki Hisaw

Ricki Hisaw is a music major. She is interested not only in the creation of music but also in the effect of music on the listener because, as in writing, the audience is of major importance. In this essay she examines Copland's levels of listening and interprets them in light of her own experience.

1   Copland begins "How We Listen" with the statement, "We all listen to music according to our separate capacities." His contention is that we listen to music on three separate planes: the sensuous plane, the expressive plane, and the sheerly musical plane. Copland says that we do not listen on just one of these planes, but that we correlate them. However, there is going to be one plane on which we focus. I feel that as we grow as individuals, our focus shifts.

2   I have a fairly musical background: when I was five years old I started singing solos in church; at eight, I began formal violin lessons; at sixteen, I started singing radio commercials. I have played with numerous symphonies, and have sung in diverse ensembles. Does this mean, however that I hear music on a different plane than the musically untrained? At this point in my life, perhaps. But I haven't always listened on the plane that I do now.

3   As a child, I listened to music purely on the sensuous plane. My enjoyment of the music consisted of "hearing" the music only. I saw music as an addition to "nap time," church, musical chairs, and Christmas. Copland expresses this as, "a kind of brainless but attractive state of mind [which] is engendered by the mere sound appeal of the music." I saw music as an accompaniment to everyday life.

4   In middle school I was asked to listen to a symphony and describe exactly what I heard happening within the piece. My teacher returned my paper with a huge "D – " emblazoned across the top and the comment, "You are the most insensitive listener in my class." What did I do wrong? I followed the instructions to the letter; I described exactly what I had heard:

> A breathtaking quiet, interrupted by sharply accented forte-pianos; crisp staccatos throughout the strings while the low brass created long, smooth lines; magnificent crescendo-decrescendos; violinists racing up the neck of their instruments with fingers climbing wildy over each other until, at last, with a single unison note played by the entire section, the piece was complete.

How could she not find that expressive? I had listened to the symphony from a "sheerly musical plane," as Copland would say, which was obviously not what my teacher desired. I was so conscious of the notes, the ensemble, the dynamics, that I missed completely the "expressive plane." I was listening from a "musical point of view," as opposed to "the music's point of view."

5   I have not played with any symphonies in the last year; I have sung only on rare occasions. I have always enjoyed performing but I find it quite refreshing to be performed to. I have attended many concerts, and have gone to hear quite a few vocalists. My musical plane has shifted.

Without dwelling on the technical aspects, I can enter the piece and look objectively at the different tones; I can feel the composer pouring his life blood into the piece, only to find his quiet indifference around another corner. I don't search for the technical aspects of the music; I feel it.

6   Copland quotes Stravinsky as saying his music was an "object," a "thing," with a life of its own, with no meaning other than its own purely musical existence. The first time I heard Stravinsky's "Firebird Suite" I was completely absorbed; the melody hung throughout, and wove completely through the piece and was so eerie and mysterious that muted pictures slipped through my mind. I did not look for meanings— I merely felt the life of the piece.

7   Copland says that all music has meaning, but the meaning can never be stated correctly. For example, the meaning that I get from a piece may be very different from the meaning the composer foresaw as he created, and quite different again from what one of my friends might receive. Also, Copland says, "music which always says the same thing to you will necessarily soon become dull music, but music whose meaning is slightly different with each hearing has a greater chance of remaining alive."

8   I am listening again to my favorite pieces, consciously switching planes. The music now has three different dimensions for me, and listening is a more pleasant experience. Copland says, "The ideal listener is both inside and outside the music at the same moment, judging it and enjoying it, wishing it would go one way and watching it go another— almost like the composer at the moment he composes it." If you can become Copland's "ideal listener," you will not only understand more completely what you are hearing, but you will also become, as he says in his last sentence, "someone who is listening for something."

The "Western"—A Theological Note

Alexander Miller

Alexander Miller (1908–1956) was a professor of religion at Stanford University and the author of *The Renewal of Man,* a study of Christian sociology. In the following selection, taken from *The Christian Century* (1957), Miller analyzes one reason for the appeal of westerns.

1   A while ago I had a week-end visit from a fellow theologian who made it clear early on the Saturday that he would accept no engagements that clashed with *Gunsmoke* on TV. Since I watch *Gunsmoke* myself, come hell or high water, I knew I had a kindred spirit as well as a fellow apostle. So we spent the early part of the evening analyzing the appeal of the show, which is not wholly to be explained by its undeniable quality. For not only do I find myself maneuvering to watch TV westerns of lesser quality than *Gunsmoke,* but I discover that through the long years I retain an unabated zest for every kind of western yarn, in print or in picture. And while I'm glad of quality when I can find it, a western has to be pretty bad before I find it intolerable. Enough for me if the hero runs to type, if there is the scent of sage and the squeak of saddle-leather, if the high hills are high enough.

2   At one level the attraction of the thing is obvious. I am professionally involved with the high matters of speculation and the deep matters of theology; and nothing is more relaxing after a bout with Hegel or Niebuhr than a vicarious ride into the sage. And there is the practical advantage that this particular escape-mechanism costs but twenty-five cents in paperback (plus one cent sales tax in some states). It's rarely necessary even to buy a new one. An old one will do equally well, since nothing of it sticks in the mind, and the formula is constant.

3   My friend wanted to go deeper. "If just once," said he, "I could stand in the dust of the frontier main street, facing an indubitably bad man who really deserved extermination, and with smoking six-gun actually exterminate him—shoot once and see him drop. Just once to face real and unqualified evil, plug it and see it drop . . ." None of this complex business of separating the sin from the sinner, of tempering justice with mercy, of remembering our own complicity in evil. To blow, just once, an actual and visible hole in the wall of evil, instead of beating the air with vain exhortation and the nicely calculated less and more of moral discrimination and doleful casuistry. To see something actually drop, as the gospel says Satan once fell as lightning from heaven.

I

4   Yet there must be more to it than that, and there *is* more to it than that. Another theologian friend of mine, whose specialty is Christian ethics, makes a point of reading the *Saturday Evening Post* from cover to cover, since, he says, it is a transcript of American folkways; and if the gospel is to be taken into all the world, the contemporary world into which it has to be taken is between the covers of the *Satevepost.* (I know other professional colleagues who find the same illumination in the funnies, but I don't read the funnies. I can't find time to master Pogo and Kingaroo, which appear to be theological staples; and in any event,

when I'm worn out with Hegel everything is too strenuous except the westerns.) The western serial is standard in the *Post,* for the good and trite reason that it is *par excellence* the American folk tale.

5   The quality of "western" writing varies endlessly. Eugene Manlove Rhodes was a literary artist of high caliber. Ernest Haycox could and did write as well as the next man and better than most, but was apparently content to be, for the most part, the best of western hackwriters. He is only one of a number of highly competent operators. Then the stream runs out into a drab flatland of pedestrian writing (odd phrase for the horse opera!) which yet—at least for me—is never dull.

II

6   The so-called formula western is compact and predictable. It runs like this: Over the ridge of the high hills (or it may be against the backdrop of the desert) appears the maverick rider, he of the lean flanks, the taut, long-planed face, the lips stern yet capable of smiling, the dust of the trail in his clothes and on his horse. A single Colt, its butt hand-polished, hangs low on one hip (only lesser men carry two guns). His eyes miss nothing. Literally at random I take a paperback from a one-foot shelf of them:

> Cole Knapp rode through the dark-timbered passages of the La Sal Mountains and down into Paradox Valley with its high, bare walls, buff and red and white, bright-hued from the misty rain that was driven against them by a wind that was cool for June. Sage-brush, damp and dripping, gave off an odor both pungent and pleasant. A rock, loosened by rain, thundered off the rim to raise a low rumble on the valley floor.
> A big man, this Cole Knapp, but thin with riding and slim trail rations. Hide and bone and muscle, and travel-stained from the countless miles which lay between southern Arizona where he had started, and the western slope of Colorado where he now was.
> The gun at his right thigh was almost a part of him. . . . [Joseph Wayne: *Show-down at Stony Creek* (Dell), p. 5.]

7   As he drops over the last ridge, there on the flat or in the valley is the cattle town, a one-street town of clapboard—saloon, livery stable, store and sheriff's office, with a coffee-and-steak house in which the heroine (unless she is a cattleman's daughter) can be located handily, yet outside the saloon.

> Horse and rider came to a halt on the bluff overlooking Saddle-Up just as the sun dipped across the western line and began to sift into the canyon. The rider . . . hooked one leg over the saddle-horn and curled himself a cigarette, meanwhile surveying the dingy houses and the crooked dusty street

of a town whose reputation was a by-word and a reproach all along the rolling leagues of two sovereign states. [Ernest Haycox: "The Bandit from Paloma County" in *Gun Talk* (Popular Library), p. 63.]

8   There is no reason why the rider should stop longer than to find vittles for himself and his cayuse. He is headed nowhere in particular, except that somewhere in the long distance lies the "spread" of his dreams. But he doubts that he will find it, or that he could settle if he did find it, for towns stifle him (he needs "a land where a man can breathe") and he knows no peace except under the stars. Yet his horse has no sooner catfooted it into town than he feels the tension in the place, "a full dozen pairs of eyes watching him from odd coverts." A shooting, the sight of a gratuitous beating, and he is hip-deep in the range war that is tearing the community apart.

III

9   Now there is nothing for it but to see it through, and see it through he does, surviving a half-dozen knock-down-drag-outs that would finish any normal man, snaking out the gun which is his pride and torment with a speed no man can match, and finally outdrawing the hired gunman brought in by the wicked cattle baron with the unsatisfied land-hunger. The ending is open: he may either marry the baron's daughter (or the local caterer who has feminine merits lacking in the baron's daughter) and find that "spread" on an unclaimed piece of bottom land; or he may take to the road again. In the first case he puts his gun away, as he had always longed to do. In the second case it stays strapped to his thigh, since in a world like this one there is always need for the law outside the law, the law embodied only in the strength of soul and speed of hand of the incorruptible man.

10   He is a philosopher after his fashion, but at no time does he understand the whys and the wherefores. Why not keep going? It's not his fight. And yet he cannot pass it up and "go on living with himself." "A man has to play the hand he's dealt." Yet now and then he takes time out to try to make sense of it all. But he's in a world that doesn't add up.

Men were not meant for peace. Their minds, so filled with incessant wonder, would never let them alone, and their bodies were racked by feelings that eventually destroyed them; there was a form and a substance and a meaning somewhere, no doubt, but men died before they knew what any of it was. [Ernest Haycox: *Long Storm* (Bantam Giant), p. 58.]

11   The pattern is worth analysis, if only because the flood of formula westerns grows greater all the time. I'm pretty sure that they now out-

number the sexy and salacious items on the pocket-book stands, and this is no doubt to the good. The TV channels are choked with them this fall, and this too is O.K. by me, both for their own sake and in view of the alternatives. But without being too heavy-handed about it, I would say that there must be some cultural symptoms here. It is not only the bulk of the phenomenon that requires explanation, but the pervasiveness of the appeal. My ten-year-old and I are radically unequal, I pride myself, in sophistication; yet we watch *Gunsmoke* or *Cheyenne* with equal absorption, and dang-bust it if I don't join him from time to time for *The Range-Rider*. Relaxing? Sure; and the sight of good horses against the skyline alone is worth the low price of admission. But one can, I think, without forcing it, find more in it than that: can find, in fact and in simplicity, most of the working philosophy, the bothersome confusions and the perplexed yearnings of the average 20th century American—maybe the average 20th century man, since you can find the same items in Charing Cross station as in Grand Central, and I myself am no American, but an amiable alien.

12   There is, for one thing, the eternal dialectic of pilgrimage and rest. The hero of this tale seeks his Shangri-la, his Tirna nOg—which for him is a place of good grass and free water: but he doubts if the world holds such a place; it if does, he doubts if he could bed down there in peace; and if his restlessness would let him stay, sure as shootin' the bad men wouldn't. This side of that six feet of earth which is the end of everything, he will keep moving or be kept moving, though he will never quite give up his dream. A longing for the home spread does battle with what T. S. Eliot calls a "distaste for beatitude" in a fashion which is of great Christian and theological interest.

13   There is a dialectic too of justice and mercy, of war and peace, and of war for the sake of peace. The gun is cruel but the gun is necessary. Good women hate it while good men wear it. A man wants nothing better than to hang it on the hook, but if he does then evil rides rampant, and the good things—including the good women—are not safe.

IV

14   So a man does what he has to do, though never clear why he has to do it. "A man has to play the hand he's dealt." And since the things he has to do make curiously for a bad conscience, he uses the two human and perennial and contemporary "outs"—which are fatalism and moralism. The gunman has to die. But in the heart of the "good" man who smokes him down there is no real enmity, for even the bad man "does what he has to do."

About all he could make out of it was that a man was meant for motion; he was meant to hope and to struggle, to be wrestling always with some sort of chains binding him. It was true of ... Ringrose [the villain in this piece]; it was true of himself. [Ernest Haycox: *Long Storm*, p. 215.]

15   So each explosion of violence has about it an inevitability which is in a way its justification. Or if it is not justified in this fatalistic fashion, we pass over into moralism. The issues are so unambiguous, the good so firmly fixed, the evil so clearly embodied, that the bad man may be stamped out "like a sidewinder," without compunction and without regret.

> Burro Yandle! The rusty-haired, rodent-faced destroyer. Dirty inside and out. But gifted with a malignant touch that ruined men and killed them. How long before ... fundamental justice caught up with him ...? [L. P. Holmes: *High Starlight* (Pennant Books), p. 165.]

The range war becomes a Holy War.

16   "A man has to play the hand he's dealt." A man does what he has to do, and justifies it one way or another. His is the incorrigible yearning after virtue, the inevitable implication in sin, the irrepressible inclination to self-justification. Every theological theme is here, except the final theme, the deep and healing dimension of guilt and grace.

17   Talking of self-justification, I have to ask myself, in respect of westerns, whether I pretend to analyze them to have an excuse for reading them, as a man might justify a visit to a burlesque house. Could be. Anything could be, human nature being what it is, in theologians as in other men. I can only protest unconvincingly that I do read westerns and I don't go to burlesque houses—I *think* because the former have more to offer.

Content Questions

1. What are the attractions of the western for Miller?
2. What does Miller mean when he writes "A man has to play the hand he's dealt"?
3. What purpose does violence serve in a western?
4. Why does Miller feel he needs an excuse for his interest in westerns?

Questions on Presentation

1. Miller begins his essay with a personal anecdote. Why is this effective? What is its effect on the essay?
2. How does Miller state his thesis?

3. How does Miller use quotations to support his argument?
4. How would you characterize his audience?
5. How do the allusions in paragraph 12 enhance the essay?

Can a Figurative Work of Art Be Libelous?

Robin Longman

An associate editor of *American Artist,* from which this essay is taken (April 1981), Robin Longman received a BA in English from Oberlin College in 1978. She graduated Phi Beta Kappa and received the prize for outstanding senior woman in English. In the following essay, Longman explores the relationship between the fine arts and libel laws. The essay focuses on Paul Georges, a contemporary American artist whose paintings have resulted in both accolades and lawsuits. Georges, born in 1923 in Oregon, studied art at the University of Oregon as well as with Fernand Léger in Paris and Hans Hoffman in New York. He began his teaching career at the University of Colorado, but later became a Professor of Fine Arts at Brandeis University in Massachusetts and Artist in Residence at Louisiana State University. Georges' work has earned him many awards, including the Hallmark Purchase Award, the Bernard Altman Prize, the Andrew Carnegie Prize, and the art award from the American Academy and National Institute of Arts and Letters. Yet, as Longman's essay shows, Georges' art stirs controversy. Two of Georges' contemporaries filed suit against him over *The Mugging of the Muse*, the subject of this essay. Although the three artists had been friends, they parted ways over issues of artistic interpretation. In their suit, the artists complained that Georges depicted them as attackers in the painting. A New York court eventually dismissed the suit. Nevertheless, the debate continues over whether any artistic work—a painting, a musical composition, a sculpture, an essay or work of fiction—can be libelous.

1   When Paul Georges, a New York figurative painter, had his allegorical painting *The Mugging of the Muse* reproduced in *American Artist* in March 1974 ("The Teachings of Hans Hofmann: Push and Pull," by Diane Cochrane), he was confident that his work illustrated Hofmann's principle of "push and pull." It depicts three men, with knives suspended, about to mug the Muse—the goddess of artistic inspiration—on a dark city corner; a winged cherub watches as a red liquid spews forth from a hydrant. To Georges' then artist-colleagues Jacob Silberman and Anthony Siani—all three of them members of the Alliance of Figu-

Paul Georges' *The Mugging of the Muse*

rative Artists in New York—the painting represented more than the "push and pull" principle. They felt that two of the three men shown with knives, about to "mug" the Muse, distinctly bore their own likenesses, and they expressed to Georges their dismay. When, however, in November 1975 Georges showed a slide of the painting, among 50 others, to 200-250 members of the Alliance, mentioning only its title, Siani and Silberman immediately brought suit for libel, along with a request for an injunction to bar the sale of the painting; they claimed they had been "defamed" as "violent criminals" by its "publication" (the viewing of it) at the Alliance.

2   The jury's verdict of libel, handed down last fall, awarded Siani and Silberman $30,000 each in damages. As we go to press, that verdict has yet to be upheld or set aside by the Judge, but whether upheld or dismissed, the legal and artistic implications for all figurative painters will be far-reaching, for this case represents the very first time a painting (or a work of fine art) has been involved in a libel suit. As Charlie Leopardo, program chairman of the Alliance, warns, "Even if the verdict is not upheld, the implications will depend on the basis on which it's thrown out: if it's thrown out on 'technicalities,' this case could come up again.

If dismissed on constitutional grounds, this case will forever be over. But the law doesn't know how to deal with it: it may go to the U.S. Supreme Court." Harriette Dorsen, of the firm Lankenau, Kovner & Bickford, is representing Georges now that the jury's verdict has come down. Dorsen, who did not represent Geroges in the trial, agrees that this case could be around for a long time to come. Whether the verdict is upheld or dismissed, either the plantiffs (Siani and Silberman) or the defendant (Georges) might appeal. The "push and pull" of George's painting is literally pushing and pulling the artistic community apart, for this case also represents the first time an artist has sued another artist. And when push comes to shove, who will be the winner?

3 Libel suits previously in the arts have involved photographs, political cartooning, and novels, but never a painting or work of fine art. "It is important, however, to make the distinction between censorship and libel in the history of the arts," says Irving Sandler, a well-known art critic and historian. "There certainly have been cases of censorship, such as in the Soviet Union. But libel is different."

4 The only historical "precedent" that might qualify today as "libelous" is that of Michelangelo's *Last Judgment*. In that large work—at the lower right—Minos is shown, leading the damned to hell. Legend says that a cardinal, a contemporary of Michelangelo's, recognized his own face on the devil and disliked this immensely. He complained to the Pope, who told him: "If he had put you in purgatory, I could have done something about it. But he put you in hell, and so there is nothing I can do."

5 Libel suits have certainly occurred over photographs, which, unlike fiction and artworks, are "more expected" to be true. Depending on the context in which it is shown, a photograph might show a person in a "false light." An example of this would be placing a photo of a young bride-to-be next to an article on prostitution, thereby changing the "context" of the photograph and its "meaning."

6 As said earlier, libel suits have also dealt with political cartooning and humor, but humor is often considered "fair comment" or opinion, particularly when it concerns a public figure or private individual who is of public interest. Opinions are a protected form of expression under the United States Constitution. As the Supreme Court stated in *Gertz v. Robert Welch, Inc.*, "Under the First Amendment, there is no such thing as a false idea. However pernicious an opinion may seem, we depend for its correction not on the conscience of judges or juries but on the competition of other ideas." Humor, parody, and satire are often intended as expressions of ideas and not intended as literal statements of fact. David Levine, staff caricaturist for *The New York Review of Books*, has never been sued for libel, although he describes an experience he once had, depicting Governor George Wallace: "Wallace threatened to sue me for de-

picting the cleft in his chin that, he said, looked like a 'Nazi symbol.' But he backed down."

7   Libelous statements—whether visual or written—must be "of and concerning" the individual, damage his or her reputation, and must be "published" (viewed or read by a third party). Most importantly, a libel must make a false statement of fact about a person and must be made with the required degree of "fault"—that is, intentionally or, in the case of a private individual in a matter of public concern, in a grossly irresponsible manner. Since an opinion, unlike a fact, cannot be proven true or false, it is a protected expression, under the First Amendment. False facts about someone, however, are often not privileged expressions.

8   The reason why libel suits in the arts present such a knotty problem for the court is that artworks and fiction are admittedly "known falsehoods" by the very virtue of their creations, yet they are also effective means of communication of ideas to large audiences. When they depict the personalities or likenesses of real people in a "false light"—even though the work is, of course, "false" and not real—libel can be proven. The consideration for the court with such works then becomes: Was the work making a statement of fact or opinion about the person? Translated to Georges' case, was his painting representing a fact or opinion? This is the issue at hand.

9   Robert Projansky, lawyer for Siani and Silberman, thinks Georges' painting is making a statement of fact; he claims "the picture speaks for itself" and obviously shows the faces of Siani and Silberman depicted as "criminals." Dorsen, on the other hand, argues that Georges' painting represents an opinion, with the allegorical context of the painting clearly understood. Her post-trial defense of Georges claims that there was no loss of reputation on the part of Siani and Silberman; that Georges' painting was an allegorical expression of opinion and opinions cannot be defamatory; and that its context was understood by all at the Alliance who viewed it.

10   In her post-trial memorandum of law, Dorsen claims Siani and Silberman suffered no loss of reputation, because no one at the Alliance who viewed the slide believed they were actually "muggers," although Siani and Silberman claim their reputations were, in fact, damaged. Says Siani: "You can't call people 'violent criminals' or 'muggers'—especially in our times, these words are bad." Dorsen asserts, however, that the defamation that they claim to have suffered was not that they were "criminals" in the eyes of their peers, but, rather, that they were "enemies of art" attacking the Muse, and that, as artists, for them this was the real hurt. Paul Georges had expressed to Siani and Silberman the meaning of his allegory, saying: "The picture demonstrates that one cannot hurt the Muse. Those who attack the Muse only hurt themselves. The artist [Georges] believes that the painting allegorically repre-

sents his view that when you attack art, you attack yourself." If so, the opinion that they were bad artists, or artists bad for art, could not be considered libelous, but, instead, "fair comment."

11   Assuming that Georges' painting was making the statement that they were enemies of art, should this be regarded as the privilege of a critic to remark on an individual or public figure of public interest? The art critic Irving Sandler ponders: "Couldn't the artist also be regarded as a critic? Siani and Silberman are artists, not just individuals, after all. They have a public dimension in this respect. The question is: Are Siani and Silberman, as artists, mugging the Muse, or are they, as individuals, mugging the Muse?" David Levine also muses on this case of the Muse: as a caricaturist, he says, "I draw someone who steps into the public arena. I've done authors, politicians, stars, and people in the arts. Artists, like authors, politicians, and stars, step into the public arena. So why can't an artist draw another artist this way?"

12   A major defense of Dorsen's is that Georges' work is an allegory, which is defined in *Webster's New Collegiate Dictionary* as: "the expression, by means of symbolic fictional figures and actions, of truths or generalizations about human existence." Dorsen admits that the painting "would be harder to defend if it were not an allegory, because its context would imply truth. Even then, though, a painting should never be taken as a true statement, unless published in a context that shows it is meant to be fact." Dorsen claims that, as allegory, the context is understood by all as an expression of an idea and not a statement of fact and, therefore, Siani and Silberman suffered no loss of reputation.

13   Dorsen takes the allegorical aspect further. A truly literal "reading" of the painting, she claims, would not produce the interpretation of Siani and Silberman as muggers; instead, "even if one were to take the painting absolutely literally, it could be argued that, since the figures are wearing masks which resemble the plaintiffs, it is not the plaintiffs who are being accused of being violent criminals, but the unidentified people wearing the masks." In fact, Georges claims that some viewers thought the three men were H. R. Haldeman, John Ehrlichman, and John Mitchell.

14   While Dorsen uses the allegorical context as her major post-trial defense of Georges' work as signifying "opinion," Projanksy, Siani, and Silberman obviously interpret the allegorical aspect completely differently. For Projansky, it is instead a "veneer over the painting to give it some putative meanings, but that's not what he meant. It didn't fool the jury." Siani, moreover, asserts that the allegorical context substantiates his claim that it represents a personal attack against him. "I personally think it makes it worse," he says. "It has two meanings—one implicit and one explicit. Therefore, his changing the face wouldn't mean anything. The allegorical meaning would still be the same. By putting my

face on one of the figures, he was saying this is an archetypical face of someone attacking the Muse. He could have put a Coke bottle on the face and the allegorical meaning wouldn't change! Many people read the red liquid from the hydrant as blood, but there's no proof it's blood. So you see, because it's allegorical, it could mean anything. It makes art into nothing. It doesn't exhibit the real truth. It makes art just something to cover up the walls with. By trying to make this a First Amendment case," Siani says, "he's saying he has a right to say anything he wants. With all the freedom of being an artist, you can't abuse art. No artist, as far as I know, has attacked a peer. Why didn't he depict someone with power mugging the Muse? I have no power in the art world."

15   Another important defense of Georges' is that no "fault" was evident. Dorsen says that, even if falsity of the painting as a "statement of fact" is proven, and that it is defamatory, it must further be proven by Siani and Silberman that it was "published" with a constitutionally mandated degree of "fault" on Georges' part.

16   The requirement of "fault" evolved from the 1974 U.S. Supreme Court decision in *Gertz*, mentioned earlier, and has since become important in journalism and media libel suits. The Supreme Court, wishing to encourage free expression, wanted to protect journalists from libel suits if they had made a "reasonable mistake." For a suit involving a public figure, the "fault" proven must be malice (that is, knowledge of falsity or reckless disregard for the truth, as opposed to simply ill will). But for that involving a private individual, the Supreme Court left it up to the states to determine the degree of "fault" that there should be to constitute libel. In New York State, the plaintiff, if he or she is an individual of public interest, must prove gross departure from journalistic standards; in other words, gross irresponsibility, not just negligence in checking sources before publication.

17   If his work is said to be a statement of fact, did Georges "publish" the painting in a grossly irresponsible manner? Paul Georges says of his work and his intent: "I don't feel I put anybody in it by intent. How do you describe 'intent'? If you can, you're not an artist. Siani thinks artists should be responsible—this means you have to know what you're doing. Edward Hopper said he never ends with what he intended to do. I agree with Hopper. I try to make a transposition, not show facts. I didn't do it to make sense of it, and I've been asked to make sense of it to the courts. The law can't make a distinction between reality and fiction." Siani counters: "The fact that there are different versions of the painting proves a lie to his 'unconscious' theory. This was a painting he considered over a long time."

18   If the jury's verdict is upheld and Georges' painting is deemed libelous, then what will be the legal implications for figurative artists? Charlie Leopardo of the Alliance points out, "If one doesn't like one's face in a work, one shouldn't be able to sue you for libel. There has to be a

limit. I'm not entirely against libel laws in the arts; but art should be 99.9 percent free of getting suits." Even Dorsen paints a nightmarish scene of the consequences artists may have to face: "If a painter does a painting with a real person in it, or one that looks like a real person any-one knows, that painter runs the risk of a libel suit if anything 'criminal' was depicted. Just as journalists have to have articles cleared by libel lawyers before publication, artists may have to have their work looked at first by a lawyer, and the lawyer may have to tell the artist to make 'certain changes.' That would be unusual for an artist to do."

19   Dorsen also remarks that portraitists, although they usually get prior consent to paint a person and so are not really affected by this case, will also have to be wary of painting a "libelous background" in their por-traits, thereby making the portrait a "false statement of fact" by chang-ing the context of the painting.

20   Kenneth P. Norwick, of the firm Norwick, Raggio, Jaffe & Kayser, says that, if the verdict is upheld, the implications for the artist will be sti-fling self-censorship. Dorsen, too, warns that "artists may now go and paint out the faces they have just done."

21   Should figurative artists obtain releases from their models to avoid li-bel and invasion of privacy suits? Allan Frumkin, an art dealer who plans to show a work by Georges in a show this month called "Narra-tive Art," expressed this fear. On the question of releases, Dorsen stresses, "Photographers should *always* get releases of models in their pictures." She warns that disclaimers on the backs of paintings or art-works that say, "No person in this work is intended to be real," are not binding.

22   It would seem, however, that to have the appropriate effect, a release should set forth the circumstances in which the model's likeness is to be employed and the use to which the final work will be put. Alice Neel, a portraitist who is often considered as one who frequently paints "unflattering" portraits, shares an experience of hers. She painted a por-trait on commission of a woman in all her splendor. "It was a beautiful nude," says Neel. "When I brought it to her, she rejected it and asked that I paint a bikini on it." After Neel had done so, it was again rejected. So Neel took it back, repainted the portrait nude, and then stored the painting away for 30 years. When she finally gave it away for free to an artists' group, she thought no more of it. A few years ago, it appeared on the cover of a brochure, advertising an auction of the painting, among others. The woman who had commissioned it 30 years ago saw it repro-duced on the brochure and threatened to sue Neel, but fortunately, she didn't. Neel points out, however, the difference between portraitists and figurative painters in facing libel and invasion of privacy suits. Neel says, "Georges' painting is different. It's a narrative picture and it paints them in a certain role."

23   How much protection should the law give artistic expression? "At

most," says Norwick, "the law should only punish false statements of facts that are taken as such and that are truly injurious." Alice Neel claims the case is "a tempest in a teapot. Once you open a loophole, then you open up everything to libel. Art should have no restrictions on it. I'm against censorship."

24 The reactions from the artistic community are mostly fear and disbelief. Whereas Georges feels that, if upheld, "it will be a disaster for the future of representational art," since an artist will be expected to "make sense" of his or her work, Siani is firmly convinced that, if thrown out, "it will demean the purpose of painting, giving an artist the license to do anything."

25 The factionalism among artists is nowhere more apparent than at the Alliance itself, where the slide was first shown. Established as a forum for artists to discuss openly their opinions on art and art issues, it is ironic that, as members of the Alliance, Siani, Silberman, and Georges could not have discussed the paintings without resorting to the courts. Charlie Leopardo is struggling to keep the Alliance going. Of the Alliance members Leopardo says, "They're not really realizing the implications of what is at stake. They're more or less confused. They don't want to choose between two artists—Siani and Georges—they've known a long time. But there's a principle involved, much larger than a personal feud. The case has expanded to the point where it can affect everybody. All the Alliance artists see now is the feud, not how it affects them."

26 Some artists see some positive points in the case, along with the negative. Jack Beal, an outspoken figurative artist, says, "I will probably be obtaining releases from models in the future. But, in a way, it's complimentary to realists to have their work taken this seriously, as a situation in real life. No abstract artists will get sued like this." But Alvin Sher, a realist sculptor who has been organizing a defense fund for Georges, says, "The timing is bad. Figurative artists have been getting wider recognition lately, and to have this happen makes them feel threatened." Siani sees the positive that may come out of all this. He says, "It will make the laws more precise. It may be a good thing. An artist can caricature a public figure. But if an artist does this to an individual, what's to prevent him from doing this to groups and minorities?"

27 Quite a few artists also believe Georges' allegorical meaning, or prophesy—"when you attack art, you attack yourself"—has strangely come to realization. What was once claimed allegorical "opinion" has become artistic "fact," for the artistic community is already seriously divided over the issue, sensing that their artistic freedom hangs somewhere in the balance between the personal feud of Siani, Silberman, and Georges and the present legal feud, ultimately to be decided at the Judge's bench.

But whatever the decision, there is no question that their Muse, the goddess of inspiration, has indeed been "mugged"; figurative painting will never be quite the same.

Content Questions

1. Why did two members of the Alliance of Figurative Artists in New York object to Paul Georges' painting?
2. What is the usual focus of libel suits in the arts? Why is this case different?
3. What is Dorsen's defense of Georges' work?
4. Why does Siani feel the painting is a personal attack?
5. How much legal protection should be provided for artistic expression, according to Norwick?

Questions on Presentation

1. Longman uses several definitions in her essay. Where and why does she use them?
2. Why does Longman use the anecdote about Michelangelo in paragraph 4?
3. Does Longman make the distinction between "art" and political cartooning clear? What techniques does she use?
4. How does Longman make the potential effects of libel suits concerning art seem chilling?
5. What is Longman's purpose in paragraph 22 in using the example of Alice Neel's experience?

Who Killed King Kong?

X. J. Kennedy

X. J. Kennedy (b. 1929) is an American poet, essayist, and translator. He attended Seton Hall as an undergraduate, earned a M.A. from Columbia, and did advanced graduate work at the University of Michigan. This essay, which is taken from *Dissent* (1960), explores the reasons for the popularity of the original *King Kong* movie.

1   The ordeal and spectacular death of King Kong, the giant ape, undoubtedly have been witnessed by more Americans than have ever seen a performance of *Hamlet, Iphigenia at Aulis,* or even *Tobacco Road.* Since RKO-Radio Pictures first released *King Kong,* a quarter-century has gone by; yet year after year, from prints that grow more rain-beaten, from sound tracks that grow more tinny, ticket-buyers by thousands still pursue Kong's luckless fight against the forces of technology, tabloid journalism, and the DAR. They see him chloroformed to sleep, see him whisked from his jungle isle to New York and placed on show, see him burst his chains to roam the city (lugging a frightened blonde), at last to plunge from the spire of the Empire State Building, machine-gunned by model airplanes.

2   Though Kong may die, one begins to think his legend unkillable. No clearer proof of his hold upon the popular imagination may be seen than what emerged one catastrophic week in March 1955, when New York WOR-TV programmed *Kong* for seven evenings in a row (a total of sixteen showings). Many a rival network vice-president must have scowled when surveys showed that *Kong*—the 1933 B-picture—had lured away fat segments of the viewing populace from such powerful competitors as Ed Sullivan, Groucho Marx and Bishop Sheen.

3   But even television has failed to run *King Kong* into oblivion. Coffee-in-the-lobby cinemas still show the old hunk of hokum, with the apology that in its use of composite shots and animated models the film remains technically interesting. And no other monster in movie history has won so devoted a popular audience. None of the plodding mummies, the stultified draculas, the white-coated Lugosis with their shiny pin-ball-machine laboratories, none of the invisible stranglers, berserk robots, or menaces from Mars has ever enjoyed so many resurrections.

4   Why does the American public refuse to let King Kong rest in peace? It is true, I'll admit, that *Kong* outdid every monster movie before or since in sheer carnage. Producers Cooper and Schoedsack crammed into it dinosaurs, headhunters, riots, aerial battles, bullets, bombs, bloodletting. Heroine Fay Wray, whose function is mainly to scream, shuts her mouth for hardly one uninterrupted minute from first reel to last. It is also true that *Kong* is larded with good healthy sadism, for those whose joy it is to see the frantic girl dangled from cliffs and harried by pterodactyls. But it seems to me that the abiding appeal of the giant ape rests on other foundations.

5   Kong has, first of all, the attraction of being manlike. His simian nature gives him one huge advantage over giant ants and walking vegetables in that an audience may conceivably identify with him. Kong's appeal has the quality that established the Tarzan series as American myth—for what man doesn't secretly image himself a huge hairy howler against whom no other monster has a chance? If Tarzan recalls

the ape in us, then Kong may well appeal to that great-granddaddy primordial brute from whose tribe we have all deteriorated.

6   Intentionally or not, the producers of *King Kong* encourage this identification by etching the character of Kong with keen sympathy. For the ape is a figure in a tradition familiar to moviegoers: the tradition of the pitiable monster. We think of Lon Chaney in the role of Quasimodo, of Karloff in the original *Frankenstein*. As we watch the Frankenstein monster's fumbling and disastrous attempts to befriend a flower-picking child, our sympathies are enlisted with the monster in his impenetrable loneliness. And so with Kong. As he roars in his chains, while barkers sell tickets to boobs who gape at him, we perhaps feel something more deep than pathos. We begin to sense something of the problem that engaged Eugene O'Neill in *The Hairy Ape:* the dilemma of a displaced animal spirit forced to live in a jungle built by machines.

7   *King Kong*, it is true, had special relevance in 1933. Landscapes of the depression are glimpsed early in the film when an impresario, seeking some desperate pretty girl to play the lead in a jungle movie, visits soup lines and a Woman's Home Mission. In Fay Wray—who's been caught snitching an apple from a fruitstand—his search is ended. When he gives her a big feed and a movie contract, the girl is magic-carpeted out of the world of the National Recovery Act. And when, in the film's climax, Kong smashes that very Third Avenue landscape in which Fay had wandered hungry, audiences of 1933 may well have felt a personal satisfaction.

8   What is curious is that audiences of 1960 remain hooked. For in the heart of urban man, one suspects, lurks the impulse to fling a bomb. Though machines speed him to the scene of his daily grind, though IBM comptometers ("freeing the human mind from drudgery") enable him to drudge more efficiently once he arrives, there comes a moment when he wishes to turn upon his machines and kick hell out of them. He wants to hurl his combination radio–alarm clock out the bedroom window and listen to its smash. What subway commuter wouldn't love—just for once—to see the downtown express smack head-on into the uptown local? Such a wish is gratified in that memorable scene in *Kong* that opens with a wide-angle shot: interior of a railway car on the Third Avenue El. Straphangers are nodding, the literate refold their newspapers. Unknown to them, Kong has torn away a section of trestle toward which the train now speeds. The motorman spies Kong up ahead, jams on the brakes. Passengers hurtle together like so many peas in a pail. In a window of the car appear Kong's bloodshot eyes. Women shriek. Kong picks up the railway car as if it were a rat, flips it to the street and ties knots in it, or something. To any commuter the scene must appear one of the most satisfactory pieces of celluloid ever exposed.

9   Yet however violent his acts, Kong remains a gentleman. Remarkable

is his sense of chivalry. Whenever a fresh boa constrictor threatens Fay, Kong first sees that the lady is safely parked, then manfully thrashes her attacker. (And she, the ingrate, runs away every time his back is turned.) Atop the Empire State Building, ignoring his pursuers, Kong places Fay on a ledge as tenderly as if she were a dozen eggs. He fondles her, then turns to face the Army Air Force. And Kong is perhaps the most disinterested lover since Cyrano: his attentions to the lady are utterly without hope of reward. After all, between a five-foot blonde and a fifty-foot ape, love can hardly be more than an intellectual flirtation. In his simian way King Kong is the hopelessly yearning lover of Petrarchan convention. His forced exit from his jungle, in chains, results directly from his single-minded pursuit of Fay. He smashes a Broadway theater when the notion enters his dull brain that the flashbulbs of photographers somehow endanger the lady. His perilous shinnying up a skyscraper to pluck Fay from her boudoir is an act of the kindliest of hearts. He's impossible to discourage even though the love of his life can't lay eyes on him without shrieking murder.

10   The tragedy of King Kong, then, is to be the beast who at the end of the fable fails to turn into the handsome prince. This is the conviction that the scriptwriters would leave with us in the film's closing line. As Kong's corpse lies blocking traffic in the street, the entrepreneur who brought Kong to New York turns to the assembled reporters and proclaims: "That's your story, boys—it was Beauty killed the Beast!" But greater forces than those of the screaming Lady have combined to lay Kong low, if you ask me. Kong lives for a time as one of those persecuted near-animal souls bewildered in the middle of an industrial order, whose simple desires are thwarted at every turn. He climbs the Empire State Building because in all New York it's the closest thing he can find to the clifftop of his jungle isle. He dies, a pitiful dolt, and the army brass and publicity-men cackle over him. His death is the only possible outcome to as neat a tragic dilemma as you can ask for. The machine-guns do him in, while the manicured human hero (a nice clean Dartmouth boy) carries away Kong's sweetheart to the altar. O, the misery of it all. There's far more truth about upper-middle-class American life in *King Kong* than in the last seven dozen novels of John P. Marquand.

11   A Negro friend from Atlanta tells me that in movie houses in colored neighborhoods throughout the South, *Kong* does a constant business. They show the thing in Atlanta at least every year, presumably to the same audiences. Perhaps this popularity may simply be due to the fact that Kong is one of the most watchable movies ever constructed, but I wonder whether Negro audiences may not find some archetypical appeal in this serio-comic tale of a huge black powerful free spirit whom all the hardworking white policemen are out to kill.

12   Every day in the week on a screen somewhere in the world, King Kong

relives his agony. Again and again he expires on the Empire State Building, as audiences of the devout assist his sacrifice. We watch him die, and by extension kill the ape within our bones, but these little deaths of ours occur in prosaic surroundings. We do not die on a tower, New York before our feet, nor do we give our lives to smash a few flying machines. It is not for us to bring to a momentary standstill the civilization in which we move. King Kong does this for us. And so we kill him again and again, in much-spliced celluloid, while the ape in us expires from day to day, obscure, in desperation.

Content Questions

1. What is the first reason Kennedy suggests for Kong's appeal?
2. Why was *King Kong* popular during the 1930s?
3. What is Kong's tragedy?

Questions on Presentation

1. What does Kennedy's reference to *The Hairy Ape* in paragraph 6 tell you about his perception of his audience? What else in the essay helps you to identify the audience?
2. In paragraph 9 Kennedy asserts that "Kong remains a gentleman." Is his development of this assertion convincing?
3. Kennedy has been called a poet wishing "to be seriously funny." What evidence can you find in this essay of serious funniness?

The Excludables

Mark Shapiro

Mark Shapiro is a frequent contributor to *Mother Jones*, from which this selection is taken. In this essay he attacks the exclusionary policies of the U.S. government regarding foreign artists and writers whose views are seen to threaten the security of the United States.

1   Dario Fo, the Italian author of over 40 satirical plays, seems an unlikely threat to the security of the United States. One of Fo's plays, *Acci-*

dental Death of an Anarchist, debuted on Broadway in 1984, but the author was not allowed to supervise rehearsals. After Fo was invited by the producers, the U.S. State Department denied him a visa, deciding that his membership in a prisoners' rights organization known as Soccorso Rosso branded him a "terrorist sympathizer." After the American Civil Liberties Union and a dozen other civil liberties and theatrical groups launched a public campaign in Fo's behalf, the State Department reversed itself and gave the playwright a visa just before his play's premiere. The novel approach taken by the play's producers may have been the key to the State Department's about-face: they claimed that denying Fo a visa infringed on their ability to earn a living as investors in the play.

2   In 1983 Hortensia Allende, the widow of Salvador Allende and a resident of Mexico, was invited by several universities in the United States to speak about the role of women in the opposition to the Chilean dictatorship. But the U.S. embassy in Mexico denied her a visa; it cited Mrs. Allende's ties to the World Peace Council, which State claims is a Soviet front. The rejection of Mrs. Allende's request for a visa came at a time when the Reagan administration was considering the resumption of arms sales to Chile. The denial had a particularly ironic denouement: soon afterward, Hortensia Allende's "successor," Mrs. Augusto Pinochet, was Nancy Reagan's guest for tea at the White House.

3   In the 1960s Nino Pasti was Italy's representative to the NATO Military Committee, stationed at the Pentagon. Later he served as NATO's vice-supreme commander in Europe for nuclear affairs and, after retiring from the military, served two terms in the Italian senate. But Pasti's sentiments have changed since his days as a four-star general. Now over 70 years old, he claims to have American military documents that dispute NATO's assertion of Soviet military superiority in Europe. After Pasti was invited by peace groups to speak against the cruise and Pershing II missile deployments, his request for a visa was denied in the fall of 1983. His entry into the United States, said the State Department, would be "prejudicial to the public interest."

4   Fo, Allende, and Pasti are three among thousands of foreign intellectuals, authors, and political figures who have been denied U.S. visas because of their political beliefs. The case of Farley Mowat, the renowned Canadian writer, provides another recent example.

5   Last April, Mowat was snared by the U.S. Immigration and Naturalization Service at Toronto's Pearson International Airport before his flight to Los Angeles to kick off a publicity tour for his book *Sea of Slaughter.* The INS performed a routine check of airline passengers against its visa lookout book of "excludable" aliens and discovered that Mowat was included. The Canadian-U.S. border is supposedly open, and Mowat did not legally require a visa.

6   The INS refused to explain why it excluded Mowat, as it does with all foreign citizens denied entry. An anonymous source later issued a partial explanation: Mowat, the author of over a dozen naturalist books, was put on the INS "hot" list after being quoted in a 1968 newspaper article saying that he was ready to defy American B-52 bombers with a .22 rifle during their low-level training runs over Newfoundland. "My threat still holds," Mowat explained during an interview after the airport incident. Soon after, the immigration service made what it considered a conciliatory gesture, offering Mowat a one-shot waiver to complete his publicity tour. In a now-celebrated declaration of Canadian nationalism, Mowat retorted to the immigration service, "Stuff it." (He subsequently indicated that he would accept the offer only if it were accompanied by an apology from President Reagan and if he were flown into the country on Air Force One.) "It was a scurrilous, scatological offer," explained Mowat, who has since written a book on the border controversy, *My Discovery of America.*

7   As Mowat's case illustrates, some of the State Department's "excludables" are issued visas with highly restricted travel rights, limited to particular cities or special public appearances. Some are denied once, then admitted after another try. The practice makes the United States the only Western democracy to exclude foreign citizens on ideological grounds.

8   The Bureau of Consular Affairs' excludable list includes some of the world's most distinguished authors and artists, all of whom have experienced visa difficulties at one time or another: Nobel laureates Gabriel García Márquez, Pablo Neruda, and Czeslaw Milosz; Mexican writer Carlos Fuentes, English novelist Graham Greene, South African dissident poet Dennis Brutus, and Spanish filmmaker Luis Buñuel.

9   Every administration since Eisenhower's has abused the ideological exclusion provision of U.S. immigration law. The Reagan administration, however, has gone a step further to limit public debate—most notably concerning its Central American policies.

10   Eloquent spokespersons opposing the administration's policies have been repeatedly denied visas, preventing them from keeping speaking engagements, appearing at congressional hearings, or attending meetings with activists, business organizations, or university officials. For example, prior to last year's congressional vote on funding the Nicaraguan contras, Efraín Mondragon, a contra defector, was prevented from traveling to Washington, D.C., to tell his inside story about contra connections to the CIA. In 1983 Nicaraguan Interior Minister Tomás Borge was denied a visa, thus preventing him from making a speaking tour of the United States, although other members of Nicaragua's junta have been granted extremely limited travel rights. Opposition leaders from El Sal-

vador such as Rubén Zamora and even right-wing politico Roberto D'Aubuisson (after falling out of favor with the State Department) have been denied visas during the past three years—as were four Salvadoran women who received the Robert F. Kennedy Human Rights Award for their work on behalf of families searching for their "disappeared" relatives.

11 After Borge was barred from entering the United States, Elliott Abrams, assistant secretary for human rights and humanitarian affairs, bluntly expressed the Reagan administration's position: "We're not keeping anybody's views out. . . . We are keeping out certain officials for certain policy reasons."

12 In October 1985 Margaret Randall, the American-born feminist writer and critic of U.S. policy in Latin America, was denied permanent residency status by the Immigration and Naturalization Service. The State Department says that Randall, who has recently taken a teaching position at the University of New Mexico, renounced her U.S. citizenship 18 years ago to live in Mexico. In supporting its decision, the INS cited a series of passages from Randall's books—many of which are available in U.S. public libraries—that express support for the governments of Nicaragua and Cuba. The Center for Constitutional Rights is suing Attorney General Edwin Meese III and immigration officials. The Center is representing a group of plaintiffs including Norman Mailer, Alice Walker, Kurt Vonnegut, Grace Paley, Arthur Miller, Toni Morrison, and William Styron. They allege that their constitutional rights to associate with and receive information from Randall are being violated.

13 Representative Barney Frank (D-Massachusetts) has challenged the administration with a bill that would revamp American visa policies and prevent the State Department from considering its own foreign policy interest in deciding who is allowed to enter the United States. "Getting into the United States should not be seen as some mark of approval," says Frank.

14 The American Civil Liberties Union is challenging several of the visa denials in court. Representing some of the people who invited Hortensia Allende, the ACLU is suing the State Department for violating their right to hear her speak. The ACLU also claims that the latest rash of exclusions are contrary to congressional intent, which was aimed at barring the entry of espionage agents, saboteurs, and active revolutionaries, not those with controversial political views.

15 Gay rights groups have unsuccessfully challenged the ban on homosexuals, who are excludable under immigration law as sexual deviants. Barney Frank's bill would eliminate that provision in the law—one of the few areas of agreement between Frank and the State Department.

16 Hodding Carter III, who was assistant secretary of state for public affairs during the administration of Jimmy Carter, sees the issue as one of

the more absurd contradictions of U.S. human rights policy. "If you're in Moscow," he comments, "the Russians have made it hard for Nobel laureates to get out of the Soviet Union. We have made it hard for Nobel laureates to get into the United States." Carter describes the Reagan administration's policies as "creating its own form of electronic curtain."

17 The law keeping America pure is the 1952 McCarran-Walter Act, which forms the basis for current U.S. immigration law; it is described by playwright Arthur Miller as "one of the pieces of garbage left behind by the sinking of the great scow of McCarthyism." Miller suffered his own travel problems in reverse when Joe McCarthy's Senate committee succeeded in getting his passport revoked in the 1950s, thereby preventing Miller from legally leaving the United States. President Truman excoriated Congress after it passed the law over his veto: "Seldom has a bill exhibited the distrust evidenced here for citizens and aliens alike."

18 The McCarran-Walter Act sets out 33 reasons for excluding individuals from the United States, combining prostitutes, paupers, and the insane with ideological undesirables and homosexuals. Of the two political sections in the Act, one permits the exclusion of individuals associated with the Communist party or affiliated organizations. The other section can be used to exclude individuals considered a danger to the "welfare, safety, or security of the United States," or whose entry is deemed "prejudicial to the public interest." Both Nino Pasti and Hortensia Allende were denied visas on this basis. "Under section 27," says Charles Gordon, former general counsel to the Immigration and Naturalization Service and author of an eight-volume text on immigration law, "you don't even need to call someone a communist. You don't like Mrs. Allende, you don't give her a visa."

19 Although the State Department has repeatedly refused to publicly explain its support of the Act's political provisions, at least one staunch supporter of the government's visa restrictions remains eager to defend them: Roy Cohn, the chief architect of McCarthy's frenzied search for communists over 30 years ago. Now a private attorney in New York, Cohn's zeal for corking the flow of unfriendly ideas is unabated. "There's no basic constitutional right to enter our shores," he says. "Many times these people are not what they look like. I don't think we have the compulsion to put the Statue of Liberty at their feet."

20 Yet even Cohn is critical of the State Department for excluding authors like Dario Fo and others. "Who cares about a playwright, a poet, or a 90-year-old actress?" asks an exasperated Cohn. "Let them come and then fall of their own weight."

21 Cohn's legacy lives on in more ways than one. The State Department maintains what is probably the world's largest blacklist, a global computer network known as the Automated Visa Lookout System (AVLOS).

22   There are about a million names in AVLOS, according to the Legislative and Intergovernmental Affairs Office of the State Department. The list includes all people considered offenders under the provisions of the McCarran-Walter Act. An estimated 40,000 to 50,000 individuals have been judged excludable for ideological reasons. A classified list of "proscribed organizations" is in the *Foreign Service Manual* issued to diplomatic staff in American embassies and missions overseas.

23   According to Charles Gordon, the list of individuals and organizations is compiled from a number of confidential intelligence sources, including the Central Intelligence Agency, local informants, and a host country's police services. The Royal Canadian Mounted Police, for example, provided the information on Farley Mowat that formed the basis for his exclusion.

24   When people apply for visas at their local U.S. consulate or at border checkpoints (as is the case for Canadians), their names are automatically checked against the AVLOS memory bank. Membership in any proscribed organization is reason enough for getting on the list.

25   Most excludable aliens are ultimately "waived" in and issued visas. But once a name is added to AVLOS, it is nearly impossible to have it erased, as Mowat and others have discovered. The only guaranteed method is to prove that one's association with a proscribed organization was involuntary, or to engage in a ritual of repentance by demonstrating five years of active opposition to the principles of communism. Aficionados of this escape clause refer to it as the "Koestler Amendment," named after Hungarian author Arthur Koestler, who defected, renounced his ties to the Communist party, and wrote about his negative experiences in the Soviet bloc for the next 40 years.

26   The most haunting aspect of the Automated Visa Lookout System is that an individual may never know what activity qualifies him or her for exclusion. Like poor Josef K. in Franz Kafka's *Trial*, an alien is never informed of the specific cause of a denial. The case of Angel Rama, a distinguished Uruguayan author and literary critic, provides a case in point. Rama left Uruguay after a military coup in 1972 and became a Venezuelan citizen. Though technically excludable, he was granted waivers for periodic visits to the United States through the 1970s. But when he applied for permanent residency in 1981, after being offered a professorship at the University of Maryland, his request was denied, and his saga through a bureaucratic hallway of mirrors began.

27   Having accused Rama of "publishing, writing, or causing to be circulated writings which advocate the doctrines of international communism," the State Department refused to reveal its evidence of these activities. Rama, who was never a communist and professed admiration for the social-democratic movements of Sweden and Austria, fought unsuccessfully for two years to have this evidence revealed to him.

28   He found himself in a surreal conundrum. As Michael Maggio, an immigration attorney who represented Rama for the Center for Constitutional Rights, explains, "We were not notified [as to] what he did, where he did it, or how he did it; but if we could prove that he didn't do what they wouldn't tell us he did, he could get his permit." Rama did not live long enough to resolve his catch-22, as he was killed in a Madrid plane crash in November 1983.

29   Critics charge that U.S. visa policies violate the human rights provisions of the 1975 Helsinki accords, which guarantee the free flow of ideas between nations. Helsinki Watch, the Fund for Free Expression, the Association of American Publishers' International Freedom to Publish Committee, and more than 30 civil liberties, political, and cultural groups have organized the Coalition for Free Trade in Ideas to repeal the ideological exclusion sections of the McCarran-Walter Act. PEN, the international writers group, will hold its 48th congress in New York this January, and a score of excludable writers will be invited as a test of the law.

30   Satirist Dario Fo offers comfort to the excluded. Unable to cross the American frontier last year to address a Free Trade in Ideas conference, he spoke via satellite from a Toronto television studio. Appearing on a screen in a Washington meeting hall, Fo told the conference: "The fact that the State Department denied . . . the visa is something which makes me very proud. I took a look at the list of people denied visas to the United States, and then I realized that I am in beautiful company."

31   Carlos Fuentes, who has faced the fitful experience of applying and re-applying for waivers to enter this country since he was first denied a visa in 1961, also spoke out at the conference. In his talk, Fuentes captured the absurdity of U.S. policy. "It is hard to imagine," Fuentes declared, "that the institutions of this great republic, its democratic edifice, its vast economic and military power, can in any way be endangered by the physical presence of Graham Greene, Gabriel García Márquez, Dario Fo, or Mrs. Salvador Allende. On the contrary: experience has taught us all that it is the application of the exclusionary clause that endangers the republic, mocks democracy, demoralizes the true friends of the United States, and offers undeserved aces to the Soviet Union. . . . This is a clause that belongs to the realm of sadomasochism, not to the legal ledgers of a self-respecting, powerful democracy."

Content Questions

1. Why was Fo denied a U.S. visa? Why was the decision reversed?
2. What is AVLOS?

3. In what way has the Reagan administration gone further than others in limiting public debate?
4. What are some of the reasons under the McCarran-Walter Act for excluding individuals from entering the United States?
5. How did Carlos Fuentes "capture the absurdity of U.S. policy"?

Questions on Presentation

1. Why does Shapiro list so many people who have been excluded from the United States?
2. To whom do you believe Shapiro is addressing this essay? How do you know that?
3. What is Shapiro's tone in this essay? How does he make it apparent?
4. Define denouement (2), conciliatory (6), scurrilous (6), scatological (6), excoriated (17), proscribed (25), surreal (28), and conundrum (28).

Why Are Americans Afraid of Dragons?

Ursula K. Le Guin

Ursula K. Le Guin (b. 1929), American science fiction writer and critic, was born in Berkeley, California, and is married to historian Charles A. Le Guin. Educated at Radcliffe and Columbia University, Le Guin has been more influential in science fiction than almost any other author. Her first novel, *Rocannon's World* (1966), established her as a successful female writer in a male-dominated literary field. In 1970 she won the Nebula Award and the Hugo Award for best novel for *The Left Hand of Darkness,* a book that describes the world of winter through the eyes of the envoy Genly Ai. She has also won a Nebula Award for best short story, "The Day Before the Revolution," a Jupiter Award for best novel *(The Dispossessed),* and Hugo Awards for best novella *(The Word for World is Forest)* and best short story ("The Ones Who Walk Away from Omelas").

Le Guin's writing is not limited to science fiction however. In several of her short stories she pursues her interests in fantasy, feminism, and Taoism. She believes that imagination is a singularly human faculty that should be developed just as people develop their intellect. She is frequently concerned in her fiction with the ways her characters learn to think; in her criticism she remains fascinated with the psychological responses of readers, or nonreaders, to fiction. In this essay, originally delivered as a speech to a Northwest Library Association conference, she examines what she sees as a basic quality of American thought.

1   This was to be a talk about fantasy. But I have not been feeling very fanciful lately, and could not decide what to say; so I have been going about picking people's brains for ideas. "What about fantasy? Tell me something about fantasy." And one friend of mine said, "All right, I'll tell you something fantastic. Ten years ago, I went to the children's room of the library of such-and-such a city, and asked for *The Hobbit*; and the librarian told me, 'Oh, we keep that only in the adult collection; we don't feel that escapism is good for children.' "

2   My friend and I had a good laugh and shudder over that, and we agreed that things have changed a great deal in the past ten years. That kind of moralistic censorship of works of fantasy is very uncommon now, in the children's libraries. But the fact that the children's libraries have become oases in the desert doesn't mean that there isn't still a desert. The point of view from which that librarian spoke still exists. She was merely reflecting, in perfect good faith, something that goes very deep in the American character: a moral disapproval of fantasy, a disapproval so intense, and often so aggressive, that I cannot help but see it as arising, fundamentally, from fear.

3   So: Why are Americans afraid of dragons?

4   Before I try to answer my question, let me say that it isn't only Americans who are afraid of dragons. I suspect that almost all very highly technological peoples are more or less antifantasy. There are several national literatures which, like ours, have had no tradition of adult fantasy for the past several hundred years: the French, for instance. But then you have the Germans, who have a good deal; and the English, who have it, and love it, and do it better than anyone else. So this fear of dragons is not merely a Western, or a technological, phenomenon. But I do not want to get into these vast historical questions: I will speak of modern Americans, the only people I know well enough to talk about.

5   In wondering why Americans are afraid of dragons, I began to realize that a great many Americans are not only antifantasy, but altogether antifiction. We tend, as a people, to look upon all works of the imagination either as suspect, or as contemptible.

6   "My wife reads novels. I haven't got the time."

7   "I used to read that science fiction stuff when I was a teenager, but of course I don't now."

8   "Fairy stories are for kids. I live in the real world."

9   Who speaks so? Who is it that dismisses *War and Peace, The Time Machine,* and *A Midsummer Night's Dream* with this perfect self-assurance? It is, I fear, the man in the street—the hardworking, over-thirty American male—the men who run this country.

10   Such a rejection of the entire art of fiction is related to several American characteristics: our Puritanism, our work ethic, our profit-mindedness, and even our sexual mores.

11   To read *War and Peace* or *The Lord of the Rings* plainly is not "work"—you do it for pleasure. And if it cannot be justified as "educational" or as "self-improvement," then, in the Puritan value system, it can only be self-indulgence or escapism. For pleasure is not a value, to the Puritan; on the contrary, it is a sin.

12   Equally, in the businessman's value system, if an act does not bring in an immediate, tangible profit, it has no justification at all. Thus the only person who has an excuse to read Tolstoy or Tolkien is the English teacher, because he gets paid for it. But our businessman might allow himself to read a best-seller now and then: not because it is a good book, but because it is a best-seller—it is a success, it has made money. To the strangely mystical mind of the money-changer, this justifies its existence; and by reading it he may participate, a little, in the power and mana of its success. If this is not magic, by the way, I don't know what is.

13   The last element, the sexual one, is more complex. I hope I will not be understood as being sexist if I say that, within our culture, I believe that this antifiction attitude is basically a male one. The American boy and man is very commonly forced to define his maleness by rejecting certain traits, certain human gifts and potentialities, which our culture defines as "womanish" or "childish." And one of these traits or potentialities is, in cold sober fact, the absolutely essential human faculty of imagination.

14   Having got this far, I went quickly to the dictionary.

15   The *Shorter Oxford Dictionary* says: "Imagination. 1. The action of imagining, or forming a mental concept of what is not actually present to the senses; 2. The mental consideration of actions or events not yet in existence."

16   Very well; I certainly can let "absolutely essential human faculty" stand. But I must narrow the definition to fit our present subject. By "imagination," then, I personally mean the free play of the mind, both intellectual and sensory. By "play" I mean recreation, re-creation, the recombination of what is known into what is new. By "free" I mean that the action is done without an immediate object of profit—spontaneously. That does not mean, however, that there may not be a purpose behind the free play of the mind, a goal; and the goal may be a very serious object indeed. Children's imaginative play is clearly a practicing at the acts and emotions of adulthood; a child who did not play would not become mature. As for the free play of the adult mind, its result may be *War and Peace*, or the theory of relativity.

17   To be free, after all, is not to be undisciplined. I should say that the discipline of the imagination may in fact be the essential method or technique of both art and science. It is our Puritanism, insisting that discipline means repression or punishment, which confuses the subject. To

discipline something, in the proper sense of the word, does not mean to repress it, but to train it—to encourage it to grow, and act, and be fruitful, whether it is a peach tree or a human mind.

18   I think that a great many American men have been taught just the opposite. They have learned to repress their imagination, to reject it as something childish or effeminate, unprofitable, and probably sinful.

19   They have learned to fear it. But they have never learned to discipline it at all.

20   Now, I doubt that the imagination can be suppressed. If you truly eradicated it in a child, he would grow up to be an eggplant. Like all our evil propensities, the imagination will out. But if it is rejected and despised, it will grow into wild and weedy shapes; it will be deformed. At its best, it will be mere ego-centered daydreaming; at its worst, it will be wishful thinking, which is a very dangerous occupation when it is taken seriously. Where literature is concerned, in the old, truly Puritan days, the only permitted reading was the Bible. Nowadays, with our secular Puritanism, the man who refuses to read novels because it's unmanly to do so, or because they aren't true, will most likely end up watching bloody detective thrillers on the television, or reading hack Westerns or sports stories, or going in for pornography, from *Playboy* on down. It is his starved imagination, craving nourishment, that forces him to do so. But he can rationalize such entertainment by saying that it is realistic—after all, sex exists, and there are criminals, and there are baseball players, and there used to be cowboys—and also by saying that it is virile, by which he means that it doesn't interest most women.

21   That all these genres are sterile, hopelessly sterile, is a reassurance to him, rather than a defect. If they were genuinely realistic, which is to say genuinely imagined and imaginative, he would be afraid of them. Fake realism is the escapist literature of our time. And probably the ultimate escapist reading is that masterpiece of total unreality, the daily stock market report.

22   Now what about our man's wife? She probably wasn't required to squelch her private imagination in order to play her expected role in life, but she hasn't been trained to discipline it, either. She is allowed to read novels, and even fantasies. But, lacking training and encouragement, her fancy is likely to glom on to very sickly fodder, such things as soap operas, and "true romances," and nursy novels, and historico-sentimental novels, and all the rest of the baloney ground out to replace genuine imaginative works by the artistic sweatshops of a society that is profoundly distrustful of the uses of the imagination.

23   What, then, are the uses of the imagination?

24   You see, I think we have a terrible thing here: a hardworking, upright, responsible citizen, a full-grown, educated person, who is afraid of dragons, and afraid of hobbits, and scared to death of fairies. It's funny, but

it's also terrible. Something has gone very wrong. I don't know what to do about it but to try and give an honest answer to that person's question, even though he often asks it in an aggressive and contemptuous tone of voice. "What's the good of it all?" he says, "Dragons and hobbits and little green men—what's the *use* of it?"

25 The truest answer, unfortunately, he won't even listen to. He won't hear it. The truest answer is, "The use of it is to give you pleasure and delight."

26 "I haven't got the time," he snaps, swallowing a Maalox pill for his ulcer and rushing off to the golf course.

27 So we try the next-to-truest answer. It probably won't go down much better, but it must be said: "The use of imaginative fiction is to deepen your understanding of your world, and your fellow men, and your own feelings, and your destiny."

28 To which I fear he will retort, "Look, I got a raise last year, and I'm giving my family the best of everything, we've got two cars and a color TV. I understand enough of the world!"

29 And he is right, unanswerably right, if that is what he wants, and all he wants.

30 The kind of thing you learn from reading about the problems of a hobbit who is trying to drop a magic ring into an imaginary volcano has very little to do with your social status, or material success, or income. Indeed, if there is any relationship, it is a negative one. There is an inverse correlation between fantasy and money. That is a law, known to economists as Le Guin's Law. If you want a striking example of Le Guin's Law, just give a lift to one of those people along the roads who own nothing but a backpack, a guitar, a fine head of hair, a smile, and a thumb. Time and again, you will find that these waifs have read *The Lord of the Rings*—some of them can practically recite it. But now take Aristotle Onassis, or J. Paul Getty: could you believe that those men ever had anything to do, at any age, under any circumstances, with a hobbit?

31 But, to carry my example a little further, and out of the realm of economics, did you ever notice how very gloomy Mr. Onassis and Mr. Getty and all those billionaires look in their photographs? They have this strange, pinched look, as if they were hungry. As if they were hungry for something, as if they had lost something and were trying to think where it could be, or perhaps what it could be, what it was they've lost.

32 Could it be their childhood?

33 So I arrive at my personal defense of the uses of the imagination, especially in fiction, and most especially in fairy tale, legend, fantasy, science fiction, and the rest of the lunatic fringe. I believe that maturity is

not an outgrowing, but a growing up: that an adult is not a dead child, but a child who survived. I believe that all the best faculties of a mature human being exist in the child, and that if these faculties are encouraged in youth they will act well and wisely in the adult, but if they are repressed and denied in the child they will stunt and cripple the adult personality. And finally, I believe that one of the most deeply human, and humane, of these faculties is the power of imagination: so that it is our pleasant duty, as librarians, or teachers, or parents, or writers, or simply as grownups, to encourage that faculty of imagination in our children, to encourage it to grow freely, to flourish like the green bay tree, by giving it the best, absolutely the best and purest, nourishment that it can absorb. And never, under any circumstances, to squelch it, or sneer at it, or imply that it is childish, or unmanly, or untrue.

34   For fantasy is true, of course. It isn't factual, but it is true. Children know that. Adults know it too, and that is precisely why many of them are afraid of fantasy. They know that its truth challenges, even threatens, all that is false, all that is phony, unnecessary, and trivial in the life they have let themselves be forced into living. They are afraid of dragons, because they are afraid of freedom.

35   So I believe that we should trust our children. Normal children do not confuse reality and fantasy—they confuse them much less often than we adults do (as a certain great fantasist pointed out in a story called "The Emperor's New Clothes"). Children know perfectly well that unicorns aren't real, but they also know that books about unicorns, if they are good books, are true books. All too often, that's more than Mommy and Daddy know; for, in denying their childhood, the adults have denied half their knowledge, and are left with the sad, sterile little fact: "Unicorns aren't real." And that fact is one that never got anybody anywhere (except in the story "The Unicorn in the Garden," by another great fantasist, in which it is shown that a devotion to the unreality of unicorns may get you straight into the loony bin). It is by such statements as, "Once upon a time there was a dragon," or "In a hole in the ground there lived a hobbit"—it is by such beautiful non-facts that we fantastic human beings may arrive, in our peculiar fashion, at the truth.

Content Questions

1. Does Le Guin's definition of *imagination* differ from a dictionary definition of the word?
2. Why are detective thrillers, hack westerns, sports stories, and pornography "hopelessly sterile"?
3. What does Le Guin think are the uses of fiction?

Questions on Presentation

1. Le Guin begins the essay with a disclaimer. Why? Is this effective?
2. Le Guin relies heavily on rhetorical questions. What is the effect of this on the reader? On the development of the essay?
3. How does Le Guin support her assertion that rejection of fiction is related to "several American characteristics"?
4. Le Guin defines a number of terms in the essay. How do these definitions differ in form? Which is most effective?

One Rejection Too Many

Patricia Nurse

Canadian Patricia Nurse was born in England and currently makes her living in the very competitive world of professional writing. As any professional writer can attest, rejections come more frequently than acceptances. Nurse, who understands the feelings that come with an editor's rejections, takes a humorous look at writing, writers, and editors in the following selection from *Isaac Asimov's Science Fiction Magazine*, Nurse's first professional sale.

1 Dear Dr. Asimov:

Imagine my delight when I spotted your new science-fiction magazine on the newsstands. I have been a fan of yours for many, many years and I naturally wasted no time in buying a copy. I wish you every success in this new venture.

In your second issue I read with interest your plea for stories from new authors. While no writer myself, I have had a time traveler living with me for the past two weeks (he materialized in the bathtub without clothes or money, so I felt obliged to offer him shelter), and he has written a story of life on earth as it will be in the year 5000.

Before he leaves this time frame, it would give him great pleasure to see his story in print—I hope you will feel able to make this wish come true.

Yours sincerely,
Nancy Morrison (Miss)

2 Dear Miss Morrison:

Thank you for your kind letter and good wishes.

It is always refreshing to hear from a new author. You have included some most imaginative material in your story; however, it is a little short on plot and human interest—perhaps you could rewrite it with this thought in mind.

Yours sincerely,
Isaac Asimov

3   Dear Dr. Asimov:

I was sorry that you were unable to print the story I sent you. Vahl (the time traveler who wrote it) was quite hurt as he tells me he is an author of some note in his own time. He has, however, rewritten the story and this time has included plenty of plot and some rather interesting mating rituals which he has borrowed from the year 3000. In his own time (the year 5015) sex is no longer practiced, so you can see that it is perfectly respectable having him in my house. I do wish, though, that he could adapt himself to our custom of wearing clothes—my neighbors are starting to talk!

Anything that you can do to expedite the publishing of Vahl's story would be most appreciated, so that he will feel free to return to his own time.

Yours sincerely,
Nancy Morrison (Miss)

4   Dear Miss Morrison:

Thank you for your rewritten short story.

I don't want to discourage you but I'm afraid you followed my suggestions with a little too much enthusiasm—however, I can understand that having an imaginary nude visitor from another time is a rather heady experience. I'm afraid that your story now rather resembles a far-future episode of *Mary Hartman, Mary Hartman* or *Soap*.

Could you tone it down a bit and omit the more bizarre sex rituals of the year 3000—we must remember that *Isaac Asimov's Science Fiction Magazine* is intended to be a family publication.

Perhaps a little humor would improve the tale too.

Yours sincerely,
Isaac Asimov

5   Dear Dr. Asimov:

Vahl was extremely offended by your second rejection—he said he has never received a rejection slip before, and your referring to him as "imaginary" didn't help matters at all. I'm afraid he rather lost his temper and stormed out into the garden—it was at this unfortunate moment that the vicar happened to pass by.

Anyway, I managed to get Vahl calmed down and he has rewritten the story and added plenty of humor. I'm afraid my subsequent meeting with the vicar was not blessed with such success! I'm quite sure Vahl would not understand another rejection.

Yours truly,
Nancy Morrison (Miss)

6 Dear Miss Morrison:

I really admire your persistence in rewriting your story yet another time. Please don't give up hope—you can become a fairly competent writer in time, I feel sure.

I'm afraid the humor you added was not the kind of thing I had in mind at all—you're not collaborating with Henny Youngman by any chance are you? I really had a more sophisticated type of humor in mind.

Yours truly,
Isaac Asimov

P.S. Have you considered reading your story, as it is, on *The Gong Show*?

7 Dear Dr. Asimov:

It really was very distressing to receive the return of my manuscript once again—Vahl was quite speechless with anger.

It was only with the greatest difficulty that I prevailed upon him to refine the humor you found so distasteful, and I am submitting his latest rewrite herewith.

In his disappointment, Vahl has decided to return to his own time right away. I shall be sorry to see him leave as I was getting very fond of him—a pity he wasn't from the year 3000 though. Still, he wouldn't have made a very satisfactory husband; I'd have never known where (or when) he was. It rather looks as though my plans to marry the vicar have suffered a severe setback too. Are you married, Dr. Asimov?

I must close this letter now as I have to say goodbye to Vahl. He says he has just finished making some long overdue improvements to our time frame as a parting gift—isn't that kind of him?

Yours sincerely,
Nancy Morrison (Miss)

8 Dear Miss Morrison:

I am very confused by your letter. Who is Isaac Asimov? I have checked with several publishers and none of them has heard of *Isaac Asimov's Science Fiction Magazine*, although the address on the envelope was correct for *this* magazine.

However, I was very impressed with your story and will be pleased to accept it for our next issue. Seldom do we receive a story combining such virtues as a well-conceived plot, plenty of human interest, and a delightfully subtle brand of humor.

Yours truly,
George H. Scithers,
Editor,
Arthur C. Clarke's Science Fiction Magazine

Content Questions

1. Why does the editor reject Morrison's story?
2. How does Morrison react to the rejection?

Questions on Presentation

1. Could this story have been effectively presented in a form other than letters?
2. How does the tone change as the series of letters progresses?
3. What type of person is Miss Morrison? How do you know this?

Questions for Discussion and Writing

1. Many of the essays in this section present art as being controversial. Write an essay in which you analyze what makes art controversial.
2. Most of the selections in this section are arguments. Write an essay in which you analyze the effectiveness of one of those arguments. What makes it effective?
3. These readings concern primarily popular art; however, some concern more formal or traditional art. Write an essay in which you establish a method of discriminating between popular and traditional art.

Appendix

WRITING THE RESEARCH PAPER

The skills you use in writing a research paper are the same as those in any shorter essay; the differences are length, time alloted to the assignment, detail, and the incorporation of supporting material from external sources. The first of these issues, length, is usually included in the assignment; your instructor will give you a range of pages, say ten to fifteen, as the length of your paper. The time is also built into the assignment; most research paper assignments are made early in the term and are due at the term's end. You may also be given a list of sources from which you are required to take your supporting evidence; if so, the paper is usually called a "resource paper." For the research paper, however, you will be given a broad area or subject as your field of research, and it becomes your responsibility to narrow that area or subject to a workable topic and to do the research yourself.

GETTING STARTED

You must, of course, in narrowing your focus do all those things discussed in Part One: An Introduction to Reading, Thinking, and Writing: find a topic, determine approach, and identify your audience. Additionally, you must undertake the actual research, finding other authors and other materials with which to support and develop your thesis. This investigation can be the most intimidating aspect of doing a research paper.

USING THE LIBRARY

Although the sheer volume of material available to you may be intimidating, understanding how your library works will make your research much easier. Therefore, you should familiarize yourself with your library's facilities. All libraries have a reference section. It is here that you will find the encyclopedias, handbooks, dictionaries, indices, and bibliographies where you will begin your research. In most libraries this material cannot be checked out, but must be used in the reference room. The major part of your research will be in books, journals, magazines, and newspapers. These are housed in separate sections of the library, and there are various aids to help you find specific works. These include the card catalog and periodical indices, also usually found in the reference room.

Card Catalogs

The card catalog is divided into author/title lists and subject lists. These are arranged alphabetically, and each card contains information about the book, including author, publisher, and publication date, what the book contains, and a call number showing where it is located in the library. There are two systems of classification, the older Dewey Decimal system and the Library of Congress system; all new works acquired by the library are classified according to the latter. Each system categorizes books by broad topics and within those broad areas provides for finer classifications.

The Dewey Decimal system uses a number system to classify books into one of ten categories:

000–099 General Works
100–199 Philosophy
200–299 Religion
300–399 Social Sciences
400–499 Language
500–599 Natural Science
600–699 Technology
700–799 Fine Arts
800–899 Literature and Belles Lettres
900–999 History and Geography

These are further subdivided by groups of ten to classify areas within the broad field; for example, 810–819 includes all American literature, and the specific number 810 identifies American essays. Additional numbers and letters identify a specific book; for example, you will find Van Wyck Brooks's *The Confident Years*, one of the books used by the author of the student essay following this section, under the Dewey Decimal number:

810.9
B791c

The Library of Congress system begins with a finer classification system, using letters to identify twenty-one broad categories:

A   General Works
B   Philosophy, Psychology, and Religion
C   Auxiliary Sciences of History
D   History (General)
E–F American History (North and South)
G   Geography, Anthropology, and Recreation
H   Social Sciences
J   Political Science and Official Documents
K   Law
L   Education
M   Music
N   Visual Arts
P   Language and Literature
Q   Science
R   Medicine
S   Agriculture
T   Technology
U   Military Science
V   Naval Science
Z   Bibliography and Library Science

As with the Dewey Decimal system, these categories are further subdivided; thus, PN indicates General Literature, and within this section you will find Raymond Williams' *Modern Tragedy*, another book used by the author of the student essay, listed as:

PN
1897
W5

Here the number 1897, indeed all numbers between 1600 and 3299, indicates that the subject of the book is drama.

Periodical Catalog

The card catalog lists books and pamphlets; to find the location of journals, magazines, and newspapers you must use the library's periodical catalog. This may be in a card catalog of its own, or, more probably, will be found on microfiche, small transparencies that contain microphotographic catalog entries which, again, will have call numbers indicating location. The library will provide the necessary equipment to enable you to read this material. Most libraries house periodicals of all sorts separately from books, and the periodical catalog may be housed either in the periodicals section or in the reference section.

Periodical Indices

Knowing which periodical you wish to read is not sufficient, however, because some periodicals have been published for more than a century. You must know which volume, even which pages you wish to retrieve. For this you must turn to one of the periodical indices, among them

Art Index
Business Periodicals Index
International Bibliography of Periodical Literature
MLA International Bibliography
The New York Times Index
Readers' Guide to Periodical Literature
Social Sciences Index

These indices are arranged by subject and will provide the titles of articles that may be useful in your research, as well as the volume, number, and pages of the periodical where the article will be found.

Microfilm and Microforms

You will find that many of the journals and periodicals your library owns are on microfilm or microforms. These, like the microfiche, are microphotographic records on either long strips (microfilm) or sheets (microforms). The libraries use these as a way of saving space and will provide you with appropriate equipment for reading this material.

On-line Computer Searches

In order to enhance their own catalogs, many libraries subscribe to one or more bibliographic data base services. Most libraries require that you submit a request for a computer search to the reference department so the librarian may make the search; for this service they will charge a fee, often only the fee charged to the library for the search; sometimes, however, the fee may be substantial, including payment for the librarian's time. There are several services that provide on-line or computer searches; among them are

Bibliographical Retrieval Services (BRS)
DIALOG

Educational Research Information Center (ERIC)
Research Libraries Information Network (RLIN)
On-line Computer Library Center (OCLC)

Journals in many fields have published articles about on-line bibliographic searches, and for more information on specific fields you should
check the indices for those fields. For general information, however, one
of the best sources is a journal called *On-line Review;* this will provide
you with a great deal of information on the subject.

Interlibrary Loan

Libraries cannot own all books and periodicals published, so they are all
part of a system known as interlibrary loan. This system allows your library to borrow from another library—for a limited time—a book or article you need. You do not need to do the search; the librarians will do
this for you. You need only give the author, title, page numbers, and as
much publication information as possible; they will discover what library owns the material and ask that it be sent. There may be a fee for
this service, usually the cost of mailing the material and any copying
that is done.

Government Publications

Some libraries are depositories for government publications, and such libraries hold vast quantities of government records and publications that
may be useful in your research. All libraries, however, should hold the
indices to these publications, and can acquire material through interlibrary loan. The indices include

American Statistics Index
Congressional Information Service
Government Publications Index
Index to International Statistics
Index to U.S. Government Periodicals
Monthly Catalog

BUILDING A BIBLIOGRAPHY

Once you are familiar with what is available to you in the library, you
will need to begin to organize your research. One way to make the project less intimidating is to have an organized system of taking notes before you begin your research.

Many people use 3×5 or 4×6 cards to record their notes and references. These have the advantage of being easily portable, and can be

shuffled in various combinations when you reach the point of arranging material. Another system is to use loose-leaf paper to organize all your notes from one text. This has the advantage of being lightweight and portable, but, if the research is extensive or complicated, subdividing notes can be difficult; additionally, loose-leaf paper is not as durable as note cards. If you are fortunate enough to have a lap-top computer, you can use that in the library to enter information directly to a data base. Whatever system you use, you must proceed in an orderly manner.

Having decided upon your system of taking notes, you must begin to create a working **bibliography** and to take notes. Ideally these should be separate activities, with your bibliography complete before you begin taking notes. In practice this rarely happens; you will probably find that you are building your bibliography while you are taking notes. Generally this is because you will discover new references while you are reading.

The first thing you must do when creating a bibliography is to make careful note of all publication data. If you are taking a bibliographic entry from an essay in another text, as soon as you find the book or article (the title of which you have written down), check the publication data; the data on the title page is always your final authority. Do not assume that the information in another place is accurate. If you are using a note card system, write all the information on the face of one card, one bibliography card to each text. You should also give each bibliography card a number and use that number to identify notes taken from that source; this will simplify sorting your cards for **documentation,** final list of works cited, or bibliography.

Encyclopedias

Another way of making the research process less intimidating is to have a plan of action, and, as in writing itself, the best plan is to move from the general to the specific. To this end, first investigate encyclopedias. When you examine single volume encyclopedias you will discover short articles that provide basic information; among these reference works are

The New Columbia Encyclopedia
Random House Encyclopedia

Multivolume works provide more detailed articles and are more completely cross-indexed to related topics than the single volume works. These multivolume general references include

Collier's Encyclopedia
Encyclopedia Americana
Encyclopedia Britannica
Funk and Wagnall's New Encyclopedia

These and other general encyclopedias offer articles related to your topic and, more importantly, bibliographies for additional reading. You should also investigate specialized encyclopedias, which provide more detailed articles about your topic; these include such works as

Cassell's Encyclopedia of World Literature
Encyclopedia of Advertising
Encyclopedia of American History
Encyclopedia of Physics
Encyclopedia of Psychology
An Encyclopedia of Religion
Encyclopedia of World Architecture
The Reader's Encyclopedia of World Drama
World Encyclopedia of Film

Handbooks

Other general references you will find valuable are handbooks related to specific fields. Among these are

Crowell's Handbook of World Opera
Handbook of Chemistry and Physics
A Handbook of Literature
Handbook of Modern Marketing
Political Handbook and Atlas of the World

Dictionaries

Finally, among the general works, you should not ignore the specialized dictionaries such as

Bryan's Dictionary of Painters and Engravers
Dictionary of American History
A Dictionary of Economics
Dictionary of Education
A Dictionary of Literary Terms
A Dictionary of Science Terms
The Oxford Dictionary of the Christian Church

All of these general works will provide you with references or terms with which you will begin your major research.

As you search the encyclopedias, handbooks, dictionaries, card catalogs, and indices your library provides, you will find additional references to works that may prove useful. At every step, update your notes.

Bibliographic Form

As you add to your bibliography cards, you will find it most convenient to make bibliographic notes in the form in which you will use them in your research paper. There are many bibliographic styles; however, two of the most widely used are the *Modern Language Association Handbook for Writers of Research Papers* (MLA) and the *Publication Manual of the American Psychological Association* (APA). Deciding what style your bibliography should take depends on what type of essay you are writing and who your audience is. If you are writing an essay that criticizes a story or novel, you should use the MLA, a style manual commonly used in the humanities, languages, and fine arts. If you are analyzing a problem in psychology, business, or anthropology, you should consult the APA, a style manual often used in the social sciences.

Scientific or technological essays, such as those that report the results of an experiment and compare the findings with published results, use variations of numbering systems or author/date systems, depending on the field. For example, biologists often use the *Council of Biology Editors Style Manual* compiled by the Style Manual Committee of the Council of Biology Editors; chemists use the *Handbook for Authors of Papers in American Chemical Society Publications* by the American Chemical Society; and physicists use the *Style Manual for Guidance in the Preparation of Papers* by the Publication Board of the American Institute of Physics. Even though readers from various disciplines prefer different forms of reference depending on their disciplines, all readers will expect you to record your source's name, the title of the source's work, the place and date of publication, and the appropriate page numbers from the work.

The bibliography you list at the end of your research paper is usually called a list of works cited or a selected bibliography, because a true bibliography is exhaustive in nature and lists all the works that deal with your topic. Below is a brief style sheet detailing how to format a list of works cited according to both the MLA and APA styles.

Works Cited—MLA Style

In your bibliography or list of works cited, arrange all the entries alphabetically by the last name of the author or authors or by the name of the work if no author is mentioned. In general the information in the reference is ordered as follows: author's name, title of the work, place of publication, name of publisher, and date of publication. You will find this information on the copyright page or in the table of contents if you have cited an article from a journal. Double-space all of the entries in your list of works cited. Indent the second and subsequent lines of an entry five spaces.

Work by one author: If you cited an entire work by an author in your essay, give the author's last name, then first name, the title of the work, the place of publication, the publisher, and the date of publication. Put periods after the author's name, the title of the work, and the date of publication.

> Rodriguez, Richard. <u>Hunger of Memory</u>. Boston: David R. Godine, 1981.

If you cited an article from a book, give the title of the article before the title of the book in your documentation.

> Gould, Stephen J. "Were Dinosaurs Dumb?" <u>The Panda's Thumb</u>. Cambridge, MA: W. W. Norton, 1980.

Two or more works by one author: If you cited more than one work by an author, alphabetize the titles. For your second reference, substitute dashes for the author's name.

> Smith, Adam. <u>The Money Game</u>. New York: Random House, 1976.
> ———. <u>Paper Money</u>. New York: Summit Books, 1981.

Work by two or more authors: If the work you cited in your essay has two or three authors, begin your documentation with the last name of the first author. Then list the other authors' names in regular order. If the work is an article from a journal with continuous pagination, give the name of the journal, its date, and the page numbers of the article. Put a colon between the date and the page numbers.

> Gould, James L. and Carol Gould. "Can a Bee Behave Intelligently?" <u>New Scientist</u> 98 (1983): 84–87.

If the work you've cited has more than three authors, use the first author's name and the Latin abbreviation *et al.* ("and others"). Put a comma between the author's name and the abbreviation.

> Turco, Richard P., et al. "The Climatic Effects of Nuclear Winter." <u>Scientific American</u> August (1984): 33–43.

Works Cited—APA Style

In your reference list or list of works cited, arrange all the entries alphabetically by the last name of the author or authors or by the name of the work if no author is mentioned. Indent the second and subsequent lines of an entry three spaces.

If you've quoted or paraphrased an author from an article in a journal, you must include the name of the journal, its volume number, and the page numbers of the article. You do not need to put quotation marks around the title or put the abbreviations *p* or *pp* before the page numbers. Single-space the entries in your list of works cited, and double-space between the entries.

Work by one author: If you cited an entire work by an author in your essay, give the author's last name, then the author's initials, the date of publication, the title, the place of publication, and the name of the publisher. Put periods after the author's initials, the date of publication, the title, and the name of the publisher. Put a colon after the place of publication.

Rodriguez, R. (1981). <u>Hunger of memory</u>. Boston: David R.
   Godine.

Two or more works by one author: If you have more than one reference by the same author, give the author's name for each entry. List the references in chronological order beginning with earliest publication date.

Smith, A. (1976). <u>The money game</u>. New York: Random House.
Smith, A. (1981). <u>Paper money</u>. New York: Summit Books.

Work by two or more authors: List all of the authors' names, last names first, for a work with multiple authors. Put a comma between the authors' names and an ampersand (&) between the last two authors' names.

Gould, J. L., & Gould, C. (1983). Can a bee behave intelligently?"
   <u>New Scientist, 98</u>, 33—43.

If the article you have cited comes from a journal that numbers each issue separately, put the issue number in parentheses after the volume number.

Turco, R. P., Toon, O. B., Ackerman, T. P., Pollack, J. B., & Sagan, C. (1983). The climatic effects of nuclear winter. Scientific American, 251 (2), 33–43.

Deciding on Types of Sources

As you discover sources, you will find that there are a number of types. Not only are there books, articles, lectures, reviews, and interviews, but these sources can range from scholarly and professional to exploitive and polemic. Sources that are serious in nature, either scholarly or professional, are always acceptable. Many popular sources, such as newspapers, magazines, or documentaries are often acceptable; you must remember, however, that sources of this nature are informal and will lower the tone and value of your paper. Sources of an exploitive or polemic nature, such as *The National Enquirer* or publications by the Ku Klux Klan, are acceptable only as examples of exploitive or polemic literature and should not be cited as supports for your argument.

Narrowing Your Bibliography

When you have what you consider to be an adequate working bibliography, you may decide that you have more sources than are useful or practical for your ten to fifteen page paper. You must now determine which are the most useful. Rather than reading all of each work, which can consume more of your time than you can perhaps afford, you should scan the table of contents, the index, and the general introduction to a book. If your source material is an article, you should read both the introduction and the conclusion carefully. In this way you gain a good sense of what is in the text and can decide upon its usefulness. Do not discard those bibliography cards at this time, however. You may decide later to use a source you had first decided against, or you may find a reference to that work in another source. If you have retained the card you will not need to look up the document again.

TAKING NOTES

You are now ready to take notes. When you make notes it is wise to write down the entire section you feel will be useful, even if this requires more than one note card. If the passage is very long, consider photocopying the passage and then taping it to cards or to your notepaper. Remember that if you use more than one page or card for an entry you must number them consecutively. You should include the entire text rather than a paraphrase in order to guard against unwitting plagiarism and to prevent another trip to the library should you later decide you want to quote the author exactly in your essay. Another danger arises when you are taking notes: you may write down an idea, not fully understanding what you're writing, and later forget whether it was your idea or someone else's. You should take notes carefully; this way you can document your sources easily. Whatever style manual you follow, your citation must provide your readers with enough information to find the source.

Avoiding Plagiarism

Failure to give credit for the information you borrow is called **plagiarism;** it's literally stealing someone else's words or ideas. For professional writers the consequences of plagiarism are serious: a writer may lose a publishing assignment, have the essay rejected for publication, or face a lawsuit for the theft. For students the consequences of plagiarism are equally serious: a student will receive a failing grade on the plagiarized essay and may be expelled from the course or, in some cases, the college or university.

Careful planning and sound documentation allows you to understand exactly what you have to document and to avoid the dangers of plagiarism. You do not have to provide a citation or bibliographic reference for every idea in your essay because most of the analysis and argumentation will be yours or will be commonly held ideas with which people in the field are familiar. However, when you quote someone else, restate someone's idea, paraphrase a concept, or summarize someone else's main ideas, you must identify whom you are quoting, paraphrasing, or summarizing.

Plagiarism is obvious when we encounter it, but it is sometimes difficult for students to avoid it when doing research because they do not understand exactly what it means. Consider the following passages:

Original Passage from Nicolson's "Romance of Scholarship"

"Scholarship," I have said, seems a hard word. The layman has inherited from literature, particularly from satire, a picture of the scholar as pedant, an elderly man (usually with thick glasses) spending his life in a dusty library, reading books which only a bookworm has visited before him, a man, as has often been said, who devotes his life to knowing more and more about less and less. . . .

Plagiarized Version

People often have a stereotyped vision of a scholar. Their picture is one they have had handed down to them, especially through satire, but in fact through centuries of literature. His usually thick glasses, through which he reads books which before only were visited by bookworms, the dusty, moldy library in which he seems to live are part of the stereotype.

Here the student has simplified Nicolson's expression of the idea of the pedant. Still there is too much that is the same. The student has used the phrase "handed down to them," but the idea of "inherited" remains; "especially" is not very different from "particularly," and it is most noticeable because it is used in the same context. The idea, metaphor, and language of "visited by bookworms" comes directly from Nicolson's passage.

An acceptable student passage would be the following:

> People often have a stereotyped vision of a scholar. Marjorie Hope Nicolson, in "The Romance of Scholarship," summarizes this stereotype by identifying him as pedantic, elderly, nearsighted, and "reading books which only a bookworm has visited before" (in *The Humanities at Scripps College* 17).

This time the student has attributed the idea to Nicolson, has summarized the idea in as few words as possible, and has directly quoted a phrase that the student finds particularly descriptive and humorous. All this, combined with the parenthetical notation which allows the reader to search out the quotation, means that the student has endeavored to use the material appropriately.

DOCUMENTING YOUR ESSAY

Having completed your research, you begin to write your essay, incorporating your research into your own argument or analysis. You must now begin to document sources. Unlike other questions about writing, questions about what to reference and how to write references are relatively simple. When you write an essay or research a paper in which you use the language, approach, or original ideas of another writer, you must include a citation, a parenthetical reference identifying the source of your quotation or paraphrase. Parenthetical citations have replaced footnotes as the way of documenting quotations and paraphrases.

Including citations shows your audience that you are a careful scholar, one who has credited the authors who contributed to your ideas. The citations in your essay should always be brief yet clear; that way your references won't interfere with the flow of ideas in your essay. Citations should be inserted at appropriate points in your text, usually following a quotation or paraphrase or at the end of a sentence. Below is a brief style sheet showing you how to complete citations in both MLA and APA style.

Parenthetical Citations—MLA style:

Entire Work: When you refer to an entire work and its author in your text, you do not have to provide a parenthetical citation.

> Richard Rodriguez in <u>Hunger of Memory</u> describes how a teacher's view of his students can be colored by his experiences.

If you do not include the author's name in your text, you must provide it in the citation.

> <u>Hunger of Memory</u> traces one man's experience of the conflicts between two cultures (Rodriguez).

If you are citing a section of an article from a longer work, you must include the author's last name and the page number for the reference.

> The strict correlation of brain size to intelligence is misleading because it neglects differing ratios of brain to body size in various species (Gould 261).

Work by one author: If you use a specific passage from a work by an author and you mention that author's name in your text, you need only mention the page number in the citation.

> Smith suggests how this model would explain rising oil costs by criticizing "how far off the great Economics, Inc. model was" (34).

However, if you don't refer to the author in your text, you should add the author's last name to the page number. You do not need any punctuation within the citation.

> The complexities of contemporary economic theory can be illustrated by analyzing a hypothetical response to rising oil costs (Smith 34).

Two or more works by one author: If you are using several works by the same author, you should provide a brief title in your citation so your readers can find the appropriate work in your endnotes. Again, you do not need any punctuation within your citation.

> Adam Smith illustrates the complexities of contemporary
> economic theory in his discussion of how a fictitious company
> would respond to rising oil costs (<u>Paper Money</u> 34).

Work by two or more authors: If you use a specific passage from a work written by two or three authors in your text, give all of their last names and the page number of the passage in your citation.

> One argument used to discredit the criteria for insect
> intelligence is that proposed criteria are unreliable (Gould and
> Gould 84).

If you use a specific passage from a work written by more than three authors, give the first author's last name, the abbreviation et al., and the page number of the passage.

> Concerned scientists argue that the leaders of the superpowers
> should reevaluate their political stances because "the long-term
> destruction of the environment and disruption of the global
> ecosystem might in the end prove even more devastating for the
> human species than the awesome short-term destructive effects"
> (Turco et al. 37).

Parenthetical Citations—APA Style

Work by one author: If you use a specific passage from a work by an author and you mention that author's name in your text, you should mention the date of the publication and the page number of the passage if you have quoted that passage. Put a comma between the date and the page number.

> Smith suggests how this model would explain rising oil costs by
> criticizing "how far off the great Economics, Inc. model was"
> (1981, p. 34).

However, if you don't refer to the author in your text, you should give the author's last name and the date of publication. Put a comma between the author's last name and the date. Notice that when you paraphrase a general idea from a work, you do not include the page numbers.

> The complexities of contemporary economic theory can be illustrated by analyzing a hypothetical response to rising oil costs (Smith, 1981).

Work by two authors: If you quote or paraphrase a work written by two authors, give both authors' last names each time you cite their work.

> One argument used to discredit the criteria for insect intelligence is that proposed criteria are unreliable (Gould & Gould, 1983).

Work by three or more authors: If you use a specific passage from a work written by three or more authors, give the last names of all the authors and the date of publication the first time you cite the work. Use an ampersand (&) between the last two authors' names. In subsequent citations use the first author's last name, followed by the abbreviation et al., the date of publication, and the page number of the quotation.

> Concerned scientists argue that the leaders of the superpowers should reevaluate their political stances because "the long-term destruction of the environment and disruption of the global ecosystem might in the end prove even more devastating for the human species than the awesome short-term destructive effects" (Turco, Toon, Ackerman, Pollack, & Sagan, 1984, p. 37).

If you've referred to an author's ideas in an article, you must include the name of the magazine or book you found the article in and the page number of the article.

PREPARING YOUR PAPER

When you have completed your research, written a rough draft, identified the sources for quotations and paraphrases, and polished your essay's mechanics, syntax, organization, and language, it is time to do your final draft. Your instructor may have given you special instructions, but generally certain rules apply.

TITLE PAGE.   You should have a title page that includes the title of your essay, your name, the course for which you wrote the paper, and the date on which it is due. The title of your essay should appear 20 lines down from the top of the page. After typing the title, double space and type *by*, then double space again and type your name. Four spaces below your name, on separate lines, double-spaced, type the name of the course, the name of your college or university, and the date the essay is due. All of this information should be centered (i.e., between the left and right edges of the paper) on your title page.

TYPING.   You should type your essay on one side of the page only; you should use nonerasable 8½×11 white 20-pound paper; you should leave a margin of 1 1/2 inches on the left margin and 1 inch on the remaining sides; you must use a good ribbon in your typewriter or printer; if you use a word processing program and printer, use either letter quality or near-letter quality type and standard fonts.

PAGINATION.   You should number pages consecutively, but the first page of your essay and the first page of your list of works cited should not be numbered; numbers should appear in the upper right-hand corner 1/2 inch from the top edge of the paper and in line with the right margin.

BLOCK QUOTATIONS.   Long quotations of more than fifty words or five lines of poetry should be set off by indenting the entire quotation ten spaces from the left margin; you do not use quotation marks around indented quotations.

EDITING BRACKETS.   You may edit quotations to fit the grammar or syntax of your own work by changing language and placing the change in square brackets [   ]; you may also add one or two words to clarify a passage, especially pronouns, by placing them in square brackets.

ELLIPSES.   You may also edit quotations by leaving part of them out; indicate omissions by the ellipsis (. . .). The following essay provides a model, in MLA form, for a research paper. The essay shows manuscript form for the insertion of quotations, the use of parenthetical documentation, the insertion of illustrations or figures into a text, the insertion of your editorial comments into a quotation, and the list of works cited.

American Drama in
the Progressive Era

by

Douglas V. Blackwater

Recent American History

Center City University

May 1,1988

American social and intellectual history has gone through numerous shifts, even convulsions. But there has been none so important, in terms of succeeding years, as the Progressive Era.
— general background material

This era was remarkable for its revolution in thought, which was, in large part, a reaction against a new lifestyle engendered by an increasingly complex industrial society. It can be said that Progressive reform was the imposition of "order on change that seemed incomprehensibly rapid. . . . the widening gap between rich and poor and the radicals who pointed to it endangered social stability"
— insertion of a quotation so it becomes part of your own sentence

(Bedford and Colbourn 327).
— parenthetical citation of short quotation where author is not named in the text

While progressivism began as a social movement in intent, it was not long limited to that. The tenets of Progressivism, as far as they could be articulated, soon began to color all aspects of American life; reform, the search for ways to express values in a new world, and an increasing rejection of industrial materialism appeared as ever-widening circles in American society.
— narrowing of topic

American theatre was no exception; although the Progressive Era was well under way before there was any great impact on American drama, when the impact came it was profound.
— student's controlling idea for essay

Playwrights and designers desired to find a new order which would express the new world. Old forms were not rejected out of hand, but were laid aside to be taken up again when and if the situation warranted. As
— statements paraphrased from a number of sources—commonly held information in the field

2

a result the course of American drama was irrevocably
changed. The excitement which spread through the
theatres of America prior to World War I was in many
ways more intense than that which spread through the
country as a whole. Manifested in many ways, from new
dramatic forms and purposes to new production styles,
the new drama spread across the country on a grassroots
level.

further
statements
paraphrased from
a number of
sources

　　　The Progressive Era had its roots in the late
nineteenth century. At a time when scientific thought
was producing technological changes with increasing
rapidity, there was a rebellion against that technology
and the thought behind it. This intellectual rebellion,
however, was part of a greater dualistic pattern of
intellectual history. Mordecai Gorelik has summarized
this pattern and its appearance at the beginning of the
Progressive Era:

use of the author's
name in the text

　　　　　thought has developed along both subjective
　　　　　and objective lines. . . . A kind of rivalry
　　　　　develops, and any move made by one kind of
　　　　　thought is quickly checkmated by the other. .
　　　　　. . The latter half of the nineteenth century
　　　　　was remarkable for the crumbling away of a
　　　　　whole superstructure of thought. All those
　　　　　theories . . . which envisioned a mechanical
　　　　　world, proved inadequate. . . . The way was

ellipses show
location of
material you have
eliminated from
the quotation

insertion of long
quotation—
quotation marks
are not used
because long
quotation is
indented

3

now open for subjective thought to reassert

itself. (185-86)

parenthetical citation of long quotation when author is named in text

Objective thought, which had sparked scientific develop-

ment of the preceding two centuries, had overstepped

itself. Objective, scientific thought could deal with

vast technological changes, but the changing lifestyles

were an entirely different matter. Subjective thought,

in the form of pragmatic idealism, was necessary here.

student provides analysis of quotation to advance argument

Objective thought could deal very capably with new

technologies; however, removed from their traditional

environments, people were faced with new needs: they

needed to know how to deal with people from different

backgrounds; they needed to know how to get and hold

jobs; they needed entertainment; in short, they needed

to go through an entire acculturation process. Mass

culture resulted in mass identity, and only subjective

idealism could give any measure of individuality.

conclusions drawn by student based on previous material

To deal with this aspect of technological impact,

women such as Jane Addams worked in settlement houses,

trying to humanize industrial society. In "The

Subjective Necessity for Social Settlements," Addams

wrote of the motives behind the creation of settlement

houses as being "the desire to make the entire social

organism democratic . . . to bring as much as possible

of social energy and the accumulation of civilization to

those portions of the race which have little" (Lasch

29).

author of an essay in a book by another author

citation of secondary author

4

The new industrial society had, by its very nature of competition and spectacular advance, engendered an atmosphere of excitement. Those opposed, for whatever reason, to the new society, created their own atmosphere of excitement and partook of that which already existed: "people were showing a disposition to look about them with fresh eyes, to investigate what was going on, and to decide to do something immediate and practical" (Allen 88-89). And the excitement grew to a fever pitch. Ezra Pound, in a letter to Harriet Monroe in 1912, wrote of the (expected) end to American industrial crassness and materialism, saying:

> Any agonizing that tends to hurry what I
> believe in the end to be inevitable, our
> American Risorgimento, is dear to me. That
> awakening will make the Italian Renaissance
> look like a tempest in a teapot! The force we
> have, and the impulse, but the guiding sense,
> the discrimination in applying the force we
> must wait and strive for. (qtd. in Brooks 492)

citation when an author is quoted by another author—with indented quotations the period comes before the citation

The development of dramatic art echoes the Progressive movement, although it lags somewhat behind in time. The intellectual revolt in American theatre was tardy, not appearing in full force until the war years. The "new theatricalism," an all-inclusive term for the many different styles of theatre of the first

5

quarter of the twentieth century, appeared fairly early
in Europe; the first symbolist production, for example,
was Georg Fuchs' production of Goethe's <u>Faust</u> in 1908.
It was not until 1915, with Robert Edmond Jones' set
designs for the New York production of <u>The Man Who
Married a Dumb Wife</u>, that the impact of the new theatre
was seen in this country.

information about
dates may be
found in any text
dealing with the
subject; therefore,
citation is not
necessary

Prior to this time the theatre had been dominated
by Neo-Romanticism and, more importantly, by
Naturalism. Naturalism on the stage purported to show
the audience a "slice of life"; what the audience saw
was not actors playing parts, but presumably real people
with real problems. The space in the proscenium arch
became a transparent fourth wall, and the audience was
placed in the position of voyeurs. The theatre became,
as Georg Fuchs put it, "a vulgar peep show" (qtd. in
Gorelik 178). Realism was the key to dramatic production at this time. So highly esteemed was absolute
realism that it was on occasion carried to ridiculous
extremes; director-producer David Belasco, for example,
imported Japanese furniture from Japan for a New York
production of <u>The Darling of the Gods</u> in order that the
actors might move in a Japanese environment (Marker 61).

use of paraphrase
and its citation

Naturalism, with its "canon of literal realism and
dependence of dramatic action on material circumstances
and events" (Gassner and Quinn 828), was, in part, a

citation of a
quotation which
appears in the
middle of a
sentence

6

product of the new industrial society. Naturalistic dramas revealed people who could not cope with the world in which they found themselves; the characters of many Naturalistic dramas, such as Ibsen's The Master Builder, found themselves in conflict with industrialism or, if not industrialism per se, with the materialism and other values of industrial society. What is important about this conflict, however, is that while it stems from and is a comment upon society there is no successful attempt to alter society, or to truly take a stand against it. The protagonist is victim and nothing can change that. This determinism results in an atmosphere of deep pessimism.

Even though Naturalistic drama drew themes from the new society, it did not partake of the excitement of the industrial age; there was no room for any variation or experimentation in Naturalism. This is not to say that there was no impact other than thematic in the late nineteenth and early twentieth centuries; there were technological advances in production techniques, the most obvious and important of which was the introduction of electrical lighting systems. It was not, however, until the rise of the new theatricalism that light became more than realistic illumination.

In the new theatres light became a means of creating mood, of enhancing non-realistic designs and

7

action. The greatest achievement of the experimental theatres in the use of light came with the Provincetown Players' construction of a plaster dome. This dome, which backed the stage, was based on German models and was the first constructed in this country. It was built specifically for the first production of The Emperor Jones and created a sense of infinity greater than that possible with an ordinary cloth cyclorama.

> The light rays strike along this curve and are reflected in millions of directions. Every light ray, as it strikes the small particles of sand finish, casts its shadow as a complimentary color. The mingling of colored light with its complimentary shadow produces, with the constant curve of surface, the effect of distance, and makes the dome appear what in reality it is--a source of light. It changes all our ideas of setting plays. (Deutsch and Hanau 61-62)

The results of this new control of light was highly praised by critics who reviewed the opening of The Emperor Jones. Although the quality of the light cannot be determined, the illustration below gives some idea of the success and visual impact the new design gave to the silhouetted dumb shows which occur throughout the play.

introduction of an illustration which appears below

8

Insert Illustration #1 Here   shows placement
                                                          of the picture

Fig. 1 <u>The Emperor Jones</u>, scene 6. Designed by Cleon   illustration is
                                                          numbered and
Throckmorton.   identified

    Naturalistic productions would never have attempted
anything of this sort. Indeed, as years passed prior to
World War I, Naturalism became ever more "realistic"
and less imaginative and creative. The American
commercial theatre rejected the excitement and change
occurring in the world beyond Broadway, and there were
no small, independent theatres at this time, no outlet
for a new generation of playwrights and designers. That
there was a need for such an outlet was certain. Eugene
O'Neill, recalling the early theatrical experimentation
of the Provincetown Players wrote in 1924 that: insertion of
                                                          editorial
      To us their [the naturalists'] old audacity is   clarification of
                                                          pronoun reference
      blauge; we have taken too many snap-shots of

      each other in every graceless position; we . . .

      are ashamed of having peeked through so many

      keyholes, squinting always at heavy,

      uninspiring bodies--the fat facts--with not a

9

> nude spirit among them . . . we "wipe out and
> pass on" to some as yet unrealized region
> where our souls, maddened by loneliness and
> the ignoble inarticulateness of flesh, are
> slowly evolving their new language of
> kinship. (qtd. in Deutsch and Hanau 192)

This new generation of playwrights and designers struck out in small groups, experimenting on their own, trying to find expression for their world, responding to what they saw. The year was 1915 and it appeared that, almost as a concerted action, small theatres devoted to experimentation sprang up all across the country. "Something was stirring. . . . flocks of little theatres were launched in America. . . . They were in revolt against the commercial theatre and they were in earnest" (Deutsch and Hanau 4).

quotation may stand separately because the ideas are closely linked to preceding statement and expand upon it

The most important and influential of these new theatres was the Provincetown Players. The founders, including Susan Glaspell, Eugene O'Neill, and Edna St. Vincent Millay, drew up a constitution which set forth their philosophy and purposes:

> The present organization is the outcome of a
> group of people interested in the theatre. .
> . . The impelling desire of the group was to
> establish a stage where playwrights of
> sincere, poetic, literary and dramatic

10

purpose, could see their plays in action.

(qtd. in Deutsch and Hanau 17)

Out of this simple statement grew the new theatricalism
which changed the course of American theatre.

The types of productions done by these companies
reflected the tremendous excitement and activity of the
Progressive Era. Productions sought to show the world
through internal images. Kenneth McGowan summarized the
scenic philosophy of the new theatre as:

> simplification of effect and means: a proper
>
> relationship of actor to background;
>
> suggestion, as when a single candlestick
>
> serves to give the whole quality of the
>
> Baroque period for La Tosca; and synthesis. .
>
> . . (qtd. in Gorelik 188)

These requirements grew out of the need to find and
affirm the essence of life in an increasingly confused
world. To satisfy them, the designer saw the stage as a
sculpture which could reveal on an emotional level the
entire production. They used skeletal settings, strange
lighting effects, and distortion in perspective because
the world which they revealed was a distorted world.

We can see this clearly in Robert Edmond Jones'
design for a Broadway production of Macbeth:

11

Insert Illustration #2 Here

Fig. 2. <u>Macbeth</u>. Designed by Robert Edmond Jones.
Here we see the skeletal effects, the fragmentation and
distortion. This is the world as it reflects Macbeth's
soul and mind. The set itself hovers over the actors at
times; at other times, when the lighting changes, it
becomes shadowy, almost intangible. The important
thing, however, is that this created world appears the
way the individual perceives it. This emphasis on the
individual grew directly out of the concerns of
reformers and intellectuals at the time.

Most of the American plays written during and
immediately after the war years "directed ... protests
against the crass economic materialism of [America] and
its resultant cultural philistinism. It was a protest,
in other words, against a remediable aspect of the community, not a blanket condemnation of society" (Gassner
and Quinn 260). The industrial society with all its new
values and problems was here to stay; Progressive
reformers knew it and the creators of the new drama knew

insertion of editorial alteration to quotation

student begins conclusion

12

it. Neither group wished to actually return to the
earlier world; they merely wished to retain some of the
old values as a way of imposing some order on what
appeared to be mass confusion.

Everyone shared in the excitement of the age,
shared in the confusion. In a world where the
individual had lost his place, there was always hope
that he would reassert himself. It is this which
sparked the Progressive Era and the new theatricalism.
As Eugene O'Neill wrote in 1917:

> The struggle of man to dominate life, to
> assert and insist that life has no meaning
> outside himself where he comes in conflict
> with life, which he does at every turn; and
> his attempt to adapt life to his own needs, in
> which he doesn't succeed, is what I mean when
> I say that Man is the hero. (qtd.in Williams
> 116)

student uses a quotation to sum up the ideas of the essay

Works Cited

Allen, Frederick Lewis. The Big Change: America
     Transforms Itself, 1900-1950. New York: Harper &
     Row, 1969.

Bedford, Henry, and Trevor Colbourn. The Americans: A
     Brief History Since 1865. New York: Harcourt Brace
     Jovanovich, 1972.

Brooks, Van Wyck. The Confident Years: 1885-1915. New
     York: Dutton, 1952.

Deutsch, Helen, and Stella Hanau. The Provincetown: A
     Story of the Theatre. New York: Farrar & Rinehart,
     1931.

Gassner, John, and Edward Quinn, eds. The Reader's
     Encyclopedia of World Drama. New York: Crowell,
     1969.

Gorelik, Mordecai. New Theatres for Old. New York:
     Dutton, 1962.

Lasch, Christopher, ed. The Social Thought of Jane
     Addams. New York: Bobbs-Merrill, 1965.

Marker, Lise-Lone. David Belasco: Naturalism in the
     American Theatre. Princeton: Princeton UP, 1975.

Williams, Raymond. Modern Tragedy. Stanford: Stanford
     UP, 1966.

Glossary

Allusion   Reference to a person, place, or thing that enhances or clarifies a writer's idea (not to be confused with *illusion*).

Analogy   Comparison of two dissimilar objects or ideas for the purpose of clarifying the more unfamiliar, for example, comparing an onion to a bureaucracy because both come in layers and both have nothing at the center. The more points of comparison there are, the stronger the analogy.

Anecdote   Short retelling of an event or single incident used by a writer as an example or illustration of a point.

Argument   Line of reasoning leading to a specific and inevitable conclusion.

Assertion   Declaration that must be proven to be valid. See **Thesis**.

Assumption   Something taken for granted or presumed to be true.

Attitude   Position taken in regard to a subject that is defended by argument.

Audience   Reader or group of readers of a text. An author has a specific audience in mind (identified by cultural, economic, educational, and other characteristics) when he or she writes. The actual audience may or may not correspond to this perceived or intended audience.

Authority   Reliable source of information whose power, whether a person, institution, or document, comes from proven reliability in the past, detailed research, or sound logical investigation. The appeal to authority is a rhetorical device which strengthens your own argument by showing that others have thought in ways similar to you.

Balanced sentence   Sentence in which the syntactical elements are equal or balanced. A balanced sentence appears to the reader to be reasonable and graceful.

Bibliography   List of works about a specific subject. In a research paper the bibliography usually takes the form of a list of works consulted in the course of research. A comprehensive bibliography is exhaustive, listing all works concerning the subject.

Character   The actors in a story. Usually humans, but in science fiction or fantasy literature may be animals or imaginary creatures.

Classification   A way of organizing an essay which establishes mutually exclusive categories and places concepts or objects within those categories.

Cliché   Overused expressions or ideas that do not enliven writing. For example, writers evaluating MBAs might criticize them because "the bottom line" is that MBAs have not learned through "the school of hard knocks."

Colloquial language   Conversational and informal style that is inappropriate for most written texts.

Comparison   A way of organizing an essay which examines the similarities between concepts or objects. See **contrast**.

Concession   Rhetorical device in which you recognize arguments or views differing from your own. Concessions are intended as your protection against charges that you have not considered everything in developing your line of argument.

Conclusion   Assumption that must be arrived at based on the facts or reasoning provided. Structurally, the conclusion is the paragraph or section ending a work, in which you introduce no new material but only state what facts are evident from your analysis or research.

Conflict   Device that drives the development of a narrative. Of three types: person against nature, person against society, and person against self.

Connotative meaning   Those emotional, intellectual, or cultural attachments to a word that expand or illuminate the user's intention.

Contrast   A way of organizing an essay which examines the differences between concepts or objects. See **comparison**.

Critical reading   Reading that is done not only for information, but also for an understanding of how that information is imparted.

Deduction   Pattern of reasoning in which a generalization is tested against specific facts or circumstances. For example, a trial jury measures a generalization that an indictment is valid against the specific facts of a case. See **Induction**.

Definition   A way of organizing an essay by moving from general to specifics; also, the process of establishing the parameters which separate one concept or object from another.

Denotative meaning   Commonly agreed upon definition: the dictionary definition.

Diction   Level and style of language, ranging from informal to formal, clichéd to inventive.

Documentation   Process of identifying the sources for ideas or quotations in your text, usually a research paper.

Draft   Rough version of an essay that precedes the polished or final drafts.

Editing   Process of correcting problems in expression, syntax, or grammar. See **Proofreading**.

Empirical research   Research based on direct observation by the researcher of quantifiable data, phenomena, or events. See **Primary research**.

Essay   Structured written response to a topic, distinguished by an **introduction** in which the topic is identified, a **body** in which information about the topic is developed, and a **conclusion** that summarizes the information, identifies what conclusions may be reached from the information, or otherwise ends the essay. Of three types: **analytic,** which analyzes information or a process, **expository,** which brings certain information to light, and **argumentative,** which attempts to prove a point.

Evidence   Information, data, or facts that support a conclusion. See **Fact**.

Example   Supporting idea, fact, or illustration that proves the validity of a generalization.

Fact   Information presented as true, either because of direct or indirect observation, or because of logical understanding.

Fallacies   Logical errors that impede the development of a logical argument. There are several major fallacies:

Argumentum ad hominem   Attempt to discredit an argument by attacking the individual making the argument.

Argumentum ad ignorantiam   Claim that a statement must be true because the opposite cannot be proven false.

Argumentum ad populum (also called **bandwagoning***)* Appeal implying that everyone with credibility accepts a position regardless of the evidence presented for or against the position.

Argumentum ad verecundiam   Appeal based on someone's authority or standing rather than to the merits of the argument.

Begging the question *(petitio principii)*   Assumption that the premise for an argument can also be the argument's conclusion.

Composition   Assumption that the parts function equally well in all combinations. Often considered the opposite of **division**.

Division   Assumption that what is true of something as a whole is true of its parts. Often considered the opposite of **composition**.

Equivocation   Deliberate hedging in a text by using ambiguous language whose purpose is to mislead the audience about your true intent.

False analogy   Analogy that is carried too far and results in a suspect appeal rather than a convincing argument.

False dilemma (also called **black and white** fallacy)   Either/or proposition wherein you ignore possibilities that lie between the extremes.

Hasty generalization (converse accident)   Argument based on insufficient evidence.

Oversimplification   The basing of an argument on only a few of the important issues.

Post hoc ergo propter hoc   Assumption that because two events occur sequentially the first causes the second.

Special pleading   Attempt to influence an audience by presenting only favorable evidence.

Focus   Restriction of a subject to one aspect or point of view. To focus an essay, a writer relies on his concept of audience, his intention or purpose, and the complexity of the subject matter.

Generalization   Assertion proved valid through specific evidence, examples, or logic.

Hyperbole   Obvious or deliberate overstatement for dramatic effect. For example, in the musical *Oklahoma* we are told that "the corn is as high as an elephant's eye."

Hypothesis   Proposition presented as an explanation for a set of phenomena: also a premise for an argument.

Idea Thought or conception existing in the mind that generates arguments and support for them.

Illusion Erroneous or fanciful belief.

Image Figure of speech that produces a sensory response or mental picture for readers.

Induction Pattern of reasoning in which a generalization is made based on a number of specific instances. For example, a grand jury may indict an individual based on circumstantial evidence because they have heard a series of similar cases in which there was concrete evidence of guilt. See **Deduction**.

Information In writing, the knowledge or content of a message communicated from writer to reader.

Irony Device used by a writer to convey a meaning that is opposite of the literal or denotative meaning. There are two basic types of irony:

situational irony is the difference between how a situation appears and how it actually is.

verbal irony is the difference between what a speaker says and what the speaker means.

Issue A matter under discussion or a point of dispute.

Jargon Language of a special discipline or profession which is used inappropriately outside that field.

Logic A specific way of arguing or discussing a point, identified by its structured approach and presentation.

Metaphor Descriptive form of analogy that compares two usually different items for the purpose of clarifying one of them.

Narrative Manner of expression that focuses on events. In simpler terms, **narratives** are stories.

Narrator Character telling a story.

Non sequitur Latin term meaning "it does not follow." Although not considered a logical fallacy, people write non sequturs when they present two successive statements without apparent logical connection. Close to a fallacy called **ignoratio elenchi,** an argument that fails to show a relevant connection between an argument's premises and its conclusion. For example, when a prosecutor says the defendant must be the murderer because murder is such a horrible crime, the prosecutor is using a non sequitur.

Objective writing Writing that presents information without apparent emotional overtones.

Paradox An apparently contradictory statement that is held to be true; for example, an event may be "incredible but true."

Paraphrase The putting of another person's ideas into your own language.

Periodic sentence Sentence in which the most important information is at the end; it is used to create suspense or add emphasis.

Plagiarism Use of another person's ideas or language without giving credit to that person.

Plot   The series of events that make up a narrative.

Point of view   Writer's mental or emotional perspective.

Premise   Proposition on which an argument is based. A **major premise** is the most important proposition; a **minor premise** is one of secondary importance.

Primary research   Material presented as experiments, interviews, or any study that is generated and conducted by the researcher.

Proofreading   Correction of mechanical and typographical errors in a text. See **Editing**.

Reason   Idea offered in support of another idea; it is often in response to an understood question of "why?"

Revision   Major reworking of an essay; it goes beyond editing to include a re-envisioning of the structure, development, or approach to the subject.

Rhetoric   The study of stylistic or structural elements that speakers and writers use to create meaning.

Rhetorical question   Unanswerable question a writer asks in an essay. Writers use rhetorical questions either to focus their audience's attention on the essay's point of view or to add emphasis to the essay's analysis or argument.

Secondary research   Research in which information is gathered from books, magazines, dictionaries, and so on.

Sentence   Group of words with a subject and predicate (i.e., a verb and its modifiers, complements, or objects).

Setting   Location, context, or environment where a story takes place.

Stereotype   Generalization in which specific characteristics of an individual are applied to an entire group.

Structure   Framework showing the relation between ideas. In an essay, traditional structure moves from a beginning, which identifies the subject and related issues, through a middle, which develops the ideas or argument, to an end.

Style   Use of language, approach, ideas, syntax, and so on, which characterizes a text as being that of a specific writer.

Subjective writing   Writing that records an author's emotional responses as well as factual information.

Subjunctive   Special verb form that indicates conditional, theoretical, or contrary-to-fact conditions. For example, instead of the indicative verb form *was* in the sentence "I wish I was rich," writers use the subjunctive form *were* to form "I wish I were rich."

Summary   Brief statement of the major points of a text, the order of their presentation, and their purpose.

Syllogism   Logical argument supported by a major premise and a minor premise.

Syntax   Order of words in a sentence.

Thesis   Proposition proven by an argument or the subject of an essay.

Thesis statement   A sentence, often at the end of an essay's first paragraph, which controls and directs the body of the essay.

Tone   Component of **style** that creates and reveals mood or attitude. Also called tone of voice.

Topic sentence   A generalization that will be developed and proven valid in the course of a paragraph.

Transition   Link between two ideas, statements, or paragraphs showing the relation between them. It may be a single word or phrase, the echoing of key language, or, in long works, a short paragraph.

Understatement   Ironical use of language by a writer. Writers use understatements to downplay an idea or issue or to create an intentional lack of emphasis.

Acknowledgments

Gloria Anzaldua, "Movimientos de rebeldia y las culturas que traicionan" from *Borderlands/La Frontera: The New Mestiza*. Copyright © 1987 by Spinsters/Aunt Lute Book Company, PO Box 410687, San Francisco, CA 94141. Reprinted by permission of the publisher.

Isaac Asimov, "The Shape of Things" from *Adding a Dimension*. Copyright 1962 by Mercury Press. Reprinted by permission of Doubleday & Company, Inc.

John Barth, "Welcome to College—And My Books" from *The New York Times Book Review*, September 16, 1984. Copyright © 1984 by John Barth. First published in *The New York Times*. Copyright © 1984 by The New York Times Company. Reprinted by permission of the publishers and International Creative Management.

Yvonne Baskin, "The Way We Act" from *Science 85*, November 1985. Copyright © 1985 by the American Association for the Advancement of Science. Reprinted by permission from the November issue of *Science 85* magazine.

Carl Belz, "Rock as Folk Art" from *The Story of Rock, Second Edition*. Copyright © 1972 by Oxford University Press, Inc. Reprinted by permission of the publisher.

William Bennett, "What Value is Values Education?" from *American Educator*. Copyright © 1980 by American Federation of Teachers. Reprinted with permission from the Fall 1980 issue of the *American Educator*, the quarterly journal of the American Federation of Teachers.

Michael Brown, "Epilogue: The Road Back" from *Laying Waste: Love Canal and the Poisoning of America*. Copyright © 1979 and 1980 by Michael Brown. Reprinted by permission of Pantheon Books, a division of Random House, Inc.

Pearl S. Buck, "America's Gunpowder Women" from *Harper's Magazine*, July 1939. Copyright 1939 by Pearl S. Buck. Copyright renewed 1966 by Pearl S. Buck. Reprinted by permission of Harold Ober Associates Incorporated.

Hortense Calisher, "Il Plœːr Dã Mõ Kœːr" from *The Collected Short Stories of Hortense Calisher*. Copyright © 1975 by Hortense Calisher. Reprinted by permission of Arbor House Publishing Corporation.

Ethan Canin, "The Emperor of the Air" from *The Atlantic Monthly Magazine* (1984). Copyright © 1984 by Ethan Canin. Reprinted by permission of the author.

Willa Cather, "Paul's Case" from *Youth and the Bright Medusa*, published by Alfred A. Knopf, Inc. Originally published in *McClure's Magazine*, April 1904.

Bruce C. Catton, "The Way of the Liberated" from *Never Call Retreat*. Copyright © 1965 by Bruce Catton. Reprinted by permission of Doubleday & Company.

Samuel L. Clemens, "Letter 2" from *Letters From Earth*, edited by Bernard De Voto. Copyright 1942 by The President and Fellows of Harvard College. Copyright 1962 by The Mark Twain Company. Reprinted by permission of Harper & Row Publishers, Inc.

Aaron Copland, "How We Listen to Music" from *What to Listen for in Music*. Copyright 1964 by McGraw-Hill Book Company. Reprinted by permission of the publisher.

Hector St. John Crevecoeur, "Reflections on the Manners of Americans" from *Sketches of Eighteenth Century America*, edited by Henri L. Bourdin, Ralph H. Gabriel, and Stanley T. Williams. Copyright © 1925 by Yale University Press. Reprinted by permission of the publisher.

Dorothy Parker, "Good Souls" from *Vanity Fair Magazine,* June 1919. Copyright 1919 by Dorothy Parker. Reprinted by permission of *Vanity Fair.*

Thomas J. Peters and Robert H. Waterman, "Analytic Ivory Towers" from *In Search of Excellence.* Copyright © 1982 by Thomas J. Peters and Robert H. Waterman. Reprinted by permission of Harper & Row, Publishers, Inc.

Henry Petroski, "Design as Revision" from *To Engineer is Human.* Copyright © 1985 by Henry Petroski. Reprinted by permission of the author and St. Martin's Press, Inc.

David R. Pichaske, "What You Wish You'd Learned in English 101." First printed in *Nutshell Magazine,* 1977–78. Copyright David Pichaske. Reprinted by permission of the author.

Beam H. Piper, "Omnilingual" from *Analog Science Fact & Fiction.* Copyright © 1962 by H. Beam Piper. Reprinted by permission of the author and the author's agents, Scott Meredith Literary Agency, Inc., 845 Third Avenue.

Plato, "The Parable of the Cave," reprinted from *The Republic of Plato.* Translated by F. M. Cornford 1941 by permission of Oxford University Press.

Richard Rodriguez, "The Achievement of Desire" from *Hunger of Memory.* Copyright © 1982 by Richard Rodriguez. Reprinted by permission of David R. Godine, Publisher, Boston.

Carl Sagan, "The Nuclear Winter" from *Parade Magazine,* October 30, 1983. Copyright © 1983 by Carl Sagan. Reprinted by permission of the author and the author's agents, Scott Meredith Literary Agency, Inc., 845 Third Avenue, New York, NY 10022.

Robert J. Samuelson, "The Budget Masquerade" from *Newsweek Magazine,* February 20, 1984. Copyright © 1984 by Newsweek, Inc. All rights reserved. Reprinted by permission of the publishers.

Irwin Shaw, "The Eighty-Yard Run" from *Mixed Company.* Copyright © 1950 by the Estate of Irwin Shaw. Reprinted by permission of Arthur B. Greene, executor.

Adam Smith, "Why Not Call Up the Economists?" from *Paper Money.* Copyright © 1981 by George J. W. Goodman. Reprinted by permission of Summit Books, a division of Simon & Schuster, Inc.

Lewis Thomas, "The Hazards of Science" from *The Medusa and the Snail.* Copyright © 1977 by Lewis Thomas. Originally published in *The New England Journal of Medicine.* Reprinted by permission of McGraw-Hill Book Company.

Robert Thomas, "Is Corporate Executive Compensation Excessive?" from *Seeing With A Native Eye.* Copyright © 1976 by Walter Holden Capps. Reprinted by permission of Harper & Row, Publishers, Inc.

Barre Toelken, "How Many Sheep Will It Hold?" from *Seeing With A Native Eye.* Copyright © 1976 by Walter Holden Capps. Reprinted by permission of Harper & Row, Publishers, Inc.

Richard P. Turco., et al. "The Climatic Effects of Nuclear War" from *Scientific American,* August 1984. Copyright © 1984 by Scientific American, Inc. All rights reserved. Reprinted by permission of W. H. Freeman and Company, Publishers.

David Vogel, "Business Without Science" from *Science Digest,* July 1981. Copyright David J. Vogel. Reprinted by permission of the author.

Subject Index

Index of Names and Titles